THE NEW POLITICAL ECONOMY
OF EMERGING EUROPE

Second, revised and extended edition

THE NEW POLITICAL ECONOMY OF EMERGING EUROPE

Second, revised and extended edition

By

László Csaba

AKADÉMIAI KIADÓ, BUDAPEST

ISBN 978 963 05 8459 3

Published by Akadémiai Kiadó
Member of Wolters Kluwer Group
P.O. Box 245, H-1519 Budapest, Hungary
www.akkrt.hu

Printed in Hungary

To my wife

CONTENTS

1. FOREWORD TO THE SECOND, REVISED AND EXTENDED EDITION

It is a great honor and pleasure for me that the Publisher has agreed to bring this second, extended edition of my monograph on emerging Europe to the international audience. The first edition has aroused considerable interest, over a dozen of reviews have been printed in Hungary and abroad, including Japan, Germany, Russia, Great Britain, the Czech Republic and Bulgaria.The book has won the Award of the Publisher in 2005, granted on the base of majority voting of the Section for Law and Economics of the Hungarian Academy of Sciences. The book has been in classroom use at several universities. Besides Hungary, I am aware of French and Japanese schools using it in their various curricula. Owing to the generosity of the Publisher a substantially revised and also extended and updated Hungarian edition has also been launched in 2006 (Csaba, 2006). The latter version has also recieved considerable attention, both in the electronic and printed media. Finally the present edition is an in-between: it retains much of the original text, but *complements it with two new chapters, unsurprisingly, on the European Union.* Certainly, wherever needed, especially in globalization and EU-related issues, updating of the bits and pieces, reflection on some of the new developments in the literature and 'in the world out there' complement the original version. I tried to improve some of the shortcomings pinpointed by the dozen reviews published so far. But I consciously refrained from re-writing the entire empirical-statistical source material, or from introducing brand new theoretical models. Both requirements may make perfect sense, perhaps in a different project, not however in a revised edition.

Why bother with an *extended and revised new edition* instead of the usual reprint? First and foremost: the basic structure and the line of argument of the previous edition, that was sold out, is still valid. None of the numerous reviewers to date have questioned the fundamental logic of my reasoning, or the major conclusions, which is truly good news for such a contested area as new political economy. Meanwhile, since the previous edition went to press, *the European Union has undergone a major crisis.* The Constitutional Treaty has been rejected in two founding nations, while several others, including Britain and Poland decided to adjourn the referenda over its ratification. In 2004 the European Court of Justice repelled the Ecofin decision on suspending the Stability and Growth Pact, while the Council in March 2005 agreed to re-interpret those rules that guide the coordinated fiscal framework for the single currency.

These two changes required a specific reflection. Chapter Nine therefore analyzes the controversies over the *new fiscal framework* in the light of economic theory, as exemplified by the Nobel prize laureates of 2004, Kydland and Prescott, who were awarded for their pioneering work over time inconsistency (Kydland and Prescott, 1977), the issue behind the conflict between short and long term incentives for policy makers. Under this angle the chapter analyzes if, and through what mechanisms, the more flexible reading of the Pact can, and indeed will, be conducive to *higher and more sustainable economic growth in Europe.* The re-launch of the Lisbon Strategy in 2005 reqired the inclusion of such analysis from a long run perspective, while the changes in the rule prompted us to take a stance on the merits of the modified fiscal framework.

Chapter Ten, yet another new inclusion, brings us to those broader debates that have been triggered by the original texts, as well as by a series of conferences I had the chance to attend. In October 2005, just a few months after the first edition came out of print, *accession negotiations have been launched with Turkey and Croatia.* This implies an interesting paradox. For one, rejection of the Constitutional Treaty has resulted not so much from the actual contents of the text, or the lack of its meaning, but from the *percieved* threats in terms of economic insecurity and social stress, from *potential future enlargements.* The median European citizen wishes that the EU first consolidates, at least for a decade, and only later engages in future enlargements. Meanwhile the logic of Europeanization does require immediate and continuous action, since the *convergence of economic and political systems* in those areas which used to be called the European periphery, do not emerge spontaneously, *without an anchor.* The anchor - often by default - has been the European Union, and in operational terms the European Neighborhood Policies of 2005, offering a number of new forms of cooperation for all the countries around the EU, i.e fom Morocco through the Palestinian Authority, Moldova, Georgia and from Kyrgizstan to Belarus. In the new Chapter Ten, an attempt is being made to assess the *potential of these new policies in a strategic perspective.* We analyze if, and to what degree, *institutional innovation* may contribute to overcoming the current dead alley. Certainly the bits and pieces of further enlargement require further elaboration, however it falls outside the scope of the current volume (Csaba, 2007).

Otherwise the main line of argument, as well as the *overall pattern of the project remains unchanged.* The chapter on the Comparative overview of emprirical evidence provides the basics needed for meaningful theorizing. In letting the statistics to run, by and large, as they used to be, my intention is to show that the process of differentiation among transition trajectories *has long been observable.* Commenting on the upcoming new data has, certainly, got its inherent merits, irrespective of the more abstract claims of the present project – a good quality example of the former is presented by Gligorov et al (2006), published right at the time of concluding the present edition. Their findings point, in a number of ways, in the same direction as did the conclusions of our comparative empirical chapter, in terms of policy implications and statistical trends alike. This is good news, as it means that our findings are not time-constrained, nor unnecessarily limited by our reliance on the selected sources, *and survive even closer scrutiny and the control for the newer numbers*. Thus it might be legitimate for us to jump to the more abstract issues instead of further number gazing. Given that failures are much more frequent than successes – ever since – the *developmental issues* and reflections on *transnationalization* follow, which put the transition experience in a global context.

In this global approach the chapters on the EU and its influence on the emerging economies follow. Having arrived in what used to be percieved as safe haven, the frontrunners among the emerging economies are confronted with a series of crises, in the institutional and policy domains alike. *How to avoid the marginalization of European structures*, especially, though not exclusively in finances, is the unifying theme of these chapters.

Having adopted a normative approach to explaining the ways and means to success, intellectual honesty reqires us to address what seems to be *the two counter-examples of success* in the 2000s: the institutionless development of authoritarian regimes registering high growth. Interestingly, none of the reviewers so far has questioned the legitimacy of including China, the developmental paradox of the past decades. Moreover in several of the classes and conferences, unrelated to China, such as on the role of money, banking and rule of law, or property rights, the Empire of the Middle comes up as an example. Also, a reflected inter alia, on the pages of *American Economic Review, Journal of Political Economy* and the *Journal of Economic Perspectives,* the focus of interest of mainstream analysts has also been gradually re-focused, at least in part, on China. And the two mainstream-adjusted outposts of comparative economic research, *Economics of Transition* and even more its US counterpart, *The Journal of Comparative Economics* abound with contributions analyzing and interpreting the Chinese paradox. But attempts to decipe Russian successes under both Putin Presidencies are also in no short supply in similarly prestigous fora of academic analyses (besides the traditional area studies and international relations [IR] journals). This is a more conventional option. However our purpose is to show, *how different the Russian trajectory has been* from the Central European mainstream. For this reason Russia is no longer an emerging economy in the same sense as the new EU members are.

Finally, a neo-institutionalist approach can not but reflect in some detail, i.e in the two concluding chapters on the role of *regulation and regulatory agencies* in democracies, as well as on the *role of institutions*. Which institutions matter and how do they matter? This is the big unknown, for which a temporary and partial answer is being provided. Suggestions for reforming available national and European institutions in order to foster competitiveness conclude, together with more theoretical reflections on institutions and economic development. In the latter, vein changes in the natural sciences, allowing for the better understanding of the workings of the brain, perceptions and of reasoning, do call for changes in social sciences in general and economics in particular, in terms of overcoming the mental constraints imposed by the predominant analytical frame bequeathed by Newtonian physics and its mathematical arsenal (North, 2005). This has developed into an entire research paradigm over the past years in the leading academic journals in the UK and the USA, with empirical studies documenting the prevelance of *incoherent* behavior and the ensuing *inability of ordering of preferences* in vast numbers of economic decisions (Cohen, 2005). Individual irrationality may, but does not have to, bring about sizable changes in *aggregate* outcomes, rendering mechanistic extrapolation (and linear modelling) largely irrelevant (Fehr and Tyran, 2005). Measurable items of income relate only losely to happiness, rendering conventional hedonistic economic hypotheses, such as mobility and more consumption being axiomatically good, as questionable, *especially for public policy applications* (Layard, 2006). Components previously abstracted away, such as trust, good governance, lack of corruption and workplace security/job satisfaction all may, and often do, matter more than an additional unit of monetary income (Helliwell, 2006). And yet another Nobel winner is in the forefront in the attempt to measure *well-being*, rather than material *output* as the end-result of economic activity (Kahneman and Krueger, 2006) – an issue we recurringly discuss in various chapters on development, governance, success indicators and the role of institutions in the democratic development alternative. *The broader approaches*, including new political economy, *no longer count as esoteric outgrowth* of a serious, technocratic and socially blind analytical discipline, some of the mainstream departments let economics to be learnt.

All in all, as the above sketch of the structure may have illustrated, this book is *not* a collection of previously published papers, but an *old-fashioned monograph, following a single line of argumentation*. Though most chapters have been presented to several conferences and also to several readers, the integrity of the overall line of the argument has hopefully remained intact. The inclusion of the two new chapters is justified by the nature and weight of changes that have taken place in the past two years, that require reflections on specific issues. But the *normative insights remain unchanged.* It is perhaps the field of development economics where these new normatives have become most pronounced, as recent analyses of the field (Szakolczai, 2006, Szentes, 2006) have illustrated.

This is certainly *not a mainstream book*, as one of the reviewers of the first edition aptly noted. But, as Professor Alexandre Lámfalussy writes in his recommendation to the Hungarian edition, this has to do with the conscious attempt of the author to avoid *clichés* and intellectual quick fixes. In so doing it is my hope to have contributed to *a number of open-ended debates that run in parallel but on different levels of abstraction*. One is the level of *economic theory and methodology*, an attempt to come up with propositions of how to conduct economic research in a socially responsible and relevant fashion. A second level is that of *area studies*, by shedding light on what tansition has meant on a global scale, and how to interpret local developments in a global perspective. Third, at the level of *European Studies*, the overdue reform of the *European Union* may be more effective, if policy debates make use of the insights from more academic analyses. Fourth, understanding big countries, outside the scope of self-contained area or country studies, is an important task for *comparative approaches*, which may shed light on some of the less trivial aspects of these specific paths of development. Finally, as fifth, the role of *institutions* and regulatory *agencies* is perhaps one of the most relevant, still the least elaborated area of modern social science research, *way beyond the boundaries of economics.*

Therefore, it is at least my sincere hope, that not only various strands of the economics profession, but perhaps also people working on improving public administration, on setting up and reforming international agencies, civil groups interested in defending human rights and privacy in the era of internet revolution, legal scientists, political scientists and specialists of IR may, perhaps to a different degree, profit from confronting our insights with theirs. In so doing a *cross-fertilization* of approaches may emerge, which, for the present author, would translate into *a more relevant* brand of economic research than the one currently dominating many of the manistream departments.

Last, but not at all least, it is my duty to express my gratitude to those who facilitated my work on this second edition. The International Relations and European Studies Department of the Central European University under then Chair Julius Horvath and its doctoral program, the CEU facilities, library and staff, have all been of great assistance. The doctoral school at the Faculty of Economics and Business at the University of Debrecen with colleagues and students have also provided intellectual stimulus. It is a great pleasure to see so many of them, from both doctoral schools, developing into mature and independent researchers and civil servants, already publishing their ideas, and not only in Hungary, but also abroad. Zoltán Ádám, István Benczes, Pál Czeglédi, Matthias Gruber, Dóra Győrffy, László Jankovics, Zdenek Kudrna, Balázs Pálosi-Németh are perhaps the most promising, though this list is fortunately far from complete. MA students from the Budapest Corvinus University, taking my class on Emerging Markets have contributed, through comments and criticism, to improving the preliminary texts. I tried to heed most of the critical commentary of the dozen reviews of the first edition and yet another dozen reviewers of the revised Hungarian edition, without sacrificing the overall line of my argument. And needles to say, the endurance and supportive love of my family, my wife Csia/Gabi, our grown-up, university student children, Zoltán and Orsi/Hedgehog, has been a source of endless inspiration and provided the purpose of the entire exercise.

Budapest, 31 July 2006.

László Csaba

References

CSABA, L. (2006): *A fölemelkedő Európa* (Europe on the rise). Budapest: Akadémiai Kiadó.

COHEN, J. D. (2005): The vulcanization of the human brain. *Journal of Economic Perspectives*, vol.19.no.4. pp3–24.

CSABA, L. (2007): The eastward enlargement of the EU: a great success story or a last nail in the coffin of the EU? In: YAGI, K.–MIZOBATA, S. eds: *Melting the Boundaries: Institutional Transformation in a Wider Europe.* Kyoto: Kyoto University Press (in print).

FEHR, E.–TYMAN, J.-R. (2005): Individual irrationality and aggregate outcomes.*Journal of Economic Perspectives,* vol.19.no.4. pp43–66.

GLIGOROV, V.–PODKAMINER, L. et al (2006): Broader-based growth resilient to global uncertainties. Vienna: *WIIW Research Reports,* no.328 – (July).

HELLIWELL, J. F. (2006): Well-being, social capital and public policy: what's new? *Economic Journal,* vol.116.no.510. pp34–45.

KYDLAND, F.–PRESCOTT, E. (1977): Rules rather than discretion: the inconsistency of optimal plans. *Journal of Political Economy,*vol.85.no.3. pp473–492.

KAHNEMAN, D.–KRUEGER, A. B. (2006): Developments in the measurement of subjective well-being. *Journal of Economic Perspectives,*vol.20.no.1. pp3–24.

LAYARD, R. (2006): Happiness and public policy: a challenge to the profession. *Economic Journal,*vol.116.no.510. pp24–33.

NORTH, D. (2005): *Understanding the Process of Economic Change.* Princeton, New Jersey: Princeton University Press.

SZAKOLCZAI, GY. (2006): A gazdaságfejlődés elméletének megújulása: az első, a második és az új generáció. (Renewal of the theory of economic development: the first, the second and the new generation). *Valóság,* vol.49.no.2. pp1–35.

SZENTES, T. (2006) : Az állam szerepe a felgyorsult globalizáció korában (The role of the state in the age of accelerated globalization). *Köz-Gazdaság* (a quarterly of the Budapest Corvinus Univerity), vol.1.no.1. pp15–46.

2. FOREWORD – WHY THIS BOOK?

It is not the time to venture for anything longer than 3–4 pages, or a 40-second-long interview clip in the evening news. Still, with the time passing there emerges a need to take stock of what we have learned. The personal history of the author and the evolution of science often call for taking stock and looking ahead. If done in good time, the outcome might be of interest to a wider readership, and may even contribute to the promotion of knowledge in a particular field. Also knowing that there are no such things as 'finally settled matters' in any of the sciences, passage of time per se may justify our reassessment of the state of art in a given area. This area for me has been the study of Central and Eastern European economies and societies in a comparative, preferably global, perspective.

Preliminaries and Background

Two decades ago, when working on *Eastern Europe in the World Economy* (Csaba, 1984/1990) the question of the time was if and how command economies of the Soviet type can *survive* the fundamental changes that had been evolving in technology, warfare, economy, trade and also finance. The *puzzle* was that despite obvious shortcomings and the ever more pronounced signs of ossification, the system of the Soviet empire and related economic structures and political institutions still survived. While the insight of Ludwig von Mises (1920/1976) on the non-viability of any economic system lacking capital markets and the resultant misallocation of resources obviously held, the prophecy of the imminent collapse of Communist economies has not, at least for over 70 years (cf. e.g. Hanson, 2003). Our finding at the time, though packaged in what was feasible under contemporary Byzantine language, had been that the cumulation of strains was clearly observable. Moreover changes in the international embeddedness of the system were largely unfavorable for its continued existence. By the time the English language edition of the volume appeared, this insight was already turned into practice, with the disintegration of the Soviet block in 1989–91.

More than a decade ago, working on *The Capitalist Revolution in Eastern Europe* (Csaba, 1994/1995) there were *three basic puzzles* to be solved. One related to the fact that the collapse of the old regime has not triggered that imminent welfare improvement what has been expected not only by the population in the region, but also by mainstream economics[1] as well as a sizeable body of the analytical and policy-making literature (e.g. Collins and Rodrik, 1991). Instead, disorganization and contraction proved to be much more lasting than most contemporary agents, both in policy-making and the academe, would have expected. The thesis on the 'crisis of transformation' has established itself (Köves, 1992; Lavigne, 1995; van Brabant, 1998; more recently in Bogár, 2006). Against this contemporary mainstream, my monograph argued that path dependence and the nature of institutional change both require years, rather than months, if changes are to be meaningful and lasting.

The second puzzle had been, at the time, how little mainstream economics – journals and analysts alike – took note of what has been an epochal change in the history of mankind. Also, as Djankov and Murrel (2002, pp. 740–741) rightly stress, this has been a unique opportunity to experiment and *test competing economic theories*. This had not been the way contemporaries tended to see affairs. Calls for studying and translating existing/established textbooks, as well as of institutions were the main propositions. The – over-optimistic – expectations of EU accession only contributed to the advocacy of institutional imports as shortcut solutions (e.g. Portes, 1991). While some may consider it just professional inertia, the experience of the past fifteen years has shown that both during European accession negotiations, and even following the Enron scandal, the tendency of *benchmarking* and of trying to *impose/import 'first best' practices* has never subdued. My argument at the time stressed the historic uniqueness of the process and called for more innovative solutions. With the benefit of hindsight, and given the increased influence of benchmarking as a component of global governance practice, re-examination of the issue seems warranted. The third puzzle thus may be that with the increasing distance of the Communist heritage in terms of time transition countries *may lose their uniqueness*. They may become more like other emerging economies – if successful – or to underdeveloped economies, if state failure and market failure is their dominant feature.

Yet, a decade later the long engagement with the EU has become a formal marriage, with 10 countries of the region plus Malta and Cyprus joining in. The insight that like in medicine, not each individual survives the same therapy, thus knowledge of analytical insights do not replace *specific investigations and applications*, in terms of institutions and policies, has become part and parcel of established wisdom, also at the level of international financial institutions and the policy-making community (e.g. Krueger, ed., 2000; Meier and Stiglitz, eds, 2001). Looking through the major academic journals as well as catalogues of major Western publishing houses, we do not find anybody of stand-

---

[1] Once artificial distortions are eliminated, efficiency must improve, by and large of itself, short of interventions that account for the contrary.

ing who would not devote, with more or less regularity, time, space and money to analyzing the experience of systemic transformation.

Currently there are *several new puzzles* to be solved. First, the explanation for *success and failure* of once Communist economies should be provided *within a single analytical framework*.[2] Second, the experience of China, and more recently Russia, seems to defy the odds: an authoritarian political system can co-exist with largely decentralized economic controls with foreign direct investment (FDI) playing a major role in shaping economic structures and competitiveness. Finally, much of what used to be subject of transition literature increasingly merges with more general *development studies* (Ofer, 2001). This is the case in the larger number of not very successful cases, and with European studies, with a smaller number of success stories. These puzzles may also objectively call for stock-taking anew. These also require reflection on the experiences of growth and the lack of it, of *financial sustainability* and the lack of it, of political conditions favoring the emergence and *taking root of institutions of the civilized market economy*; last but not least, *conditions for good governance* and the lack of those. The latter term – used sometimes as a buzzword by the international agencies – means no less than the *return of the political* into economics. The devil, exorcized by the Walras–Samuelson line, now returns through the backdoor. This justifies our sticking to the term 'political economy', despite the unfavorable connotations burdening these as a legacy from the Communist period.

What Is New Political Economy?

What is then the *new political economy*, the approach wishing to merge the analytical insights of mainstream with the major role played by institutions and policies in implementing these? There is no easy answer, since in the social sciences, unlike in natural sciences, the evolution of generally accepted terms and analytical frameworks is less than uniform. In the 18–19th centuries, when the study of the economy emancipated itself from administrative sciences and law, the generally accepted term was *political* economy. National economics or public economics (*Nationalökonomie*) focused interest on macro-processes rather than on the individual household, that was to be studied by business management. While the Walrasian revolution implied a microeconomic angle, the then mainstream of the profession, centering around Alfred Marshall and John Maynard Keynes sustained the rigorous delineation between micro and macro. This holds to the point that modern macro-economics is normally originated with Keynes (a reason why Lucas [1996] in his triumphant counter-revolution declared the death of macro).

However, with the breakthrough of Nobel winner Paul Samuelson, first in terms of teaching, then in terms of analytical approach, and further with the

---

[2] For such attempts cf. e.g. Roland (2002) and Falcetti et al (2002) and Blanchard (1997), more recently Kolodko (2006).

victory of the counter-revolution led by Robert Lucas[3] and Gary Becker, both awarded by a Nobel Prize for their work, the study of economic processes has become increasingly technicized, formalized in mathematical equations, and separated from the social sciences. This had to do with the quest for methodological rigor and for quantitative results. The term, introduced generally by the ever revised textbooks of Paul Samuelson (and William Nordhaus, 1992), *economics* reflects the discipline's self-delineation, a demarcation line against the soft and qualitative social sciences, that do not attribute the same significance to methodological rigor, as economic professionals do. Following Lucas, the quest for micro-foundations of macroeconomics, i.e. the need to base macro-analyses on micro-economic insights and results rests on two premises. One is the need to formalize presentation. The other is the consequent application of *methodological individualism*, most radically applied by the extension of microeconomic approaches to all human activities especially following the path-breaking work of Theodore W. Shultz (1973) and Gary Becker (1976 and 1996) (for an assessment cf. Lazear, 2000).

The self-contained – and often self-referential – evolution of mainstream economics resulted in a theory, capable of explaining erratic and chaotic changes via models, be that chaos or the stock exchange. On the other hand, insights from these theories are often at *conflict with practical exigencies*, most extremely shown by the 1998 autumn crisis of the Long Term Capital Management hedge fund, where the previous year's Nobel winner was a major analytical advisor.[4] More problems emerged when academic insights were to be translated into universally valid policy packages, that were dubbed by John Williamson (1994, pp. 17–19) as the Washington Consensus. The per se valid insights had a long and arduous journey into policy implementation. As documented in our previous monograph, as well as in the *Transition Reports* of EBRD, there used to be a tendency to use abstract models and insights, applying under certain conditions and levels of abstraction only, as immediate policy guidelines. This has backfired. By the 2000s common wisdom, both in the academe and in the international financial institutions, has become aware of the need to take into account *the context* and of the fundamental role *institutions* play in shaping actual outcomes. For instance the role of fixed exchange rates cannot be understood in separation. Likewise private property though is in general more efficient than public or mixed forms of ownership, but only if side conditions for a long chain of bringing about efficiency is being observed (an issue we shall analyze in separate chapters). And the growing *literature on*

[3] For a concise assessment of the terms 'counter-revolution' and 'death of the macro' cf. the excellent survey of Júlia Király (1998).

[4] This paradox does not denounce Myron Scholes and Robert Merton. The LTCM was caught not so much by the Russian crisis proper than by its spill-over. As B. Pálosi–Németh called to my attention, LTCM did not hold Russian bonds, but had encountered a series of difficulties from the early months of the year. The spillover that was sudden and not justified by the size of the Russian market or the share held by Russian papers in total global investment portfolios, was the final drop in the fate of the hedge fund. The crux of the misjudgement was timing and location, not a matter of academic quality. More on this cf. (Edwards, 1999).

policy reform, stemming from the 1980s and 1990s has been confronted with the need to include institutions, policies and public preferences/choices, that have been often contradictory to what mathematical models would have suggested as rational. Only the works of Kahneman and Tversky (1979) awarded by a Nobel Prize in 2002, have provided scientific (psychology-based, empirically tested) observations on such issues as why risk-taking and risk aversion is *not* symmetric (as postulated by a model).[5]

Evolution of economics, as well as of its interaction with practice (i.e. testing of theories) have triggered a development that is most important from our perspective. The 20th century's academic development tended to de-emphasize institutional, historic and generally speaking contextual factors and stressed rigor and *analytical coherence, even at the cost of social relevance* (cf. more on that in Baumol, 2000). By contrast, experiences with policy reform in developing countries, as well as with the multiplication of policy failures in post-Communist transformation have *triggered a contrarian move*. The need to *integrate* the insights of other social sciences, of context and to create a better *interaction* with the policy-making and business community laid the groundwork for an approach that we call *new political economy*. As elaborated in detail elsewhere (Saint-Paul, 2000: Hibbs, 2001; Csaba, 2002) this approach does not question the validity of insight and relevance of the mainstream theories. It attempts, however, to *integrate these in policy-relevant insights*, and wishes to incorporate the feedback to and from the institutional and policy processes. This line of research has constantly been present in mainstream journals up to the point of analyzing electoral competition and the impact of heterogeneous pattern of districts on the outcomes (Collender, 2005).

It is interesting to note, that also in the more applied version of *international studies* literature *a similar turn*, away from abstract grand sociological theories of the 1960s, towards more economically informed analyses, based on rational choice models, and generally a view quite resembling to *homo oeconomicus* could be observed ever since the 1970s. In his overview of the postwar development of American political science and developmental literature, Richard Higgott (2004, chapters 2 and 4) describes in great detail the emergence of *new political economy as a discipline and an academic approach*. He calls it as a mixture of rationalist politics, public choice and policy analysis, that together have injected the previously missing economic component in the development debate from the early 1970s.

One may wonder if, and to what degree, this change of the heart implied an attempt at revenge, that is to re-conquer those fields where mainstream economics has been marching into, due to its immense ability to *generalize and formalize* questions (as well as suggesting at least testable and falsifiable hypotheses). The latter approach is present with a number of journals published under this name, such as *Review of International Political Economy*, or *New Political*

---

[5] It is hardly surprising that an application of this empirical insight was extended to the workings of the capital markets, cf. Barberis, Huang and Santos, (2001). A broad analytical assessment of the work of Kahneman is offered by Hámori (2003).

Economy, or the *Review of International Studies* and more recently *Global Social Policy*. However, as the above quoted book of Higgott proves with a detailed literature review, the US brand of new political economy, having emerged in development studies, emphasizes though the importance of collective choices and institutions, still remains clearly within the liberal tradition (if for no other reason, because of its methodology). In our analysis the case for multi- or cross-disciplinary approaches can be taken as given.

It is equally important to note what William Tabb (1999) rightly calls as the *two cultures in economics*. In his broad review of the history of economic thought the above cited volume proves that besides the formalized mainstream, an equally powerful presence of institutionalism and structuralism could be observed over the past hundred years or so. Moreover many of the major breakthroughs in social sciences and economics have been produced by the heterodox approaches. Therefore, the clear dominance of formalized approaches in the leading journals and in professional pecking orders may represent more a *fashion trend* than a *sound academic judgement*, based on generally accepted methodology/scientometrics/of the sciences in general. If we were to judge by the number of citations, it would be hard to consider the influence of such authors as Mancur Olson, Friedrich August von Hayek, Lord Peter Bauer or Walter Eucken, Albert Hirschman or Amartya Sen as second rank, marginal or not having contributed to the evolution of what is considered to be the hard core of the profession. It is interesting to observe that in recent years 'outdated' institutionalist approaches regained academic respectability. In 2005 the Richard Ely lecture of the American Economic Association (AEA) was held by Oli Williamson (2005), the iconic figure of the old school. In 2006 a special section of the AEA annual meeting and of the *American Economic Review* was devoted to issues of political economy, and yet another section or issues analyzing lessons from China, India and Russia.

In venturing into new political economy, therefore we are not at all entering un-chartered waters. In the second half of the 20th century several *school-molding personalities* of the economics profession have contributed to this line of thought. Let us recall only the Nobel-winning oeuvre of James Buchanan (1992) and his public choice theory, called in the European continent as constitutional political economy. A rallying point of this line of thought, across the Atlantic, is the journal *Constitutional Political Economy*, where the Freiburg tradition of intensive interaction between law and economics is being sustained at a high professional level. The stronghold of European mainstream political economy, particularly international political economy is the Swiss quarterly, *Kyklos*, bravely declaring itself the only socially relevant economic journal, not written by referees and editors, but authors themselves. Similarly interdisciplinary orientation features two other international political economy journals, the libertarian *CATO Journal* and the understandably left-leaning two manistream developmental fora, *Third World Quarterly* and *World Development*. Meanwhile the *Journal of Development Economics* is a stronghold of a variety of approaches applying mainstream techniques and analytical angles to issues of development. By contrast, the editorial policy of *The World Economy* defines it as a policy forum, though several academic papers have been published by the editors in the recent years. Several political economy papers have been published in the two leading journals of the American Economic Association, *The Journal of Economic Literature*, as well as the intentionally less technical *Journal of Economic Perspectives*. Yet another American quarterly, having changed editors and taken over by Palgrave, *Comparative Economic Studies* moved from area studies to political economy, and carries interesting contributions to the area.

Another Nobel-winner, Douglass North has been constantly stressing the importance of institutions in longer term economic development, as well as the interaction with political institutions. Likewise, from among the 2001 Nobel winners, George Akerlof (1970) and Joseph Stiglitz (1993) have long emphasized the consequences of *imperfect information* for the *applicability* of models based on full information and unlimited capacity to process these. And let us not forget one of the first Nobel-winners, Kenneth Arrow (1950), much of whose output relates to social costs, political selection and welfare issues. In recent years the expansion of 'economic imperialism' political economy analysis has come back to the mainstage. It may be sufficient to cite to recent contributions to the *Quarterly Journal of Economics:* one on the liberal bias of US media (Groseclose and Milyo, 2005) and one on the causes of state religion (Barro and McClearly, 2005). Gone are the days when some colleagues could afford to disqualify these approaches as 'poetry', falling outside the scope of the economics discipline proper. Moreover the Nobel lecture of Ed Prescott (2006) comes back to the traditional way in demonstrating how new policy experience and formalized research methods have been interactive also during those decades, when it was not in vogue.

Many people would contest our choice. Neo-institutionalists, a school aiming to build a bridge between the methodological individualism and formalism of the mainstream on the one hand, and more traditional, historically informed institutionalists on the other, often try, without much success, to ally in one church in order to reintegrate broader approaches. Structuralist and neo-Marxian approaches try to do the same.

The term *'new political economy'* (NPE) in the sense we use it is reflecting the American developmental literature parlance, as explained in Higgott (2004). This usage is also akin to the German ordoliberal economic tradition. This has been sustained primarily around two yearbooks – *ORDO* and *Jahrbuch der Neuen Politischen Ökonomie*. In so doing, a liberal approach to *economic systems* is combined with historically informed institutional analysis. Furthermore, matters of *public choice* (such as the choice between a high tax – high service versus a low tax – low service economy) are being treated as *endogenous* variables, rather than exogenous factors, as in the mainstream. While any choice is contestable, in my view the term best conveys to the English speaking audience of what can be expected. The up until recently marginal position of institutionalism in the English speaking academic economics is an additional argument against the usage. In his presidential address providing a broad overview of the area Paul Joskow (2003) of MIT singled out *public policy applications among the weak points* (or limited success areas) of new institutional economics.

In particular he listed economic development, corporate governance, globalization and network liberalization among the issue areas, where the shortcoming is manifest – and these are crucial for the focus of this book. New political economy, by contrast captures exactly these features. This is also the research project of Yale professor T. N. Srinivasan, a leading figure of development economics. His term 'neoclassical political economy' (Srinivasan, 2001, p. 510 and 522) implies basically the two salient features of our approach: *endogenizing the state* and collective action, as well as introducing these in the *standard analysis* in order to produce policy relevant and interesting new outcomes.

Finally we must admit, that many scholars, also in the English speaking world, use *NPE in a different meaning*. Scholars of *international relations*, having fought a long time the dominance of the 'neo-liberal paradigm' attempted to regain ground by an alternative called 'political economy' (a good quality example is Gilpin, 2001). This approach is, by and large, a reinvention of classical political economy, or, in most other cases, constitutes an attempt to apply *political science paradigms on economic matters*. Understandably, their findings tend to be at odds with those of the economics mainstream, though not necessarily implying a 'turn to the left'. If for no other reason, the different methodological approach allows for a *limited, if any interaction with our understanding of new political economy*, as defined above in terms of a subchapter of broadly defined general economics discipline. Neo-Marxist authors gathering around the journal *Review of International Political Economy*, as well as radical/critical analysts contributing to the Carfax journal *New Political Economy* produce completely different pieces on different paradigmatic grounds.[6] The eldest journal, carrying such a name, *The Journal of Political Economy* is being edited in Chicago, and unsurprisingly, has evolved into a typical mainstream journal over the past four decades. On the other hand, the *European Journal of Political Economy*, published by the Dutch academic publishing house Elsevier, brings articles that could be denoted in German parlance the economic theory of politics. Rather than working on the interaction of economic and political processes, authors of this journal adopt the mainstream economic angle and arsenal, analyze political processes, such as pension reform or tax evasion through the lenses of the mainstream paradigm. This approach adopts *one level higher abstraction* in analyzing issues than we do. Our choice, not competing with any of the former, but complementing these, attempts to highlight *developmental, regional and post-Communist specific features* of economic processes. However, since there is no single 'right way', the only sincere method for us is to remain straightforward in stating our aims and scope also in terms of using the core term *new political economy* in ways and for the purposes described above.

---

[6] In the former pieces what I would call institutionalist modelling, in the latter radical policy analyses are offered; both legitimate on their own right, still being a different genre from our output.

Why Not Eastern Europe/Transition Economies?

Finally the term *Emerging Europe* needs to be defined. As in so many other instances, new concepts evolve with the resurgence of new phenomena. Following the Second World War, development economics emerged as a revolutionary sub-discipline, swimming against the tide of contemporary mainstream (cf. the broad overview of Waelbroek, 1998; Szentes, 2002). Reflecting the normative approach of the '40s and '50s the new states having emerged on the ruins of colonialism tended to be called 'developing' countries. However, their problem, as described in a voluminous literature, has remained to date *underdevelopment,*[7] i.e. the inability to enter a path of financially, environmentally and socially sustainable growth. Reckoning with this fact, from the 1960s, also reflecting the non-aligned movement of Nehru, Nasser, Nkrumah and Tito, the term 'third world' was introduced. However, in the 2000s with the irreversible demise of the bipolar system, the term 'third world' is a hollow one. *Non-OECD countries differ more substantially from one another than they are unlike of OECD economies.* Furthermore, differentiation among non-Atlantic countries is much bigger than most analytical terms would allow (such as 'developing country', with Korea, Turkey and Mexico already being members of the OECD).

Facing realities, the financial literature of the 1980s introduced the term *emerging markets* for those non-Atlantic nations, where development was *not just a polite diplomatic euphemism for backwardness.* Especially following successful stabilization in countries like Chile, Spain, Israel, Mexico, coupled with the growth miracle of East Asia in the 1970s and '80s it made no business sense to lump up decaying and disintegrating quasi-states with the ones having registered the highest growth rates globally, owing to their outward looking industrialization policies. Therefore this term reflects a *long run growth*, potential and real, but by no means cyclical in nature. In emerging markets, to put it shortly, the *trend rate of growth is palpably above the average of OECD countries.* Therefore, for them catching up is not just a mirage, a promise too frequently misused by nationalist politicians for the sake of state building (while disregarding the preferences and interests of the poorest and the middle-classes alike).

In a similar vein, it is high time to get rid of the term *transition economies* (in some extreme neologisms we could read even transitional economies, that imply, grammatically the ephemeral nature of these). One of our fundamental hypotheses, to be proven across the present monograph, is that the 28 – and with the independence of Kosovo and Montenegro already 30 – post-Communist countries cannot and *should not be lumped into a single analytical category.* The Communist legacy, that used to mold their common experience fifteen or twenty years ago, no longer count as decisive. Some of them are integrated in

---

[7] As Higgott (2004, Chapter 3) rightly emphasizes, the theory of underdevelopment emerged as a reaction to both neo-Marxist and liberal views, but received moderate attention and appreciation in mainstream academe. More on that in Szentes (2002).

the EU, others disintegrate into smaller entities in Southeast Europe and the Caucasus (perhaps also in Central Asia). Yet some other countries follow specific, national models of capitalism (that is count among the less successful developing nations).[8] As we shall show in the next (and following) chapters, even if we disregard the entirely different experience of China, these countries have shown *markedly different trajectories of development* over the past 15 years and longer. These have to do with path dependency, culture, policies, geography and many other matters. *In proper perspective, the Communist interlude of 40 or 70 years can hardly be taken as the sole defining moment of history.*

As a consequence, Kyrgyzstan is unlikely to be more similar to Slovenia, than to other Central Asian countries, only because of several decades of Russian rule. It is common knowledge, that the Soviet structures, imposed arbitrarily from above since the late 1920s, failed to create post-capitalist conditions. Nowadays the Central Asian societies struggle against typical features of *post-colonial situations,* such as dual society, nation building, captive state, corruption and despotism. These are clearly *not* the problems faced by the Central Europeans. With the time passing these *differences are likely to increase, rather than decrease.* Therefore it may be plausible to suggest at this point that divergence is likely to be the defining feature of the times to come; a point that is to be cross-checked across the various chapters, empirical and theoretical alike.

If there is a modicum of truth in our hypothesis, it does make academic sense to apply a new analytical category, *emerging economics.* This term stresses the commonality of issues in terms of market reforms and democratization both with *Southern European,* now EU nations like Spain, Portugal and Greece, as well as with *non-European* countries having entered a phase of sustaining growth as a trend, such as Chile, Mexico, Taiwan, Korea. The big challenge for the coming decades will see the following: if how and when the countries among the Mediterranean basin, starting up with Turkey and Morocco, can transform themselves in emerging economies.

Thus *the focus of this book* is, like that of its predecessors, what once used to be called, mistakenly, but then politically correctly, Eastern Europe. *The angle of analysis* is the global economy. Today the defining processes, such as the information and communications technology (ICT) revolution, the new economy, the evolution of such previously unknown forms of organization as the virtual firm or the virtual bank, are added to the centuries-old processes of industrial, trade, financial and organizational intertwining, that carry most recently the misnomer of *globalization.* While disagreeing with the over-emotional and politicized uses, we may also refer to this as a shorthand form in describing/ alluding to the many novelties that together constitute *a brand new environment* for an ever growing competition among localities.

In the following pages we attempt to provide empirical evidence and theo-

[8] For a regular comparative overview of facts and figures proving this point in great empirical detail cf. *Transition Report, 2006.* London: EBRD and *Economic Survey of Europe,* no. 2. (2005). Geneva and New York: a publication of the UN Secretariat, that was regretfully discontinued whit the cited issue.

retical insights of *what has changed* and contribute to solving our three puzzles listed above. If we manage, it might be a contribution to a better understanding of both the *region* and the potentials (and limitations) of *economic analysis*. Many of the chapters emerged from various conference initiatives, from which I benefitted, especially from open exchanges with my colleagues. Still I do hope that *an overall structure* emerges, that proves the points raised. The book contains original research and I hope to contribute to the international debate on these contentious issues, not aspiring for a 'final say' or a 'defining moment' in offering my insights for critical commentary of the readers.

The Map of the Project

The present monograph starts in Part One with the comparative overview of *previously available evidence*. This is done in two parts: empirical and theoretical. Starting with *statistical* evidence and its interpretation we can address some of the traditionally controversial issues of transition theories. We can assess progress and failure and test the empirical and policy relevance of competing theories. This long-term view allows for grouping the transition economies and answer the question if the Communist legacy is still dominant. Following up this overview we try to put the transition experience in a broader perspective of *development*. This stresses the role of institutions, the quality of regulations and the importance of external anchors, as well as of consensus building.

Part Two is devoted to *global issues*. This is an attempt to overcome the somewhat parochial nature of many transition analyses that tend to remain hostage to traditional area studies approaches. In so doing the challenge of the ICT revolution as well as the various processes transgressing the border and the regulatory capacities of nation states come to the fore. We address the interaction of global, regional and local processes in bringing about policies and outcomes. We also ask if and *to what degree European integration*, the present arrangements of the EU, allow for meeting its Lisbon goals, that is becoming *the most competitive community of the globe*. We find that the two challenges overlap only partly. By the same token, so the argument in the chapter on the limits of EU driven transformation, new member states must take advantage of the *specifics of Europeanization*. The latter means that instead of the previously dominant copying new, innovative and constructive approaches are needed both at the national and European levels. Two chapters are devoted to the Stability and Growth Pact (SGP), an institutional reflection of economic insights on the uses of the rules-based conduct. It has come under severe criticism both from old and new member states. The present monograph addresses this controversy from the point of view of long-term growth and finds that monetary and *fiscal solidity allow for growth to sustain for long periods*, that is for decades rather than months. And this is precisely what is the task to be mastered by the new members through their adoption of the accomplishments of ICT and institutional innovation alike. In this context we address in a new chapter the impact of EU enlargement to its broader neighborhood. How far can Europe be stretched, and under what conditions?

Having drafted what is seen as the mainstream of development in Part Two, the following Part Three is devoted to analyzing two *control cases* that seem to defy all economic theories, that of Russia and China. Russia experts tend to be absorbed, up until today, in the view dating back to the Slavophile writer Tutchev claiming that "Russia is by definition unfit for rational reflection". By contrast we claim to be able to interpret Russian stagnation under the Presidency of Boris Yeltsin and recovery under Vladimir Putin in terms of standard economic theories. In our China chapter we are looking for analytical answers to the mystery of sustaining economic growth despite the fact that China follows unconventional policies and disregards the role of formal institutions, considered to be focal in the post-Washington Consensus and in modern economic theory alike. Putting the Chinese experience *in comparative perspective* we try to offer a solution in terms of conventional growth theory, claiming that *there is no Chinese puzzle.* Countries with a potential for major structural changes in favor of more productive activities do have a chance for lasting growth as long as this one-time factor sustains, that is for a decade at least.

Having addressed the case and counter-case, Part Four is on the potential *theoretical inferences.* Here some of the basic policy relevant issues of economics are being addressed. In one chapter the issue of *privatization and regulation* is being addressed. The more the market is seen as an institution, the more important the quality and the form of regulation becomes. Relying on the experience of OECD countries and new public management literature the argument comes up in favor of more competition/market coordination in ever growing areas, while sustaining regulation that allows for transparency and observance of the public good. Finally the big theoretical questions of *how exactly institutions matter for growth, which of them and through what mechanism* are being addressed. In this summary chapter the experience of frontrunner transforming economies and those of other OECD economies are being compared. The importance of *formal* institutions in turning the market a modern and *civilized* arrangement is being underscored.

As can be seen, the attempt is to produce an *overview of major issues*, even without trying to be exhaustive. Not only constraints of time and space, but also the open-ended nature of development calls for temporary, rather than definitive conclusions. Such unexpected crises, as the 1997–99 financial contagion, the burst of the IT bubble, or the implications of software terrorism have shaken the once over-confident mood of analysts. I am sure that the present overview is only one among the possible competing interpretations. If this revised book further triggers professional controversy in the spirit of *sine ira et studio*, all the better.

In writing the monograph I have benefited from the excellent facilities, the library and the intellectual aura of the Central European University. Discussions with my colleagues at the Department of International Relations and European Studies allowed me to improve many shortcomings of the original version of the individual chapters of this book. Most of these have additionally been presented for critical comments to one or more international conferences in Hungary and abroad. The intensive feedback I received from participants allowed me to overcome a number of shortcomings of the original/first/second drafts.

I have profited from working in a multi-disciplinary environment at the CEU with highly motivated post-graduate students in a culture of controversy. My special thanks go to Julius Horvath, Erin Jenne, Róbert Becsky, and Dóra Győrffy, who have read various chapters of my piece line by line, and provided regular critical feedback on style and substance. With the usual caveats their support is greatly appreciated. The publisher improved my text significantly through careful editing. My special indebtedness is due to the late József Kormányos. Some other colleagues working on the specific fields volunteered to read and comment chapters related to their area of specialization. I benefited from these and tried to accommodate most of the criticism that I could. I also benefited from working with my colleagues and PhD students at the Faculty of Economics and Business at the University of Debrecen. While trying to accommodate the inflow of new pieces of information and critical commentary alike, I hope to have managed to keep the structure of the argument of the monograph clear-cut and self-contained. Last but not at all least, the devotion of my family (my wife, Csia/Gabi, our kids, Zoltán and Hedgehog/Orsi) has been a source of energy and inspiration, which I can hardly reciprocate.

Budapest, 28 July 2004

References

AKERLOF, G. A. (1970): The market for 'lemons': quality uncertainty and the market mechanism. *Quarterly Journal of Economics,* vol. 84. no. 3. pp. 488–500.

ARROW, K. J. (1950): A difficulty in the concept of social welfare. *Journal of Political Economy,* vol. 58. no. 2. pp. 328–346.

BARBERIS, N. – HUANG, M. – SANTOS, T. (2001): Prospect theory and asset prices. *Quarterly Journal of Economics,* vol.116. no.1. pp. 1–53.

BARRO, R. – MCCLEARLY, R. (2005): Which countries have state religions? *Quarterly Journal of Economics,* vol. 120 no. 4. (nov) pp. 1331–1370.

BAUMOL, W. (2000): What Marshall did *not* know: The contribution of the 20th century to economics. *Quarterly Journal of Economics,* vol. 115. no. 1. pp. 1–44.

BLANCHARD, O. (1997): *The Economics of Post-Communist Transition.* Oxford: Oxford University Press.

BECKER, G. (1976): *The Economic Approach to Human Behavior.* Chicago and London: The University of Chicago Press.

BECKER, G. (1996): *Accounting for Tastes.* Cambridge/Mass: Harvard University Press.

BOGÁR, L. (2006): *Bokros újratöltve* (Bokros refilled). Budapest: Kairosz Kiadó.

BRABANT, J. van (1998): *The Political Economy of Transition.* London and New York: Routledge.

BUCHANAN, J. M. (1992): *Piac, állam, alkotmányosság* (Market, state and constitutionalism). Budapest: Közgazdasági és Jogi Könyvkiadó.

COLLINS, S. and RODRIK, D. (1991): *Eastern Europe and the Soviet Union in the World Economy.* Washington D. C.: Institute for International Economics.

COLLENDER, S. (2005): Electoral competition in heterogeneous distincts. *Journal of Political Economy,* vol. 113. no. 5. pp. 1116–1145.

CSABA, L. (1984): *Kelet-Európa a világgazdaságban.* Budapest: Közgazdasági és Jogi Könyv-kiadó – revised and extended English edition was subsequently published under the same title as: *Eastern Europe in the World Economy.* Cambridge and New York: Cambridge University Press, 1990.

CSABA, L. (1994): *Az összeomlás forgatókönyvei.* (Scenarios of a collapse). Budapest: Figyelő Kiadói Rt. – an English version was published under the title *The Capitalist Revolution in Eastern Europe.* Cheltenham/UK and Northampton/USA: Edward Elgar Publishing Co., 1995.

CSABA, L. (2002): Transformation as a subject of economic theory. In: BÖNKER, F. – MÜLLER, K. – PICKEL, A. eds: *Post-Communist Transformation and the Social Sciences: Cross-Disciplinary Approaches.* Boulder, Colorado/USA: Rowman and Littlefeld, pp. 39–58.

DJANKOV, S. and MURREL, P. (2002): Enterprise restructuring in transition: A quantitative survey. *Journal of Economic Literature,* vol. 40. no. 3. pp. 739–792.

EDWARDS, F. (1999): Hedge funds and the collapse of LTCM. *Journal of Economic Perspectives,* vol. 13., no. 2. pp. 189–210.

FALCETTI, E. – RAISER, M. – SANFEY, P. (2002): Defying the odds: initial conditions, reforms and growth in the first decade of transition. *Journal of Comparative Economics,* vol. 30. no. 2. pp. 229–250.

GILPIN, R. (2001): *Global Political Economy: Understanding the International Economic Order.* Princeton: Princeton University Press.

GROSECLOSE, T. – MILYO, J. (2005): A measure of media bias. *Quarterly Journal of Economics,* vol. 120 no. 4. pp. 1191–1238.

HANSON, Ph. (2003): *The Rise and Fall of the Soviet Economy (1945–1991).* London: Pearson Education.

HÁMORI, B., (2003): Kísérletek és kilátások – Daniel Kahneman. (Trials and prospects – D. Kahneman). *Közgazdasági Szemle,* vol. 51. no. 9. pp. 779–799.

HIBBS, D. (2001): The politicization of growth theory. *Kyklos,* vol. 54. no. (2–3), pp. 265–286.

HIGGOTT, R. (2004): *From Colonialism to Globalization: a Genealogy of Extraterritorial Politics.* Cambridge: Cambridge University Press.

JOSKOW, P. (2003): 'New institutional economics: a report card' – plenary closing address of the outgoing President to the 7th convention of the International Society for New Institutional Economics, entitled '*Institutions and Change*', Budapest Corvinus University, 11–13 September.

KAHNEMAN, D. and TVERSKY, A. (1979): Prospect theory: An analysis of decisions under risk. *Econometrica,* vol. 47. no. 2. pp. 263–291.

KIRÁLY, J. (1998): A makroökonómia vége, avagy egy megkésett Nobel-díj. (The end of macro-economics, or a belated Nobel Prize). *Közgazdasági Szemle,* vol. 45. no.12. pp. 1082–1095.

KOLODKO, G.W. (2006): *The World Economy and the Great Post-Communist Change.* New York: Nova Science Publishers

KÖVES, A. (1992): *Economic Transformation in Eastern Europe: The International Dimension.* Boulder, Colorado/USA: Westview Press.

KRUEGER, A. ed. (2000): *Economic Policy Reform: The Second Stage.* Chicago and London: Chicago University Press.

LAVIGNE, M. (1995): *The Economics of Transition.* Basingstoke and London: MacMillan.

LAZEAR, E. (2000): Economic imperialism. *Quarterly Journal of Economics,* vol. 115. no. 1. pp. 99–146.

LUCAS, R. E. (1996): Nobel lecture: Monetary neutrality. *Journal of Political Economy,* vol. 104. no. 3. pp. 661–682.

MEIER, G. and STIGLITZ, J. eds (2001): *Frontiers of Development Economics: The Future in Perspective.* Oxford and Washington: Oxford University Press for the World Bank.

MISES, L. von (1920/1976): Economic calculation in the socialist commonwealth. In: NOVE, A. and NUTI, M. D. eds (1976): *Socialist Economics: Selected Readings.* Harmondsworth/UK – New York – Auckland: Penguin, pp. 75–91.

OFER, G. (2001): Development and transition: emerging but merging? In: Ten Years of Transition in Eastern European Countries. *Revue d' Économie Financière,* special issue, no. 10. pp. 107–145.

PORTES, R. (1991): The path of reform in Central and Eastern Europe. *European Economy,* special issue, no. 45. pp. 1–23.

Prescott, E. (2006): The transformation of macroeconomic policy and research. *Journal of Political Economy,* vol. 114. no. 2. pp. 203–235.

ROLAND, G. (2002): The political economy of transition. *Journal of Economic Perspectives,* vol. 16. no. 1. pp. 29–50.

SAINT-PAUL, G. (2000): The new political economy: Recent books by Drazen and by Persson and Tabellini. *Journal of Economic Literature,* vol. 38. no. 4. pp. 915–925.

SAMUELSON, P. and NORDHAUS, W. (1992): *Economics,* vols I–III. New York: McGraw-Hill.

SCHULZ, Th. W. (1973): The value of children: an economic perspective. *Journal of Political Economy,* vol. 81. no. 2. part 2 (March-April), pp. S2–S13.

SRINIVASAN, T. N. (2001): Neoclassical political economy, the state and economic development. In: SRINIVASAN, T. N.: *Economic Policy and State Intervention.* (edited by V. S. Narayana). Delhi: Oxford University Press, pp. 504–530.

STIGLITZ, J. E. (1993): *Economics.* New York: W. W. Norton.

SZENTES, T. (2002): *A Critical Theory of International and Comparative Economics.* Budapest: Akadémiai Kiadó.

TABB, W. K. (1999): Two cultures in economics. In: TABB, W. K.: *Reconstructing Political Economy.* London: Routledge, pp. 1–16.

WAELBROEK, J. (1998): Half a century of development economics. *World Bank Economic Review,* vol. 12. no. 2. pp. 323–352.

WILLIAMSON, J. (1994): In search for a manual for technopols. In: WILLIAMSON, J. ed.: *The Political Economy of Policy Reform.* Washington, D. C., Institute of International Economics, pp. 9– 47.

WILLIAMSON, O. (2000): The new institutional economics: Taking stock, looking ahead. *Journal of Economic Literature,* vol. 38. no. 3. pp. 595–613.

WILLIAMSON, O. (2005): The economics of governance. *American Economic Review,* vol. 96, no. 2. pp 1–18.

3. A COMPARATIVE OVERVIEW OF EMPIRICAL EVIDENCE

Our aim in this chapter is to provide an overview of *facts and figures*. This is necessary both as a preliminary to broader theoretical analyses, as well as a means of tackling some of the issues that have been controversial in the literature. In the following we first look at the distance – if and to what extent catching up is taking place. Then we look at the most basic indicators of economic performance, such as the production and utilization of GDP, social costs of change, the embedding of the transforming countries in the global processes as reflected by trade, finance and investment. Finally we ask if there is anything to be concluded. Our hypothesis to be tested is that *diversity is dominant over common features, thus the Communist past no longer serves as a defining moment* in shaping the quality of economic development. Testing this hypothesis is relatively straightforward: if Communism still is dominant, signs typical of decaying regimes, such as transformational recession, weak core state, and the ensuing corruption, low level of economic activity, structural lagging behind, limited role of FDI, the resource curse, neglect of the information and telecommunication revolution (hereafter ITC), high levels of inflation/shortages, formal, if any, reliance on institutions congruous with those in the EU should be observable in each or most of the cases. If, however, divergence is indeed the name of the game, moreover, if differences that emerge add up to qualitative dissimilarities, path dependence (i.e. the dominant role of the Communist heritage) can no longer be subsumed.

In order to provide a uniform overview, we rely on the comparative regional statistical data series provided until recently by the UN Economic Commission for Europe (ECE), and we support it, when needed, with data provided by the European Bank for Reconstruction and Development (EBRD). This choice, like any other, is contestable. But we do not aim a methodological piece, while official comparative statistics does serve as a starting point for most analytical and policy assessments. Both institutions are intergovernmental, and national authorities have the opportunity to cross-check data, without, however, being able to manipulate them directly. On the other hand, the production of internationally comparable data sets is anything but trivial, given the continuing diversity in national reporting practices. While being aware of the limitations imposed upon us by reliance on borrowed data, *coherence and reliability,* that is good quality of these *may compensate for standardization and loss of 'couleur locale'.* Needless to say, that our assessment may or may not overlap with those of the data providers.

On Catching Up

Overcoming backwardness[1] and catching up with more advanced nations has been a dominant concern over the past two centuries in Central and Eastern Europe.[2] Also, when transition started the belief of immediate welfare gains had been strong, both in the profession and by the public at large. Favorable consequences of discontinuing distortive practices were seen to be trivially at hand. As it is known, instead of the immediate improvement a period of unprecedented recession evolved, that lasted longer and was more costly in terms of jobs and output than most analysts would have expected (more on that in Kornai, 1994 and Winiecki, 2002). As can be seen from *Table 2* in the Appendix, only Central European countries, i.e. a minority from among the transforming economies that managed to surpass the pre-crisis levels of output by 2002.

But it is well known, and documented in numberless sociological surveys, that in open societies, and especially in the age of the information and communications technology revolution people no longer judge their lot on the basis of past experience. The constant comparisons to the Jones', i.e. to neighbors both within the society and across societies is an everyday experience, amply documented by Eurobarometer and many other public opinion surveys. Thus it is equally important to assess if the level of development is now closer to that of the West or not.

If we just glimpse at *Table 1* in the Appendix we see that *'the West' in total has never seen a recession in the 1988–2002 period,*[3] despite frequent statements to the contrary end. If we disentangle numbers we see one single year, 1993, when output in the European Union contracted, by 0.3 per cent. As growth in Western Europe was positive between 0.1 and 4.1 per cent in each of the years, whereas in the United States growth was between 0.4 per cent and 4.4 per cent

---

[1] Several authors have attempted to clarify the meaning of this concept, such as Gerschenkron, Olson, Berend, Landes, and Szentes. Typically the broader the category the less it fits to empirical cases. For our purpose backwardness is defined as the opposite of modernity in the Weberian sense (the totality of social and economic relations in the most advanced countries of the time). Or as Albrow (2002, pp. 21–23) puts it, in contemporary debates the term 'globalization' replaced the term ' modernization' meant to "incorporate hithero excluded countries along the course of which rich countries were already far advanced".

[2] In this book we define as Central Europe the 2004 EU members plus Croatia, Eastern Europe the European New Independent States (NIS), and Southeast Europe and Central Asia as the rest.

[3] Recession is understood to imply four quarters of consecutive contraction at the macroeconomic level, reaching at least 0.75 per cent in the time span of 12 months. This is the definition of the European Central Bank, based on a number of theoretical and practical considerations.

in each year except 1991 (when a drop of 0.6 per cent was recorded), thus *developmental gaps generally widened in the 15 years under scrutiny.* The absolute distance, measured in dollars, grew both between the US and Western Europe, as well as between Western Europe and Central Europe in the longer run. For instance, in 2001 per capita gross national income in Austria was $27 080, while that of Hungary $12 500, of Poland $9 280 and of Russia $8 660 (as reported in the IBRD: *World Development Report, 2003.* London: Oxford University Press, pp. 234–235). Since these numbers already reflect those corrections which are needed for purchasing power parity adjustment, the problem of *distance* is palpable indeed.

Looking at Western Europe the very slow growth of the defining economies of the European Union, particularly of Germany, France and Italy comes to the fore. By contrast the *fastest GDP growth is recorded by the richest EU nation*, Luxemburg. Signs of the much-discussed Irish miracle can be seen, and Finland too, overcoming the crisis of 1992–93, triggered by a poorly timed financial liberalization (Paunio et al, 1993), registers high growth, though a volatile one. All in all, it is telling that *size and success do not seem to correlate* (refuting the literature's obsession with scale economies).

Looking at the Southern members, one observes Greece catching up since 1997, i.e. since the successful switchover from profligate to sound finances (that culminated in this country's joining the euro-zone in 2001). By contrast, numbers of Portugal show the consequences of the Guterres Government neglecting structural reforms and fiscal prudence in 1999–2002. Therefore growth in Portugal, *since 1999, has not been faster than in the core EU.*

In the case of Spain, one of the latecomers both to EU and euro-zone, we can observe a period of serious adjustment in 1992–97. Prior to this period, the Spanish catching up was based on a closed market that was gradually liberalized. Following the 'cure' Spain entered the club of countries with sound money, and growth, this time non-inflationary, also resumed since then. The conservative Aznar Government of 1996–2004 has adhered to fiscal prudence and instituted structural reforms at good times. As a consequence, Spain is one of the few big EU countries that do not struggle for meeting the criteria of the Stability and Growth Pact and is not advocating the softening up of the Pact. Meanwhile, Spanish growth is above the EU average, thus *here catching up continues.*

Already a sketchy overview of the numbers should make us agnostic in terms of a variety of economic theories. *Signs of convergence are not observable*: some countries do catch up, others don't, the richest ones show no sign of decline, whereas poorer ones either must adjust and grow quicker or not. *Size of the country*, often involved by advocates of regional economic integration, *does not seem to matter* that much for success. On the other hand, as we shall elaborate in detail in the concluding chapter of this monograph, the proper mix of policies and institutions do matter. Lacking these, as in German reunification, has indeed lead to ossification and slowdown in the period following 1997. Growth thus is not given either by history or by country size, furthermore *membership in the EU may or may not result in catching up.*

What is also observable from *Table 1* is that sound money does not hibernate growth as suggested by some old-fashioned theories. In Western Europe and in North America in the 15 years under scrutiny *there is no observable trade-off between high growth and low inflation.* As seen in the Greek, Irish and Spanish cases, disinflation based on structural reforms may cost for a while, but not on the long-term growth path. Also conversely, low inflation per se is not a panacea for growth, if other structural factors inhibit innovation and organizational change, as in Germany, France and Italy.

There does not seem to exist a nexus between developmental level and good policies (as first explained by Rüdiger Dornbusch, 1993). Less advanced countries do not seem to be pre-judged for inflationary policies. By contrast, adopting a sound fiscal stance, based on structural reforms, does allow less developed countries to grow quickly. Actually, in the longer run they may grow more quickly than leading economies. Thus catching up, is though not predetermined, still *a potential* for them. This *'conditional convergence'* seems to hold for countries at the higher medium level of development/income. Leading countries, on the other hand *do not seem to lag automatically behind,* as the secularly slower productivity growth in their economies might imply, only for it is more difficult for them to grow. The United States, possessing with the deepest and broadest system of financial intermediation, plus with the centers of innovation/endogenous growth, is not bound to lose out. Nor do less developed countries possess an unlimited access card to prosperity. In a way, there is empirical evidence for selecting more relevant economic theories and delineating these from less relevant ones, at least for own analytical purpose.

Production and Performance of the Transforming Economies

Overall economic performance is measured, despite difficulties,[4] by GDP growth and level, since this is accepted as a synthetic indicator for all activities that have a price.[5] Despite some de-modernization in the first transition years, when self-sufficiency ventures proliferated, transforming countries are *typically unlike developing countries* owing to their higher level of industrialization, urbanization and human capital formation (emphasized esp. in Ofer, 2001, pp. 118–128). Therefore it does make sense to apply this measure for the subject or our analysis.

---

[4] It is common knowledge that each indicator, especially ones expressed in money terms, has drawbacks. This is the reason why the World Bank in the above cited publication uses a series of indices, based on the Human Development Indicators, developed originally by a competing agency, UNCTAD, uses purchasing power parity (PPP) adjustments, as well as Gross National Income. Furthermore GDP, especially for long run comparison, is vulnerable to structural changes. Most glaringly, 100 per cent in our ECE tables is qualitatively different in 1989 than in 1999. But no overview is possible without compromises, even if there always is a cost.

[5] Household activities, that account for about 30 per cent of all human activities related to wealth creation and subsistance, do not carry a price. Production for own uses, home care of the elderly and of the sick, for instance do not carry a price, while the same services provided in a hospital do so.

In terms of GDP, recovery and growth, Poland, Slovenia, Albania and Hungary take the lead[6] with only Poland being obviously better off (if we, following Jánossy, (1966), allow for the trend rate of growth that would have occurred under non-crisis circumstances). The group of laggards was composed of Serbia, having fought three wars and suffering disintegration of the state structures, followed by Latvia and Lithuania, all carrying the Soviet heritage. In a way, this empirical finding runs counter to the perception of the Baltic wonder, but is in line with what was to be expected from economic structures torn out, after six decades, from the unified Soviet space. Also, economic structures in the Baltic States had been planned, for decades, under all-Soviet considerations. Therefore self-sufficiency, or viability in a different state construct surely had not figured among the priorities of planners. The disruption of relationships with the former Soviet Union and disorganization in general must have played a major role. Inflow of foreign direct investment (FDI) has been less, up until the late 1990s, than to Estonia, and reform policies in both countries have been less radically reformist/free marketeer.

By contrast, *radical therapy did work in Poland and Eastern Germany, though with a different degree of efficiency*. It was these two countries where recession was the shortest, and both activity levels and income started to recover, already in 1992 (two years ahead of the rest of the frontrunner group). The radical approach, for which shock therapy has been a misnomer (more on that in Murrel, 1992), implied that growth resumed already after a short initial period, from 1992 in East Germany and from 1993 in Poland. The respective societies *had to suffer for less protracted periods* than, say in Ukraine or Romania, where soft policies wanted to avoid the initial sharp fall in output and employment. In the longer run, however, other factors than the initial policies shaped outcomes. In case of Eastern Germany, already from 1997 onwards, catching up has come to a halt, much earlier than equalization of development level (a politically set, economically never justified, goal) could have materialized. As a vast German and English language literature had proven, conditions for self-sustaining growth have not materialized in the new provinces. This had to do primarily with the politically set exchange rate between Eastern and Western Mark and the politically pre-ordained equalization of wages irrespective of productivity. This situation was only exacerbated by the employment destroying consequences of transplanting West German corporatism to the new provinces. Therefore continuation of *transfers*, adding up to 5 per cent of West German GDP, *could not replace lacking endogenous sources of growth*. By contrast, Poland entered a path of sustaining growth, with only 2002 being a first year where this period has come to a temporary end. Whereas the extreme fall of output in ex-GDR can be accounted for the combination of an overvalued exchange rate and a wage hike, completely detached from productivity gains. In Poland the fall of output *had not been deeper, but lasted shorter* than in fellow-traveller countries.

[6] Mind that some countries have different starting points, thus the numbers, such as Bosnia-Herzegovina's staggering 280 p.c actually reflect the very low starting level, not a return to the Yugoslav normalcy levels.

Looking across the region, we can observe the resumption of growth from 1994 onward. The true dividing line is, however not this year, but the longer run view: if this has proven *sustainable* (as in Hungary and Poland and Slovenia, in Bulgaria and Albania after 1997) or not, as in the case of Romania and the Czech Republic. The onset of growth took much longer in the New Independent States (NIS),[7] thus despite impressive current growth rates in the post-1999 period both Russia and even more Ukraine have still a long way to go in regaining their lost output levels, thus incomes.

Our *Table 2* also shows that the recovery of growth is by no means automatic, and countries like Croatia, Bulgaria and Ukraine seem to struggle with the resultant problems, both in the economy and in society. What we can also observe, rushing ahead for a moment to *Table 5*, that *there is no single case where growth could have been resumed without stabilization.* This finding, with the benefit of hindsight, depreciates contemporary suggestions aiming at 'alternative economic policies', that is a combination of Keynesian demand management with growth generating policies, at the cost of de-emphasizing stabilization and liberalization. Meanwhile, stabilization does not automatically trigger growth, especially not lasting and robust growth needed for catching up. In other words, the options of delaying stabilization, of slowing down privatization and other institutional reforms, of trying to save old jobs and corporations, *has not paid off in any single case,* in terms of wealth and income. We abstract from the extreme case of Belarus, where the quality of economic reporting, plus available information does not allow for giving a solid picture.

Moving to the *Commonwealth of Independent States (CIS)* the truly important first insight is that though the performance of the post-Soviet space is obviously dominated by Russia,[8] thus the two co-evolve, the overlap is less than complete. Contrary to the impression one may gain from studying Russian sources of the 1990s, *Russia is not an outlayer, a representative of catastrophic failure.* It is important to call attention to the optical misperception caused by the regional standardization by the ECE Secretariat. The fact that 1989 is taken as a baseline year covers up the important fact that in Russia the *contraction of economic activity started already in 1989, and 1992 was a year of disintegration.*[9] Thus a 21.2 percent drop of activity should by no means be attributed to transformation, whatever we think about the merits and de-merits of contemporary poli-

---

[7] The reasons for this delay are explained by the fact that transformation in the NIS started two years later; strictly speaking the years 1992–1994 have been spent on state building, NOT reforms. While there was talk of reforms in each of the new independent states, in reality, crisis-management was dominant. More on that in our Russia chapter, and the literature quoted therein.

[8] Russia alone accounts for about two thirds of the joint GDP of NIS/CIS, two terms used interchangeably.

[9] Let us recall: in 1992 no reform policies were instituted in Ukraine or Kazakhstan. For Russia, keeping the ruble area and a restive Supreme Soviet, managing monetary policies towards hyperinflation obviously dominated those reform endeavors that used to stand in the focus of attention of contemporaries, as well as of retrospective theorizing. For a broad empirical substantiation of this point (cf. i.e. Dabrowski, ed. 1993 and Gaidar, ed. 1998.)

cies. As a matter of fact this Russian – and the comparable Ukrainian – figure is indicative of *a recession evolving without any transformation-related policies.* In other words, the old regime had not been in any kind of equilibrium. Its decay started before anybody touched the basics of the Soviet economy. In yet other words, *not all of the decline* could and should be accounted under the heading of *transformational* recession.

If we take account of this circumstance, the truly *transformation-related* recession in Russia and Ukraine had been neither deeper nor more protracted than in Central and Eastern Europe. On the other hand, given that the two contractionary factors were added together, the recovery of the Putin/Kuchma years must be seen in proper perspective. Russia in 2002 was still only at 68 per cent of its pre-crisis levels, Ukraine at 47.3 per cent only. First: these are *by no means identical performances.* Knowing the procrastination and foot-dragging in Ukraine, the superior performance of Russia per se is a proof of reform-oriented policies delivering better results on the same grounds/ruins. In other words: whereas in the early 2000s these two countries may have looked as truly emerging growth poles in Europe, the level of activity should not be forgotten.[10] If we rely on ECE numbers, Russian economic activity in 2006 should be still below pre-crisis maximum.

It is an important follow-up insight from this analysis, supported by monographic assessments of the empirical detail (e.g. Réthi, 2003; Mau and Starodubrovskaia, 2001) that in the period of 1991–1994 there emerged a major drift between discourse and reality in Russia. Whereas discourse – and related discourse analysis – focused on competing reform projects, on monetarists and structuralists, centrists and those searching for a national model of the economy, reality had been dominated by day-to-day *crisis management coupled with state building.* It is much too easily forgotten that Russia did not use to have its own administration, that state borders had been undefined and contested, that CIS countries could (mis)use the ruble until 1994. As contemporary insider reports (Aslund and Layard, eds, 1993) testify, the hectic reformist program-writing co-existed with daily crisis management run by parallel power structures. Moreover, a lack of elementary co-ordination among various dimensions and activity levels within the partly reformed, partly inherited Russian government apparatus has sustained during 1991–1994. Many analysts attribute the outburst of the first Chechen War in 1994 to the erosion of central command structures all across the state, thus letting the spontaneously privatizing generals loose.

Only after the conquest of the Supreme Soviet in October 1993 and the subsequent elections of December 1993 had an anchor, in the form of an elected

---

[10] These numbers are disputed in the literature, most intensively by Aslund (2002, chapter 3). He provides a detailed – though contested – methodology of showing how much of production was unwanted, useless for consumers etc. While much of his arguments may hold, at least to a degree, it looks over-ambitious to me to discard all official reporting, national and international, while aspiring for coherence in the long-run analysis. Technical assistance has certainly improved the quality of most regional statistics during the 1990s.

and universally accepted Presidency (and a much weakened legislation), emerged. At the level of practical policies only from 1994 onwards could one conceive a policy of stabilization, with the monetary monopoly of *Centrobank* re-introduced (and the ruble zone dissolved), with the central bank and government acting in concert, and a government having at least some formal powers to collect revenues from the subordinated federal subjects. Therefore it is legitimate to take 1994, rather than 1989, as a starting point of Russian market reforms, if real processes rather than discourses/history of thought is the subject of analysis.

Under this angle, the cumulated output loss of 17 percentage points, spread over five years until 1998, is fully in concordance with the Central European experience. *Neither depth nor length is extreme.* Following the devaluation of the Russian currency in August 1998, triggered by the contagion in Asia, *the Russian economy tended to react much in a textbook-like manner,* by increasing exports, making use of protection, thus utilizing import substituting opportunities, and benefiting from the windfall oil revenues in 2000–2004. It has long been devoted to what extent this recovery is a result of one-time measures, and to what extent represent just changes on the margins (cf. Hanson, 2003; Csaba, 2002; Yasin, 2003). More recent econometric evidence (Voigt, 2006) has shown the importance of institutional measures limited and subordinate to windfall at best. But these facts are supportive of earlier findings (Rostowski, 1997, pp. 230–231) highlighting: it is misleading and inappropriate to compare the post-Soviet collapse to the Great Depression of 1929–1933, since the *components, causes and mechanisms are unlike.*

It is equally mis-perceived to rehash without commentary the contemporary talk about the crisis of transformation, for much of this decline had to do with economic *consequences of imperial disintegration.* The latter has been taking place in mostly unreformed or only marginally reformed environments. The fact that much of contemporary production used to be, at more realistic prices, value-deducing at the macroeconomic level, thus their discontinuation has been desirable, was no secret to contemporary analysts (e.g. Winiecki, 1991; Hare and Hughes, 1992). Thus it cannot and should not be taken as ex post rationalization of suffering on ideological grounds. If this holds, Anders Aslund does have a point in stating that part of the collapse is a statistical artifact (though it is not settled as yet, on exactly how large a part of it is that). All in all, Russia looks more like any *small open economy* in transition than the unique creature postulated by Slavophile intellectual heritage.

To sum up the Russian experience: 1989–1993 should be treated in terms of disintegration of the Soviet Empire and the one party state. Economic disintegration, having started already during the Soviet era, had been continuing in these years, despite the recurring crisis-management programs of Ryzhkov, Pavlov, Gaidar, Chernomyrdin One and Two Governments in a row. Creation of a nation-state and a presidency, avoidance of disintegration along Yugoslav lines were the priorities that had been accomplished. In 1994–1998 we observe five years of *transformational recession* that can be interpreted, by and large, along the theory distilled from Central European experience.

The major difference is twofold: one is the federal structure and the ensuing fiscal federalism (first implicit, later more explicit), and the second is the 1996 Presidential election. It took place just in the middle of the period, thus recreating what Lenin used to call the 'primacy of politics'. As long as the Constitution of December 1993 has turned Russia into a Presidential Republic, while Boris Yeltsin has never won free elections before 1996, the stakes were high indeed. Finally the 1999–2006 period represents a single unit. Here *consolidation of power* is reflected by the first ever peaceful hand-over of power in Russian history, the following strengthening of the central state (both against subject of the Russian Federation and against business interest), a resulting improvement of tax collection (from 8 to 21 per cent of GDP to the federal coffers according to EIU (2006) estimates). This 'grace period' has greatly been assisted by sustainingly high oil prices on the world market (a windfall, since Russia has no leverage over them), as well as by the restructuring of international alliances following the terrorist attacks on the United States on 11 September 2001. The strategic appreciation of Russia as an ally of the West assisted the centralizing tendencies of the Presidency, and saved it from the international backlash that otherwise could have been expected. Rushing to *Table 11*, however, indicates, that the inflow of FDI has hardly exceeded the levels that emerged since 1995, thus *the overall business climate and the quality of economic system can hardly be judged as fundamentally improved.*

Let us recall: the NIS should, by no means, be equated with its internationally most exposed member, Russia. Looking at *Table 2* we can observe the *real bottom cases.* These are *Georgia*, plagued by a civil war and tendencies toward disintegration (Abkhazia, Pankisi Gorge, Osetiia and the spillover of the first and second Chechen wars). According to ECE, activity levels stand at one third of the pre-crisis levels, which is worse than in war-torn Yugoslav successor states.

Another bottom case is the *Republic of Moldova.* Here again civic unrest, the unresolved problem of the internationally non-acknowledged, still defiant Transdniestrian Republic, as well as soft policies and state failure, that catapulted in 2001 the Communists back to power, explain much of the failure. The outlayer position of the country may also have contributed, and so did slow privatization and miniscule FDI.

The third poorest performer within the NIS is *Tajikistan.* Here civil war lasted for several years and could be concluded only thanks to a Russian understanding with Tehran, with the latter limiting the support of the Islamist rebel forces. While war is over, borders are still protected by Russian, rather than Tajik, troops. The spillover of the ongoing civil strife in Afghanistan, though no longer in the focus of the international press, poses a severe threat to the integrity of this country. We must take into account that Tajikistan, like other Central Asian states, is basically an artificial creature of the Soviets. Ethnic Tajiks live, to a large degree in other countries, including Afghanistan. Nation building, following the European middle-class model has not even started. Markets are at the level typical of underdeveloped countries. In sum, it is no surprise to see weak overall performance sustaining. The landlocked and distant position of the country is no lure for FDI.

Last but not at all least, a country of France's population, *Ukraine* needs to be mentioned. It could be seen from the very outset (van Selm, 1997) that there is a puzzle inherent in Ukrainian independence. On the one hand, all endowments, natural and human factors would have predestined the country for prosperity. On the other hand, the *inappropriate policies, weak institutions, corroding corruption and lasting inaction* could develop into factors seriously hindering development. Stabilization took much longer, privatization was much slower, and according to the regular surveys of the EBRD (2006), institution building much less successful than in Russia, let alone Poland. The impressive growth rates of the post-1999 periods have still left the Ukraine with about half of its pre-crisis GDP levels, that is comparable to a post-war situation. Low activity levels are known to be harmful to social capital and a divided oligarchic power structure breeds developmental vicious circles, much discussed in the literature.

We should address some of the *queer success stories* of the NIS. These are led by Uzbekistan, followed by Turkmenistan. Uzbekistan, having palpably surpassed the pre-crisis level of activity figures on par with Central Europeans, and also the performance of Turkmenistan is much better than that of the Baltics. Last but not at all least, mention should be made of the pariah state of Europe, Belarus, led by the populist leader, the re-elected President Lukashenka. Surprisingly, the economic indicators are not so bad[11] as the name of the country is, and the traditional explanation, of Russia paying the bill, also does not seem to be supported by ECE data for the post-2000 period.

In order to explain these cases, the role of *special circumstances* needs to be considered. First, as long as a – despotic, but somehow still functioning – state is in existence, this allows those in power to co-ordinate economic processes via bureaucratic co-ordination, much the same way as Communists managed to eschew open crises in the 1970s and 1980s. A couple of further factors need to be considered, that apply basically to the two Central Asian cases.

1. The *resource-based*, mono-cultural economy allows for the continued existence of centralized systems, as evidenced inter alia by the Middle East. Such a structure does not require and allow for more sophisticated forms of control.

2. The *traditional society*, based on clans and the extended family, the authority of the elder is still around. This is a fertile ground for centralized policies.

3. *Nation building from above*, as typical in post-colonial settings, is in the making. This state and nation building is often perceptible to the cult of the leader, who embodies the nation. The dynastic marriage between the Kazakh and the former Kyrgiz rulers have already let a taste of it to be felt. But the Uzbek and Turkmen leadership is of the same genre.

4. Both countries entertain *special relationship* to the former colonial power, *in*

---

[11] In so far as Belorussian indicators, without exception, are above the average of the NIS, this may seem as a relative success in its own category.

terms of security and in terms of the latter's tolerating non-payments. The penetration of the US at the turn of the century and following 9/11 appreciated the local leaders as 'bastions and guardians of stability in the region', in the fight against terrorism.

5. Finally we should not forget what is an established fact (cf. Drábek, 1986; Rosefielde, 2003) that statistics *do tend to be manipulated, the more centralized the political system, the stronger*. A post-despotic government will have to spend a lot of time and energy on settling this problem, as experiences in the former East Germany, Bulgaria, Albania and Romania have amply demonstrated.

Summary View

Overviewing macroeconomic performance from the production side has shown *distinct categories* among the post-Communist countries. Only Central Europeans may qualify as a success. It is surprising and runs against the widespread perceptions to see the Baltic States, Southeast Europe and Russia in the same – *medium* – category.

It is hard to overlook that *historic* and *political processes*, leading to the disintegration of formerly existing, and somehow still functioning states *dominate over economic strategies*.[12] Whatever 'system designers' or advisors or changing elites conceived and theorized, this remained subordinate to such processes as war, disintegration, un-settled armed conflicts and the legacy of the eroding imperial bureaucracy. Kirgyzstan, having adopted several times radical policies, may be a case in point.

Colonial heritage does seem to matter. The longer a country spent in the Soviet Empire, the more it adapted its institutions, strategies and behavioral norms to Soviet needs/commands, the higher these costs were to be (Winiecki, 1991). And indeed, if we look at the numbers of the Baltic States, or the depth of the transformational recession in Eastern Germany, it is hard to eschew this conclusion.

The *resource base* also seems to matter, though much less than traditional trade theories and endowment-based views would have suggested. In case of sophisticated, industrialized, urbanized countries like Ukraine, availability of these was of no big help. By contrast, in the traditional Central Asian societies, at least in the first 15 years, resource abundance helped to avoid the worst, even if it seems to carry the danger of resource curse for the future.

We cannot identify any common trajectory, especially not along the lines of policies adopted. Circumstance mattered, as did choice, but their interaction has proven to be much more complex than abstract theories and initial policy suggestions would have had it. Since this point has been neatly elaborated in the literature, with reliance on a broad analytical-econometric arsenal (de Melo et al, 2001) let us just reiterate, that the concept of 'optimal policy mix', or 'opti-

---

[12] A refreshing new inititative, trying to revert the vicious circle is offered by the normative-analytical book by (Collier et al, 2003).

mal transition trajectory' does not seem to carry analytical value,[13] if applied to empirical processes rather than narrowly defined models. In other words, *there is no common standard against which the success of post-Communist transitions could be measured*. Optimality therefore, unlike in general economics, is not a relevant conception for our subject matter.

As we have seen, except for Russia, *the European NIS is not part of emerging Europe* in the sense we defined this term in the Foreword. This might be an important finding and a message to policy-makers on both sides of the Atlantic. The crux of the matter is that the collapse of the 'evil empire' has not, by itself, led to the solution of problems created by it. Rather *a multiplication of local conflicts in poorly researched areas might* be probable. Elaborating a meaningful good neighborhood policy for the EU has already been suffering delays, and the version published in July 2004 – 'anything but instituions' – was a declaration of good will, rather than an operational policy strategy.

In the area of Central Asia typical *post-colonial economies and societies* emerged with problems typical for these (including oppression, ethnic strife and the vulnerability to Islamic fundamentalism). It is important not to mistake the formal stability of despotic regimes for actual strength, a fallacy that was widely spread in the late 1980s, when Gorbimania dominated analytical insights. Outside observers (Sachdeva, 2003, pp. 250–253) highlighted the vulnerability of these regimes and attribute partial success to the geo-strategic appreciation of the region, however not to sound or improving fundamentals. This may not bode well for the long term future. Let us also add, that the *countries in the Caucasus* may be even more of a problem, with a history and evolution resembling to a large degree to what we observe in the Balkans. Euro-Atlantic involvement may already be too little and too late for paving the way for peaceful economic development. European NIS also deserve more attention than the tendency of 'passing over responsibility to Moscow, the regional leader' would imply.

In a way, our findings are supportive of Leo Tolstoy's introductory words to Anna Karenina, explaining that while all happy marriages are the same, all unhappy ones are different. As already the first overview suggests, and later analysis will elaborate, this has indeed been the case with the transforming economies, where failure has been more widespread than success. In the following we turn to the decomposition of performance, first looking at how GDP has been utilized, thus how living conditions have changed during the years of transition, therefore how societies are likely to assess the process of 'great transformation', to borrow Karl Polányi's over-used phrase (1964) for the evolution of the market order.

---

[13] Optimality is a concept that relates to the objective function, that is *externally* given, either by value maximization, or through public choice, or via an analytical concept/model valid for all countries (as early modernization theories of American political science tended to assume in the '50s and '60s). As the comparative survey quoted above shows in great detail, some countries, like Mongolia and Kirgyzstan, have actually outperformed their 'trend rate', despite weak overall performance in quantitative-statistical terms.

Utilization of Gross Domestic Product

Moving to *Table 3* and *4* in the Appendix gives us an idea about how GDP produced was utilized. This matters on both accounts. On the one hand, consumption is the final goal of economic activity, and in the longer run, especially in democratic societies, voters judge the economic performance (and in part, the governmental efficiency) of those in power by the material progress these have or have not brought about. On the other hand, consumption and investment, i.e. the future consumption and current consumption by definition compete in each moment of time. Therefore a major dilemma for any policymaker, and particularly for those acting under grave uncertainty (due to the institutional vacuum and new rules of the game), *is how to balance between now and the future.*

Our *Tables* present a long-term process, thus allow for some generalizations. Under this angle, Poland, Slovenia and Croatia take the lead (in case of Estonia numbers run only from 1993, which must have been the bottom year of transformational recession, thus the indicator is not comparable with the rest of the table). Poland and Slovenia are among the star performers, whereas in the Croatian case the 1991 starting year (presumably about 10 per cent below the pre-crisis level a decade later) does not make the picture that impressive. Moreover, as Croatia has not assumed any responsibility for Yugoslav debt, this amplified the elbow room for governmental policies. In sum, in the frontrunner country group *economic performance and consumption growth has been strongly correlated.*

Among the poorest performers we find Kirgyzstan, Latvia and Kazakhstan, not however Russia. In case of Kirgyzstan poor economic performance, in case of Kazakhstan also the concentration of wealth may have played a role, that is characteristic of resource dependent authoritarian regimes. In the Latvian case the cost of reorientation was high. The banking crises of the mid-90s have shaken confidence in the financial sector. Finally, political turbulence (governmental instability) remained deterring factors.[14] The inclusion of Latvia *warns us from lumping all Baltic countries together*, just because they happen to be small nations.

It is important to see that several countries *have still to achieve the pre-crisis consumption levels;* in other cases it took nearly a decade to regain lost levels. The major exception is Poland, where by 1993 (sic!) consumption levels regained their previous (though not very impressive) levels. Also in Eastern Germany consumption grew quickly, mostly unrelated to economic performance, by way of transfers and artificially low prices, e.g. for housing. This was strengthened by the widespread occurrence of two pension households (in West Germany one pension households are dominant).

---

[14] One may wonder, if this was another case of state failure leading to market failure; with state failure the deep divisions in the elite groups as well as the drift of society into Latvians and Russians (by half) might have contributed to the unfavorable outcome. The resulting weak institutions, banking crises and governmental fragility, of course, only add to this chain of mishaps.

Interestingly, and in line with what we observed with overall activity levels, the bottom year in terms of consumption *seems to be largely unrelated to initial policies*. This means no more and no less that the *debate* on shock therapy versus gradualism, radical or socially sensitive alternatives, *has been largely misplaced*. In case of Bulgaria 1997, in case of Latvia 1995, in case of Slovakia 1994, in Russia 1999 and in Kyrgizstan 1997 was the worst in terms of personal consumption. This finding indicates that also in terms of consumption, the end result of economic activity is a function of a variety of factors. The contribution (or the responsibility) of policies of the government, especially measures related to transforming the economic system, might well have been heavily overemphasized in explaining the outcomes. What is clear from available evidence is that *countries that have been delaying their reforms, for whatever reasons, suffered more and longer*, than ones that managed to implement sound policies. This means no more and no less, that *policies also matter* (cf. Havrylyshyn and van Rooden, 2003, arguing in the same line).

Last but not at all least, consumption levels do not immediately and fully correlate to activity indicators. This reflects the circumstance that the decision between consumption and investment, growth and debt, saving and consumption is always and everywhere a *political/public choice*. Weak governments in Moldova, might well be unable to withstand pressures for more redistribution and government sponsored consumption. On the other hand, strong governments, as the Czech or the Hungarian ones in the 1990s, could effectively withstand the usual pressure for more immediate consumption.

Turning to *investment*, it needs to be stressed that economic science knows precious little about the way investment and growth is correlated (Blomström et al, 1996; Solow, ed. 2001; Erdős, 2003 offers a broad analysis of the literature and competing interpretations). What is clear is that investment and growth *are related*, that the relation is conditioned largely by the system of *financial intermediation* and that growth is finally a function of *innovation*, that may or may not be endogenized, depending on the theory concerned. The role of *allocation* has particularly been highlighted by the failure of the socialist experiment, with the East European economies requiring 5–7 per cent more investment per annum to attain similar or even less growth in the 1950–1985 period, than their West European counterparts did (Heitger, 1991 provided detailed statistical evidence for this point). Since the interconnection between growth, policies and institutions is one of the focal points in economic theory, we shall come back to these broader issues in the concluding chapter of this monograph, on 'Institutions and growth.'

What we know currently more than in previous monographs is twofold. One that *the size of* investment is positively related to growth, it does matter. Thus sustainingly low investment levels do not allow for high growth rates to sustain (a point proven on general considerations for Hungary e.g. by Darvas and Simon, 2000). Second, that high rate of investment, on their own, do not guarantee the 'everlasting' growth, as the East Asian crisis of 1997–1999 has amply demonstrated. In other words, in line with established insights from economic theory, the *allocation mechanism* and related institutions also matter for success.[15] These are the points under which we survey the investment data presented in *Table 4* of the Appendix. In this latter respect we also are aware that the idea of creating capital markets quickly, of making the *equity market the major mechanism of capital allocation,* as advocated by adherents of mass privatization, *has nowhere materialized in the region*. Therefore, the efficiency of allocation does remain a problem, even though reliance on external capital market financing in countries where FDI and resultant asset ownership by foreigners is substantial, does alleviate the problem.

These considerations prop up when we look at *Table 4*. The leading country is Croatia, where again the later starting point needs to be considered. Still, even accounting for that we can observe a high investment–low growth scenario, that is in line with what we know of continued state dominance of the Croatian banking system (until the 2001–2002 period). The second in the ranking is Poland, known for its high investment-high growth scenario. However, the slowdown in 2002–2003 is indicative of the limitations of growth by more factor accumulation alone. The third in the ranking is Slovenia, another quickly growing transition country. Interestingly, and in line with macroeconomic theory, *in the long term perspective more investment and more consumption go hand in hand* (and vice versa).

In the group of laggards we find Armenia, where *state failure* and the still largely *unsettled military conflict* with Azerbaijan, the role of Russian troops and the resultant *lasting uncertainty* are no good signs for investors. In the second worst place, unsurprisingly, we find Ukraine, where overall conditions are known to be generally business hostile. This is dominant despite recurring lavish tax exemptions granted by a cash-strapped government, wishing to create an independent, westward-looking economy (van Zon, 2000). *Capital flight* in the last few years also emerged. Last but not at all least this group includes Russia, where capital flight in the 2000s account for 25 to 30 (!) per cent of recorded export intakes. The latter number excludes shuttle traders, *chelnoki*, accounting for a substantial part of Russian trade and the social safety net alike. This fact allows for at least two conclusions to be drawn. First, the emphasis in international fora on rescheduling Soviet debt as a major policy component (alternatively as a leverage) has been grossly *overrated* in the entire post-1992 period.[16] Second, the Putin presidency, despite a number of measures at structural reforms instituted in 2000–2006, fell short of convincing Russian domestic investors of the virtues and profits of *investing at home* rather

---

[15] This should have been self evident following the Communist experience when lastingly high rates of investments could only temporarily compensate for consequences of mis-allocation of resources – a major cause of the slowdown of Soviet growth.

[16] This is trivial, since the officially reported amounts of capital flight/current account surpluses, cumulated since 1992, would have more than sufficed to pay back all Soviet time outstandings. On the other hand, as Sutela (2004, chapter 2) unfolds, the first years of Russian transformation have been dominated on how large an injection of external money could allow for even softer fiscal policies than could be observed. The latter thus seems to have been fully misplaced in view of the numbers we have.

than abroad.[17] If we take account of the still existing home bias in international financial flows, this must be taken as a warning sign in terms of the *savings-investment-growth chain* in the longer run. This also implies that import substitution and oil windfalls rather than long-term measures that accounted for the growth of the 1999–2006 period.

Summing up of what has been said of the utilization of GDP, we see a recovery of investment activities in most of the region. The robustness of this is at great variance among the individual cases. Investment levels in Southeast Europe and the NIS are *still quite low*, even if we accept the argument that the initial levels must have been inflated, largely predetermined by the system-specific needs of the Soviet imperial structures and the resultant inefficiency. Meanwhile, the co-evolution of investment and consumption in the longer run is yet another testimony of the Central European economies 'becoming normal countries'.[18] On the other hand, the extreme numbers for Azerbaijan, showing 500 per cent of the investment level and 105 per cent of the consumption level of the pre-crisis period in 2002 are clear indications of over-investment. This holds even if statistical series start in 1992, not in 1989, thus the numbers are not automatically comparable with the rest. The very high investment rate in GDP is hardly questionable, and its efficiency looks doubtful. In other words, not even FDI is a panacea. Also the very high Slovenian number might reflect low investment efficiency, that is congruent with what we know of a basically non-privatized, insider dominated banking system in that country.

The Social Side of Transformation: Inflation and Unemployment

There emerged a clear consensus by now, with the subduing of 'non-conventional' and 'experimental' economic approaches of the early years of transformation, that not only growth and private property matter, but so do inflation and unemployment; sound policies controlling both are at the heart of policy tasks in any country in the region (cf. the account of Kolodko, 2001). Not many analysts would doubt by now that high rates of inflation, especially from over the moderate levels of 20–30 per cent per annum, are harmful for savings and investment calculation, lead to misallocation of resources and distort normal incentives to economic agents, thereby undermine possibilities for a non-bureaucratic co-ordination of macroeconomic processes. As inflation, by its very nature, constitutes a hidden redistribution of income and wealth, it is particularly harmful for the socially weak and vulnerable, such as pensioners and

[17] Retroactive levying of 1.5 bn $ taxes on BP/TNK, one of the biggest investor, was a recent example as reported in: *Financial Times*, 1 December, 2006.

[18] It is quite important, since the more abstract transition literature, generalizing basically the Russian/NIS experience considers the collapse of investments and their sustaining inefficiency as a major proof of the failure of overall transition strategies *grosso modo*. Our intention is to highlight the marked and empirically proven *difference* among the various country groups, with only Central Europeans becoming 'normal' and the rest drifting into 'developing' economies.

others living on transfer incomes. This insight has lead even those who used to be more lenient on inflation to adopt a conservative line (Fischer and Burton, 1998), calling for an organic but continuous disinflation, and considering *low levels of inflation an accomplishment on its own right*. Likewise, unemployment is not treated any longer with the ease of the early years, when many analysts believed that the tertiary sector and the rebound of the new private sector will simply absorb any amount of people sacked from the eroding state industry and from public sector payrolls. As can be deduced from *Table 5* in the Appendix, *average unemployment levels in Central and Eastern Europe by the first half of the 2000s has exceeded 15 per cent*, or fifty percentage points higher than in the eurozone, where this is understood to be the major social challenge. Unemployment is known to be a threat to the social fabric, undermining social capital, and leading to vicious circle phenomena. Whether or not the natural rate hypothesis of the 2006 Nobel winner Edmund Phelps holds, according to this the value of it for the USA should be in the range of 4 per cent,[19] thus the numbers registered in the transforming economies is legitimately considered to be *extreme*.

One of the most contested issues of course has been if and to what extent massive unemployment is a price for disinflation to sustain, or in other words, if and to what extent the Phillips curve holds for post-Communist countries. The applicability of the idea had been advanced (Rostowski, 1999, chapter 1), however comparing *Table 5* and *6* does not lend support to this claim, as we shall explain below, in line with the original insight of Milton Friedman (1968) as well as of its reformulation by Robert Lucas, quoted in the Foreword.

A glimpse at *Table 5* allows to recall some basic features of *inflation under post-Communist conditions*. Without reiterating country experiences, regularly reported by the *Transition Report* of EBRD, as well as the analytical chapters of *Economic Survey of Europe*, some defining features come to mind.

First, in line with global experience in the 20th century, *if and when formal institutions disintegrate*, especially if federal states fall apart, *inflation is on the increase*. Actually, as Latin American countries have shown, but also the disintegrating African states, when there is no central authority, price rises are not to be stopped. Very few counter-examples are known, such as the introduction of the Czechoslovak crown in 1918 that registered even years of deflation. Normally, while only one (or none) of the central fiscal authorities collect revenues, several of the new authorities spend, among others on arms and creating new administrative structures. Thus the eruption of inflation is by and large inevitable, and the post-Soviet and post-Yugoslav experiences are both cases in point. But if one thinks of the rise of local powers, both in Russia and Ukraine, inside Serbia, or of the power vacuum that existed after the collapse of formal authority in Albania or in Bosnia, the eruption and sustaining of inflation is by no means surprising. At the end of the day there are two fundamental reasons for inflation. First, the government finances its expenditures

---

[19] Niskanen (2002, p. 193) puts it to 3.7 per cent with zero inflation; a formal proof is presented in the article.

by printing money or credit emission, irrespective of the macroeconomic consequences. Second, being weak, the central authorities are unable to resist pressure groups calling for more outlays (subsidies) debt forgiveness. Thereby they spend more than it originally intended. The outcome is either shortage or inflation (in extreme cases, as in the last years of socialism, both).

Second, if controls are lifted, while prices had been distorted, for a long time, and shortages prevail, a one-shot *corrective inflation* is by and large inevitable, if for no other reason than because of technical difficulties of and information-al shortages in managing money supply under the new conditions. This does not need to last longer than a few months. But under conditions of transition from dictatorship to democracy, and also while new states emerge, central authority often had eroded. Law enforcement had, by definition, weakened by the revolutionary changes, as well as by the lack of formal, universally accept-ed legitimacy of new powers. This obviously held in Russia, Ukraine and in most post-Yugoslav cases. Abolition of shortages and finding new price rela-tives happens via trial and error, thus the rise of price levels is practically inevitable.

Third, especially for NIS countries, *money creation had remained decentralized* for much too long. As explained by contemporary accounts (Aslund and Layard, eds, 1993; Michalopoulos and Tarr eds, 1994) the political priority of preserving the leading role of Russia within the NIS and the trade policy con-cerns, also supported by IMF, of saving intra-NIS trade, allowed for this situa-tion to sustain for nearly three years in 1992–1994. Parallel money creation happened also if and when *independent commercial banks were created*. These are technically capable of money creation via credit granting. The more the gov-ernment was concerned about sustaining employment in the socialist dinosaurs, the big one town – one factory establishments, or electorally motivat-ed to buy votes of agricultural interests, the higher the probability of lastingly soft crediting, of tolerating non-payments, of the re-emergence of barter.

A fourth factor contributing to inflation is *backward-looking indexation*,[20] that tended to be quite widespread. Not only public sector wages, but pensions, insurance rates, mortgages and many more contracts tended to be indexed, with a tradition of backward rather than forward looking contracts. This cre-ated inertia.[21]

Finally mention should be made of the sustaining *soft budget constraints* (Kornai, 1996 and 2001; Kornai–Maskin–Roland, 2003) that have been counter-vailing a variety of governmental efforts to introduce financial discipline in state finances and among inter-firm payments alike. As long as bankruptcy

---

[20] This is a practice when changes (of pensions, of insurance rates, of transport tariffs or what-ever) are not determined by a view of current and future market situation, but by automatically adjusting these variables to the actual rate of inflation registered in the preceding year. Understandably such an arrangement fuels inflationary expectations and does not allow for decelerating price rises, even at times when the market supply would warrant for that.

[21] An all-encompassing theoretical treatise analyzing major components of inflation in gener-al and post-Communist inflation in particular is offered in the bulky volume of Tibor Erdős (1998).

and liquidation rules tend to be soft, this feature survives. The latter has been the case in most of the region, for fear of political consequences of centrally non-controlled restructuring, divestiture, asset stripping and layoffs.

In the individual cases, the interaction of these factors varied, but these sum up the most important components of why, contrary to early expectations cherished by politicians and advisors alike, inflation has come down much slower in the transforming economies. What we do observe, with the benefit of hindsight, is that *no growth could sustain in the emerging economies with high or even moderate inflation.* This runs counter to the traditional views held in reform economics and in parts of developmental literature, but is in line with mainstream convictions. A less general, more country-specific issue follow, namely the way *how do we get to low inflation.*[22] In explaining this, we are likely to see if the categorization offered above, as well as the *divergence* among post-Communist economies is *an empirically testable* hypothesis.

If we look at *Table 5*, we see a first group, composed of Armenia, Tajikistan, Georgia and of course, more than once, Yugoslavia. In these cases disintegration took the form of *armed conflict,* civil strife, and in certain periods the lack of central government. Thus the central bank could exert no control over the processes. War, especially in poor countries, tend to be financed by money emission, which had been the case in the examples listed.

A second group of countries had been grappling with the consequences of *Soviet disintegration.* Haphazard, mostly improvised policies of crisis management and state building add up in the very poor performance of Russia, Ukraine, Kazakhstan and Turkmenistan in the 1992–1994 period.

A third group of countries is saddled by the inability and/or the *unwillingness of the central government to control processes.* It is not always clear, if and to what degree we can delineate the two. For a weak government may be tempted – or indeed, forced – to inflate away those nominal incomes that had been pressurized out of it by activist lobby groups of various kinds. Belarus and Romania are the prime examples, where the reactive policies of the government have born resemblance to practices known from Argentina and Brazil in their respective pre-reform economic histories.

A fourth insight is that *disinflation does not require a flourishing economy, not even a strong state,* as postulated by much of the policy-oriented and political science literature, especially in area studies. Successful stabilization in Bosnia in 1995–1996, in Latvia in 1998–2002, or in tiny and vulnerable Macedonia in 1996–2002 all are proving our point.

Fifth, as we could see from the *Table, sustainable disinflation is not a matter of months in democracies,* and if state building is also around, it may even last longer. For it is hard to overlook, that democratization implies the emergence and organization of formal structures of interest representation. These include not only postmodern political parties, but also quite traditional lobbies, corporate networks, regional pressure groupings. Since it is their job

---

[22] A broad overview of the relevant global experience is available in (Fischer, et al, 2002)

to resist if the interest of members is threatened, they do so, slowing down what otherwise would be economically more rational. Competing rationalities, such as the myopic media/political rationality versus long term macroeconomic rationality, must be accepted as a fact of life once the multiparty system emerged.

Finally, as a sixth insight the *lasting disinflation since 1997–1998 should not come as a surprise*. In mature urbanized economies based on complex structures, bureaucratic co-ordination of processes is clumsy. Fine-tuning of economic processes does require relevant money, that buys everything, and *authorities that can refrain from micro-managing business affairs*. Therefore, as long as the issue of power is settled (in the sense that a central government is in place), *it is its prime interest to be able to macro-manage*. This can happen via fiscal and monetary policy, that is meaningful and efficient only if money is sound. Thus Russia since 1997 does constitute a mainstream, with the August 1998 devaluation acting in a textbook-like manner, and with the return to fiscal prudence reflecting the new market order that emerged in that country. In a way, the exceptions are Romania until 2005, Belarus and Uzbekistan, but even in those countries moderate, rather than high rates of inflation exists. Since many developing countries co-existed with moderate inflation for longer time, this experience is also in line with what we knew beforehand.

Turning to *unemployment,* the big question, from the very outset of changes had been *if there exists a soft/socially sensitive option* that could save societies from the manifold troubles of this phenomenon. It is common knowledge, that one of the big lures of the 'Czech miracle' of 1992–1996 had been the promise and practise of avoiding double digit unemployment and the resultant disruptions. The big unknown, also for economic modelling, had been if the tertiary sector and new private business could absorb those laid off from the public sector.

Looking at *Table 6* in the Appendix we find that, not unrelated to activity levels, unemployment in the post-Communist world has *nowhere* remained a transient phenomenon as hoped for by the optimists. Moreover, in the 1997–2002 period *a worsening of the situation* could be observed, and 2003 has seen only partial improvements (in Slovakia, but not in Poland). Low activity levels alone cannot be invoked to explain the story. Some of the very good performing economies, namely Poland and Slovakia, but also the third star performer, Slovenia has been registering even higher levels of registered unemployment than the stagnant NIS economies. This is a reflection, in all three cases, of *insider dominance*, that is a rigid labor market structure disfavoring new entries and slowing down layoffs. The problem, known as the insider-outsider dilemma also in the European Union, is very clearly present here, and not only as a minor issue. By contrast, Hungary's good performance until 2005 has been only partially explained by recovery, and to a larger degree the *liberalized labor market* contributes to the favorable outcome. Hungarian unemployment, standing below 6 per cent at the time, was a third of its Polish counterpart, despite the marked slowdown of the 2000–2005 period.

In the NIS it had long been a claim that stagnant reforms are showing up in the inability and unwillingness of corporations to lay off redundant workers. While this point used to be valid in the first transition years, since 1997, i.e. a year when Russian reforms turned serious, and also other countries started to stabilize, joblessness developed into a serious macroeconomic problem. It is interesting – and quite reassuring, indeed – to observe that *economic rebound,* even if limited, *immediately translates into the creation of jobs.* This gives ground for hope, namely that the spontaneous liberalization of labor markets may deliver socially more acceptable outcomes than in some West European countries, in Central Asia and in the high unemployment country group. The reverse side of the same coin is that in the NIS, except the traditional big family countries of Central Asia, social protection is very limited, thus the problem of poverty is a serious one. This needs to be mentioned, even if its analysis would go beyond the limits of the present chapter.

Looking at the unemployment numbers of South-East Europe *we can observe the single major peace-time problem of the area.* Obviously, it is not only the destruction of war and lack of FDI, but also the *remnants of the Yugoslav self-managed enterprise,* strongly protective of insider interests, that make each post-Yugoslav successor state so poorly performing, even in intra-transformation perspective. This circumstance is both a cause and a consequence of the lasting criminalization of the Balkan economies; as one observer succintly summed up, 'once a state goes into the business of crime, it can be difficult to get out of the business' (Andreas, 2004, p. 7). In an environment where politics, the administration and criminal networks intertwine, the incentive to invest, but also to provide and find a decent regular job, has been limited indeed.

From among the *best performers* Hungary, Latvia and Estonia, that is countries with free market labor policies can be mentioned. The decisive role of insider control seems to be supported by the group of worst performers. This leads everywhere and always to high unemployment rates. True, the case of Bosnia may be explained by special circumstances. However, the most advanced and richest transforming economy, the former German Democratic Republic also suffers from sustaining high rates of unemployment. Here copying West German labor market arrangements has made hiring and firing next to impossible.[23] Wages were set according to the political criterion of quick equalization between East and West, not according to productivity and profitability levels. Furthermore, centralized bargaining – called *Tarifautonomie* – per se is known to be strongly discouraging *new* employment. Unlike in the West, high wages and social security coupled with limited purchasing power constrain the growth of bottom-up small-scale private sector, that accounted for a larger part of 'privatization' in Poland and many other transforming soci-

---

[23] Reviewing the first edition Jan HŘICH (2006, p. 102) criticizes as ideological prejudice what continues to seem a straightforward observation to us: wherever insiders dominate, open unemployment is bound to skyrocket and for a long time. Thus we continue to caution any emerging economy from emulating corporatist practices, irrespective of their ideological orientation.

eties.[24] Likewise, the other three countries with the poorest record, Poland with 18.1 per cent, Croatia with 21.5 (!) per cent and Slovenia, with 17.5 per cent are known of their labor markets where insider interest dominates. Since the two best performers in terms of growth and consumption register the highest unemployment, both societies are saddled with increasing inequalities and growing social strains. This reinforces our earlier insight, namely that *growth is though a pre-condition for social progress, however, in itself is not a panacea.* The type of growth matters as well, i.e. if it is creating jobs, if equity is improving, and environmental and financing constraints are properly observed. Under this angle *deregulation is needed* not only from the point of view of efficiency, which is trivial, but also *from the point of view of equity*, that might seem less so.

Turning to the NIS, we enter a certain time journey. The best performers in terms of unemployment are Azerbaijan, Moldova, Turkmenistan and Kyrgyzstan, that is, societies where change from Soviet patterns has remained the least impressive. Worst case scenarios are represented by Armenia and Russia, where low activity levels and ongoing state desertion (not to be equated to privatization) explain the outcome. Firms are no longer held responsible for keeping people on their payrolls only in order to retain their Moscow residence permit, or access to public health care, irrespective of the value they add to the firm. In the latter cases we see the reverse side of the same coin, i.e. without attaining sufficiently high activity levels deregulation alone is unable to take care of the labor market. Still, in comparison with Southeast Europe the virtues of more, rather than less, liberalized labor markets become palpable.

Summing up our findings, statistics did reveal some theoretically important insights. First, *disinflation has been a must;* there is no way to eschew stabilization. It is in the interest of central state power, of investors, of savers, of the socially vulnerable alike. We have not encountered any single case where growth could be resumed without – even less prior to – stabilization, as so-called 'alternative economic policy' advocates suggested in the first half of the 1990s. There is also *no trade-off between growth and price stability:* on the contrary, those countries that tried to grow irrespective of inflation suffered more in cumulative terms.

Second, *activity levels do matter.* As we have seen economic growth is the answer to many problems, including social ones. It is also an exigency, since societies in post-Communist countries have revealed their public choice in favor of high, rather than zero or low growth scenarios. One of the reasons why societies are disenchanted is, that delivering on this promise was rudimentary in all countries except Poland and Slovenia. Experience of the latter, together with Slovakia, however, cautions us from taking growth as a panacea; its qualities also matter.

---

[24] For a detailed theoretical and empirical overview on conditions for bottom-up growth of the small business sector see (McIntyre and Dallago, eds, 2003).

Related to this is our third finding, namely that *insider control is socially harmful*. At the outset of transition it looked (Dabrowski, 1994, pp. 29–30.) that the controversy against self-management and worker participation/control of corporations is mostly an ideological one; what matter is getting the state administration out of business. Our survey of post-Communist empirical evidence is suppportive of a finding, long observed in Western Europe, that *insider control is detrimental* not only to privatization and related dynamic efficiency increases, *but also to social equity.*[25]

Fourth, experience of some of the NIS shows that large scale *unemployment though can temporarily be avoided, it may, however not be a lucrative option*. If firms continue to act according to the old Soviet standards and norms, they do take people on their payrolls, irrespective of performance. However, this circumstance may directly be seen at the root of stagnant economic performance, lack of structural change, in the end of the day, lack of performance, of incomes that could be distributed in one way, or another.

We have seen, fifth, that unemployment is even *more serious a problem in most transforming societies, than it is in Western Europe*. However, it needs to be added that official numbers reported in our *Table 6* often cover up the true size of the problem. The rise of agricultural employment, in some cases, as in Romania, Bulgaria and Poland over 20 or even 30 per cent of total employment – does not imply, in the majority of cases, productive employment. It means a *regress into rural self-sufficiency ventures*, where the logic of the traditional peasant family predominates. This is, indeed a cheap way, and also an efficient way of avoiding extreme poverty and sowing the seeds of entrepreneurship (Bauer, 2000). However, once a society reached a stage of urbanization, such regressive defense mechanisms hardly create dynamic comparative advantages at the micro- and the macro-levels. If for no other reasons than the *constraints* put by backward societies and lacking infrastructure *on human capital formation*, this strategy is likely to backfire already in the medium run. This is trivial as long as *sources for long run growth are simply not being brought about* by these defensive – survival rather than future-oriented – strategies of crisis management. The extreme numbers of early retired and on disability pensions are also likely to burden additionally public finances of many, mostly Central European, countries for decades to come.

As our empirical evidence has indicated, there has been *no trade-off between inflation and unemployment* in transforming societies in the 20 years under scrutiny. This lends additional support to the original insight of Milton Friedman (1968) about the Phillips curve being vertical. In other terms, post-Communist economies have developed into quite normal market economies, rather than specific creatures, as the term 'East European capitalism', preferred

---

[25] One may well wonder, how socially-minded analysts can so easily forget about the equal right/access to labor as one of the fundamental social rights. The more it relates to young people – in some countries up to 40 per cent of people under 25 are without jobs, despite the buffer role played by mass enrollment to public universities – the deeper a problem it is likely to be for the entire social fabric.

54

by a part of the international sociological and political science literature, would have indicated.

Our seventh finding is that there is *a potential,* though by no means an iron law, for growth generating employment and thereby *becoming efficient and equitable at the same stroke.* Especially the experience of Hungary, but more recently of Slovakia and Russia, is indicative of this opportunity. Our analysis above would therefore very strongly *caution against taking over the initiatives* to adopt wide co-decision rights and other corporatist practices that are to blame for much of Western European unemployment. Instead, a liberalization of labor markets and de-emphasizing insider dominance where it still prevails, seems to be the normative conclusion.

External Trade and Finance

If seen in a global perspective, it makes sense to interpret fifteen years of transformation through the eyes of development economics. In this area of economics the earlier much debated issue of inward-looking self-sufficiency against outward orientation seems to have been settled. Let us refer to more established literature that, alas, does contain references to the exchanges of the earlier debates (Greenaway–Morgan–Wright, 2002; Winters, 2002; Bruton, 1998; Pitlik, 2002). Without reiterating the regional dimension of the debate that had been documented in our previous monographs, let us just mention that *sustainability of economic growth is intimately related to constantly growing exports.* This creates a revenue base for an ever wider range of imported goods and services, which in turn allows for more, structurally competitive products and services to be produced. Let us recall also that *import substitution has proven to be deleterious to endogenous sources of growth,* innovation and spreading knowledge. If anything the bad experiences of the Czech Lands and Eastern German provinces clearly illustrate this broader point. The first has been degraded from the number three industrial power of inter-war Europe into an average post-Communist industrial society. The latter suffered even more, from being the industrial heartland of Germany into a lasting trouble-spot until long times to come. In both cases the extinction of sources of endogenous growth mattered much more than ad-hoc policy mistakes. And conversely, outward orientation should not be equaled with simplistic measures of promoting export sales. It is based on the equal treatment of exports and imports, further that external competition is seen as a major instrument of preserving the contestability of domestic markets in small open economies. As has been indirectly proven by the twin crises of debt and implosion in the Soviet block, steady growth of export revenue is a sustainability condition for economic progress in small open economies. If we rush to *Table 10,* we can observe that some countries, though starting with no debt (for instance, because of not assuming any part of former federal debts) have already accumulated sizeable external dues. Furthermore, countries with stagnant export intakes do face financing constraints in the long run that may well trigger the stop-go cycles well known from underdeveloped economies.

Trade – Exports

The global indicator for the growth of East European exports from $61 bn in 1992 to $157 bn in 2001 reflects a 2.5 fold increase, which is a respectable performance, both on its own, but even more against the background of two decades of unsuccessful attempts to improve foreign trade performance in the 1970s and 1980s. The group of *best performers* is led by Estonia, with exports growing from 400 m to $3.3 bn, i.e. 8 times, reflecting a very successful re-orientation and structural change as a result of free market policies. In the second place we find Lithuania, with exports growing from 850 m in 1992 to $4.6 bn a decade later, a growth of 6 times. This is all the more impressive, since Lithuanian reforms started only with a delay of over two years. In the third place we find the Czech Republic, the most closed economy in the Communist period. Czech exports grew from $8.7 bn in 1992 to 33.4 bn a decade later, that is four times. Finally, the often disregarded Slovak Republic comes as the fourth, from $3.5 to 12.7 bn, a growth of 3.5 times. These are *truly impressive numbers*, in terms of dynamics, also in international and historical comparison.

Some remarks are certainly due to interpreting these numbers. First, as relying on the approach of new economic geography, Soós (2000) has proven, geography does matter for trade. In concrete terms, he found the closeness to the axis of Stuttgart–Milan to have more explanatory power than other conventional considerations of trade theory, thereby explaining up to 70 per cent of the impressive Slovak performance in the 1990–1997 period, i.e. *prior to* the victory of the radically reformist Dzurinda government. Second, it is hard to overlook that Estonian exports peaked in 1998 and never recovered since then, since this is likely to pose a severe constraint on future growth on this small open economy. Slovenian exports also stagnate, casting doubt over the long-term growth potential of the current star performer. On the other hand, the Czech economy, much criticized for its slow structural change in the 1990–1997 period, has been showing signs of *extraordinary dynamics* in the post-1998 period. This is indicative of the results of structural reforms implemented during the Grand Coalition period.

Among the *weakest performers* we find Serbia, with exports contracting from $2.5 bn in 1992 to a mere 1.9 bn a decade later. This is followed by Macedonia, also declining from the low $1.2 bn in 1992 to $1.1 bn, and, surprisingly for many of us, Croatia, with exports growing from $4.3 bn to a mere $4.6 bn a decade later. It is hard to overlook, that the *heritage of the Yugoslav model* of inward-looking industrialization and self-management (insider dominance, supported by regional seclusion) seems to have exerted a major influence. This is an extreme case of path dependence, since not even Slovenia is immune from its repercussions.[26]

---

[26] This point is elaborated in the empirical analysis of Simonetti (2001) showing the direct – and politically motivated – continuity from the Yugoslav self-managed firm to the de facto management-owned Slovenian large firms.

Turning to the *NIS*, it seems reasonable to restrain our analysis to the non-NIS exports and imports, since intra-NIS trade is still state controlled and accounted for in clearing currency, thus numbers are not truly comparable with the rest. Also from the point of view of re-integration in the global economy the non-NIS numbers are more meaningful. Total NIS exports to non-NIS (far abroad, *dalnee zarubezhie*) increased from $51 bn to $113.6 bn, less then twofold, which is not very impressive if we take account of the dominant role of fuel and energy that experienced a major price hike in the post-1999 period.

Interestingly, the star performer of the NIS in the decade under scrutiny was Kazakhstan, increasing (basically fuel) exports from $1.4 bn to $6.0 bn, a fourfold increase. The second best is Tajikistan, increasing its $100 m exports to $440 mn, a 4.4 times increase, reflecting, of course, also the very low starting level. The third best is no one else but Ukraine, increasing its non-NIS exports from $3.3 to 11.6 bn, a 3.5 times increase, comparable thus to Slovakia, one of the best in the Central European group. Finally the leaders include Azerbaijan, increasing exports from $0.75 to 2.1 bn, less than threefold in a decade.

In the middle group we find Russia, with its Western exports growing from $42 bn in 1992 to $86 bn, twofold in a decade, despite the sizeable oil windfall and related natural gas price increases. This number already foreshadows *major problems in Russian industrial competitiveness*. It is no secret that, owing to the large military-industrial complex, there could have been a sizeable potential, both in terms of human capital and in terms of technology, for restructuring and creating a modern, manufacturing-based export sector.[27] And while nobody doubted the gargantuan difficulties of managing the process, a decade should have been enough for getting the process started. This has not happened, allowing for calls, inter alia, by then Presidential chief advisor Illarionov (2003) to caution against resource curse. If industrial restructuring does remain a slogan, the repercussions for Russia's long term growth rate are bound to be dim (closer to the 3 than the currently planned 6 per cent per annum despite the current low activity levels).

The *worst performer* of the NIS in terms of exports is Turkmenistan. It is not only the initial and final points of $0.9 and 1.3 bn deserve attention, but the very big volatility showing up in export revenues. This is a clear indication of underdeveloped, weather-dependent economy. The fluctuation by a factor of 4 is extreme even compared to developing countries.

NIS countries, excluding Russia, register *generally weak export growth* (less than a twofold increase). By contrast, the Baltic states, coming from the same Soviet economic space stand out for their exemplary fourfold increases in exports. This is a real performance reflecting the judgement of international markets on policies and structures that emerged over the past fifteen years. Central Europe in this dimension takes the middle ground only, with *Southeast Europe being stagnant, thereby recording a performance that is inferior even to that of the NIS countries*. As long as all the Balkan countries are also small open

[27] We shall come back to the broader implications of this in the Russia and China chapters.

economies, this must be seen as a warning sign in terms of their long-term growth potential. Lacking export revenues there is, in terms of simple arithmetic (preceding economic analysis), no way to fund their modernization process. This is followed by the general insights, elaborated in great detail in the general development theory and literature quoted at the beginning of this subsection, why outward orientation is the only way for small open economies to flourish (which, of course, a world of difference from claiming a unilinear development path). The more one believes that lasting peace should rest on improved economic performance, the more disturbing the inability of Southeast Europeans to improve their export performance may look. Indeed, if there is an operational role of *EU Neighborhood Policies* this would require active involvement, in terms of market opening and technical assistance alike in helping the region overcome its economic stagnation, an issue we shall expand in Chapter Ten.

Import Markets: Potential or Problem-Field?

One of the eldest insights of international economics has been that country size is not determined by its territory, military might or the number of the population. Economically, the *size of a country equals,* in the first approximation, *its import capacity.* In the second approximation the *capacity to absorb foreign – direct and portfolio – investments* that comes to it. Therefore, such big capital importing country as Belgium, matters more for the world economy, as the entire Sub-Saharan Africa, and Canada, with its 31 m population is much bigger than, say, India with its own, which counts exactly one thousand million more human beings (according to World Bank, op. cit. p. 234). Therefore, from the point of the global economy, it does matter if transforming economies developed into important product markets and capital importers or not. And conversely, the growth of import penetration is one of the most widely used proxies for opening, since this is sustainable only if export revenues grow fast enough to sustain this line.

Looking at *Table 8* allows us to get an overview. Here again, for NIS we analyze non-NIS imports, that being indicative of the processes we survey for other countries as well.

Looking at the *Table* we see East European imports growing from $72 bn to $201 bn in the decade following 1992, which is an increase of 2.5 times. This is in line with the dynamics of overall export growth analyzed in the preceding sub-chapter. In case of the NIS, imports grew from $42 to 48 bn only, that is by a mere 20 per cent. These numbers indicate, that the *broad debate about excessive opening has been by and large filthy talk,* it is not born out by statistics. Import growth has not been excessive either in comparison to exports, or to international standards. Suggestions blaming 'one-sided' or 'premature' opening might well represent industrial, agricultural or labor interest, adversely affected by the change but without aspiring for academic rigor.

The biggest opening in the region has been registered by Estonia, from $0.4 to 4.2 bn, which is a ninefold increase, representing a very radical re-orientation of economic relations from the Soviet Union. In the second place we find Lithuania, with import growth from $0.6 to 6.3 bn in the post-1992 decade, followed by Latvia, registering a 4.5 times increase from $0.8 to 3.5 bn. Only the fourth is the leading country in Central Europe, the Czech Republic, that needed to overcome a legacy of seclusive policies in the entire communist period.

The countries registering the smallest/least successful opening happened to be, as was to be expected on the grounds of export numbers, the successor states of the former Yugoslavia. In Macedonia imports grew from $1.2 to 1.7 bn, whilst in Serbia from $3.8 to 4.8 bn. The growing indebtedness of these states, showing up in *Table 10* is therefore worrying, since these reflect an unhealthy trend. Namely, *not even this moderate opening is sustainable on the basis of export revenues*, which foreshadows a vicious circle scenario, well known in stagnant developing nations. The need for international action is given (even if the bits and pieces need further elaboration, that fall outside the scope and genre of this volume). If we compare the three groups, it is hard to avoid the conclusion that *overall success in economic change is related to opening, empirically as well as theoretically.*

Turning to the NIS the importance of country-specific factors comes to the fore. The biggest opening was registered in the decade under scrutiny by Turkmenistan, starting from a negligible $0.03 bn and ending with $1.4 bn, registering thus a 43 times increase. This is followed by Armenia, starting with an equally small $0.05 bn in 1992 and ending with $0.65 bn a decade later, meaning a 13 times increase. The third best performer is Kazakhstan, with imports rising from $0.47 bn to $3.05 bn, i.e. by a factor of 6. It is worth noting that Kazakhstan also registers a surplus, that is a sign, most probably, of oil and gas related *capital flight.*

The least open economy, contrary to anecdotal evidence by frequent Moscow travellers, remained the Russian Federation. Imports in 1992 accounted for $37 bn, that decreased (!) to $30 bn a decade later (this is not a coincidental, one-time figure, indeed). The minus 20 per cent implies a *diminishing openness in Russia at the macro-level.* The second worst performer is Tajikistan, with imports hardly growing from $0.13 bn in 1992 to $0.15 bn a decade later.

Summing up the NIS experience we can observe the *difference of Central Asians*, not only in terms of history and cultural heritage, but also in trade terms. Reorientations were different by the country groups, the Baltic countries' being the most successful.

It is hard to overlook the *small size of the NIS markets,* as a decades-long reality. This is worth re-iterating as a feature standing in stark contrast to the ritual talk about the huge post-Soviet market and its potentials. For the 2000s Poland alone has become a bigger market than the entire NIS. The Russian market prior to the new oil boom had become smaller than the Czech or the Hungarian market alone. This is a hard fact of life setting severe constraints on what Russia can or cannot attain, especially in economic terms, i.e. in the dimensions of the WTO or EU. It is also sobering if we are to assess what to think of the next 'deal of the century', promulgated under ceremonial circumstances, in the presence of top-level politicians.

In case of the NIS it is also observable that stagnant imports reflect stagnant exports and *resulting slowdowns in structural modernization via imports and competition alike*. This gives room for import substituting activities, that are able to improve activity indicators, however, only in the short to medium term. The cementation of import substitution, in line with international evidence quoted above (Bruton, 1998), is a relatively secure sign of *limited long run growth potential for the decades to come*. Catching up is therefore likely to remain more of a slogan than an empirically observable reality in the NIS.

If we turn to *trade by direction*, reflected in a summary form in *Table 9* in the Appendix, we must come to the more than surprising insight that re-orientation of trade from within the Soviet block *has been accomplished more completely by NIS countries than by their Central and Eastern European counterparts*. For a number of reasons, including the comparative advantage of Russia in the energy sector and the existence of a pipeline system, Central Europe continues to rely on Russian supplies. Meanwhile, Russians, if they do not save abroad, have become extremely selective in choosing their import sources. Thus a structural trade imbalance emerged, which is neither good nor bad, just a fact of life. It is ironic to suggest that it should be overcome by governmental activism. Futile attempts of changing Hungarian governments, for instance, to change the tide, and counteract, via trade promotion, what basic Russian interest is, were bound to fail.

Looking from a different angle, the mere 10 (!) per cent share of Central and Eastern Europe in Russia's imports is a clear indication, to what a degree the Soviet empire had become economically hollow by the last years of its existence. It reflects that former allies can by no means be seen as an asset, even from a Great Russian perspective, since they can hardly contribute to Russian modernization. It also shows how *fundamentally disinterested Russia is and will remain in any reconquest*, as Russian interest in modernization ties the country to Western Europe and the United States. The reliance, in the order of two thirds, on supplies from OECD countries also indicates that the continued discourse over Eurasianism, Eurasian options, that is focusing on China rather than on the US, lacks any empirical footing and *runs directly counter to Russian economic interest*. This is an important insight, also for future foreign policy analyses.

These longer run time series also disprove claims (e.g. van Brabant, ed., 1999; Welfens, 1999) that NIS and Eastern Europeans allegedly undertrade among themselves. The 16–18 per cent of intra-Eastern European trade that emerged by the 2000s is entirely in line with what most gravity models, calculated diligently in many places, have been forecasting for over the last 15 years or so.

If there is anything surprising, it is the continued *under-representation of developing countries*, both on the export and on the import side of Central and Eastern European countries. Many of these nations registered spectacular trade growth in the last quarter of a century, and this region seems to have missed out on the ensuing potentials.

It is equally interesting to observe, that Central and Eastern Europe has remained much more important for Russia as a market than the other way around. Eastern Europe, as we saw, has been an important source of funding Russian activities, most importantly imports from the West. This feature is unlikely to change in the future, that implies that for Russia Central Europe remains a politically underrated, though economically important area.

Summing up the findings of the trade section, the comparison of NIS and Eastern Europe has proven to be fruitful. The *dissimilarities* among the major groups, but also within them could be *demonstrated on empirical material.* In trade terms the Baltic countries take the lead, and only Central Europeans can claim success, though to a lesser degree. By contrast, both NIS and Southeast Europe has been shown to be stagnant, where trade inefficiency, slow restructuring, more state intervention and less restructuring, that lead to import substitution, form a classical developmental vicious circle. For prospects of growth in small open economies are not unrelated to trade performance.

From among the Visegrád countries, Slovakia and the Czech Republic are the best performers in the longer run, however their accomplishments do not match that of the Baltic states. Meanwhile, structural analyses also support our claim that the Baltic miracle has reached its limitations in the past few years. This, notwithstanding is no doubt, especially on the basis of import statistics, that *only the Baltic states and Central Europeans are underway to global economic integration,* whereas the 'Rest' is unlikely to join the 'West' unless the processes described in this chapter fundamentally change.

As final conclusions to the trade chapter we must recall what had been presented on activity and consumption levels of the Baltic countries. Success in trade, therefore, should not be directly equated to economic progress in general, though the two are related. Also we should recall that *Central Asia is also on the road to globalization, but this is a very unilateral, one-dimensional process,* constrained to the financial and fuel sector, and unlikely to have the broader stimuli and trickle down needed for a successful modernization of those societies.[28] This also implies very low levels of joining both international trade and finance, even compared to Central Europeans (that trade much less in absolute terms than comparable countries in terms of population, such as Switzerland or the Netherlands, for that matter).

External Finance

External finance is a basic concern for any small open economy. Especially socialist and developing country experience indicates that unless sound policies are sustaining, the inability to finance imports regularly becomes a constraint on growth (the earlier mentioned stop-go cycle emerges). This is basically because of the phenomenon of *twin deficits,* where governmental overspending, sooner rather than later, translates into current account deficits. The latter may well be bridged for a while, but only for a finite time span. Thus, unless general government revenues and expenditures are structurally balanced, so economic theory goes, external finance will become a constraint on growth. *Table 10,* especially if considered jointly with *Table 7,* allows the reader

---

[28] This is a long established insight in international economics, see Kádár (1984) and Török (1986).

to obtain an overview on the post-transition years. The most important insight we gain is *that external finance is, indeed, becoming a constraint on growth in post-Communist countries once again by the middle of the first decade in the 2000s.*

In case of Eastern Europe, it is hard to overlook that ever since 1997 a serious disequilibrium emerged and has been sustaining. In other words, the growth of export revenues does not keep pace with import demand any longer, a problem generated primarily, but by no means exclusively, by Poland. The NIS, by contrast, is faced by an opposite problem, that of capital flight. *This has been increasing since 1999* despite harsh measures to discipline entrepreneurs and control capital outflows. Given that the big outflows happen from countries where activity levels are very low, this is a sign of *dis-saving at the national –* though by no means at the household or corporate – *level.*

In case of the East European country group a sizeable deficit, in the range of 10–15 per cent of regular export revenues sustains, which is clearly unhealthy and cannot be sustained without serious repercussions. In case of the NIS, this time clearly dominated by Russia, *the size of the capital flight* is even more embarrassing than its evolution: in certain years – not just one – up to 30 per cent (!) of export intakes land abroad. This is serious disinvestment from the national economic perspective. If we compare the size of capital flight, reflected in current account surpluses, with inward foreign investment, we see that *the outflow of money is eight to ten times that of the inflow.* This is hardly an encouraging sign for such ambitious long-term development projects as the Gref Plan of 2001 forecasting 6–7 per cent annual growth rates for Russia for a decade. Also one wonders – joining the earlier quoted Andrei Illarionov (2003) – *if indeed, capital shortage is the crux of Russian economic ills.* We may also ask, what if the Paris and London Club of official and private debtors had written off Soviet era debts, whether or not it could indeed have contributed to Russian economic recovery. The ritual references to debt and capital shortage seem, in the light of the summary numbers, rather oft-repeated, than well substantiated. For there is no such thing as an investment need abstracted from conditions of return and financing. Furthermore, if domestic investors, best informed about investment conditions, flee, it is not very rational to expect less informed foreigners to fill that vacuum.

From among the non-Russian NIS countries two deserve special analytical attention. The first one is Ukraine, where country size and the positive growth rates in the post-1999 period created interest in it as an investment spot. However, what we observe is not a big inflow of FDI, that could, for instance, capitalize on import substitution and a 50 m people strong market, say, in the consumer goods industry. Instead, a *small but steady capital flight* is registered, with repercussions similar to Russia. Also, it is noteworthy that the investment boom in Azerbaijan is over, which is the case for Uzbekistan as well.

Turning to Eastern Europe the biggest deficit is registered by Poland. Since this feature is dominant since 1998, *it is hard to agree with those who consider the slowdown in the Polish economy as cyclical.* Indeed, Polish debt started to balloon after 1995, when the Polish and London Clubs agreed to write off 95 per cent of Communist era debt. However, as can be seen from the numbers, this has *not* led to the expected increase of *competitiveness*. On the one hand, the deal did provide breathing room for the contemporary Polish government and, beyond doubt, contributed to the country's achieving the best growth performance in the successive years. On the other hand, the fundamental problem of creating *regularly and sufficiently growing export revenues*, which is at the heart of the outward orientation, could not be mastered.

In an important change against its conservative traditions, the Czech Republic started to use first indebtedness and since 2000 also the above mentioned *twin deficit* to bridge costs of structural adjustment. Bulgarian deficits though look small, especially compared to Polish deficits, still if measured against export performance, they give grounds for concern. A real problem case seems to be Latvia, the new EU member, where deficits stabilized at 25 to 30 per cent of export revenues. This development is in sharp contrast to Romanian figures, where exports have continuously grown since 1999. Among the new problem cases, we may mention Hungary, where the populist policies of the 2001–2006 period have created a current account problem that ceased to exist since 1995. Perhaps even more worrying is the situation in Croatia, a country often seen, ever in Brussels, as leap-frogging Romania and Bulgaria in the process of EU accession. Actually (Bank Austria, 2004, p. 6) external debt of the country has grown from 59.9 per cent of GDP in 2000 to no less than 83.9 per cent by 2003 and further to 89.6 per cent by the end of 2004. *This is worse than the Jugoslav debt boom of the 1970s.* All the more so, that most of this debt is private, investments grew double digit in 2001– 2004 and unemployment, despite this massive injection of money (also reflected in continuously over 5 per cent general government deficit), has never gone under 19 per cent. Exports in the same period grew from 8.5 to barely $13 bn only. Thus the notoriously low efficiency and limited competitiveness of Croatian investments hardly allow for the scenario of 'growing out of debt', as the East Asian tigers did.

Summing up our findings: we have to establish that *finance has become a structural constraint on growth again.* This statement applies in the three major country groups in three different manners. In the case of the Central European countries, current account problems seem to be mostly cyclical in nature, with the important exception of Poland. Such imbalances are, at least technically (though not always politically) easy to manage. In case of Russia and to a lesser extent in Ukraine, *capital flight seems to reflect deeper structural problems,* that are likely to have serious repercussions on long-term growth potential of both countries. Inadequate savings, that are not turned to national investments (or transfigure to investments in other nations) may contribute to global welfare, however not to local welfare improvements.[29] Finally, in Southeast Europe the stabilization of current account deficits at 20 per cent of export revenues is, by its own right, a sign of grave difficulties, of *structural constraints* of these countries to join global economic processes. The two most probable scenarios, if

---

[29] Certainly, these sums could well have been wasted for such adventures as the second Chechen war, that is in its tenth consecutive year at the time of writing. Against this opportunity capital flight is a superior option, but only a second best in normative terms.

extrapolating current trends, is a move towards aid dependence (the Bosnian model), or alternatively, heading toward trouble. Foreign investments may be useful, but in order to become realistic, *first domestic conditions must be stabilized* following the Central European pattern. The international community is both morally obliged and materially interested in extending broad assistance to this problem, otherwise a recurring set of problems, including armed conflicts and the spread of organized crime is likely to spill over to core Europe. In a way, foreign direct investment seems to be the key in all three different cases.

Foreign Direct Investment – Do We Possess a Key?

There is a near consensus view in the literature on development that FDI is good for growth in more than one dimension (cf. Blomström, et al, 2000; Kalotay, 2003; Inotai, 1989; Hamar, 1995; Hansen and Rand, 2006). *FDI is good for a number of reasons*, basically by providing physical and human capital, tacit knowledge, network externalities and relational capital to previously outsider players in the world economy. It is also known that the favorable tendencies do not emerge by themselves, but require governmental policies and regulatory environments that need to be brought about by a variety of comprehensive measures, whose enumeration fall outside the scope of this book.

Our starting point is that due to ideological and systemic reasons, the region simply was left out from the revival of global capital flows in the period following World War II. Up until the 1990s, despite previous efforts to lure capital, the post-Communist countries were heavily under-invested. This explains, in part, their poor export performance. It is relatively easy to establish, even by comparing the numbers in *Tables 7* and *11*, but also on the basis of sectoral and corporate level evidence, that *there is an immediate relationship, in the longer run, between FDI and export growth.* The micro-foundation of this insight is that most markets in the region are too small to be interesting for big investors. Furthermore, in the era of global sourcing, it is next to impossible to join in the multi-dimensional, multi-layer web of inter-firm relations if the old socialist habit of 'do it yourself' dominates. If anything, the failure of the Russian defence sector to convert its capacities to civil industries, such as of refrigerators, vacuum cleaners, watches, civic aircrafts, photo machines and the like, is clearly indicating how important is the *constant and intimate intertwining with the markets* and those managing them (possessing labels, outlet chains, services etc.) is. If Russian failure is to be traced back to the lack of FDI and thus lack of market access and market capabilities, *export performance of the country can indeed test the efficiency of transformation,* checked by international markets. In order to provide empirical evidence, as well as to control the ability to lure capital, it makes sense to take the long term perspective. *Table 11* may serve as a starting point. It does ensure cross-national comparability of statistical reporting, which is otherwise not the case in the region.

One observation relates to the sporadic numbers that could be collected ever since the early transition period. Accordingly, Eastern Europe started from a low of $476 m and grew to $163 bn by 2001, that is a growth of 35 times. Russia started also from a low $100 mn in 1991, and recorded a growth of 25 times, to 2.5 bn in terms of annual inflows. These numbers indicate that the region remained a marginal player in the 1500 bn (2000) and 500 bn (2002) global capital flows, with Poland, the biggest recipient of a mere $7 bn in 2001 (cf. also the insightful analysis of Kalotay, 2003).

The biggest recipients in the region have been Poland, the Czech Republic, Hungary and Slovakia, with the pioneering role of Hungary gradually vanishing from 1999 onward. Large scale privatization in Poland, the Czech Republic and Slovakia have all overcome previous ideological and political barriers, while Hungarian privatization has come to a halt in the 1998–2004 period. This is an interesting insight, since in the general FDI literature and business experience would forecast that capital invests where it has already invested; for experience and search costs push business executives in a conservative direction. However, the strengthening locational competition and the strong decline in FDI in the early 2000s have not allowed for once acquired advantages to sustain without additional efforts.

In per capita terms the overall picture changes. This indicator corrects for country size and shows the 'net efficiency' of capital importing strategies. In this second approach the leading countries are Estonia, Slovakia and Lithuania, whereas the laggards are the successor states of former Yugoslavia (except for Croatia and Macedonia). Whenever the independence wars ended, *the post-Yugoslav states have remained outliers*, even measured against the Central Europeans. The drift between normative and descriptive analysis, what we would like to see and what we do observe in the Balkans, is sizeable indeed. Explaining this outcome Gligorov (2004, pp. 96–98) draws attention to the crucial role of nationalism, in part derived from self-management ideology, and the lack of liberalization among the factors delivering this outcome. Pure economic logic may, and often does, get subordinated to other considerations.

From amongst the NIS countries, where big hopes have been cherished, little of these were realized. The leading countries are Russia and Kazakhstan with *small numbers of inward FDI*, Russia for instance lagging behind Hungary, even in absolute terms, for several years. This is clearly a sign of an unfriendly business climate that sustains amidst annual new initiatives at favorable treatment, tax brakes and the like. Russia and Kazakhstan could, in theory, import much more FDI, if we take GDP and country size in terms of geography and population. In reality these countries remain in a marginal position in the global economy. Their quest for 'national capitalism' has proven to be successful from the point of view of veto players, however not from the point of view of macroeconomic development.[30] Also by the nature of affairs, these structures are quite resembling to East Asian and Latin American *political capitalism*, in a neologoism re-baptized to 'crony capitalism'. This means, in short, that meeting the expectations of the political class and of state bureaucracy is

---

[30] This paradox is going to be expanded in greater detail in our chapter on 'Transnational markets and local politics'.

much more of a component of business success, than meeting consumer needs, domestically and abroad.

Turning to Ukraine, it is surprising to see that a country of France's population regularly receives only as much FDI as the two tiny Baltic states, Latvia and Lithuania taken together. This implies an *FDI intensity of one tenth* of the two pioneering states. Interpreting this sad outcome one may recall a general insight, namely that endowments though allow for success, do not guarantee them. Writing at the time of Ukrainian independence a book, published three years later, Bert van Selm (1997) has rightly invoked this insight for Ukrainian economic perspectives. He underscored the puzzle that exists between the technically quite favorable Ukrainian starting position and the weak institutional and social capital that preconditioned soft and incoherent policies. The latter left Ukraine in a bad shape and much more dependent on Russian markets than the much less favorably starting Baltic countries. Given the common starting positions, it is hard to overlook the different trajectories and not to relate these to policy choices. This finding is supported by later broader institutional analysis by Havrylyshin (2006) stressing the need for further structural reforms if growth is to survive into the post oil-boom years.

Central Asia, that could, in terms of development theory, become an object of major investments in a modernization drive that was to follow, according to official projects, the East Asian miracle. However, all this remained in the realm of poetry. Centralized power structures on their own, lacking all additional conditions that make the business climate investment friendly, do not guarantee success. As we have shown on the example of several countries, *only experimental*, rather than strategic investment materialized in the region.[31] This, regretfully makes *pessimistic scenarios*, well known from traditional developmental literature as vicious circle models, quite probable for the decades to come. Should the spillover of Islamist fundamentalism spread over the countries, for instance as a revolutionary reaction to despotic and corrupt regimes, replicating the experience of the Middle East, this would further worsen the situation. A choice for seclusive policies is not a promising one for societies with high fertility rates and already confronted with serious environmental problems, such as the spread of deserts, lack of water, and soil erosion, partly as an outcome from earlier emphasis on heavy industries.

If we look at *Table 11* it is interesting to observe that there is no trend in FDI inflows, it takes place in waves. The process started with the joint venture legislation of the 1970s and 1980s, then accelerated via privatization (first in the small business sector, later also via large privatization, when strategic foreign owners were allowed to step in). This process continued by *follow-up investments into privatized firms*, and more recently also *outward foreign investment*. The latter process has proven to be macro-economically significant for Hungary and Slovenia by the 2000s, changing the policy perception, that tend-

---

[31] Fabry and Zenghi (2002, p. 300) establish a similar feature for FDI to Russia, also in the Putin period, and warn of the resulting potential marginalization.

ed to relegate FDI into yet another item of the capital account, that may – and should – counterbalance current account deficits.

The growth of outward direct investment is, in a way, the headache of success, since inward FDI decreasingly may serve to offset trade deficits. Thus the current account position needs to be improved by further increasing export performance. This is, however, a minor nuisance, pertaining to the frontrunner country group. The real trouble is with the laggard countries, where the question of *national versus transnational developmental model* sustains and remains unsettled for many years to come. It is not only the NIS, but also Slovenia and perhaps Romania until 2004 that seem to have opted for such a line. Less FDI is also a sign of lastingly inward looking strategy, one that has been shown to remain an inferior option by the broader developmental literature quoted earlier.

It is worth mentioning that in the frontrunner group, i.e. those joining the European Union in 2004 the opening of capital accounts has already taken place. This is known to be a source of additional financing as well as of potential instability. Joining in the regulatory framework of the EU will certainly enhance stability, calculability as well as crisis-resistance of the respective national regulatory systems. In turn the EU enhances the lure of these countries as investment spots. And indeed, in the 2000–2006 period capital markets tended to treat the new accession countries as their darlings, overlooking a variety of macroeconomic loopholes and policy errors, such as the softening up of fiscal stance amidst no clear social pressure, in the hope of long-term convergence.

Let us emphasize however, that *EU membership does not replace sound domestic policies, also with regard to FDI*. The less than convincing experience of Portugal and Greece, or more recently of Hungary indicate that a good business climate and generally investment friendly measures, also in terms of education and physical infrastructure, are needed for the continued involvement of FDI. This circumstance may explain why some empirical analysts (Jensen, 2006, pp 897-8) find evidence for an 'automatic' trickle-down fragmentary and inconclusive. This has never been the original claim, not the major finding, rather the ideological simplification of a complex interrelationship. The latte explains why failure is also not preordained. The mirror image of the same story is Slovakia, where the extremely unfavorable heritage of the Meciar period could be overcome by the resolute market-oriented policies of the Dzurinda governments in the post-1998 period. Latvia too seems to have come out of the nadir.

Summing up our findings on the subject, we hope to have been able to illustrate (and perhaps prove) that *inward FDI is indeed a good summary indicator of the overall progress made in systemic change* and international competitiveness (on the latter cf Csáki and Szalavetz, 2004 relying on a broad survey of business literature). In doing, so stock numbers reflect history, per capita numbers correcting for country size, and flow numbers represent cyclical processes and an evaluation of perspectives. FDI, by its very nature, tends to be *forward-looking*, whereas usual assessments by international agencies and scholars tend to be backward-looking by their very nature. This is not so much of a surprise if we look for a micro-foundation, that suggests that people deciding on their own money (or even more acting under fiduciary responsibilty) are likely to be sounder in passing their judgements. Moreover, their stake is greater in sustaining sunk costs inherent in any real asset investment over years (in face of sharply changed conditions) than say, that of journalists, rating agencies, common people or politicians, who all might easier fall victim to intellectual fashions. The role of FDI declines at times when populism dominates the economic agenda, and in turn, increases when policies are sound, even if current indicators are poor.

Some Preliminary Conclusions from Empirical Evidence

A comparative statistical analysis is time-limited/ephemeral by its very nature. Also a lot depends on the quality of numbers. However, it is impossible to talk about theory without having presented empirical evidence. In doing so, we hope to have managed to answer some of the recurring controversial questions in and for the theory of transformation, at least in the way these questions emerged in the literature and in the policy debates. The decade since the publication of our preceding monograph required that we start with 'facts and figures' before addressing theory. Looking at these did allow to answer some important issues. Let us offer a summary of preliminary findings.

A) The hypothesis that transition trajectories differ substantially, and *there is no such thing as common or optimal trajectory* has been proven in a variety of dimensions. In all the areas analyzed we managed to group countries in a similar fashion, thus our interpretation of what is and is not *emerging Europe* is not a subjective, coincidental one, but rests on facts. Trajectories of change do differ in a lasting fashion. Similarly, we validated the starting hypothesis, that with time passing the relevance of the Communist legacy diminishes. Moreover, that *the Communist legacy is no longer a defining factor of longer term development* seems already plausible[32]. Long- term path dependencies, geography, culture, and yes, policies also shape the outcomes for the longer run more than does the heritage of Communism, both favorable and unfavorable.[33] This also implies that the specifically post-Communist type of transition is indeed over. If for no other reason *no future convergence can be expected* among those countries that are currently analyzed together, for reasons of convenience and tradition, not only by the UN agencies, but a large part of the analytical literature as well. This finding received support from a slightly unexpected corner, when a Russian analyst (Kudrov, 2006, pp. 113–114) also related the divergent macroeconomic perfor-

---

[32] This insight was contested, inter alia, by Lajos Bokros at the book launch of the Hungarian edition by the Hungarian Association for New Institutional Economics, BCU, 7 November 2006, with reference to setbacks and the large number of failures. Let us stress: if it were Communist, rather than very long term historical and institutional memories, that are at work, commonalities in patterns (of regress and progress) should dominate over divergences. This is, however not the case in any of the areas we investigated.

[33] This is a more radical version of the findings of de Melo et al (2001), in line with Havrylyshyn and van Rooden (2003).

mance in NIS and Central Europe not only to different policies, but also to dissimilar *very long term* factors, including *social intangibles*.

B) Some of the thirty countries studied in the *Tables* do emerge, others do not. Various indicators mostly, though not always, *co-evolve*. This is a good sign, supportive of the coherence of our grouping. Development and progress, contrary to utopian and revolutionary views, is not at all pre-ordained, not even at times of 'globalization'.

C) Especially our analysis of foreign trade, finance and FDI has shown, that *success is indeed directly related to joining the global processes*, whereas failure is intimately related to staying out. This might well be involuntary, imposed on societies by their inability to finance their needs for modernization.

D) *Growth remains of paramount importance for development.* We do not find any case (even in the World Development Report quoted several times) where *human* development indices would lastingly have improved where *economic* indicators deteriorated. Activity levels in most of the countries in the region are still at very low levels, thus social and economic considerations all dictate further growth. There is no room for calling for less growth along the lines of the Club of Rome thinking in these countries, as long as they still have to find their way back to where they once used to be, in terms of consumption and welfare in general.

E) It is possible to interpret success and failure in economic change *within a singular theoretical framework.* This is though a trivial scientific requirement, that is most often not met by the rather postmodern transitology literature, but also much of the broader developmental literature lacks such a focus. The story can be arranged around the now canonical SLIP (stabilization, liberalization, institution building and privatization). Those who follow this line have changed reality, not only new discourses have been constructed about what success is and what qualifies as failure.

F) *Soft policy options have not proven socially more sensitive or sensible.* On the contrary, long-term data unambiguously show that those following a non-SLIP line, experimenting with 'alternative' and 'national' models have been faring unanimously worse, also in terms of social indicators. Cumulative costs, in terms of lost welfare, lost jobs and, in a forward-looking manner, social capital formation, have been significantly higher in countries who have opted for – or merely drifted to – a non-radical line of transformation (with slow stabilization, limited liberalization, and insider privatization only).

G) *Finance, especially savings, investment, banking, current account FDI all matter for development.* There is no way to break out of recession if and when the savings–intermediation–investment–reinvestment chain is not recreated. Capital markets and banking, all other allocation mechanism matter for growth. FDI does act as a pace-maker, small but very important for the overall modernization process. Reinvestment also matters.[34] In other words, the post-

---

[34] Antalóczy and Sass (2002), based upon their study of corporate reporting, have established reinvestment to run at 2–2.5 per cent of GDP in some of the Central European countries. Reporting practices of the National Bank of Hungary have accordingly been corrected since 2004, adding this to the previously reported current account deficit figures.

Communist context *does not call for an entirely new brand of economic thinking*, as suggested in several of the broad overviews quoted in the Foreword and in this chapter, and advocated in the monograph by Kazmer and Konrad (2004). Standard economics will do, at least serve as a basis for analysis and recommendation. The analytical frame, describing the post-Communist experience in terms of market failure (Andor and Summers, 1998) is therefore simply flawed.

H) Once regular market institutions are in their place, *a different quality emerges that can be elaborated and solved in a context-specific manner*. From corporate governance to health care systems areas where public choices need to be made, where trial and error solutions emerge will prevail. *Joining the European Union therefore is unlikely to solve the peculiar tasks that each of the thirty societies face.* There remains a sizeable market for further analysis as well. This is an issue to be discussed in a separate chapter.

References

ALBROW, M. (2002): Globalization and modernization: A new paradigm for development studies. In: SCHURMAN, F., ed.: *Globalization and Development Studies: Challenges for the 21st Century.* London: Sage, pp. 21–30.

ANDOR, L. and SUMMERS, M. (1998): *Market Failure: Eastern Europe's 'Economic Miracle'.* London: Pluto Press.

ANDREAS, P. (2004): Criminalized legacies of war: The clandestine political economy of the Western Balkans. *Problems of Post-Communism,* vol. 51. no. 3. pp. 3–9.

ANTALÓCZY, K. and SASS, M. (2002): Magyarország helye a közép- és kelet-európai működő-tőke beáramlásban: statisztikai elemzés. (Hungary's role in the inflow of FDI in Central and Eastern Europe: A statistical analysis). *Külgazdaság,* vol. 46. no. 6. pp. 33–53.

ASLUND, A. (2002): *Building Capitalism.* Cambridge and New York: Cambridge University Press.

ASLUND, A. and LAYARD, R. eds (1993): *Changing the Economic System in Russia.* London: Frances Pinter Publishers.

ASLUND, A. and LAYARD, R. eds (1995): *Russian Economic Reforms at Risk.* London: Frances Pinter Publishers.

Bank Austria/Creditanstalt (2004): *CEE Report,* no. 2. Vienna (a business information and analysis publication).

BAUER, P. T. (2000): *From Subsistence to Exchange and Other Essays.* Princeton, New Jersey: Princeton University Press.

BLOMSTRÖM, M. – KOKKO, A. – ZEJAN, M. (2000): *Foreign Direct Investment: Firm and Host Country Strategies.* Houndmills: MacMillan.

BLOMSTRÖM, M. – LIPSEY, E. – ZEJAN, M. (1996): Is fixed investment the key to economic growth? *Quarterly Journal of Economics,* vol. 111. no. 1. pp. 269–276.

BRABANT, J. van ed. (1999): *Global Trade Policy and Transition Economies.* London and Basingstoke: MacMillan.

BRUTON, H. (1998): A reconsideration of import substitution. *Journal of Economic Literature,* vol. 36. no. 2. pp. 903–936.

COLLIER, P. – ELLIOT, V. L. – HERGE, H. – HOEFFLER, A. – REYNAL-QUEROL, M. – SAMBANIS, N. (2003): *Breaking the Conflict Trap: Civil War and Development Policy.* Washington, D. C.: a World Bank Policy Research Report.

CSABA, L. (2002): Russia's political economy. In: BUGAJSKI, J. ed.: *Toward an Understanding of Russia: New European Perspectives.* Washington, D. C.: a book published by the Council on Foreign Relations, pp. 27–44.

CSÁKI, Gy. and SZALAVETZ, A. (2004): A működőtőkevonzó-képesség mint a nemzetközi versenyképesség mércéje (The ability to draw FDI as a measure of international competitiveness). *Külgazdaság,* vol. 48. no. 3. pp. 58–75.

DABROWSKI, M. (1994): The role of government in post-Communist economies. In: CSABA, L. ed.: *Privatization, Liberalization and Destruction: Recreating the Market in Central and Eastern Europe.* Aldershot (UK) and Brookfield (Vermont, USA): Dartmouth Publishing Co., pp. 21–34.

DABROWSKI, M. ed. (1993): *The Gaidar Program.* Warsaw: a book published by the Friedrich Ebert Foundation and CASE.

DARVAS, Zs. and SIMON, A. (2000): Capital stock and economic development in Hungary. *Economics of Transition,* vol. 8. no. 1. pp. 197–224.

DORNBUSCH, R., ed. (1993): *Policymaking in the Open Economy.* EDI series, Oxford: Oxford University Press for the World Bank.

DRÁBEK, Z. (1986): New trends in East-West trade: a trade diversion or a statistical aberration? *Comparative Economic Studies,* vol. 28. no. (2–3). pp. 17–31.

EBRD (2006): *Transition Report.* London, November.

EIU – Economist Intelligence Unit (2006): *Country Report Russia update,* statistical annex, November (online edition).

ERDŐS, T. (1998): *Infláció.* (Inflation). Budapest: Akadémiai Kiadó.

ERDŐS, T. (2003): *Fenntartható gazdasági növekedés.* (Sustainable economic growth). Budapest: Akadémiai Kiadó.

FABRY, N. and ZENGHI, S. (2002): FDI in Russia: How the investment climate matters. *Communist and Post-Communist Studies,* vol. 35. no. 3. pp. 289–303.

FISCHER, S. and BURTON, D. (1998): Ending moderate inflations. In: COTTARELLI, C. and SZAPÁRY, Gy. eds: *Moderate Inflation.* Washington and Budapest: a book jointly published by the International Monetary Fund and the National Bank of Hungary, pp. 15–96.

FISCHER, S. – SAHAY, R. – VEGH, C. (2002): Modern hyper- and high inflations. *Journal of Economic Literature,* vol. 40. no. 3. pp. 837–880.

FRIEDMAN, M. (1968): The role of monetary policy. *American Economic Review,* vol. 58. no. 3. pp. 1–17.

GAIDAR, Ye. T. ed. (1998): *Ekonomika perekhodnogo perioda.* (The economics of the transition period). Moscow: a book published by the Governmental Institute for Economic Reform.

GLIGOROV, V. (2004): The economics of disintegration and reintegration: the case of Yugoslavia. In: MUNGIU-PIPPIDI, A. and KRASTEV, I., eds: *Nationalism after Communism.* New York and Budapest: Central European University Press, pp. 83–100.

GREENAWAY, D. – MORGAN, P. – WRIGHT, P. (2002): Trade liberalization and growth in developing countries. *Journal of Development Economics,* vol. 67. no. 1. pp. 259–280.

HAMAR, J. (1995): Tendenciaváltozások a közvetlen tőkebefektetések nemzetközi áramlásában: Elmélet és gyakorlat. (Changing trends in the flow of FDI in the global economy: Theory and practice). *Külgazdaság,* vol. 38. no. (7–8). pp. 49–68.

HANSEN, H. and RAND, J. (2006): On the casual link between FDI and growth in developing countries. *World Economy,* vol. 29. no. 1. pp. 21–42.

HANSON, Ph. (2003): The Russian economic recovery: Do four years tell us that the fundamentals have changed? *Europe-Asia Studies,* vol. 55. no. 3. pp. 365–382.

HARE, P. G. and HUGHES, G. (1992): Trade policy and restructuring in Eastern Europe. In: ROLLO, J. and FLEMING, J. eds: *Trade, Payments and Adjustment in Central and Eastern Europe:* a book published jointly by the Royal Institute of International Affairs and the European Bank for Reconstruction and Development, London, pp. 181–209.

HAVRYLYSHIN, O. and van ROODEN, R. (2003): Institutions matter in transition, but so do policies. *Comparative Economic Studies,* vol. 45. no. 1. pp. 2–24.

HAVRYLYSHIN, O. (2006): Growth and institutions in transition: How do Belarus, Russia and Ukraine compare to others? Warsaw: *TIGER Working Paper,* no 97 (October), available online: www.tiger.edu.pl

HEITGER, B. (1990): Wirtschaftliches Wachstum in Ost und West: Ein Vergleich. *Die Weltwirtschaft,* no. 1. pp. 173–192.

HŘICH, J. (2006): The new political economy of emerging Europe. *Perspectives – the Central European Review of International Affairs,* no. 26 (summer), pp 98-104.

ILLARIONOV, A. (2003): 'Russian economic reforms and prospects for growth' – distinguished lecture given to Collegium Budapest, 20 March.

INOTAI, A. (1989): *A működőtőke a világgazdaságban.* (Foreign direct investment in the world economy). Budapest: Kossuth Könyvkiadó.

JÁNOSSY, F. (1966): *Das Ende des Wirtschaftswunders.* Frankfurt: Neue Kritik.

JENSEN, C. (2006): FDI and economic transition: panacea or painkillers? *Europe-Asia Studies,* vol. 58. no. 6. pp. 881–902.

KALOTAY, K. (2003): Működőtőke – válságban? (Foreign direct investment in crisis?) *Közgazdasági Szemle,* vol. 50. no. 1. pp. 35–55.

KAZMER, D. and KONRAD, M. (2004): *Economic Lessons from the Transition: The Basic Theory Re-Examined.* Armonk, N. Y.: M. E. Sharpe.

KÁDÁR, B. (1984): *Structural Changes in the World Economy.* New York: St. Martin's Press.

KOLODKO, G. W. (2001): *Post-Communist Transformation: The Thorny Road.* Rochester and London: Rochester University Press.

KORNAI, J. (1994): Transformational recession: the major causes. *Journal of Comparative Economics,* vol. 19. no. 1. pp. 37–52.

KORNAI, J. (1996): The evolution of financial discipline in post-communism. *Kyklos,* vol. 46, no. 3. pp. 315–336.

KORNAI, J. (1998): Soft budget constraint and market discipline in transition. *Journal of Comparative Economics,* vol. 23. no. 4.

KORNAI, J. (2001): Hardening the budget constraint: The experience of post-communist countries. *European Economic Review,* vol. 45. no. 9. pp. 1573–1600.

KORNAI, J. – MASKIN, E. – ROLAND, G. (2003): Understanding the soft budget constraint. *Journal of Economic Literature,* vol. 41. no. 4. pp. 1095–1136.

KUDROV, V. (2006): Strany Tsentralnoj i Vostochnoi Evropi i opit systemnoi transformatsii (Lessons from systemic change in CEE). *Voprosy Economiki,* vol. 77. no. 5. pp. 97–114.

MAU, V. and STARODUBROVSKAIA, I. (2001): *Revolutionary Changes in Russia and Europe.* Cambridge and New York: Cambridge University Press.

MCINTYRE, R. and DALLAGO, B. eds (2003): *Small and Medium Enterprises in Transition Economies.* Basingstoke and London: Palgrave.

de MELO, M. – DENIZER, C. – GELB, A. – TENEV, S. (2001): Circumstance and choice: The role of initial conditions and policies in transition economies. *World Bank Economic Review,* vol. 13. no. 1. pp. 1–32.

MICHALOPOULOS and TARR, D. eds (1994): *Trade in the New Independent States.* Washington: The World Bank.

MURRELL, P. (1992): Evolutionary and radical approaches to economic reform. *Economics of Planning,* vol. 25. no. 1. pp. 79–95.

NISKANEN, W. (2002): On the death of the Phillips curve. *CATO Journal,* vol. 22. no. 2. pp. 193–198.

OFER, G. (2001): Development and transition: converging but merging? In: Ten Years of Transition in Eastern European Countries, a special issue of *Revue d' Économie Financiere,* pp. 107–146.

PAUNIO, J. – HONKAPONJA, S. – KOSKELA, E. (1993): A finn gazdasági válság (Recession in the Finnish economy). *Külgazdaság,* vol. 37. no. 10. pp. 46–61.

PITLIK, H. (2002): The path of liberalization and economic growth. *Kyklos,* vol. 55. no. 1. pp. 57–80.

POLÁNYI, K. (1946): *Origins of Our Time: The Great Transformation.* London: Victor Gollanz Ltd.

RÉTHI, S. (2003): *Gazdasági transzformáció Oroszországban, 1992–2001.* (Economic transformation in Russia, 1992–2001). – Ph. D. thesis defended at the University of Debrecen, Faculty of Economics, June.

ROSEFIELDE, S. (2003): The riddle of post-war Russian economic growth: Statistics lied and were misconstructed. *Europe-Asia Studies,* vol. 55. no. 3. pp. 469–483.

ROSTOWSKI, J. (1997): Comparing two depressions: 1929–33 and 1989–93. In: ZECCHINI, S. ed.: *Lessons from the Economic Transition.* Kluwer Academic Publishers for OECD, pp. 225–240.

ROSTOWSKI, J. (1999): *Macroeconomic Instability in Post-Communist Economies.* Oxford: Oxford University Press.

SACHDEVA, G. (2003): Understanding Central Asian economic models. In: JOSHI, N. ed.: *Central Asia: The Great Game Replayed.* Delhi: New Century Publications, pp. 198–256.

SELM, B. van (1997): *The Economics of Soviet Brake-Up.* London: Routledge.

SIMONETTI, M. ed. (2001): *Investment Funds in Transition.* Aldershot: Ashgate.

SOLOW, R. ed. (2001): *Landmark Papers on Economic Growth.* Cheltenham/UK and Northampton/Md/USA: Edward Elgar Publishing Co.

SOÓS, K. A. (2000): Structural upgrading in manufacturing under transition: A comparative analysis of eight countries. In: BARA, Z. and CSABA, L. eds: *Small Economies' Adjustment to Global Tendencies.* Budapest: Aula Publishing House for the European Association for Comparative Economic Studies, pp. 245–274.

SUTELA, P. (2004): *The Russian Market Economy.* Helsinki: Kikimora Publishers.

TÖRÖK, Á. (1986): *Komparatív előnyök – újabb elméleti megközelítések.* (New theoretical approaches to comparative advantage). Budapest: Közgazdasági és Jogi Könyvkiadó.

UN Economic Commission for Europe (2005): *Economic Survey of Europe,* no. 2. Geneva and New York: a publication of the UN Secretariat.

YASIN, Ye. (2003): Ekonomicheskaia transformatsiia i sistema tsennostei Rossii. (Economic transformation and the system of values in Russia). *Voprosy Ekonomiki,* vol. 74. no. 4. pp. 1–35.

VOIGT, P. (2006): Russia's way from planning to market – a success story? *Post-Communist Economies,* vol. 18. no. 2. pp. 123–138.

WELFENS, P. (1999): *EU Eastward Enlargement and the Russian Transformation Crisis.* Heildelberg and New York: Springer Verlag.

WINIECKI, J. (1991): *The Distorted World of Soviet-Type Economies.* London: Routledge.

WINIECKI, J. (2002): An inquiry into the early drastic fall of output in post-Communist transition: An unsolved puzzle. *Post-Communist Economies,* vol. 14. no. 1. pp. 5–30.

WINTERS, L. A. (2002): Trade liberalization and poverty: What are the links? *World Economy,* vol. 25. no. 9. pp. 1139–1168.

ZON, H. van (2000): *The Political Economy of Independent Ukraine.* Basingstoke and London: MacMillan.

Table 1.

Real GDP in Western Europe, North America and Japan, 1988–2002
(Percentage change over preceding year)

	1988	1989	1990	1991	1992	1993	1994	1995	1996	1997	1998	1999	2000	2001	2002
France[a]	4.6	4.2	2.6	1.0	1.5	-0.9	2.1	1.7	1.1	1.9	3.4	3.2	3.8	1.8	1.0
Germany[b]	3.7	3.5	3.2	2.8	2.2	-1.1	2.3	1.7	0.8	1.4	2.0	2.0	2.9	0.6	0.2
Italy	3.9	2.9	2.0	1.4	0.8	-0.9	2.2	2.9	1.1	2.0	1.8	1.6	2.9	1.8	0.4
Austria	3.4	4.2	4.7	3.3	2.3	0.4	2.6	1.6	2.0	1.6	3.9	2.7	3.5	0.7	0.7
Belgium	4.7	3.5	3.1	1.8	1.5	-1.0	3.2	2.4	1.2	3.6	2.0	3.2	3.7	0.8	0.7
Finland	4.7	5.1	–	-6.3	-3.3	-1.1	4.0	3.8	4.0	6.3	5.3	4.1	6.1	0.7	1.4
Greece	4.3	3.8	–	3.1	0.7	-1.6	2.0	2.1	2.4	3.6	3.4	3.6	4.2	4.1	3.5
Ireland	5.2	5.8	8.5	1.9	3.3	2.7	5.8	9.9	8.1	10.9	8.8	11.1	10.0	5.7	3.3
Luxembourg	10.4	9.8	5.3	8.6	1.8	4.2	3.8	1.3	3.7	7.7	7.5	6.0	8.9	1.0	0.1
Netherlands	3.0	5.0	4.1	2.5	1.7	0.9	2.6	3.0	3.0	3.8	4.3	4.0	3.3	1.3	0.2
Portugal	7.5	6.4	4.0	4.4	1.1	-2.0	1.0	4.3	3.5	3.9	4.5	3.5	3.5	1.7	0.7
Spain	5.1	4.8	3.8	2.5	0.9	-1.0	2.4	2.8	2.4	4.0	4.3	4.2	4.2	2.7	1.9
Euro area[c]	4.2	3.9	2.9	2.0	1.5	-0.8	2.3	2.3	1.5	2.4	2.9	2.8	3.5	1.5	0.8
United Kingdom	5.2	2.2	0.8	-1.4	0.2	2.5	4.7	2.9	2.6	3.4	2.9	2.4	3.1	2.0	1.6
Denmark	1.2	0.2	1.0	1.1	0.6	–	5.5	2.8	2.5	3.0	2.5	2.3	3.0	1.0	1.7
Sweden[a]	2.6	2.7	1.1	-1.1	-1.7	1.1	4.2	4.0	1.3	2.4	3.6	4.6	4.4	0.8	1.6
European Union[d]	4.3	3.5	2.5	1.4	1.2	-0.3	2.8	2.5	1.7	2.6	2.9	2.8	3.4	1.6	0.9
Cyprus	8.5	7.9	7.4	0.6	9.8	0.7	5.9	6.1	1.9	2.5	5.0	4.8	5.2	4.1	1.8
Iceland	-0.1	0.3	1.2	0.7	-3.3	0.6	4.5	0.1	5.2	4.6	5.3	3.9	5.0	1.5	-0.6
Israel[a]	3.4	1.4	6.3	5.7	6.8	3.4	6.9	8.3	4.5	3.3	2.7	2.6	6.4	-0.9	-1.0
Malta	8.4	8.2	6.3	6.3	4.7	4.5	5.7	6.2	4.0	4.8	3.4	4.1	6.1	-0.8	2.5
Norway[a]	-0.1	0.9	2.0	3.8	3.3	2.7	5.3	4.4	5.3	5.2	2.6	2.1	2.4	1.4	2.1
Switzerland	3.1	4.3	3.7	-0.8	-0.1	-0.5	0.5	0.3	1.7	2.4	1.5	3.2	0.9	-0.2	
Turkey	2.1	0.3	9.3	0.9	6.0	8.0	-5.5	7.2	7.0	7.5	3.1	-4.7	7.4	-7.4	3.7
Western Europe	4.1	3.4	2.8	1.3	1.4	0.1	2.4	2.6	1.9	2.8	2.9	2.4	3.6	1.2	1.0
Canada[a]	5.0	2.6	0.2	-2.1	0.9	2.3	4.8	2.8	1.6	4.2	4.1	5.4	4.5	1.5	3.3
United States[a]	4.2	3.5	1.8	-0.5	3.0	2.7	4.0	2.7	3.6	4.4	4.3	4.1	3.8	–	3.2
North America	4.2	3.4	1.6	-0.6	2.9	2.6	4.1	2.7	3.4	4.4	4.3	4.2	3.8	0.4	2.4
Japan	6.5	5.2	5.2	3.3	1.0	0.3	1.0	1.9	3.4	1.8	-1.1	0.1	2.8	0.3	-0.7
Total above	4.5	3.7	2.6	0.8	1.9	1.2	2.9	2.5	2.8	3.4	2.9	2.9	3.6	0.7	1.4
Memorandum items: 4 major West European economies[e]	4.3	3.2	2.3	1.2	1.3	-0.3	2.7	2.2	1.3	2.1	2.5	2.3	3.1	1.4	0.7
Western Europe and North America	4.2	3.4	2.2	0.4	2.1	1.3	3.3	2.7	2.7	3.6	3.6	3.3	3.7	0.8	1.7

[a] Annual changes are calculated from chained national currency series.
[b] West Germany, 1988–1991.
[c] Twelve countries above.
[d] Fifteen countries above.
[e] France, Germany, Italy and the United Kingdom.

Source: UN ECE Survey, no 1/2003. p. 213.

Table 2.

Real GDP/NMP in Eastern Europe and the CIS, 1980, 1989–2002
(Indices, 1989=100)

	1980	1989	1990	1991	1992	1993	1994	1995	1996	1997	1998	1999	2000	2001	2002
Eastern Europe	–	100.0	93.4	83.3	78.1	76.9	84.4	87.9	90.4	92.5	93.9	97.5	100.5		103.4
Albania	79.4	100.0	90.0	64.8	60.1	65.9	71.4	80.9	88.2	82.0	88.6	95.0	102.4	109.0	113.9
Bosnia and Herzegovina	–	–	–	–	–	–	–	100.0	154.2	210.7	231.6	256.2	267.6	273.7	280.0
Bulgaria	76.2	100.0	90.9	83.3	77.2	76.1	77.5	79.7	72.2	68.2	70.9	76.4	79.5	82.9	
Croatia	99.0	100.0	92.9	73.3	64.7	59.5	63.0	71.3	76.2	76.1	77.4	79.6	82.6	86.4	
Czech Republic	–	100.0	98.8	87.3	86.9	86.9	88.9	94.1	98.2	96.4	96.9	100.0	103.3	105.8	
Estonia	74.5	100.0	91.9	82.7	71.0	65.0	63.7	66.4	69.0	75.7	79.2	78.7	84.3	88.6	93.6
Hungary	86.3	100.0	96.5	85.0	82.4	81.9	84.4	85.6	86.8	90.7	95.1	99.1	104.3	108.2	111.7
Latvia	68.5	100.0	102.9	89.9	61.1	54.1	55.3	54.7	56.8	61.5	64.4	66.3	70.6	76.2	80.6
Lithuania	64.7	100.0	96.7	91.2	71.8	60.2	54.3	56.1	58.7	63.0	66.2	63.6	66.0	70.0	74.1
Poland	91.1	100.0	88.4	82.2	84.4	87.6	92.1	98.6	104.5	111.7	117.1	121.8	126.7	128.0	129.6
Romania	88.5	100.0	94.4	82.2	75.0	76.2	79.2	84.8	88.2	82.8	78.8	77.9	79.3	83.5	87.4
Slovakia	–	100.0	97.5	83.3	78.0	75.1	79.0	84.1	89.0	94.0	97.7	99.0	101.2	104.5	108.7
Slovenia	98.9	100.0	91.9	83.7	79.1	81.4	85.7	89.3	92.4	96.6	100.3	105.5	110.4	113.6	117.3
Macedonia	93.3	100.0	89.8	84.3	78.7	72.8	71.6	70.8	71.6	72.6	75.1	78.4	81.9	78.2	78.5
Yugoslavia[a]	95.7	100.0	92.1	81.4	58.7	40.6	41.7	44.2	46.8	50.3	51.5	42.4	45.1	47.6	49.5
CIS[b]	77.5	100.0	96.9	91.0	78.3	70.7	60.6	57.1	55.2	55.8	54.2	56.6	61.3	65.0	68.0
Armenia	73.5	100.0	94.5	83.5	48.6	44.3	46.7	49.9	52.9	54.6	58.6	60.5	64.1	70.3	79.3
Azerbaijan	79.6	100.0	88.3	87.7	67.9	52.2	41.9	37.0	37.4	39.6	43.6	46.8	52.0	57.1	63.1
Belarus	65.7	100.0	96.1	96.7	87.4	80.8	71.4	63.9	65.7	73.2	79.4	82.1	86.8	91.0	95.2
Georgia	79.4	100.0	84.9	67.0	36.9	26.1	23.4	24.0	26.7	29.5	30.3	31.2	31.8	33.3	35.1
Kazakhstan	87.0	100.0	99.0	88.2	83.5	75.8	66.2	60.8	61.1	62.1	60.9	62.6	68.7	78.0	85.4
Kyrgyzstan	69.1	100.0	104.8	96.5	83.2	70.3	56.2	53.1	56.9	62.5	63.9	66.2	69.8	73.5	73.2
Republic of Moldova[c]	72.1	100.0	97.6	80.5	57.2	56.5	39.0	38.5	36.2	36.8	34.4	33.2	34.0	36.0	38.6
Russian Federation	78.1	100.0	97.0	92.2	78.8	71.9	62.8	60.2	58.2	58.7	55.9	58.9	64.2	67.4	70.2
Tajikistan	80.8	100.0	100.2	91.7	62.1	52.0	40.9	35.8	29.8	30.3	32.0	33.10	35.9	39.5	43.1
Turkmenistan	80.7	100.0	101.8	97.0	82.5	83.7	69.2	54.2	68.5	60.7	65.0	78.0	83.6	90.3	98.4
Ukraine	75.	100.0	96.4	88.0	79.3	68.0	52.4	46.0	41.4	40.2	39.4	39.3	41.6	45.4	47.3
Uzbekistan	76.0	100.0	99.2	98.7	87.7	81.2	80.5	81.9	86.1	89.9	93.9	97.6	102.0		106.3
Total above	–	100.0	95.8	88.7	78.2	72.5	66.2	65.2	64.9	66.0	65.5	67.6	72.0	75.4	78.4
Memorandum items: Baltic states (BS-3)	678	100.0	97.6	89.2	68.4	59.3	56.4	57.7	60.1	65.0	68.2	67.4	71.1	75.5	79.9
Central Europe (CE-5)	–	100.0	93.2	84.0	83.7	85.0	88.5	93.5	97.9	102.4	106.0	109.3	113.6	116.1	118.5
South-East Europe (SEE-7)	89.0	100.0	92.9	80.8	70.7	66.8	69.2	74.4	76.6	75.1	74.5	73.1	75.6	79.0	82.4

[a] Gross material product (1980–1989 for Croatia, 1980–2000 for Yugoslavia). Yugoslavia: since 1999, without Kosovo and Metohia.

[b] Net material product for 1980–1990 (until 1992 in the case of Turkmenistan).

[c] Excluding Transdniestra since 1993.

Table 2 (continued)

	1980	1989	1990	1991	1992	1993	1994	1995	1996	1997	1998	1999	2000	2001	2002
SCIS without Russian Federation (CIS–11)	76.4	100.0	96.6	88.8	77.3	68.2	56.1	51.0	49.3	50.1	50.8	52.2	55.6	60.3	63.8
Caucasian CIS	78.6	100.0	87.7	77.7	51.1	39.3	34.3	33.0	34.9	37.3	39.8	41.8	44.7	48.3	52.9
Central Asian CIS countries (CACIS–5)	81.9	100.0	99.9	92.5	82.7	76.8	67.5	63.4	64.2	65.2	66.3	69.6	74.9	81.9	87.8
Three European CIS countries (ECIS–3)	73.4	100.0	96.7	89.1	79.7	69.6	54.9	48.6	45.2	45.4	45.7	46.1	48.7	52.5	54.8
Former GDR[d]	–	100.0	84.5	68.3	73.3	80.1	87.9	91.9	94.9	96.7	97.7	99.0	100.0	99.9	100.0

Source: UN ECE *Survey,* no 2/2003. p. 112.

Table 3.

Real total consumption expenditure in Eastern Europe and the CIS, 1980, 1989–2001 (Indices, 1989=100 or earliest year available thereafter)

	1980	1989	1990	1991	1992	1993	1994	1995	1996	1997	1998	1999	2000	2001
Bulgaria	–	100.0	100.6	92.3	89.4	86.2	82.3	80.7	74.1	67.1	69.8	75.9	80.2	83.9
Croatia	–	–	–	100.0	87.2	85.3	92.0	106.6	106.5	117.1	117.4	116.1	118.8	121.1
Czech Republic	–	100.0	104.9	85.5	88.4	90.2	94.5	97.2	103.7	104.3	101.8	103.7	105.3	108.4
Estonia	–	–	–	–	100.0	101.9	109.0	115.7	122.7	128.0	126.9	133.0	138.4
Hungary	92.2	100.0	97.3	92.2	92.8	97.9	95.6	89.3	86.1	91.7	95.6	99.1	102.6	
Latvia	–	–	100.0	76.7	49.2	46.5	47.4	47.0	50.6	52.4	53.7	55.2	57.9	60.4
Lithuania	–	–	–	–	–	–	–	100.0	108.2	116.4	125.4	122.4	126.8	129.0
Poland	108.0	100.0	88.3	94.9	98.2	103.0	107.0	110.5	118.4	125.6	130.8	136.6	140.0	142.3
Romania	83.9	100.0	108.9	96.0	90.7	91.8	95.3	105.5	112.9	108.1	109.3	106.5	107.7	113.8
Slovakia	–	100.0	103.3	76.9	75.6	74.2	72.6	75.1	83.6	85.8	92.4	92.5	91.6	95.5
Slovenia	–	–	100.0	91.6	88.8	99.1	102.6	110.2	112.7	116.3	120.9	127.7	129.5	132.2
Macedonia	–	–	100.0	93.9	84.2	89.7	95.9	94.3	98.5	101.8	105.6	114.0	–	
Armenia	–	–	100.0	97.4	84.9	66.4	68.9	74.5	76.8	81.7	85.4	86.6	93.3	98.6
Azerbaijan	–	–	–	–	100.0	77.4	62.2	60.4	65.3	72.2	80.4	88.1	96.9	105.8
Belarus	–	–	100.0	93.5	84.1	78.8	70.0	63.4	65.7	72.3	80.9	87.7	94.2	107.1
Georgia	–	–	100.0	79.2	77.1	45.4	42.4	46.1	–	–	–	–	–	–
Kazakhstan	–	–	100.0	96.8	96.2	84.9	67.7	55.0	51.3	51.8	50.4	51.1	52.5	57.6
Kyrgyzstan	–	–	100.0	-83.5	72.8	64.3	51.8	43.4	46.2	42.4	42.8	49.3	47.9	48.6
Republic of Moldova	–	–	–	–	–	100.0	82.6	90.3	99.7	111.5	109.3	92.0	107.8	112.5
Russian Federation	–	–	100.0	93.9	89.0	88.1	85.4	83.1	80.5	82.9	81.7	79.7	85.6	90.9
Ukraine	–	–	100.0	94.7	88.7	72.1	65.1	62.7	57.5	56.4	54.3	55.4	60.5	

Source: UN ECE Common Database, derived from national and Interstate Statistical Committee of the CIS statistics
Source: UN ECE *Survey,* no 2/2004. p. 44.

[d] Excluding the former East Berlin since 1998.

Table 4.

Real gross fixed capital formation In Eastern Europe and the CIS, 1980, 1989–2001
(Indices, 1989=100 or earliest year available thereafter)

	1980	1989	1990	1991	1992	1993	1994	1995	1996	1997	1998	1999	2000	2001
Bulgaria	–	–	100.0	80.0	74.1	61.2	61.9	71.8	56.6	44.7	60.5	73.1	84.4	101.1
Croatia	–	–	–	100.0	88.5	94.5	93.6	108.2	148.8	183.5	188.1	180.8	173.9	190.7
Czech Republic	–	100.0	97.9	71.1	82.8	83.0	90.5	108.4	117.3	113.9	114.7	113.5	119.5	128.3
Estonia	–	–	–	–	–	100.0	106.3	110.6	123.2	144.8	161.1	137.4	155.7	169.9
Hungary	114.7	100.0	92.9	83.1	81.0	82.6	92.9	88.9	94.8	103.6	117.3	124.2	133.8	137.9
Latvia	–	–	100.0	36.1	25.7	21.6	21.8	23.7	29.0	35.0	50.4	48.4	58.0	67.9
Lithuania	–	–	–	–	–	–	–	100.0	117.6	143.6	157.8	147.9	142.2	154.6
Poland	124.6	100.0	75.2	71.9	73.6	75.7	82.6	96.2	115.1	140.1	160.0	170.9	175.6	160.2
Romania	163.7	100.0	64.4	44.0	48.9	52.9	63.9	68.3	72.2	73.4	69.2	65.9	68.9	73.5
Slovakia	–	–	100.0	74.8	71.5	67.7	66.0	67.1	87.9	100.4	111.5	90.9	92.0	100.8
Slovenia	–	–	100.0	88.5	77.1	85.4	97.4	113.8	123.9	138.2	153.9	183.6	180.2	
Macedonia	–	–	100.0	95.8	79.9	73.6	67.3	74.1	79.0	75.6	73.6	72.5	70.2	–
Armenia	–	–	100.0	67.0	8.6	7.9	11.5	9.5	10.5	10.7	12.0	12.1	14.0	14.6
Azerbaijan	–	–	–	–	100.0	61.0	115.3	94.5	199.8	333.7	410.4	402.2	412.7	497.7
Belarus	–	–	100.0	104.2	84.8	78.3	67.6	47.6	46.1	56.2	61.8	59.3	60.7	59.3
Georgia	–	–	100.0	67.3	49.2	18.5	133.4	219.9	–	–	–	–	–	–
Kazakhstan	–	–	100.0	74.2	61.9	44.2	39.2	24.3	18.5	19.1	17.8	17.9	20.7	26.0
Kyrgyzstan	–	–	100.0	89.4	63.2	49.4	35.1	56.4	49.1	34.6	34.0	43.6	55.3	54.3
Republic of Moldova	–	–	–	–	–	100.0	56.50	50.8	63.8	60.4	66.0	50.8	46.4	54.4
Russian Federation	–	–	100.0	84.5	49.4	36.7	27.1	25.1	20.8	19.1	17.3	18.2	20.8	22.5
Ukraine	–	–	100.0	79.1	67.4	46.8	27.6	19.1	14.8	15.1	15.5	17.4	18.5	

Source: UN ECE *Survey,* no 2/2004. p. 44.

Table 5.

Consumer price indices in Eastern Europe and the CIS, 1990–200
(Annual average, percentage change over preceding year)

	1990	1991	1992	1993	1994	1995	1996	1997	1998	1999	2000	2001	2002
Albania	–	35.5	193.1	85.0	21.5	8.0	12.7	33.1	20.3	-0.1	–	3.1	5.3
Bosnia and Herzegovina	594.0	116.206	4 218.338	825.1	553.5	-12.1	-21.2	11.8	4.9	-0.6	1.7	1.8	–
Bulgaria	23.8	338.5	91.3	72.9	96.2	62.0	121.7	1 058.3	18.7	2.6	10.2	7.3	5.8
Croatia	597.1	124.2	663.6	1 516.6	97.5	2.0	3.6	3.7	5.2	3.5	5.4	4.7	1.8
Czech Republic	9.9	56.7	11.1	20.8	10.0	9.1	8.9	8.4	10.6	2.1	3.9	4.7	1.8
Estonia	18.0	202.0	1 078.2	89.6	47.9	28.9	23.1	11.1	10.6	3.5	3.9	5.8	3.5
Hungary	28.9	35.0	23.0	22.6	19.1	28.5	23.6	18.4	14.2	10.1	9.9	9.2	5.4
Latvia	10.9	172.2	951.2	109.1	35.7	25.0	17.7	8.5	4.7	2.4	2.8	2.4	1.9
Lithuania	9.1	216.4	1 020.5	410.1	72.0	39.5	24.7	8.8	5.1	0.8	1.0	1.5	0.4
Poland	585.8	70.3	45.3	36.9	33.2	28.1	19.8	15.1	11.7	7.4	10.2	5.5	1.9
Romania	5.1	170.2	210.7	256.2	137.1	32.2	38.8	154.9	59.3	45.9	45.7	34.5	22.5
Slovakia	10.4	61.2	10.2	23.1	13.4	10.0	6.1	6.1	6.7	10.5	12.0	7.0	3.3
Slovenia	551.6	115.0	207.3	31.7	21.0	13.5	9.9	8.4	8.1	6.3	9.0	8.6	7.6
Macedonia	596.6	110.8	1 511.0	352.0	126.6	16.4	2.5	0.9	-1.4	-1.3	6.6	5.2	–
Yugoslavia	580.0	122.08	926.0	2.2E+14	7.9E+10	71.8	90.5	23.2	30.4	44.1	77.5	90.4	19.3
Armenia	6.9	174.1	728.7	3 731.8	4 964.0	175.5	18.7	13.8	8.7	0.7	-0.8	3.2	1.0
Azerbaijan	6.1	106.6	912.6	1 129.7	1 663.9	411.5	19.8	3.6	-0.8	-8.6	1.8	1.5	2.8
Belarus	4.7	94.1	971.2	1 190.9	2 219.6	709.3	52.7	63.9	73.2	293.7	168.9	61.4	42.8
Georgia	4.2	78.7	1 176.9	4 084.9	22 266.1	261.4	39.4	7.1	3.5	19.3	4.2	4.6	5.7
Kazakhstan	5.8	114.5	1 504.3	1 662.7	1 880.1	176.3	39.2	17.5	7.3	8.4	13.4	8.5	6.0
Kyrgyzstan	5.5	113.9	854.6	1 208.7	278.1	42.9	31.3	23.4	10.3	35.	18.7	7.0	2.1
Republic of Moldova	5.7	114.4	1 308.0	1 751.0	486.4	29.9	23.5	11.8	7.7	39.3	31.3	9.8	5.3
Russian Federation	5.2	160.0	1 528.7	875.0	309.0	197.4	47.8	14.7	27.8	85.7	20.8	21.6	16.0
Tajikistan	5.9	112.9	822.0	2 884.8	350.3	682.1	422.4	85.4	43.1	27.5	32.9	38.6	12.2
Turkmenistan	5.7	88.5	483.2	3 128.4	2 562.1	1 105.3	714.0	83.7	16.8	–	–	–	–
Ukraine	5.4	94.0	1 485.8	4 734.9	891.2	376.7	80.2	15.9	10.6	22.7	28.2	12.0	0.8
Uzbekistan	5.8	97.3	414.5	1 231.8	1 550.0	76.5	54.0	58.8017.7	29.0	24.9	–	–	

Source: UNECE Database, derived from national statistics.
Source: UN ECE *Survey*, no 2/2004. p. 45.

Table 6.

Registered unemployment in Eastern Europe and the CIS, 1990–2002
(Per cent of labour force, end of period)

	1990	1991	1992	1993	1994	1995	1996	1997	1998	1999	2000	2001	2002
Eastern Europe	–	–	11.7	13.4	13.1	12.3	11.7	11.5	12.3	14.3	14.8	15.3	–
Albania	9.5	9.2	27.0	22.0	18.0	12.9	12.3	14.9	17.6	18.2	16.9	14.5	–
Bosnia and Herzegovina	–	–	–	–	–	–	–	39.0	38.7	39.0	39.4	39.9	–
Bulgaria	1.8	11.1	15.3	16.4	12.8	11.1	12.5	13.7	12.2	16.0	17.9	17.9	16.3
Croatia	–	14.1	17.8	16.6	17.3	17.6	15.9	17.6	18.6	20.8	22.6	23.1	21.5
Czech Republic	0.7	4.1	2.6	3.5	3.2	2.9	3.5	5.2	7.5	9.4	8.8	8.9	9.8
Estonia[a]	–	–	1.6	5.0	5.1	5.0	5.6	4.6	5.1	6.7	7.7	7.7	6.8
Hungary	1.7	7.4	12.3	12.1	10.9	10.4	10.5	10.4	9.1	9.6	8.9	8.0	5.6
Latvia	–	–	2.3	5.8	6.5	6.6	7.2	7.0	9.2	9.1	7.8	7.7	7.6
Lithuania	–	–	3.5	3.4	4.5	7.3	6.2	6.7	10.0	12.8	12.9	10.9	
Poland	6.5	12.2	14.3	16.4	16.0	14.9	13.2	10.3	10.4	13.1	15.1	17.5	18.1
Romania	1.3	3.0	8.2	10.4	10.9	9.5	6.6	8.8	10.3	11.5	10.5	8.8	8.1
Slovaki	1.6	11.8	10.4	14.4	14.8	13.1	12.8	12.5	15.6	19.2	17.9	18.6	17.5
Slovenia	–	10.1	13.3	15.5	14.2	14.5	14.4	14.8	14.6	13.0	12.0	11.8	–
Macedonia	–	24.5	26.2	27.7	30.0	36.6	38.8	41.7	41.4	44*	45*	42*	–
Yugoslavia[b]	–	21.0	24.6	24.0	23.9	24.7	26.1	25.6	27.2	27.4	26.6	27.9	–
CIS	–	–	2.7	3.8	4.6	5.8	6.6	7.6	9.0	8.3	7.1	6.2	5.6
Armenia	–	–	3.5	6.3	6.0	8.1	9.7	11.0	8.9	11.5	10.9	9.8	9.1
Azerbaijan	–	–	0.2	0.7	0.9	1.1	1.1	1.3	1.4	1.2	1.2	1.3	1.3
Belarus	–	–	0.5	1.3	2.1	2.7	4.0	2.8	2.3	2.1	2.3	3.0	
Georgia	–	–	0.3	2.0	3.8	3.4	3.2	8.0	4.2	5.6	–	–	–
Kazakhstan	–	–	0.4	0.6	1.0	2.1	4.1	3.9	3.7	3.9	3.7	2.8	2.6
Kyrgyzstan	–	–	0.1	0.2	0.8	3.0	4.5	3.1	3.0	3.1	3.1	3.1	
Republic of Moldova	–	–	0.7	0.7	1.0	1.4	1.5	1.7	1.9	2.1	1.8	1.7	1.5
Russian Federation[c]	–	–	5.2	6.1	7.8	9.0	10.0	11.2	13.3	12.2	9.8	8.7	7.1
Tajikistan	–	–	0.4	1.1	1.8	1.8	2.4	2.8	2.9	3.1	3.0	2.6	2.7
Turkmenistan	–	–	–	–	–	–	–	–	–	–	–	–	–
Ukraine	–	–	0.3	0.4	0.3	0.6	1.5	2.8	4.3	4.3	4.2	3.7	3.8
Uzbekistan	–	–	0.1	0.2	0.3	0.3	0.3	0.3	0.4	0.5	06.	–	–
Memorandum items: Baltic states	–	–	2.1	4.5	5.3	6.6	6.4	6.4	7.3	9.1	10.1	10.2	9.1
Central Europe	–	9.7	11.3	13.3	12.9	12.0	11.2	9.8	10.3	12.5	13.4	14.7	–
South-East Europe	–	9.3	14.2	15.1	14.6	13.6	13.3	15.0	16.1	17.8	17.8	17.2	–
Russian Federation[d]	–	–	0.8	1.1	2.1	3.2	3.4	2.8	2.7	1.7	1.4	1.6	1.8
Former-GDR	–	–	13.5	15.4	13.5	14.9	15.9	19.4	17.4	17.7	17.2	17.6	18.4

Source: UN ECE Survey, no 2/2004. p. 46.

[a] Job seekers until October 2000, therafter – registered unemployed as percentage of the labour force.
[b] Since 1999, excluding Kosovo and Metohia.
[c] Based on Russian Federation Goskomstat's monthly estimates according to the ILO definition, i. e. including all persons not having employment but actively seeking work.
[d] Registered unemployment.

Table 7.

Merchandise exports of Eastern Europe and the CIS, 1992–2001
(Billion dollars)

	1992	1993	1994	1995	1996	1997	1998	1999	2000	2001
Eastern Europe	61.472	66.872	77.261	100.621	107.084	115.895	127.933	141.892	157.131	
Albania	0.072	0.123	0.139	0.202	0.213	0.137	0.207	0.352	0.260	0.305
Bosnia and Herzegovina	–	–	–	0.024	0.058	0.193	0.352	0.518	0.675	0.799
Bulgaria	3.992	3.769	3.935	5.345	4.890	4.940	4.194	4.006	4.825	5.113
Croatia	4.353	3.709	4.260	4.633	4.512	4.171	4.541	4.302	4.432	4.666
Czech Republic	8.767	14.463	15.882	21.273	22.180	22.779	26.351	26.265	29.052	33.369
Estonia	0.444	0.802	1.305	1.838	2.079	2.934	3.236	2.938	3.176	3.305
Hungary	10.681	8.921	10.701	12.867	15.704	19.100	23.005	25.012	28.092	30.498
Latvia	0.843	1.401	0.988	1.304	1.443	1.673	1.812	1.723	1.865	2.001
Lithuania	0.852	1.994	2.031	2.705	3.355	3.860	3.711	3.004	3.809	4.583
Poland	13.187	14.202	17.240	22.887	24.440	25.756	28.229	27.407	31.651	36.092
Romania	4.363	4.892	6.151	7.910	8.085	8.431	8.302	8.487	10.367	11.385
Slovakia	3.500	5.458	6.714	8.585	8.822	9.640	10.775	10.277	11.908	12.704
Slovenia	6.681	6.083	6.828	8.316	8.310	8.369	9.050	8.546	8.732	9.252
Macedonia	1.199	1.055	1.086	1.204	1.147	1.237	1.311	1.191	1.319	1.155
Yugoslavia	2.539	–	–	1.531	1.846	2.677	2.858	1.493	1.730	1.903
CIS: total	–	–	89.991	110.622	121.936	122.913	104.716	104.179	143.691	143.474*
CIS to non-CIS	51.242	52.547	62.652	80.007	87.897	88.698	76.757	82.346	114.949	113.613*
Armenia	–	0.156	0.216	0.271	0.290	0.233	0.221	0.232	0.301	0.339
Non-CIS	0.026	0.029	0.058	0.101	0.162	0.138	0.140	0.175	0.227	0.252
Azerbaijan	1.484	0.725	0.653	0.637	0.631	0.781	0.606	0.929	1.745	2.314
Non-CIS	0.754	0.351	0.378	0.352	0.341	0.403	0.374	0.718	1.510	2.091
Belarus	–	–	2.510	4.707	5.652	7.301	7.070	5.909	7.331	7.428
Non-CIS	1.194	0.789	1.031	1.777	1.888	1.922	1.910	2.287	2.927	2.958
Georgia	–	–	0.156	0.154	0.199	0.240	0.193	0.238	0.330	0.320
Non-CIS	0.068	0.069	0.039	0.057	0.070	0.102	0.085	0.131	0.198	0.176
Kazakhstan	–	–	3.231	5.250	5.911	6.497	5.436	5.592	9.126	8.647
Non-CIS	1.398	1.501	1.357	2.366	2.732	3.515	3.266	4.100	6.750	6.015
Kyrgyzstan	0.137	0.396	0.340	0.409	0.505	0.604	0.514	0.454	0.505	0.476
Non-CIS	0.077	0.112	0.117	0.140	0.112	0.285	0.283	0.271	0.297	0.308
Republic of Moldova	0.470	0.483	0.565	0.795	0.875	0.632	0.464	0.472	0.570	
Non-CIS	0.166	0.178	0.159	0.279	0.252	0.267	0.203	0.211	0.196	0.224
Russian Federation[a]	–	–	66.862	79.869	86.889	86.627	73.000	73.700	102.796	100.653*
Non-CIS	42.376	44.297	53.001	65.607	70.975	69.959	58.800	62.800	89.068	86.213*
Tajikistan	0.193	0.350	0.492	0.749	0.770	0.746	0.597	0.689	0.784	0.652
Non-CIS	0.109	0.227	0.399	0.497	0.439	0.473	0.394	0.374	0.411	0.440
Turkeminstan	–	–	2.145	1.881	1.682	0.751	0.594	1.190	2.500	2.700
Non-CIS	0.908	1.049	0.494	0.951	0.610	0.300	0.442	0.700	1.200	1.300

[a] Russian Goskomstat data exluding trade by physical person (shuttle trade), but including trade flows not crossing the Russian borders such as off-board fish sales and natural gas deliveries under debt repayment agreements with former CMEA countries.

Table 7 (continued)

	1992	1993	1994	1995	1996	1997	1998	1999	2000	2001
Ukraine	7.415	7.817	10.272	13.128	14.401	14.232	12.637	11.582	14.573	16.265
Non-CIS	3.297	3.223	4.653	6.168	6.996	8.646	8.435	8.329	10.075	11.589
Uzbekistan	–	–	2.549	2.821	4.211	4.026	3.218	3.200	3.230	3.110
Non-CIS	0.869	0.721	0.966	1.712	3.321	2.689	2.425	2.250	2.090	2.050
Total above	–	–	167.252	211.243	229.019	238.808	232.649	229.702	285.584	300.605*
Memorandum items: Baltic states	2.1394	4.197	4.324	5.846	6.877	8.467	8.759	7.665	8.851	9.890
Central Europe	42.816	49.127	57.365	73.928	79.456	85.644	97.410	97.508	109.436	121.916
South-East Europe	–	–	–	20.848	20.751	21.785	21.764	20.350	23.606	25.326
CIS without Russian Federation	–	–	23.129	30.753	35.047	36.286	31.716	30.479	40.895	42.821
Caucasian CIS countries	–	–	1.025	1.062	1.120	1.253	1.019	1.399	2.376	2.973
Central Asian CIS countries	–	–	8.757	11.110	13.079	12.625	10.358	11.125	16.145	15.585
Three European CIS countries	–	–	13.347	18.581	20.848	22.408	20.339	17.955	22.375	24.263

Source: UNECE secretariat calculations, based on national statistical publications and direct communications from national statistical offices.

Source: UN ECE *Survey,* no 2/2004. p. 47.

Table 8.

Merchandise Imports of Eastern Europe and the CIS, 1992–2001
(Billion dollars)

	1992	1993	1994	1995	1996	1997	1998	1999	2000	2001
Eastern Europe	70.190	80.386	91.379	125.033	145.996	159.004	173.259	167.553	185.483	201.589
Albania	0.524	0.421	0.549	0.650	0.913	0.620	0.795	0.903	1.059	1.317
Bosnia and Herzegovina	–	–	–	0.524	1.204	1.55	2.120	2.431	2.290	2.340
Bulgaria	4.530	5.120	4.272	5.638	5.074	4.932	4.957	5.515	6.507	7.261
Croatia	4.346	4.166	5.229	7.510	7.788	9.104	8.383	7.799	7.887	9.147
Czech Republic	10.368	14.617	17.427	25.265	27.919	27.563	28.789	28.126	32.183	36.504
Estonia	0.406	0.896	2.540	3.231	4.441	4.786	4.108	4.256	4.291	
Hungary	11.123	12.648	14.554	15.466	18.144	21.234	25.706	28.008	32.080	33.682
Latvia	0.794	0.961	1.240	1.818	2.320	2.724	3.189	2.946	3.189	3.507
Lithuania	0.602	2.244	2.352	3.649	4.559	5.644	q5.794	4.834	5.457	6.353
Poland	16.141	18.758	21.566	29.043	37.137	42.314	47.054	45.911	48.940	50.275
Romania	6.260	6.522	7.109	10.278	11.435	11.280	11.838	10.57	13.055	15.552
Slovakia	3.889	6.332	6.634	8.777	11.112	11.622	13.006	11.265	12.660	14.689
Slovenia	6.141	6.501	7.304	9.492	9.421	9.367	10.098	10.083	10.116	10.148
Macedonia	1.206	1.199	1.484	1.719	1.627	1.779	1.915	1.776	2.085	1.688
Yugoslavia	3.869	–	–	2.665	4.113	4.826	4.830	3.290	3.721	4.837
CIS total	–	–	63.137	79.576	86.960	94.316	81.747	62.005	70.693	81.729*
CIS: from non-CIS	42.297	33.696	36.743	45.678	49.205	57.780	50.560	37.571	38.652	48.875*
Armenia	–	0.255	0.394	0.674	0.856	0.892	0.902	0.811	0.885	0.869
Non-CIS	0.050	0.087	0.188	0.340	0.578	0.593	0.672	0.624	0.711	0.655
Azerbaijan	0.940	0.629	0.778	0.668	0.961	0.794	1.077	1.036	1.172	1.431
Non-CIS	0.333	0.241	0.292	0.440	0.621	0.443	0.673	0.711	0.797	0.986
Belarus	–	–	3.066	5.564	6.939	8.689	8.549	6.674	8.574	8.049
Non-CIS	0.843	1.119	0.974	1.887	2.369	2.872	2.995	2.385	2.551	2.443
Georgia	–	–	0.338	0.385	0.687	0.944	0.884	0.602	0.651	0.684
Non-CIS	0.228	0.167	0.066	0.231	0.417	0.603	0.617	0.377	0.423	0.433
Kazakhstan	–	–	3.561	3.807	4.241	4.301	4.350	3.687	5.051	6.363
Non-CIS	0.469	0.494	1.384	1.154	1.295	1.969	2.290	2.089	2.295	3.057
Kyrgyzstan	0.421	0.448	0.317	0.522	0.838	0.709	0.842	0.600	0.554	0.467
Non-CIS	0.071	0.112	0.107	0.168	0.351	0.273	0.401	0.341	0.256	0.210
Republic of Moldova	0.640	0.628	0.659	0.841	1.072	1.172	1.024	0.587	0.776	0.897
Non-CIS	0.179	0.184	0.183	0.272	0.420	0.567	0.584	0.345	0.517	0.557
Russian Federation[a]	–	–	38.661	46.709	47.373	53.568	44.600	31.000	33.769	41.237*
Non-CIS	36.984	26.807	28.344	33.117	32.798	39.365	32.500	22.200	22.171	30.121*
Tajikistan	0.254	0.630	0.547	0.810	0.668	0.750	0.711	0.663	0.675	0.688
Non-CIS	0.132	0.374	0.314	0.332	0.285	0.268	0.265	0.148	0.115	0.150
Turkmenistan	–	–	1.468	1.364	1.011	1.183	1.008	1.500	1.780	2.250
Non-CIS	0.030	0.501	0.782	0.619	0.450	0.531	0.530	1.000	1.100	1.400

[a] Russian Goskomstat data exluding trade by physical persons (shuttle trade), but icluding trade flows not crossing the Russian borders such as off-board fish sales and natural gas deliveries under debt repayment agreements with former CMEA countries.

Table 8 (continued)

	1992	1993	1994	1995	1996	1997	1998	1999	2000	2001
Ukraine	6.892	9.533	10.745	15.484	17.603	17.128	14.676	11.846	13.956	15.775
Non-CIS	2.049	2.652	2.907	5.488	6.427	7.249	6.779	5.103	5.916	6.943
Uzbekistan	–	–	2.603	2.748	4.712	4.186	3.125	3.000	2.850	3.020
Non-CIS	0.929	0.958	1.202	1.630	3.195	3.047	2.256	2.250	1.800	1.920
Total above	–	–	154.516	204.609	232.957	253.320	255.006	229.558	256.176	283.318*
Memorandum items:	1.802	4.101	5.251	8.006	10.110	12.809	13.768	11.888	12.901	14.151
Baltic states										
Central Europe	47.663	58.856	67.485	88.043	103.733	112.100	124.653	123.393	135.979	145.298
South-East Europe	–	–	–	28.984	32.154	34.095	34.838	32.271	36.603	42.140
CIS without Russian Federation	–	–	24.476	32.867	39.587	40.748	37.147	31.005	36.924	40.492
Caucasian CIS countries	–	–	1.510	1.727	2.503	2.630	2.864	2.449	2.708	2.984
Central Asian CIS countries	–	–	8.496	9.251	11.470	11.129	10.034	9.449	10.910	12.788
Three European CIS countries	–	–	14.470	21.889	25.614	26.989	24.249	19.107	23.307	24.721

Source: UN ECE *Survey,* no 2/2004. p. 48.

Table 9.

Merchandise trade of Eastern Europe and the Russian Federation, by direction, 1980, 1990–2002 (Shares in total trade, percent)

	1980	1990	1991	1992	1993	1994	1995	1996	1997	1998	1999	2000	2001	2002
Eastern Europe, to and from:														
Exports World	100.0	100.0	100.0	100.0	100.0	100.0	100.0	100.0	100.0	100.0	100.0	100.0	100.0	100.0
Eastern Europe and the CIS	48.5	38.1	28.5	23.0	30.7	28.5	28.6	28.5	28.6	24.7	20.8	20.7	21.0	20.8
CIS	27.1	22.3	17.9	12.4	11.4	10.0	9.8	10.0	10.6	7.4	4.2	4.1	4.3	4.6
Eastern Europe	21.4	15.8	10.6	10.7	19.3	18.5	18.7	18.5	18.0	17.3	16.6	16.6	16.7	16.2
Developed market economies	35.7	49.5	59.8	63.0	57.5	61.9	62.6	63.5	63.6	68.3	73.4	73.0	72.9	72.6
Developing economies	15.8	12.4	11.7	14.0	11.8	9.6	8.8	8.0	7.8	7.0	5.8	6.3	6.1	6.6
Imports World	100.0	100.0	100.0	100.0	100.0	100.0	100.0	100.0	100.0	100.0	100.0	100.0	100.0	100.0
Eastern Europe and the CIS	42.0	26.6	25.5	24.7	29.9	26.2	25.8	24.7	23.1	20.0	20.6	23.6	23.0	24.7
CIS	26.8	18.3	20.2	17.9	16.5	14.0	13.0	12.0	11.0	8.6	8.5	11.4	10.6	12.0
Eastern Europe	18.8	14.3	8.1	6.8	13.4	12.2	12.9	12.7	12.1	11.4	12.1	1.22	12.4	12.7
Developed market economies	38.7	53.3	58.3	64.4	61.2	65.1	65.6	66.2	66.7	70.2	69.7	66.6	66.1	66.2
Developing economies	19.3	20.1	16.1	10.9	8.9	8.6	8.5	9.1	10.2	9.8	9.7	9.8	10.9	9.1
Former Soviet Union/Russian Federation, to and from:														
Exports World	100.0	100.0	100.0	100.0	100.0	100.0	100.0	100.0	100.0	100.0	100.0	100.0	100.0	100.0
Eastern Europe	34.5	21.8	25.9	22.3	18.1	15.1	16.8	18.2	19.5	18.1	17.8	20.0	19.4	17.2
Developed market economies	42.2	49.5	56.5	57.9	59.7	66.6	60.6	58.1	58.6	60.0	58.0	55.6	55.2	55.6
Developing economies	23.3	28.7	17.6	19.8	22.2	18.3	22.6	23.7	21.9	21.9	24.2	24.4	25.4	27.2
Imports World	100.0	100.0	100.0	100.0	100.0	100.0	100.0	100.0	100.0	100.0	100.0	100.0	100.0	100.0
Eastern Europe	31.5	24.7	26.0	15.9	10.6	14.1	15.5	12.6	13.7	12.0	9.6	10.9	10.1	10.0
Developed market economies	46.4	52.9	58.1	62.4	60.6	70.3	69.5	67.8	68.3	68.2	68.3	69.3	67.6	65.4
Developing economies	22.1	22.4	15.9	21.7	28.8	15.6	15.0	19.6	18.0	22.1	19.8	22.3	24.5	

Source: UN ECE *Survey,* no 2/2004. p. 49.

Table 10.

Current account balances of Eastern Europe and the CIS, 1990–2001
(Million dollars)

	1990	1991	1992	1993	1994	1995	1996	1997	1998	1999	2000	2001
Eastern Europe	–	–	–	–	–3.377	–3.814	–15.587	–18.969	–21.120	–24.124	–20.731	–20.152
Albania	–118	–168	–51	14	–43	–15	–62	–254	–45	–133	–156	–218
Bosnia and Herzegovina	–	–	–	–	–177	–193	–748	–1.060	–794	–839	–957	–1.126
Bulgaria	–1.710	–77	–361	–1.098	–32	–198	164	1.046	–61	–652	–702	–842
Croatia[a]	–621	–589	329	637	711	–1.407	–956	–2.512	–1.453	–1.398	–439	–617
Czech Republic	–122	1.708	–456	456	–787	–1.369	–4.121	–3.564	–1.255	–1.462	–2.718	–2.625
Estonia	–	–	36	22	–167	–158	–398	–563	–478	–247	–294	–340
Hungary[b]	123	267	325	–3.455	–3.911	–2.480	–1.678	–981	–2.298	–2.081	–1.328	–1.105
Latvia	–	–	191	417	201	–16	–279	–345	–650	–654	–493	–732
Lithuania	–	–	321	–86	–94	–614	–723	–981	–1.298	–1.194	–675	–574
Poland[b]	716	–1.359	–269	–2.868	677	5.310	–1.371	–4.309	–6.841	–11.533	–9.952	–7.166
Romania	–3.337	–1.012	–1.564	–1.174	–428	–1.774	–2.571	–2.104	–2.917	–1.437	–1.355	–2.223
Slovakia	–767	–786	173	–532	759	511	–1.960	1.827	–1.982	–980	–702	–1.756
Slovenia[a]	518	129	926	192	575	–75	56	51	–118	–698	–548	31
Macedonia[a]	–409	–259	–19	–83	–263	–299	–340	–286	–269	–32	–75	–235
Yugoslavia	–	–	–	–	–400	–1.037	–600	–1.279	–660	–764	–339	–624
CIS[c]	–	–	–538	10.267	4.696	3.888	5.228	–6.309	–7.368	23.544	48.001	33.834
Armenia	–	–	–50	–67	–104	–218	–291	–307	–403	–307	–278	–196
Azerbaijan	–	153	488	–160	–121	–401	–931	–916	–1.365	–600	–168	–52
Belarus	–	–	131	–435	–444	–458	–516	–859	–1.017	–194	–323	–275
Georgia	–	–	–248	–354	–277	–216	–275	–375	–416	–195	–262	–211
Kazakhstan	–	–1.300	–1.900	–641	–905	–213	–751	–799	–1.236	–236	675	–1.241
Kyrgyzstan	–	–	–61	–88	–84	–235	–425	–138	–364	–184	–80	–19
Republic of Moldova	–	–	–152	–155	–82	–95	–192	–275	–335	–64	–105	–92
Russian Federation[d]	–6.300	2.500	1.142	12.792	7.844	6.963	10.847	–80	219	24.616	48.839	34.842
Tajikistan	–	–	–53	–208	–170	–89	–75	–61	–120	–36	–62	–74
Turkmenistan	–308	447	926	776	84	23	0	–580	–934	–	–	–
Ukraine	–	–	–526	–765	–1.163	–1.152	–1.184	–1.335	–1.296	1.658	1.481	1.402
Uzbekistan	–	–	–236	–429	118	–21	–980	–584	–102	–164	184	50*
Total above[c]	–	–	–	–	1.318	74	–10.360	–25.278	–28.488	–581	27.270	13.682
Memorandum items: Baltic states	–	–	548	353	–59	–788	–1.400	–1.890	–2.426	–2.095	–1.462	–1.646
Central Europe	469	–41	698	–6.207	–2.687	1.897	–9.074	–10.630	–12.493	–16.775	–15.246	–12.621
South-East Europe	–	–	–	–	–631	–4.922	–5.113	–6.449	–6.200	–5.255	–4.022	–5.885

[a] Exludes transactions with the republics of the former SFR of Yugoslavia: Croatia (1990–1992), Slovenia (1990–1991) and The former Yugoslav Republic of Macedonia (1990–1992).
[b] Convertible currencies. Hungary until 1995; Poland until 1992.
[c] 1999–2001 totals include estimates for Turkmenistan.
[d] 1990–1992 exclude transactions with the Baltic and CIS countries.

Table 10 (continued)

	1990	1991	1992	1993	1994	1995	1996	1997	1998	1999	2000	2001
CIS without Russian Federation	–	–	–1.680	–2.525	–3.148	–3.075	–5.619	–6.229	–7.587	–1.072	1.162	–1.008
Caucasian CIS countries	–	–	190	–581	–502	–835	–1.497	1.597	–2.184	–1.102	–708	–460
Central Asian CIS countries[c]	–	–	–	1.324	–589	–957	–2.231	–2.163	–2.756	–1.371	817	–1.584
Three European CIS countries	–	–	–547	–1.355	–1.689	–1.705	–1.892	–2.469	–2.647	1.401	1.053	1.035

Source: UN ECE *Survey,* no 2/2004. p. 50.

Table 11.

Inflows of foreign direct investment in eastern Europe and the CIS, 1990, 1992–2002
(Million dollars)

	1990	1992	1993	1994	1995	1996	1997	1998	1999	2000	2001	2002	2003
Eastern Europe	–	–	–	–	–	11 413	15 142	20 043	22 231	23 983	22 866	26 669	18 636
Albania	–	20	68	53	70	90	48	45	41	143	207	135	178
Bosnia and Herzegovina	–	–	–	–	–	–	–	67	177	146	119	268	382
Bulgaria	4	41	40	105	90	109	505	537	819	1002	813	905	1419
Croatia	–	16	120	117	114	511	533	932	1467	1089	1559	1124	1956
Czech Republic	132	1004	654	869	2562	1428	1300	3718	6324	4986	5641	8483	2683
Estonia	–	82	162	215	202	151	267	581	305	387	542	284	891
Hungary	311	1471	2339	1146	4741	3291	4166	3344	3311	2777	3949	2869	2519
Latvia	–	29	45	214	180	382	521	357	347	410	164	382	359
Lithuania	–	8	30	31	73	152	355	926	486	379	446	732	179
Poland	89	678	1715	1875	3659	4498	4908	6365	7270	9341	5713	4131	4225
Romania	–	77	94	341	419	263	1215	2031	1041	1037	1157	1146	1840
Serbia and Montenegro	–	–	–	–	–	–	740	113	112	50	165	475	1260
Slovakia	18	100	195	269	308	353	220	684	390	1925	1579	4012	571
Slovenia	4	111	113	117	151	174	334	216	107	136	370	1645	179
Macedonia	–	–	–	24	9	11	30	128	33	175	442	78	95
CIS	–	1777	1876	1770	4064	5313	9035	6780	6749	5439	7290	8982	14 397
Armenia	–	–	1	8	25	18	52	221	122	104	70	111	121
Azerbaijan	–	–	60	22	330	627	1125	1023	510	130	227	1392	3285
Belarus	–	7	18	11	15	105	352	203	444	119	96	247	171
Georgia	–	–	–	8	6	40	243	265	82	131	110	165	338
Kazakhstan	–	100	228	635	964	1137	1321	1152	1472	1283	2835	2590	2058
Kyrgyzstan	–	0	10	38	96	47	83	109	44	–2	5	5	46
Rep. of Moldova	–	17	14	12	67	24	79	76	38	136	146	117	58
Russian Federation	–	1454	1211	690	2065	2579	4865	2761	3309	2714	2748	3461	6725
Tajikistan	–	9	9	12	20	18	18	25	21	24	9	36	32
Turkmenistan	–	11	79	103	233	108	108	62	–	–	–	–	–
Ukraine	–	170	198	159	267	521	623	743	496	595	792	693	124
Uzbekistan	–	9	48	73	124	90	167	140	121	75	83	–	–
Total above	–	–	–	–	–	16 726	24 176	26 823	28 979	29 422	30 156	35 651	33 033
Memorandum items:													
Baltic states	–	119	238	460	454	685	1142	1863	1139	1176	1152	1399	1429
Central Europe	555	3364	5015	4275	11 420	9 744	10 929	14 327	17 402	19 165	17 253	21 140	10 077
South-East Europe	–	–	–	–	–	984	3070	3853	3690	3642	4461	4130	7130
CIS without Russian Federation	–	323	665	1080	1999	2734	4170	4019	3439	2725	4542	5521	7672
Caucasian CIS countries	–	–	61	38	361	685	1419	1509	715	365	406	1669	3744
Central Asian CIS countries	–	129	374	861	1289	1400	1697	1488	1747	1510	3102	2796	2276
Three European CIS countries	–	194	229	181	349	649	1053	1022	978	850	1034	1057	1653

Source: UN ECE *Survey*, no 2/2004. p. 95.

4. THE DEVELOPMENTAL DIMENSION OF POST-COMMUNIST CHANGE[1]

In the preceding chapter we have offered an empirical overview of transition in comparative perspective. Doing so allowed us to address some of the hotly debated theoretical issues with the benefit of hindsight and on the basis of statistical evidence. We also have shown that accession to the EU though does mark the end of an era in terms of externally led adjustment policies, however, it leaves several issues, that are of major importance for long-term development, open. Last but not least, addressing the issue of 'globalization' allows us to highlight the importance of transnationalization, a feature that is strengthened by various new forms of international intertwining brought about, and fostered by, the new economy and the spread of ICT in the traditional sectors as well as in services. Allowing for these orients us to the fundamental issues of development. In the upcoming chapter, we shall offer an *overview of theories* that may explain development and transition in countries that join the process of European integration.

Our major *puzzle* in the chapter follows from the fact that contrary to the widespread belief of professionals and political actors alike, joining the EU does not solve major issues of development, although it creates more favorable side conditions than staying out would. We shall show, in chapter, that transition specific tasks and EU specific tasks do not fully overlap. On the other hand, we have also shown that several transition countries do not emerge from their quasi-developing status, therefore they do not qualify as integral parts of emerging Europe. Therefore, it remains a challenge, both for policy making in the EU in terms of proximity policies, and in terms of more general developmental theory, how to tackle the lot of the lagging behind.

We do not address in this chapter the conditions of digression from the 'mainstream' in successful transformation. Moreover, we shall address in a chapter 12 the true strategic alternative, that of market socialism (or state led catching-up model), most palpably represented by the post-1979 China, and

---

[1] Useful comments by G. W. Kolodko on a previous version of this chapter are appreciated, with the usual caveats.

leave for the moment aside the intricate question if such an alternative has been open, particularly for the less successful transforming economies.

In the present chapter our major hypothesis, to be tested, goes as follows: with the gradual emergence of market-type institutions and policies that are in line with these, once Communist economies are becoming gradually akin to any market economy typical of the medium level of income. Therefore, it is likely that the major policy challenges and development tasks they face are also similar to those observed in other emerging nations and transition specific tasks, the SLIP agenda gradually loses its weight. The recent turn in development economics toward institutions also allows for a degree of *convergence*.

On the other hand, as discussed in detail in several chapters, East and Central European societies continue to exhibit important *dissimilarities* to underdeveloped countries in terms of urbanization, human capital, location, social intangibles and the like (Ofer, 2001). Therefore it may still make sense to start our investigation from an endogenous point of view, that of systemic transformation. This choice is needed to address the path dependence issue in due course. For it is hard to deny that the Communist past is likely to exert some, if not dominant, influence in many countries of emerging Europe and even more so in countries that have been lagging behind, such as Moldova or Ukraine or Belarus for that matter. True, for these countries systemic change might have had a different content than for the frontrunners, but this issue falls truly outside the scope of the present analysis.

In answering the question of 'what has been left' or alternatively, 'what we have learned' we adopt the following approach. First we survey some salient findings of transitology proper. Then we attempt to put these in the context of new development economics (Todaro, and Smith, 2006; Meier and Stiglitz, eds, 2001), interpreting the ups and downs of poor countries within the context of general economics. Our focus is thus on the overall landscape and theoretical novelties, while detailed substantiation of some of the points is left to the references.

The Thorny Path to Growth

According to conventional wisdom in economics, and also in the predominant view in historiography, the collapse of the Soviet empire was built into the system and has been inevitable. Still its speed and timing, as well as its very occurrence remained a surprise to the overwhelming majority of analysts. The situation is best reflected in the fact that the G7 meeting of Houston, convening in December 1990, entrusted the tasks of analyzing and assisting the Soviet economy to institutions whose only common denominator was that the red superpower was no member to any of them. The joint effort of these (IMF, OECD, IBRD, 1991) – and the parallel endeavors of the European Communities (EC, 1990) – produced weighty volumes; however, by the time of their publication, the object of research – the Soviet Union – had ceased to exist.

Even in more academic analyses, the confusion was considerable. Sovietologists, on the one hand, tended to be versed in the languages and customs of the region, not so much, however, in standard economics and its applications. Likewise, academic – and especially macroeconomic – departments had little idea, if any, about command economy in general, and the societal context of Central and Eastern Europe in particular.

This applied, basically, also to the international agencies, as their – limited – experience with Hungary and Romania was of little assistance in managing the problems of a disintegrating Soviet Empire or a collapsing communist economy in Poland. As a contemporary survey (Murrel, 1995) neatly proved, the lack of knowledge of the specific post-Communist context tended to be 'remedied' by reliance on shallow analogies to the experience of international financial institutions (IFIs) in developing countries, or a direct application of textbook solutions, without much care about the institutional or historic context into which these insights were to be transposed. *The holistic nature of post-Communist change has often been denied or neglected.*

At the level of policy advice, reliance of simplistic adaptations of otherwise elaborate policy conceptions proved to be even more widespread. Ideological leanings, experimenting spirit and mechanistic application of what the current wisdom on poor countries suggested were combined to produce quick fixes.

Uncritical reliance on standard, pre-cooked solutions, coupled with ideological postulates stressing speed over quality, and instrumentalizing the concept of spontaneous institution emergence for trivial political ends, often swept away any attempt at analyzing local conditions on their own right. This led – as Stiglitz (2000, pp. 552–557) retrospectively illustrates – to a neglect of those *contextual circumstances* which decide about the success or failure of the application of a proven theoretical insight to policy-making. Thus the quest for speed and the resultant policy improvisation (lacking a systemic coherence) has often brought about partial reforms yielding paradoxical outcomes, with unintended side-effects dominating over desired and planned objectives.

Correct theories translated into haphazard policy implementation thus produced perverse outcomes in a number of cases. Suffice it to mention some of the better known cases: in Hungary, public utilities were privatized with a stroke of a pen in late 1995, without, however, their prior regulation. Thus public monopolies were simply transformed into private (or, in some cases, foreign public) monopolies. With 'real owners' established, the chances of further liberalization and deregulation (called for by the EU single market) are slim, and low efficiency has been built into the system for many years. The introduction of voucher privatization in Russia in 1992–1994, at the height of hyperinflation, could not stand a chance of testing the Coase theorem, nor could it build a reform constituency. Similarly, introducing a fully funded private pension system in Kazakhstan in 1999 – while the capital market was lacking – could hardly bring about those benefits on which the general arguments for pension privatization are based.

On the other hand, it would be wrong to ignore the fact that local economists – of a great variety of persuasions – have been, as a rule, poorly equipped to deal with the theoretical and policy challenges of transformation. The contemporary vogue – reform economics – functioned within a self-constraining framework of market socialism, which never addressed questions related to a real market order (like capital market regulation, banking crises, credit crunches or the conflicting demands of exchange rate policy; cf. Wagener, ed. 1998; Antal, 1999; Kaase et al, eds, 2002). Its positive message – over and above the critical account of the *status quo ante* – has evaporated in the face of the in-between solutions and *ersatz*-solutions left behind by the political drive toward real markets and real democracy.

Even in Hungary, where by the mid-1980s economics had long overcome any form of socialism and focused on such issues as capital market, private property and opening up the economy (cf. Kornai, 1990; Kornai, 2001), these insights had only inadequate influence on policy decisions and institutional options. Until late 1989, the state administration held more radical transformation projects to be politically infeasible. Later, the daily struggle for retaining the solvency of the country dominated any broader consideration, at least until 1992. The former opposition (post-transition ruling parties), stepping in the footprint of the 1956 revolution, called for a third road, based on self-management solutions, with private property and competition playing a subordinate role at best (Laki, 1991; Lányi, 1996). As the two analyses quoted above show in detail, the program of democratic parties was populist rather than pro-market, on occasion going back on the radicalism of the projects adopted by the outgoing socialist administration.

These critical and self-critical remarks do not imply that the entire economic profession were unable to interpret and solve real-world puzzles. Already the earliest analyses (Blommestein, Marrese and Zecchini, 1990) highlighted the focal role of *stabilization* and large-scale *privatization*.[2] In calling for trade reform and *outward looking policies*, including currency convertibility, local analysts joined forces with the leading authorities of the time and elaborated common propositions in line with the mainstream of the day (Köves and Marer, eds, 1991). Consulting has been involved, with a fair degree of overzealousness, making these activities a favorite topic of local humor. But jokes apart, international agencies, private actors, governments, and – predominantly – *the EC/EU played a formative role in the transformation process*, through PHARE, the Europe Agreements and the resultant harmonization of legal systems to the acquis communautaire. The EC has never shied away from an independent role; its policy advice represented a special line in providing guidance for new democracies (Portes, ed., 1991). The latter – despite the latter-day legend of colonialism – had been, from the very outset, a *co-operative endeavor*: local experts were involved, their output was published – although policy advice was furnished by the incumbent apparatus.

In hindsight, the early transitological literature can be divided into two major categories. The *policy oriented* category tended to be dominated by issues

---

[2] Quite a heated debate went on in several transition countries (especially in Russia and in Southeast Europe), centered on the claim that stabilization was nothing more than an IMF straightjacket or a product of ideological over-zealousness. Thus many people (publishing e.g. in *Acta Oeconomica* and other Sovietological journals) called for policies that downplayed stabilization, i.e. advocated a 'growth first, financial discipline later' approach.

that later proved to be irrelevant or misleading. These included the debate over shock therapy versus gradualism, the theories of how to escape recession, how to increase the number of domestic owners, how to create capitalism without large capitalists, restitution and reprivatization, and, finally, the search for the optimal technology of privatization. In the more *theoretical category*, an attempt was made to apply the Western economic theories currently in vogue. These included an early version of the political economy approach, portraying the building of *reform coalitions* and providing compensation for losers as the major feasibility conditions of successful change (Roland, 1991). Others highlighted the relevance of *fiscal federalism* for finding new equilibria in Russia (Schneider, 1993), and also highlighted the role of *corporate governance* as the link between ownership change and efficiency gains (Dallago, 1994).

Analysts from transition countries tended to see privatization as an exclusively or predominantly political issue of power redistribution. Their major aim was to break the backbone of the old guard and create stakeholders in the new arrangements (Chubais and Vishievskaia, 1995). From this angle, classical economic and business considerations and the related success indicators, such as the number of successful corporate *turnarounds*, or the share of companies with improved performance in total output, have been by definition *secondary* at best. If the considerations inherent in economic analysis – such as wealth creation, welfare improvement, growing efficiency, better combination of factors – are openly de-emphasized, the resultant absence of these is *hardly a surprise* (and even less of a proof of the inefficiency of economic theories).

Anybody familiar with the dismal performance of economic reforms of the socialist period, doomed by recurrent recentralization waves, would subscribe, even in hindsight, to the need for radical solutions in order to attain the *point of no return*. The more we conceive the Soviet empire as a rent-seeking society, with large numbers of perceived or real beneficiaries having no clue about the real cost of their welfare (and not interested in securing its sustainability with their own effort), the more we may condone revolutionary options. However, already early analysts, sympathetic to this point of view (Malle, 1994/2001) have underscored the fact that both the economic efficiency and social acceptance of privatizations are crucially dependent upon the quality of those *institutional and regulatory changes that accompany* (or not, as the case may be) the transfer of property rights. These will decide whether the transfer of property to private owners is tantamount to the introduction of a *competitive order* and an open society, or public monopolies and the profits accruing to them are merely passed over to private persons. The prosperity of the latter is conditional upon their success in preserving *entry barriers* that preclude any new effort to combine factors in a more efficient manner. If monopolist rent-seeking works, there is no reason to expect privatization to be efficiency enhancing and welfare improving, not even in the long run.[3]

---

[3] This insight had been explicitly formulated by the liberals (Böhm, 1982/1933; Eucken, 1948) in Germany and by the theory of collective action (Olson, 1982) in the US, well ahead of the East Asian crisis or the debacle of the NIS in the 1991–1999 period.

Seen from this angle, the dismal performance of the Newly Independent States is anything but surprising, and can by no means be attributed to an overdose of 'monetarism' or 'neoliberalism'. Likewise, a privatization based on favors and aimed at nominating a new *clientele*, while state activism and regulation remain all-pervasive – as is the case under the Putin presidency – will not improve performance; the oil-boom fed upswing can only be transient (lasting for a few years only). This does not prove, contrary to what is usually asserted, the uniqueness of Russia, but the *universal relevance* of the economic laws formulated above. A state-led monopolistic economy cannot be expected, on the basis of available theories, to be *more efficient*, if changes are restricted to property structure, while all other incentives, allocational mechanisms and the overall economic environment remain hostile to any major innovation (as explained in more detail in our chapter on Russia).

Since the mid-1990s, two new features have dominated transitological literature. One of them is the *transformational recession*, described in our comparative and empirical chapter at length. The second is the *return of successor parties* and the related perception of a threat of societal regression – a point studied mostly in the political science literature (Körössényi, 1995).

With the benefit of hindsight, it is hard to overlook the fact that the fears pertaining to both developments proved exaggerated. Growth did resume, in East Germany already in 1991, in Poland in 1992, and in the rest of the region in 1993–1994, but only from 1999 in the NIS. True, growth proved to be sustainable only in those countries which not only preached, but also implemented the agenda of stabilization, liberalization and privatization (SLIP), and, moreover, complemented these steps with *institution building* and solid *macropolicies*. This point has been most forcefully proven by the World Bank (1996) but also by analysts from within the region (Kolodko, 2000b, pp. 57–86).

What *structural reforms* were needed to get on the path of sustained growth? These included changes in the banking system (i.e. the establishment of financial intermediation proper), and the creation and efficient regulation of capital markets (these are needed to improve allocative efficiency). The latter factor has proven decisive in bringing about success, or conversely, failure. As the overview of Berglöf and Bolton (2002) indicates, the 'great divide' among the country groups follows their performance in financial sector reform. Their insight goes thus in the same direction as our own findings in the Comparative and empirical as well as in the Transnational markets and local politics chapters. But further reforms were needed in the inherited welfare systems, immediately related to the focal issue of long-run *fiscal sustainability* (through the problem of intergenerational accounting and the implicit debt of the pension system).

In other words, handling a prime economic problem – the sustainability of the general government position[4] – required interdisciplinary analyses, as is

---

[4] 'General government' is a broader category than fiscal balance if we take it to cover not only the central budget, but also pension funds and other items not figuring in the state's central budget, approved or unknown ex ante by parliament (but constituting public spending). This is the macro-economically significant variable, not parliamentary debt.

richly documented by one of the pioneering volumes on the subject (Nelson et al, eds, 1999). The underlying issues here are all related to value judgements and, ultimately, to matters of worldview: the scale and ways of ideal redistribution, the role of state versus civil society in providing public goods and services, the share of centralized versus municipal self-financing in covering the costs of public activities, the new mix of solidarity versus self-care, or the economic value of health.

In a pluralistic society, based on the coexistence of competing values and life strategies, it is by definition impossible to expect a full professional consensus to emerge. *Public choices* are needed, and these have to be anchored in constitutional arrangements, i.e. laws that cannot be changed by a new legislation adopted by a simple 50 per cent plus one vote majority. Until a consensus is reached, it might be in vain to expect successor governments to sustain commitments assumed by their predecessors without having taken into account their objections. Unless it is *sustained over several election cycles*, no change in the health and pension systems is likely to be successful, and the same goes for the municipalities' role in the economy ('Europe of Regions'). Those reforms are likely to continue long after the EU accession of the frontrunner transition countries. Thus no decision is helpful that is based exclusively on financial or narrow professional considerations, but does not enjoy wide public endorsement.

As far as the return of *successor (post-Communist) parties* is concerned, the related fears proved to be unfounded. Global comparisons of the experience of the 1980s and early 1990s (Williamson, John 1994) had already proven by that time that leftist parties turned out to be quite efficient promoters of market-oriented reforms (years before New Labor was conceived). This had to do with their high level of organization as well as their social embeddedness. To the examples provided by the volume quoted above, one could add those of France since the mid-1980s or Italy and Greece in the mid-1990s. From among the transition countries, we may list the governments of Hungary in 1994–1998, Poland in 1993–1997 and the Czech Republic in 1998–2002 (under a minority government). It seems that these have been setting the trend, rather than constituting deviations in need of special (culture- and history-based) explanation.

This outcome is hardly surprising if we take into account the fact that left wing parties in Central Europe (but not in the NIS) represent mostly the *winners of the transformation*, such as entrepreneurs, civil servants, individuals benefiting from their cultural and social heritage and the like. The more we accept the relevance of inherited skills and starting positions as determinants of privatization outcomes, the less surprised we are to see this. Those in small and micro-business, unsuccessful entrepreneurs (oriented towards local markets only), losers in the transition process, and strata permanently *dependent on transfers* (e.g. pensioners or farmers) tend to group around right-wing parties in protest to the outcomes of the changes. This has lead to the revival of *splits according to the interwar lines*, with unreconstructed, statist conservative parties becoming a lasting feature of the scene. This may solidify a *division of economic platforms* which runs *contrary* to what is observed in most core countries. In Central and Eastern Europe, the left calls for deregulation and privatization, while the right demands more redistribution and state protectionism. In empirical terms, such a division clashes with the models prevailing in political science, still quite widely represented in continental Europe.

At the turn of the millennium, transitology took yet another twist. Primarily in the context of EU accession, external performance measurements have become formal and continuous, while competition for foreign investment has also intensified. In this dimension, the increasing *differentiation* among transition countries has come to the focus of attention among analysts. This growing divergence has been regularly documented using a wide array of indicators by all institutions dealing with the region, from the *Transition Reports* of EBRD, to the since 2005 defunct *Economic Survey of Europe* of the UN Economic Commission for Europe in Geneva, to publications of various regional research institutes, banks and rating agencies. This analytical material, which has been widely presented in our Comparative and empirical chapter, divides transition countries into three different categories, confronted with *three different research programs*.

First is the *frontrunner group*, where the SLIP agenda has been concluded, the system of financial intermediation and the rule of law are in place, not contingent upon particular political forces remaining in power. These economies are on a *secular growth path*, even though the rate of growth is naturally volatile by the country and period. EU membership has been accomplished. Here the question is how to *accelerate welfare reforms*, how to build up a social consensus around the major trends of change and how to secure better professional foundations for these processes. The issue is to orchestrate sustainable growth that realizes the potential for catching up, or real convergence, to use the EU parlance. The subject of the debates is thus no longer what needs to be done, but *how and at what speed*.

In the *second group*, EU membership remains a medium to long-term objective. Still, for the same reason, day-to-day decisions are hard to reach. In this group there is a demand for an answer why transition has remained only a partial success. Social and political forces call for normative approaches that should lead to more successful policymaking and institution-building solutions. A typical case was Romania, where in the elections of 2000, over 70 (!) percent of the electorate turned their back on various Westernizing forces. The returning post-Communist party never enjoyed an absolute majority in the legislative, thus proved unable to institute any step to change the status quo. There is a serious *gap* here between *economic rationality and social acceptability*, which is also the case with other members of this group. It is a situation for which the greater part of the literature on policy reform offers little or no remedies, since no society can be led to prosperity against its revealed preferences. On the other hand, a weak government is usually unable to institute major structural reforms, since such steps involve by their very nature imminent and certain costs, whilst benefits are uncertain and can be reaped only in the future[5]. Thus democratic processes may or may not lead to the selection of a more viable, more efficient institutional setting; the 'law' of natural selection may or may not apply in socio-economic processes (Hoff and Stiglitz, 2001, pp. 394–397). In societies which lag behind, there is a tendency to reinterpret the path dependency insight of North (1990) in terms of *the inevitability of governance failures* in less developed countries and to put the entire blame on those informal institutions which replace the defunct or mismanaged formal ones. While anyone familiar with the original argument would clearly see this as perverting a valid scientific claim, it is hard to overlook the fact that references to path dependence are often used instrumentally to justify interventionism in policy-making and the quest for national models of economic development (which is, in the end, no less than a relapse to the historicism of Gustav von Schmoller).

A *third group* of countries consists of the NIS and Southeast European states, where the level of per capita GDP, according to official and internationally comparable data, by and large, still lags at about 70 per cent of the Soviet-era level, and in some cases – like Georgia, Bosnia and Moldova – it is even lower, closer to 40 per cent of the pre-crisis value. In these societies, daily *crisis management* is the name of the game and all the *rest*, including wider-ranging structural reform projects, tends to belong to the realm of poetry. Here the major task of research is to find the reasons – over and above incidental factors, like civil wars or corrupted régimes – for the failures and the *inability to correct*. Unilaterally cultural explanations are obviously unsatisfactory for an analytical economist. Good analytical answers are badly needed in such cases as Ukraine, Belarus – comparable in size to Greece or Austria – not to speak of the Caucasian and Balkan countries. These constitute the real puzzles not only for the EU wider neighborhood policy, but also in academic terms – an issue we shall try to address in our chapter on Transnational markets.

To wrap up what has been said, transitology is becoming an ever *narrower field on its own right*. One part of the countries under discussion 'qualifies' for European studies; another one shows a striking affinity to the traditional topics of development economics. While the latter branch of study – as will be shown – has made important advances in understanding the dynamics of less developed and less successful economies, the learning process (of transition countries looking South) is still in its infancy, partly in consequence of the early improvisation. Still, it is hard to overlook the fact that such *traditional topics* in development economics as vicious circle phenomena, or the ways to create an outward-oriented economy or to fight corruption, might have a *direct bearing on countries lagging in transition*.

---

[5] It is important to add that the 2004 elections produced a reformist President-reformist government alliance, which despite its internal divisions managed to gain EU membership by 2007. The impact of Europeanization would be hard to negate.

Emerging Economies or Developing Societies?

Development economics was born right after World War II as an antidote to the neoliberal mainstream, reflecting revolutionary ideas and showing little appreciation for the type of formal approaches that has come to dominate major departments and journals ever since[6] (for an excellent summary, cf. Meier, 2001). This has made it a bestseller among many policy-makers in the Third World, and likewise in the leading departments of major world universities. *Desarrollismo* is a shorthand for anti-American, import-substituting nationalist and populist policies in South America, though literally it means only 'supportive of development'.

The *original paradigm* of development economics was based on the negation of Western market-oriented concepts and policies, and of the laissez-faire of the colonial period. It emerged as a rejection of the materialist West, equated with moral decay, political oppression, racism, and a free market culminating in the Great Depression of 1929–1933 and its dire consequences for the periphery. In order to overcome dependence, it advocated state planning (even if no Soviet advisors were around). The contemporary official statistics of the Soviet Union tended to be taken at face value, which resulted in a sincere admiration for the non-capitalist alternative. It also took for granted the idea of import substitution as a means of nation building and state building – an idea that has acquired global appeal ever since Friedrich List, under the banner of economic nationalism. Furthermore, it took for granted that the state must play a leading role in accelerating economic development (based on various theories of the big push, originating with Rosenstein-Rodan, 1943). The central state administration (in the hands of the vanguard) – rather than civil society, municipalities, private capital of domestic or foreign origin – was to become the sole *owner, regulator* and *organizer*, constrained only by its own ideological beliefs. The central state was to become the driving force and guarantor of accelerated change.

The more heavily the strategy relied on priorities which deliberately limited the scope of the market – or ones which were just incongruous with, say, the long-time priorities of the market agents, or made recoupment uncertain – the more inevitable it became to *repress the financial sector* by means of highly inventive regulatory measures and justifications (Lal, 1993). It seemed obvious that monetary processes must be (or are by their very nature) instrumental, subordinate to 'real processes', which were to be co-ordinated basically by the bureaucracy.

It is common knowledge that the more sophisticated an economy and society is, and the higher its development level is, *the greater the role of prices is as the major instrument of co-ordinating* millions and tens of millions of individual decisions, if welfare is to be increased. Therefore, it was inevitable and predictable

---

[6] For this reason some of the pioneers in the area, such as the first editor of the first Handbook on the subject. Holis Chenery, Evsey Domar or Simon Kuznets qualified as growth theorists (owing to their quantitative orientation that ensured canonic acceptability).

that the more the financial system is repressed and the longer this repression lasts, the higher the costs in terms of lost (sacrificed) welfare are at any point of time. The longer such an arrangement persists, the greater the lag it leaves behind.

The dominance of bureaucratic co-ordination caused, as it did in the Soviet-type economy, first efficiency losses and later on stagnation. Alternatively, countries tried to borrow in order to bridge the revenue shortfall. But the more money was lent, in the absence of domestic corrective and absorption mechanisms, the less growth could materialize, and adjustment was merely postponed (Easterly, 2001, pp. 101–120). Recurring *payments crises* – and the high visibility of interrupted and never finished grand prestige projects – had a sobering effect. Experience opened up the way to the 'monetarist counterrevolution' of the 1970s and 1980s, leading to the gradual change of paradigm in most developing countries.

The *new paradigm* is built upon the appreciation of market-led growth and overcomes the ideological elements derived from the principle of negating everything resembling the Western experience. It is generally acknowledged that the same *principles*[7] of solid macro- and micromanagement that work in OECD countries should be valid for less developed countries, and cultural differences can no longer be invoked to justify profligate or simply unprofessional policies. Development is conditioned by public policies ensuring price stability, export-led growth and providing investments for such public goods and externalities that private agents tend to undersupply (more on that in: Behrman and Srinivasan, 1995, pp. 2467–2496).

What has been said implies a *Copernican turn* in development economics. On the other hand, the story just means that the discipline of *standard economics has returned into the discourse about poor countries*, and nothing more. Underdevelopment and ways of overcoming it can now be discussed in standard economic terms, following the logic and procedures of standard economic analysis. This return of economics took place in a slow, evolutionary manner, through a substantial amount of trial and error as well as open scientific exchanges – as documented in rich detail by the four volumes of the *Handbook* quoted above. In most of the cases and throughout this process, there was no sign of the oft-alleged dictates of the IMF,[8] wrongdoings of the Chicago boys,

---

[7] Harberger (2001, pp. 549–557) highlights the need to avoid rigidity, especially doctrinaire approaches to policy issues where *discretion* and *common sense* (e.g. in assessing administrative capacities) cannot be substituted with general references to textbook solutions or to abstract theoretical models. Thus this insight by no means implies the mechanistic copying of even 'best practices' or an indiscriminate use of benchmarking. The May 2003 Basle Two agreement is a nice example of how and why decentral assessments – differently tailored within the same logic – may be the only practicable solution. More on Basle Two in (Szabó-Morvai, 2003).

[8] Even authors sympathetic to the international financial institutions (e.g. Krueger, 1998; John Williamson, 2000) consider as by and large *unsuccessful* most of the attempts by the IFIs to be involved in *institution building* in developing and transforming countries. Currently also the IFIs themselves stress the need for domestic 'ownership' of reform packages. Moreover, the quoted authors consider the mere emergence of a common language, a common intellectual framework for discussing issues, and personal contacts among wide segments of policy-makers – also on the second and third levels – as the single most *lasting accomplishment* of the IFI-sponsored structural reform projects of various sorts.

tricky stockbrokers and fund-misusers from Harvard, corrupted media multi-pliers and other folkloristic elements still dominating much of the social science discourse on transition in large parts of the globe. But even if in some individual cases such discourse is substantiated (which is very rarely the case), anecdotal evidence and the related incidental factors can hardly explain the turn of the tide in an entire strand of international intellectual endeavors. As we have seen – and our references prove this *in extenso* – this turn can by no means be attributed to the Western triumphalism that followed the collapse of the 'evil empire', as it had taken place a *decade earlier*, in the 1980s. The largely pragmatic and policy-level agreement among the various trends of thought came to be known as the Washington Consensus, and later on – with reference to lessons from transition failures, and with a new emphasis on institutions – as the post-Washington Consensus (John Williamson, 2005; Kolodko, 2000a, pp. 119–140).

Development economics has long been studying phenomena that propped up as queer novelties for transitology or Sovietology. This applies *a fortiori* to cases when the transformation failure is rooted in the *disintegration of formal institutions*, regulatory arrangements, or even the core state itself. Fuzzy property rights, the lack of independent judiciary and the inability to enforce private contracts by an impartial third agent, rampant corruption, malfunctioning of formal institutions and the resultant informalism, the dominance of traditional networks over imported arrangements, or the impacts of a sizeable irregular economy are all among the evergreens of development studies.

The encounter of the 'neoliberal' mainstream with 'exotic' themes proved to be quite productive. One of the fortresses of formalized approaches, growth theory, and the wide and sophisticated econometric arsenal could now become *applied to real-world issues*. Moreover, these instruments facilitated the settlement of debates. In comparative analyses, quantitative methods helped clarify the contribution of various factors to economic success. Applications often allowed the relevance of specific theoretical or methodological propositions to be verified. All in all a variety of contradictory observations, successes and failures could be interpreted within a *single theoretical framework*. Moreover, by reliance on analytical concepts and quantitative methods several long-debated issues could be settled. One of these was the ancient dispute over *import substitution versus export orientation*.

Especially following the second oil price hike of 1979, the superiority of export-led policies became evident: the countries adopting this line were disadvantaged in terms of natural endowments, and yet their growth proved *sustainable*, whereas the windfall tended to create 'Dutch disease' symptoms and temporary booms in the resource-rich economies in the Middle East. The sustainability of outward orientation went hand in hand with the broad concept of *market orientation* and supportive *institutions*, over and above the narrow prioritizing of external sectors (Santos-Paulo and Thirwall, 2004). Recent analysis has disproved the conventional counter-argument, based on a mythical belief of the East Asian tiger economies being state-led interventionist development models based on industrial activism (Paldam, 2003). Long-term analyses have shown that export-led growth is not based on the financial support of sectors selling abroad, but implies a broad liberalization strategy extending beyond the trade sectors. Its intensity, sequencing, timing and overall professionalism explains the cases when this option proved successful and sustainable (Dollar and Kraay, 2004). Indeed, this long established insight that emerged from the debates of the 1970s has recurringly been reinforced by findings supportive of the crucial role of outward orientation in bringing about sustainable economic advancement and, as a consequence, a reduction of poverty in all countries entering this path (but making the lagging behind even more desparate in relative terms; see the survey of Winters et al, 2004). Empirical analyses have helped to substantiate this turn of the tide. In recent summary, considering the accounting problems, Sala-i Martin (2006) has demonstrated the existence of both income convergence and diminishing *absolute number* of poor people, by about 500m, in the 1970–2000 period, notwithstanding population explosion. In sum, the paradigmatic turn of the 80s and 90s did yield clearly favorable empirical outcomes.

In order to test the above finding, several analyses have been carried out, probing into the causes of the inefficiency of import substitution policies. These indicated *governance failures* as a major reason, inherent in the original state-centered paradigm (relying heavily on the right choices by the vanguard as opposed to the use of decentrally available social knowledge). This problem has been exacerbated by the frequency of *state capture*.

Third, it proved unjustified to assume that the *core state* would by definition stand for the *public purpose*. State administrations, especially in weak states and under non-democratic arrangements, still predominant in the majority of developing countries, tend to *fall victim to the redistributory tendencies of traditional societies*. State jobs are used to boost employment and serve as rewards for political loyalty rather than to function on meritocratic principles. Cases which fit into a typical public choice model, where public policy players maximize their own personal welfare and power rather than any abstract public good, are hard to find, especially in Africa, Central Asia and Latin America. This tendency can be reversed if the state becomes *decreasingly involved* in protecting palpable interests (the protective state should only guard unambiguous public goods, such as price stability, competition, rule of law, public security – but not individual producer interests or pre-set redistributory outcomes). On the other hand, the smaller the size of the productive state is, i.e. the scope of goods and services provided by the central state, the lower the propensity is (or: the weaker the motivation is) to abuse it.

From this angle, it can be clearly seen how *insufficient* the reliance on such traditional models of growth is, where development is primarily based on *physical capital accumulation*. These models – which were invoked to justify import substitution – tended to downplay or neglect a key element of endogenous growth, which is the *accumulation and spread of knowledge* in societies (Bruton, 1998). While the accumulation of physical capital may be managed by governmental action – at least in the short and medium run – the accumulation and spread of knowledge can at best be *lubricated, but not created* by the authorities.

These insights have lent additional weight to an approach that has always emphasized, albeit sometimes from a minority position, the *social conditioning* of the market as a system. In contrast to the simplistic reading of the Harrod-Domar model, it considers the market as the fundamental coordination mechanism through which the vicious circle of poverty can be overcome (Hayek, 1989; Bauer, 2000). Adherents to this approach interpret as a revolution in development economics the movement from state-led approaches, emphasizing physical capital accumulation, towards a broader, more realistic and socially conceived version of *growth promoting mechanisms*. In this framework, the market rules and institutions – which occasionally emerge spontaneously, but are largely man-made – lead the countries *out* of the low-level steady-state equilibria, relying on the related incentives, allocation and accumulation mechanisms (Dorn et al, eds, 1998). Empirical analysis of the following decade (Hoekman and Javorick, eds, 2006) have shown a limited and rather narrow role of the state in the direct provision and generation of technological change, as opposed to creating side conditions for this change.

It is worth emphasizing that a market-based approach to development is by no means equivalent to the revival of the 'night watchman state' ideal. Instead of preaching the minimal state, a *strong state* is required: one constrained by constitutional, legal, procedural and other democratic checks and balances (Buchanan, 1977). A civilized market is one constitutionally constrained and protected, where the state is a *regulator* and an arbitrator, but *by no means a day-to-day manager of affairs*, producer or protector of individual concerns. Reliance on self-interest of market actors alone will hardly guarantee the respect for those cultural and civilizational norms that have evolved over centuries, whereas the constitutional rules that secure the latter are setting the rules of the game, but not its pre-determined outcomes (Vanberg, 2001, pp. 2–36).[9]

It is interesting to recall that these 'new' insights *were already available by the time systemic changes had started* in Central and Eastern Europe. In a volume published on the occasion of the 25th anniversary of the Harvard Institute of International Development (Perkins and Roemer, eds, 1991), the contributors came out against a unilateral emphasis on trade liberalization as a panacea and called on public authorities to supplement these steps with institution-building measures. True, this call implied something different from what is actually seen in the region, namely, the state replacing (in a Gerschenkronian way) the

---

[9] A *strong* state thus should not be confused, as is often the case, with an *activist* one, with interventionism and aggressive wielding of power, as the Putin administration has been interpreting this call. It is worth noting that the ordo-liberals of the 1930s developed their theory as a reaction to limitless and arbitrary state interventionism in Germany that ended up in totalitarian rule. In opposition to it, they call for *cutting back discretion to the minimum* and for a rule-based government (Böhm, 1982/1933; Eucken, 1948). In the United States a similar debate over rules versus discretion took place in the 1970s in the context of monetary policy with the conclusive paper by Kydland and Prescott (1977) awarded by the Nobel Prize in Economics in 2004. Later on, the victorious position of rule-based management was modified somewhat, with reference to drawbacks of too rigid interpretation of any of the golden rules for policy-making and theories alike (DeLong, 2000).

market. Instead, it advocated a market-supportive state, where interventions build market institutions and overcome co-ordination and information failures, much the same way as it was put forward later by Hoff and Stiglitz (2001, pp. 397–412). This requires, in the HIID view, a slim, but well-paid (rather than cheap, thus underpaid) state administration, based on meritocracy and transparency, which refrains from interventionism and day-to-day crisis management. Such an administration may become the *anchor for those reforms* that may lead stagnant societies out of their vicious circles. The timing of sectoral reforms and their pace in this normative view are conditioned by the ability for and speed of social learning, collective choices and interactions in the democratic process of deliberations.

Thus we have come to what a contemporary classic, Robert Bates and Anne Krueger (1993, p. 463) called the *orthodox paradox*. This means that extending the scope of the market requires strengthening the core state, while the policy of grievances and individual rationality (of buying clients) must be *subordinated to collective rationality* (geared towards, e.g. transparency and accountability). In concrete terms this requires financial discipline (such as the balanced budget proviso for the constituent states of the USA), limiting the scope of redistribution (especially if carried out on discretionary basis or in a non-transparent fashion), strengthening the rule of law in the economy, and, last but not least, enhancing the role of *technocratic agencies*, which are not subject to daily political pressures – an issue we shall explore in the chapter on Privatization and regulation.

As we can see, this broad approach abandons the previous narrow interpretation of reforms embraced by IFIs and most of the literature, restricted to changes in some sectors or policy areas. In the 1990s, reform came to imply deep changes pertaining to the macroeconomic *allocation* mechanism, *decision-making* structures at the macrolevel, and the way *legislation* works (a classical area of political science).

It is in this context that representatives of standard macroeconomics also call for reinterpreting the role of the state as a precondition for stabilization to sustain. In order to attain this, Dornbusch (1993) advocated improving the *administrative capacity* by way of decentralization, by empowering local municipalities with financial competences, with improved transparency and accountability at all levels and in all areas.[10] Reform policies should ensure that support goes indeed to the most needy. They can create mobilizing visions, build a consensus around focal issues, ensure consistency among reforms running in parallel, and thereby contribute to the social acceptance of economic change. In this way, thorough *reform policies may sustain a single electoral cycle and thus deliver.* This is, trivially, a side condition of such undertakings as a successful pen-

---

[10] Discussing this point, a leading authority of institutional economics, Oliver Williamson (2000, p. 611), noted that the functioning and embeddedness of bureaucracy largely remained a mystery for the social sciences. Neither formalized approaches, nor political science, could come up with an interpretation that could be accepted as a new paradigm. By the same token his institutional approach remains also open-ended.

sion reform, and also brings considerable benefits in terms of improving administrative capacities, strengthening the rule of law, or *changing informal institutions* such as social norms (e.g. the (un)acceptability of taking bribes or applying kinship criteria in making appointments).

Importantly, the institutional focus of the new political economy of development is *by no means a rehash of the state-centrism* of the old paradigm. This is, to a large degree, a generalization of the experiences of three decades of statist developmental strategies. Such an insight follows directly from the experience of non-capitalist development initiatives in sub-Saharan Africa (Paulson, ed., 1999), where the state turned out to be more of a problem than an agent of solution. The volumes quoted above, non provide ample empirical evidence how and why governments trapped within various vested interests proved *unable to perform the elementary functions of public policy,* thus *aggravating* the situation that had already been critical anyway. State failure in these cases *lies at the heart of market failure,* which is only aggravated by non-neutral redistributory practices. If foreign investors with a large bargaining power come in, they may further distort the outcomes.

The deeper the distrust in the abilities of the state as a provider, the stronger the case for large-scale privatizations; this does not depend on the level of development. The best empirical overview of comparative country experiences to date (Meggison and Netter, 2001, esp. pp. 380–381) proves that private corporations tend to outperform their publicly-owned competitors and mixed-ownership firms alike. This experience is global and the tendency is overwhelming.

It is true, however, that the *change of ownership,* as seen above, *does not lead on its own,* and in the absence of other conditions, *to improved efficiency:* privatization works in a context. According to the survey quoted above, mass privatization proved to be the least efficient form of ownership change. Its popularity is derived from exigency situations, at least in political terms. A preferential treatment of employees was observed in 91 per cent of cases. Privatization technologies and terms often emerged as an outcome of competing regional, employment, financial, organizational and prime political strategies. As a rule, a privatization proves lastingly efficient if it also contributes to the *broadening of the local capital markets,* by the public quotation of shares. This is the best indicator of whether or not corporate governance has improved, that is, whether a new combination of factors will lead to greater efficiency or just to a changed distribution of rents. Further requirements are the introduction of international accounting standards, the enforcement of disclosure rules and the improvement of the *quality of macroeconomic governance.*

These findings corroborate the conclusions of Joseph Stiglitz (2000, p. 577). He blames the reformers in transition countries not only for the neglect of the contextual factors listed above, but also for their tendency to downplay the *feasibility constraints* of any major reform under *democratic conditions.* The further we get beyond the elementary SLIP phase, the more involved we become in administrative and welfare reforms, i.e. in the *modus operandi of the power structures and of the daily lives of millions of people.* Changes in these areas shape the nature of societies. Thus the *public may choose something different from an option*

103

derived from comparative institutional or economic studies. The more willing we are to acknowledge that backtracking is often a result of half-hearted or incoherent reforms, the less likely we become to be taken by surprise. In this context, the literature typically mentions the liberalization of East Asian financial markets: carried out without sound institutions and regulation, but with a fixed rate of exchange. Such conditions invited the crisis (cf. also Kaminsky, Reinhart and Vegh, 2003). In turn, liberalizing strategies may well have lost their popular appeal irrespective of their substantive features. This experience has triggered research on the conditions for successful liberalization. The broad empirical survey of Bosmann et al (2006) has found the *institutional quality* in terms of freedom, as explained in our concluding chapter, to be the key. This includes, surprisingly, even the political legitimacy of these institutions.

Varietas delectat?

Variety pleases – holds the old Roman proverb. Indeed, if any prediction can be safely made, it is the lasting nature of institutional and policy diversity among the emerging economies (more on that in: Daianu, 2004; Kowalik, 2003). This follows not only from the path dependent nature of post-Communist developments that ended up in diverging trajectories of change in the fifteen years that followed. It also is supported by the insight portraying the Communist modernization strategy as an *aborted development project* leaving a series of structural legacies behind (Szentes, 2004, pp. 205–209).

As we argued in the previous and present chapters both the pattern of legacy and the policy responses to the transformational recession have been sustainingly different across the post-Communist countries. Therefore any approach should be comfortable, at the level of description at least, with observing this feature. Making further inferences, however, is anything but simple/uncontroversial.

We might be less at ease when trying to *apply* the two major *insights* from our first two chapters – the relevance of global processes/approaches and of lasting diversity – *into our analytical and normative view of emerging economies.* There are *several, closely interrelated issues that require deeper consideration.* First, how does international orientation – the local response to globalization – relate to developmental success? This is the subject of our chapter on Transnational markets and local politics. Second, how does EU membership, accomplished by the frontrunners, foster sustainable development and support global catching up? This is the subject of our chapter on the Limits to accession driven transformation. Third, there emerges the follow-up question of how global and European challenges interact? This is the subject of the chapter on Globalization and Europeanization. Fourth: are there any exceptions to the new developmental paradigm that seems to hold for most of the once Communist economies? In order to test the hypothesis we examine the control cases of Russia and China. The first, often portrayed as a textbook case of failed transition, thus allegedly defies the mainstream theory of development. The second control case is of

China. In this country, market socialism seems to have been a viable alternative in the past quarter of a century. Moreover, it often seems to be a successful alternative to the mainstream, the new developmental paradigm. If this is indeed the case, the current policy mainstream – the post-Washington Consensus – does not have paradigmatic nature, since its insights are not universally valid. Finally, in conclusion we should come back to the more general issues of which institutions bring about sustainable development.

The latter is the implication of our broadening of the interpretation of post-Communist change from the traditional 'plan to market' trajectory to the broader developmental dimension. If we succeed in providing a plausible interpretation, a half-way coherent reading of contradictory empirical evidence, we may have made a step towards the better understanding *of the nature of emerging economies* constituting a specific phenomenon in global development. Under this angle it is crucial to retain both features: *the global (uniform) standard* as an ordering principle, and the ability to appreciate – and interpret – *lasting differences,* diversity and divergence across the individual cases surveyed. This also implies that there is no more room, even in abstract terms, for the grand old theories of underdevelopment, stressing the focal role of the state in overcoming backwardness, or the search for the single optimal way to prosperity, (Ricz, 2005, pp. 121–2). In other words, the era of development studies, as distinct from standard economics, seems to be over.

References

ANTAL, L. (1999): What is left of 'reform economics'? *Acta Oeconomica*, vol. 50 nos (1–2) pp. 89–102.

BATES, R. and KRUEGER, A. (1993): Generalizations arising from the country studies. In: BATES, R. and KRUEGER, A. eds: *Political and Economic Interactions in Economic Policy Reform.* Oxford: Basil Blackwell, pp. 444–472.

BAUER P. (2000): The disregard of reality. In: BAUER, P.: *From Subsistence to Exchange and Other Essays.* Princeton New Yersey: Princeton University Press, pp. 15–27.

BEHRMAN, J. and SRINIVASAN, T. N. eds. (1995): Introduction to policy reform, stabilization, structural adjustment and growth. In: BEHRMAN J. and SRINIVASAN, T. N. eds: *Handbook of Development Economics,* vol. 3B, Amsterdam: Elsevier, pp. 2467–2496.

BERGLÖF, E. and BOLTON, P. (2002): The great divide and beyond: Financial architecture in transition. *Journal of Economic Perspectives,* vol. 16. no. 1. pp. 77–100.

BLOMMESTEIN, H. – MARRESE, M. – ZECCHINI, S. (1990): *Centrally Planned Economies in Transition.* Paris: OECD.

BOSMANN, A. – BUSSE, N. – NEUHAUS, S. (2006): Institutional quality and gains from trade. *Kyklos,* vol. 59. no. 3. pp. 345–368.

BÖHM, F. (1982): The non-state ('natural') laws inherent in a competitive economy. In: STOZEL, W. – WATRIN, C. – WILLGERODT, H. – HOHMANN, K., eds: *Standard Texts on the Social Market Economy.* Stuttgart: G. Fischer Verlag, pp. 107–113 (originally published in German in 1933).

BRUTON, H. (1998): A reconsideration of import substitution. *Journal of Economic Literature,* vol. 36. no. 2. pp. 903–36.

BUCHANAN, J. (1977): Law and the invisible hand. In: BUCHANAN, J.: *Freedom in Constitutional Contract*. College Station: Texas A(M University Press, pp. 2–39.

CHUBAIS, A. – VISHIEVSKAIA, M (1995): Russian privatization in mid-1994. In: ASLUND, A. ed.: *Russian Economic Reform at Risk*. London: Frances Pinter and New York: St. Martin's Press, pp. 89–99.

DAIANU, D. (2004): Policy/institutional diversity and economic development. *Competitio* (Debrecen), vol. 3. no. 1. – special English language edition, pp. 5–31.

DALLAGO, B. (1994): Some reflections on privatization as a means to transform the economic system: The Western experience. In: WAGENER, H.-J. ed.: *The Political Economy of Transformation*. Heidelberg and New York: Physica Verlag, pp. 113–144.

DELONG, B. (2000): The triumph of monetarism? *Journal of Economic Perspectives*, vol. 14. no. 1. pp. 83–94.

DOLLAR, D. and KRAAY, A. (2004): Trade, growth and poverty. *Economic Journal*, vol. 114. no. 493. pp. F22–F49.

DORN, J. – HANKE, S. – WALTERS, A. eds (1998): *The Revolution in Development Economics*. Washington: The CATO Institute.

DORNBUSCH, R. (1993): *Stabilization, Debt and Reform: Policy Choices for Developing Countries*. New York: Harvester Wheatsheaf.

EASTERLY, W. (2001): *The Elusive Quest for Growth*. Cambridge/Mass. and London: The MIT Press.

EC–European Commission (1990): Stabilization, liberalization and devolution. Assessment of the economic situation and reform process in the Soviet Union. *European Economy*, no. 45. (special issue).

EUCKEN, W. (1948): On the theory of the centrally administered economy. An analysis of the German experiment. Parts I and II, *Economica*, new vol. 15. no. 1. pp. 79–100 and no. 2. pp. 173–193.

HARBERGER, A. (2001): The view from the trenches: Development processes and policies as seen by a working professional. In: MEIER, G., and STIGLITZ, J. E., eds: *Frontiers of Development Economics*. Oxford University Press for the World Bank, pp. 541–561.

HAYEK, F. A. (1989): *The Fatal Conceit: Errors of Socialism*. Chicago: The University of Chicago Press.

HOEKMAN, B. – SMARZYNSKA-JAVORCIK, B. eds (2006): *Global Integration and Technology Transfer*, Washington – N. Y. a co-publication of the World Bank and Palgrave/Macmillan.

HOFF, K. and STIGLITZ, J. (2001): Modern economic theory and development. In: MEIER, G., and STIGLITZ, J. E. eds: *Frontiers of Development Economics*. Oxford: Oxford University Press for the World Bank, pp. 389–459.

IMF/OECD/IBRD (1991): *A Study of the Soviet Economy*, Vols. I–III, Washington, D. C.: Government Printing Office.

KAASE, M. – SPARSCHUCH, V. – WENNINGER, A. eds (2002): *Handbook of Three Social Sciences in Central and Eastern Europe: Political Science, Economics, Sociology (1989–2001)*. – a book published jointly by Collegium Budapest – Informationszentrum Berlin/GESIS – Fifth Framework Program of the EU Commission/Brussels.

KAMINSKY, G. – REINHART, C. – VEGH, C. (2003): The unholy trinity of financial contagion. *Journal of Economic Perspectives,* vol. 17. no. 4. pp. 51–74.

KOLODKO, G. W. (2000a): Ten years of post-socialist transition: The lessons for policy reforms. In: KOLODKO, G. W.: *Post Communist Transition: The Thorny Road*. Rochester, N. Y.: University of Rochester Press, and Boydell&Brewer Ltd., Woodbridge/Suffolk/UK, pp. 57–86.

KOLODKO, G. W. (2000b): The Washington Consensus Revisited. In: KOLODKO, G. W.: *From Shock to Therapy*. Oxford etc.: Oxford University Press for the UN WIDER, pp. 119–142.

KORNAI, J. (1990): *The Road to a Free Economy*. New York: W. W. Norton.

KORNAI, J. (2001): Ten years after the 'Road to a Free Economy': the author's self-evaluation. In: PLESKOVIC, B. and STERN, N. eds: *Annual Bank Conference on Development Economics, 2000*. Oxford and Washington: Oxford University Press for the World Bank, pp. 49–66.

KOWALIK T. (2003): Systemic variety under the conditions of globalization and integration. In: KOLODKO, G. W. ed.: *Emerging Market Economies: Globalization and Development*. Aldershot/UK: Ashgate, pp. 205–220.

KÖRÖSSÉNYI, A. (1995): Reasons for the defeat of the Right. *East European Politics and Societies,* vol. 9. no. 3.

KÖVES, A. and MARER, P. eds (1991): *Foreign Economic Liberalization: Experiences of Socialist and Market Economies*. Boulder/Col./USA: Westview Press.

KRUEGER, A. (1998): Whither the IMF and the World Bank? *Journal of Economic Literature,* vol. 36. no. 4. pp. 1983–2002.

KYDLAND, F. and PRESCOTT, E. (1977): Rules rather than discretion: The inconsistency of optimal plans. *Journal of Political Economy,* vol. 87. no. 3. pp. 473–492.

LAKI, M. (1991): Economic programs of the ex-opposition parties in Hungary. *East European Politics and Societies,* vol. 5. no. 1. pp. 73–92.

LAL, D. (1993): *The Repressed Economy*. Aldershot/UK and Brookfield/USA: Edward Elgar.

LÁNYI, K. (1996): Szociális piacgazdaság – nálunk, most? (A social market economy for Hungary, now?) In: *2000,* vol. 8. no. 4. pp. 8–17.

MALLE, S. (1994): Privatization in Russia: A comparative study in institutional change. In: CSABA, L. ed. *Privatization, Liberalization and Destruction*. Aldershot/UK and Brookfield/USA: Dartmouth Publishing Co. pp. 71–101. – reprinted also In: PEJOVICH, S., ed.: *The Economics of Property Rights,* vol. I. Cheltenham/UK and Northampton/MA/USA: Edward Elgar, 2001, pp. 403–433.

MEGGISON, W. and NETTER, J. (2001): From state to market: A survey of empirical studies on privatization. *Journal of Economic Literature,* vol. 39. no. 2. pp. 321–389.

MEIER, G. (2001): The old generation of development economists and the new. In: MEIER, G. and STIGLITZ, J. E., eds: *Frontiers...,* op. cit. pp. 13–50.

MURRELL, P. (1995): The transition according to Cambridge, Mass. *Journal of Economic Literature,* vol. 33. no. 1. pp. 164–178.

NELSON, J. – TILLY, Ch. – WALKER, L. eds: (1999): *Transforming Post-Communist Political Economies*. Washington: The National Academy Press.

NORTH, D. (1990): *Institutions, Institutional Change and Economic Performance*. Cambridge etc.: Cambridge University Press.

OFER, G. (2001): Development and transition: converging but merging? *Revue d'Économie et Financière,* vol 10. (special issue), pp. 107–146.

OLSON, M. (1982): *The Rise and Decline of Nations: Economic Growth, Stagflation and Social Rigidities*. New Haven: Yale University Press.

PALDAM, M. (2003): Economic freedom and the success of the Asian tigers: An essay in controversy. *European Journal of Political Economy,* vol. 19. no. 3. pp. 453–478.

PAULSON, J. A. ed. (1999): *African Economies in Transition*, Vols. I–II. New York: St. Martin's Press.

PERKINS, D. and ROEMER, P. eds. (1991): *Reforming Economic Systems in Developing Countries*. Cambridge/Mass: The Harvard University Press.

PORTES, R. ed. (1991): The path of reform in Central and Eastern Europe. *European Economy,* special issue no. 2. pp. 2–23.

RICZ, J. (2005): Paradigmaváltás a fejlődés-gazdaságtanban (Paradigm shift in development economics). *Competitio* vol. 4. no. 2. pp. 109–123.

ROLAND, G. (1991): The political economy of sequencing tactics in the transition period. In: CSABA, L. ed.: *Systemic Change and Stabilization in Eastern Europe*. Aldershot/UK and Brookfield/USA: Dartmouth Publishing Co. pp. 45–64.

ROSENSTEIN-RODAN, P. (1943): Problems of industrialization in Eastern and South-Eastern Europe. *Economic Journal*, vol. 53. no. 212. pp. 202–211.

SALA-I MARTIN, X. (2006): The world distribution of income: falling poverty and ... convergence period. *Quarterly Journal of Economics*, vol. 121 no. 2. pp. 351–398.

SANTOS-PAULO, A. and THIRWALL, P. (2004): The impact of trade liberalization on exports, imports and the balance of payments of developing countries. *Economic Journal*, vol. 114. no. 493. pp. F4–F21.

SCHNEIDER, F. (1993): The federal and fiscal structures of Western democracies as a model for a federal union in former Communist countries? In: WAGENER, H.–J., ed.: *On the Theory and Policy of Systemic Change*. Heidelberg and New York: Physica Verlag, pp. 135–154.

STIGLITZ, J. E. (2000): Reflections on the theory and practice of reform. In: KRUEGER, A. ed. *Economic Reform – The Second Stage*. Chicago and London: The University of Chicago Press, pp. 551–581.

SZABÓ-MORVAI, Á. (2003): Az új bázeli tőkeszabályozás és a belső minősítésen alapuló megközelítés. (Basle Two and the internal rating approach). *Közgazdasági Szemle*, vol. 50. no. 10. pp. 881–890.

SZENTES, T. (2004): *The Political Economy of Development, Globalization and System Transformation*. Budapest: Akadémiai Kiadó.

TODARO, M. and SMITH, S. (2006): *Economics of Development*, 9th edition. New York: Addison Wesley.

UN Economic Commission for Europe (2005): *Economic Survey of Europe*, no. 2. Geneva and New York.

VANBERG, V. (2001): *The Constitution of Markets: Essays in Political Economy*. London and N. Y.: Routledge.

WAGENER, H.-J. ed., (1998): *Economic Thought in Communist and Post-Communist Europe*. London: Routledge.

WILLIAMSON J. (1994): In search for a manual for technopols. In: WILLIAMSON, J. ed., *The Political Economy of Policy Reform*. Washington, D. C.: Institute of International Economics, pp. 9–47.

WILLIAMSON, J. (2005): Differing interpretations of the Washington Consensus. Warsaw: *Tiger Distinguished Lectures*, no. 17. (July) – available online: www.tiger.edu.pl

WILLIAMSON, O. E. (2000): The new institutional economics: Taking stock, looking ahead. *Journal of Economic Literature*, vol. 38. no. 3. pp. 595–613.

WINTERS, L. A. – MCCULLOCH, N. – MCKAY, A. (2004): Trade liberalization and poverty: The evidence so far. *Journal of Economic Literature*, vol. 42. no. 1. pp. 72–115.

WORLD BANK (1996): *From Plan to Market*. Special edition of the World Development Report. Washington and Oxford: Oxford University Press For IBRD.

5. TRANSNATIONAL MARKETS AND LOCAL POLITICS – THE POST-COMMUNIST DIMENSION

In this chapter we shall try to explain how the interaction between what is often termed as 'globalization' and local politics shape the evolution of institutions and policies. While our empirical evidence comes basically from post-Communist countries, we hope to be able to arrive at generalizations that may apply to all emerging economies. Our central contention is twofold. First, since most of the procedures that define processes for emerging economies are not global in their nature, but these do transcend the nation states' border, we propose to call these, in line with the vocabulary of international relations, as *transnationalization*. This term differs from the 'internationalization' term of the Marxists in that it rejects the focality of nation states and 19th century visions of sovereignty. It also aims at the delineation from the overused, non-specified and emotionally loaded concept of 'globalization', that has become a much too widespread label. For instance, the defining factor of the international environment for emerging Europe has been the European Union, thus we devote five chapters to it and its implications. However, the EU is though relevant for the global economy and polity, it is still a *regional structure*. Therefore EU influences should not be discussed under the term 'global influences'.

Our second major claim is that transnational processes themselves are not decisive. It is the *way local politics interacts with these that shapes the outcomes in the longer run, and not only in the economy.* Therefore it is vital for the quality and the outcome of systemic change, especially in the second and third generation tasks of transformation, on how these interactions evolve.

State Desertion, State Failure or Subversive Globalization?

Much has been written on the vices of *state desertion* in the process of post-Communist transformation. Some go as far as describing the erosion of the empire as an outcome of deliberate efforts of a neo-liberal camp, mostly interested in destroying the old regime and not caring much about the creative component of Schumpeterian destruction (cf. eg. Poznanski, 2002; Ellman and Kontorovich, 1999; Stiglitz, 2002). These authors blame the radical reformist camp of neglecting institutions in theory and institution-building in policy. Comparative analysis of facts and figures, e.g. a glimpse at the degree of income centralization at the macroeconomic level, available from the country analyses of the *Transition Report*, as well as our overview presented in the chapter on 'Comparative overview of empirical evidence' and the chapter on Russia may prove, that this claim is only widespread, not well substantiated. While it may apply to many developing countries, and also it contains a modicum of truth when confined to the state of central/federal government coffers, on balance the statement is misleading. If we accept, following the terminology of the IMF Code of Good Fiscal Practices, that it is *general government, rather than the central government budget what matters for the macroeconomic outcomes,* there can be no talk of state desertion. While the scope of central budgets in some years and some countries – notably in Russia – has indeed shrunk below levels customary in all developed economies, local/regional budgets and other covert forms of state intervention, regulation and redistribution are alive and well in all emerging economies including the New Independent States. In transition economies – including Russia – the state has remained all-pervasive: not only a major *owner* of assets, a major – often the sole – *regulator*, but also a source of *revenue* for some, and a source of excise taxes for many others.

In reality, the consolidated level of all public revenues collected in post-Communist countries, that is revenues raised by all local and central organs, in the form of levies, fees, health and social security contribution, customs and down payments of various sorts, *the levels of public spending and public revenues are by no means extreme:* it oscillates between 30 and 52 per cent of GDP. The lower number is the amount collected in Ireland or the United States, the higher reflects the norms of Scandinavia. If we do see worn down infrastructure, underfunded homes of the elderly and many other signs of neglect, these are likely to reflect the combined effect of socialist under-investment and capitalist mismanagement at times when the division of responsibilities as well as of revenues have hardly followed any master plan, least the ones promulgated at the political levels. Spontaneous capitalist development is known to have its seamy sides.

Our *puzzle* is by and large the inverse to the one postulated by the authors of the literature, cited above. In short, if public spending is 'normal', still its outcomes are depressingly weak, what we observe is more likely to fall under the category of *state failure*.[1] While literature on the latter, especially in the context of corruption, but also on failed states, and the role of state collapse in explaining the developmental tragedy of many poor areas abound, we hypothesize, that in some of the less successful post-Communist countries a *peculiar brand* of state failure emerged. It has nothing to do with the complete lack of formal institutions, as in some countries of sub-Saharan Africa, but with the ways inherited information were transformed and distorted. In our hypothesis

---

[1] On the terminology – definition of state failure versus market failure – see more detail in our chapter on Russia.

local power holds the key,[2] that remained well and alive after so many reforms at deregulation and decentralization.

Intertwining between local states and corporations located in their territory is well and alive (on Russia cf. Radygyn, 2001). This creates a business-unfriendly overall atmosphere, and recreates problems of bureaucratic co-ordination, this time at the local level. Thus we assume that, at the end of the day, state failure *lays at the heart of market failure, while the latter reinforces and calls for more central/bureaucratic intervention.*[3] This insight may be generalized for countries like Ukraine and Serbia, more broadly even for NIS and Southeast Europe, in an attempt to explain why these countries could not deliver even as much as the frontrunner transition economies, whose performance is anything but impressive, as documented in the chapter on Comparative and empirical evidence. If the hypothesis holds, events in the two laggard groups of post-Communist economies are likely to be interpreted along the lines of traditional development economics. If this procedure works, social science is unlikely to be in the need of a new brand of economics called upon by great many observers of the scene. Then insights from the literature on underdevelopment and poverty alleviation may become more policy relevant for these countries than much of the transition-specific economic theorizing.

By contrast, more successful, frontrunner or emerging economies do experience the spread of market relations, primarily through *transnationalization.* This term reflects the fact that the broad net of global sourcing, global norms, the spread of the IT economy and related forms of organization transgress the national boundaries in unprecedented degrees and forms. Not only in economic, technological and information levels do we observe the emergence of virtual communities creating actual value added (a process to be analyzed later in this chapter). What is even more important is that the previously dominant *inter-national or inter-state* features of exchanges are relegated to the background. In part global, in part local, in part meso-level regulations emerge, and not only in codes of conduct, but in terms of enforceable law (on the latter cf. Teubner, 1997). State borders as well as state controls have become permeable. Controls, such as taxing capital flows, or limiting cash-withdrawals simply founder on new technologies (for instance, for transferring huge amounts via leveraged deals we need just a push of a button, no coffers, no bodyguards etc.). This process is complemented by informalization, both at the top and the bottom level of providing goods and services, also in the most advanced

[2] Local power – in the original Russian term *mestnichestvo* – has nothing to do with federal structures. It means that the traditionally over-centralized but weak Russian state could not control the peripheries efficiently. 'Moscow is far away' as the proverb in the 19th century went. This implied that non-elected local bosses could re-interpret laws and regulations in an arbitrary fashion. This feature has, of course, survived the Soviet period. By appointing presidential envoys – *gubernatori* – President Putin tried to put an end to this as one of the first measures of his rule in 2001. However, besides enhancing formal centralization, it has not resulted in more coherence in legal and economic practices. Similar 'local power' has been observable in the last two centuries of the Ottoman Empire as well.

[3] I tried to document this idea on Yeltsin's Russia in (Csaba, 2000).

societies (Sassen, 2002, pp. 111–115).Therefore it may make sense to stick to this term despite its business flavor.[4]

Thus in the second half of our hypothesis we assume that *the more successful* are those countries that, indeed, managed to *cut the umbilical cord between state administration and the firms,* primarily by joining in the process of transnationalization, via FDI,[5] via the privatization of banks, via reliance on parent company financing. Globalization of finance has thus overwritten the path dependent forms of recombinant property (Bruszt and Stark, 1998), thus relational capital and the reproduction of old structures could not happen. Once corporations mind their businesses, and the economy is becoming more regular, the state can also raise more revenues via normal channels. This may develop into a *virtuous circle,* where the virulence of a transnational market serves as a base for an ever stronger state, that is able to provide a wider variety of public services, starting up with the rule of law. By doing so the state may counteract the more extreme income differentiation and the reproduction of the vicious circles of poverty, already emerging in the form of digital divide and exclusion, especially of some social groups, also in the transforming country group.

It is important to differentiate, following the non-transition specific policy reform literature (e.g. Krueger, 2000, p. 595) between the state in general and the *core state,* as defined by the literature on policy reform, in terms of major regulatory functions.[6] Starting from a stage of quasi-total nationalization under Communism it has only been natural to call for de-statization, privatization, getting the political class and the administration out of business etc. On the other hand, developing country experience, surveyed inter alia, in the collection of papers quoted above, indicate that failure of well meant and often technically also well defined reforms is often attributable to the *lack of local capacity to administer these.*

[4] Richard Higgott (2001, p. 91) describes it as 'the core question besetting international political economy' how do we understand and explain the relationship between increasingly non-territorial and globalized economic system on the one hand, and the extant territorially delimited hierarchical state system on the other?

[5] As Keren and Ofer (2002, esp. pp. 36–37) explain, FDI matters primarily as an agent of transnationalization; the more it takes place in the financial sector and commercial services, the higher the probability of positive spillover effects is. Certainly better governance and less corruption also aided Central Europe in its relative success against the NIS. The claim is tested in detail via formal analysis in their article.

[6] Some political science theories on embeddedness question the existence of a core state as different from interest groups. However, in policy relevant terms, it would be lethal to give up the idea, developed in the Middle Ages in Western Europe, namely that the ruler is also subject to the laws, that checks and balances exist, further that public purpose and functions (of the ruler), as different from its capacity as an individual or a representative of a group, in other words, the public purpose exists. More recent theorizing in the US political economy, primarily in the works of James Buchanan (more recently in Buchanan and Congleton, 1998) and the late Mancur Olson (2000) have highlighted the importance of this issue. Likewise, in the literature on policy reform it is hard to be meaningful without postulating the core state and the function of public policy, pursuing the interest of the community, rather than its constituents. Further elaboration of this point would lead us to democratic theory, a different subject matter and discipline.

112

This circumstance alone calls for *strengthening*, rather than weakening of the core state, while interventionism and *micro-management should certainly be rolled back* if efficiency is to be increased. This is an issue we explained in the preceding chapter comparing transition and development theories. What we propose in this chapter is that *strengthened market co-ordination allowed for an improved bureaucratic co-ordination*, creating the virtuous circle in the pioneering economies. By contrast, a weak state 'embedded' in terms of direct intertwining with vested interest groups, but lacking checks and balances that could hold public officials accountable, has been shown to be at the root of failure in most reforms in Latin America over the past decade (Manzetti, 2003, pp. 359–360).

What we experience in the post-Communist context is puzzling, indeed. If one looks at a bird's eye view, economic science tends to take the dichotomy, even the polarity of market and bureaucratic co-ordination as given, by such diverse authors as Smith, Marx, Keynes or Friedman. At very general level, the history of economic thought is a shuttle movement between advocates of more and less state involvement, thus the idea of *co-evolution of state and market power*, rather than these forming antipodes, is anything but trivial.

Policies and Erosion in Emerging Economies: What Is the Nexus?

The starting point of systemic change has been the erosion of power structures of the Soviet Empire. In a nutshell, neither sticks nor carrots remained in the hands of the old regime. It is no secret by now that it is not the collapse that requires explanation, but rather why the Soviet system survived for so long. It is hard to overlook the importance of one-time factors, such as the two oil price hikes in 1973 and 1979, both representing a windfall.[7] Also, the long period of cheap credit, that reflected the recycling of petrodollars as well as the blind faith of creditors in the controlling abilities of the command economy contributed to a one-off injection of money.

In the Soviet empire formal institutions collapsed. This was documented by such extreme phenomena as the eruption of shortages leading to open inter-regional strike movements in 1989 in the Soviet Union, or to the defeat in Afghanistan (and by proxy, in the first Gulf War in 1991). Therefore, *the role of formal policies*, decaying Soviet institutions, and by implication, of much discussed reform projects *has become marginal*. This state of art only gained momentum in 1991–1994, when state formation and crisis management dominated policies and institutions alike. While reform projects were diligently produced (and analyzed), their impact was next to nil. The dominant trend of disintegration culminated in the ongoing decay of the Soviet army and its slip-

---

[7] As the Soviet Union, as now Russia, is in no position to influence prices, not even contribute to their shaping, it is a *price taker*, to use Scitovsky's term. This means the small economy feature as well as policy-makers' innocence in letting this happen or not. In business terms, gains resulting from factors outside the control of the agent's action is called windfall.

ping into the first Chechen War in 1994. It happened not by a conscious policy decision taken in Moscow. Rather it emerged basically by way of illegal dealings and decisions by the local commanders. Finally mention should be made of the inability to control the capital account of the Russian Federation,[8] that is in a country where until the late 1990s cash was the only accepted payment method. All in all, disintegration and decay had been the name of the game. Thus *spontaneity* had been, by necessity, *the dominant trend* over contemporary projects (regulations) concepts of various sorts.

If we follow Douglass North (1990), the collapse of formal institutions inevitably invites the emergence of *informal institutions* to fill the vacuum. These fulfil the coordinating functions inherent in the viability of any society that avoids starvation. In other words, the growing *informalization* should not have been seen as a sign of crisis in the post-Communist economies, but as much of a natural phenomenon as pain is following a surgery.

Seen from this angle, *the mismatch between planned and actual* processes, that had been anything but unknown in 'countries of real socialism', has been a sustaining feature of transformation policies all across the countries. Illustrative facts can be listed at length: budget deficits never meet the targets, inflation is under- or overshooting, exchange rates and interest rates do not behave well, unemployment does not follow governmental programs, the return on private pension funds do not follow expectations, nor do agriculture evolve according to the most recent five-year-plans. If our view, of erosion being dominant and *informalization*, at least temporarily, *inevitable,* there is not much to be surprised at these, frequently reported and discussed phenomena. This, of course, is fundamentally different from the uncertainty inherent in any – business or policy – decision also in Western societies, that may explain regular discrepancies between planned and actual processes.

The concept of *'state desertion'* emerged in Central Europe and several authors may claim priority. The term implies that *certain functions inherent to the core state remain unattended.* The term is used by those, having coined it in the normative, in so far as it suggests, that should right people be in the right place, the problem would not have emerged or could/should be solved. A most important area where the concept gained legitimacy was the financial sector. Analyzing the processes of financial intermediation, it has been found that lacking regulation (alternatively: the unwillingness to regulate) created situations of *state capture,* where the administration fell hostage to a clearly defined interest group. The Czech Republic and Russia of the mid-90s were prime

---

[8] We can only re-iterate that the recurring surplus in the Russian current account, that has long been a puzzle for external observers, has emerged not as an outcome of conscious decisions taken in the central bank or in the ministry of finance. If the latter were the case, surpluses would be used for servicing Soviet outstandings. In reality, this has been capital flight and money ended up in private pockets (more often than not in offshore centers). While the Russian governments, especially following the August 1998 currency crisis, attempted to control capital flight, they never managed. As documented in our tables on current account, surpluses in the post-1999 period reached unprecedented magnitudes.

cases for this point (Bruszt, 2002; Meyerdorff and Thakor, eds, 2002).[9] Also looking at deregulation and privatization, lack of regulation was shown to serve special interest and result in inefficiency (Lányi, 1995).

One way of looking at these phenomena would portray this outcome as a by and large inevitable side effect of the neglect of institutions, or in other terms, of *the blind faith in the market* (Stiglitz, 2000; Stiglitz and Ellerman, 2001). Adherents to this approach blame 'system designers' for their under-performance and insufficiently enlightened policies.

The other camp (e.g. Mau, 2000; Dabrowski et al, 2001a and 2001b) adopts different premises. The starting point for them is chaos, and in a figurative sense, they interpret transition in terms of *chaos theory*. Informalism as well as compromises with vested interests, were a price to be paid for the peaceful nature of post-Communist change.[10]

In our view, the concept of state desertion is a tricky one and lends itself too easily to political instrumentalization. Whereas in cases of regulating the stock exchange in the Czech Republic in the 1992–1997 period, or in the much publicized and criticized loans for shares privatization in Russia in 1995, or the non-regulated voucher privatization in both countries the term may be appropriately applied. By contrast, the broadening of this interpretation to the degree done by Joseph Stiglitz (2000) and rightly criticized by the three Polish economists (Dabrowski – Gomulka – Rostowski, 2001 a, b) carries the danger of over-estimating what can be centrally managed in a modern complex economic system, especially when even its physical-legal boundaries are in question.

In any analysis, it is ritually raised whether and to what degree the international financial organizations, and more generally, Western advice extended much too diligently (and accepted much too readily locally) can be held responsible for the meager outcomes reported earlier in this book. Ever since the Nobel-winner Joseph Stiglitz (2002) introduced IMF bashing in the good manners of policy analysis, critical voices amplified.[11]

---

[9] In the case of the Czech Republic of 1992–1996 financial investors close to the ODS party of Václav Klaus, in the Russian case, the oligarchs close to (actually financing) President Yeltsin constituted the group capturing the state in the traditional sense. One can establish by 2007 that the crusade of Putin has brought no more than the redistribution of one group of oligarchs – having emerged from nowhere under Yeltsin – to a different group – originating mostly in the secret services.

[10] Colonial wars that have been happening in parallel, have as little to do with transition, as Algeria had with the economic changes in the Fourth French Republic, or de-colonialization with British nationalization in the 1950s. Coincidence and cause should not be mixed up.

[11] This is not to suggest that critical voices did not use to be around in the pre-Stiglitz period. On the contrary, in less developing countries IMF bashing has always been the norm, and blaming the IMF or the World Bank for any unpopular measure has been in use for decades. Many of these criticism has been valid, as appreciated by the Fund's current leaders (Krueger, 1998). However, it does require careful scrutiny, if we want to prove – rather than merely allege – that a given measure was IMF *inspired*, *-imposed*, or merely *-initiated*. For instance the 1997 Hungarian pension reform was a basically domestic issue. As insiders would testify, it was Péter Medgyessy who made it as a condition to take up a job as minister of finance in 1996, rather than external pressure, that convinced the Socialist Premier Gyula Horn to bow in. Later – also in governmental papers – ritual reference was made to the IMF, though the country was no longer under a stand-by, thus the leverage of the IFIs was minimal over moral suasion.

One should avoid the temptation to simplistic answers, despite the heritage of the 'who is to blame' question in intellectual life. It is hard to believe, and even harder to *demonstrate,* that countries with a strong bargaining position, such as Russia, could be pressured into anything that would have gone *against the real will and serious professional convictions of the government* and its experts. Also in the cases of small countries, like Hungary, the IMF has proven unable to pressure the government into publishing regular and credible statistics on external debt and government finances up until 1995 (the country joined the IMF in December 1981). In general, similarly to developing countries, any decision in crisis is the result of compromises and deals. *One player* to this comprehensive game is the IMF, whose bargaining position has been crucially dependent upon the host country's standing on international financial markets. Thus the *interaction of transnational and local* politics and economics cannot be denied.[12]

Broadly speaking, in the more theoretical literature on the transition experience, there emerged a tendency to over-generalize. Strong positions, as the ones voiced in the Stiglitz – Ellerman (2001) versus Dabrowski et al (2001 a, b) debate, are voiced and repeated, while substantiation, especially one based on prime sources is scanty at best. Therefore, it is perhaps *impossible* to answer the question in its entirety with a simple yes or no.

On the one hand, we do not abstract away from the fact of collapse and erosion from the disintegration of formal institutions. Moreover, we appreciate that it takes many years of evolution of any new institution would require. Thus if we follow the approach of Douglass North, the 'political' view seems to be biased, as it tends to overstate the potential of any government in a modern post-industrial economy. On the other hand, local institutionalists tended to be those who advocated less radical platforms. As we have seen from the numbers, *less radical policies have not delivered better results anywhere.* Therefore, it should be clear, that an *analytical and policy-level distinction is needed* between advocating less radical policies/slower pace of changes on the one hand, and appreciating the role of institutions on the other. The differentiation, long established in a variety of neo-institutionalist approaches, such as German ordo-liberalism or even some radical transition economists,[13] here gains analytical importance. It seems that in all frontrunner countries *success rested on the combination* of radical policies with appropriate institution-building, allowed for by an emerging (EU-based) policy consensus over long run issues.

This might explain the emerging new consensus or policy mix, that we may dub post-Washington Consensus, or New Washington Consensus, where the role of both policies and institutions are stressed, and the art of orchestrating

---

[12] It may well be postulated that the more assertive bargaining style, or better professional foundations IMF has, people make the impression of an imposition even at cases when no direct pressurizing is demonstrable.

[13] Balcerowicz (1995, chapter 3) for instance clearly distinguished short term/stabilization-related tasks/shock therapy/ from institution building and privatization. The latter was, also in his view is to take years.

the appropriate mix is left to policy-makers.[14] If this is the case, the interaction with local actors, also incorporated in the slogan of *'local ownership of reforms'* already during the Wolfensohn Presidency at the World Bank, is indeed the name of the game. Moreover, we need to appreciate the *cutting back of activities* of both the Fund and the Bank following the deliberations of the Meltzer Commission in 2000, and followed up by the neo-conservative Republican administration in the US.[15] Thus it might be hard to conceive, let alone to document, cases where the strawmen of the IMF-bashers, of an almighty Fund and a powerless local leadership, delivered defenseless to the mercy of international bureaucrats, would make practical analytical sense.

The Experience of Frontrunners

One of the few points on which there might be a consensus among analysts of transition experience is *the formative role played by the EU and the perception of European expectations* in shaping local politics, institutions, self-perceptions and to a degree even the rules of the game. Such measures as the conquest of the Supreme Soviet in October 1993, or ethnic cleansing by Serbs, Bosniaks, Albanians and Croats, or even a return to hyperinflationary policy or even just postponing regular elections when these are due, were simply out of question[16] for the decision-makers in Central Europe. If we look at it from the point of view of *consensus-building,* so crucial in modern theories of economic policy, or gaining *credibility,* those making promises in line with revealed EU preferences have obviously been much better equipped with winning cards, than those disagreeing, whatever the substance of the matter was. This has been clear, since especially in the early years of transition 'joining Europe' has figured among one of the few uncontestable preferences across the political spectrum, and the competition was only in terms of who is the better European. In sum, local politics has become European, and European politics/perceptions local – an issue we shall discuss in two separate chapters.

[14] Some analysts (Higgott, 2000, pp. 148–152) consider even the post-Washington Consensus too feeble, being 'managerialist, top-down, non-sensitive to issues of wealth distribution and justice, and downplaying democratic legitimacy and participation'. These features, however, may derive from the nature of IFIs and their mandate; on participation it would be hard to prove that this would be perhaps the only field where the maxim 'the bigger the better' would indeed apply. On the contrary, Srinivasan (2001) reports of several cases where more participation implied the enforcement of priorities of more vocal, rather than more vulnerable groups in water management projects in India.

[15] The Budapest office of the IBRD, for instance, was first moved from the pompous Bank Center to a less impressive premise; later it was transformed to an advisory agency; further it was transformed to a regional office, and finally closed down at the time of writing of the first edition of this book.

[16] If for no other reason, because of the perspective of EU-membership, that was seen as realistic ever since the adoption of the Copenhagen criteria of accession in June 1993.

On the other hand, the lack of a palpable, realistic EU perspective has indeed been having disorienting local politics. Belarus, Ukraine and Serbia are only extreme cases in point. When the European option is not given, or at least a large part of the elite is unconvinced of its virtues, *the role of experimentation has grown*,[17] and the influence of Europeanization diminished. Lacking consensus-building, such as in the cases of Serbia, Turkey, the Ukraine for that matter, allow for more *couleur locale*, more experimentation and less convergence, in economics and politics alike. Since their stage of transformation has been shown to be still dominated by the un-mastered SLIP agenda, such diversity could not play the favorable role, otherwise, diversity as such plays in evolutive processes.

The process of converging to Europe played a formative role in at least two dimensions. First, in countries where *creation of democracy and state* had been on the agenda, it helped to manage both processes in a self-sustaining, mutually reinforcing manner. This is anything but trivial, since state formation, as in NIS, often requires more centralization, and democracy often is relegated to lip service to international organizations (not only in Central Asia). Second, the process of implementing *the Europe Agreements*, with a clear view to full membership, then applying the *White Book of 1995*, explaining the sectoral technicalities of EU requirements, finally *the acquis screening*, the phase when the EU Commission checked *implementation on the ground*, not mere promulgation of EU law, have all paved the way to eventual membership.

In a way, and also including the *accession agreements proper*, that contain a large chunk of commitments taken, but still to be delivered, from monetary policy to environmental regulations, *have acted as formative components of state building in the new EU countries*. By doing so, the EU has played a most useful role in *lending institutional credibility* to newly established formal institutions, rules and procedures. This was correctly seen, by early transition literature, as a missing element in autochtonous development models. The latter, observable in the NIS and Southeast Europe, have clearly been struggling with the lack of an anchor, around which policy consensus could be built, as well as with the low if any credibility of imported institutions. Borrowing without control and perspectives has not proven to be more efficient than in the average of developing nations. Also, the Kosovo and Bosnian cases call attention to the otherwise also proven fact, that external assistance (and surveillance) alone cannot *replace* domestic institutional and policy development.

We have indicated in the comparative empirical chapter that inward FDI can and should be seen as a success indicator of systemic change. In other words, we extend this insight into theory, and claim that the successful *entry of transnational corporations has laid the micro-foundations for macroeconomic success* in the frontrunning countries. By now it should be clear, that differences are merely in terms of *timing* and *circumstances*, rather than in strategies (as suggested in

---

[17] Such as adopting lax fiscal policies for the long run; or mass privatization; or applying policy mix that is contrary to the mainstream, as in Ukraine or Moldova.

the early debates). All countries, including the late starters, like Slovakia, Lithuania and Slovenia, have adopted a path of outward orientation, of open door policies, and of privatizing structurally important assets to foreigners.

True, it takes two to tango, that is a favorable assessment on the side of investors of the country in the long run, and in broad terms, to adopt a strategy that allows for upgrading. As the good summary of corporate strategies by Czakó (2003) explains, foreign firms may well be tempted to squeezing out one-shot games or to strategies leading to downgrading rather than upgrading local R+D and other capabilities. This is likely if the feedback they receive and the related perceptions are indicative of insecure property rights, non-transparent regulatory frames, lasting industrial conflict or a re-surge in inflation. This, at the end of the day, is yet another sign of why FDI can, indeed, be taken as a success indicator of systemic change.

It might well be superfluous to re-iterate both empirical evidence and the literature processed earlier to support our claim that *structural upgrading*, thus lasting *ability to earn sufficient revenue* to sustain growing imports, that lead domestic overall modernization are *the keys to sustaining growth* in the emerging economies. We have seen the great dividing line across countries. A large number of well publicized examples, from VW in Bratislava to the relocation of Nokia's R+D center to Hungary, the big investments in Czech banking all indicate a similar pattern of long-term orientation in corporate/investor behavior. Accordingly, transnationals *do not remain islands in the domestic economy*, as is the case when growth is resource dependent, or reliant on agriculture or cheap labor only.

Transnationalization implies a joining in the process of global sourcing, not only of inputs, but of competences, all across the entire chain of management, sales, R+D, and of course production (more on that in Szabó and Kocsis, 2003). By the same token, *structural adjustment is managed at the firm level*, not via central industrial policies.[18]

Perhaps even more contentious has been *the entry of foreign strategic owners in the financial sector.* This has long been a contested issue, at least since the Great Depression of the 1930s, and the distrust in markets as well as the overall 'strategic' handling of the financial sector have become parts of conventional wisdom in policy-making. This inherited approach long survived the monetarist counter-revolution of Milton Friedman and Robert Lucas, who fought to revive the trust in the market in general and financial markets in particular as an efficient institution of resource allocation. By contrast deep distrust of markets is still dominating much of the *regulatory practices* in the countries in the old continent, as the inability of the EU to enforce common regulation of banking and capital markets – following the suggestions of the Lámfalussy Committee (2002) – has clearly indicated in recent years. Therefore, in part owing to the traditionally

---

[18] Industrial policy is a contentious term in Western Europe. Whereas some still conceive it as setting sectoral priorities, others see it more in terms of competition policy, subsidy control, educational measures and support of human infrastructure. Our criticism is directed to the first interpretation only, and is aware of the relevance of the second.

strong *benchmarking* that has always been typical of the conservative bankers, the idea of quick privatization of banks has always remained a contested issue in emerging Europe.

Interestingly, *the more radical suggestion* of quick/early bank privatization to foreigners *has come from within the region* (Mizsei, 1993, p. 176), not from the international community. While this position has always remained in the minority, the pressures of banking crises, the resultant loss of capital and loss of confidence, the obvious lack of professional knowledge (especially tacit knowledge), the political relevance and scale economies in the retail banking have all prompted governments of the frontrunner accession countries to drift to a *more radical policy position* than the majority of the contemporary academic and financial profession would have had it.

It can be demonstrated empirically (Várhegyi, 2002; Szapáry, 2002; Kudrna, 2004), that the great privatization drive of the 1995–2000 period had been an outcome of a variety of factors. These included daily crisis management, policy improvisation and finally interaction with the international financial community. The latter implied not only, after 1997 *not even primarily, the interface with the international financial institutions.* As long as the Central European countries consolidated their debt position, they did not have to rely on Fund/Bank assistance either. This changed situation, progress with EU accession talks, as well as changes in the domestic balance of political forces that resulted by the late 1990s and early 2000s in the biggest bank privatization in European economic history.[19]

As soon as the attempt to create 'national capitalism' has proven unsustainable, and the political second thoughts about the German *reconquista* ebbed, in the context of accelerating accession process to the European Union, the large-scale sell-out of Polish, Czech, Slovak, Slovene banks have become a reality. Knowing the four freedoms of the EU, that do require national treatment for EU banks by new entrants, the fight against foreign penetration has turned into a lost battle. This happened by the mid-90s, when such crises, as the Latvian, the Czech, the Albanian, the Russian, but also the individual big scandals in the Hungarian banking sector all called for prudent, solid, domestically non-corruptible banking.

This is not the place to repeat the story of banking reforms and privatization by the country (cf. e.g. Petrick, ed., 2000; Sevic, ed., 2002; Várhegyi, 2002). What really matters is their outcome. Looking at these at the abstract level of stylized facts, privatization to strategic foreign owners did imply *a fundamental change in the rules of the game*. If in the Communist period, by definition, and later by

---

[19] Traditionally, in Antiquity and in the Middle Ages money lending had, by definition, been a private activity, that was sparsely regulated by the state. Even if rules were introduced, these tended to be avoided, and the self-regulation among private market agents, similar to *lex mercatoria*, had been dominant. Even the Bank of England was run on private market principles until the Great Depression (more on these intricate issues in the excellent monograph of Spahn, 2001). By the same token privatization, that is the act of transforming publicly owned assets into private hands, made no sense at all.

default, the closed economy model was relevant, since nobody invested big amounts into chaotic transforming economies. This situation has changed with the selling off the big financial institutions country by country. In a closed economy it is easy, and to some degree also inevitable, that *cosy relationships emerge between banking and industry, as well as between banking and the state administration.* As long as these sustain, the model of recombinant property, developed by László Bruszt and David Stark (1998) is relevant, thus domestic intertwining between big banks and big industry remains formative for the new market economy. By the same token, path dependence is likely to dominate newly imported institutions. This is the model of the laggards, from Ukraine to Romania and to Serbia. Unlike in the latter listed countries the sell-off of banking, especially if followed by capital account liberalization, deprives domestic policy-makers from their leverage. Business calculation will dominate over inherited relations, else the chief executive officer and his associates must, sooner than later, say good bye to their jobs.[20]

This implies no more and no less than the emergence of textbook-like *principal-agent relationships in the allocation of resources.* Managers thus lose their extreme independence, gained either in the reform socialist period, or during the institutional vacuum, or informalism of the early transition years. Even those managers, who could hand-pick their eventual owners could be, and indeed, had been sacked (starting up with our example in the footnote). When big corporations can afford financing from the global capital markets through their parent company, the demand for banking and related financial services is unlikely to grow within the transforming economies. There is a situation where banks are gradually 'crowded in' the retailing business, when they have to do more than broker state bonds and serve a few selected VIP clients from among the blue chips.

Similarly, politicians are unlikely to lose interest in cosy, cheap funding (especially if hypocritical[21] party funding laws do not secure survival of any party in a media democracy). However, their possibilities are getting limited. Even under golden share rules, outlawed by the EU only by 2003, the state as a minority shareholder can hardly influence each and every major decision, not even personnel decisions. Furthermore, as long as banks live on something else than managing state directed credit, or selling state bonds, *there is not much that the political class can reciprocate* (the more protectionism is diminishing, the

---

[20] This has actually happened, following the privatization of one of the largest Hungarian banks, *Magyar Hitel Bank* in the post-1995 period. Following its take-over by *ABN AMRO Bank*, one of the most aggressive retail bankers in the globe, each year a new management was appointed, finally the Dutch, being disappointed with sustaining poor business results simply sold off the institution to their competitor, *Kredietbank* of Belgium. None of the top managers could survive, in leading position, any of reorganizations.

[21] Party finance limitations do not take account of the actual costs of, say, buying prime time on television, or spreading giant posters, as they follow a populist approach of 'poor' or 'serving' politicians. Those taking the rules literally do not survive, those who survive are unlikely to observe the rules, as in ancient Sparta.

less so). Since everybody else, the media, and all public personalities try to get banks sponsoring them, politicians are becoming just one competitor for the limited funds available for the process. There is no way to stop the shrinkage of the pie. Thus *the main 'front' of fighting for resources becomes the market*, definitely not a shrinking public sphere.

Also the spread of ICT, of virtual services of various kinds, and availability of the global capital market limits the relevance of banking. In a way, what used to be trivial under Communism is now becoming *next to impossible:* that is for politicians to decide over major *allocation* issues. The interface among many players renders their influence much less, than it used to be. If TNCs decide over major investment, the role of policy-makers is bound to diminish. Moreover, to use the slogan of the *perestroika* period: there is no way back,[22] in part because of transnationalization, in part because of the supranational legislation that emerged in the EU. If this insight holds, the *differences between transnationalizing and inward-looking transition countries is bound to grow in the future*, and not only in business terms. The variety of market models that emerges in a national/closed economy model is likely to be significantly dissimilar to a transnationalized one, where the role of the central state is likely to change and diminish. This finding is immediately supported by the research by Piatkowski (2003) on the role of the new economy in emerging economies. He finds that the grouping of these corresponds to our classification, because it is the institutional infrastructure rather than the inherited R+D potential or the publication record of academic personnel that is decisive for the spread of ICT in the respective economies.

Once we accept the *pivotal role played by the capital markets* in resource allocation in the contemporary economy, it is hard to avoid the above conclusion. In a nutshell, global capital markets do discipline national policies that do not follow the logic of theirs. Meanwhile at the microeconomic level, only those firms will be able to finance their expansion from cheap international money markets, that also adapt to the logic of transnational markets. In other words, structural change, taking place at the micro level is oriented by the logic of global capital market, rather than by other considerations (be those political, production, locational or else). The largest Polish, Czech and Hungarian corporations already trade their shares on the New York and London Stock Exchanges, that applies *a fortiori* for the transnationals, contributing already to 50–70 per cent of export revenue for the Central European economies. This path of development is no longer an abstract theory-inspired option, but an *accomplished fact that therefore molds the nature of the economic order* in the new EU countries of the region.

Finally, mention should be made of the *virtuous circle* that has demonstrably emerged, in terms of development theory, and contrary to many pessimistic views that used to dominate the social science output in the first, and some-

---

[22] Certainly, as extreme cases like Belarus or Myanmar remind us, social science laws are not iron laws; thus at a high price the opposite of everything, stated in normative terms, is feasible. The likelihood of closing down a country like the Czech Republic must therefore be seen as minimal, short of an other Stalin.

times in the second half of the 1990s. Joining transnationalization has been considered *a contradiction in terms* of several theories that are still well represented in development studies. Neo-Marxism, structuralism, post-Keynesianism, a variety of network theories and the narrow interpretation of path dependence, as well as old institutionalism would all predict an inevitable failure. I do not think it would be fair to quote authors by their names and point to the fallacies. However, it would be hard to deny the interdependence of various sides of the success story.[23] This is so, as we do have their *interplay* in all cases observed and do not have any single control case, in which *only one* of the components of the chain of virtuous circle would have been present.

In other words, experience of emerging Europe is supportive of the mainstream view of development, emphasizing that *there is an inherent logic in transnationalization,* that may, and does, come to effect only if local policies allow for it. How local policies are formed is a different matter, and will be discussed in separate chapters. However, what we have indeed seen, that these *local policies are formative* to a variety of components that decide if joining the global process will be a road to 'immiserising growth' (Bhagwati, 1991 and 1998), or conversely, to a process of gradual catching up.

The Same Seen from the Angle of the Mouse: Laggards in Transition

As we have seen in the empirical chapter, there are many more failures than success in the transition history, thus it makes sense to try and offer a framework explaining the diverse experiences. Our hypothesis is that transnationalization and local politics interact in these cases as well. *It is the nature of this interaction which differ* and that might explain the dissimilar outcomes, as we shall elaborate in this chapter.

If there is anything common among the laggard countries, this is the *drift* in policy-making and a search for a peculiar *national model of development* at the level of theorizing. The drift implies no more and no less than an ongoing emphasis on various crisis management projects, short term emergency measures and improvisation, that is coupled with a lack of comprehensive approach to issues of the economic order, and a de-emphasis issues of the long run.[24] It is

---

[23] This point is particularly strongly emphasized in the habilitation theses of Péter Mihályi (2001) applying this insight to the Hungarian case. Similar conclusion is reached, with less of a triumphalist tone by King and Váradi (2002).

[24] In a typical manner the poorly digested quibble of Keynes is invoked, 'in the long run all of us are dead', which related to the need of crisis management policy in the given context of the Great Depression. Also, it is not very well known that Keynes himself never considered his *General Theory* to be anything else but a summary of his policy experiences in the Treasury. Alas, in the same vein, his personal friend and intellectual adversary, Hayek equally tended to see *The Road to Serfdom* as a policy pamphlet written in preparation for the post-war years, with the advent of state interventionism as an established policy (and not, as during both wars, as a set of mere emergency measures).

hardly surprising for anybody with an economic background that a series of improvisations can only lead to the reproduction of old strains and inefficiencies. While this is, to some degree, understandable under democratic conditions, the vast literature on policy reform, partly already quoted, is devoted to the conditions and ways under which major changes in inherited arrangements *can and should* be brought about. Whereas the tendency to appeasement with bad conditions is psychologically well justified, in terms of academic analysis we need to be more ambitious in setting our standards. The *post hoc, ergo propter hoc* approach is though widespread, and not only in historical science, still an analytical discipline can never put up with this methodological nihilism.

What is the typical mindset in a laggard country that sets the environment in which policy decisions are being made? *Backwardness is always and everywhere path dependent.*[25] Thus there has been a long established tendency to blame history for every ill. Furthermore as blame is, by definition, put on the shoulders of outside world (which is yet another form of psychological rationalization), the logic as well as the intellectual climate of the latter is described as *inherently hostile to late-comers.* There is only one further step from here to make a virtue out of weakness, by declaring the outside world as invalid / unworthy / inferior, and the 'world from within' as the only source of legitimacy, higher quality and superior. A search for a 'national model of the economy', as well as the rejection of Western mainstream thinking is, at the end of the day, part and parcel of the broader intellectual climate in the laggard societies the world over. The more intellectuals know about such, once fashionable, still non-Marxian (though nationalist) theories as of *dependencia*, structuralism or historicism, the higher the probability of canonizing one (or several) of these theories to the level of an official dogma is. Being that this is taught in secondary schools and at universities, the more the entire intellectual environment is likely to be receptive to these.

Under these circumstances, any suggestion on universally valid rules of say, microeconomics, or of supply and demand, or of sound public and private finances, or on the lack of corruption being a value on its own right, tends to be branded as ideological bias, an instrument serving only and exclusively the interest of currently successful/core countries.[26] The hostile explicit policies of host countries have long been shown (Lucas, 1990) to be a major cause of why capital is not flowing from rich to poor countries.

We have already introduced such concepts as the 'core state' and 'state capture'. In concrete terms this implies, that similarly to developing economies, the laggard transition countries are saddled with *large but ineffective state apparatuses.* This public sector is over-extended, but not very target oriented. In the

[25] This point is expounded, relying on a broad literature, in the insightful monograph of Daniel Daianu (1998).

[26] A good example of this line of thought is offered by the chapters written by the Provost of New Delhi University, also editor of the volume in Nayyar (ed. 2002, published by Oxford University Press), or from my own country Bogár (2003).

language of administrative science, functionality is low, thus similar results are achieved at higher cost or similar costs deliver less impressive results.[27] International comparisons on physical units, like the number of civil servants employed to get the same output, or even the number of medical doctors needed to get a certain level of health in terms of human development indicators; or even comparing the number of people employed in state-owned hotels or airlines to that of their private sector competitors, are all clear indications of this point.

Let us recall that it is not just weak administration or hostile policies that account for the investment unfriendly environment. It is the entire *governance infrastructure* that matters: it covers the legal infrastructure, independent and efficient courts, enforceable property rights (enforceable at reasonable costs), a credible, honest administration and public policies that promote rather than limit competition and new entry in all markets. Globerman and Shapiro (2002, esp. p. 1915) find significant and robust correlation between the above defined governance infrastructure and FDI inflows in over forty countries. Moreover, tax rebates have proven insignificant, while environmental protection significantly positive factors promoting inward FDI; in their words FDI and public goods show remarkable *complementarities*.

In our hypothesis, it is the big and inefficient state and governance structures that lay at the heart of the *chain reaction*, that leads to weak markets, the latter triggering still *more state intervention*. This suggestion is in line with current mainstream development economics (cf. Stiglitz, 2000; Krueger, 2000; Carment, 2003). If this suggestion holds, the defensive stance of these economies – and societies – against transnationalization is given, namely by the poor quality of their domestic market, as well as of the regulation of these, and thus *the regular and inevitable breach of the rules of the game*, as defined by the global players in the 'outside world'.

A common thread among the various failures is the *inability* (and unwillingness) of the political class to adopt a minimal *consensus view* on major strategic issues of the economy and society. If we take Hungary, it is clear that all major political forces represented in the legislation agreed in the 1989–2002 period on such fundamental issues as joining NATO and the EU, private property and regular elections, but also on several other matters. By contrast, in Ukraine, for instance, the orientation of the country to the EU is anything but uncontested (since Ukrainian membership in the EU/NATO has not been within easy reach in the post-1991 period). A large body of the political class still favors strong – actually ever stronger – relations to Moscow. The major constraint on this road, like in Belarus, is Russian economic and geo-strategic interest, that caution against too close political integration, say, in the form of a federal state.

---

[27] Introducing measurable performance criteria for various public services has been one of the major thrusts of the burgeoning literature on new public management. Still, it is non-trivial to define what is or is not an accomplishment in public service. For instance, university admissions (as a proportion of student body for the secondary school) in countries with limited entry possibilities is one such indicator. However, some analysts consider this to be a biased ad partial measurement (which is, in the end, still better than no measurement at all).

Similarly, some other major issues, such as the market economy, or the need to join WTO with its disciplines, has been a subject of fierce debate. On the one hand, under the foreign policy angle, everybody favors Ukrainian membership in the WTO. On the other hand, the disciplines, limiting state arbitrariness and requiring transparency, run counter to the prime interest of politics based on serving the needs of various lobbies (particularly in the area of tax rebates and import/export arrangements). Therefore, the voicing of support can and does co-exist with limited progress toward streamlining the bureaucratic arbitrariness haunting the trade regime and public finances. Lacking consensus does not allow to adopt long term positions (more on that in: Hoffmann, ed., 2000).

A similar lack of consensus is observable in a number of other countries, from Romania to Turkey. *It cannot be answered at a level of a general question* if, and to what degree local politics is to blame (mostly, exclusively, in part) for this outcome, which itself is a result of interaction between local and transnational forces. For instance chances of (being delayed in) EU membership have long played a formative role in the behavior of local political classes.[28] A case by case answer, that might be due, does not invalidate the common feature.

A next, and partly resultant feature of the laggards is the tiny, mostly less than adequate, *structural change* that has occurred in the pattern of production as well as in the system of institutions. While in the frontrunner countries new industries, often based on FDI, account for the bulk of exports, in laggard countries only partially reconstructed industries of the socialist period continue to shape most of the output. Likewise, while in the financial sector foreign owned banks and the stock exchange dominates in the frontrunners, mostly domestic industries continue to own local banking in the laggards. No surprise that the latter continue to finance their owners, thus considerations of return can hardly influence allocation of resources. This explains much of the sluggish performance in the latter countries. As documented in the empirical chapter, the major divide between success and failure runs along their foreign trade performance. The growth of exports was shown to relate to production pattern, and the latter to privatization, banking and capital markets, as well as to the presence of FDI or the lack of the three latter factors. All in all inadequate structural change, in some cases even regression to the patterns of monoculture, does create the well-known *trap of under-development*, elaborated at great length in the development literature. In these cases insufficient export revenues lead to import restrictions, that in turn will constrain domestic activity levels.

These are not abstract insights. Signs of the resource curse (Ross, 1999) are clearly observable in the Russian,[29] Ukrainian and Central Asian cases. In the latter, as well as in the Southeast European countries signs of de-industrializa-

[28] Allowing for Hungarian language universities in Romania, or the very moderate changes brought about by the Islamists in the public life of Turkey in 2003–2006 are examples for this.
[29] Kalotay (2004, p. 136) observed the intimate relationship between insider privatization and the search for 'breeding local capitalism that ended up in a failure'.

tion have become manifest, with employment growing in farming as well as a self-sufficiency oriented service sector. The re-primitivization of society might, in the short run, have been rational. Perhaps, this remained the only feasible option if mass starvation was to be avoided when formal institutions collapsed and the economy has shrunk to half of its pre-crisis peaks. Still, long-term trends in international trade do not show a single case when countries could grow over decades while relying exclusively or mostly on primary commodities. Not even the countries of the Middle East managed to turn oil wealth and the resulting windfall into a pattern of sustaining growth. Therefore the *regress in economic patterns is indeed a cause for grave concern*, and even more so from a long-term development perspective.

A further problem, that is both a reflection of the resource curse and an underlying reason for the lack of sufficient level accumulation and financing is the *underdeveloped state of the financial sector*. This state of affairs can no longer be ascribed to the Communist heritage, since this has been overcome in a number of countries also starting from centralized banking patterns. On the other hand, developing country experience suggests that bureaucratic and political domination of the financial sector, called *financial repression* is an important reason for why so many countries have proven unable to grow (more on that in Lall, 1993). If arbitrary allocation, thus misallocation of scarce resources continues, it does not really matter if Communists, liberals, nationalists, or reconstructed modern left wing parties, or despotic clans rule. The fundamental weakness of the *ancient regime* will not change as it cannot change: the mechanism of allocating resources remains an arbitrary, bureaucratic bargaining process without any market control.

This is already the well-known *vicious circle of underdevelopment*, broadly analyzed in the general literature on backward countries. Once banking is subordinate to 'the political', broadly defined, there is no security for people to save.[30] It is a problem, since as the late Lord Peter Bauer (2000) demonstrated, already at the lowest level, that of households, surpluses may emerge that can be re-channelled by tradesmen, who thereby improve *efficiency* and *welfare*. If this does not happen – actually, private intermediation still counts as a criminal act punishable under laws inherited from Communist times – there are only three ways to react. The first is to put money into state controlled banks, but here the credibility problem is enormous (either for the too low or for the too high interest rates, and because of the prohibitive spreads coupled with lack of services). The second alternative, for big business at least, is capital flight. Money is thus saved, however not invested. A new phenomenon, called *disintermediation* in the financial jargon emerges. Finally, as in all other poor countries, there might be an incentive *not to save at all, or not in financial form*. This is a well-researched phenomenon of traditional societies, where patrimonialism

---

[30] Such extreme examples as the currency confiscation of the Pavlov (1991) and Primakov (1999) Governments in Russia, the recurring freezing of assets (including hard currency deposits) in Argentina, or an obviously bankrupt state managed pension system (with negative returns on current payments) are just some of the more obvious cases.

dominates over private property and division of powers. A set of safety nets exist in the form of the extended family, the incentive to produce more and save it for rainy days, however is missing. Thereby we arrive at a point long observed by students of the poor countries, that is the *chronically inadequate level of financial savings*. These, according to economic theory, immediately limit investment, which in turn, limits economic growth. And this is where the models of *low level steady state equilibria* come in.

This problem is not related to the financial sector only. The under-funding of enterprises, the inability of the state to tax/collect revenues, the resulting low level of public services and law avoiding behavior, the ensuing lack of trust, that is known to lay at the foundation of market economy and society.[31] There is no microeconomic incentive to produce more and save, thus additional production potential, that may be calculated by an econometric model might not be forthcoming at all. Since only a small part of free resources are allocated on a market base, the high spread earns a bad name to money managers. Intertwining with the administration, also known as crony capitalism, hardly improves resource allocation. Therefore entry of foreign banks is rightly seen as an important component of overall modernization, at least in normative terms, also outside the post-Communist context (Sanchez, 2003).

There are no easy answers to the age-old question of *how to overcome* the low savings-low investment trap, exacerbated by financial repression. Much of the development literature, produced more recently, and already quoted, call for gradual institution building, an active regulatory role of a non-corrupted state, ensuring property rights, allowing for a gradual entry of foreign banks, opening up the capital markets *after the regulatory framework and institutions are in place*.[32] Last but not at all least, rule of law considerations also matter, when confidence building is a priority item of the policy-making agenda.[33] It is hardly surprising that the business community takes *rule of law* more of a priority than the granting of preferential treatments (which, of course, they never reject). The latter in fact, as seen in the case of Ukraine or Serbia, can never replace or compensate for the lack of the former.

To sum up this subchapter we may conclude that the differences among the frontrunners and laggards *are by no means dictated by political fashions*, such as liberalism or the neighborhood policy of the European Union. In fact, with the emergence of the 'Coalition of the Willing' and the resulting de-emphasis

---

[31] This point has been emphatically raised by Francis Fukuyama (1995) many years before corruption indices has become fashionable at the international agencies. It also is in contrast to the simplistic free marketeer/anti-state approach of the early transition ideologies.

[32] This was, by no means, the majority view of the 1990s, when any call for re-regulation was greeted with ideological skepticism. By the early 2000s, this has become the predominant position in the profession, and represented by the contributions to Caprio et al (eds, 2002).

[33] This allows for fighting corruption as well. As Lambsdorff (2003, pp. 468–469) explains and empirically proves, it is the quality of bureaucracy, rule of law and stability of government that is vital for the fight of corruption and result in efficiency increases; in his calculations this may be as large as 20 per cent of GDP, should corruption be extinct.

on NATO the strategic position of several laggards might appreciate. This, however, does not overshadow (or improve) the *cumulatively negative developmental features* of the respective societies – a challenge that is yet to be faced by the Atlantic community.

The New Economy – A Defining Feature of 21st Century Development

It is impossible to talk about transnationalization without addressing the issue of the new economy. What really matters here is, of course, not so much the dot.com bubble that burst in 2000, but the rather lasting influence of ICT on the traditional sectors, such as industry, trade, finance, transportation, tourism and the rest (more on that in Szabó, 2002). It is next to impossible to sum up what changes by the new economy era, but basically everything that relates to the fundamentals of economics. It is hard to model the creation of wealth through the interaction of labor, land and capital, when the boundaries of these are becoming permeable. Up until very recently macroeconomic statistics produced across the globe have fallen short of taking into account the contribution of the IT sector properly, while in the 1996–2002 period about half of the growth of the USA originated from the IT sector (Jorgenson, 2004).

Moreover, there are some qualitative changes as well that need to be considered. It is not shortage of the factors that defines economic activity. There is *abundance*, in some sectors rather an over-abundance of factors, goods and services. In the new, knowledge-based economy it is not physical capital, but *information* that sets the pace and other side conditions for wealth creation. It is not scarcity, but *oversupply*, and it is not lack of access, but the *inability* of human beings *to cope with* the plethora of information that constrains the possibilities for progress. It is not the place to recapitulate all related aspects (the best and broadest summary is offered by Salzberger, 2002), but it might be useful to highlight some of those aspects that relate directly to our subject matter.

First, as we have seen, the boundaries of nation states are becoming – actually have already become – ever more permeable, the more a country succeeds in keeping pace with the challenges of transnationalization, the more so. This process started way back in the 19th century, and has been strengthened immensely by financial innovation and the spread of ICT. The flow of capital as well as the flow of information *render the flow of people largely superfluous*, at least for purely economic conditions as traditionally represented in economic models of migration. The value of trade, recorded exports and imports taken together, exceed the value of GDP already in several emerging economies, such as Hungary or Estonia. Under these circumstances the *closed economy models* used in the period of national economic planning, but also the mental mindsets shaping perceptions and public discourse, that relate to the nation state as a unit, become *largely obsolete*. The small open economy view of macroeconomics already reflects this fact of life at the academic level, calling attention to the limitations of state sovereignty, with very few potential exceptions as the United States or perhaps the EU.

A similar process is observable at the firm level. The corporation is decreasingly identical with the smoke-screen factory, employing thousands of people in three shifts. Nor does it bear resemblance to the traditional movie view of the City of London, where black suited professionals rush to their respective large-scale financial factories. *The border of the firm is becoming relative*, depending on taxation, sourcing, human capital, physical infrastructure and services, all organized along a global scheme, where asset value is maximized. Toyotism is the management name for the more flexible lean hierarchies, where traditional 'commanding heights' give way to lateral coordination of activities and team work. Outsourcing and subcontracting are global, thus the location of the firm is becoming somewhat arbitrary (dictated by the size of corporate taxes).

Flexible forms of work replace traditional contracts, a feature that poses a heavy burden to welfare state built on employee/employer social security contributions (more on that in Szabó and Kocsis, 2003 chapter 6). It is hard to establish with certainty how big/small a firm is, since it might be seasonally quite different. Moreover, it is hard to locate the place where wealth creation occurs, thus it is hard to decide where public dues (especially the major employer contributions to social security) should be levied. The growing *dematerialization of production and wealth creation* does not allow conventional excise taxes, value added taxes and social security contributions to be collected so conveniently as in industrial societies. Only through *voluntary compliance*, that may only come with privatization of health and pension services, where incentives are direct and sizeable, can this situation be remedied.

Except for top personnel, corporations may virtually recruit employees from all around the globe. Jobs are no longer advertised in newspapers, but through the web. Purchases of inputs, including air tickets, may be decentralized. The head office may often become virtual, and we do know of virtual banking (not only from the crime stories reported by the press, but as prestigous ventures, primarily in Britain and the United States). Once the corporate boundaries become permeable, the term 'capital flight' might no longer be appropriate. Nor do such concepts as 'protection of jobs', or relocation of employment/ social dumping may be meaningful.

Let us add, that *transnationalization and localization of the regulatory frame is also taking place*. This proceeds along the experience of *lex mercatoria* (Teubner, 1997)[34] and the understandings that used to govern money lenders in the period before the classical gold standard, as referred above. Let us mention the emergence of the Basle Two Accord on sound banking, the IMF Principles of Good Fiscal Practices, the International Accounting Standards, or the OECD

---

[34] In his monograph on international economic law a leading authority (Vörös, 2004, volume II, pp. 56–61) describes the strongly growing presence of this form of transnational co-ordination of behavior that would otherwise fall victim to colluding national rules. He also highlights the non-state character of the arrangement, which renders the usual concept of 'inter-national' hollow at best.

130

Code of Conduct for Transnational Firms (practically outlawing corruption,[35] allowed by several national legislation, if applied to poor countries only). These all indicate a sea change in the direction of *transnational control*. References to different traditions, different national accounting habits, different cultural valuation of, say, corruption no longer count as valid counter-arguments. These deliberations, as well as the ever broader and deeper WTO disciplines are enforceable by courts, thus there is no reason to treat them less serious as than, say, human rights convention or the Kyoto Protocol. The role of national sovereignty, as defined in the 19th century, has been hollowed to a large degree by these and other changes, as we shall further elaborate on our chapter on Privatization and regulation.

In this respect the *emergence of virtual communities* is a major socio-economic change that is likely to transform 'world society' (or as in an other place discussed, 'global polity') in previously unknown ways and intensity. For the time being, the emergence of multiple identities has developed into a mass phenomenon. Not only members of professions, say neuro-biologists, form clans, but a variety of people join a variety of networks. The *territorial community of state, that legitimates law and thus the rule of law, becomes only one of these* Salzberger, op. cit. stresses the complexities this causes for legal and democratic theory alike). For political legitimacy and the resultant legal framework continues to be shaped via territorial communities, while the transnational networks evolve and function according to the (different) logic of their own. Recurring – futile – attempts to police the contents of internet or of civil groups organized via e-mails, and rendering, say the security apparatuses protecting G8 summits lame, are cases in point.

To cut a long story short, while the political process and thereby institutions, decision-making and *legitimacy* remains lastingly within the boundaries of the *nation states*,[36] all corresponding processes, be that economic, intellectual, information or technological, tend to be organized on *a global scale*[37]. The growing *virtualization* of the process of wealth creation, of community building and of organization of activities is likely to be at odds with those processes that continue to be orchestrated along the national lines. Therefore the co-existence of transnationalization and local politics is anything but harmonious. There is no trivial way or mechanism through which the iteration, typical of both the democratic and the market processes, would emerge and produce viable outcomes. The spontaneous emergence of transnational regulatory regimes is only a *partial answer* to the challenge.

---

[35] Collier et al (2003, pp. 174–175) observe major successes in this area. They also report of the Kimberley process in which there is a partially successful attempt to shut out rebel organizations from the diamonds market, thereby switching off the taps for civil warfare (op. cit. pp. 178–180)

[36] The very low turnout at the elections to the European Parliament, scarcely exceeding the 35 to 40 per cent thresholds, or the often surveyed fact that 8 out of 10 West Europeans could not identify their representative in the European Parliament, or the fact that most elections are fought on local issues, all point to this direction.

[37] This insight is expounded in great detail in the recent monograph by Imre Lévai (2006).

Last but not least, the consequences of *the digital divide* must be addressed. In those societies where *centralization* of management is a virtue on its own right, be that because of traditions, ideology, or the interaction of both, *there is little room for making use of the new dimensions of ICT.* Most of the social consequences, but also the economic ones, triggered by this sea change in production and organization, based to a large degree of non-profit elements and decentrality/lack of controls,[38] thus those societies, built, for instance, around the traditionalist-fundamentalist interpretation of Islam, cannot fully profit (Kuran, 2004). For decentralized, independent decisions and lack of controls cannot be restrained to areas deemed necessary by those in power – this is one of the unambiguous lessons from the erosion of Soviet power in the 1970s and 1980s.

Once ICT is equated with 'evil' and Westernization, thus is constrained, the drift between those making use of it and those lacking access is bound to increase. As it is well known, the development of market economy has been featured by an exponential growth of accumulation, whereas the 'Rest', to use the term of North (1990) is lagging behind by way of stagnation, of non-participation, rather than positive falling behind in absolute terms – a point richly documented in the long-term historic survey of Angus Maddison (2001). Therefore, the likelihood of *further differentiation among the transforming societies, primarily along the already existing dividing lines, that relate them to transnationalization* is a most likely phenomenon.[39] As we have documented in the chapter on Comparative empirical evidence, the dividing line does emerge along more and less open societies in emerging Europe. The entry of foreign banks, the transnationalization of the corporate sector, reliance on FDI as a pace-maker of development and participation in global institutions (including the adoption of global standards of various sorts) do *constitute a single chain*, as has been shown to be the case in the region under scrutiny. The dividing line between emerging and non-emerging/submerging post-Communist societies goes along these general lines, replicating the main findings of development literature. This is unlikely to remain without repercussions for the political setup and the institutions of those – an issue both NATO and EU is likely to be confronted in their neighborhood policy.

On the Co-Evolution of the State and Market

Our line of reasoning attempted to prove, both in general terms, and later by the comparison of the stylized models of frontrunner countries and laggard countries that it is possibile to *establish a link between transnational markets and local politics*, therefore the interaction between the state and the market is no

---

[38] On this aspect and the economic consequences of the gratis element see the unconventional book of András Kelen (2001).

[39] A similar conclusion is reached by Tamás Szentes (2002, p. 163. and pp. 193–194).

longer coincidental. Though our empirical material related to transforming countries, if the ideas in our preceding chapter on the Developmental dimension hold, the interrelationship may well be generalized to *all emerging economies*. The interface of transnationalization and the patterns of local reactions bear close resemblance to those observed in emerging developing countries. Therefore, in line with the more general insights of the post-Washington Consensus, we may venture to establish, that *strong, though not interventionist, core state and strong transnationalization, especially of markets are mutually supportive phenomena*. In turn, weak state, captured state, overextended but inefficient administration is often at the root of weak, poorly performing, 'perverse' market relations. In both cases *self-reinforcing processes* are likely to evolve in theory, and are indeed demonstrably observable in empirical cases.[40]

This finding of ours in part reinforces the insight of László Bruszt (2002) about the nature of interrelationship between state and market: only an independent, non-captured state is able to regulate market processes so that these could result in improved welfare and socially equitable income distribution, both being side conditions of the sustainability of market order and democracy. But we can be more specific on the 'lean state' that is strong enough to resist and to be self-restraining when calls for daily intervention are echoed. We also can explain that an extended, much intervening, *dirigiste* state is not the same as an efficiently regulating one. The regulation of entry (Djankov et al, 2002; Török 2003) is vital for instance for the efficiency of privatization and of contestability of markets.

It is important to recall the positive shaping role played by the EU in the formation, legitimating and technical operation of new institutions in the frontrunner countries. However, this role is secondary at best against the fundamental role played by *the perception and prospect of their becoming fully-fledged Europeans*, a label that was distributed by the EU (and by NATO) through a series of conditionalities. From the need to abolish capital punishment to civil control of the army, from the need to respect minority rights and make efforts to integrate the Roma, to the point of committing relatively poor societies to the virtues of environmental protection, *the EU has indeed provided* transition societies *with a specific set of measures*. The latter orientated not only general approaches but as the technicalities and substance of regulation.

The EU has also been playing an important *signalling function to the global players*, primarily to FDI and also the corporations, and portfolio investors, about the type of expectations that were to be formed against the frontrunners. This indirect influence is certainly above the macro-economically insignificant sums, that following the Copenhagen compromise of 2002 is

---

[40] This concept is a long way from the similarly sounding proposition published by Geoffrey Underhill (2003, pp. 756–757 and 761–767) describing the state and market as a *condominium* of authority and governance. As can be expected, his perception is more an extension of the governance literature that would, so to say, absorb the market as an integral part of the former (so on p. 779). This is contrary to the mainstream economic paradigm of the market we try to adhere to and apply in this analysis.

likely to flow into the accession countries. Not only because the flow of private money is currently 50 to 100 times that of the official flows, but also because of the strong component of confidence building, that was shown to be crucial in our discussing the savings-investment chain as well as the role of financial markets. Thus the *developmental dimension of the EU should not be measured by the amounts of official flows*. Moreover, being marginal in macroeconomic terms, the latter may be a positively misleading indicator for the overall process.

As we have seen, transnationalization *has not led and will not lead to homogenization,* neither in terms of economic policies, nor in terms of institutions shaping the economic order, even less in terms of social structures. Whereas in frontrunner countries the tendency to internalize Atlantic values is likely to increase, in the laggard group the 'Jihad versus McWorld' (Barber, 1995) approach may better capture the long-term intellectual environment, that also translates into policies. The culture of monetary stability, particularly highlighted by the Germans, could be transplanted to countries, like Spain or Bulgaria, where it did not use to be the case. By contrast, laggards tend to see the political instruments of this culture of stability, such as the Maastricht criteria and the Stability and Growth Pact as mere straightjacket on the freedoms of democratically elected governments.

Finally, mention should be made of *path dependence*, an issue that is particularly important in understanding how rule of law, good quality state administration, and many other signs of modernity/globality in the sense of Max Weber (as defined in the first chapter) come about in areas called 'transition economies'. It is perceptible that the frontrunners did have a favorable historical legacy in terms of legal infrastructure and *memories of the market*.[41] Also the role of geographical proximity needs to be highlighted, since as *new economic geography* would suggest, distance matters, agglomeration of activities is a fact of life. But policies can certainly change a lot: as Finland or Singapore could emerge, in only four decades from backwardness, the *determinist* interpretation of path dependence is *not analytically helpful*. It is the interaction with policies that create the outcome. In analytical terms we do not have to choose between the two: counter-posing them is an empty word-play.

Finally, the question of *democracy* needs to be addressed, since transnationalization may or may not breed democracy. This is of course a broad issue falling outside the scope of the present chapter. However, as the insightful and controversial analysis of Hernando de Soto (2000) has proven, the interrelationship is non-trivial and aspects of rule of law, often downplayed by some economic policy advisers, may matter more than it is customary to assume. If this is the case, the importance of the EU as *a community of democracies, thus a community of values* by definition prevails over those trade theory and financial

---

[41] Empirical and econometric evidence to this point is provided in the article of Berkowitz et al (2003) studying the impact of legal transplants in latecomer countries. They find that antecendents, that is familiarity with the logic of these has been more important for success, than the choice (i.e. from which family of legal arrangements countries borrowed). Lack of prior familiarity rendered 'optimally designed' projects futile in the course of implementation.

bargaining approaches, that regretfully have come to the fore in the public debate. In this approach the *cultural anchor function of the EU* may, historically, but also economically, be much more relevant than any amount of assistance that is or is not forthcoming in any period of time.

References

BALCEROWICZ, L. (1995) *Socialism, Capitalism, Transformation.* London-Budapest-New York: CEU Press.

BARBER, B. (1995): *Jihad versus McWorld.* New York: The Free Press.

BAUER, P. Th. (2000): *From Subsistence to Exchange and Other Essays.* Princeton, New Jersey: Princeton University Press.

BERKOWITZ, D. – PISTOR, K. – RICHARD, J.-F. (2003): Economic development, legality and the transplant effect. *European Economic Review,* vol. 47. no. 1. pp. 165–195.

BHAGWATI, J. (1991): Immiserizing growth. In: BHAGWATI, J.: *Political Economy and International Economics.* Cambridge/Mass. and London: The MIT Press, pp. 209–234.

BHAGWATI, J. (1998): The theory of immiserizing growth: further applications. In: BHAGWATI, J.: *Writings on International Economics* (edited by V. N. Balasubramanyam). Delhi: Oxford University Press, pp. 75–84.

BOGÁR, L. (2003): *Magyarország és a globalizáció* (Hungary and globalization). Budapest: Osiris.

BRUSZT, L. (2002): Market making as state making: Constitutions and economic development in post-communist Eastern Europe. *Constitutional Political Economy,* vol. 13. no. 1. pp. 53–72.

BRUSZT, L. and STARK, D. (1998): *Post-socialist Pathways.* Cambridge and New York: Cambridge University Press.

BUCHANAN, J. and CONGLETON, R. (1998): *Politics by Principle, Not Interest: Toward a Nondiscriminatory Democracy.* Cambridge and New York: Cambridge University Press.

CAPRIO, G. – HONOHAN, P. – STIGLITZ, J. eds: (2002): *Financial Liberalization: How Far? How Fast?* Cambridge and New York: Cambridge University Press.

CARMENT, D. (2003): Assessing state failure: Implications for theory and policy. *Third World Quarterly,* vol. 24. no. 3. pp. 407–427.

COLLIER, P. – ELIOT, V – HEGRE, H. – HOEFFLER, A. – REYNAL – QUEROL, M. – SAMBANIS, N. (2003): *Breaking the Conflict Trap.* Oxford and Washington: Oxford University Press for the World Bank.

CZAKÓ, E. (2003): Globalizáció – vállalati stratégiai megközelítésben. (Globalization through the lenses of corporate strategy). In: BLAHÓ, A, ed.: *Elmaradottság – fejlődés – átalakulás.* (Backwardness – development – transition). Budapest: a book published by the Department of World Economics of Budapest Corvinus University, pp. 99–110.

CSABA, L. (2000): A decade of transformation: Russia and Hungary compared. In: BRZESKI, A. – WINIECKI, J. eds: *A Liberating Economic Journey.* London: The Cromwell Press for CRCE, pp. 99–140.

DABROWSKI, M. – GOMULKA, S. – ROSTOWSKI, J. (2001a): Whence reform? The critique of the Stiglitz perspective. *Journal of Policy Reform,* vol. 4. no. 4. pp. 291–324.

DABROWSKI, M. – GOMULKA, S. – ROSTOWSKI, J. (2001b): Our main criticism remain unanswered. *Journal of Policy Reform,* vol. 4. no. 4. pp. 339–348.

DAIANU, D. (1998): *Transformation as a Real Process: An Insider's Perspective.* Aldershot/UK – Sidney etc: Ashgate Publishing Co.

DJANKOV, S. – La PORTA, R. – LOPEZ-de SILANES, F. – SHLEIFER, A. (2002): The regulation of entry. *Quarterly Journal of Economics,* vol. 117. no. 1. pp. 1–38.

ELLMAN, M. and KONTOROVICH, F. eds: (1999): *The Destruction of the Soviet Economy*. New York: M. E. Sharpe.

FUKUYAMA, F. (1995): *Trust*. London: Penguin Books.

GLOBERMAN, S. and SHAPIRO, D. (2002): Global FDI flows: The role of governance infrastructure. *World Development*, vol. 30. no. 11. pp. 1899–1919.

HIGGOTT, R. (2000): Contested globalization: The changing context and normative challenges. *Review of International Studies*, vol. 26. no. 5. pp. 131–153.

HIGGOTT, R., (2001): Taming economics, emboldening IR: The theory and practice of IPE in an era of globalization. In: LAWSON, S., ed.: *After the Fall of the Wall: Rethinking International Relations*. London: Polity Press, pp. 91–108.

HOFFMANN, L. ed. (2000): *Ukraine: On the Road to Europe*. Heildelberg and New York: Physica Verlag.

JORGENSON, D. W. (2004): 'Economic Growth in the Information Age': paper presented to the conference of the Committee on Economics of the Hungarian Academy of Sciences, Budapest, 20 May.

KALOTAY, K. (2004): Will FDI take off in the Russian federation? *Journal of World Investment and Trade*, vol. 5. no. 1. pp. 119–138.

KELEN, A. (2001): *The Gratis Economy*. Budapest–New York: The CEU Press.

KEREN, M. and OFER, G. (2002): The role of FDI in trade and financial services in transition: What distinguishes transition economies from developing economies? *Comparative Economic Studies*, vol. 44. no. 1. pp. 15–45.

KING, L. P. and VÁRADI, B. (2002): Beyond Manichean economics: FDI and growth in the transition from socialism. *Communist and Post-Communist Studies*, vol. 35. no. 1. pp. 1–21.

KRUEGER, A. (1998): Wither the IMF and the World Bank? *Journal of Economic Literature*, vol. 36. no. 4. pp. 1983–2002.

KRUEGER, A. (2000): Agenda for future research, or what we need to know. In: KRUEGER, A. ed: *Economic Policy Reform: The Second Stage*. Chicago and London: The University of Chicago Press, pp. 585–594.

KUDRNA, Z. (2004): 'Getting the institutions right: Reforms of banking sectors in the Czech Republic and Romania' – MA Thesis, Department of Political Science, Central European University/Budapest, June.

KURAN, T. (2004): Why the Middle East is economically underdeveloped: historical mechanism of institutional stagnation. *Journal of Economic Perspectives*, vol. 18. no. 3. pp. 71–90.

LALL, D. (1993): *The Repressed Economy*. Oxford etc.: Oxford University Press.

LAMBSDORFF, J. (2003): How corruption effects productivity. *Kyklos*, vol. 56. no. 4. pp. 457–474.

LÁMFALUSSY, S. (2002): Gondolatok az európai értékpapír-piacok szabályozásáról (Reflections on regulating European stock markets). *Közgazdasági Szemle*, vol. 49. no. 3. pp. 181–192.

LÁNYI, K. (1995): A dereguláció és az újraszabályozás nemzetközi környezete. (The international environment and deregulation and re-regulation). *Külgazdaság*, vol. 38. no. (7–8). pp. 4–21.

LÉVAI, I (2006): *A komplex világrendszer evolúciója* (Evolution of the complex global order). Budapest: Akadémiai Kiadó

LUCAS, R. (1990): Why doesn't capital flow from rich to poor countries? *American Economic Review*, vol. 80. no. 2. pp. 92–96.

MADDISON, A. (2001): *Monitoring the World Economy, 1850–1995*. Paris: OECD

MANZETTI, L. (2003): Political manipulations and market reform failures. *World Politics*, vol. 55. no. 3. pp. 315–360.

MAU, V. (2000): *Russian Economic Reforms as Seen by an Insider: Success or Failure?* – a monograph published by the International Economics Program of the Royal Institute of International Affairs, London.

MAU, V. and STARODUBROVSKAIA, I. (2001): *The Challenge of Revolution: Contemporary Russia in Historical Perspective*. Oxford etc.: Oxford University Press.

MEYERDORFF, A. and THAKOR, A. eds: (2002): *Designing Financial Systems in Transition Economies*. Cambridge/Mass. and London: The MIT Press.

MIHÁLYI, P. (2001): Foreign direct investment in Hungary: The post-communist privatization story reconsidered. *Acta Oeconomica*, vol. 51. no. 1. pp. 107–129.

MIZSEI, K. (1993): Hungary: gradualism needs a strategy. In: Portes, R. ed.: *Economic Transformation in Central Europe: A Progress Report*. London and Brussels: a book jointly published by the Center for Economic Policy Research and the EU Commission, pp. 131–186.

NAYYAR, D. ed. (2002): *Governing Globalization: Issues and Institutions*. Oxford etc: Oxford University Press for WIDER.

NORTH, D. (1990): *Institutions, Institutional Change and Economic Performance*. Cambridge and New York: Cambridge University Press.

OLSON, M. (1996): Big bills left on the sidewalk: Why some nations are rich, while others are so poor? *Journal of Economic Perspectives*, vol. 10. no. 2. pp. 3–24.

OLSON, M. (2000): *Power and Prosperity: Outgrowing Communist and Capitalist Dictatorships*. New York: Basic Books.

PETRICK, K. ed.: (2000): *Banking and Financial Stability in Central Europe: Convergence Between the EU and Central and Eastern Europe*. Cheltenham/UK and Northampton/MA/USA: Edward Elgar Publishing Co.

PIATKOWSKI, M. (2003): The 'new economy' and catching up potential of transition economies. *Prague Economic Papers*, vol. 12. no. 1. pp. 37–56.

POZNANSKI, K. (2002): The crisis of transformation as a state crisis. In: BÖNKER, F. – MÜLLER, K. – PICKEL, A. eds: *Post-Communist Transformation and the Social Sciences: Cross-Disciplinary Approaches*. Boulder/Colorado/USA: Rowman and Littlefield, pp. 55–76.

RADYGIN, A., (2001): Sobstvennost' i integratsionniie protsessi v korporativnom sektore. (Property and mergers in the corporate sector). *Voprosy Ekonomiki*, vol. 70. no. 5. pp. 22–39.

ROSS, M. (1999): The political economy of resource curse. *World Politics*, vol. 51. no. 2. pp. 297–322.

SALZBERGER, E. (2002): Cyberspace, governance and new economy. In: SIEBERT, H, ed.: *Economic Policy Issues of the New Economy*. Berlin and New York: Springer Verlag, pp. 169–208.

SANCHEZ, S. (2003): Foreign bank entry: Experience, implications for developing economies and agenda for future research. *World Bank Research Observer*, vol. 18. no. 1. pp. 25–60.

SASSEN, S. (2002): The demise of Pax Americana and the emergence of informalization as a systemic trend. In: TABAK, F. and CRICHLON, A. eds: *Informalization – Process and Structure*. Baltimore and London: The Johns Hopkins University Press, pp. 91–115.

SEVIC, Z. ed.: (2002): *Banking Reform in Southeastern Europe*. Basingstoke and London: Palgrave.

SOLOW, R. ed.: (2001): *Landmark Papers on Economic Growth*. Cheltenham and Northampton: Edward Elgar Publishing Co.

de SOTO, H. (2000): *The Mystery of Capital: Why Capitalism Triumphs in the West and Fails Everywhere Else?* New York: Basic Books.

SPAHN, H.-P. (2001): *From Gold to Euro: On the Theory and History of Currency Systems*. Heidelberg and New York: Springer Verlag.

SRINIVASAN, T. N. (2001): *Economic Policy and State Intervention*. New Delhi: Oxford University Press.

STIGLITZ, J. (2000): Wither reform? Ten years of the transition. In: PLESKOVIC, B. and STIGLITZ, J. eds: *Annual Bank Conference on Development Economics, 1999*. Oxford etc: Oxford University Press, pp. 27–56.

STIGLITZ, J. (2002): *Globalization and Its Discontents*. Oxford: Oxford University Press.

STIGLITZ, J. and ELLERMAN, D. (2001): Not poles apart: A reply. *Journal of Policy Reform*, vol. 4. no. 4. pp. 325–338.

SZABÓ, K. (2002): Az információs technológia szétterjedésének következményei a hagyományos iparágakban. (Consequences of the spread of ICT in traditional industries). *Közgazdasági Szemle,* vol. 49. no. 3. pp. 193–211.

SZABÓ, K. and KOCSIS, É. (2003): *Digitális paradicsom vagy falanszter?* (A digital paradise or a phalanster?) Budapest: AULA Publishing House.

SZAPÁRY, Gy. (2002): Banking sector reform in Hungary: What have we learned and what are the prospects? *Comparative Economic Studies,* vol. 44. no. (2–3). pp. 103–124.

SZENTES, T. (2002): *Globalizáció, regionális integrációk és nemzeti fejlődés korunk világgazdaságában.* (Globalization, regional integration and national development options in the contemporary world economy). Szombathely: Savaria University Press.

TEUBNER, G. (1997): Global Bukowina: legal pluralism in the world society. In: TEUBNER, G. ed.: *Global Law Without a State.* Aldershot/UK and Brookfield/Vermont, USA: Dartmouth Publishing Co. pp. 3–28.

TÖRÖK, Á. (2003): A piacra lépési korlátok átalakulása és a világgazdaság kibontakozása. (Changing barriers to entry and the evolution of the world economy). *Közgazdasági Szemle,* vol. 50. no. 3. pp. 195–208.

UNDERHILL, G. (2003): States, markets and governance for emerging market economies: Private interests, public good and the legitimacy of the development process. *International Affairs,* vol. 79. no. 4. p. 755–782.

VÁRHEGYI, É. (2002): *Bankvilág Magyarországon.* (The world of banking in Hungary). Budapest: Helikon Kiadó.

VÖRÖS, I. (2004): *A nemzetközi gazdasági kapcsolatok joga, I–III.* (Law of international economic relations, volumes I–III). Budapest: KRIM Bt.

6. 'GLOBALIZATION' AND 'EUROPEANIZATION': A DOUBLE CHALLENGE FOR EMERGING EUROPE

Following the by and large successful completion of their transition from the Soviet model to the European type of market economy, the countries of Central Europe have been confronted with new challenges by the first decades of the 2000s. On the one hand, the evolution of global processes and the growth of challenges that emerge on world scale, from terrorism to the ICT revolution, question the foundations of all established societies. This is all the more demanding, since these challenges pertain to the foundations of the European model of social market economy, that has just been emerging as an outcome of multiyear efforts. On the other hand, the European Union – often mistakenly labelled for shorthand as 'Europe' – poses immediate and concrete demands on the new members. This applies not only to the *acquis communautaire*, where living up to the commitments taken by the Copenhagen Council of December 2002 will take at least another decade in such areas as environmental protection or rural development. The *acquis* itself is an ever broadening set of rules and regulations, whose precise meaning and interpretation evolves over time in the interplay between governmental and non-governmental actors (more on that in the reference book by Wallace and Wallace, eds, 2000). By the same token it would be misleading to characterize the relevance of the EU by the maximum 1.27 per cent (in reality, in 2000–2003 1.13 per cent, from 2004 0.97 per cent) of EU GDP redistributed via the Community funds. Especially in such areas as environment, social policy, common foreign and security policy and legal rulings the presence of EU policies and regulations has been constantly on the increase. Therefore, the enlargement of the EU in 2004 *does not mean a conclusion of adjustment for the emerging economies*. On the contrary, the more difficult part has only begun – a feature that could though be foreseen (Csaba, 1998) but one that has hardly motivated the considerations of policy-makers, as the stagnant institutional reforms testify.

In the following chapter we try to address four major issues. First, what 'globalization' means for the emerging economies. Second, we try to address some of the peculiar stresses that follow from the speedy adjustment of the *acquis* where the Amsterdam and Nice Treaties have foreclosed any further opt-outs, over and above the ones negotiated by the incumbents (such as the

Danes, the British, the Irish or the Swedes). Third, we try to overview salient features of a new round of institutional and structural reforms that are yet to come, *if emerging economies wish to continue to emerge* (from poverty and the heritage of the Soviet Empire) rather than being a stagnant periphery. Given that growing role of enhanced co-operation, the prospect of second rank membership is a very real one. But over and above this, conditions of sustainable growth are not given forever by the reforms of the early and mid-90s, that have not been followed up by similarly broad measures in the first couple of years of the 2000s. Thus it is primarily the self-interest in sustaining growth and avoiding the ramifications of being integrated into a non-dynamic part of the global economy that may trigger further radical changes in the Central European region. Finally, we conclude with a normative subchapter on how to harmonize the need for more competitiveness with social equity – a major issue in the new political economy of development.

Global Challenges – Transnational Processes

The term 'globalization' is one of the ideologically most loaded and academically least meaningful ones. It is a product of the debates that have been taking off since the East Asian and Latin American financial crises and contagion, primarily by the social movements and academics sympathetic to these.[1] It replaces the older terms of 'imperialism', or 'the rule of financial capital', or 'capitalism' unbridled. It is often portrayed by its adherents as the final source of all evils that plague humankind, from famines to environmental decay, thus there is a majority view in the policy discourse that it should be 'tamed', or at least 'reshaped' (cf. most contributors in Krizsán and Zentai, eds, 2003). During the Clinton Administration high level working groups have been convened to elaborate what was then called 'the new financial architecture', an arrangement that was to replace or at least in major points correct the workings of free capital markets (cf. on the latter Csikós–Nagy, 2002. pp. 314–331).

It is worth noting how little constructive results these discourses have brought, both in intellectual and policy terms, let alone institutions. At *one level* the outcome is that no conference or convention on the world economy may be convened without triggering massive and previously unknown violent protests on the streets, and that in a row. At *a second level,* the talks on further liberalization of world trade, the so-called Doha or Millennium Round, have been thwarted, first in Seattle in 1999 then in Cancún in 2003 and finally in Geneva in July 2006.[2]

---

[1] The best survey of this broad literature is offered in the critical essay of Lányi (2003).

[2] Well informed sources in the business press tended to blame, on both occasions, poor preparations and domestic concerns in the EU and the USA, respectively, rather than the demonstrators for the cessation of world trade talks. By 2006 this has come to the open, when the EU Commissioner Peter Mandelson publicly accused his US counterpart for the failure. As a consequence not even those concessions that would have helped the poorest (and had been negotiated in Hong Kong) could enter into force. cf: *Neue Zürcher Zeitung,* 28 July, 2006.

Despite the fact that developing countries were to gain the most (and thus stand to lose the most) from the success or failure of these, respectively (Pangariya, 2002). In *the third level*, in international finances, besides cutting back the activities of the World Bank in middle income countries, and besides focusing IMF activities more on its original focus of current account adjustment (at the cost of more ambitious projects on multi-year structural adjustment programs) not much has changed. Some initiatives, like the HIPC, took off, some calls for more transparency have been made, the Good Fiscal Practices Code was condoned. But the accounting scandals of 2000–2001 have swept away the more formal initiatives to change. Moreover, the Republican Administration has withdrawn support from the idea of the new architecture, engaged in a series of unilateralist actions – from steel duties to withdrawal from the Kyoto Protocol, and requiring waiver from the jurisdiction of the International Criminal Court in the Hague. In sum, not much has happened, and the profession of accountants, lawyers and financial economists are equally divided internally over how to avoid the replication of similar mishaps. Therefore, not much progress in terms of constructive or positive initiatives has happened.

In terms of including *environmental and labor standards* in international trade agreement, this claim is known to be misplaced and harmful for developing countries (Bhagwati, 1998). Moreover, the mandate of the WTO is such that it cannot be extended to cover these, per se serious, concerns. What we are confronted with at the moment, is a situation where contracting parties, in their bulk, democratically elected, representative governments, balk off from the forward looking commitments taken back in 1994 and are unwilling to subscribe even to those 'concessions' that were agreed back in 1994. True, implementation of the 1994 agreements has been inadequate, and market protection disproportionally stuck the poor. However, this misbehavior does not invalidate the insight, proven in detail in the literature (Greenaway et. al, 2002; Winters, 2002) that trade liberalization is welfare improving and in the long run is good for the poor. The latter – often controversial point – has been proven by a detailed long run analysis of Dollar and Kraay (2004). Therefore, if social groups call for the reform of the global order, these may have a point, but *the WTO is the wrong door to knock at.* 'Globalization' as critical analyses (Szentes, 2004, pp. 319–322) also maintain, create potentials for convergence, even if turning this opportunity into reality requires a number of pre-conditions. The latter include as appropriate and supportive public policy, the development of technological capabilities and the underlying human capital allowing for the latter.

In fact, as can be proven (Whalley, 2003, pp. 188–192) it would have been *primarily in the interest of poor countries* to facilitate a success of the ambitious Millennium or Development Round. Tariffication of quantitative restrictions, for instance, is a major way of overcoming protectionism of the advanced countries. The issue of special and differentiated treatment in a number of areas is also of major importance for the developing nations, and so is the issue of liberalization in the farming sector. Moreover, the built-in agenda from the Uruguay Round has been also to a large degree about compliance, implementation and dispute settlement, that is the areas where complaints of the poor remained unaddressed. Turning the table to its head might have been a useful tactical device in Cancún, but not as a strategy.

These deliberations may sound commonsensical, should we not have a broad academic line of reasoning calling for global regulation and global social rights (Deacon, 2002), or opposing the global market via social mobilization and inter-state regulation (Yeats, 2002). Even the European Union sponsored a multi-year multi-country project on how it is the best to fight globalization as a pressure on the welfare state (Manning and Palier, 2003). In more mainstream sources, like the influential journal of Chatam House analysts (Underhill, 2003, pp. 779–780) call for the explicit subordination of global markets to new forms of interstate control. This, as we have seen, proved impossible, if for no other reason than the decentralized nature of the market and financial innovation, relying on ICT, that has lead to the dematerialization of major transactions. Thus such ideas as the age-old Tobin tax are simply impossible to implement.

In a way, it seems, if the talk is about globalization, it results, willy-nilly in *diverting attention from truly global issues,* such as terrorism, the spread of infectious diseases, migration, child poverty, the tens of millions of displaced persons and the ever growing number of failed states. These are the truly global issues, together with the environment, that relate to the fate of all humankind and require action on a global scale. Some radical analysts (Brassett and Higgott, 2004, p. 34) go as far as talking of 'global polity' in three main dimensions:

a) policy interconnectedness (including supra-, sub- and non-state actors in an interchange);

b) the interlocking networks of global networks and sites of decision-making where *policies of quasi-global nature* are being made (as in rating agencies);

c) the increasingly global thinking, enhanced by ICT, global gatherings, global media and the ensuing convergence of values.

By contrast, as could be proven in detail in the empirical chapter, new features of international economic intercourse, though do transcend the national borders, these, however, rarely take place at the global scale. Starting up with the European Union and its regulatory frame global and local processes take place in parallel. These may, and often do transcend national borders, without necessarily being on the world scale. The regional belt that emerged around Frankfurt and spreads until Brussels, the newly formed Euro-regions and many examples are cases in point. Here, what critics mean with a degree of justification, is the *declining significance of the territorial state* and thereby the diminishing democratic/popular legitimacy of actors, as long as the political process of control continues to be organized along the national lines.

Therefore, as we argued before, it seems more appropriate to term these processes as *transnationalization,* as long as both from the organizational and the regulatory perspective the crux of the matter is the emergence of a variety of forms not relating to national legislation. If one thinks about the international accounting standards, which are rules of a profession that are being applied in the regime of self-enforcement, it is clear, that national authorities have clearly lost a piece of their sovereignty, and that forever. Whatever a government may think appropriate in terms of accounting – and the principles as well as applications are subject to controversy within the accountancy profession and amongst regulators alike – it is unlikely to get along if it follows its own ways. On the macro-level the Code of Good Fiscal Practices, or the ESNA-95 standard, enforced by the EU Directorate of Fiscal Affairs, on the micro-level the IAS or similar codes of conduct, approved by the profession, rather than formally legislated, will take the lead.

It is hardly by chance that following the East Asian and Latin American financial crises and contagion, the issue of *transparency* has become a leading theme on the agenda of policy-makers and regulators alike. This implies, on the one hand, standardization of procedures and the international support for the diffusion mechanisms that enforce these against the vested interests (Hanson, 2003, pp. 63–64). In doing so, both the *rules of the game* and the *enforcement mechanisms* are increasingly originating and located (or at least anchored) in institutions *transcending the national borders*. In the case of accounting standards and anti-corruption drives, it would be hard to demonstrate the 'heavy hand of the Americans'. In other cases, such as the advocacy of general human rights as part of the expected civilized code of conduct by any nation, the move is clearly transnational, without however being global.

In sum, *financial vulnerability and embeddedness in global trade flows* have been shown to constitute major components of economic globalization. However, it is correct to recall (Harley, 2000; Bell, 2003) that the extension of international economic relations to the entire globe is by no means a product of the late 1990s. It has been a long historic process that has been typical of the spread of capitalism ever since the 16th century. As the quoted sources document, financial globalization, measured against GDP, reached only by 1995 the levels once attained in 1913; the same is the case with international commodity flows. Therefore, it does require some detailed scrutiny what, if anything, is new in the processes that ensue from the geographical extension of trade and other exchanges.

What is new in this respect thus may boil down to *three major factors:*

a) financial vulnerability, that has rendered the retaining of national currencies in a luxury good available to the largest players only;

b) the breakdown of liberalization along the WTO disciplines at an early point when free trade is more of a slogan (or a four letter word) than reality in a number of markets;

c) the spread of electronic trade and ICT in general, whose regulation along the logic of WTO disciplines is less than perfect at the moment (more on that in Matteo and Schuchknecht, 2002).

It would require separate monographs to elaborate each of these points, thus let me restrict myself to a couple of observations. First, all these issues pertain to *all players* of the world economy, thus it is legitimate to call them *global*. This holds even if the dependence of individual players is different and often asymmetric; it is more important to those who are more deeply involved in the transnational processes. Second, the spread of derivatives and dematerialized deals has lead to an ever growing volume of financial flows that are completely *detached* from what used to be called *'fundamentals'*. Thus the available set of

143

regulations – national and international, especially at the level of elected governments – is becoming increasingly ineffectual. Third, there are some areas where states still retain some control rights. This includes the regulation of commodity flows, of the transfer of intellectual property rights, in setting some of the conditions for major cross-border investment flows, or equally importantly in the regulation of services, especially those that relate to the flow of people. In each of these, the threat of regressing into inter-war patterns of bilateralism, or even *unilateralism* is perceptibly on the increase. In other words, regulators try to catch what they are unable to catch and what they could regulate in a co-operative fashion, is being left unregulated, at least at the level of multilateral understandings. The *latter* are known to benefit the small and the less mighty, as the emerging European economies are.

Let us just mention – as *first among the global challenges* – that the internet – and more generally the ICT revolution – has created new opportunities and *new threats*. Lot has been written on the new opportunities, thus let me just mention the threats. On the one hand, terrorist and other groups hostile to the Western type of democracy could already make good use of this new dimension in *coordinating* their activities. This applies not only to armed attacks, but money laundering and quite conventional criminal activities, like the trafficking of human beings or of drugs. Global co-ordination of police and security activities is obviously lagging behind, it is ad-hoc and in rudimentary stages, mostly stuck in the narrow constraints defined by 19th century interpretation of national sovereignty. Furthermore, as the ever more frequent attacks by global hackers have uncovered the *second main problem*: the extreme *vulnerability* of the global ICT network against non-political but non-cooperative minorities. Finally, entries into such well protected areas as the Pentagon or NASA, or of banks have also uncovered the inadequate protection of sensitive information. But also in more general terms, as Geruschkat (2002) correctly underlines ICT poses an insurmountable challenge to all sorts of traditional regulation, be that on product or factor markets, or in the realm of inter- or intra-state affairs.

As *the third major problem*: the state of affairs what Kolodko (2002, pp. 84–90) rightly terms global markets without global government is unlikely to change. The difficulties listed above do not call, as the above quote also suggests, to more interventionism in general. However, there is a world of difference between petty meddling into affairs or micro-management on the one hand and lack of regulatory institutions on the other. One possible option to overcome vulnerability, at least for small countries, is to join currency blocks – a suggestion well elaborated in the literature (Horvath, 2004). Finally, *self-regulation*, that has been dominant in the financial sector and in the ICT community is also known to be an efficient form of regulation, without necessary calling for the creation of inter-state organizations and endowing these with the authority to police whatever they wish to.

Actually, if global problems – i.e. the challenges pertaining to all humankind – are indicative of anything, it is the need to *re-assess traditional concepts of international law and economics*, both tending toward an over-emphasis on nation states and the regulatory activities of these. As Crocker (2003, pp. 43–44) right-

144

ly emphasized, the need to be engaged more in what are currently termed *failed states*,[3] to foster their re-integration in the international community, the spreading of universally accepted – UNO sanctioned – *codes of conduct* of civilized behavior. These should include the disengagement of criminal networks from the polity, include the opposition, termination of *civil wars*, inter alia via switching off the sources of funding, or the already mentioned enhancing of overall *transparency* all require co-operation at the global level, and not exclusively among governmental actors.

In sum, if we are to address the *fourth* global problem, *terrorism* by more elaborate and deeper going means than the War on Terror (Byman, 2003; Freedman, 2003) new forms and means of transnational co-operation and co-ordination are required. These should by no means be equal to the age-old attempts to create a global supra-government, whose legitimacy thus efficacy can only be questionable. As long as the object of the fight is not a nation state, *traditional concepts of military security are of little avail*. Likewise, the more these groups are organized along the network principles – the most modern in management science – the less efficient the government and formal military focus in fighting these can be. Coping with failed states and with the terrorist groups located in their territories would call for much more co-operation among security and police organs than is observable these days in the framework of Interpol and Europol, still much constrained in their respective activities by 19th century concepts of sovereignty.[4] Similarly the network organization follows a different logic than the still predominant traditional military doctrines, that pre-suppose the existence of a well defined enemy, normally a hostile state, that follows a rationality of its own that is easy to model in game theory. Therefore our understanding of a different logic, *different rationality, that does not follow either wealth maximizing or power maximizing principles under constraints of customary financial and political rationality* needs to be developed in order to enable us to develop preventive measures of various kinds. In these areas, social sciences seem to have little to offer to policy-makers at the moment.

The *fifth* important follow-up problem, also closely related to failed states is the *spread of infectuous diseases* and many other crippling repercussions of lasting poverty. A state can be considered failed when basic functions remain unattended, such as securing public security and elementary public services including health care. As the Human Development Indices, regularly published by the World Bank in its annual reports testify, in a number of states these are not being regularly provided, and also in the long run a tendency toward deterioration can be observed. This is a problem in so far as this is a main area of the vicious circle of poverty, where *undernourishment leads to diminishing capabilities*, the latter to crowding out of labor markets, further marginalization, and exposition to crime. With the massive migration that is

---

[3] This problem has been emphatically stressed – as public enemy number one for democracies – by Francis Fukuyama (2004).
[4] Repeated denials of German courts to extradite suspects of armed terror, on grounds of citizenship law, in 2005–2006 are cases in point.

unlikely to be controlled by police methods only, the spread of these is a very real eventuality, as the HIV virus or the re-emergence of tuberculosis in advanced countries has testified. The SARS panic already foreshadowed that the modern interconnected world carries enhanced risks for each individual, thus facing these challenges is not the job of policy-makers only.

A *sixth* global problem is the *crisis of the welfare state*. It relates to migration in a fairly straightforward manner. If the crux of the matter is, as shown by numerous analyses, the gap between limited revenue raising capabilities of the state and unlimited demand for its services provided as entitlements, there is no solution for the crises of the pension systems within the framework of a closed national economy. The trivial solution may sound migration (Hewitt, 2002), that is allowing the young and enterprising people of the underdeveloped countries to move according to economic criteria. Let us note, that migrants should not be mixed up with refugees. While the latter are normally displaced persons that need to be assisted on humanitarian grounds by any civilized society, the former tend to be healthy, young and enterprising persons. Their taxes and contribution to social security is perhaps the only conceivable way how the current implicit debts of pension systems could be bridged in the medium run. Let us also remember (Lipton and Ravallion, 1995) that migration used to be a major source of alleviating the demographic problems of the old continent: in their calculation in the 1863–1933 period no less than 45 per cent of the population increment of the British Isles migrated outwards. Once labor remains a factor of production it is hard not to see its inherent capabilities for wealth creation, especially in societies where, allegedly, incentives are right. Moreover, as the broad overview of Saskia Sassen (1999, pp. 155–157) has demonstrated, it is ahistoric to portray migration as an unregulated form of mass migration. In reality, not even in the 19th century, with border controls being nearly non-existent has this been the case. Moreover, the policies and regimes pertaining to this have long become transnationalized themselves, allowing for battles in terms of human rights, involvement of courts and new arrangements in terms of citizenship as well.

But it is not migration that poses the major challenge to the welfare state. Over and above the fundamental problem (limited revenues – unlimited demand) the slowdown of trend rate of growth and the ICT revolution exacerbate difficulties. In the 1950s and '60s annual 7–8 per cent growth rates allowed for more lavish options, than the current 1.5–2 per cent. Furthermore, when activity levels were high, and employment tended to be in the wage earning sector, the revenue raising capacity of the state could be taken as given. The latter has fundamentally changed due to major changes in industrial organization and employment, brought about by ICT (Kocsis, 2000; Szabó, 2000). These changes turned what previously used to be called 'non-traditional forms of employment' the norm. These include contract work, distant work, part time employment, multifunctional, multi-task employees and many others. The common thread of consequences is the loss of fixed jobs in large organizations, where the collection of social security contribution is secured by an elaborate bureaucracy. Irregular employment per se is an incentive to dodge public dues, and control costs are soaring. *The less private provision of health and old age services occurs, the higher the incentive to avoid self-care measures on a massive scale is.* The re-emergence of poverty among the elderly and among the small business people in the West is an example of this.

Let us be explicit on this point. It is the change in the type of *wealth creation* and economic *organization,* rather than financial liberalization that has triggered this change. As recently Dreher (2006) has empirically documented, the burden of taxation has not moved towards labor: in fact capital taxation even increased by several percentage points in the OECD area. For this reason limiting financial markets or empowering the EU with tax police prerogatives would be of no avail. Experience in the Western countries is mixed. On the one hand, political processes have clearly revealed a preference of the majority in European societies to preserve salient features of the post-war welfare state. On the other hand, while some countries avoided any major changes, and ended up with stagnation and soaring public debt, as in Germany, Italy and France, others have made incremental reforms. Sweden, Finland and the Netherlands are perhaps the best examples where the fundamentals of the welfare system remain, though *their functioning has changed tremendously.* True, most changes contribute to easing budgetary burdens, while other considerations of sustainability may not always be observed. While this gradualism does enhance legitimacy – rule by persuasion allows for insights to be turned to consensus – most observers would certainly qualify these changes as falling short of what is needed for sustaining growth. Nobel Laureate Robert Mundell (2003) formulated this through the following maxim: *'Europe needs a supply-side revolution'.* Recent measures in Germany, France and Italy, though triggering major social unrest, surely still fell short of heeding his call. Thus, it is rational to expect that their impact on improving macroeconomic performance in Western Europe is also likely to remain limited at best.

It is important to recall: not each form of the welfare state is under equal stress. As the more theoretical piece of Sapir (2006) and the rather empirical piece of Aiginger and Guger (2006) explain, those who manage to put the supreme maxim of *fiscal sustainability first* are alive and well, while those who treat it as secondary tend to stagnate for long periods to come. Last but not at all least, *as seventh,* the new global problem of *localization* needs to be addressed. Not only does it mean the ever growing share of the tertiary sector, which is often immobile and provides mostly non-tradables. But also in the political and information flows there is a tendency to focus on the funny, at the cost of the important. Infotainment is dominant over analyses, and the survival of public broadcasting stations, as well as of major quality papers has been questioned.[5] This implies a serious challenge, insofar as the global challenges

---

[5] In 2002–2003 two leading papers in Germany, the left-centre *Süddeutsche Zeitung* and also the center-right *Frankfurter Allgemeine* barely escaped bankruptcy. Even the business oriented *Financial Times* has become much slimmer than it used to be; and the *Neue Zürcher Zeitung* is also facing financial difficulties. In September 2004 the left-wing *Frankfurter Rundschau* was bailed out by the ruling Social Demociatic Party.

are crowded out by local news. Public opinion is in the hands of tabloids and popular show-biz, thus in a number of cases *informed decisions are unlikely to be forthcoming.*

The more we are convinced of the need to make public choices on reforming the welfare state, the more dangerous the process of super-localization of the media may seem. For *it is unlikely that uninformed voters can make forward-looking decisions,* especially if temporary welfare losses are also part of the longer run solution. The more the Republican Government of the US is involved in populist fiscal policies, the less one can think about the customary 'do what I say, not what I do' in the context of welfare state reform, as a solution to the emerging problems. Similar myopia could be observed in the rejection of the Constitutional Treaty of the EU by the French and Dutch voters, as discussed in chapter 10. For this reason Lámfalussy (2005, p. 8) rightly qualifies as the misuse of the idea of the referendum to put complex and ambiguous issues at popular vote in mass democracies.

Since the emerging economies of Central Europe are already confronted with the problem of greying population, negative birth rates, slowdown of growth and limited immigration, while their welfare system remained basically unreformed, the challenges apply, *ceteris paribus* to them as well. Some of the direct consequences will be discussed in chapter 8 on the Stability and Growth Pact (SGP) of the EU.

'Europeanization' as a Special Challenge

Europeanization is a term that comes from the political science and European studies literature. It denotes a process of *mutual* adjustment of national and EU-wide systems in a variety of planes, including the economy, regulation, legislation, political systems and institutions.[6] There are several examples of this. For instance if the EU takes a decision, by qualified majority voting, to impose a strict environmental regulation, citizens of the non-compliant country can launch court cases to foster enforcement. The fact that the given country has not voted for it, is no excuse. Likewise, the initiation of warnings and later excessive deficit procedures against the non-compliant governments, such as Portugal, Ireland, Germany and most recently France, and even the Netherlands, trigger adjustment processes in the respective countries. In part this follows the feedback of markets, in part from the public debate/peer pressure.

There is understandably a reverse flow as well, with European institutions and policies reflecting to a large degree the domestic policy outcomes of the member-states. The conversion to monetary orthodoxy in the '70s and '80s, or the turning away from centrally financed big prestige projects to co-financed, regionally managed smaller ones are all clear examples of the feedback process.

---

[6] For a broad overview cf. eg. Kutter and Trappmann, eds (2006).

It would be hard to overlook, that in a number of areas, primarily in economic philosophy and also in fiscal approaches, there has been a fair degree of *convergence* between global mainstream thinking and policies adopted at the European level (Lányi, 1997 and 2001). However, it would be a mistake to identify the two processes; the European Union is to a large degree a closed economy, a unit of its own, with specific policies and institutions that require more and to some extent different things than the global markets in general do. As the broad survey in the volume edited by Kuklinski and Skuza (2003) illustrates, values, governance structures, visions, policy-formation – in terms of procedures and implementation – all *differ considerably* in the two planes. Thus both common and different features must be addressed, with the present subsection devoted to the latter.

For the emerging European economies talking of the process of 'Europeanization' is particularly something of a misnomer. On the one hand, these economies have always been located in Europe, in economic, political, geographic and cultural terms. On the other hand, their accession to the EU, up until now, has been a process of unilateral adjustment, of their – controlled – taking over of the Community laws and regulations in the process of harmonization, that preceded enlargement. Also the way the *acquis* was re-interpreted in the Amsterdam and Nice Treaties did not allow for opt-outs, like some current incumbents have. On the other hand, the sheer possibility of 'enhanced co-operation' allows for the emergence of second class membership.

Similarly to 'globalization', the challenge of 'Europeanization' also comes from a circumstance that is different than the name would imply. The real challenge comes from *the drift between normative and actual processes*. In normative terms, one of the few consensus points of the more academic and policy-oriented literature used to be the need for intra-EU reforms *prior to* enlargement. However, the inter-governmental conferences of Turin and Nice and the Convention at Laeken *fell short of producing an algorithm* that would allow for the enhanced diversity and the ensuing divergence in preferences among member-states and even more among the citizens. In one of the big paradoxes of history, while in economic terms enlargement adds only slightly more than 5 per cent of GDP to the incumbent EU, in terms of population an additional one third of voters is added. Thus, the more the EU moves towards overcoming its democratic deficit, the more its institutions reflect the normative claim of being closer to the citizens, the higher the immediate repercussions of enhanced diversity are likely to be. This could, in theory, be a source of inspiration, not however for institutions where unanimity and informal decision-making used to be the name of the game.

Following the debacle of the Constitutional Treaty it is no longer contestable that the attempt at overcoming the democratic deficit via 'politicization of the EU' was the misperception from the very outset (Bartolini, S. (2006). If the 'political' translates into populist / antiliberal, this is only to exacerbate the hardships of operating a Community of 27. Dumping the domestically failed public figures in the Commission, creating portfolios without appropriate assignments, or to oversee areas where the EU has no jurisdiction (like R+D or taxation) were bound to backfire.

A second major challenge of the enlarged EU is the unreformed state of *redistributory policies.* Most of the EU literature that focuses on the technicalities of integration is devoted to various forms of solidarity, primarily expressed in the Common Agricultural Policy and the various forms of regional spending via the structural funds. The fundamental problem here is twofold. On the one hand, enlargement by ten, mostly poorer members has been decided without *either* redefining the priorities of spending, *or* by revising capping of common funds to 1.27 per cent of GDP (in actual practice even less, to a mere 0.94 per cent). While the decisions are understandable on grounds of vested interest politics, this is a clear reflection of the lack of orientation. Either expenditure priorities need to be redefined as proposed by the Commission, but rejected by the member states in February 2004, or conversely, the limited lavishness of net contributors need to be reassessed. If none of these happen – as is the case for the transitory period of 2004–2006 – the evolution of *first and second rank membership* becomes inevitable. For it is justified to question the entire rationale, for instance, of direct income supports spread over 14 years following the MacSharry reforms, but only across the board. The option, elaborated in Copenhagen, that new members are gradually phased in until 2014, is obviously contrary to the elementary principle of equal treatment among members.

A third area where the European Union is seriously challenged is *regionalism.* In short, with the evolving decentralization of previously unitary states (Hrbek, ed., 2001) the idea of regional development based on central redistribution of resources and central policies in general has been questioned. This applies to the member-states, like Spain or even Great Britain in the Blair period, so it applies a fortiori to the EU. To put it bluntly, while the tendency of member-states to get back 'their money', as Baroness Thatcher once exclaimed, seems to have been dominant over any other considerations. Thus it has not been EU structural funds and related institutions that were the driving forces of European regionalism, but rather the other way around. The emerging European regionalism has rendered EU-level structural spending largely irrelevant. And this is a major difference to the period of Southern enlargement, when in some years Portugal, Ireland or Greece received up to 4 per cent of their GDP in terms of EU transfers, mostly in regional spending (that overlaps with CAP transfers as well).

This implies, among others, that *the structural funds and related EU policies are decreasingly relevant both for incumbents and new members alike.* In a way, this is the clearest example of why accession driven transformation is over and a new, more innovative phase is to come in designing and implementing institutional and structural reforms in the new members (as indicated in the chapter on the 'Limits to EU-driven transition'). The ongoing policies of re-tailoring territorial organization in the hope of official transfers that are either not forthcoming or may be negligible at the macroeconomic level is a case in point.

A *fourth,* perhaps even more challenging factor is the *slow if any progress in the Lisbon Strategy* of the EU. It is known that in March 2000 the EU adopted a ten-year-strategy to accelerate the use of ICT, productivity and flexible organization of labor. One of the novelties has been that progress reports need to be presented to the Council every year on the implementation of decisions. One of the few things that we do observe is that progress in this area, most relevant for the long-term growth of the European continent, is limited at best. This means, among other things, that the new members cannot rely on a dynamically growing market in the EU that would, by and large automatically, produce spillovers and generate demand and thereby long-term growth potential for them. This finding is directly contradictory to the normative view (Langhammer and Wössmann, 2002) that see the EU as a forum to elaborate a regulatory environment which is globally more competitive than alternative arrangements. Unsurprisingly the authors quoted above consider credibility to be a major condition for this to materialize.

Last but not at all least, as *fifth,* mention should be made of what is usually referred to as the second pillar of the European Union, that is *Common Foreign and Security Policy (CFSP).* It would be hard to overlook, how important this dimension should be, provided the EU does take its own global aspiration, as reflected in the Lisbon Strategy seriously. There are three areas where progress should be palpable: the policy on the West Balkans, the Barcelona process and neighborhood policies vis-à-vis the NIS.

As far as the West Balkans is concerned the gradual disengagement of US-led NATO troops has taken place at a period when the economic reconstruction does not seem to have gathered momentum. Nor EU military capabilities seem to have been built up to a level needed for a judge that must, willy-nilly, be involved in peace creation, not only in peace keeping. The EU has fallen short of providing financial assistance on the grand scale. It has fallen even more behind in *providing a European perspective to the westward-looking, democratically committed leaders of the region.*

As far as the NIS are concerned the EU has yet to develop a policy that would go beyond the level of declarative diplomacy. On the one hand, the EU is the largest trading partner for Russia, and also a major player in Russian foreign policy. On the other hand, it found itself marginalized, first in the 1990s behind the international financial organizations, and later in the 2000s with the emergence of the War on Terror and of the Coalition of the Willing. The Union has proven unable to come up with an operational strategy on the Orange Revolution in Ukraine and the democratic turn in Georgia in 2004–2005. Neither could it react to the ongoing autocratic practices in Belarus and Moldova. The collapse of the EU-Russia energy summit over the ban on importation of Polish meat in November 2006 was just a tip of the iceberg.

Last but not at all least *the Barcelona process* should be mentioned. It is vital for the EU, not least because of historic ties and because of the geographical pattern of migration to entertain special good relations with countries of the Mediterranean. The process, started in 1993 aims at closer co-operation in all the mentioned areas, including free trade or even association agreements. Turkey is a candidate since 1999, for full EU membership.

However, it would be hard to overlook, that not least because of the violent nature of the conflict in the Middle East, with the Intifada going on for several years, the inability of the EU to develop a defense arm, have led to *continued US dominance and European marginalization*. Over and above conferences and declarative diplomacy, there remained precious little room for a peculiar EU accent in managing these affairs.

It goes without saying that the drift between the very real challenge of migration, economic and social insecurity, of the consequences of suppressed but elementary social strains, as reflected in the ongoing civil war in Algeria, in the Kurdish insurgency in Turkey in 1995–99, in the violence in tourist receiving Morocco and Egypt, are but a few of the manifestations of the troubles. All in all, the EU has a strong interest in developing something more meaningful than its proximity policies used to be. In so doing, the new members have a *shared interest, and perhaps some additional regional competence* to share with the incumbents.

New Members:
The Challenge of Third Wave of Transformation

One of the pre-conditions for the post-Communist countries to join the EU has been, according to the Copenhagen criteria of 1993, their successful completion of transition to a market economy. With joining the OECD in the period of 1995–1997 the three frontrunners have actually over-fulfilled this plan target, insofar as the OECD, unlike the EU, did require commitment to full *capital account liberalization*. Membership followed by a test and intensive scrutiny, where the market economy characteristics of the respective countries underwent a severe professional test.

Looking from this perspective the entry in 2004 to the EU is rather delayed. On the one hand, at least in the thinking of the EU, enlargement contributes to *the lasting stabilization* in a previously restive post-Communist neighborhood and the Mediterranean *at a ridiculously low cost* (of 0.15 per cent of the GDP of incumbents). On the other hand, one of the motives that prompted the EU for the long engagement, could have been the idea of thereby providing additional incentives to structural reforms in a number of post-Communist economies (more on that in Balázs, 2001, chapter 8). If one considers the phases of acquis screening and the detailed discussions over the 31 chapters that paved the way to accession this hope does not seem unfounded.

In reality, in the Central European countries the first phase of transition, characterized by stabilization, liberalization, institutional reform and privatization (SLIP) was concluded by the mid-90s. Following this stage in several countries so-called second generation reforms were initiated, such as re-tailoring the welfare system, privatization of network industries, pension reforms to address the inter-generational implicit debt, as well as administrative reform.

This is not the place to replicate the detailed assessment of institutional reforms provided regularly by the *Transition Report* of the EBRD, one of the first among analysts that have traditionally laid great emphasis on institutional progress. Whatever we think about the merits and weaknesses of the indicators developed by the London-based analysts, it is clearly relating to economic performance and observed changes in national policies. Being an international agency, even-handedness is more secured than in the case of national self-assessments.

It might suffice to glimpse on these tables to be convinced that structural reforms, especially second generation reforms though have been launched, however their pace of implementation *has been suffering severe setbacks in the period between 1997–2006 in all the emerging European economies except Slovakia and Estonia.* Pension reforms, where initiated, were slowed down, on occasion reversed. Utility privatization though started, have not been completed. In other network industries, as well as in transport privatization, has been tiptoeing. Also in the more conventional tradable sectors no new initiatives occurred, while Slovakia, Estonia, the Czech Republic and Lithuania were catching up with Hungary of the mid-90s. In the latter country the center-right government stopped the process, and the center-left successor basically spent the first two years of talking rather than acting in privatization.

It would be hard not to relate *the secular slowdown in the economies of Central Europe to the stagnant institutional and structural reforms.* In a way, the convergence among economic systems took place around the level reached by Hungary by 1997, and except for Slovakia and Estonia, no further progress is observable. In the first years of the 2000s we could observe old-fashioned Keynesian attempts, by both left and right wing governments, to sustain growth by expanding domestic demand – an attempt that could only bring transient results in small open economies. Therefore, it is hard to see how else these economies could regain their growth, in degrees required by conditional convergence models, than by instituting a new wave of reforms that aim at creating conditions of sustainable growth and its financing.

One of the reforms that have long been dodged in the post-Communist countries – though not only there – has been in the area of *public finances.* For the time being some elementary conditions of fiscal sustainability are not being observed. *Transparency* of government expenditures requires much to be desired, both from the point of view of publicity and of legislative control. Also in terms of *assignment* of tasks, traditions and compromises on daily political matters, rather than any more general considerations that set expenditure priorities. In the area of revenue raising such simple maxims as those of few and low tax rates coupled with broad tax bases and effective enforcement have a long way to go. In the populist outbursts of the 2000–2006 period *discretionary elements* of both the tax and expenditure sides have increased tremendously. It is very rarely asked if any task, currently attended and financed publicly, do serve specific national interest on *public goods* grounds, or if there is an alternative for these to be *outsourced.* One extreme example is the monopoly firm testifying of precious materials (not a tax collecting, but a quality control authority), which is loss making, but is still publicly owned in Hungary, once a champion of privatization. Sustaining national carriers at the time of big international mergers in the airline industry is yet another example. And the cases know no end.

It is relatively easy to see that for broad coalitions, be these within a single broad-based party (*Volksparteien* in German terminology) or as formal coalition of competing forces, the temptation to spend more, and that in discretionary fashion is on the increase. Likewise, if the economy slows down but social pressure to hand out more pork is on the increase it is certainly easier to give in and blame 'the straightjacket of Maastricht', and 'the cold-heartedness of monetarists', than to rationalize expenditure and stick to old-age norms of solid housekeeping.

One of the major obstacles to fiscal reforms in the Central European economies is the *institutional integration of local municipalities* in the system of general government finances. This implies that any conceivable cut is immediately politicized; the more individual constituencies weigh in the electoral policies (and they do), the higher the probability is that any attempt to fiscal cuts will be resisted and reverted in behind the scenes bargains. As long as the limitations on public involvement in the economy are not constitutionally regulated and politically clearly delineated, the tendency to overspend – once called Wagner's Law in classical economics – is hard to revert.

The *size of public sector* is rarely a subject of considerations revolving around any concept of optimality or social cost, as postulated by the theory of optimal economic policy. Rather *ad-hoc coalitions,* 'policy of grievances', and continuous improvisations in managing local crises that shape the outcomes. This leads, by necessity, to a growing state involvement, not necessarily through nationalization, but also via a set of regulations and other covert forms of state involvement. Analysis of the Hungarian experience (Voszka, 2003) is indicative that reference to – bad – EU practices can reinforce monoplistic, re-distributory and anti-competitive practices.

Reform of public finances is thus hard to implement without *a reform of public administration.* In the view of Attila Ágh (2003, pp. 68–69) the institutional transfer of the EU harmonization period be followed by a phase of policy transfer. This may, indeed, be the easier part of the story, since as we tried to show above, the EU *does not possess operational policies that would be conducive to radically improved performance in the new member countries.*

It would be hard to find a cookbook to go by, insofar as cultural and historical factors also shape the pattern of public administration in all societies of the globe. In the new member-states the problems differ substantially, with Malta being a small island and Poland a middle-size power. For the majority of new members, a relatively high degree of public services is a revealed preference of the electorate, as parties offering more, rather than less redistribution tended to be elected over the past 15 years.

The basic question to be addressed in this respect remains the following: *to what extent the provision of public services requires public ownership and delivery,* and to what extent it could be outsourced to a variety of non-profit organizations, that may be private or co-operatives or else. The bad experience in Britain has somewhat diminished the previous enthusiasm favoring public-private partnerships, although this may be a misreading of outcomes of a clear regulatory failure.

Reform of *territorial administration* overlaps only in part with government reform. It is a matter of deliberation and debate what pattern suits best to a decentral and territorially democratic development, providing equal opportunities also for people living at long distances to the capital cities and other major cultural centers. For the time being the restructuring seems to follow the logic of how best receive potential EU inflows. This is of course a clearly *exogenous consideration* (even if funds comparable to those following the Southern enlargement were forthcoming). A major challenge in this respect derives from the fact that political structures, including electoral districts are drawn along territorial lines (as will be discussed in the chapter on the 'Limits of accession-driven transformation'). Unless the single round voting applying party lists only, as adopted in Italy, becomes the rule, local power is most likely to sabotage any major change. This, however, might well not be a drawback, if top-down reforms follow non-realistic or arbitrary priorities. *Regionalism* within the EU, as shown above, *does not come from Community policies*, the causal link works rather the other way around.

A fourth component of reforms to be implemented is the *re-structuring of welfare provision*. In this respect not much can be added to the overall considerations unfolded in the context of West European economies. The new members are strikingly similar to incumbents in terms of their social structure as well as in terms of the public provision of a variety of services through state-owned units. The exigencies explained there apply to these economies in the same way.

Here some structural problems will be hard to overcome. On the one hand, health services in post-Communist societies tend to be relatively *cheap at the macroeconomic level,* while provision is general. This is a fortunate mix, and many observers, both at the macro- and the micro-levels agree that it is an accomplishment. On the other hand, the cost explosion in medical technology and the lengthening of human lives, with the concomitant funding requirements clearly calls for introducing economic incentives. These include not only the customary cost dampening measures like co-financing, but also more investment into *prevention*, spreading healthier *life styles*, as well as incentives for *private savings* for medical purposes.

A different problem props up with pension reforms. Here the credibility of financial institutions has been limited over the past decades. Due to wars and changes in systems, as well as the recurring inflationary periods in all countries except for the Czech Republic and Slovakia, have shortened the time horizon of citizens well below the normal levels. Experience in the West, especially in Britain and the US has been indicative of the wide spread *myopia of the median citizen,* that makes the fully funded mode unattractive and public presence highly likely (on grounds of market failure). This unfavorable situation has been exacerbated by regulatory mistakes, allowing for enormous diversity of profitability of private funds (allowed to invest basically in government bonds only). Furthermore, the political controversy, like the one initiated by the center-right government of Hungary in 1998–2002, have further eroded trust in these, by definition very long-term investments. With the low level of development of long term securities market (the longest government bonds run to 10 years only, against 30 years in the USA) *the idea of long-term saving in forms other than housing or similar fixed assets is not very widely accepted.* Since trust is not something that one can declare or import from abroad, there will be a long period until the market for pension and health care funds and life insurance will be developing. Until then typical shortcomings of a basically publicly run pay as-you-go system, with the relegation of most pensions into subsistance allowances, unrelated to performance, is likely to prevail. That will further *constrain the propensity for long-term savings,* and thereby diminish growth rates as well.[7]

Environmental protection is yet another area where lots of good intentions have been declared with quite limited practical implementation. The surveillance mechanisms of the EU may play a pivotal role in appreciating this area among the competing policy areas in the new member states. Implementation of a number of innovations, including the greater reliance on private financing and private provision on such areas as waste management, water supply, and reforestation may open up completely new perspectives for the new member countries. Here we have to do with an area where the EU has though *explicit policies and requirements, but no common funds,* a feature that is likely to figure high in the future of EU integration.

Last but not at all least the importance of *enhancing social cohesion* needs to be mentioned. In the traditional theories of economics and in some political science approaches this is taken as given. What we have experienced during the transition and accession years is a warning sign that societies find it hard to put up with growing inequalities in wealth, income, life-styles, potentials and perspectives. The *rise of populism,* both within and outside the established parliamentary parties is a clear sign of the stress that is reflected in these processes. The *low turnout* in elections may undermine the legitimacy of governments. Without having *shared values* the insitutions of democracy can hardly function effectively. Without providing a minimum of equity, whatever way the majority defines this term, European type of consensual democracies and societies are unable to function.

Therefore, additional efforts are needed to *strengthen everything* that traditionally used to be called as *social intangibles.* These partly come from the system of education, partly from the media and from the norms represented and spread by the elite through their practices. If robbers and other outcasts are the role models for the youth, as in some countries and some periods it could be surveyed, it does not bode well for the type of society we visualize, if we talk of European common values.

It would be hard to overlook that what is called the Bologna Process in the EU will contribute to the further *deterioriation of the adjustment of higher education*

---

[7] On the intimate interaction between the economic and social components of change see in detail (Csaba, 2006).

to the labor market needs. This is a problem, since the world of labor is known to be the strongest integrating component in any society. All the more so, if other integrating factors, such as religion, national consciousness, family values, commitment to locality and altruism in general are losing rather than gaining momentum, for a number of reasons that fall outside the scope of the present monograph. What remains is a clear normative conclusion to *spend more and more efficiently on education* in the broad sense so that an ever growing number of citizens could profit from the processes of transnationalization and the enlargement of the European Union, despite its paradoxical features.

On Social Stress: No Pain, No Gain?

When discussing the chances of those far-reaching changes that we advocated in the preceding sections we can rely on a rich international literature on policy reform. This literature, drawing on the experience of mostly developing, more recently also of transition, economies allows for *more optimistic conclusions than the mechanistic extension of the rational choice model,* currently dominating political science, would allow. At the bottom line, rational choice extrapolates the dominance of short-termism and of immediate economic interest on macro-economic and macro-social decisions, which often is a legitimate approach. However, from this it follows, at the level of definition, that those reforms that aim to change salient features of the status quo can never materialize. However, in reality 'out there' we do see successful reforms, not least in the countries joining the EU from 2004. Therefore, we must venture into a field where the customary arguments from rational choice school are not taken at face value, although this approach is indeed able to explain the policy derailments of the past few years.

One of the many paradoxes of democracy is its reliance on *a strong 'core state',* as well as of *trials and errors.* While democracy does have a tendency to be myopic, it also has been able to overcome these features whenever major challenges were faced, be that totalitarianism or terrorism. Therefore it is only right if we do not dispute away the possibility of 'rule by persuasion' from the new democracies either.

It would be hard to overestimate the importance of the 'first things first' approach. In order to move towards such advantages that show up in the longer run, like free trade, solid public finances, or improved environmental management, what is needed is perspective coupled with actions *on the home front.* In other words, these changes should ideally begin immediately, not waiting for the EU, for the improvement of international climate, or for the miraculous revitalization of economic activity. Policies aiming at the improvements in the sense outlined above should be *endogenous, or domestically owned.* As demonstrated, most recently in Afghanistan and Iraq, previously in Bosnia, Rwanda and Somalia, attempts to construct democracy, market economy and multiculturalism from abroad are bound to fail.

At this point of time, there is a grave danger that the far from best practices of large EU countries may be easier to emulate than to launch a vigorous policy aiming at economic vibrancy and sustainable growth in the long run. Instead, at least in normative terms, 'Europeanization' should become *the window of opportunity* to launch a series of reforms, whose implementation will take decades. The EU, in most of the new member states, may become the *rallying point* of modernization, along which *social consensus could be built* at least in a number of issues of principle, such as long-term goals. These may pave the way to more prospective policies also in reality.

The new EU members have to tackle an entire broad development agenda, that of *participatory growth.* For the time being they face a next to insurmountable dilemma. In periods when foundations for sustaining growth have been lain, economic strains were transformed to social strains and growing inequality. By contrast, in those periods when social strains were about to be addressed, governments relapsed into old fashioned populist policies that are obviously harmful to growth, already in the short to medium run. The normative way-out, following the development agenda, would be participatory growth, i.e. a platform where public sector reforms and institutional change bring about transparency and welfare gains *at the same time,* an issue we shall consider in detail in the concluding chapter of this book.

Let us be clear: while not being a trivial option participatory growth is a feasible option in the new EU members, as long as they have already mastered the elementary agenda of creating market institutions and disinflation while retaining and strengthening the democratic setup. By allowing for a *broader based growth*, that requires the support of SMEs rather than big public work projects, sustaining disinflation rather than extending services as entitlements, irrespective of costs, and generally speaking *sincere public discourse instead of the infantile manipulation of the public opinion* that has emerged over the past few years. The state would by no means be relegated to a night watchman, but would be actively shaping outcomes, primarily in its capacity as *a regulator and supervisor*. Deepening the capital markets, for instance, definitely requires more active public policy involvement than before.

What has been said about developing countries applies to emerging economies as well in terms of the millennium or development round of the WTO. It is not in the interest of these small open economies that bilateralism and unilateralism, the practice of 'might is right' would overwhelm those dispute settlement mechanisms that are by no means perfect, but do provide some backing to the weaker and the poor. It would be an important contribution to the evolving EU if they could add, in a constructive fashion, to shaping a *more co-operative European negotiating stance,* rather than joining the 'coalition of the nasty' trying to sabotage any reform that would diminish redistribution inside the EU. However, the latter scenario may be more realistic in the medium run, despite its obvious moral and economic drawbacks.[8]

---

[8] This forecast materialized by the debacle of the Doha Round in July 2006. Where the good news is, that following a year of elections, compromise solutions will perhaps stand a better chance at a later stage as suggested by: *Frankfurter Allgemeine Zeitung,* 26 July 2006.

Finally, it would be hard to eschew *the fundamental question of non-inflationary and sustainable growth* which is in the self-interest of the emerging markets. Quite irrespective of what EU funds will or will not be available, it is not a subject of debate any longer in economics that only non-inflationary growth is sustainable. And these economies are still at 38–77 per cent of the average of the EU-15, at times when the citizens have already acquired the four freedoms of the EU, and when transnationalization has permeated most of these economies in internationally unprecedented degrees.

It is important to face the tough realities: convergence of less developed countries, also within a market-led integration, can only be conditional. In other words, *there is a potential, however no certainty.*[9] Growth rates of emerging Europe that would exceed the trend rates of the EU countries are though conceivable, but by no means given. While new EU members, unlike the NIS, are not suffering from too low levels of savings, the efficiency of their system of financial intermediation thus of *macroeconomic allocational efficiency has still a long way to improve.* Deepening and broadening of capital markets is a condition for innovation to turn into embodied technological change. Without more extensive financial services the SME sector is unlikely to grow. *Unless the state ceases to crowd out private investment,* that is unless general government turns into equilibrium in normal years of growth, *there is no scope for funding the new establishments.*

In order to master these tasks, well known insights of the new developmental agenda, stressing the need for investment into *human capital,* the importance of supporting SMEs, of the need to create productive jobs (including self-employment), of the need to spread computer literacy at early ages, or the need to spend on *integrating* marginalized minority groups need to be heeded.

What has been said in normative terms echoes broadly accepted insights in the global literature on policy reform. However it certainly would require a sea change in the way policy is formulated, communicated and generally conducted in the new EU member-states. The need to differentiate between what looks, and what is in reality, socially sensible, what is and what is not financeable, what does and does not require public intervention *run counter to the practice of media-led policy-making.*

It would be hard to overlook that in the need to switch styles and substances the new EU members have already converged to the incumbents. Most of the issues on the agenda, the need to overcome short-termism, or the need to better co-ordinate welfare needs and financing possibilities are largely overlapping. Similarly the need to face the challenges of global nature and that of transnationalization, is common, indeed. If they wish to overcome those strains what Attila Ágh (2003/2004, p. 24) described as lack of effective (rather than formal) membership, they need to heed the advice and *formulate their national interest in terms of reforming inefficient EU governance structures,* rather

---

[9] These complex issues are analyzed at great length in a forthcoming volume (Winiecki, ed., 2007).

than in terms of myopic official transfer bargains, as would follow from the current dominance of low politics in old and new members alike.

One of the gravest dangers new EU members face is the *negative spillover scenario*. A decade ago it seemed customary to maintain that the EU is likely to gain from enlargement, if for no other reasons than the vibrancy and vitality these may add to an ossifying Western structure (Daianu, 1996). However, a decade later the situation *may well be reversed*. Less than enlightened practices of incumbent EU members are easy to emulate. Reference to EU standards, real rather than normative ones, may undermine efforts to introduce policies with a longer horizon.

While the future options are open it is hard not to conclude on an optimistic note: once we are able to call a spade a spade, it should be possible to orchestrate the consensus that is needed for the successful completion of the third round of transformation in the new EU member countries. If the EU is able to provide, at least in part, the rallying point around *domestically owned* policy platforms, delivering credible regulatory environment, promote the evolution of independent regulatory agencies, and of course, sustain monetary stability via the single currency, *it has already contributed to its historic mission of re-unification of Europe* in the name of democracy and market economy, welfare and social consensus, co-operation and peace. As a formal model demonstrated (Roland and Verdier, 2003) EU accession, even without any external infusion of money, *provides a mechanism for overcoming bad equilibrium* resulting from poor law enforcement, provided that a new member is small enough, relative to the EU. Since this is the case, the formal analysis is supportive of our finding on what EU membership may contribute to the sustainable development of emerging economies. Contributing to the latter could, indeed be their best service, *provided through example,* to the less successful countries of the post-Communist transition.

References

ÁGH, A. (2003): *Anticipatory and Adaptive Europeanization in Hungary.* Budapest: a book published by the Hungarian Center for Democracy Studies.

ÁGH, A. (2003/2004): Smaller and bigger states in the EU-25: The Eastern enlargement and decision-making in the EU. *Perspectives – The Central European Review of International Affairs,* (Prague), no. 21. pp. 5–26.

AIGINGER, K. – GUGER, A. (2006): The ability to adopt: why it differs between the Scandinavian and continental European models. *Intereconomics,* vol. 41. no. 1. pp. 14–25.

BALÁZS, P. (2001): *Európai egyesülés és modernizació.* (Unification and modernization in Europe). Budapest: Osiris Könyvkiadó.

BARTOLINI, S. (2006): Politicization of European institutions. *Zeitschift für Staats- und Europewissenschaften,* vol. 4. no. 2.

BELL, D. A. (2003): History of globalization: Reflections on temporality. *International Affairs,* vol. 79. no. 4. pp. 801–814.

BHAGWATI, J. (1998): Trade liberalization and 'fair trade' demands: Addressing the environmental and labor standards issues. In: BHAGWATI, J.: *Writings on International Economics* (edited by V. N. Balasubramanyam). New Delhi: Oxford University Press, pp. 134–151.

BRASSETT, J. and HIGGOTT, R. (2004): Building the normative dimensions of a global polity. *Review of International Studies*, vol. 29. no. 1. pp. 29–55.

BYMAN, D. (2003): Scoring the war on terror. *National Interest*, no. 72. pp. 75–84.

CROCKER, Ch. (2003): Engaging failed states. *Foreign Affairs*, vol. 82. no. 5. pp. 32–44.

CSABA, L. (1998): On the EU maturity of Central Europe: Percieved and real problems. In: CASSEL, D. ed.: *Europäische Integration als ordnungspolitische Gestaltungsaufgabe*. Berlin: Duncker und Humblot, Schriften des Vereins fuer Socialpolitik, Band 260. pp. 240–265.

CSABA, L. (2006): Social change in Central and Eastern Europe: regional patterns and national characteristics. Warsaw: *Tiger Working Papers* no. 98 (October), available online: www.tiger.edu.pl

CSIKÓS–NAGY, B. (2002): *Közgazdaságtan a globalizálódó világban – II.* (Economics in a globalizing World, vol. II). Budapest: a book published by the Center for Social Science Research of the Hungarian Academy of Sciences.

DAIANU, D. (1996): *Vitality and Viability: A Double Challenge for Europe*. Frankfurt am Main: Verlag Peter Lang.

DEACON, B. (2003): Global social governance reform. *Global Social Policy*, vol. 3. no. 1. pp. 6–17.

DOLLAR, D. and KRAAY, A. (2004): Trade, growth and poverty. *Economic Journal*, vol. 114. no. 493. pp. F22–F49.

DREHER, A. (2006): The influence of globalization on taxes and social policy: an empirical analysis. *European Journal of Political Economy*, vol. 22. no. 1. pp. 179–201.

FREEDMAN, L. (2003): Prevention, not preemption. *Washington Quarterly*, vol. 26. no. 2. pp. 105–115.

FUKUYAMA, F. (2004): The importance of state building. *Journal of Democracy*, vol. 15. no. 2. pp. 17–31.

GERUSCHKAT, R. (2002): Elektronischer Welthandel, Wettbewerb und staatliche Handlungsmöglichkeiten. In: SCHÜLLER, A. and THIEME, H. J. eds: *Ordungsprobleme der Weltwirtschaft*. Stuttgart-Jena-New York: Lucius & Lucius, pp. 158–178.

GREENAWAY, D. – MORGAN,W. – WRIGHT, P. (2002): Trade liberalization and growth in developing countries. *Journal of Development Economics*, vol. 67. no. 1. pp. 229–244.

HANSON, M. (2003): The promotion of transparency in emerging markets. *Global Governance*, vol. 9. no. 1. pp. 63–80.

HARLEY, K. H. (2000): Global history (a review of O' Rourke and Williamson). *Journal of Economic Literature*, vol. 38. no. 4. pp. 926–935.

HEWITT, P. (2002): The end of the post-war welfare state. *Washington Quarterly*, vol. 25. no. 2. pp. 17–34.

HORVATH, J. (2004): Comments on unilateral euroization. In: HEIDUK, G. and HORVATH, J. eds: *On Some Currency Regime Considerations for the Visegrád Countries*. Berlin: Duncker und Humblot, pp. 113–124.

HRBEK, R. ed.: (2001): *Jahrbuch des Föderalismus*. Baden-Baden: Nomos Verlag.

KOCSIS, É. (2000): Networks as boundary-less organizations. In: BARA, Z. and CSABA, L. eds: *Small Economies' Adjustment to Global Tendencies*. Budapest: Aula Publishing House for the European Association for Comparative Economic Studies, pp. 53–68.

KOLODKO, G. W. (2002): *Globalizáció és a volt szocialista országok fejlődése*. (Globalization and the development of post-Communist countries). Budapest: Kossuth Könyvkiadó.

KRIZSÁN, A. and ZENTAI, V. eds: (2003): *Reshaping Globalization: Multilateral Dialogues and New Policy Initiatives*. New York-London- Budapest: The CEU Press.

KUKLINSKI, A. and SKUZA, B. eds: (2003): *Europe in the Perspective of Global Challenge*. Warsaw: Oficyna Wydawnicza 'Rewasz' for the Polish Association for the Club of Rome.

KUTTER, A. and TRAPPMANN, V. eds (2006): *Das Erbe des Beitritts. Europäisierung in Mittel- und Osteuropa*. Baden-Baden: NOMOS Verlag.

LANGHAMMER, R. and WÖSSMANN, L. (2002): Erscheinungsformen regionaler Integrationsabkommen im weltwirtschaftlichen Ordnungsrahmen: Defizite und Dynamik. In: SCHÜLLER, A. and THIEME, H.–J. eds: *Ordnungsprobleme der Weltwirtschaft*. Stuttgart etc.: Lucius&Lucius, pp. 373–397.

LÁMFALUSSY, A. (2005): Challenges ahead for the European Union. *Competitio*, vol. 4. no. 2. pp. 7–13.

LÁNYI, K. (1997): A globális konvergencia változatai: Washington és Maastricht, I–II. (Varieties on global convergence: The Washington Consensus and the Maastricht criteria). *Külgazdaság*, vol. 41. no. 11. pp. 5–29 and Part II, ibidem, vol. 41. no. 12. pp. 4–19.

LÁNYI, K. (2001): Vázlat a globalizációnak nevezett jelenségkör értelmezéséről (A draft on interpreting the issues termed commonly as globalization). *Közgazdasági Szemle*, vol. 48. no. 6. pp. 498–519.

LÁNYI, K. (2003): A globális rendszer változó arculata az újabb irodalom tükrében. (The changing profile of the global system through the eyes of the new literature). *Európa Fórum*, vol. 13. no. (3–4). pp. 3–26.

LIPTON, M. and RAVALLION, M. (1995): Poverty and polity. In: BEHRMAN, J. and SRINIVASAN, T. N. eds: *Handbook of Development Economics, vol. 3B*. Rotterdam etc.: Elsevier Publishers, ch. 4.

MANNING, N. and PALIER, B. (2003): Globalization, Europeanization and the welfare state. *Global Social Policy*, vol. 3. no. 2. pp. 139–152.

MATTEO, A. and SCHUCHKNECHT, R. (2002): A WTO framework for the new economy. In: SIEBERT, H. ed.: *Economic Policy Issues of the New Economy*. Heidelberg-Berlin-New York: Springer Verlag, pp. 143–168.

MUNDELL, R. (2003): One global economy – one world currency? Warsaw: *TIGER Distinguished Lectures*, no. 12.

NAYYAR, D. (2002): Limits to migration and the WTO framework. In: NAYYAR, D. ed.: *Governing Globalization: Issues and Institutions*. Oxford etc.: Oxford University Press for WIDER, chapter 6.

PANGARIYA, A. (2002): Developing countries at Doha: A political economy analysis. *World Economy*, vol. 25. no. 9. pp. 1205–1234.

ROLAND, G. and VERDIER, Th. (2003): Law enforcement and transition. *European Economic Review*, vol. 47. no. 4. pp. 669–685.

ROTHBERG, R. (2002): The new nature of nation-state failure. *Washington Quarterly*, vol. 25. no. 3. pp. 85–96.

SAPIR, A. (2006): Globalization and the reform of the European social models. *Journal of Common Market Studies*, vol. 44. no. 2. pp. 369–390.

SASSEN, S. (1999): *Guests and Aliens*. New York: The New York Press.

SZABÓ, K. (2000): Learning firms and their adjustment to global tendencies. In: BARA, Z. and CSABA, L, eds: *Small Economies' Adjustment to Global Tendencies*. Budapest: AULA Publishing House for the European Association for Comparative Economic Studies, pp. 31–52.

SZENTES, T. (2004): *The Political Economy of Development, Globalization and System Transformation*. Budapest: Akadémiai Kiadó.

UNDERHILL, G. (2003): States, markets and governance for emerging market economies: Private interests, the public good and the legitimacy of development policies. *International Affairs*, vol. 79. no. 4. pp. 755–782.

YEATS, N. (2002): Globalization and social policy: From global neo-liberal hegemony to global policy pluralism. *Global Social Policy,* vol. 2. no. 1. pp. 69–91.

VOSZKA, É. (2003): *Versenyteremtés – alkuval.* (Creating competition via bargains). Budapest: Akadémiai Kiadó.

WALLACE, W. and WALLACE, H. eds: (2000): *Policy-Making in the European Union.* Oxford etc.: Oxford University Press, 4th edition.

WHALLEY, J. (2003): The WTO and the new development-oriented trade round. In: Krizsán, A. and ZENTAI, V. eds: *Reshaping Globalization: Multilateral Dialogues and New Policy Initiatives.* New York-London-Budapest: The CEU Press, pp. 181–196.

WINIECKI, J. ED. (2007): *Competitiveness of New Europe,* London: Routledge (in print).

WINTERS, L. A. (2002): Trade liberalization and poverty: What are the links? *World Economy,* vol. 25. no. 9. pp. 1339–1368.

7. LIMITS TO ACCESSION-DRIVEN TRANSFORMATION IN CENTRAL EUROPE

In the previous chapter on 'Transnationalization', as well as in the empirical chapter, the anchor role of the European Union has been highlighted in more than one dimension. Both in terms of intellectual development and institutional change, the EU has played a role of a model that was to be emulated and approximated. By the accession in May 2004, this process became by and large a matter of history. In this chapter our puzzle is if, and to what degree, 'catching up with European standards', or Europeanization can continue to serve as a point of reference for structural reforms that are yet to be instituted if economic growth is to sustain. Our hypothesis is that a negative answer is probable, since the EU itself is in need of reform if it is to cope with enlargement and the challenge of transnationalization. To put it bluntly, *in the post-2004 period, the policies based on copying/transplanting EU institutions are no longer feasible, nor would it be rational for the new members.* In order to prove our point we look at converging European institutions from both sides, issues of standardization and of multi-level governance are discussed, and finally the genre of reforms, i.e. a normative part concludes.

Transition and EU Integration: Do They Fully Overlap?

When the Soviet empire collapsed, to a large degree unexpectedly in terms of time and peacefulness for most observers, the emerging new democracies have been confronted with the tasks of large-scale institutional rearrangement at the macroeconomic level. While this unique historic opportunity provided a lot of food for thought, and academics advanced a variety of normative visions of 'the type of capitalism' they deemed best suited for their respective societies, at the political and bureaucratic levels this sudden freedom triggered fear and bewilderment. Aligning themselves with the vast majority of the population, the newly elected leaders tended to opt for safe ways. As Communism used to constitute, among other things, a grandiose attempt at social engineering, and later on socialist reforms added up to further experimentation at the macro level, millions of people tended to be fed up with the trials and errors that had been going on for decades. Experimentation with social engineering has earned a particularly bad name in the region, actually ever since the end of the First World War.

Much has been written on the contemporary atmosphere of 'returning to Europe'. Reliance on this phrase – and the related discourse – also reflected a belief, that once the artificial, ideology-inspired social experimentation is discontinued, there is an easy way to improve the economy in terms of efficiency and welfare (Collins and Rodrik, 1991). For it is straightforward in economic theory, that once distortive, inefficient practices are discontinued and the mechanisms of misallocation of resources abolished, welfare improvement must be imminent.

This overall approach of mainstream thinking could be translated into specific policy advice on how to replace and/or reshape collapsing old institutions in Central and Eastern Europe. Rather than experimenting with various untested theoretical models, or relying on third road solutions, that used to enjoy particular popularity at the time of erosion of the old system, the best option seemed to be the copying of already existing institutions in the EU and its member states (Portes, 1991). In a more sophisticated version, all that the post-Communist countries needed was the re-introduction of monetary co-ordination, by monetizing and opening up the closed command and control systems (Dietz, 1991). Let us observe that this sort of policy advice and social expectations originating from within the societies concerned largely overlapped in and for the economies in transition.

The operationalization of this approach has been fostered by the publicly voiced desire of the freely elected governments of most, if not all, new democracies to capitalize on the stipulations of the Treaty of Rome. Adopted in 1957, just a couple of months following the brutal crushing of the Polish and Hungarian uprisings of 1956 against Communist rule and Soviet domination, the Treaty deliberately kept the door open in front of 'all democracies in Europe'.

True, by 1990 the EC had become fully preoccupied with its deepening project, the adoption of economic and monetary union, culminating in the Maastricht Treaty.[1] Additionally, and by no means marginally, the challenge of German reunification, basically settled with the currency union of 3 October 1990, did imply the first Eastward enlargement of the EC, absorbing a country of 17 m people, without, however applying any transition period (as in previous enlargements had been the case). Notwithstanding this circumstance all new democracies in Central and Southeast Europe *considered the European Communities as their natural anchor* (cf. Kulcsár, ed., 1998), irrespective of the timing and other conditions of eventual membership.[2] What a modern, civilized market economy is/should be, has been represented for them by the EC

---

[1] For a detailed analysis of EU structures cf. the monograph of Tibor Palánkai (2004).

[2] Being aware of the Copenhagen compromise of December 2002, it is quite obvious, that the frequently drawn parallel to German reunification is entirely misplaced, in political and financial terms alike (cf. Sinn, 1999).

and its member states. The explicit reference in the preamble of the Treaty of Rome on the possible admission of all European democracies also supported this claim.

The interaction of democratic change within the new democracies and their adaptation to EC/EU policies in general, and the *acquis communautaire* in particular is now generally termed as 'Europeanization' in the political science and the European studies literature.[3] This term denotes a process in which EU institutions and policies shape, or at least immediately influence, the formation of policies and institutions within the borders of a nation state. For the post-Communist countries, having applied for full EC/EU membership in the 1991–1996 period the Copenhagen Council of June 1993 was setting *explicit criteria for entry*. These included political democracy, market economy, the ability and willingness of the candidates to implement the legal framework of the Union, and finally the Union's ability to cope with enlargement. In short, a set of explicit political criteria, relating to the fundamental features of political and economic systems of the applicants have been formulated and promulgated.

In short, the stronger partner – that is the EC/EU – practically *prescribed* the take-over of the *acquis*, and the component of mutual give and take, inherent in any deal in international law/business, and not least on previous occasions of enlargement[4] – had been flatly excluded from the agenda. This followed from the priority of the deepening project, adopted just a year and a half before the accession criteria, and which looked to a large degree normative and overly optimistic for most contemporary observers. Thus the EC/EU wanted to protect its newest achievements from watering down by enlargement.

The component of unilateral adjustment was also strengthened by a series of further steps. In these the EU assisted accession by specifying the entry criteria. On the other hand, since the exact formulation of these also lacked elements of iteration, this boiled down to further *severing of the interpretation*. The story started with the introduction of *structured dialogue* in Essen in 1994. In this process a regular semiannual consultation ensured, that ministers from accession countries see to it, that they could report in the progress made by their respective administrations in adopting EU law. The second step was the *White Book of 1995* specifying the sectoral tasks of adjustment, following, of course, the internal setup of the Commission, rather than the macroeconomic or social significance of individual issues.[5] Last but not least, a previously unknown phase of *acquis screening* had been introduced, when officials of the Commission checked, on the field, if harmonization of laws and policies is implemented on the ground, or only in the books. This represented a fairly investigative scrutiny of administrative and policy practices of not yet members.

---

[3] More on that in Palánkai (2005)

[4] For instance the inclusion of fisheries, Mediterranean crops, Trans-Alpine transport or the concern over de-populated areas all reflected national agendas by various new entrants.

[5] In an extreme case, the safety instructions of water boilers were put on the same rank as creating monetary stability or not allowing for individual tax exemptions (a wide-scale practice of luring in FDI).

The process of bargaining on conditions of accession could only be launched when the preceding steps were declared complete by the EU. In the latter process, primarily, though by no means exclusively, through the Regular Reports, published by the Commission, and approved by the Council. These Reports presented a wide coverage of developments in the accession countries, and contained specific, often controversial assessment of particular policies. Interestingly for an international bureaucracy, these Reports have not been standardized. Thus the report on Romania included longish sections on orphan houses, while the report on the Czech Republic did not cover the same issue area.[6] This was only one, formal sign of the Commission seeing itself in the role of a policy entrepreneur.

Overall, Regular Reports tended to be overly specific, entering into debates of purely domestic nature, where the Community has no competence whatsoever, even with its incumbents. Such examples included gender equity, the way public media is being financed and controlled, or the way waste management is organized. On the other hand, this patronizing approach has been much less resisted than could be expected from countries that had just regained their sovereignty after several decades. Many analysts have portrayed EU accession as a unique opportunity to attend those tasks that were deemed necessary anyway, from territorial reorganization to fiscal decentralization (Ágh, 2001).

It is hard to reject out of hand the latter approach of voluntarily overdoing EU demands, as there has been a rationale to it. Global experience with policy reform has long been highlighting the problem of *credibility* and *lacking consensus*, as major impediments to change. Knowing the emergence of an institutional vacuum (or as we labelled previously, informalism), coupled with the formalization of vested interest as an inherent feature of democracy, the conditions for successful reforms in Central and Eastern Europe could not be taken as given (Nunnenkamp, 1995). A conceivable way of bridging the gap between ambitions and capabilities could be the voluntary acceptance of the institutional and policy anchor role of the EU. The EU, for its part, could see this as a contribution to stabilizing its own backyard.

As long as EU accession has figured among the very few consensus points across the political spectrum in the region, adopting the entirety of EU accomplishments/laws, institutions and policies, commonly referred to as the *acquis* could provide both the importation of credibility for the new institutions, and play a consensus-building function, that could ensure a degree of much needed policy continuity over and above a single electoral cycle.[7] As demonstrated in the empirical chapter, both the democratic and the economic performance in countries where such anchor function existed far exceeded those, where the

---

[6] Reports by the OECD, IMF or WTO typically follow the same internal pattern in evaluating each country, and this is the practice of rating agencies and other opinion forming organizations, such as the *Economist Intelligence Unit*.

[7] This feature – and its predominantly favorable role – becomes quite conspicuous if compared to Russian transformation, where a similar external anchor has been missing, thus the across the board consensus on fundamentals is still missing (Sutela, 2004, p. 53. and pp. 73–75).

anchor (and thus the minimal consensus) was lacking. Agreeing on the fundamentals and on the terminus – full membership in the EU – has allowed to pass
non-popular legislation (such as abolishing the capital punishment) and to
sustain policies that, at least in the short run, contradict the immediate interest
of pressure groups, such as lasting disinflation or equilibrating the budget. In
fact, this insight is in line with what the policy reform literature distilled from
studying the example of Latin America in the '80s and the '90s.

With the advent of EU accession in 2004, a set of new questions emerged.
First, are Central European emerging economies acceding to the most competitive regulatory system globally possible and available? Second, to what extent
is the continued reliance on copying rather than inventing allowing for managing specific and development related tasks? Third, what lessons can we draw
from studying the Europeanization processes in the incumbent EU countries?
Last but not least, *does enlargement call for more standardization within the EU* (the
level playing field argument would suggest so), or conversely, is it more and
lasting diversity (as the theory of regulatory competition would have it) is the
name of the game for a future European architecture? We shall address these
issues in detail below.

European Governance in Global Perspective

The quality and efficiency of the EU regulatory framework have not been typical subjects for critical analysis during the process of enlargement. On the one
hand, for tactical and substantive reasons, it makes no sense to criticize a club
where we are just about to enter. This is all the more so, if new entrants know
of the major divisions of strategies/opinions among the incumbents, as the
miniscule progress successive inter-governmental conferences (IGC) of Turin,
Nice and the Convention in Laeken have clearly been indicating. Implications
of the intra-European divisions on Iraq have been by no means fatal (Crowe,
2003), however these added to already present disagreements and *mutual
distrust* that emerged since the unlawful boycott of Austria by the 14 members
in 2000– 2001.[8] Therefore, at least at the level of operational policy making, new
members were well advised not to antagonize any of the incumbents, each
with a veto power on allowing applicants, in or rejecting them.

On the other hand, the EU had been more than reserved to admit a group of
nations, whose joint economic significance in terms of additional GDP is below
a potential single candidate, that of Switzerland. This reflects the fact that their
per capita GDP at purchasing power parity is between 48.2 per cent (Latvia),
49.2 (Poland) and 83.3 per cent (Cyprus) of the EU-25 (purchasing power parity in euros in 2005).[9] Moreover, six of the ten applicants are dwarfs – the three
Baltic States, the two Mediterranean islands and Slovenia – have populations

---

[8] More on the legal status and the political background of this event in Merlingen et al (2001).
[9] ECB: *Statistics Pocket Book.* Frankfurt/M, November, 2006, p. 38.

below 2.5 million. Admitting these under unchanged conditions would have offset the workings of EU bureaucracy and would have stretched the problems ensuing from the over-representation of small countries in decision-making to the extreme. Therefore, contrary to the widespread public perception originating in the daily press, it is *not economic matters that delayed enlargement from 1989 to 2004*. Economically, these nations can neither trigger major changes in incumbent EU economy, nor can they pose major threats to the arrangements of the incumbents. They might have caused some trouble to the management of EU funds, that accounted, taken together, 1.1 per cent of the common GDP of the EU-15 in the 1990s. But this is also marginal in macroeconomic terms, indeed.

What, if not the commonly invoked economic argumentation, lays at the heart of delaying Eastward enlargement way beyond any reasonable political and economic timetable? It had been rather the above discussed fear of watering down, a prospect cheerfully embraced by the British administrations, traditionally deeply suspicious of any deepening that goes beyond a free trade zone. The unwillingness to spend more on a fuzzy European project, the diminishing interest in, and enthusiasm for, the European integration initiative, expressed by the median voters in the EU in the past decade were additional rather than constitutive elements. The British exhilaration for enlargement must have been real, since growing diversity is a best recipe against centralization and standardization of any kind – an issue reflected by the Nice Treaty allowing for 'enhanced cooperation' among the more committed members.

By 2004 this game was over. The *deepening project has been implemented*, despite occasional setbacks and the surrounding skepticism. The single currency is a major player in the international arena, also in capital markets, with its market value at the time of writing being back to and often quite above the levels where it had been launched. The tree pillar system, strongly debated on legal grounds in the Convention, has crystallized. During the accession process, Central Europeans adjusted themselves to the stronger player's 'take it or leave it' approach, and agreed to join even EMU from the very outset, true, with a timely derogation. Unlike in previous enlargements, when such new concerns as Trans-alpine transport, or the need to support, from common coffers, sparsely populated areas, have been put on the Community agenda, the new members had to adopt existing rules. Moreover, the Amsterdam and Nice Treaties excluded the previously widely practiced option of opt-outs, when new members could distance themselves from ongoing EU projects in a negotiated fashion, also ex ante. Therefore, by 1997 a strange situation emerged in terms of equal treatment within the EU, since some (incumbent) members continue to enjoy privileges not open to new members.[10] Moreover, no new concerns that would reflect transformation specific or region specific issues were put on the EU agenda.

---

[10] Ireland for instance opted out from common foreign and security policy, the second pillar; Denmark voted down in September 2001 the single currency, and the British are not members of the Schengen Agreement (basically opting out from the third pillar, while not adhering to the crux of the first pillar, the euro).

This might be all very well, should EU regulations represent 'the best of all possible worlds'. With the benefit of hindsight it can perhaps be established that in the institutional vacuum and lack of credibility, having dominated the aftermath of Soviet rule, exacerbated by the disorganization of its formal institutional structure, *unilateral adjustment did have its virtues*. When compared to the broad literature on state failure in developing countries, as well as with similar experiences in the NIS and Southeast Europe, these benefits may be seen as truly positive, not only in terms of a 'second best' line of argumentation. Following that period, however, when the SLIP agenda has been settled, and market institutions and democracy firmly established as part of the social order, some of the fundamentals need to be addressed.

First, international economics has established that major processes in the world take place basically *either on the global scale, or at the local level* (Krugman, 1997). This is in line with our independent analysis and outcomes presented in both preceding chapters. In other words, the regional dimension is being gradually but irreversibly de-emphasized,[11] a feature only underscored by factors we examined in terms of the new economy and the global architecture of finances. This process unfolds, as was documented in the preceding chapter, in regulation, the evolution of standards and norms, media or in the environment and its urgently needed protection. These trends, as can be demonstrated in detail – relying on game theory and institutional insights most elaborately in the bulky volume by Aoki (2001) – produce a *lasting co-existence and competition of economic models*, both at the micro- and at the macro-economic levels.[12]

While the literature – especially in management and finances – tended to favor the Anglo-Saxon model of market-led finance, the series of scandals, starting from Enron and World.com in 2001 and ending with Parmalat in 2004, have shaken this confidence. At the end of the day, nobody guards the guardians, thus basic pieces of information may be manipulated.

The accounting scandals thus relate to some of the fundamental features of 'stock market capitalism', based on the publicity and reliability of information, serving the decisions of millions of economic actors. The quality of the latter have been repeatedly questioned.

Once the lasting variety of economic models is taken as given, the follow-up question of *comparative efficiency* is hard to escape. After the adoption of the new Lisbon Strategy of the EU in March 2005 one does not need to go out at great length demonstrating that *currently existing EU arrangements are not the globally most competitive ones*. The need to de-emphasize traditional redistribution, the urgency to lessen the role of funding for primary branches, the need to roll

[11] This insight is over two decades old, as documented in the book of Inotai (1986, original Hungarian edition in 1980).

[12] The bottom line of his sophisticated argument, summarized in the closing pages is, that while rules are global, knowledge, especially managerial and other decision-relevant knowledge is always contextual and tacit, thus the interchange can by definition *not* produce similar outcomes. A formal proof is also presented, that I will not replicate here.

back welfare reducing protectionism in favor of ICT, flexibility and innovation is very real. Thus at the normative level the Lisbon Strategy seems to apply. However, progress along these lines has proven minimal at best in the first half time. This is best illustrated by the commissioning of former Dutch Premier Wim Kok in the Brussels Council in April 2004 to conduct a study on the causes for this lack of progress. His soul-searching self-assessment as of November 2004 must have alerted public awareness of these major delays.

If we look at the current practice of the EU, as formalized in the 2007–2013 Financial Perspective and the annual financial guidelines, it is hard to oversee the *prevalence of traditions and vested interest politics over the more normative considerations* of the EU, summarized above. About 40 per cent of common spending is still directed to agriculture, where cost-controlling considerations have created an ever growing regulatory intensity, as well as a great incentive to fraud (Brümmer and Köster, 2003, pp. 87–89), due to lack of enforceablility and bureaucratic over-regulation. Moreover, as Imre Fertő (2004) has shown, these policies continue to favor the rich 20 per cent where 80 per cent of the subsidies go; the latter are paid basically by the poor urban population. For the latter food constitutes a major item of outlays. Furthermore, fraud is put regularly to the range of 10 per cent of total outlays of the CAP, basically due to lack of controls and the strong incentive for farmers to manipulate the data. It goes without saying that adopting this extremely complex, but inefficient and often misaligned, scheme might imply only some improvement over current practices of the Central European countries. However, it is unlikely to produce the desired effects, if for no other reason, than because of the limited administrative capacities of the new EU member emerging economies. The oft-voiced (and truly needed) re-orientation of common agricultural policies to environment-friendly and rural development projects is, however, crucially dependent upon the countries' administrative capacities. Regular failure to cope with its stipulations by the incumbent Southern member states already indicate severe potential problems for the future.

One may wonder, at a more general level, if and to what extent the adoption of a *highly complex but quite inefficient scheme* is in the best interest of newcomers. This question is all the more legitimate, since the share of agriculture in GDP is below 4 per cent in the Central European economies, in terms of employment its share is 5–7 per cent except for Poland (where this number is 18 per cent). Is it not, at least in comparative terms, a waste of scarce administrative and financial resources, especially if measured against an equally feasible deregulatory option, like the one adopted in Estonia?

Yet another 40 per cent of community spending is directed to the structural funds. These, at least in theory, aim at fostering regional development by way of overcoming regional income disparities within the European Union. However, empirical studies (Boldrin and Canova, 2001; Midlefart-Kravnik and Overman, 2002) *could not establish any positive correlation between the amounts drawn from EU funds and the relative position of the recipient regions.* On the level of the regions, unlike at the national levels, there is no sign of actual convergence and catching up, postulated by many trade theories.[13] In terms of the individual large projects, the analyses quoted above have established several cases of perverse incentives, of R+D misallocation, and even neglect of trans-border regional co-operation opportunities.

This is a warning sign. But it is even more of a warning sign for new EU members, that are about to reshape their territorial organizational set-up with an eye on prospective major transfers from community coffers. In the case of Poland the territorial reorganization, resulting in territorial units overlapping with NUTS-2 regions in the EU, has already taken place. Empirical surveys of these changes (Baun, 2002; Yoder, 2003) have underscored the formal and ad-hoc nature of these changes. As a consequence these have not produced, according to the analyses quoted above, more efficient and more independent management levels at the new regions. The slogan of multi-level governance has thus remained largely on paper. Ferry (2003) described regional reform in terms of 'Europeanization' in the sense that he gives a detailed account of the Commission being directly involved in shaping outcomes, as one of the bargaining parties. However, as the analysis shows, the limits to such involvement have become very clear at the early stage.

In the case of Hungary, territorial reform has remained largely stagnant. The regions constructed in 1996 are mechanical additions of previously available counties, whereas the 2003 revision, envisaging only 6 regions instead of the 19 counties is only a slightly edited version of the former. This is easy to comprehend, in so far as the entire Hungarian political class is disinterested in a major change that would upset the meticulously circumscribed electoral districts, as defined in 1989. As national legislation is composed of a combination of regional lists and individual constituencies, any change in the territorial setup immediately influences the political landscape at the national level (not least because of the majoritarian element of the system, that rests with the territorial principle). Furthermore management issues, be that of schools, hospitals or of the unemployed, rests with the regional organizations (a feature derived from the Constitution). Thus re-tailoring these would equal to a revolution to millions of people. Moreover, there is no clear vision and rationale, that would mobilize agents of change. Furthermore, there is no economic logic behind the new setup: the Northern shore of Lake Balaton, for instance, continues to be on par with one NUTS region, while the Southern beach belongs to another.[14]

It is less than surprising to observe that political forces, sabotaged any major change and voted down the governmental project in July, 2006 in the new legislation, since the electoral system, both nationally and for municipal power, was organized along county lines in 1990. Diminishing the numbers

[13] In a less radical fashion the formal test by Carrington (2003, pp. 390–391) has also shown the importance of the factor of *location* rather than *policies* shaping the outcomes. This is in line with earlier findings by Soós (2000) establishing the same for Central European countries.

[14] In issues of practical significance these continue to join forces in the Balaton Development Association, covering all those municipalities where the major source of revenue is the big tourist lure of the largest lake in Central Europe.

of MPs and local representatives, or setting up new boundaries for political competition is certainly not a popular task. Moreover, many public administration officials believe that if only 'the bigger the better' is the aim, present counties (themselves merged in 1919 from smaller historic counties) could serve the purpose equally well.

It is worth noting that Hungarian governments of the 1998–2006 period radically diminished the financial room for manoeuvre of the regional organizations Centralization of revenues, particularly of personal income taxes, the planned abolition of local 'industry tax' (*iparűzési adó*) as advocated by the big investors, will further undermine their standing. Meanwhile, a growing number of expensive tasks are being delegated to the regional organs (such as paying out increased wages followed by the arbitrary increase of minimal wages by over 100 per cent in 2001–2003).

The EU, in reality, *has not acted as a catalyst of regionalism*, but as one, that is supportive of retaining the 'gate-keeper function' of central governments. In the case of Hungary the center-left government of 2002–2006 attempted to delegate the management of regional development projects involving EU funding to the newly set up meso-level regions. However, out of administrative convenience, the Commission strongly resisted the idea of dealing with seven (later six) Hungarian projects.

This development seems to lend support to the cautioning words of the leading Polish analyst (Winiecki, 2002, chapter 5) advising Central Europeans not to subordinate to current EU arrangements much too keenly their specific tasks, also in the area of regional development, to the Scylla of maximizing EU funds. While tapping somebody else's resources may seem to be rational from the national/political perspective, *it may well not be the case if these resources are being allocated on a bureaucratic and political logic and end up wasting your own resources as well.* This consideration is only strengthened, if the external funds in question constitute a macro-economically negligible, miniscule share of total investment outlays. In the case of Hungary, the Copenhagen compromise of 2002 envisaged a net transfer of 1.4 bn euros spread across three years, which amounts to 0.5 per cent of GDP, provided all available funds can could drawn.[15] Whereas the sum actually earmarked for Hungary may well be justified, its *limited macroeconomic*, that is developmental *impact is also beyond doubt.*

European Standardization and Developmental Tasks

This is not the place to replicate the multi-dimensional arguments and the literature review proving that, following accession, Central European countries will continue to face a series of developmental tasks. Let us just consider that in 2005 PPP terms the most advanced among the new entrants, Slovenia stands around 81,6 per cent of the average GDP level of EU-25, with Hungary at 61,4

---

[15] The preliminary number is about 85 percent for 2004–2006.

per cent and Latvia barely over 47,2 per cent[16], furthermore as shown in the empirical chapter, convergence is by no means automatic. At the regional level, the studies quoted earlier have *not* shown convergence, not even in the incumbent EU. Thus, if catching up is taken seriously by the new members (in EU terms: real convergence is a priority), the challenge is given.

As already indicated in preceding chapters, the experience of Spain, Greece and Portugal should caution against the mechanistic, simplistic interpretation of convergence theories. Being at a lower level of development though allows for *a potential*, that may or may not be realized, in terms of higher growth rates. In the case of Southern EU members a *slight slowdown* followed EU accession. Introducing sound finances where profligacy used to be the standard, did have a transitory cost in terms of growth (whereas those not paying this entry fees pay in terms of sustainingly slow growth). Therefore, it is *positively misleading to portray EU accession as a universal panacea for the growth problems of the new members.* While improved credibility of institutions, in the long run, may indeed translate into higher growth rates, this potential, however needs to be made use of, for which appropriate side conditions and policies need to be brought about. Thus we may join Daniel Daianu (2003, pp. 196–201) in seeing early signs of *growth fatigue* (also for reasons described in the empirical chapter). We also share his claim that adopting the *acquis* does not replace much more traditional factors of growth as domestic ownership of reforms, high savings rates, rule of law and sizeable inward-FDI.

Let us try to specify these general insights! We have just seen that the major spending channels of the Union, that is the common agricultural policy and the structural funds supporting regional development, together accounting for over five sixth of Community spending, *do not contribute in a trivial manner to the generation of growth and a business friendly environment.* For instance, labor, social regulations and indeed, technological and industrial polices, or even SME supports at the EU level, have improved by little the growth performance of the member states in the past decades. Taking over, for one, overly complex and provenly growth-inhibiting German tax arrangements, with reference either to social justice or to tax harmonization (level playing fields inside the EU), would be simply catastrophic. Therefore, *there is no reason to suppose that by way of mere copying the new EU countries can ensure sustainingly high growth rates in their economies.* The stagnation of several core economies in the EU, particularly in Germany, caution against the idea that a sheer import of 'advanced' policies and institutions will ensure development.

The limitations of the mainstream EU approach, that used to dominate perhaps inevitably the period of accession negotiations, that is the focus on copying, has become a subject of intensive scrutiny in the international literature. Alas, in the context of policy reform, this issue is of immense practical and academic significance. A multi-country study of the World Bank (Pistor et al, 2003) indicated that legal transplants have a tendency *to stagnate for long periods of time*

---

[16] ECB: op. cit. p. 38

in the new environment. Formal law may prove largely irrelevant in a different context. Alternatively there may be little demand for the specific brand of service/conflict resolution offered by these. A good example illustrating the validity of this insight may be the case of EU competition law in Hungary. While it was hoped that taking it over will leave 'no room for anti-competitive practices and policies to survive' (Dieringer, 2001, p. 63), in reality that caused little if any harm to anybody. As will be discussed in some detail in our chapter on 'Privatization and regulation', considerations of competition (that is to create competitive market order) played little if any role in the decisions on how to privatize in the emerging economies. The number of annual cases on mergers and market domination, that ended with the reversal or prohibition of previous market practices has been less than a dozen in the past twenty years. The amounts of fines actually collected could not even cover the operating costs of the managing personnel of the competition agency in any year in the 1990–2002 period, though it has markedly changed since then.

The World Bank study, quoted above, lists such areas as corporate entry and exit, finance and governance, as well as reorganization among the issue areas where transplants have proven to be notoriously ineffective. These happen to be the fields that are of greatest significance for economic adjustment, or in other words, *that create micro-foundations of sustaining growth at the macroeconomic level.*

Studying the mechanisms of Europeanization in the core EU countries has also been indicative of the limitations of the simple copying approach (Schmidt, 2002). Automatic taking over by EU guidelines or policies has been shown to be *the exception,* rather than the rule. The dominant form has been an *interplay* between the guidelines adopted at the EU level, transnationalization processes, domestic policy priorities and traditions, that all acting together shape the final outcome. France, for that matter, by making its ritual references to the considerations of *service publique,* could sabotage most of the liberalizing initiatives in a variety of sectors over the past twenty years, and not only in the energy sector. Reference to the public interest covered up protection of incumbents rather than any serious consideration at the macroeconomic level, be that efficiency or security of supply. By contrast, the British could conduct much more transnationalizing/globalizing policies than the wording of the EU stipulations could have called for, or even allowed for. This insight is likely to apply to the new entrants as well.

EU regional policy usually presupposes the pre-existence of *a strong meso-level management organ* at the level of NUTS-2 regions, as discussed above. This has indeed been the case in, say, Finland, but much less in Greece or Portugal. This circumstance alone may account for most of the paradoxical outcome in which Finland could rely much more on EU funding than Greece in alleviating its regional difficulties. This renders the cohesion philosophy (and the reference to solidarity) in the EU an empty word. As seen in the detailed studies, it has been *administrative capacity* – usually directly related to the higher level of development – rather the idea of *solidarity,* that is helping the poorer more, that has been dominant. It is hardly by coincidence that Commission initiatives to re-focus regional spending on the poorest regions only were flatly rejected for the 2007-13 period, despite the obvious needs originating from Bulgarian and Romanian membership.

Analyzing the Hungarian case highlighted the lack of empowerment of local organizations and municipalities, as well as the weak linkages, especially in terms of R+D, that characterize old industrial districts (Szalavetz, 2002). Remedying both of these ills requires national level treatment. Although, as the author of the above cited analysis notes, this would be in line with EU guidelines, however *it is not the primary reason* why decentralization, empowerment and improving the R+D linkages in old industrial districts need to be improved.[17] It is the need for organic local and regional development, the need to counteract agglomeration effects, finally the territorial component of democracy and equity that would amply justify similar measures.

Meanwhile, if we adopt the concept of *efficient membership* developed by Nicolaides (2003), then the maximizing of the national benefits from EU membership would call for reforms that go actually *deeper than required by the Union*: such as the modernization of public services, strengthening the capacity for policy implementation, improving the process of *impact assessment*, currently hardly in existence in most new EU member states. Setting up the Office for Controlling Subsidies has remained mostly a formality (definitely in Hungary in the 1999–2006 period).[18] Here again, EU membership in triggering these reforms may serve as a politically skillful, yet *complementary argument supportive of core considerations*. The latter relate to the need to be accountable when using public funds, to have an effective public administration, transparency, or the arguments that may or may not be invoked for further reduction of public dues and the related expenditure cuts.

This leads us to the next question, namely if, and to what extent, experience in the present European Union implies and requires a tendency toward institutional and *policy uniformity* (in areas like tax rates, or provision of social services). This is a fundamental assumption of many policy suggestions, made domestically and internationally alike, favoring shortcut solutions. Also, in the practice of policy-making there is a tendency to justify each and every step, especially non-popular ones, with references to the 'requirements of the EU', also in areas where the Community has no competence. For instance, increasing value added tax rates in Hungary, or joining the so-called Bologna Process in (standardizing) higher education (at a low level and irrespective of labor market ramifications), this reference has been used by the Hungarian Government in justifying its options.

---

[17] The Dutch experience for instance has shown that municipalities often find the acquisition of EU funds burdensome, too costly in terms of time and administrative duties, furthermore disadvantageous the practice of retroactive financing. Retroactive punishment once funds are not used according to EU priorities makes reliance on these more of a burden than a blessing. Interest in raising EU money has been on the steady decrease over the past decade in the Netherlands.

[18] Voszka (2006, p. 16) notes that most subsidies were not under the Ministry of Finance jurisdiction anyway – a circumstance we continue to find ironic and hard to square with the idea of transparency, accountability and constitutional control.

Europeanization:
Is There a Move to a Single Standard Solution?

There is no easy answer to this truly fundamental question, raised in the subtitle. It is hard to overcome the impression, that at least at the normative level, a sort of European social market economy model does exist. It is often contrasted to a sort of American brand of 'unbridled capitalism'. Representatives of social policy analysis, as well as those studying the ever thicker body of EU environmental legislation, often present their views in unambiguous terms on what constitutes a European standard and what does not.

In the early years of transformation this all-encompassing vision of 'European standards' played a useful role as *political shorthand*. Such standards implied, among other things, calls for regular and free elections, limited governmental domination of the public media, civilian control over the armed forces and intelligence agencies, or social safety nets at the times when full employment ceased to exist and double digit rates of unemployment sustained.

With the first things of transformation – stabilization, liberalization and much of privatization – settled, however, this reference tended to be diluted, or conversely, invoked for covering intellectual laziness. In one of the most frequently voiced claims the trend toward deregulation and privatization makes, allegedly, all economies more similar, dismantling social protection. Accordingly, convergence takes place around the American model of 'cowboy capitalism' or 'casino capitalism' that needs to be counteracted, according to this line, by more global interventionism. This lays at the heart of various global governance projects, especially ones advocating new financial architecture and global policy agencies, over and above a strengthened IMF (cf. e.g. Nayyar, ed., 2002). In the European discourse the EU is often portrayed as a bastion of defense against the cold winds of 'globalization' (Krizsán and Zentai, eds, 2003).

Empirical analyses have never lent support to these claims that tend to spread via repetition rather than via rigorous empirical testing. Empirical surveys of regulation regimes in the OECD have found that, in contrast, following privatization and deregulation, *national systems have actually become more dissimilar*. They also have found entry barriers to be at the heart of lagging productivity and lagging innovations in the ICT intensive industries of Europe (Nicoletti and Scrapetta, 2003).

A broad summary of a multiyear project on how EU level regulation influences change in the national models in the long run, has found *comprehensive interactions rather than top down motions* in the process (Thatcher, 2002). Accordingly, it is ideational considerations (such as what is perceived as efficient and equitable), the strength of interest representation, as well as institutional traditions that constitute an interface. The interaction of these, rather than any idea constructed at a desktop, that mold actual economic systems in Europe. Thus historic coincidences, compromises and many other shape regulatory regimes, not just abstract considerations of various sorts (one of them being in conformity to EU standards). With moving away from public ownership these *interfaces become less trivial and more differentiated* in the meantime. All embracing central regulation becomes less frequent, thus regional and sectoral specifics become more varied.

Similar findings emerge from the comparative analysis of social security systems. Though many countries embarked upon the partial privatization of a variety of services, this has almost nowhere amounted to an overall retreat of the welfare state, expressed in welfare provisions as a percentage in GDP. Rather a more integrated, financially and also socially much better controlled set of provisions has emerged.[19] Variations are explained by the institutional heritage, as well as by country specific socio-political constellations, and innovations addressing these. Bahle (2003) also concludes that *growing diversity undermines broad theories of the welfare state* and the related *over-generalizations* dominant in the policy literature. In concrete terms there is hardly any sign of survival of the welfare states in an unchanged fashion, nor of their 'withering away' as a consequence of 'neo-liberal reforms' and 'globalization'.

Should these conclusions hold, these were certainly to imply that the diversity of interests and preferences in a pre-enlargement EU had already been so broad and diverse, that the customary *attempt at standardization* must be seen as *principally mis-conceived.* Save for bureaucratic convenience, there is no ground to accept the 'level playing field' argument behind the standardization ideas more than to subscribe to a Ptolemaian view of the world: both look evident, while being plainly wrong.

In this view, the enlargement of the EU by another twelve members *does not pose a qualitatively new challenge.* Rather, it just reinforces previous insights about the virtues of abiding the rules of any game (instead of trying to gain yet more goodies by way of intergovernmental bargains). It reinforces the insight derived from the theory of regulatory competition that the EU should aspire to become an *additional rather than the single* regulatory frame. Roger van den Bergh (2000, pp. 451–459) provides examples from environmental law, competition law, corporate law and consumer protection to operationalize his concept. Full harmonization, in this approach, should serve as *ultimum remedium* only, for competing legislations are likely to meet a much larger set of preferences than any single framework.

This means nothing less than that in the long enlargement process *an important opportunity has been missed.* Preparing for enlarged membership could well have triggered those long overdue reforms within the EU that could have paved the way to rolling back purely tradition-based redistribution. These could have re-focused community spending *exclusively on matters of common concern,* such as peace keeping, control of external borders, or improvement of transit between the member states. This were entirely feasible if competing ongoing projects, serving no more than 'buying in' certain reluctant partners would simply be discontinued. The room for this, in both major spending areas, of agriculture and regional development, is sizeable, indeed.

---

[19] Means testing at unemployment and other social benefits has become widespread in Britain and Sweden under the social democratic governments. Likewise targeting of welfare programs, introducing charges for previous entitlements, private contributions to pensions were introduced in Holland, Germany, Spain and Greece.

In this genre, the challenge of enlargement is a mere quantitative one, in which *principles and qualities of incumbent EU-15 did not need to be adjusted. Policies,* however, reflecting not only the fundamentals, but also tactical matters, are still in need to be *brought in line with enhanced diversity.* Since there is nobody to foot the bill of meeting claims based on mechanistic extrapolation of past inefficient practices, the calls for re-nationalization of some of the farming and regional support will be hard to ward off in the period of following the 2009/2010 overhaul of expenditure as agreed in December 2005 Brussels Council.

Toward Multi-Level Governance – By Default?

What has been expounded until now, sets clear limits to the continuation of European integration based on sectoral policies and centralized management, as it has emerged since the 1950s. This model was based on the Franco-German administrative tradition and the contemporary mentality of planning centrally everything that was deemed as 'strategic'. Normative and practical limitations to this concept have become obvious[20] by the time of adoption of the Maastricht Treaty at latest (in 1992). Adoption of this Treaty, at least in its original form, has been rejected by the Danish electorate. Special opt-outs (from monetary union and common justice and home affairs) needed to be secured in order to get it passed. Likewise the British were partly forced (by the pound crisis of 1992) and partly volunteered (through opt-outs) to stay out from the most important institutional innovations of the day. *Thereby the idea of two speed Europe has become a reality, and not only in policy practice, but also in terms of institutional design.* The project of the single market with a single currency would have called for a series of deregulating reforms. These, however, have remained limited at best. Even in the area of labor market reform, that has been technically most closely correlated to the mechanism of the single currency, non-members have been outperforming the members of the euro-zone (van Poech and Borghijs, 2001).

It is interesting to see that some current EMU members, not having a strong tradition of fiscal prudence, like Spain, or non-EMU members, like Sweden, Denmark encounter no difficulties in meeting the Maastricht/SGP criteria, while other core members, having fought for the single currency, do. This insight is indicative of the overall importance of finding the *nationally appropriate, different ways of delivering the same* – a point often raised in labor and environmental legislation. The reason, as documented in the articles quoted above is straightforward: good results have been attained by incumbent (old) EU-12 members through a variety of ways, quite in line with the EU principle of subsidiarity.[21]

---

[20] More on this point in the inaugural lecture of Tibor Palánkai (1997).

[21] For instance labor markets have been deregulated in Britain, whereas the 'polder model' in the Netherlands applies a variety of active labor market instruments (such as supporting part time work via tax incentives) to achieve high levels of employment.

This implies that while new members should continue to improve their ability to apply the *acquis*, this *is no longer the main focus of their institution building exercise*. Once we appreciate that European policies, in reality, are half way between merely influencing and full emulation, moreover that common EU policies tend to be a composite of the constituents (Padgett, 2003), it is trivial that new members will continue to have specific tasks. This relates not only to their lower level of development, but also to the culturally and historically conditioned institutional and policy arrangements.

First, they should be capable of coming up with conceptual innovations, instead of sticking to the outlived arrangements (that seem to work to their benefit in the short run). For instance, while short term fiscal and PR interest would call for sticking to the current, rigid and outdated arrangements of the CAP, they could contribute to the elaboration of such concepts of rural development at the EU level, that could take account of their concerns about additional needs of investment in physical infrastructure and education. Likewise, it could be easiest to blame 'Brussels' for every unpopular measure, whereby they could and actually managed in 2002–2006, foster hostility towards anything relating to EU.

Second, they should learn how to get their priorities through, even when policies do not center around redistributing macro-economically insignificant amounts. *Third*, new members may have to learn to much better co-ordinate the activities of their domestic agencies in formulating what is, at the end of the day, their properly re-defined national interest to be represented in Brussels and Strasbourg. *Fourth*, they have to learn a new culture of co-operative games, since each of them is simply too small to be relevant in bringing about major EU decisions on its own (with the exception of Poland). The fact that the period of unilateral adjustment is over and the room for representing national priorities emerged do call for *innovative solutions, not only for the extrapolation of practices based on low politics, as is the case with the old members*. Rather, the new members are well advised to contribute to further reforms of established EU structures and policies, among others in advocating the case of further enlargement, good governance and improved enforcement (more on that also in Ágh, 2004).

With the size of centrally redistributed funds, as a percentage of GDP shrinking, and the number of claimants rapidly growing, the *EU policies will become growingly decentral*. This will enhance the political and interest articulating role of the regions, as well as of corporations and chambers and other lobby groups, as well as the increasingly local media. This follows both from the secular trend toward decentralization in general, and from the marginality of financial flows that are available via EU-level bargaining in particular. Such forms of co-operation as the Euroregions, public-private partnership in financing the development of physical infrastructure, common training programs for graduate and post-graduate institutions, the emergence of the European research area are among the forms that will be the name of the game in the enlarged EU. By contrast, such *traditional issues* as farm produce quotas and prestige projects of the central state administration *will gradually be crowded out of the policy domain*. If for no other reason, by default. Following the repeated warnings of the six net contributors on capping the common spending at 1.045 per cent of GNI in the Brussels Compromise of December 2005 does not allow for the extension of grand projects of various sorts, already in 2007–2013[22] unless the latter are *nationally financed*. The latter has, indeed, been a long established practice in environmental policy, justice and home affairs, as well as in the common foreign and security policy domain. The latter three items are likely to become the defining ones for overall EU policies in the years and decades to come.

This implies that new members should be explicitly *warned against transforming their territorial administration and their rural development schemes or higher education establishments with keeping an eye on availability of EU funds*. This seems to be a very real danger in all new members except for the two Mediterranean islands of Cyprus and Malta. By emulating the inefficient practices of the present period, and misdirecting scarce resources along bureaucratic, rather than efficiency criteria, the new members could *positively diminish their contribution to a future, more competitive Europe*. The fundamental insight in this respect is that the nation state will be though more transparent and less constraining, however its dominance will *not* give way to various amorphous schemes of regionalism (Nolte, 2006).

References

ÁGH, A. (2001): The Euro-capacity of small ECE states. *Central European Political Science Review,* vol. 2. no. 5. pp. 98–117.

ÁGH, A. (2004): Hungarian accesion to the EU in a Central European context. In: ÁGH, A., ed.: *Europeanization and Regionalization: Hungary's Accession.* Budapest: a book published by the Hungarian Center for Democracy Studies, pp. 7–42.

AOKI, M. (2001): *Toward a Comparative Institutional Analysis.* Cambridge/Mass. – London: The MIT Press.

BAHLE, Th. (2003): The changing institutionalization of social services in England and Wales, France and Germany: Is the welfare state on the retreat? *Journal of European Social Policy,* vol. 13. no. 1. pp. 5–20.

BAUN, M. (2002): EU regional policy and the candidate states: Poland and the Czech Republic. *Journal of European Integration,* vol. 24. no. 3. pp. 261–280.

BERGH, R. van der (2000): Towards an institutional legal framework for regulatory competition in Europe. *Kyklos,* vol. 53. no. 4. pp. 435–466.

BOLDRIN, M. and CANOVA, F. (2001): Inequality and convergence in Europe's regions: Reconsidering European regional policies. *Economic Policy,* no. 32. (April) pp. 205–245.

BRÜMMER, B. and KÖSTER, U. (2003): EU enlargement and governance of the CAP. *Intereconomics,* vol. 38. no. 2. pp. 86–94.

CARRINGTON, A. (2003): A divided Europe? Regional convergence and neighborhood spillover effects. *Kyklos,* vol. 56. no. 3. pp. 381–394.

COLLINS, S. and RODRIK, D. (1991): *Eastern Europe and the Soviet Union in the World Economy.* Washington D. C.: Institute of International Economics.

---

[22] For a widely optimistic reading of these opportunities cf. Terták (2006), who does not even consider the consequences of fiscal retrenchments already adapted at the time of writing.

CROWE, B. (2003): A common European foreign policy after Iraq? *International Affairs*, vol. 79. no. 3. pp. 553–546

DAIANU, D. (2003): Is catching-up possible in Europe? In: KOLODKO, G. W., ed.: *Emerging Market Economies: Globalization and Development*. Aldershot/UK and Burlington/VT/USA: Ashgate Publishing Company, pp. 187–204.

DIERINGER, J. (2001): Wettbewerbspolitik im Transformationsprozess. In: STURM, R. – DIERINGER, J. – MÜLLER, M. eds: *Rediscovering Competition*. Opladen: Leske&Budrich and Budapest: HVG/Orac, pp. 51–66.

DIETZ, R. (1991): The role of Western capital in the transition to the market: A system's theoretical perspective. In: CSABA, L. ed.: *Systemic Change and Stabilization in Eastern Europe*. Aldershot/UK and Brookfield/Vermont, USA: Dartmouth Publishing Co., pp. 103–123.

FERRY, M. (2003): The EU and the recent regional reform in Poland. *Europe-Asia Studies*, vol. 55. no. 7. pp. 1097–1116.

FERTŐ, I. (2004): 'Agrárproblémák és agrárpolitika a modern gazdaságban' (Farm problems and policies in the contemporary economy) – habilitation thesis defended at the Faculty of Economics, University of Debrecen, April.

INOTAI, A. (1986): *Regional Integrations in the New World Economic Environment*. Budapest: Akadémiai Kiadó.

KRIZSÁN, A. and ZENTAI, V. eds: (2003): *Reshaping Globalization: Multilateral Dialogues and New Policy Initiatives*. New York and Budapest: Central European University Press.

KRUGMAN, P. (1997): *Pop Internationalism*. Cambridge/Mass. and London: The MIT Press.

KULCSÁR, K. ed.: (1998): *Az integráció: történelmi kihívások és válaszkísérletek*. (Integration: Historic challenges and attempts at answering these). Budapest: a book published in the series 'Europe Studies' by the Institute of Political Science of the Hungarian Academy of Sciences.

MERLINGEN, M. – MUDDE, C. – SEDELMEYER, U. (2001): The right and the righteous? European norms, domestic politics and the sanctions against Austria. *Journal of Common Market Studies*, vol. 39. no. 1. pp. 364–394.

MIDLEFART-KRAVNIK, H. and OVERMAN, H. (2002): De-location and European integration: Is structural spending justified? *Economic Policy*, no. 35. (October) pp. 323–358.

NAYYAR, D. ed.: (2002): *Governing Globalization*. Oxford etc.: Oxford University Press for WIDER.

NICOLAIDES, Ph. (2003): Preparing for EU membership: The paradox of doing what the EU does not require to do. Maastricht: European Institute for Public Administration, *Working Papers*, April – available online in: *Euractiv*, 11 April.

NICOLETTI, G. and SCRAPETTA, S. (2003): Regulation, productivity and growth: OECD evidence. *Economic Policy*, no. 36. (April) pp. 11–72.

NUNNENKAMP, P. (1995): Wirtschaftsreformen in Entwicklungslaendern – Anreizprobleme, Glaubwürdigkeitsdefizite und die Erfolgschancen umfassender Reformen. *Die Weltwirtschaft*, no. 1. pp. 99–116.

NOLTE, P. (2006): Shifting boundaries: the rise and fall of European nation-states in comparative perspective. *Zeitschift für Staats- und Europawissenschaften*, vol. 4. no. 1. pp. 9–27.

PADGETT, S. (2003): Between synthesis and emulation: EU policy transfer in the power sector. *Journal of European Public Policy*, vol. 10. no. 2. pp. 227–245.

PALÁNKAI, T. (2004): *Az európai integráció gazdaságtana*. (Economics of European integration) 4th edition. Budapest: Aula Publishing House.

PALÁNKAI, T. (1997): Az európai integráció mérésének néhány elméleti és gyakorlati problémája. (Some theoretical and practical problems in measuring European integration). *Jogtudományi Közlöny*, no. 2. pp. 3–17.

PALÁNKAI, T. (2005): Európai egyesülés – integrációelmélet (European unification and integration theory). *Magyar Tudomány*, vol. 165. no. 10. pp. 1221–1235.

PISTOR, K – KEINAN, Y. – KLEINMEISTERKAMP, P. – WEST, M. (2003): Evolution of corporate law and the transplant effect: Lessons from six countries. *World Bank Research Observer*, vol. 18. no. 1. pp. 89–112.

van POECH, A. – BORGHIJS, A. (2001): EMU and labor market reform: Needs, incentives, realizations. *World Economy*, vol. 26. no. 10. pp. 1327–1347.

PORTES, R. (1991): Introduction. In: The Path of Reform in Central and Eastern Europe. *European Economy*, special issue, no. 45. pp. 1–23.

SCHMIDT, V. (2002): Europeanization and the mechanics of economic policy adjustment. *Journal of European Public Policy*, vol. 9. no. 6. pp. 894–912.

SINN, H.-W. (1999): EU enlargement, migration and lessons from German unification. London: *CEPR Discussion Papers*, no. 2174 (October).

SOÓS, K. A. (2000): Structural upgrading of manufacturing under transition: A comparative analysis of eight countries. In: BARA, Z. and CSABA, L. eds: *Small Economies' Adjustment to Global Tendencies*. Budapest: Aula Publishing. Co. for the European Association for Comparative Economic Studies, pp. 245–274.

SUTELA, P. (2004): *The Russian Market Economy*. Helsinki: Kikimora Publications.

SZALAVETZ, A. (2002): European policy lessons in the process of regional transformation in Hungary. *Acta Oeconomica*, vol. 52. no. 2. pp. 205–219.

TERTÁK, E. (2006): About the EU financial perspective for the years 2007–2013. *Public Finance Quarterly*, vol. 51. no. 2. pp. 152–173.

THATCHER, M. (2002): Analyzing regulatory reform in Europe. *Journal of European Public Policy*, vol. 9. no. 6. pp. 859–872.

VOSZKA, É. (2006): Uniós támogatások – a redisztribúció új szakasza? (Do EU supports trigger a new wave of the redistribution?), *Külgazdaság*, vol. 50. no. 6. pp 8–30.

WINIECKI, J. (2002): *Transition Economies and Foreign Trade*. London: Routledge.

YODER, J. (2003): Decentralization and regulation after communism: Administrative and territorial reforms in Poland and the Czech Republic. *Europe-Asia Studies*, vol. 55. no. 2. pp. 263–286.

8. A NON-STABILITY AND ANTI-GROWTH PACT FOR EUROPE? AN UPDATE ON THE BASICS[1]

It is common knowledge that sustainable growth requires sound public finances. Furthermore the single currency requires a coordinated fiscal framework. Still, this framework has come under increasing criticism, both in the academe and in policy making in the 2000s.

What Is at Stake?

The first years of the 2000s have produced an interesting *puzzle*. On the one hand, the single currency has proven to be a success story. It could replace 12 national currencies, first as an accounting unit, later also in the cash form. The switchover was managed without major derailments, the *upsurge of inflation*, feared and forecast by many, *has not materialized*. This is an established statistical fact, contrary to widespread popular claims, amplified by media reports.[2] The decentralized system of the European System of Central Banks has been functioning well (for detailed empirical evidence cf. ECB, 2004). The single currency has become a global player, else the gains in value against the US dollar (and a faster growing US economy) could not be explained. Having started from a parity of 1.17 US $, the value of the single currency first plummeted to a low of 85 cents, then regaining strength to over 1.15 $ by the fall of 2003 and surged to 1.30 by January–March 2004, then fluctuating between 1.20 and 1.30 until October 2006, for about three years in a world of floating. Meanwhile, the headline inflation target of the ECB, though narrowly missed in quantitative terms in each year, but were by and large attained with inflation never exceed-

---

[1] Useful comments by J. de Haan, G. Oblath and G. Peli as well as of I. Hetényi and É. Voszka are appreciated, with the usual caveats.

[2] The sizeable price adjustment, experienced by any traveller, is better explained by the potential created by mass tourism. While travelling, few of us have time and energy to be involved in arbitraging, such as visiting suburban shopping malls, while spending a day or two abroad. Thus, sooner rather than later any price may go in downtown shops and restaurants, that, however, would be wrong to equate with the overall price level of the host country (which is a macro-variable).

ing 2.3 per cent, with 2.1 per cent in 2000, 2.3 per cent in 2001 and 2002 and reaching 2.1 per cent in 2003 2.1 in 2004, 2.2 in 2005 and 2.3 in the first half of 2006 (source: ECB: *Statistics Pocket Book*, Frankfurt, June, p. 36). This has been achieved, despite major international economic disturbances, such as the burst of the IT bubble, the accounting scandals, the new hike of oil prices, the terrorist attacks on the US and the war in Iraq, just to name a few. Thus in essence the promise that the euro will be 'just as strong as the Deutsche Mark' has surprisingly, but undoubtedly, been heeded.

Moreover, as von Hagen and Hoffmann (2003, pp. 24–25) explain, ECB policies have *not created a contractionary bias*, nor did these result in a liquidity trap or higher unemployment. Finally, it also has not brought about increasing economic divergence due to inflation differentials according to the evidence provided by these two authors. Contrary to frequent claims, the ECB has been one of the *more open and accountable organs* of the Union, with their regular public assessments of the situation and regular reporting to the European Parliament. In a recent comparison based on nine indicators (Eijfinger – Gerraats, 2006 , p. 18) the Bank was found to be as transparent and communicative as its American counterpart, the FED.

Against this background, it may be surprising to observe, that there are *few less popular* phenomena in Europe than the single currency. The rejection of the single currency by the Danish referendum in September 2001 was followed up by the Swedes in the fall of 2003. Here the vast majority of votes casted against the euro was breaking news, and analysts tended to see this as a signal of overall dissatisfaction with the outcomes of the entire European project of deepening integration over and above a free trade zone, that is all what the single currency stands for.[3]

Yet another puzzle follows up with the enlargement of the European Union. While two of the richest members of the EU have sustained their opt-out from the monetary union, the new members are obliged, first by the Amsterdam and later by the Nice Treaties, to adopt the single currency. This measure, seen widely as a measure of self-defense by incumbents, implies that the 'if' is not a matter of choice, only the 'when' in terms of joining the euro-zone. From among the new member countries, Estonia, Lithuania and Slovenia have adopted the fast track, by entering the ERM-2 regime in June 2004 and stick to it, despite their debacle in 2006. By contrast, the cautious Polish and Hungarian governments were happy to give up any deadline in 2006. Anyway, the difference seems to be more of sequence and tactics than of strategic nature: in forseeable time period new EU member-states will become full members in EMU. Thus the question emerges if, and to what degree, *this implies a cost in terms of growth.*

The *puzzle* emerges in two basic ways. First, if frontrunners, the Paris–Berlin axis joined more recently in by Rome and London, prove unfit or unwill-

---

[3] Risse (2003) explains in political science terms how the single currency plays a major role in bringing about previously non-existing forms of European identity.

185

ing to meet the criteria of the single currency, why should it be a good idea for the less developed newcomers to adopt it? And second, even if it were a good idea per se, *how will nominal and real convergence relate to one another*? Is there not a danger of stagnation or slow growth, that will bring about incessant calls for transfers, as evidenced by Eastern Germany?

In the following, we shall try to address if and to what degree the Stability and Growth Pact (from now on SGP), which is formally not part of the Treaty on the European Union, only one of its annexes,[4] is indeed a straightjacket on *the economic dynamism of the incumbents*. All the more so, since new members joined the EU with a timely derogation, rather than with an opt-out. Thus their non-adherence to SGP can be temporal only. Moreover, missing the targets of the SGP does trigger *a review procedure*, first by the Commission and then by the Ecofin Council of finance ministers.

This is based on a binding legal obligation, derived from terms of their accession treaties, of the new members, entails components of assessment and discretion. It does contain a possibility of a public reprimand, even though fines specified in the excessive deficit procedure of the SGP are not yet applied on non-euro members. These procedures of 'naming and shaming' have proven efficient in triggering corrections in Portugal and Ireland and even launching reforms in Germany. *Ex post control of delivery*, rather than promulgating vague promises and declarations of good intent is the name of the game. These features do not allow, as much of the political class in Central Europe tended to, interpret the SGP as 'just another nuisance from Brussels'.

In the following, therefore, we shall investigate if the narrow interpretation of monetary stability will slow down the catch-up process in the East. Finally we shall look into the question *if the Stability and Growth Pact is a forward-looking arrangement*, or a matter of the past that, under ideal conditions needs to be fundamentally revamped or even scrapped entirely. While in this chapter we try to understand the logic of the *original* European coordinated *fiscal framework*, in the *next chapter* we shall analyze what the reinterpretation of 2005 implies for economic theory and policy.

The Stability and Growth Pact and the Single Currency

It is not the place to reiterate the emergence of European monetary integration and the way the 'monetarist' model prevailed over the model of the 'economists', i.e. the Keynesians (cf. e.g. Pentecost, 2001). The bottom line of the story is a process of decades long *learning by doing*. The first attempt at monetary integration, the Werner Plan collapsed with the abolition of Bretton Woods and the ensuing international financial instability. The second attempt, the snake

[4] Since the basic document of the EU, including SGP, is freely and easily accessible in printed and online forms (eg. on the site *EurActive*), and my text is not one of legal analysis, I took the liberty of not citing these word by word, also in the current edition. Checking the validity of commonly available references should not pose a problem to any reader.

and related quasi-fixed parities stumbled on the consequences of the second oil price hike. Finally, ERM-1 collapsed when an overvalued lira and pound had to leave the system by 1992.

To cut a long story short, the reasons for the non-sustainability of attempts at monetary integration rested with the *divergent national economic priorities* that resulted in different inflation rates, thus in regular exchange rate realignments. While this happened, and theory tended to condone lax practices, the pegging by small economies like Austria and Finland, but also the Netherlands and later also in Belgium, gained acceptance. The bottom line of their approach was the policy of *hard currency* and importing stability via *fixed exchange rates*.

Let us underscore: it has not been the theory of economic integration, nor abstract theorizing on the optimal financial institutions, that resulted in such an arrangement. Rather it has been a long period of *trials and errors* that ended up in the practice of the hard currency policy. Thus the conversion to 'monetary orthodoxy' has *not* been, as much of the political science literature would have it, an outcome of adjustment to external pressures, for shorthand, 'the straightjacket of Maastricht'.[5] On the contrary, the latter emerged on the basis of *gradual and basically self-imposed adoption* of solid fiscal and monetary practices (for a description of the system cf. ECB, 2004). Likewise the strengthening of Franco-German relationship allowed for a *climate of trust* in which de facto subordination of French – and later Spanish and Italian – monetary policy to that of the Bundesbank could be formalized as a monetary union.

Let us also highlight, that this conversion can hardly be attributed to *any school of economic theory* (more on that in Issing et al, 2001, chapters 1–3). On the one hand, the collapse of Bretton Woods allowed for the testing of floating rates, an option that has always been advocated by monetarists. This has indeed enhanced the sovereign nature of the conduct of macroeconomic policies. But the latter is precisely the underlying assumption of Keynesianism, that was modelling policy-making in the frame of a basically closed national economy. Hardly surprisingly, the 70s saw a resurgence of Keynes-inspired macroeconomic adjustment programs, trying to preserve full employment and avoid painful structural adjustments.

Meanwhile, it was precisely this feature, the lack of co-ordination among macroeconomic policies that *undermined* European integration in the '70s and '80s. Domestically the emergence of stagflation reminded policy-makers and the public of the limitations of anti-cyclical policies when faced with a structural

---

[5] Surveying the international literature on how rules can replace discretion Benczes (2004. pp. 25–29) shows that adopting common numerical targets, rather than common budgetary procedures, let alone common fiscal institutions, is the only option that is in line with the principle of subsidiarity. Particularly the third option would equal to fiscal federalism, an idea rejected vigorously already in the debates on the EU Constitution, thus it clearly lacks political foundations. By the same token, as common numerical targets allow for the difference of expenditure and revenue structures, dissimilar procedures and diverse policy platforms, thus in reality this is *the least constraining option* on national sovereignty. Differently put: this is a *minimal* version of any 'straightjacket' aimed at insitutionalizing fiscal sustainability that is available in the political economy literature.

challenge. This experience gave birth to the insight that monetary stability, supported by fiscal prudence is *a key achievement* and precisely this is the road to successful adjustment and *sustaining* growth. With the conversion of the Mitterrand Administration in France to the policy line of *franc fort* the policy debate had been settled. Only Greece, for a while, and Portugal, also for a while, experimented with demand management – both with a major failure (Nagy, 1999; Boltho, 2000).

Once France, and subsequently Spain, and in the '90s even Italy decided *autonomously on pegging* their respective currencies to the German Mark, the idea of monetary integration became feasible. If for no other reason than the difference between mutually pegged and unified/single currency became *notional*, nominal. The true difference, that does matter, is *irreversibility*. There is no exit from the single currency. *The road back to old fashioned demand management policies has been blocked*. It happened perhaps because it could be foreseen, that in intellectual terms, the moving back of the shuttle from stability oriented policies to more growth orientation had become inevitable by the late '90s.

When the introduction of the single currency was already a close eventuality, and the 1997 Amsterdam Treaty strengthened the political component – the three pillar structure – of the EU, there was some fear that some members, then mostly the Club Med, would not meet the Maastricht criteria. The latter were seen by some as too much tailored to the voluntary and already established Franco-German-Benelux policy coordination. The SGP established *procedures* and *quantitative targets* in order to allow the market participants (globally) and voters (locally) *to check* if and to what degree the government of each EU member state sticks to its guns. The Broad Economic Policy Guidelines in general, and the medium-term stability Convergence Plans[6] in fiscal terms, should reflect publicly and in quantitative terms the medium term orientation *and in detail the actual conduct of national economic policies*, that may or may not overlap with general policy statements and declarations of intent. In his generally critical account of EMU Charles Wyplosz (2006) also highlights the *political economy nature* of both the single currency and of SGP. In the course of its formation, both the window of opportunity considerations and political *practicalities* have clearly dominated over any *academic* consideration. For this reason the name of both arrangements in the academe has always been much worse than actual delivery would have justified it.

It is a bizarre, though by no means entirely surprising, turn of history that Germany, once having advocated the SGP the most, fell short of living up with the quantitative targets set by the SGP. Given that the first Schröder Government did little to address the cumulated institutional rigidities of the German economy – termed *Reformstau* in the country (more on that in Franz, 2003) – the slowdown of activity and the growing financing needs of the state exploded the fiscal 'straightjacket'. Similarly, the once overheated Irish econo-

---

[6] Having joined the single currency member-states no longer elaborate Convergence Plans but Stability Plans, reporting basically on the same macro-variables. I am indicted to one of my reviewers, Dr. T. Halm, who drew our attention to this important distinction in his meticulous assessment of the Hungarian edition in: *Public Finance Quarterly*, vol. 2. no. 3 (2006), p. 378.

my has had to live temporarily with higher inflation than envisaged by Maastricht, once the Balassa–Samuelson effect is taken into account.[7] However, it was not the inflation criterion, but the *pro-cyclical policies* of the Irish government that triggered the public reprimand by the EU Commission in 2001. This may remind us of the fact that fixing exchange rates, especially in small open economies is an act of *dirigisme*, which may well run counter to the exigencies confronting these. *However, economic theory is split in evaluating how important this consideration may be.* In single but diverse economic spaces as the USA, or in any larger country, significant growth differences may emerge among regions applying a single currency (thus not having separate exchange rates).

On the other hand, the Balassa–Samuelson effect, if relevant at all under the arrangements of ERM-2, may well be a concern of the *very quickly catching up* economies, not those on similar levels of development and with integrated economies, forming an optimal currency area à la Mundell, as the core EU has been, less Italy. Therefore neither this, nor the much discussed asymmetric shocks, posed a big policy challenge for the euro-zone. The latter is explained by the fact that the EU is composed of basically diversified economies, thus the very problem of asymmetric shocks that would need a remedy, if capital flows were not free, simply has not arisen (Horvath, 2003).

If our starting point is macroeconomic statistics rather than the current policy debate, it is hard to find reasons to be deeply dissatisfied with the SGP. On the one hand, we find member countries like Spain, Austria, the Netherlands or Finland, or even Britain and Denmark, for that matter, that easily met the criteria and grew above the EU average – a mere 1.7 p.c.p.a. for the 2001-2005 period (according to ECB: *Statistics Pocket Book*, Frankfurt, June 2006, p. 36.). On the other hand, we find member states, where growth was sluggish, reforms have been dodged for decades, and these were – unsurprisingly – not being able to meet the SGP criteria either. These include Italy, France and Germany. In the first two, governments in the 2000s followed a combination of tax cuts and expenditure increases, which is rather populist than Keynesian. In the latter, the slowdown and the inability to control expenditure, partly due to political divisions of the legislature – different majorities in lower and upper houses of Parliament – resulted in the same.

Global experience is supportive of the ideas, that – following the quibble of Keynes – haunt with a delay of 25 years policy-makers. Fiscal activism, once believed to be conducive to generating additional growth, could be seen as detrimental, that is producing exactly the opposite effect. In a broad empirical survey conducted by Fatas and Mihov (2003) a panel of 91 countries has been analyzed. They find, that countries using fiscal policy agressively induced

---

[7] The Balassa–Samuelson effect means that if a country is catching up through productivity gains, prices for non-tradeables grow quicker, than those of tradeables. This drives up the price level, the exchange rate, or both. Once the Irish pound is merged to the euro, there remains no room for exchange rate adjustment. For this reason the *temporary* quick productivity gains of the second half of the '90s produced a large and controversial literature on how this process may effect the enlargement process; cf. Kovács (2004).

significant macroeconomic volatility. Each percentage point of this translated into a loss of 0.8 per cent of aggregate growth. The prudent use of fiscal policy, on the other hand, never resulted from pure economic insights; *it needed anchoring in the political processes (fiscal planning procedures as well as in institutions).* These findings are in line with the broader literature on fiscal sustainability. Therefore the idea of creating at least some soft form of a 'straightjacket', that is *institutional anchoring and procedural rules* for the EU, especially if stability of the single currency is a supreme joint objective, may hardly be questioned on academic grounds. What may be questioned are the actual numbers, procedures and interpretations that shape policy practice. But this is a different cup of tea from the populist calls for *just doing away with any rules* and return to discretionary practices of the past, in the name of poorly understood 'democratic legitimacy'. Quite in line with this, a similar finding results from the empirical analysis of inactive policies of the ECB. Countries with previously activist monetary policies such as Spain benefited most from the stabilizing role of ECB (Mafi-Kreft and Sobell, 2006).

If we take into account that in the period since 1999 some major shocks took place in the global economy, whose nature must have been only partly cyclical, the good performance of the euro becomes all the more remarkable. Interestingly, as long as the policy consensus lasted, the challenges discussed in the theoretical literature have not become divisive. Let us address seven of the *non-opportunistic, theory-driven criticisms of the SGP,* without, however aiming to be exhaustive![8]

1. The EU does not have an instrument to *co-ordinate macroeconomic policies.* Ecofin does not have a sanctioning mechanism against those disobeying its deliberations. Typically in world history, monetary integration has been a *concluding rather than starting phase* of a political union. By contrast, the EU, remains politically divided, void of real supra-nationality. Not having the right – even less the monopoly – to tax and to use force, the EU is *far from being the 'super-state'* regularly attributed to it by the British press. This, however means that fiscal policies are not joined, thus a major condition of a stable single currency seems to be missing (Berthold, 1993).

   In reality, the common code of conduct that is needed to sustain monetary stability (Braga de Macedo, 2001) has not – yet – been openly questioned. In the first seven years national fiscal policies were tuned, by and large, to the policies of the European Central Bank. With the exception of the two Latin countries no government questioned publicly the line of ECB. Temporary conflicts have not exceeded the ones customary in any democracy, where both the monetary and the fiscal authority are located in the same city. In this period the trends in public borrowing and spending went at least in line with the spirit of the Convergence/ Stability Plans, even though quantitative targets were missed by a num-

---

[8] Orbán and Szapáry (2004, pp. 2–4) provide a different but valid categorization: a/ lack of analytical foundation; b/ lack of symmetry; c/lack of flexibility; d/ disregard for the quality of fiscal consolidation (that is if it comes from one-off measures); e/ enforceability.

ber of countries. The improving tendency explains how Greece could join the euro in 2001.

2. A further problem was raised in the context of *implicit and intergenerational debt* that burden most West European states (Kotlikoff and Ferguson, 2000). To cut a long story short, a greying population coupled with immigration controls result in structural deficits in public pension funds, that are likely to turn into explicit deficits with the passage of time. This correct observation, however, has been less relevant than it looked. For one, this is a *very long-term* story, whose relevance shows up in 15–20 years. Second, *gradual privatization* of public pensions have been launched in many EU countries, from Greece to Sweden and the Netherlands. These unpopular measures *do diminish the implicit debt* and the related financing burden. Immigration, too, could not be contained, as any observer of the Champions' League could testify. This is yet another good news for the recipient nations, from our perspective.

3. Lack of track record implies *lack of credibility* in any new currency. At the time of introduction the fear was widespread that the euro starts a free fall, and its acceptance as a store of value by capital markets will be limited at best (Detken and Hartman, 2002; Cohen, 2003). Despite the decline in the first year, the euro has regained its relative strength, although it is no concern to the ECB, whose task is to keep the domestic purchasing power of the single currency. However, the accumulation of the sizeable current account deficit of the USA, and even more the accounting scandals have appreciated Europe as a safe heaven for investors. This change of the tide of financial flows has restored the value of the euro, more importantly has established it as a global currency, as part of a portfolio hedging against currency risks.[9]

4. Other analysts (Bofinger, 2003) claim that the original SGP was too rigid, as long as high and low inflation countries lastingly co-exist within the EU. In this view, *quantitative targets do not allow for the necessary flexibility* to compensate for the inevitably rigid, non-country-specific line of the ECB. The counter argument may consider that any public target is a measure of credibility, that should rest on a few well defined numbers. Otherwise, *it is not controllable* either by a global investor – the much-quoted housewife from Indiana buying stocks on the Internet – or by the median voter at home. Typically, countries where governments do not follow populist policies find it possible to come to terms with the ECB line, and as seen above.

---

[9] If the Obstfeld–Rogoff (1996) view of exchange rates holds, depicting these as derivatives of financial flows rather than representing fundamentals, it makes no sense to talk of 'strong' or 'weak' currencies per se. Moreover, the ECB has an exclusive inflation target (and so does, alas the NBH). This means that the central bank is not (and therefore should not be) concerned with the external value of the currency. Consequently it cannot be charged with/blamed for a given exchange rate level, that may be beneficial to some and detrimental to other agents. However, the relative value of the single currency has always been a matter of intense political concern, thus it is an issue to be discussed. In the period of 1999–2006 the above quoted theoretical doubt over the potential of the euro as a store of value has proven empirically unfounded.

5. Still others (Buiter and Graffe, 2004) advance the argument that the SGP is flawed insofar as it does not distinguish between *'good' and 'bad' deficits*. In other terms, it is only about the size, not about the nature of the deficits. For it is known that a deficit brought about by structural reforms, such as in public pensions, or by dynamic public investments supportive of market activities, like modernization of railways, have a different economic meaning than deficits arising from inflated public sector payrolls.

This is a valid point in theory. *However, this is not the actual dividing line across EU nations.* For it is not an extreme reform zeal that drives up French or German deficits. Likewise, it is not a public investment drive that creates headaches for the Italian Treasury. In all the three countries consumption related expenditure, unwillingness to re-tailor the welfare state that lay at the heart of the problem.

It is equally important to add, that complex measurements, like the ones suggested by Buiter and Graffe, are though intellectually stimulating and academically elegant, however they tend to be *unfit for policy purposes*. As the article by de Haan, Berger and Jansen (2003) demonstrates, opening up the 'straightjacket' to interpretations has resulted, even until now, to big differences, basically due to the *large variations in the calculated output gap*, and also due in big revisions that have been regularly taking place between first and 'final' estimates of these. This was the case even when big countries, in their majority, have not yet had a direct incentive to blur performance criteria. *Simplicity and transparency are interrelated*, especially if a large number of non-connected players must judge complex processes, as well as their outcomes. Thus being operational is a plus, rather than a minus of SGP. Furthermore, Peffekoven (2003) having surveyed the critical suggestions rightly underscores the need for a 'first things first' approach in policy-making, since there is *no alternative to symmetric fiscal policies within a monetary union* (short of formal co-ordination, that is ruled out for political reasons in the present stage).

6. Finally, the most popular objection to SGP is that it *inhibits growth*. As we can see from statistics of the Economic Commission for Europe (*Economic Survey of Europe*, 2005, no. 2.), there is a different type of correlation especially in the long run, than the ones postulated by Keynesians. It is monetary stability that establishes conditions for growth (as in Spain, recently in Greece) rather than growth conditioning monetary stability. Let us recall again, that it is not the SGP that created monetary stability, rather the other way around. Likewise, the detailed analytical study by Gali and Perotti (2003) has illustrated, that while Maastricht has diminished the propensity to run deficits, it has NOT affected public investment negatively; nor did it constrain the stabilizing role of fiscal policy (whenever the government wished to resort to the latter).[10] While their findings are

---

[10] It is a different story, that if governments (of France and Germany) have missed the good times for fiscal consolidation, in bad times they do not find the leeway. But it would be hard to blame the mirror for the image.

hotly debated by von Hagen (2003) as well as Hughes-Hallet et al (2003), independent empirical tests conducted by Andrikopoulos et al (2004) have repeatedly re-confirmed the findings of Gali and Perotti quoted above. Namely, that the presence of a political business cycle could not be proven for the EU-15 in the 1970–1998 period, whereas the presence of stability oriented policies, induced both by conviction and the fear to be left out of the EMU, has been demonstrable. It was born as an *institutionalization of insights* that had been derived from the trials and errors of the '70s and '80s. It is true, that some countries, like Germany may well not grow with monetary stability, while others do. Still, as even previous adherents to soft stance on inflation (Burton and Fischer, 1998) admit, it is a global experience that no country can grow *sustainingly* with high or even moderate inflation. Thus the reference to SGP, as the mother of all problems, may often cover intellectual laziness, inability to face structural constraints on growth, weak innovation and many other ills (neatly analyzed in the soul-searching new Lisbon Strategy of the EU).

7. Finally Wyplosz (2006) claims that the simplistic number-fixing itself has created an incentive to flout, and disregarded the macroeconomics of debt and medium-term orientation. This criticism is in part valid. Brück and Stephan (2006) have found overwhelming evidence for the spread of creative accounting, especially in large countries. On the other hand, as we shall elaborate in the next chapter, it is perhaps overambitious to expect any piece of soft (EU) law *to create, rather than register,* the commitment to certain values, such as fiscal sustainability. For this reason Buti and Franco (2005) call for strengthening the *national* framework for fiscal sustainability.

The Stability and Growth Pact and the New EU Members

For the new member states, it is inevitable to look into the challenges posed by the SGP. The negative votes in Scandinavia and the foundering of the two traditional engines of EU integration may create the false impression, that the fiscal stance does not really matter and that the abolition of the SGP is just a matter of time. This may well be a dangerous signal, since the period 2001–2006 has seen some of the new member countries' getting seriously out of track from the euro. As the early public warning of the EU Commission already, back in September 2003 and several times since then noted, the average fiscal position in accession countries was regularly out of the line of SGP targets. The reasons for these deficits, as the Commission noted, is not so much the excessive zeal in terms of institutional reforms and restructuring measures than *old-fashioned populist policies* in Poland, Hungary and the Czech Republic alike. This derailment lends support to earlier fears (Eijfinger et al, 2004, p. 190) that the accession of new members to the ECB Board and ESCB may weaken the orientation of ECB to eurozone-wide aggregates. This fear has lead to the proposal (Reform…, 2002) to re-weight the voting rights along economic power. Contrary to Nice, this suggestion has been adopted by the time the new members acceded, *thus their integration to EMU may be basically smooth and swift, from the perspective of the system as a whole.* The basic reason for this is the small economic size of the new members (a mere 5 per cent of EU-15) that precludes any major destabilizing impact on the euro-zone. Once the UNO-like coalition of the dwarfs is pre-empted, the potentially assertive stance of new members no longer count.

But what motivates expansionary fiscal policies in the new members, once this stance can be viewed as contrary to their own best interest, that relates to sustainable growth, or in EU parlance, real convergence?

In a way this situation is easy to understand. As I tried to show earlier, front-runners in transition managed to keep wages down and keep investments high, as a centerpiece of their strategy of overcoming transformational recessions. By contrast, laggards wanted to eschew social strains, kept current consumption high, but as long as the pie was understandably shrinking (with investment shrinking), the outcome was even worse. Now, what is rational from the *macroeconomic point* of view has been a source of strain from the *social point* of view. All the more, so since previously egalitarian income and wealth distribution has changed dramatically towards the less egalitarian end of the European spectrum, the difference between upper and lower decile earning an 8 times difference in Central Europe. Therefore governments, both on the left and the right, felt compelled to conduct policies, where a broad spectrum – the electoral majority – is assisted directly in profiting from the boom. This of course worsened the debt and the fiscal indicators, prompting the central banks in Poland and Hungary, and less so in the Czech Republic to counter fiscal expansion by monetary stringency. This in turn means that basically all criteria of Maastricht are being violated. *Previously attained levels are being lost,* without however of any sign of having laid the groundwork for future improved performance.

Under the prevailing mood of Central European politics, replicating the competition among populist platforms, so typical of Germany and Italy across the political landscape[11], there is a great danger of *instrumentalizing* the seven valid theoretical counter-arguments against the SGP. The bad example of the big guys and observing the lagging behind of regional competitors may convey the false impression that fiscal stringency is just an unnecessary exercise,[12] trying to over-fulfill the criteria of the EU. Moreover, as de Haan et al (2003) elaborate, the political economy of bargaining and the ensuing ambiguity has

[11] In her succinct analysis Győrffy (2006) originates the economic myopia in the lack of trust among major political forces – a point obulovsly valid for the French, German and Italian cases as well.

[12] So the Chairman of the Board of the ruling Socialist Party, as reported in: *Népszabadság,* 25 September 2003. With the benefit of hindsight, this early sign already foreshadowed the successive decision to give up entry to the Eurozone. On giving up the 2010 deadline the first official acknowledgement came from the Minister of Economy in: *Figyelő net,* 27 July 2006.

created incentives for large countries to dilute the SGP. This is bad news, since balanced budget rules are, according to evidence (Shugart et al, 2003), *more often violated in cases when vested interest politics dominates the scene*, that is in cases when parties representing specific concerns of constituencies, rather than following overall rules and the public purpose govern. According to the empirical evidence provided by the article quoted above this type of policy yielded *higher Gini coefficients and lower productivity* against the practices of more rule-based practices of other states in the USA.

Let us be clear from the very outset: it is hard to imagine, either in theory or in practice, an arithmetic that would allow government deficits to sustain *without creating a crowding out effect for private investments*. This is demonstrably true also in recession times for the longer run (cf. Erdős, 1993). Therefore it would be hard to build a solid economic argument explaining why should it be in the best interest of the new members to let their fiscal balance, lastingly be in disequilibrium. Likewise, it needs to be proven why it should be a good idea to revert to old fashioned inflationary policies that failed in Western Europe in the 1970s and in Central and Eastern Europe across the 1980s and l990s. All the less so, if the latter is not the outcome of a deliberate policy choice, as some analysts suggested a decade ago, but *the unintended side effect of overall drifting*, of polices following the signals of weekly opinion polls only.

If deficits do turn into crowding out, then it would require a very strong belief in the *above average efficiency of public investments* to construct a credible argument favoring a negligent, or benign attitude on general government deficit. Moreover, it is hard to overlook the fact that in case of Hungary, for instance, debt servicing constituted 4.5 per cent of GDP in 2004–2006 against 3.5 per cent spent on public investment. What we observe in the 2001–2006 period has been the return of covert ways of consumption related and institution-supporting forms of public spending, not reported transparently in the budgets to be presented to the national legislation (sometimes to the international organizations either). Creative accounting is well and alive, thus the true size, and what is more important, *the actual pattern of public spending* becomes known only ex post facto. This is a danger, since it may become quite hard to develop *rational expectations* concerning any macroeconomic variable and their prospective development trajectory. The low credibility of the governments is reflected in the high real rates of interest in many new members, including Poland and Hungary.

By contrast, countries like Slovenia and Estonia, conducting vigorous market-oriented reforms in the past couple of years, do not face major problems in terms of deficit, while their economic growth is dynamic. In terms of annual per capita FDI, shown to be one of the immediate success indicators in terms of business climate, these two countries have overtaken both Hungary and the Czech Republic in the 1999–2006 period. It is hard to believe that investors would really be typically after the Estonian or the Slovene market. Therefore outward FDI is likely to generate the revenue that will be needed for continued modernization in both nations in the future. Moreover, sustaining growth with low and simple taxation should generate, according to public finance theory, lastingly high government revenues as well. Therefore, the need for deficit spending/financing is unlikely to emerge.

In a way, *the numbers in the SGP*, often described as arbitrary by its critics, *may come quite handy in assessing the situation in the new member states*. It is hardly by chance that Polish Constitution stipulates legislative debates and procedures if public debt exceeds 50 per cent of GDP, which currently is in the making. Likewise, in Hungary public debt has gone down from 84 per cent of GDP in 1995 to a mere 53.5 per cent by 2001. Since then debt started to grow, despite the historic lows of the costs of financing[13] and according to ECB reached 58.4 per cent by 2005 and the corrected figure for 2006 is 68.5 pc.[14] This trend is just the opposite of what we observed in the case of Spain,[15] (a decline from 52.2 to 43.2), Belgium (from109.1 to 93.3) (ECB: *Statistics Pocket Book*, June, 2006, p. 43.)

Without getting into the nitty-gritty of country experience let me just list a few features of the Hungarian experience that makes it strikingly comparable to that of Germany, France and Italy. In the 2001–2004 period the expenditure side of general government has run out of control. Wages, especially in the public sector, exploded. The minimal wage grew from 19 thousand forints to 55 thousand forints by 2003, pushing up the wage scale across the board. In the national economy, wages grew *annually* by over 13 per cent in 2001–2003, while economic growth decelerated from 5 to 2.9 per cent. The re-emergence of the twin deficits of the '80s and '90s, with fiscal expansion translating into current account deficits (in 2003 to 6.6 per cent of GDP)[16] was inevitable. Even more warningly, the debt/GDP ratio is to grow to about 70 pc until at least 2009, rendering the euro-adoption a very long term potentiality (MNB, 2006)

These developments do no support the claim (Eichengreen, 2003, p. 8–9) that the efficiency of using numerical, rather than procedural measures of fiscal sustainability were a matter of size, with Poland being a large country and Hungary being a small one, still facing equal difficulties. He has a valid second argument; that the numbers of the Stability and Growth Pact are somewhat arbitrary. – It means that the reference members are not embedded in, or derived from, academic arguments. Eichengreen argues, that these features of SGP may undermine the credibility. We think that he may miss the point in the

---

[13] The prime rate of FED at the time of writing has been, for several months, kept at a mere one per cent, the yen rates are even below that. This has been the lowest in 46 (!) years despite the US economy growing about twice as fast as its trend rate in 2003–2004.

[14] Convergence Program of the Hungarian Government for 2007–2009, December, 2006. available online: www.pm.gov. hu.

[15] By contrast, Orbán and Szapáry (2004, pp. 10–11) give 40–45 per cent as the long-term optimal debt burden that can be financed, despite the dramatically deteriorating age structure of the population and the resultant surge in health and pension payments.

[16] Source: MNB. (November 2003), calling attention to the change in methodology, that adds two percetage points to previously reported numbers by the National Bank of Hungary, as it covers reinvestments and repatriation, following the EU methodology, arriving at 8.6 per cent for 2003 and a 9 per cent for 2004. This renders the 2006 figure of 9.6 per cent and the 2007 forecast of 8.5 per cent of the trend rate, rather than exception. On the latter of MNB: *Stability Report*, April, 2006 (online) and retroactive acceptance by the minister of finance in: vg.online, 26 July, 2006.

light of the Central European experience of the 2000–2006 period – a point we shall elaborate in detail below.

On the one hand, as we have seen above, the evolution of the policy of hard currency and the conversion to fiscal orthodoxy in the 1980s had been an outcome of spontaneous *learning by doing*, not of immediate theoretical enlightenment. Second, being a policy document, simplicity is a precondition of its feasibility, else there is no way for the public and for investors to check it. Third, the German experience has been quite convincing over the decades, and this makes emulation of it even then *politically desirable*, if success was attained for 'the wrong reasons'. The inclusion of targeting money supply among the policy variables of ECB has clearly shown the importance of traditions and psychological factors.

While Eichengreen is right in underlining the importance of *fiscal procedures* in the final assessment of whether and to what degree a fiscal stance of a country is sustainable[17], the example of all the four Visegrád countries is indicative of the *continued significance of numerical indicators* or target numbers. Although in theory, it could be conceived that these countries run deficit for 'the right reasons', in reality it is not the case. Moreover, if the doors were opened to complex and democratically non-controllable interpretation and re-interpretation of the criteria of stability, it is more than certain that policy-makers in the accession countries were at least as much tempted to arbitrary, lax and only politically handy opportunistic readings, as it has been the case in France and Germany.[18] Needless to say, that though the core argument of Eichengreen, namely that the focus on the fiscal causes of potential inflation is too narrow, of course holds. Still, *the political context already cautions from turning his argument into policy,* documents or binding international legal documents (by re-writing the SGP).

It would be hard to overlook *the political economy context* of Eastward enlargement (more on that in Palánkai, 2004). In short, traditional *bargains over macro-economically insignificant amounts of official transfers have entirely been dominant over any broader considerations.* The latter might have related to more efficient decision making or introducing elementary rationality in terms of established public finance principles in Community spending. If the above observation holds for issues where, at the end of the day, only prestige is at stake, it is rational to expect *even more foot-dragging* when macro-economically

---

[17] More on the concept and the institutional features of fiscal sustainability in the EU in von Hagen et al (1997).

[18] A Franco-German summit, for instance, has already expressed the view that investment outlays should be deduced from fiscal spending numbers, further that growth promoting direct subsidies should not count on the expenditure side (as reported in: *Népszabadság*,19 September 2003). They may easily be joined by the new members, who may argue that, e.g. outlays related to the need to invest for meeting, the environmental *acquis* should equally be deduced. And the snowball could only grow. For an academic version of this claim cf. Blanchard and Giavazzi (2004). In this context, von Hagen (2003, point 2.1) notes, these factors do not act, in the excessive deficit procedures, as trigger of punitive action, just as triggers of analysis, that may well take into account the above factors, if these be predominant.

important amounts, and issues related to retaining or losing government *power is at stake*, as with the national budgets, that equal to vote of confidence in each country.

As long as EU membership is seen, not only by the public at large, but also by policy-making elite, basically in terms of finding yet another milking cow, the Copenhagen compromise of December 2002 and the ensuing limited inflow of official transfers to the new members were likely to produce a *political backlash*. Following the established patterns, governments that have led their countries to EU membership were to lose the next elections. The new government was not only likely to be less pro-European, but also more likely to be tempted to revolt against 'the straightjacket of the EU'. This indeed has been observable in the Visegrád Four in 2004–2006. Since the nature of the disgruntlement was economic, the pressure to increase rather than control spending, moreover to focus on consumption rather than investment with long gestation and recoupment periods, as in environmental protection or physical infrastructure, are likely to re-emerge. This is a serious concern that is better to be addressed *in advance*, than retroactively.

While ascribing all inflationary pressures to fiscal laxity only is indeed simplistic, it is equally wrong not to consider the political economy of introducing the euro. For the experience of the Southern European members has been clearly indicative of the *potential* created by the then non-existent single currency, *to introduce structural reform and fiscal consolidation that were favorable for the long term economic health of the respective economies*. With the experience of the successful management of euro, the introduction of the cash version, the smooth transfer of the ECB Presidency and the lasting appreciation of the single currency against the US dollar may have provided a much better chance to use the euro as a *new anchor for the medium term economic policy* in the new member countries.

Let us recall, that it is precisely the – somewhat arbitrarily chosen – numerical targets that make *the public and the media aware* of the fact that the governments of the Czech Republic, Hungary and Poland have turned away in the post-2004 period from the previous policy line that may be termed 'euro-conformity', despite their continued preaching of the contrary. Lacking the anchors the media, especially the electronic media, thus the vast majority of the electorate, could not be conveyed, the message long available in analytical papers of the central banks or of independent researchers. Moreover, as Benczes (2003, p. 213) correctly observes, if stable monetary frame is to be preserved, a *severing* of the institutional anchors, rather than their relaxation may be justified. His idea at the time was to institute a *quasi-independent fiscal planning authority* publishing regularly macroeconomic forecasts needed for fiscal sustainability and actually plan most of the needed measures.

It is precisely the availability of numerical, obligatory targets that may *trigger a debate* on the nature of increasing public debt in each of the new members. It is the availability of the deficit criterion that may bring about a more meaningful debate on public finances, on expenditure priorities and on *sustainability*. And it is the existence of the long-term interest rate criterion that may draw

198

attention to the excesses of monetary policy in certain periods, or to the lack of credibility of fiscal policies at times when domestically seen, everything is on the right track. In short, the SGP may prove to be *an irreplacable instrument of re-introducing long-term economic rationality* in societies where media democracy pushes many decision makers to an extreme form of short-termism.

In sum, both the *size and the dynamics* of change are worrying. None of the countries are involved in major *investment projects* improving the physical or human infrastructure. Nor do these experience conditions of *recession*, where even the SGP would call for deficit spending to counter cyclical effects. In all the three cases, expenditures grow in part because of consumption related outlays, in part for covering up losses made by public companies (such as the banks, sold under a debt takeover scheme in the Czech Republic, or the railway company in Hungary, or the mines in Poland). By contrast, analysis of Benczúr et al. (2003, p. 26) has demonstrated that fiscal savings, if allowing for externalities that are likely, may well produce a return up to 20 per cent (!), well above the industrial average profit rate of 6–8 per cent. Knowing this there is *no immediate reason* to underwrite the academic doubts on SGP *as policy relevant* suggestions to be followed by policy-makers in the new EU members. On the contrary, Kopits and Székely (2003, pp. 293–294) call for *more, rather than less, formal rules* that would orient policies toward EMU reference values, such as limits on primary expenditure, a structural balanced budget requirement and limits on public debt ratio.[19]

Once the frame defined by the SGP is no longer a subject of dispute in terms of the fundamentals, there is more room to discuss the optimal size of public expenditure, the improved pattern of public spending, of ways of improving corporate competitiveness and on how regulation may create an investment friendly environment. *These debates are much more needed than the narrow evaluation* if, and to what degree, missing of the inflation criterion by say, 0.2 per cent is a threat to the stability of the single currency. These findings support the call by Robert Mundell (2003) for retaining the SGP in an environment, where federal *functions* are already transferred to the federal/EU level, without, however, having established the *institutions* that could perform these functions. Others (de Haan et al, 2003; Inman, 1997) also mention *the lack of enforcement mechanisms* that allow for balanced budgets to sustain in individual states of the USA, without any federal intervention, though under strong public control.[20] Meanwhile, capital markets do punish ruthlessly and immediately lax fiscal policies via capital flight (from Germany), or limiting the quantity and simultaneously pushing up interest rates at which any government debt may be placed at all (as for Poland and Hungary).

---

[19] As a matter of fact, Poland and Germany do have much of these arrangements. These two countries have also indicated the limited efficiency of constitutional and other rules once the policy consensus, as advocated by adherents of fiscal prudence, is gone or replaced by a populist type of consensus.

[20] Unlike in the EU, in the US individual citizens can bring the state government to court if that refuses to play by the rules (of balanced budget).

The Gradual Adoption of the Euro?

While the timing and trajectory of introducing the single currency in new EU states will be dealt at some length in the next Chapter, adoption of the euro as part of the SGP is not a mere technicality *that could and should be discussed in monetary terms only* (for the former approach the best summary is offered in Szapáry and von Hagen, eds, 2004). Therefore, we may well skip the extended debate on why and how new members could unilaterally adopt the euro. Though proponents may be right in pointing out that counter-arguments of ECB were unconvincing (Bratkowski and Rostowski, 2000), *still the ECB has proven politically right and* forward-looking. Once the euro were unilaterally adopted, most of the fiscal and institutional adjustment required by SGP could have been dodged. But as explained above, it would not have been a bright idea, for such options to apply to colonies or quasi-states like Bosnia, where the currency board or using foreign currency is a way to restrain the misuse of monetary system by corrupt local politicians.

However, the context of EU accession is fundamentally different. The basic aim, in the long run, is institutional convergence, as follows from the Single European Act, the supra-national European Court of Justice, or the environmental and fisheries acquis, developed through QMV. All these imply, already at the present stage, a broad set of actions and measures, shaping the entire social and economic model, the European types of market economy. It calls for co-operation among social partners, agreement on broad economic policy guidelines that set quantitative frames for the free flow of ideas and policy initiatives. All in all, the single currency is not to be equalled to the establishment of whatever regime of payments. Let us recall again, that it has also been the case in the incumbent Western European and Southern European EU members.

Meeting the SGP criteria, at the end of the day has at least three benefits. One is the institutionalization of *low inflation and solid public finances*. These are known to be *virtues on their own right*, no longer questioned in the academic economics or policy reform literature. The second is bringing about conditions for long-term growth, through an *investment friendly climate*. The latter follows from low inflation, low interest, and credible institutional and regulatory frame. Third, not least important is the political dimension. Those staying out of EMU become, willy-nilly, *second rank members in the European Union,* as they are not involved in the most important fora of decision making and policy co-ordination. The deliberations of the Nice Treaty, explicitly call for 'enhanced co-operation', that allows for the less enthusiastic to be left out as we shall explore in Chapter Ten on the future options for EU reforms. Likewise, the strengthening of the position of large countries in both documents make especially dangerous for small and medium sized members, such as the Czech Republic or Hungary, to abstain.

These EU-related arguments are supported by the global insight, following from the experience of the 1997–1999 East Asian and Latin American financial crises, that the national currencies of small states have become extremely vulnerable. Therefore *it may well count as a luxury to stick to a separate currency at the age of global financial instability,* which is perhaps the strongest argument in favor of a quick adoption of the single currency by new members (Oblath, 2003). It would be hard to deny that the destabilization of the exchange rate can turn a variety of 'real economic' processes upside down, from travel plans of families to subsidy requirements of publicly supported foreign medicines. Thus the arguments that led to the adoption of hard currency-fixed exchange rates in the EC at times of much less global capital mobility apply *a fortiori* for the new members, transacting over 75 to 85 per cent of their trade with other EU countries, including now CEFTA.

Under this angle, optimal currency area considerations and insights from financial economics are equally supportive, also in the case of Hungary, of the idea to join the euro-zone as early as possible. Empirical evidence, provided by a partly new methodology presented in Darvas and Szapáry (2004) call attention to the lasting dissimilarities among the new members. While Hungary, Poland and Slovenia are shown to be even more in tune with the business cycle of the euro-zone than many current members, such as Portugal, the Baltic States are clear outlayers in terms of harmonized cycle. Therefore, the arguments relate only to those countries, that do qualify as OCA members. However, as the study also indicates, *the policy of joining does orchestrate expectations and finally realities,* so that synchronization takes place, in part after and because of joining in.

Needless to say, the quick adoption of the single currency is an ambitious task and skeptic voices have already been heard immediately upon making the statement public. Let us consider *seven of the major counter-arguments,* that go beyond re-iterating the insider doubts discussed in the preceding section.

1. The most frequently voiced among the counter-arguments is the one stressing the unnecessary costs in terms of slowing down growth, known in the international debate as the *growth sacrifice* argument. According to this, fiscal restriction is by definition contractionary. All the more so, if public investment is a sizeable share of overall demand. Furthermore, if current economic growth is, to a large degree, fuelled by public spending on wages and the ensuing consumption spree, the influence may be even stronger.

   Let us recall the point, long proven in the international literature, and evidenced by the Hungarian experience of the mid-60s, mid-70s, mid-80s and the mid-90s alike, namely that in a small open economy domestic demand-led growth leads, sooner or later to a surge of imports, that in turn triggers fiscal and import restrictions, which flatten activity levels. Signs of the latter happening were already present in the 2002–2003 slow-down of the Hungarian economy to a rate of 3.5 and 2.9 per cent, respectively, from over 5.2 per cent in 2000. In other words, long run growth can by no means rely on demand management – a lesson learnt by the Mauroy and Papandreu Governments in France and Greece. In short, if there is a growth sacrifice, *it is short-lived and leads to adjustment pressures.* In their empirical study on the growth sacrifice of fiscal consolidations Hughes-Hallett et al (2003 pp. 43–44) have found that *in OECD countries this cost was next to nil* (although the contrary case of non-Keynesian, that is expansionary effects dominating fiscal consolidations could also not be empirically proven). Likewise, the broad analysis of Benczes (2007) shows, that fiscal stabilization if properly managed, has never been contractionary over the past 25 years in Europe. It can, if appropriately orchestrated, be expansionary, though it does not have to. Quantitative estimates of experts of the National Bank of Hungary suggest the likelohood of a *mildly expansionary* (non-Keynesian) impact in the medium term perspective (Horváth, Á et al, 2006)

2. Second, fiscal adjustment is described as harmful to investment, since in a transition economy, so the argument goes, additional efforts are needed to polish up infrastructure, education and law enforcement. While the second part of the argument is clearly valid, *it does not follow that these outlays, in their entirety, or even in their majority should be financed from public coffers.* Plans of the Hungarian Ministry of the Economy to rely more on public-private partnership, in line with EU practices, point in the right direction. Similarly deregulation, say of the air transport market, or privatization of environment-related services, as waste collection, are already in advanced stages. The idea to spend more on 'non-productive' activities and the call for more public spending do not overlap.

3. It has long been a contentious issue if, and to what degree, *price stability* can be brought about in the emerging economies. It is common knowledge, that the share of administered prices is still significant and their adjustment has been rather gradual. *Administered prices* cover a number of items where social policy and plain *redistributive considerations* dominate over microeconomic rationality in many democracies, but especially in post-Communist societies. These include public transport – with an item of environmental sustainability consideration –, medical services, drugs[21], housing, energy prices, education, some foodstuffs and many others.

It goes without saying that adjusting all these items to microeconomic rationality/market clearing prices in any real world economy is usually an outcome of public choices to be made in a political process, deciding over *timing, sequencing and dosing* these correctives. For this reason it is no surprise to see that, especially during the populist 2000s, such adjustments have slowed down, became sporadic and ad-hoc. Meanwhile, as a *second* factor, global energy prices, that have climbed from 30 dollar a barrel for oil in the early 2000s to 75 dollar at the time of writing, and perhaps will be approximating 100 dollars in a few years to come. At the same time, gradual but inevitable corrective inflation from adjusting administered prices continue to put upward pressure on the consumer price index in emerging economies. This is counteracted, if liberalization continues, by increased competition from new entrants, domestic and external alike, and also by a policy of strong currency. Still, *the upward pressure seems to be*

[21] According to the Green Book of the Hungarian government, published in July 2006 subsidies for medicines in 2005 exceeded the outpays on primary, secondary and higher education. Available at: www.magyarorszag.hu/zöldkönyv, downloaded: 25 July, 2006.

given, even if no populist wage hikes and ensuing pension explosions were created by the governments.

Third, the *taxation system* of new democracies is though far superior to those of the NIS and many developing nations, however, they suffer from a number of weaknesses. Tax evasion is widespread and enforcement is often selective and inefficient. The irregular economy is still in the range of 20-23 per cent of GDP in Central Europe and 30 to 40 per cent in Romania, Bulgaria and other Southern European members. This means that attempts at ensuring financial sustainability often translate into enhancement of statutory tax rates, without caring about better implementation, broader base and improved enforcement. Such tax measures, but also measures aimed at introducing the flat tax in a number of emerging countries, have resulted in tax-based price increases, such as in Slovakia, Hungary and the Baltics.

Fourth, in some countries with *unilaterally pegged exchange rates*, high and constant productivity gains (due to low starting levels) and stagnant export patterns, the earlier mentioned Balassa-Samuelson effect may also be relevant in driving up prices, since the other channel of adjustment, that of the exchange rate is given up. This has been a relevant concern for the Baltics, where inflation started to *accelerate* in 2004-2006, rendering their joining the single currency impossible. For instance Estonian inflation has though come down from 8.8 to 3.5 per cent in the 2001-2005 period against the previous five years, which is still more than a full percentage point above the Maastricht number. Moreover, the 2004 figure of 3.0 per cent gave way to as much as 4.1 per cent by 2005 and even 4.3 for mid-2006 (ECB: op.cit.p36). This is not only high but is on a *different track* than required by the financial architecture of the EMU. Therefore the Estonian government in April 2006 withdrew its application to the eurozone. Similarly in Lithuania, though inflation for 2001-2005 was only 0.9 per cent against 8.2 in the preceding quinquinnum, but in the run-up period to EMU unfavorable digressions happened. The inflation in 2004 grew to 1.2 pc, in 2005 accelerated to 2.7 per cent and in the first months of 2006 accelerated to 4.3 per cent. This is not only way above the Maastricht reference number of 2.4 per cent, but the trend was more disquieting. For this reason the Ecofin in May 2006 rejected the Lithuanian application to join the single currency. Let us note, that quite apart from the daily twists and turns of politics, the Slovak performance in the same period was 8.2 per cent in 1996–2000 and 5.8 in 2001–2005, the Hungarian 15.1 and 5.8 per cent respectively. This is a clear indication that disinflation is much harder a nut to crack, especially in a sustainable fashion, than mainstream theory and textbook models would have it. At the time of writing, therefore all Visegrád Four countries seem to have given up their earlier projects to join the euro-zone at any time soon (i.e. by the period of 2009–2010 as predicted by previous convergence plans).

What has been said should not be read as our condoning this outcome with the shallow *post hoc, ergo propter hoc* type of argumentation. This is simply inadmissible in analytical social science, despite its widespread popularity. What we are driving at is a different insight. Namely: *in new but full-blown democracies carrying some of the legacies of the past, disinflation may be more protracted than it would be good/optimal for these countries under a purely economic logic.* The latter equals to our priority of sustainable development coupled with price stability and solid, sustainable public finances. If and when, for whatever reason, disinflation is not organic, thus can not be sustained, joining the euro-zone would, though technically be feasible, however it will not materialize. Incumbents do have political and credibility consideration at stake. Thus – as we shall explain in the next Chapter – the interpretation of both Maastricht and the SGP are likely to be, if anything, *more restrictive than for incumbents of the euro-zone*[22]. This, coupled with the poor inflation record, and sometimes even with a poor fiscal record, is a weighty *economic* counter-argument against a possible quick adoption of the single currency.

4. Some observers contend, that retaining *sovereign monetary* policy is an *indispensable instrument* to fine tune convergence to core EU, both in nominal and real terms.[23] This argument, however, disregards the lessons from the 1997–1999 contagion of financial crises stemming from East Asia and its repercussions. While the East Asian and Latin American countries in their majority did have monetary policy sovereignty (constrained only by their unilateral peg to the US dollar), this *has not proven to be an efficient instrument in warding off the consequences of misconceived policies.*

Let me recall again: quick adoption of the single currency is needed and useful not only for the convenience of not having to pay commission when travelling abroad. The latter deduces, on occasion 2–5 per cent of the purchasing power of any unit of the local currency, that is equal to domestic profit margins on most activities outside the financial sector, but for

    a) overcoming the chronic problem of *crowding out,* and

    b) in order to *abolish the vulnerability of finances of emerging economies, especially exchange rate and interest rate risks and shocks.*

5. A related argument highlights the need to *retain fiscal autonomy* at times of major structural adjustment. In part, this is the replication of the Bofinger argument discussed above, in part it relies on general arguments why it may be tough for poorer countries to adopt financial stability. Let us remind, however, of the fact that the opening of Hungarian trade took place in the

[22] Inflation rate in Portugal, e.g. was 2.4 per cent in 1996-2000, but climbed up to 3.2 per cent in 2001-2005. The respective performance of Greece was 4.6 and 3.5 per cent, that of Spain 2.6 and 3.2 per cent, and of Ireland 2.6 and 3.4 per cent (ECB:op.citp36). Since we refer to five year averages, these countries have clearly been in violation of the Maastricht criteria, not merely digressing for cyclical reasons. This, however, even in the apalling case of *accelerating trend rates,* has not resulted in being excluded, suspended, or any way punished, for similar tresspassings rightly identified also in the new member-states.

[23] By contrast, having weighted the arguments for and against, the monograph of Tibor Erdős (2003, p. 443) concludes that 'giving up monetary sovereignty has next to negligible consequences under Hungarian conditions'.

first half of the '90s, of capital account in the period between 1996–2001. Similar processes could be observed in both the Czech Republic and Poland while these countries joined, together with Hungary, the OECD in 1995–1997. Therefore *adjustment to opening has already taken place, unlike in Southern Europe* where much of this adjustment had to be made after EU accession.

Let us recall (more on that in Issing et al, 2001) that the centralized conduct of monetary policy and the related rejection of discretionary interventions *is one of the basic advantages of the single currency*, thus should not be depicted as a drawback. Structural measures cannot be substituted for monetary easing – this is a lesson from the stagflation period. Furthermore, if it follows that fiscal policy remains the only instrument of fine tuning, it also follows that *fiscal policy needs to be endowed with the elbow room that is needed to address cyclical issues*. This is one of the main reasons why the SGP does require balanced budget in 'good times' of growth, but does allow deficit spending during recession.

It should be clear from the above sketched rudimentary summary that, for the time being, fiscal policy in the Czech Republic, Poland, Slovakia and in Hungary *is not yet endowed* with the freedoms required by the centralized conduct of monetary policy at the level of ECB. In short, entitlements and other policy-related expenditure items *over-determine the spending side*, rendering it extremely rigid, even in 'normal times' of 2–4 per cent of economic growth. This follows from the structure of expenditures, where – especially following the wage hikes of 2001–2006, payrolls, obligations to sustain various public organizations and firms cannot be changed by economic growth alone. A major re-tailoring of expenditure priorities (for shorthand: fiscal reforms) were needed to remedy this situation. Resorting to seigniorage is no longer an option, and the acceleration of inflation is already seen as a warning sign both by the public at large and by the investor community.

If this is the case, than domestic considerations – such as the need to attain sustainability in public finances, low inflation and high investment rate, based on private investment – as well as the technicalities of EMU point in the same direction: this is fiscal adjustment. Short of this, it is already clear that the sizeable increase of public dues, observable since 2001 will be the name of the game. *No economy in the world could sustainingly grow with an increasing tax burden and with lastingly growing redistribution by the government.*

6. A further argument calls for the need of *better co-ordination between fiscal and monetary policies* as a precondition for fiscal adjustment to make sense. This observation is though valid, one should not neglect the fact that in a small, open and extremely transnationalized economy, like the Hungarian, or the Czech, not to speak of smaller economies like the Latvian or the Maltese, the elbow room of the monetary authority is very limited. Capital flows and the policy options adopted by other leading central banks, such as the FED, ECB and the Bank of England constrain the theoretically available options in the practical management of affairs. Therefore *the initiative*

should come from the fiscal side. All the more so, since unilateral rate cuts in face of expansionary budgets fuel additional inflation over and above the one stemming from the cost side (energy prices) and the wage push.

7. Let us mention in passing that the *Balassa–Samuelson effect, extensively discussed in the literature, does not seem to be a policy relevant factor in the period under investigation,* if for no other reasons than due to the slowdown in activity levels of the new members. According to what we know about growth theory, this is unlikely to be a mere cyclical slump; the trend is on the change. For low innovation, low investments in R+D, palpable regress in the development of the stock markets, the ensuing weaknesses in financial intermediation, and also low net savings rates of the households together do not allow for the quick catching-up scenarios that would make Balassa–Samuelson relevant. Also, the experience of Southern enlargement indicates that *joining the EU is not a means to accelerate growth about the levels of the trend rate.* Finally, as Clausen and Donges (2001, p. 1322) noted, the Balassa–Samuelson effect is a typical regional effect that the ECB should *not* take into account, in view of the regional focus of its monetary targeting.

This finding received support from Eijfinger et al (2004) reviewing the extensive literature of the Balassa–Samuelson effect, once the sexiest topic for EU related analyses. They underscore the *methodological weakness* of these, that is inevitable as long as the demarcation line between tradables and non-tradables does not have any theoretical or methodological ground. It rests on statistical conventions or *arbitrary classification* conducted by the model builder. Technological change and transnationalization also has been constantly changing the borderlines. The authors of the above quoted book find that the size of the Balassa–Samuelson effect varies between 0.4 per cent and 4 per cent per annum. It is remarkable that the bigger numbers derive from the earlier, ruder measurements, whereas the later, more sophisticated studies yield much smaller numbers (when they account for previously unobserved factors). Closer analysis of the issue when dual inflation – that is when tradable and non-tradable sector show different price increases – has shown to be built upon *strong presumptions,* such as price discrimination, highly unionized (thus sticky) wage setting and sticky prices in local currencies (Világi, 2004, pp. 42–43). These are not realistic – policy relevant – assumptions. Also, the Balassa– Samuelson effect would be sizeable, if currencies were to depreciate strongly – *this is exactly the opposite of what has been observed* (and is the trend to be expected in the run up to single currency).

Last but not at all least the + or – 15 per cent *(altogether 30 per cent) width of the fluctuation band should be broad enough to accommodate any productivity-related upward pressures in economies operating with price stability* in the sense of the ECB, that is 2 per cent headline inflation as maximum. Provided the central parity is right (around the equilibrium rate of exchange), *it would take 35 (sic!) years of appreciation,* due to Balassa– Samuelson, to get out of the band. Likewise convergence analyses tend to adopt a perspective of 25–45 years. Thus, even if there is indeed an upward pressure on the price level, due to remaining price convergence, *its size is spread over several decades*. For instance, if we take price level equal to the level of development, Hungary in 2005 is 61.4 per cent of EU average (ECB: *Statistics Pocket Book*. Frankfurt/M, November, 2006, p. 38.). This would mean, that provided convergence does take place – which has not been the case in 2001–2004 in any significant degree – the remaining 46 per cent price increases are spread along 45 years. Therefore those who believe that the Balassa-Samuelson effect is much bigger than the empirical studies we cite would let us believe, may want to advocate the sober (non-prestige-driven) choice of central parity that may well accommodate adjustment of prices for over a decade after accession (de Grauwe and Schnabl, 2005).

Practical and empirical considerations all point to the same direction. In their extensive re-assessment of the potential size of Balassa–Samuelson, Égert et al, (2003, p. 569) call attention to the fact that numerical results depend crucially on the way tradables and non-tradables are classified. They do not find any robust correlation either to producer or to consumer prices, whereas if they do find a relation that is to changes in *administered prices*. The latter account for up to 25 per cent of prices, their changes are, however, erratic, determined by domestic *policy compromises* rather than by *productivity* gains. Likewise, the broad quantitative survey of Mihajlek and Klau (2004, p. 85) also finds that the size of this effect is inevitably on the decrease. In their wording, not even in an extreme case can this be the determining factor in the ability of the new members to satisfy the SGP criteria. As their argument is based on the observable slowdown of productivity catch-up, this is congruous with our findings published several years ago (Csaba, 2001).

More recent analyses at the sub-sectoral level for Visegrád countries (Cincibuch et al, 2006) have found the *quality* changes actually *dominated* productivity trends. This factor contributes to the volatility of exchange rates and lack of trend therein.

But even then, one may ask, if price convergence is a realistic assumption. Empirical studies show that though prices do not diverge, *they also fail to converge in the real world economies*, such as the United States (where factor mobility is larger than in Europe). While bond yields may and do converge with the passage of time, other prices, especially of non-tradables hardly do. It does not justify the customary 1–1.5 per cent additional inflation hypothesis.

By the same token this consideration surely does not weigh strongly in the 5–7 years run-up period to the adoption of the euro. Furthermore, as Eijfinger and associates (2004) also contend, that higher inflation is *by no means inevitable* in quicker growing economies – an insight strongly supported by global evidence over the past fifteen to twenty years.

Productivity gains used to be associated with upward pressure on prices at times – during the Bretton–Woods era, and only then – when capital flows were constrained and exchange rates used to be fixed, thus *only prices could carry the entire burden of adjustment*. This was indeed the case when Béla Balassa (1964) advanced his thesis, but is obviously not under the ERM-2 system with wide bands of fluctuations and free capital mobility. Also, let us add, that it remains to be seen if double digit gains in productivity should be taken as a baseline forecast. *Such exceptional gains apply only in cases, described in growth theory as 'transition path',*[24] when productivity levels move from one trajectory to the other. Once it is over – normally in 5 to 7 years at best – the trajectory, that is the rate of additional productivity *gains,* as *distinct* from productivity *levels,* can by no means be postulated to be the same. It seems that overlooking this elementary and well-established finding of modern growth theory has made the way for the proliferating econometric business that have yielded only those results that were implicit in the (false) assumptions, but have *misled the policy debate* for a substantial amount of time.[25]

It is outside the scope of this monograph to discuss the technicalities of how the single currency could and should be introduced to Central Europe. What really matters is that *it is not transition-specific tasks that make early adoption difficult.* Rather, redistributory, social and political concerns, well known in established democracies, including incumbent members, that limit the freedom of actors in the sphere of decision-making. For this reason Orbán and Szapáry (2004) also concluded, that the SGP should not be changed with reference to transition specific tasks, as attaining the *sustainable levels of public debt burden* would require fiscal adjustment anyway, exactly in the same direction This is in their view, in the range of 1.9 per cent per year, or four times more ambitious than that of the Ministry of Finance in its contemporary Convergence program. This finding is, inter alia, yet another proof of the Central European countries' having become 'normal economies', where it is no longer the Communist past that is the major defining component of their socio-economic behavior. Rather it is factor endowments, geography, and not least *the quality of the institutions and of the ensuing policies* as well as low politics that decide over their long-term rates of economic growth. This conclusion may well hold even if some of the slowly changing informal institutions, such as rule-abiding or solid financial behavior are obviously slower to evolve than formal institutions do.

Conclusions

We have tried to elaborate *two interrelated points.* On the one hand, we addressed the issue, hotly debated in the academe and in the policy literature alike, if and to what degree the original Stability and Growth Pact, with its focus on numerical numbers for fiscal sustainability, is a *rigid instrument* constraining growth and adjustment. Surveying the experience of incumbent EU and the controversies in the literature we have found no compelling evidence to this end. On the contrary, *academically* valid critical arguments have proven *politically* misleading. All countries of core EU, currently facing difficulties,

---

[24] This is elaborated in great detail in the monograph of Tibor Erdős (2003, pp. 294–303).

[25] This in line with earlier findings by Balázs Égert (2002, pp. 306–307) explaining that productivity gains translate to price increases to a limited degree, furthermore his empirical estimates have shown the real appreciation due to productivity increases close to nil (!) in the four Visegrád countries.

struggle with unresolved *structural problems,* such as the implicit debt of the public finances that come from public pensions, rigid labor markets, insufficient innovation and low levels of entrepreneurship. These are *unlikely to be remedied by easing monetary targets and by providing a fiscal stimulus.* The global economy has not been in a recession for long as defined by ECB, nor is Europe as a whole. Those economies that adjusted themselves to the challenges by structural reforms, that include by now Finland, Denmark, Greece and Spain, managed to grow with low inflation.

Despite overwhelming academic evidence, it is correct to underscore, that it is not the extreme severity/rigidity – the oft-invoked straightjacket nature – but *softening up that poses a true challenge to SGP.* Whether reinterpretation makes SGP more realistic, as Charles Wyplosz (2006) suggests, will be the subject of the next Chapter.

What we have seen in 2000-2006 in much of continental Europe is best described is a textbook case of *non-sustainable* adjustment of public finances. The latter, at least in the short and medium run may or may not weaken the single currency. Euro-strength since 2004 is a clear illustration of this point. However, *the credibility of the entire EMU would seriously suffer. Applying the same political economy games in the new member states, as the ones that worked in the Southern members earlier may prove politically questionable,* despite its economic feasibility and obvious advantages.

Also for incumbents, as Inman (1997) has indicated, it is problematic that *balanced budget rules are not enforced by an independent authority.* This paradox stems from the *predominantly inter-governmental nature* of the EU.

The new member states of the EU experience a difficult period. The slow-down in economic growth could not be counteracted by easing fiscal policies. The latter did materialize in 2000–2006, despite repeated claims of adjusting themselves to the SGP. *The inefficiency of fiscal expansion,* clearly demonstrable on the data of the 2000–2006 period in all Central European and core EU countries, itself puts a big question mark behind ideas that portray the SGP as a straightjacket on growth.

Closer analysis has indicated the need for fiscal adjustment in Central Europe, not because of the ambitious plans to introduce the single currency, but primarily because of the need to *create the financing sources for sustaining growth.* In order to be able to master this task, the introduction of the single currency and the numerical targets enshrined in the original SGP still provide a *window of opportunity to replicate the structural adjustments* that enabled the Club Med countries to join the euro-zone. As long as the euro is basically a political construct, there is nothing wrong in playing, once again, the political economy games. Here the *external anchoring* may still allow *to orchestrate that consensus,* which is needed to manage painful and long *structural reforms* in the welfare state and in the way the state functions. This includes a wide range of activities, public firms and public institutions, not least the way public finances are conducted and controlled by the legislation and the general public alike. This insight is congruous with earlier findings by Jorge Braga de Macedo (1999) on the converging nature of transitions at the European level, that pertain to fundamental features of both institutions and policies.

If the above line of thought contains a modicum of truth, the SGP should not be seen as a straightjacket, but rather *as a handy instrument in orchestrating the political economy of a growth-oriented, perspective policy* in the new members. In this respect, the importance of *peer pressure* should also not be underestimated. This applies a fortiori in a world dominated by the electronic media. External influence did prompt finally even the German government of Gerhard Schrö- der to elaborate and legislate, with the support of parts of the opposition, health and labor market reforms that had long been sabotaged by vested interests and populist concerns. Also in France a multiyear program of fiscal sustainability was launched in 2005 to ensure balanced budget by 2009.

Thus it would, indeed, be misleading to assert, that the SGP were 'dead' since it is 'not legally binding'. *Peer pressure* is generated, among others, by the *procedures* already available for coordinating policies among EMU members. In fact, public debate – in the press and as a consequence, via reactions by the *financial markets* – on the Broad Economic Policy Guidelines, as well as on the more detailed Fiscal Stability/Convergence Plans, actually add up. The com- bined effect *exerts more pressure* on all governments, new and incumbent, than the SGP and the excessive deficit procedures therein. Market reaction does not need to go through the filtering of intergovernmental gate-keepers. And capital markets are quick in responding (in the worst case, punishing) those non- abiding the rules.

What we tried to substantiate in this chapter boils down to a simple conclu- sion. Despite the widespread claims to the contrary, *attaining nominal conver- gence may well be the safest way to real convergence,* a process that is unlikely to show up in months rather than decades. Providing the perspective might be the best service the SGP may render to the new members. But this might equal- ly hold for the incumbents as well. Under this angle we shall analyze in the next Chapter what the re-interpretation of EU fiscal framework of March, 2005 is likely to bring to the growth prospects of the enlarged Union.

References

ANDRIKOPOULOS, A. – LOIZIDES, I. – PRODROMIS, K. (2004): Fiscal policy and political busi- ness cycles in the European Union. *European Journal of Political Economy,* vol. 20. no. 1. pp. 125–152.

BALASSA, B. (1964): The purchasing power parity doctrine: A reappraisal. *Journal of Political Economy,* vol. 72. no. 6. pp. 584–596.

BENCZES, I. (2003): Tehetetlenség vagy reform? (Doing nothing or reform?) In: LENKEI, G., ed.: *Euró – érvek és ellenérvek.* (The euro – for and against). Budapest: a book published by the Center for Strategic Analyses under the Prime Minister's Office, in the series 'Stratégiai Füzetek', no. 16. (December) pp. 199–220.

BENCZES, I. (2004): Fiskális szabályok használata GMU-ban (Fiscal rules in EMU). *Külgazdaság,* vol. 48. no. 11. pp. 20–37.

BENCZES, I. (2007): *The Comperative Political Economy of Expansionary Fiscal Consolidations in Europe.* Budapest – New York: CEU Press (inprint)

BENCZÚR, P. – SIMON, A. – VÁRPALOTAI, V. (2003): Fiskális makropolitika és a növekedés elemzése kalibrált modellel. (Analyzing the impact of fiscal policy on growth through a calibrated macro-model). Budapest: *MNB Füzetek*, no. 13. (December).

BERTHOLD, N. (1993): 'Fiscal federalism' in Europa: Eine Voraussetzung für eine erfolgreiche Wirtschafts- und Währungsunion? In: GRÖNER, H. and SCHÜLLER, A. eds: *Die europäische Integration als ordnungspolitische Aufgabe*. Stuttgart: G. Fischer Verlag, pp. 147–172.

BLANCHARD, O. and GIAVAZZI, F. (2004): Improving the SGP through a proper accounting for public investment. London: Center for Economic Policy Research, *Discussion Paper* no. 4220. (February).

BOFINGER, P. (2003): The Stability and Growth Pact neglects the policy mix between fiscal and monetary policy. *Intereconomics*, vol. 38. no. 1. pp. 4–7.

BOLTHO, A. (2000): What matters for economic success? Greece and Ireland compared. In: BARA, Z. and CSABA, L. eds: *Small Economies' Adjustment to Global Tendencies*. Budapest: Aula Publishing Company for the European Association for Comparative Economic Studies, pp. 151–170.

BRAGA de MACEDO, J. (1999): Converging European transitions. in: DIMITROV, M. – ANDREFF, W. – CSABA, L. eds: *Economies in Transition and the Varieties of Capitalism*. Sofia: Gorex Press for the European Association for Comparative Economic Studies, pp. 13–42.

BRAGA de MACEDO, J. (2001): The euro in the global financial architecture. *Acta Oeconomica*, vol. 51. no. 3. pp. 287–314.

BRATKOWSKI, A. and ROSTOWSKI, J. (2000): The EU attitude to unilateral euroization. In: BRZESKI, A. and WINIECKI, J. eds: *A Liberating Economic Journey*. London: The Cromwell Press for CRCE, pp. 199–232.

BRÜCK, T. and STEPHAN, A. (2006): Do Euro-zone countries cheat with their budget deficit forecasts? *Kyklos*, vol. 59. no. 1. pp. 3–16.

BUITER, W. and GRAFFE, C. (2004): Patching up the Pact: Some suggestions for enhancing fiscal sustainability and macroeconomic stability in an enlarged European Union. *Economics of Transition*, vol. 12. no. 1. pp. 67–102.

BURTON, D. and FISCHER, S. (1998): Ending moderate inflations. In: COTTARELLI, C. and SZAPÁRY, Gy. eds: *Moderate Inflation*. Budapest and Washington: a book published jointly by the NBH and the IMF, pp. 15–96.

BUTI, M. – FRANCO, D. (2005): *Fiscal Policy in Economic and Monetary Union*. Cheltenham/UK – Northampton/US: E. Elgar.

CINCIBUCH, M. – PODPEIRA, J. (2006): Beyond Balassa-Samuelson: real appreciation in tradables in transition countries. *Economics of Transition*, vol. 14. no. 3. pp. 547–573.

CLAUSEN, J. and DONGES, J. (2001): European monetary policy: The ongoing debate on conceptual issues. *World Economy*, vol. 26. no. 10. pp. 1309–1326.

COHEN, B. (2003): Can the euro ever challenge the dollar? *Journal of Common Market Studies*, vol. 41. no. 4. pp. 575–596.

CSABA, L. (2001): The euro – a new entry barrier? In: VÉNARD, B. ed.: *Économie et Management dans le Pays en Transition*. Paris and Angers: CNRS and ESSCA, pp. 81–101.

DARVAS, Zs. and SZAPÁRY, Gy. (2004): Business cycle synchronization in the enlarged EU: Co-movements in the soon to be new and old members. Budapest: National Bank of Hungary, *MNB Working Paper*, no. 1.

DETKEN, C. and HARTMAN, Ph. (2002): Features of the euro's role in international financial markets. *Economic Policy*, no. 35. pp. 553–570.

EICHENGREEN, B. (2003): What to do with the Stability Pact? *Intereconomics*, vol. 38. no. 1. pp. 7–10.

EIJFFINGER, S. – de HAAN, J. – WALLER, S. (2004): *European Monetary Integration*. Cambridge/Mass. and London: The MIT Press.

EIJFFINGER, S. – GERRAATS, P. M. (2006): How transparent are central banks? *European Journal of Political Economy*, vol. 22. no. 1. pp. 1–21.

ERDŐS, T. (1993): Kiszorítási hatás és válságellenes politika. (Crowding out effects and anti-cyclical economic policy). *Külgazdaság,* vol. 37. no. 11. pp. 4–22.

ERDŐS, T. (2003): *Fenntartható gazdasági növekedés.* (Sustaniable economic growth). Budapest: Akadémiai Kiadó.

European Central Bank (2004): *The Monetary Policy of the ECB.* Frankfurt am Main: an official publication with a foreword by J.-C. Trichet.

ÉGERT, B. (2002): Investigating the Balassa–Samuelson hypothesis in the transition. Do we understand what we see? A panel survey. *Economics of Transition,* vol. 10. no. 2. pp. 273–304.

ÉGERT, B. – DRINE, I. – LOMMATSCH, K. – RAULT, Ch. (2003): The Balassa–Samuelson effect in Central and Eastern Europe: Myth or reality? *Journal of Comparative Economics,* vol. 31. no. 3. pp. 552–572.

FATAS, A. and MIHOV, I. (2003): The case for restricting fiscal policy discretion. *Quarterly Journal of Economics,* vol. 118. no. 4. pp. 1419–1448.

FRANZ, W. (2003): Zur Notwendigkeit wirtschaftspolitischer Reformen. *Zeitschrift für Staats- und Europawissenschaften,* vol. 1. no. 1. pp. 95–114.

GALI, J. and PEROTTI, R. (2003): Fiscal policy and monetary integration in Europe. *Economic Policy,* no. 37. (October) pp. 533–573.

DE GRAUWE, J. – SCHNABL, G. (2005): Nominal versus real convergence – EMU entry scenarios for the new member-states. *Kyklos,* vol. 58. no. 4. pp. 537–557.

GYŐRFFY, D (2006): Governance in a low-trust environment: the difficulties of fiscal adjustment in Hungary. *Europe-Asia Studies,* vol. 58. no. 2 pp. 239–259.

de HAAN, J. – BERGER, H. – JANSEN, D. J. (2003): The end of the Stability and Growth Pact? Munich *CES/ifo Working Paper,* no. 145.

von HAGEN, J. (2003): Fiscal discipline and growth in euroland: Experiences with the Stability and Growth pact. Bonn: Rheinische Friedrich-Wilhelms Universität, Center for European Integration Studies, *ZEI Working Paper,* no. B06.

von HAGEN, J. and HOFMANN, B. (2003): Macroeconomic implications of low inflation in the euro area. Bonn: Center for European Integration Studies, *ZEI Working Paper* no. B29.

von HAGEN, J. – PEROTTI, C. – STRAUCH, P. (1997): *Fiscal Sustainability.* London: a book published by the Center for Economic Policy Research.

HORVÁTH, Á. – JAKAB, M. Z. – KISS, P. G. – PÁRKÁNYI, B. (2006): Myths and Maths: Macro-economic effects of fiscal adjustments in Hungary. Budapest: National Bank of Hungary, *MNB Occasional Paper,* no 52.

HORVATH, J. (2003): The optimum currency area theory: A selective review. Helsinki: Bank of Finland, *BOFIT Discussion Papers,* no. 15. (November).

HUGHES-HALLETT, A. – LEWIS, A. – von HAGEN, J. (2003): *Fiscal Policy in Europe in 1991–2003: An Evidence-Based Analysis.* London: Center for Economic Policy Research.

INMAN, R. P. (1997): Do balanced budget rules work? US experience and possible lessons for the EMU. In: SIEBERT, H. ed.: *Quo vadis, Europe?* Tubingen: J. C. B. Mohr/Paul Siebeck, pp. 307–332.

ISSING, O. – GASPAR, V. – ANGELONI, I. (2001): *Policy-Making in the European Central Bank.* London and New York: Cambridge University Press.

KOPITS, G. and SZÉKELY, P. I. (2003): Fiscal policy challenges of EU accession for the Baltics and Central Europe. In: TUMPEL-GUGERELL, G. and MOOSLECHNER, P. eds: *Structural Challenges for Europe.* Cheltenham/UK and Northampton/MA/USA: Edward Elgar, pp. 277–297.

KOTLIKOFF, L. and FREGUSON, N. (2000): The degeneration of EMU. *Foreign Affairs,* vol. 79. no. 2. pp. 110–121.

KOVÁCS, M. A. (2004): Disentangling the Balassa–Samuelson effect in CEC–5 countries in the prospect of EU enlargement. In: SZAPÁRY, Gy. and von HAGEN, J. eds: *Monetary Strategies for Joining the Euro.* Cheltenham/Glos/UK and Northampton/Md/USA: Edward Elgar, pp. 79–105.

MAFI-KREFT, E. – SOBELL, R. (2006): Does a less active central bank lead to greater economic stability? *CATO Journal*, vol. 26. no. 1. pp. 49–70.

MIHAJLEK, D. and KLAU, M. (2004): The Balassa–Samuelson effect in Central Europe: a disaggregated analysis. *Comparative Economic Studies*, vol. 46. no. 1. pp. 63–94.

MNB (2003) (National Bank of Hungary): *Jelentés az infláció alakulásáról*. (A report on inflation). Budapest, November.

MNB (2006): Jelentés a pézügyi stabilitásról (A report on financial stability). Budapest, April. (available also on: www.mnb.hu).

MUNDELL, R. (2003): One global economy – one world currency? Warsaw: *TIGER Distinguished Lectures*, no. 12. (available at: www.tiger.edu.pl)

NAGY, A. (1999): Lessons drawn from the accession of three Southern European states and its effects on their foreign trade. *Acta Oeconomica*, vol. 50. no. (3–4). pp. 385–412.

OBLATH, G. (2003): Belül biztonságosabb. (It is safer inside). *Figyelő*, vol. 47. no. 17. pp. 20–26.

OBSTFELD, M. and ROGOFF, K. (1996): *Foundations of International Macroeconomics*. Cambridge/ Mass. and London: The MIT Press.

ORBÁN, G. and SZAPÁRY, Gy. (2004): The Stability and Growth Pact from the perspective of new member-states. Budapest: National Bank of Hungary, *MNB Working Paper* no 4. (available at: www.mnb.hu)

PALÁNKAI, T. (2004): *Economics of Enlarging the European Union*. Budapest: Akadémiai Kiadó

PEFFEKOVEN, R. (2003): Der Stabilität- und Wachstumspakt – als finanzpolitisches Rahmenwerk unverzichtbar. *Zeitschrift für Staats- und Europawissenschaften*, vol. 1. no. 2. pp. 220–229.

PENTECOST, E. J. (2001): *European Monetary Integration: Past, Present and Future*. Cheltenham/ UK and Northampton/Md/USA: Edward Elgar Publishing Co.

Reform of the decision-making rules of the ECB Council in view of EMU enlargement. (2002) *Intereconomics*, vol. 38. no. 3. pp. 116–131.

RISSE, Th. (2003): The euro between national and European identity. *Journal of European Public Policy*, vol. 10. no. 4. pp. 487–505.

SHUGART, W. – TOLLISON, R. – YAN, Zh. (2003): Rent-seeking into income distribution. *Kyklos*, vol. 56. no. 4. pp. 441–456.

SZAPÁRY, Gy. and von HAGEN, J. eds: (2004): *Monetary Strategies for Joining the Euro*. Cheltenham/UK and Northampton/MA/USA: Edward Elgar.

VILÁGI, B. (2004): Duális infláció és reálárfolyam a nyitott gazdaságok új makroökonómiája megközelítésében. (Dual inflation and real exchange rate in new open economy macroeconomics). Budapest: National Bank of Hungary, *MNB Füzetek*, no. 5.

WYPLOSZ, Ch (2006): The EMU: the dark sides of a major success. *Economic Policy*, no. 46 (April), pp. 207–247.

9. RE-INTERPRETING RULES-BASED BEHAVIOUR IN EUROPE[1]

The preceding chapter discussed the drift between the theoretical insights in support of a coordinated and rules-based fiscal framework for European monetary integration on the one hand, and the opportunistic policy-making experience of largest members- and more recent new member-states in the period since 2000. In the present chapter an attempt is being made to explain this drift and interpet the revised Stability and Growth Pact, with special emphasis on the long run development perspectives of new member-states.

When deciding over the Nobel Prize in Economics for 2004, the academic experts convened by the Swedish central bank, *Riksbank* could not disregard the fundamental challenges of the time. This is in line with its previous practice, when Nobel Prize winners always tended to be persons, having worked on what was seen as the basic challenge of the period. For instance, when issues of global poverty have come to the fore, researchers as Gunnar Myrdal and later Amartya Sen received the top prize of the profession. Following financial crises of 1997–99 analysts of asymmetric information, such as George Akerlof and Joseph E. Stiglitz were decorated. Following the collapse of the Soviet system, the symbolic figure of the institutionalist approach, Douglass C. North was acknowledged. And despite the fact that the judgement of history may or may not overlap with those of the Swedish Academy and Riksbank, as was the case in literature, it is perhaps not without use to use the Nobel as a benchmark for measureing progress in the relatively young academic discipline of economics. The award went to F.Kydland and E.Prescott, a Norwegian –American duo, having established the supreme need for applying rules and limiting policy discretion in the area of fiscal policy. The authors have proven that this is the only way to sustainable – as opposed to short run, cyclical – growth in any small open economy.

[1] Useful comments on various previous versions of this text by László Jankovics, Álmos Kovács, Alexandre Lámfalussy and György Szapáry are appreciated, with the usual caveats.

Rules-Based Fiscal Policy in the European Union

This award seems to have settled one of the most contentious issues of economic debate, an academic one with immediate policy relevance. This controversy revolved around the appropriate mix of rules versus discretion in economic policy-making. While nobody would doubt that both rules and discretion are needed, the first for setting the standard of evaluation, the second to reflect contextuality, it is far from clear what the optimal policy mix should look like. If there are no rules, a populist policy of 'anything goes' will rein.This – as evidenced from the ruinous consequences of the 1970s and 1980s – is a real danger, bequeathing sustainingly high public debts in many European countries, still crippling current fiscal decision-makers. By contrast, any policy-maker, especially former academics turned politicians – called *technopols* by John Williamson (1994) – highlight in the quoted volume and elswhere: there is no benchmark, no rule that could save sober assessment of the given situatuion and the discretion needed for managing any crisis. Politics, thus remains the 'art of posible' (*die Kunst des Möglichen*), as Bismarck once aptly described it.

Economic theory accepted this insight, thus the subject of the debate was different. Namely it is about the fine-tuning of the economy, and the ability of governments to do so. Practical applications of the Keynesian set of ideas tended to rely on the manipulation of the rate of interest as an incentive/disincentive to invest, the counter-cyclical application of public spending, especially of investment-related items, sometimes also the devaluation of the currency as an across-the-board measure to limit imports, support import substitution and promote exports, in order to overcome a current account difficulty. While Keynes himself has always gone out of his ways in elaborating the subtle set of side-conditions, under which his unconventional suggestions may work, his followers tended to be much less restrained. In reality, by the early 1970s, when Keynesianism has become part and parcel of economic good manners, policy-makers tended to see the economy much like a machinery, where pushing the proper buttons at appropriate times is bound to deliver the forseeable result, without friction and uncertainty.

It is no secret that this approach has always – continuously – had to encounter weighty intellectual opposition from such powerful schools of thought as Austrian economics, monetarism and constitutional political economy, later also public choice (Jankovics, 2004). These approaches have always doubted the validity and the general applicability of the Keynes-inspired economic policies, especially in small open economies. The common point of criticism has been directed towards the belief of the Keynesians portraying the economy working like a machinery, therefore being subject to fine tuning by the government. These approaches, deplored as 'fatal conceit' (Hayek, 1989) the idea also immanent in contemporary attempts at central planning, the economy were a carbon copy of any machinery. There the subtle and multidimensional coordination of millions of actors could be substituted by state activism, even relying on the most sophisticated forms of ICT. It is also known that it was primarily his famous work on economic history of the United States that led Milton

Friedman (1968) to conclude on the neutrality of money. The latter means that the government, already in the medium run, is unable to influence actual decisions of millions of players – households, firms, workers and employers – thus state activism in terms of discretionary fiscal policy or manipulation of the interest rate can only translate into higher inflation, not to the smoothing of the business cycle. His empirical studies have actually shown that activity by the monetary authority to lay at the root of business fluctuations, quite contrary to the assumptions, never proven by Keynes. While some may consider this to be a part of history, others (Issing et al, 2001, chapters 1–3) have shown this to be the case for the period of postwar Western Europe as well.

The stagflation experience of the 1970s has lent additional support to the doubters. Let us mention two pieces from this period, whose authors have been awarded the Nobel Prize in Economics. Buchanan and Wagner (1977) have shown with classical argumentation why *democracies are prone to overspending*. In the end, the median voter is unable to assess the actual costs of meeting all the promises made by the electioneering politicians correctly. As there is no free lunch, any additional public good or service needs to be financed from tax increases, or else the state has to rely on money emission that translates into higher inflation, thus lower consumption. As long as economic transparency is less than perfect, the median voter is unlikely to punish the irresponsible politician for his/her non-realistic promises, while politicians can maximize their power by advancing competing – non-feasible – promises. This is the final explanation of the empirical finding, documented already by then, that the counter-cyclical policies have very rarely followed the maxim of Keynes and were *seldom applied in a symmetric fashion*. In the original approach, while contractions allow for overspending, good years of high growth would require fiscal surpluses, also mentioned in Keynes. In reality, deficit spending though did occur, the 'good years' very rarely used for fiscal retrenchment, either earlier, or in the past decade or so. In years of high growth, most governments – as the Italian, the German and the French, even the British in recent years – do not restrict public spending, make no effort to reduce public debt at a substantial degree.

In order to remedy this half-sidedness, Buchanan and Wagner propse constitutional stipulations to urge the governments of the day to act in a symmetric fashion. A similar line of thought emerged in the article by Kydland and Prescott (1977) that used to belong to the most frequently quoted sources even prior to the Nobel award. They describe the policy dilemma in terms of '*time inconsistency*'. In their model, politicians are rational actors. Thus as private persons they are perfectly aware of the limitations of activism, and know that only long term goals, such as price stability or balanced budgets are worth following. However, working under the constant pressures of the minute, of vested interest politics, they just 'happen' to act the other way around. If this insight holds, central banks must be insulated from the ups and downs of democratic politics in order to allow them to act in the long run interst. Or to use the languague of the literature on policy reform, thereby legislators institute a degree of '*collective rationality*', supportive of price stability and/or fiscal equilibrium, against the 'individual rationality' of interest representations of players of daily politics, of vote maximizers or simple power opportunists. The crux of the matter is that collective rationality *needs to be institutionalized by rules* and discretion limited, in order to ensure public interest and conditions for long term growth. These insights serve as the base for the constitutional independence of the European Central Bank as well as of the Federal Reserve System in the USA.

Relying on these insights there is a burgeoning literature on the need for rules-based fiscal policy in democracies that have found their way in the legislative practice of several European countries. This is not the place to document these developments (cf Benczes, 2004, Győrffy, 2005), but the major finding is that no monetary policy can succeed on its own on the long run, without adequate support from fiscal policy. As it has been experienced both during the Reagan Presidency and under the Presidency of Bush Jr., even the largest economy with the broadest capital markets can't survive any economic policy without repercussions. Lasting fiscal expansion in the USA on both accounts has lead to inflationary pressures, serious devaluation of the currency, a palpable slowdown and even a risk factor for the global capital markets. This is why the member-states of the EU have agreed, first in the Treaty of Amsterdam, later in the Trearty of Nice, to adopt rules-based fiscal policy. The latter in part means rules at the Community level, and as seen at the end of the preceding Chapter, also *in part rules at the national level*, further procedures to dovetail the two and check the transparency and quality of information flows. At the end of the day, this is what the Stability and Growth Pact has been. When the new member states accepted the bargain in Copenhagen in December 2002 and later signed the accession treaty in Athens in April 2003, they agreed to accede to an EU which no longer knows about opting-out, at least not for the new members. While Denmark or Britain can invoke their opt-out, since their accession conditions were different, *this option no longer holds for the new members.*

Adopting rules-based systems has a meaning over and above the political compromise of the day. On the one hand, it reflects a constitutional norm typical of democracies, that compels public finances both at the revenue and the expenditure sides, is *regulated by laws*, adopted by the legislation not by governmental arbitrariness/decrees. This means that one of the basic assumptions of Keynes-inspired policies no longer hold is that the free calibration and discretionary manageability of expenditures/intakes, not even following cyclical or labor market considerations (Tanzi, 2004, p. 66.). This applies *a fortiori* for community level spending, where the seven year Fiancial Perspective set the limits, objectives and procedures. Annual agreements may, and do modify the exact numbers, such as the amounts paid, but these are in no position to change the fundamental features set by the Perspective, or change the procedure of their application.

There are at least further two points in support of the economic validity of the Stability and Growth Pact (SGP) in its original form – and as it is advocated inter alia by the European Central Bank (Trichet, 2005). On the one hand, it goes without saying that fiscal policy is no longer an 'internal affair' amongst members of a monetary union, as profligacy of one member immediately influences price stability in, and financing terms for, the other. A mismanaged member may trigger credibility losses, inflation or higher financing costs for the entire community, as financial markets decreasingly differentiate among the member states. This consideration is only reinforced by the insight that the European Central Bank (ECB) is in no position to meet its statutory target of sustained price stability unless national fiscal policies are supportive of its goals. Not taking into account the different business cycles by the members, is therefore one of the major pluses, rather than a minus of the single monetary policy and of SGP supportive of this, despite frequently voiced positions (Losoncz, 2004, p74) to the contrary. It is exactly the arrangement that secures the rules-based, rather than discretionary conduct in both monetary and fiscal affairs. The single currency is a unique phnomenon in monetary history, its functioning is based on voluntary compliance with those rules of conduct (of solid finances) that emerged during the 1980s. Multilateral surveillance mechanisms thus may complement and assist, however never replace lack of commitment. On the other hand it can be proven with a detailed model computation (Carlberg, 2003) that even if we were to follow full employment as a single European target function (and not price stability, as the ECB does), it were *coordinated rather than individualized, improvised policies* – i.e ones following daily political tricks – that could yield a better result for each of the participants.

Adoption of the SGP has been followed by ambiguous developments. On the one hand, the SGP did play a disciplinary role, bringing down deficits and debts in most EU countries, although, primarily before rather than after joining the single currency. Being left out of the euro-project was generally percieved to be such a political shame that not even countries with a poor history of fiscal discipline could afford it (Papademos, 2004). At the same time, however, economic policy practice in many EU contries gradually distanced itself from the academic normatives described above. Following the international financial crisis and contagion of 1997–99 the Democratic administation in the USA has experimented with large-scale – and lavishly funded – projects on creating a new international financial architecture. This policy initiative has created favorable conditions for a return of old-fashioned Keynesianism as an accepted policy-relevant academic approach (Krugman, 1998). This change in the intellectual fashion has not given ground, but provided a point of reference for, governments willingly eschewing major fiscal consolidation prior to its actual onset.'

Analyzing fiscal policies in the EU-15 Hughes-Hallet and associates (2003) establish a degree of 'consolidation fatigue' in most larger member states. As documented in Table 1 and 2, it were just the largest members that account for about two thirds of the total EU output, which have proven incapable of instituting broader structural reforms that could have paved the way for fiscal sustainability. Many incumbents have just signed off, being already within the Euro (the latter not having any exclusion or punishing mechanism for those not complying). As we can observe from Tables 3 and 4 this irresponsible approach was far from general, with several member states, such as Ireland, Spain and Finland easily meeting the SGP targets. The latter applies to Denmark, Britain and taking into account declining debt, also for Sweden, from among the non-members. By contrast in the three core states and also for most new members, the period 2001-2006 has been characterized by fiscal laxity that in turn translated into decelerating growth rates. In other words, *there is no trade-off between higher growth and higher inflation,* as the old fashioned Keynesian theories would have suggested.

Why has it been so that large countries could easily afford an irresponsible policy line that was openly running counter to their declared principles and binding international obligations as well? This is explained by a new political economy analysis of the SGP by Jakob de Haan et associates (2003). They underline two weaknesses of the Pact. First, reflecting the predominantly intergovernmental nature of the EU, there is no way to sanction trespassers. The Nice Treaty contains no provisions that would allow individuals or groups of individuals to bring the non-compliant governments to court, as is the case in most member states in the US. Launching excessive deficit procedures (EDP) against conutries regularly not meeting the quantitative targets, is though concievable, by no means automatic or obligatory for the Council. This injects a high degree of non-controlled and non-accountable discretion in the mechanism that is meant to ensure rules-based behavior. Moreover on the issue of launching or not launching the EDP it is the Ecofin who decides, a body composed of players working under identical incentives and *themselves being part of the problem.* For instance, the Netherlands, having adopted as combattant stance on excessive deficits in 2002-2003 has found itself in a similar pair of boots in 2004, which of course cautions from adopting rigid stances on others. This circumstance obviously leads to the erosion of the credibility of the rules and the related sanctions for non-compliants. This would be wrong to be interpreted, as in the daily press, that 'practice has defied theories', as it can never be the case, but it does reflect the lack of voluntary compliance. The latter is, at odds with the experiences of previous decades as well as with the theories underlying the special arrangements for the single currency. In reality, the *causation runs just the other way* around from populist critics of the SGP would have it. It has not been the 'stupid' arrangement, the 'straightjacket' and the doctrinaire interpretation that has been constraining the strenuous efforts of each national government to comply and generate growth. On the contrary, – as elaborated by Mayes and Virén (2004) – asymmetry within the EU arises from the fact that while some governments have indeed instituted broad reforms and pro-growth policies, others have missed this opportunity in the 1999–2004 period. This produces the *lack of synchronized behavior* in line with SGP, rather than the other way around. The repercussions of this are severe, as we shall elaborate below.

Last but not at all least, note should be made of the repercussions of *perverse incentives* that have ensued from the existence of the SGP as a common and credible fiscal framework. Markets in the period of 2000–2006 tended to see the

EU *as a single unit* with new members joining the single currency at their earliest convenience. Also in terms of the old members, the expectation that some form of consolidation to sustainable public finances will occur some day or another has been general. This expectation has allowed for a practice of brushing away detailed consideration of fiscal positions of individual member-states. In other words it allowed for free riding by the opportunistic politicians: instead of creating pressures for adjustment, it provided a room for doing nothing, postponing overdue adjustment measures indefinitely.[2] By continuing to finance Italian and Greek debt without a discount, the ECB has contributed to an implicit bailout of these governments irrespective of the *raison d'etre* of the joint fiscal framework, i.e the need to act as a bullwark against spreading the costs of overspending across the Union as a whole. However neither the political decison-making structure inside the ECB, nor the oft-invoked disciplinary eye and action of financial markets have been acting over a series of years. Thereby the drift between intention and reality has opened wide. Avaliability of *the EU framework has promoted, rather than prevented, free riding.*

Initiatives to 'Patch Up the Pact'

In the past few years, quite a number of studies and political initiatives were aimed at revising and reinterpreting the SGP. Since the overview of this burgeoning, and to a large degree technical litarature is presented in the preceding chapter, we constrain ourselves only to those suggestions that matter for the actual revision of the Pact. Our analysis thus focuses on the frequent suggestion about the 'death' or of the 'suspension' of the SGP. Furthermore we address the issue if the cure is worse than the illness, if – contrary to the explicit suggestions of President Manuel Barroso (cited in: *Neue Zürcher Zeitung*, 24 November, 2004) – entire budgetary positions may be excluded from the calculation of fiscal deficits? This is all the more important if some of the items that are not to be included do constitute *additional demand* for the Euro-zone, irrespective of their other virtues, such as costs for European reunification, or R+D spending, or assistance to developing countries, thus their *inflationary potential* can not be professionlly doubted. It also goes without saying that the modifications listed above run contrary to some of the elementary principles of public finance in general and accounting in particular, such as the need to cover the entirety of items, solidity and transparency. Similarly, allowing for the avoidance of cash flow approach and allowing for the interpretation of the benchmarks opens the door wide for opportunistic political interpretation. This renders the assessment of a macroeconomic situation and the related risks next to impossible to most market agents, such as individuals selling and buying government bonds, or the median voter, *none of which can have a clear idea*

---

[2] A broad and insightful analysis of these processes is offered in the forthcoming monograph of Győrffy (2007).

about the expansionary or restrictive nature of public policies conducted in the period preceding his decision. It eaqually goes without saying that such commendable goals, as developing the phyisical infrastructure, or creating a funded pillar for pensions are only indirectly, and on the long run, related to non-inflationary growth.[3]

The first important question is if the Pact is still an internationally binding agreement that is in force? When the Ecofin allowed Germany and France to get away with several years of non-compliance in its decision of November 2003, the Commision turned the case to the European Court of Justice. The court in Luxembourg has passed a binding ruling (*Handelsblatt*, 13 July, 2004) interpreting the SGP as part and parcel of the Treaty on the European Union and stipulated the Council to take remedying action. Therefore the Commission and the European Central Bank maintained the critical evaluation of progress by individual EU-members, including new ones, on their road to convergence and meeting the criteria. Individual member-states, notably Germany and Italy have saved no effort to present annual and medium term programs for fiscal adjustment and avoid stepping over the 3 per cent limit. Thus therefore the frequency of quotations of ex-Commission President (and now Italian Prime Minister) Romano Prodi's statement on the alleged 'stupidity' of the Pact does not allow for the position represented also in the professional literature (Rácz, 2004, p. 97) that the Pact was 'suspended', or its future was in any way doubted, or that new members could afford a laxer fiscal stance in light of the controversies discussed above.

The second part of the story is to address the shape in which the Pact is following the reinterpretation by the Council in its Brussels session of 22-23 March 2005. In laying the groundwork for the reinterpretation of the Commission proposals of September 2004[4] played a major role. The proposition reflects the economic debates of the past four years and relies on suggestions stemming basically from British and Dutch authors. These included *three major areas:* assessment of the cyclical situation, assesment of structural components and evaluation of individual circumstances.

The need to take into account the *cyclical situation* is by no means a novelty. Reflecting the concerns of the French, the Pact is to serve growth as much as stability, furthermore – as a consequence – it allowed, in its original form – for counter-cyclical measures, should a recession occur. This requires references to 'exceptional circumstances'. As the detailed analyis of Issing et al (2001) explains, this was interpreted in procedures and numbers from the very outset. Since the question of a recession is at hand, it is of operational relevance for the ECB, that is not allowed to follow a contractionary policy. Following broad

---

[3] The EU is renown for the 'cathedrals in the desert', i.e for projects that never recoup, such as the Formula One project in Lausitz, the bridge in Párkány/Sturovo, or the fact that most private pension funds in Hungary functioned with a minimal profitability in 2002-2005.

[4] European Commission (2004): Communication of the Commission to the Council and the European Parliament: 'Strengthening the governance and clarifying the implementation of the SGP', 3 September, made available in: *EurActiv*, of the same day.

deliberations this was translated into the following: recession is a situation where in *four* consecutive quarters *overall* output – not sectoral output – contracts by 0.75 per cent. In the band between 0.75 and 2 percent, an evaluation of the situation is needed, and a slump below 2 per cent allows national governments to follow expansionary policy *without consulation,* and also *obliges* the ECB to ease up its monetary stance, should this contraction occur across the entire Euro-zone.

How big a role this original interpetation allows for counter-cyclical policies? In view of one of the globally most accepted authorities on public finance, Vito Tanzi (2004, pp. 65-66) – the inflation elasticity of GDP is about 0.5 per cent. In other words, in order to reach the 3 per cent deficit spending, maximally allowed for governments by the original SGP, the country in question would have to register a drop of no less than 6 percent. There was no single case in the European Union of this according to the standardized data provided by the United Nations Economic Commission for Europe: *Economic Survey of Europe,* no2 (2005, p. 69). Thus the reference to the rigidity of the Pact is flawed. It is equally wrong to blame the one-sidedness of the Pact in terms of cyclical adjustment (e.g Losoncz, 2004, p. 75 quoting UN analysts). The solution to this problem is not to allow the asymmetric application of Keynesian policies, as referred to it in the preceding section. But this is a matter of *domestic* politics, rather than any EU arrangement.

Any important novelty of the Commission suggestion was to *assess the structure of the deficit,* which is seen as a more liberal interpretation. This holds only for those countries that spend a lot on measures paving the way for future growth, such as investments and structural reforms, but it is a toughening for those spending basically on short term issues like consumption or pensions. The latter is the case with the three big 'problem countries' as well as the new members, where transfer payments, spending on sustaining institutions of various sorts and covering the losses of public and semi-public firms play a prominent role. *None of these items provide for higher growth in the future.*

In theory, it is legitimete to delineate 'good' deficits from 'bad' ones. It is obvious, that introducing private pensions turns the previously hidden, implicit public debt open, and the same goes for allowing realistic costs – such as depreciation – to show up in the bills for health care. It is equally straightforward that environmental outlays, as required by the high EU standards, are likely to incur sizable costs and contribute to public deficits for the new members, even if we allow for the fact that not all investments need to be covered from public coffers. It is certain that a defence force that may render indeed the Helsinki headline goals realistic, with capabilities to fight terrorism and enforce peace, for instance on the Balkans, is unlikely to be cheaper than traditional armies used to be. But these factors are likely to make the case against the new members as well as against the three basic trespassers only more severe.

Outsiders may well percieve the reference to *individual circumstances* as yet another step to liberal interpretation and some politicians have indeed made such statements. In reality, being an international organization, the EU cannot choose its evaluation criteria at will. The ECB, for instance, is simply not in the position to give up its interpretation of price stability to be 2 per cent or less (as of March, 2003) only beause some politicians and commentators disagree with it. Likewise the Ecofin and the Council cannot abstract away from the meaning, the spirit and the objectives of the SGP, as supported by a binding ruling of the ECJ.

This means that in the original reading, the Commission, ECB and the Council may assess only if there was a recession in the country not abiding, i.e a drop of GDP between 0.75 and 2 per cent over four consecutive quarters when their deficit exceeded 3 per cent, or not. In assessing the performance of the new members, for instance, it may be raised, if a growth over 3.5 to 4 percent was enough for them to meet the symmetric part of Keynesian policies, requiring *fiscal surpluses* and a *decline in public debt* in the sunny years like those in 2002–2006? Put it differently, if measures to bring about the sustainability of public finances have been undertaken and brought sufficient results, is the medium-term fiscal convergence program credible? In concrete terms: when meeting the criteria, one-off measures, like tax increases, the prohibited use of privatization revenues for covering current spending, that is creative accounting, or indeed, serious structural measures allow for the higher growth of the next period?

This explains why the Vice President of the European Central Bank highlighted: the Commision proposals contained rather *clarifications and enhanced controls* over reporting, rather than a general easing in the practical management of the Pact (Papademos, 2004). Let us recall the point of the preceding Chapter: the SGP, like most other instruments of integration, is based on *voluntary compliance* and reliance on publicity by naming and shaming deviations. While inside one country, one may manipulate public opinion, international capital markets follow events in detail and, at least in the long run, punish non-obedience to what they percieve as solid finances. Capital flight and unexpected devaluations are known to be features for countries not playing by the rules – the 1997–99 and the 2001–2002 currency crises have amply demonstrated this point.

This might explain the fact that the allegedly 'dead' Pact has triggered a *series of adjustment measures in a number of core – EU-15 – countries* as well. Ireland, for instance, has given up its pro-cyclical policies of 2000–2001. Portugal, too, has limited its public deficit in 2002–2003, following a warning from the Commission. Italy, while sustaining a vocal criticism of the Pact, has not let its deficit to go over 3 per cent in any year since 2000, and even the stock of public debt declined by 5 percentage points between 2000–2005 (source of all data: ECB *Statistics Pocket Book*, Frankfurt, March 2005, pp. 41–42). In the meantime, the most indebted country of the euro-zone, Belgium has brought down its public debt by 9 percentage points, whereas in Hungary public debt has climbed from 53.5 percent in 2001 to close to 68.5 per cent by the first quarter of 2006. In Germany, despite scrious drifts within the governing Social Democratic Party, broad reforms have been launched in such areas as labor markets, health care and pensions, despite the sizable public protest. These facts do not allow to treat the reinterpreted Pact as 'yet another piece of paper' that should not bother 'serious' policy-makers, especially during election years.

In the economic litrature, several further suggestions have been raised to reinterpret the numerical targets of the SGP. It has been raised, that instead of actual deficits, operational deficits – i.e. excluding interest payments – should be considered. Others suggest the consideration of potential output, and allow for financing the output gap. Yet another suggestion calls for reliance on accrual-based and cyclically adjusted numbers and many others. Without entering the discussion of these, let us recall: the Pact has never been meant to be a scientific elaboration, where exactness and elegance are the supreme virtues. The SGP, by contrast, is an instrument of orientation for sub-optimally informed investors and for voters, whose turnout at recent European Parliament elections were a mere 37 per cent in the EU-25. Thus *simplicity* and *transparency*, as well as *unambiguity* are its basic virtues. If exchanged for other indicators, whose substance is accessible to a part of professionals only, moreover for indicators that become available usually only months after the decision is needed, this would indeed enhance academic quality, but destroy business confidence. Let us add, that substantive analyses (Hodson and Maher, 2004, Buti and Pench, 2004, p. 1032) have demonstrated that opening the door for individual interpretations render benchmarking and standardization hollow and meaningless, since *there is no way to check* in an impartial fashion if rules are adhered to, and if obligations are met or violated in numerical terms. Such an option is *unlikely to enhance rule abiding behavior*, does not produce incentives for correction of misdeeds, thus is likely to deteriorate rather than improve the final outcome. This likelihood could immediately be tested in the continued opportunistic behavior of large member states, with France and Germany, the traditional trespassers joined by Italy and yes, even Great Britain, in simply disregarding the common rules at times of moderate growth, rather than recession in 2004–2006.

For the summary of this section, let us recall: suggestions to reinterpret the SGP were *threefold*. One large part of them were obviously motivated by *opportunistic* interest of individual parites, such as the inclusion of costs for reunification, or the subtractability of assistance to developing nations, as these do not relate to Euro-zone-wide price stability and growth. The second group, by contrast, is derived from the most dynamic and most *elaborate* pieces of *academic analysis*. These follow considerations of formalized approaches, abstract considerations and practical relevance (applicability is rarely a major concern for those elaborating them, rather coherence) consistency considerations prevail. Third, we have analyzed the *intermediate* position of the Commission that contained points for *clarification* and points for severing *implementation*, while not – yet – allowing for opportunistic considerations. These also rely and enhance the enforcement mechanisms, that is peer pressure and naming and shaming, that draw on the feedback provided by international capial markets for policies where the free flight of ideas no longer correlate to the standards of solid finances. But, as Issing (2006, pp. 17–20) correctly observes, the fact, that laymen and politicians have limited understanding of the substance of the matter, *the fundamental economics of the arrangement has not been challenged by* any of these suggstions, namely that monetary union in the lack of political union, for technical and economic reasons, *does require a common fiscal framework* under any circumstances.

Re-Interpretation of the Pact

The European Council of March 22-23 2005 was devoted to the medium term strategy of the Union. Most of the time was spent on deliberations on re-launching the Lisbon Strategy, the medium term project of global competitiveness, and approved the re-interpretation of the SGP, as agreed in the last minute compromise of Ecofin in the preceding day, as a secondary issues of the agenda. Since the assessment of the Lisbon Strategy was a subject of a separate analysis (Csaba, 2005), here I focus on the salient features of the reinterpretation of the SGP only.

Looking from a formal perspective, the re-interpretation is legally questionable, as the SGP has become incorporated, in its original form in the Constitutional Treaty, that was at the time already approved by several legislations, including Lithuania and Hungary[5], while in other countries, terms of the referenda might have changed. Procedures of the decision repeatedly highlight the intergovernmental nature of the EU, including the weakened position of the Commission and other non-governmental agencies. The Council rejected the opinion of the ECB that argued for upholding the SGP in its original form, basically in line with the reasoning presented above.

Given the legal and political situation as described above, there could not be any talk about changing the reference numbers or scapping the Pact altogether, as believers in both corner positions would have had it. Meanwhile the Council accepted two major points from the majority views of criticism as voiced in the professional literature (Corricelli, F., 2005). Delineation of 'good' and 'bad' deficit was accepted, thus any temporary deficit that derives from measures improving future sustainability is seen as being in conformity with the Pact. The latter include R+D expenditures, especially for the Lisbon Agenda, privatization of pensions – altough, only until 2007 with a 20 per cent degression each year, and deficit numbers need not be interpreted mechanistically. Thus for instance Holland, having exceeded the reference number due to its costs on private pensions, is no longer subject to EDP. Furthermore, it has been accepted, that deficits are current numbers with no memory. Therefore, the second innovation highlights *the focal role of public debt and its dynamics* among the evaluation criteria, as the latter does have a memory and does have a forward-looking implication insofar as how narrow or broad the governments' room for manoeuvre may be in the future.

Meanwhile the Council decision has strongly been influenced by those considerations that we qualified above as merely opportunistic short-run points of

---

[5] By January 2007 18 member states ratified the Constitutional Treaty.

view. It entirely disregarded procedural tightening that each and every proponent of more liberal interpretation advocated as *necessary complements* to reinterpretation. Supporters of the broader interpretation advanced, e.g as a central argument (Boonstra,2005, p. 6. and p. 9) the need to exclude purely tactical bargains and decisions reflecting political sensitivities, the need for strengthening transparency. They also advocated the de-emphasis of the omnipotence of finance ministers, the main culprits, and relocate the assessment – of if and when a given country exceeded debt and deficit reference numbers – *to independent agencies* as the European Court of Auditors or the Eurostat. By the same token, more radical, though technically feasible suggestions, such as automatically depriving the trespassing country from its right to vote on economic matters in the Council and the Ecofin, as long as others do not accept its program for fiscal adjustment (Rostowski, 2005, pp. 155–156) have not even been considered. This is a pain, since it were opponents of the Pact who unfolded that the problem with the SGP is not so much in its numbers and procedural norms as its *partisan enforcement* – better to say, non-enforcement. Remedying this was not even envisioned by the Commission proposal (Eijfinger, 2005, pp. 13). This was the case despite the fact that political, technical and procedural matters can be neatly delineated as three different layers that might follow *three different* mechanisms of enforcement. As the above quoted Sylvester Eijfinger notes without addressing the issue of better enforcement, allowing the room for interpretation could only lead to softening up and even less enforcement – this was the core of the opposing argument of the ECB.[6]

As a quasi-inevitable follow up of this, the Council agreed to allow for the consideration of 'sluggish economic growth', *a concept completely unknown in academic economics.* When adopting the related arguments the Council simply disregarded the gargantuan difficulties in specifying potential output and the related output gap, the extremely high uncertainties surrounding these, as well as the usually considerable delay by the time the relevant numbers can be obtained (Antal, 2004, pp. 211–235). It is an additional danger, that *the rate of potential economic growth might be elevated to a measure of national pride,* a standard for patriotic commitment. This is a realistic problem and not only in the new member-states. For it is easiest to meet the numerical targets of the SGP by overstating the growth forecast, even if it serves a merely populist policy (Gros, 2005, pp. 16–17). This is unlikely to be remedied by the guideline that independent research institutions need to be invoked in making the growth assessment, since the government often acts as the major contracting party for these. Even if we disregard the practically non-negligible threat of *conflitc of interest situations,* researchers are also part and parcel of the domestic public discourse. Thus most of them are unlikely to position themselves as 'traitors', not believing even in the future potential of their own commuity. For instance the German economy should

---

[6] The ECB has sustained its position even after re-interpretation. Speaking on an international conference, ECB president Jean-Claude Trichet (2005) claimed the ECB support 'any measure that ensures enhanced fiscal solidity and the improved credibility of the Pact', as these represent the self-interest of the countries concerned. This is a very polite way of rejecting the re-interpretation exercise.

already be steadyly growing, should the forecasts of the 2000–2005 period of most institutes have come true. In the latter case, Germany should not be under the threat of an EDP. Buti and Franco (2005, pp. 240) find it problematic that the deadline for correcting deficits has been extended, and a *number of technical issues remain controversial*. The latter include the ways sustainability is to be calculated and how the effect of one-off measures is to be identified, or how the quality of public finances is to be assessed. All these threaten efficient monitoring, while the timing of actual fiscal adjustment might become *an ever moving target*.

Taking into account 'individual circumstances' has, from the very outset, been turned into an instrument of involving political opportunism. For instance contributions to Community budgets, or the costs of reunification has never figured among the items to be considered. Still they were included among those, giving in to German pressure. It is similarly contestable – on the base of endogenous growth theory – that all public R+D expenditure count as non-deficit items. Experiences of the central planning should have warned agaist it. It is hard to accept, even to comprehend how developmental aid – a French requirement – contribute to EU-wide financial stability and growth. Likewise, common defense expenditures do not relate to the former, no matter how commendable these may be.

Since the Council did nothing to stop the three major culprits, despite warnings of the ECB and the ruling of the ECJ, the obligation to diminish deficits by 0.5 per cent per annum automatically *does not sound credible*. Likewise assessment of individual conditions, including sluggish growth, when there is no algorithm to set trend rates, and no independent monitoring of numbers. Meanwhile transparency suffers due to the broad possibilities for interpretation and deductibility, and independent enforcement mechanisms continue to lack. Thus *a soft interpretation seems to be a done deal*. Explicating the semi-official view of the Commission Marco Buti (2006, pp. 22–23), in line with our previously voiced position highlights the need for *national rules* and national committment. All the more so since the Council has thus far, and perhaps also in the future, refrain from what he calles the 'nuclear option' of imposing fines on large country trespassers. While this remark is true on its own right, it is also a prime case of circular reasoning. Since it has indeed been exactly those countries and *lack of both committment and institutions* in those countrics that have resulted in a serial breach of the stipulations of the joint fiscal framework. Also, as Buti himself acknowledges, the basic incentive problem remains, i.e that the carrot of entry has been eaten up, while the stick of exclusion (or alternatively market punishment for individual EMU members) has not been at work. Thus the EU fiscal framework, in its re-interpreted form, provides little if any *additional incentive* over and above the conventional argumentation in favor of sound public finances, being a macroeconomic value on its own right and a side-condition for sustainable development.

Given that there is only an indirect relationship between price stability, sustainable growth and meeting of the SGP criteria (Pisani–Ferry, 2005) it would be wrong to create doomsday scenarios based on the reinterpretation of the Pact. As could be seen, the Pact has already served both the decrease of public debts and to trigger a series of measures and structural reforms that may contribute to the sustaining growth and healthy public finances of EU states, even against considerable domestic social opposition. It has contributed to price stability, that has though never been 2 per cent or below. But it has never been above 2.6 per cent despite considerable external shocks, such as the skyrocketing of oil prices, the burst of the IT bubble, or the terrorist attacks in the US, London and Madrid. Therefore *it is highly inappropriate and misleading for new members* to overstress the political compromises and ad-hoc circumstances surrounding the SGP, and *de-emphasize its proven economic logic*. It is no doubt, that a softer fiscal framework allows for more leeway for electoral politickling. However the sacrifice in terms of growth is likely to show up already in the medium run. As we have seen, some – by no means all – EU countries encounter growth slowdown. However, in none of the cases can we observe overdilligence in meeting SGP criteria, just the contrary. By re-launching the Lisbon Strategy, the EU Council itself allowed for such an interpretation. The normative conclusion is therefore for the new members is that they need to grow faster than the old ones, that in turn, requires more prudence in their fiscal stance, the promotion of savings and improvement of the investment climate. Opportunism of some of the old EU states need to be evaluated only in conjunction with their recent poor economic performance, rather than being taken unconditionally as a standard. Thus the insight (Heijman, 2006, p. 103) stressing the need for both retaining the coordinated fiscal framework *and supplementing it with supply-side measures* and stimulating long run factors of growth, such as the use of IT and more spending on R+D, remains valid for both old and new member-states.

Perspectives of the New EU Member-States

Following a previous extensive analysis by leading experts of the National Bank of Hungary (Orbán–Szapáry, 2004) advocating the retaining of the original SGP, it seems expedient to elaborate on the role the *revised* Pact may play in bringing about sustainable and financable *growth* in the new member states.

It seems to be a consensus view in the profession (Palánkai, 2005) that meeting the numerical criteria is needed for serving the interest of these countries, primarily for limiting the crowding out effects of public deficits that limit the private propensity and possibility to invest. Different analyses have also indicated that the threat from crowding out that translates into a slower actual growth rate than the trend rate would justify, is already emerging (Erdős, 2006, chapter 4). If this holds, the Pact should not be seen in itself, as one of the numerous stipulations of the EU, but rather as *a fundamental frame for macroeconomic policies* that allow for instituting those structural reforms that are needed for long run growth anyway. In so doing, the political economy of introducing the Euro is, or can be, to a large degree a carbon copy of the experiences of the Southern European member states. It is basically not the threat of falling under EDP and the fear of having to pay fines up to 0.5 per cent of

GDP that keeps new member countries on the path of fiscal solidity. Rather it is the self-interested quest for preserving the side conditions of sustainable growth, whose institutional and quantitative existence has been shown eroding already back in the the 2000–2004 period all across the Central European region (Antal, 2004). Yet differently put, by missing the targets for nominal convergence real convergence may easily come to a halt, much earlier than having attained the average of EU-15 in terms of per capita income. The fact that most analyses, including the structural and institutional indicators, reported in the EBRD *Transition Report,* (London, November 2006, annex) show a slowdown of reforms, privatization and fiscal consolidation alike, should be read as warning signs for the future. This only means that convergence is *conditional* rather than automatic – conditioned by approriate policy and institutional development in the catching up countries.

Therefore we have to deplore the flourishing 'patriotic' industry of trying to explain why the conditions of SGP should *not* be met, of trying to elaborate creative accounting techniques of *how not to report* general government deficit in full, in line with ESA and the IMF Code of Good Fiscal Practices standards. One of the more conceivable solutions would be to compel the fiscal authorities to legislate the measures that ensure the attainment of the quantitative targets on the long run, adoption of medium term fiscal perspective by the major political forces, reliance on independent expertise on growth and revenue forecasts etc. The real question is therefore how to attain the targets in a *credible and realistic fashion* under conditions of democratic competition, where the economic platform is one of the basic factors of choice for the citizens of each country.

The first question is certainly if the arguments on rules-based fiscal behavior apply for emerging economies, or should one allow for regressions in the old developmental paradigm, neomarxism or structuralism, that is into economic approaches that doubt that *less developed* countries are subject to *general economic and policy rules*? According to an authoritative and representative multi-author volume published on the issue, the rehash of old maxims is not convincing, especially under conditions of enhanced capital mobility. The growing use of IT, resultant dematerialization and delocation of international exchanges. In the argument in favor of *elevating fiscal rules to the constitutional level.* Allan Drazen (2004) highlights not only the need to resist daily political pressures, but also underscores the growing relevance of such items as *reputation and credible commitments* in managing financial flows. The more the latter are unrelated to commodity flows – such as derivates – and the less governments are able to manage these, the higher is the practical significance of reputation and credibility of commitments as a base of interaction with millions of market agents. Addresssing the relevance of these insights for less developed countries Drazen, (op.cit. pp. 28) specifically emphasizes that less developed countries are well advised to take these considerations even more seriously. Their financial institutions are less advanced thus their *vulnerability to external shocks* is even bigger, since credibility is lower. Therefore less advanced countries should conduct even *more conservative policies,* as the ramifications of eventual financial crises are even more serious for them.

The study on how these insights apply to EU accession (Coricelli and Ercolani, 2004, esp. pp. 159-160) drew attention to the warning sign of the reproduction of *disproportionately high levels of public debt* in the new member states. Moreover in several years between 1999–2004 a procyclical policy could also be observed. Therefore the real challenge for these is not how to meet the Maastricht criteria – say via creative accounting and making use of the re-interpretation of SGP – but *how to arrest the non-sustainable growth of their public debt*. The latter may translate either into slower growth rates, or in a worst scenario exchange rate shocks and a related adjustment, also a return to higher inflation and slow growth. Even the lasting uncertainty may translate into exchange rate volatility. Therefore the two Italian authors cited above suggest more reliance on the debt dynamics and a *de-emphasis of the deficit criterion* as well as of the inflation criterion for the new members. Looking from the longer perspective what really matters is whether these economies are on a sustainable growth path or not. This is better reflected in the debt dynamics, having a 'memory' and being forward looking, as explained above. Looking under this angle the data in Tables 2 and 3 are indicative, in the case of the Czech Republic and Poland debt levels way below the Maastricht reference levels may be a cause for grave concern, due to their dynamics. Analyzing these trends Scheider and Zapal (2005, pp. 84–87) conclude, that new meber states face three synergic problems. First, they *missed the opportunity* to consolidate their public finances when the environment would have been the most favorable for them in terms of growth and EU euphoria. Second, that the size of the government and the size of the recurring deficits, though two different cups of tea, still, *work in a mutually reinforcing manner,* especially in the Visegrád countries. Third, the new members already experience the softening up of the implementation of SGP rules, thus the European *incentive* to consolidate is alrady weakened.

It is therefore worth reiterating, that it is the best interest of the new member-states to follow the criteria of noninflationary growth, that is to bring about fiscal adjustment in order to create financing room for lastingly high growth rates. Only as second, but equally weighty is the argument that Central European countries have voluntarily opted for joining a monetary union with well known rules of the game. Given that that EMU is based on voluntary compliance, it is the common interest of the EU-27 to avoid even the appearance that rules are not abided, that new members contribute to watering down the existing monetary frame that used to work quite sucessfully in terms of price stability before eastward enlargement. Knowing the actual balance of power within the EU it would be hard to doubt the insight (Jonas, 2004, pp. 26–27) that the more new members require *flexible treatment* – say, with reference to the rigidity of ERM-2, or with reference to the transitory fiscal costs of structural reforms – the more that they *must* gain *strategic credibility* that is not being undermined by their emulation of the political opportunism of old members. On the contrary: the more convincing is the delivery on rules-based behavior by the new members, the higher is the chance of obtaining a flexible interpretation of rules by the majority of – that is by the old – EU members.

What is the sustainable level of public debt for the new members? This issue is of major significance for fiscal planning as well as for the realistic assessment of fiscal targets and convergence programs. Analyzing the situation of the Central European new members Orbán and Szapáry (2004) list various items of implicit public debt, low level of activity on the labor market, as well as ageing of the population, which is as bad or worse as for the old members. They come to the striking and policy relevant conclusion that the Czech and Hungarian cases sustainable debt levels are in the range of 40 to 45 per cent of GDP. Similar considerations might have prompted the inclusion of the 50% rule in the Polish Constitution, obliging the government to act and initiate parliamentary debate on how to remedy the situation. This implies that in the decade to come, a fiscal improvement in the range of 3.70 to 4.19 percent is needed only for the reasons discussed above (Orbán – Szapáry, op.cit. pp. 826-827). This number does not include the additional tightening needed for cyclical reasons as well as for overcoming consequences of several years of 'creative accounting'. The latter was put years ago by experts of the National Bank (P. Kiss et al, 2005) in the range of 8 per cent of GDP. This is the relevant number, which in macroeconomic terms is basically in line with the targets ensuing from the 'softened' version of the SGP. In reality however, Hungary has regularly been missing even those moderate improvements, enshrined in its own convergence programs, regularly produced since August 2002 by the half year, as required by the EU procedures. No explanation though, over and above the usual references to unforseen events, such as the winter cold and summer heat, has been provided.

External reviewers, such as the State Audit Office, the IMF, the World Bank, the OECD and of course the ECB, have recurringly called attention to the *lack of institutionalization in the budgeting procedure*, the regular lack of reliance on independent data and forecasts, as well as the customary overplanning of growth/revenues and underestimation of even forseeable commitments, such as pensions and health expenses, or losses of the public sector. No agent checks the fiscal plan, annual or multiyear, for its internal coherence or its relation to the medium term convergence plan. Improvisations of the government during the medium-term run-up period, such as first increasing then decreasing VAT rates (in 2004 and 2006), or multiplying the minimum wage, or increasing pension entitlements while decreasing contributions of employers and employees have only aggravated a situation[7], which had already been bad enough without such 'innovations'.

One of the basic analyses of fiscal sustainability in the EU is the book of Hughes-Hallet et.al, (2003) underscores that *high rates of growth* would be the obvious wayout from fiscal retrenchment in the EU. This may sound trivial: if the cake is bigger, a similar slice is proportionately smaller. And conversely, if everything grows, each player gets more, including the state budget. The smaller is the informal sector, the more efficient the tax administ-

---

[7] On the latter see in detail the overview of Orbán and Szapáry (2006).

ration, the more immediate fiscal improvements from growth may be. Therefore it is understandable – though by no means acceptable – that ministries of finance in old and new member states tend to overstate their growth forecasts, also year by year. As we have seen in the preceeding chapter, the *unidirectional bias in errors* – upward in growth, downward of deficits – was unmistakeable.

Abstracting for a moment from the loss of credibility that has resulted from this practice – and translated into higher yields on government bonds and higher real rates of interest – it seems *questionable* if, indeed, for the new EU members *any linear dependence* of fiscal intakes on growth would indeed hold. This has to do not only with the high share of the informal economy – set at about 20–22 per cent in Central Europe and significantly higher in Cyprus and Malta. It also is related to the fact that most *structural reforms* that are needed for sustainingly high growth *induce transitory fiscal losses* in the short and medium run partly because they make previous implicit costs and explicit debts. Tibor Erdős (2006, chapter 3) provides a detailed list of the areas where developmental projects are urgently needed, while *subtracting* from productive investment. These are however indispensable for bringig about the *side conditions for long run growth*, such as rural development to public health and public education. In the light of the theory of endogenous growth as well as of human capital, it is hard to believe that keeping R+D expenditures at the present level of 1 per cent of GDP (public and corporate outlays taken together) in 2004–2007 in Hungary could have no repercussion on the long run innovation rate, thus on the *long run growth potential of any economy*. This holds even if everybody is aware of the fact that fundamental research produces indirect benefits and on the long horizon only. Since the neglect of *high quality* higher education – not to be mixed up with student numbers and enrollment ratios – as well as the de-emphasis of R+D, both in the academic and corporate spheres, are *decades-old phenomena* in the region, there is a high probability that actual growth rates in the new member states are likely to fall below their trend rate of 2.7–3.2 per cent, as calculated by Tibor Erdős in his analysis quoted above.

The normative conclusion would call for reversing the sequence of measures, where public expenditure items and their structure would follow from a *long run program of convergence and catching up*, rather than on the base of the ratchet principle and of short term political bargains in the legislation. This would require a lot of analytical work as well as active *participation* of experts from all major political forces. It is an interesting separate issue if, following the experience of coordinated western European market economies, also civil societices, including unions, employers' associations, professional clubs and the regional municipalities should be involved. Following the latter, experience would intuitively suggest to the new member states to try and emulate earlier experiences of Southern EU members in elaborating *multiyear social contracts*. The latter would allow for elevating some of the joint insights – such as the need for a cyclically adjusted balanced budget rule for the medium run – to the level of the national fiscal framework, ideally in the wording of the national

Constitution.[8] However, more detailed analysis of the fragmented labor market and conflictual political structures of the new members caution against the usefulness/feasibility of such an imitative solution (Benczes, 2006).

Whatever form the basic understanding on the need to institutionalize fiscal prudence may actually take, this would be in line with earlier suggestions from constitutional political economy (Vanberg, 2001) of creating a stable overall framework over and above daily political fluctuations, that would allow for calculable and transparent rules, while allowing sufficient room for competing economic and political forces to shape the processes via their bargains on the short run. The latter includes such vital items as the structure of taxation, or the relation between local and central budgets, whereas the former could cover the broad guidelines, institutions and points of orientation. Such arrangements are well known also in modern mass–media democracies, from Denmark to Spain, from Ireland to New Zeeland, Canada and Sweden, and have delivered quite convincing economic results in the medium and long run in each of the cases. By contrast, the ritually invoked reference to the 'inevitable' *political business cycle*, that is an economic policy dominated primarily or exclusively by electoral considerations, have *not* been a *powerful explanation* for what empirical analysis (Andrikopoulos et al, 2004) has found in the EU-15 for the post-1980 period. Thus there is no serious excuse for the irresponsible financial policies that took media efficiency as the sole criterion of success in the 2000–2006 period in the new member states.

Theory and Practice

This chapter analyzed the pros and cons of sustaining rules-based behavior in the EU from the point of view of new members. Avoiding purely tactical suggestions, we have found that lasting growth and sustainable public finances are the *two sides of the same coin*. This is in line with findings of the international academic economic mainstream.

The basic conclusion is that retaining the SGP is not merely a legal and political nuesance that follows from its status in the Treaty on the European Union, as well as in the accession agreements, but it meets the interests of all EU members old and new. While interpreting its stipulation needs, a degree of flexibility – such as avoiding minor overruns if these follow from virtuous policy measures – the ruling of the European Court of Justice as of 13 July 2004, as well as the broader economic analytical considerations invoked above call for a *better enforcement* of its logic than before. Following the propositions of the

---

[8] The present Hungarian Constitution, itself an outcome of the 1989 round table negotiations, is tellingly silent on a number of issues that are vital for long term economic development, such as the independence of the central bank, the balanced budget rule, or the individual responsibility of those publishing the numbers of public finances, similarly to the individual responsibility of auditors and financial executives, as required by the modifications of US legislation elaborated by the Sarabanes Commission following the accounting scandals of 2001–2002.

Commission, the Council adopted a re-interpretation, that contains *elements of severing*[9] *just as much as elements of more liberal reading.* It is not in the interest of the new members to take the opportunistic behavior of some old member-states as a yardstick, since their own long term sustainable growth requires, in fact, stricter discipline in financial planning in the medium and long run than the 'Maastricht straightjacket', or even the 'stupid SGP' would have it. The 'neither stick nor carrot' perception of the Pact thus seems to have spread much quicker than reformers would have had it.[10] At the time of concluding this update, supporters of the center-left Hungarian government (Petschnig, 2006) discussed as a done deal that each of the Visegrád countries have given up even the attempt at fiscal stringency, and as a consequence, also the deadline of joining the single currency any time before 2013–2014, despite the obvious growth sacrifice of this choice.

Turning back to theory, the starting point of our elaboration, it has proven fruitful to apply the theory of time inconsistency and the suggestions of constitutional political economy, both distilled from the American experience, on European empirical material. The robustness of these theories have been proven. On the one hand the explanatory power of the theory of time inconsistency of Kydland and Prescott has not lost any of its value, rather *it has gained in policy relevance.* Applying their insights allows for a plausible reading of the softening up of the Pact, and allow for forming rational expectations for the future. Indeed, the analysis of European arrangements in a global context (Christl, J., 2006) have highlighted the importance of *convergence criteria, availability of fiscal rules and the ensuing/presupposed stability orientation* of domestic policies and their framework among the conditions for financing sustainable growth. The theory of constitutional political economy by Buchanan and followers allows us to delineate long and short run phenomena and make suggestions on policy relevant institutional arrangements for the new member states so that they could meet their convergence targets and bring about conditions of sustainable growth. Our analytical frame allows for 'if-then' predictive conclusions, also for cases when nomative considerations must give way to more pedestrian ones. It also allows for getting a hunch feeling of the costs of following a logic of populist myopia and a disregard for sustainable public finances. And while creating a *perpetuum mobile* has long been a dream of

---

[9] These include more rigorous checking of the reported statistical numbers, mobilizing a number of early warning measures, the automatic obligation to present fiscal convergence plans with improvements of 0.5 per cent of deficit/GDP ratio by the year, the need to rely on external assessment of growth prospects, and the concrete lists under which deficits are tolerated, that are completely different from the ones faced by the new members.

[10] Let us recall again: in May 2006 Lithuania was not admitted to the euro-zone, due to its high and accelerating rate of inflation, from 1.2% in 2004 to 2.7 by 2005 and still 4.3 in April 2006 (ECB: *Statistics Pocket Book*, November, 2006 pp. 36). Estonia for similar reasons withdrew its application in April 2006 with inflation accelerating from 3.0 to 4.1% by 2005 and 4.3% by April 2006 (ECB: op.cit). Reflecting on the medium run perspectives of new members other than Slovenia Commissioner Almunia aired his severe doubts on any other applicant's good chances, basically due to fiscal imbalances, as reported in: *portfolio.hu*, 13 July, 2006.

humankind, science allows us to state its impossibility. Likewise, while democratically elected politicians, working under short term incentives, have long been wishing to conduct growth promoting policies without being constrained by any rules, be those economic or constitutional, it is impossible.

Thereby we have come back to *the crux of new political economy:* the relation between market and the state and *the possible interaction of the failure of both.* In order to elaborate these complex interrelationships, two further steps will be made. First, in Chapter Ten we shall look, in a tentative and normative manner, into ways and means of improving the existing European intergovernmental regulatory frame for a market, which is increasingly transnationalized and even globalized. Then, in Chapters Eleven and Twelve we look into the possible alternatives to what we consider the mainstream of economic development. Both Russia and China have been registering high and sustaining rates of economic growth over several years, thus the viability and virtues/vices of authoritarian solutions also deserve a detailed analysis, before more general considerations over regulation and the role of institutions may conclude. As we have seen in our survey of EU affairs, it is not so much if regulations and institutions matter that is contested. What really is at stake is: which regulations, which institutions and *under what specific conditions matter for economic success?*

References

ANDRIKOPOULOS, A. – LOIZIDES, I. – PRODROMIS, K. (2004): Fiscal policy and political business cycles in the European Union. *European Journal of Political Economy,* vol. 20. no. 1. pp. 125–152.

ANTAL L. (2004): *Fenntartható-e a fenntartható növekedés?* (Is sustainable development likely to last?) Budapest: a book published by the 'Közgazdasági Szemle' Foundation.

BENCZES I. (2004): Fiskális szabályok használata a Gazdasági és Monetáris Unióban. (The use of fiscal rules in EMU). *Külgazdaság,* vol. 48. no. 11. pp. 20–37.

BENCZES, I. (2006): Social pacts: a helping device in euro adoption? *Transition Studies Review,* vol. 13. no. 2. pp. 417–438.

BOONSTRA, W. (2005): Proposals for a better Stability Pact. *Intereconomics,* vol. 40. no. 1. pp. 4–9.

BUCHANAN, J. – WAGNER, R. (1997): *Democracy in Deficit: the Political Legacy of Lord Keynes.* San Diego, USA-London: Academic Press.

BUTI, M. – PENCH, L. (2004): Why do large countries flout the Stability Pact? And what can be done about it? *Journal of Common Market Studies,* vol. 42. no. 5. (Dec.), pp. 1025–1032.

BUTI, M. – FRANCO, D. (2005): *Fiscal Policy in Economic and Monetary Union.* Cheltenham, UK – Northampton, MA, USA: Edward Elgar Publishing Co.

BUTI, M. (2006): Will the new SGP succeed? An economic and political perspective.Brussels: EU Commission, *European Economy - Economic Papers,* no. 241.

CARLBERG, M. (2003): *Policy Coordination in a Monetary Union.* Heidelberg – New York etc: Springer Verlag.

CHRISTL, J. (2006): Regional currency arrangements: insights from Europe. Vienna, Austrian National Bank, *ÖNB Working Paper,* no. 125.

CORRICELLI, F. – ERCOLANI, V. (2004): Fiscal rules on the road to an enlarged union. In: KOPITS, G. ed: *Rules-Based Fiscal Policy in Emerging Markets.* Houndmills-London etc, Palgrave/ MacMillan, pp. 146–163.

CORRICELLI, F. (2005): 'Fiscal policy and adjustment in EMU' – paper presented to the international conference of CASE entitled *Europe after Enlargement,* Warsaw, 7–8 April – the proceedings forthcoming at Cambridge University Press under the edition of A. Aslund.

CSABA, L. (2005): Poetry and reality about the future of Europe. *Intereconomics,* vol. 40. no. 2. pp. 61–66.

DRAZEN, A. (2004): Fiscal rules from a political economy perspective. In: KOPITS, G. ed.: *Rules-Based Fiscal Policy in Emerging Markets.* Houndmills etc: Palgrave/MacMillan, pp. 15–29.

EIJFFINGER, S. (2005): Reform of the SGP: evaluating the European Commission communication of September 2004. *Intereconomics,* vol. 40. no. 1. pp. 10–14.

ERDŐS, T. (2006): *Növekedési potenciál és gazdaságpolitika.* (The potential rate of growth and economic policy). Budapest. Akadémiai Kiadó.

FRIEDMAN, M. (1968): The role of monetary policy. *American Economic Review,* vol. 58. no. 1. pp. 1–16.

GROS, D. (2005): Reforming the Stability Pact. *Intereconomics,* vol. 40. no. 1. pp. 14–17.

GYŐRFFY, D. (2005): Adopting the Euro: the path to fiscal sustainability. *Acta Oeconomica,* vol. 55. no. 2. pp. 151–170.

GYŐRFFY, D. (2007): *Democracy and Deficits?* Budapest: Akadémiai Kiadó, Ph.D.dissertation series.

DE HAAN, J. – BERGER, H. – JENSEN, D.-J. (2003): The end of the SGP. München: CES/IFO *Working Paper,* no 1093.

HODSON, D. – MAHER, I. (2004): Soft law and sanctions: economic policy coordination and reform of the SGP. *Journal of European Public Policy,* vol. 11. no. 5. pp. 789–813.

HAYEK, F. (1989): *The Fatal Conceit. Errors of Socialism.* Chicago and London: The University of Chicago Press.

HEIJMAN, W. J. M. (2006): The need for a European fiscal policy. *Intereconomics,* vol. 41. no. 2. pp. 100–103.

HUGHES-HALLETT, A. – LEWIS, J. – VON HAGEN, J. (2003): *Fiscal Policy in Europe, 1989–2003: an Evidence-Based Analysis.* London: Center for Economic Policy Research.

ISSING, O. – GASPAR, V. – ANGELONI, I. (2001): *Monetary Policy in the Euro Area: Strategy and Decision-Making at the European Central Bank.* Cambridge and New York: Cambridge University Press – revised version reprinted in 2004.

ISSING, O. (2006): Europe's hard fix: the Euro area. Vienna, Österreichische Nationalbank, *Working Paper* no 120/April.

JANKOVICS, L. (2004): A modern pénzpolitika elméleti hátteréről. (On the theoretical background of modern monetary policy.) *Competitio* (Debrecen), vol. 3. no. 3. pp. 139–156.

JONAS, J. (2004): Euro adoption and Maastricht ctieria: rules or discretion? Bonn: Rheinische-Friedrich-Wilhelms-Universitaet, Center for European Integration Studies, *Working Paper* B–14.

KRUGMAN, P. (1998): Depression economics returns. *Foreign Affairs,* vol. 78. no. 1. pp. 56–74.

KYDLAND, F. – PRESCOTT, E. (1997): Rules rather than discretion: the inconsistency of optimal plans. *Journal of Political Economy,* vol. 85. no. 3. pp. 473–492.

LOSONCZ, M. (2004): A Stabilitási és Növekedési Egyezmény kérdőjelei. (Question marks about SGP). *Európai Tükör,* vol. 9. no. 2. pp. 61–78.

MAYES, D. – VIRÉN, M. (2004): Pressures on the SGP from asymmetry in policy. *Journal of European Public Policy,* vol. 11. no. 5. pp. 781–797.

ORBÁN, G. – SZAPÁRY, GY. (2004): A Stabilitási és Növekedési Egyezmény az új tagállamok szemszögéből (SGP seen from the angle of new members.) *Közgazdasági Szemle*, vol. 51. no. 9. pp. 810–830. – English version as: *MNB Working papers*, no. 4.

ORBÁN, G. and SZAPÁRY, GY. (2006): Magyar fiskális politika: quo vadis? (Hungarian fiscal policy: quo vadis?) *Közgazdasági Szemle*, vol. 53. no. 4. pp. 293–309.

PALÁNKAI, T. (2005): Magyarország modernizációja, versenyképessége és uniós fölzárkózása. (Modernization, competitiveness and EU catching up of Hungary) *Európai Tükör*, vol. 10. no. 5. pp. 25–50.

PAPADEMOS, L. (2004): 'The Exchange Rate Mechanism and the EMU' – paper presented to the joint conference of the Center for Economic Policy Research and the National Bank of Hungary, Budapest, 25 September .

PETSCHNIG, M. Z. (2006): Rövid távú áldozat? (A short term growth sacrifice?) *Figyelő*, vol. 50. no. 29.

PISANY-FERRY, J. (2005): 'Comments on Corricelli' – discussion paper at the CASE conference *Europe after Enlargement*, Warsaw, 7–8 April.

P. KISS, G. – KARÁDI, P. – KREKÓ, J. (2005): 'Az euró bevezetésével járó strukturális politikai kihívások: költségvetési politika.' (Structural challenges on the road to Euro: fiscal policy) – National Bank of Hungary, *MNB Háttértanulmányok*, no. 1. available online on: www.mnb.hu

RÁCZ, M. (2004): A Stabilitási és Növekedési Paktum érvényesítésének problémái és a lehetséges megoldás körvonalai (Enforcement problems of the SGP and ways of possible solutions). *Közgazdasági Szemle*, vol. 51. no. 10. pp. 970–986.

ROSTOWSKI, J. (2005): How to reform the Stability and Growth Pact. in: DABROWSKI, M. – ROSTOWSKI, J. eds: *The Eastward Enlargement of the Eurozone*. Heidelberg-New York etc: Springer Verlag, pp. 147–158.

Schneider, O. – Zapal, J. (2005): Fiscal policy in new member states: go East, prudent man! In: WINIECKI, J. ed: *Reverse Learning*. Rzeszów: a joint publication of the Polish Economists' Society and The University of Information and Technology (WSIiZ), pp. 55–92. reprinted also in: *Post-Communist Economies*, vol. 18. no. 1.

TANZI, V. (2004): The SGP: its role and future. *CATO Journal*, vol. 24 nos (1–2), pp. 57–70.

TRICHET, J.-C. (2005): 'Economic and financial integration in Europe' – keynote delivered to the CASE conference *Europe after Enlargement*, Warsaw, 7–8 April.

VANBERG, V. (2001): *The Constitution of Markets*. London: Routledge.

WILLIAMSON, J. (1994): In search for a manual for technopols. In: WILLIAMSON, J. ed: *The Political Economy of Economic Policy Reforms*. Washington,D.C.: Institute of International Economics, pp. 7–41.

Table 1.

General government deficit / surplus
(as a percentage of GDP)

	2002	2003	2004	2005
BE	0.0	0.1	0.0	0.1
DE	-3.7	-4.0	-3.7	-3.3
GR	-4.9	-5.8	-6.9	-4.5
ES	-0.3	0.0	-0.1	1.1
FR	-3.2	-4.2	-3.7	-2.9
IE	-0.4	0.2	1.5	1.0
IT	-2.9	-3.4	-3.4	-4.1
LU	2.0	0.2	-1.1	-1.9
NL	-2.0	-3.1	-1.9	-0.3
AT	-0.5	-1.5	-1.1	-1.5
PT	-2.9	-2.9	-3.2	-6.0
FI	4.1	2.5	2.3	2.6
Euro area	-2.6	-3.1	-2.8	-2.4
CZ	-6.8	-6.6	-2.9	-2.6
DK	1.2	1.0	2.7	4.9
EE	1.0	2.4	1.5	1.6
CY	-4.5	-6.3	-4.1	-2.4
LV	-2.3	-1.2	-0.9	0.2
LT	-1.4	-1.2	-1.5	-0.5
HU	-8.4	-6.4	-5.4	-6.1
MT	-5.6	-10.2	-5.1	-3.3
PL	-3.2	-4.7	-3.9	-2.5
SI	-2.7	-2.8	-2.3	-1.8
SK	-7.7	-3.7	-3.0	-2.9
SE	-0.2	0.1	1.8	2.9
UK	-1.6	-3.3	-3.3	-3.6
EU	-2.3	-3.0	-2.6	-2.3

Source: Euro area data: ECB; EU data and countries'
deficits / surpluses: European Commission
ECB *Statistics Pocket Book,* Frankfurt/M.,
June 2006, pp. 42.

Table 2.

General government debt
(as a percentage of GDP, unless otherwise indicated)

	Share (in%: 2005)	2002	2003	2004	2005
BE	4.9	103.2	98.5	94.7	93.3
DE	26.9	60.3	63.8	65.5	67.7
GR	3.4	110.7	107.8	108.5	107.5
ES	6.9	52.5	48.9	46.4	43.2
FR	20.1	58.2	62.4	64.4	66.8
IE	0.8	32.1	31.1	29.4	27.6
IT	26.7	105.5	104.2	103.8	106.4
LU	0.0	6.5	6.3	6.6	6.2
NL	4.7	50.5	51.9	52.6	52.9
AT	2.7	66.0	64.4	63.6	62.9
PT	1.7	55.5	57.0	58.7	63.9
FI	1.1	41.3	44.3	44.3	41.1
Euro area	100.0	68.1	69.3	69.8	70.7
CZ	0.5	28.8	30.0	30.6	30.5
DK	1.1	46.8	44.4	42.6	35.8
EE	0.0	5.5	6.0	5.4	4.8
CY	0.1	65.2	69.7	71.7	70.3
LV	0.0	13.5	14.4	14.6	11.9
LT	0.1	22.3	21.2	19.5	18.7
HU	0.7	55.0	56.7	57.1	58.4
MT	0.0	61.2	71.3	76.2	74.7
PL	1.6	39.8	43.9	41.9	42.5
SI	0.1	29.7	29.1	29.5	29.1
SK	0.2	43.3	42.7	41.6	34.5
SE	2.1	52.0	51.8	50.5	50.3
UK	11.2	37.6	39.0	40.8	42.8
EU	100.0	60.5	62.0	62.4	63.4

Source: as in Table 1., pp. 43.

Table 3.

Selected indicators for EU Member States
HICP (annual percentage changes, unless otherwise indicated)

	Share (in%; 2006)	Average 1996-00	Average 2001-05	2004	2005	2006 Mar.	2006 Apr.	2006 May.
BE	3.4	1.6	2.0	1.9	2.5	2.2	2.6	2.8
DE	28.7	1.1	1.6	1.8	1.9	1.9	2.3	2.1
GR	2.9	4.6	3.5	3.0	3.5	3.3	3.5	
ES	12.0	2.6	3.2	3.1	3.4	3.9	3.9	4.1
FR	20.3	1.3	2.0	2.3	1.9	1.7	2.0	
IE	1.3	2.6	3.4	2.3	2.2	2.8	2.7	
IT	19.1	2.4	2.4	2.3	2.2	2.2	2.3	2.3
LU	0.3	1.7	2.8	3.2	3.8	3.7	3.5	
NL	5.2	1.9	2.8	1.4	1.5	1.4	1.8	
AT	3.1	1.2	1.9	2.0	2.1	1.3	2.0	
PT	2.2	2.4	3.2	2.5	2.1	3.0	2.9	
FI	1.6	1.6	1.4	0.1	0.8	1.2	1.5	
Euro area	100.0	1.6	2.2	2.1	2.2	2.2	2.4	2.5
CZ	1.3	5.8	2.0	2.6	1.6	2.4	2.3	
DK	1.1	2.0	1.9	0.9	1.7	1.8	1.8	
EE	0.1	8.8	3.5	3.0	4.1	4.0	4.3	
CY	0.2	2.9	2.5	1.9	2.0	2.6	2.5	
LV	0.2	4.3	4.1	6.2	6.9	6.6	6.1	
LT	0.4	8.2	0.9	1.2	2.7	3.1	3.4	
HU	1.2.	15.1	5.8	6.8	3.5	2.4	2.4	
MT	0.1	3.2	2.5	2.7	2.5	2.9	3.5	
PL	4.3	11.0	2.7	3.6	2.2	0.9	1.2	
SI	0.3	8.2	5.5	3.7	2.5	2.0	2.8	
SK	0.6	8.2	5.8	7.5	2.8	4.3	4.4	
SE	1.7	1.1	1.8	1.0	0.8	1.5	1.8	
UK	17.1	1.4	1.4	1.3	2.1	1.8	2.0	
EU	100.0	2.4	2.4	2.1	2.2	2.1	2.3	

Source: as in Table 1., pp. 36.

Table 4.

GDP
(annual percentage volume changes, unless otherwise indicated, quarterly data working day adjusted)

	Share (in%; 2005)	Average 1996-00	Average 2001-05	2004	2005	2005 Q3	2005 Q4.	2005 Q1
BE	3.7	2.6	1.5	2.6	-1.2	1.2	1.5	2.2
DE	28.1	2.0	0.7	1.6	1.0	1.6	1.7	1.4
GR	2.3	3.4	4.4	4.7	3.7	3.8	3.7	4.1
ES	11.3	4.1	3.1	3.1	3.4	3.5	3.5	3.5
FR	21.4	2.7	1.5	2.3	1.2	1.4	1.1	1.5
IE	2.0	9.7	5.2	4.5	4.3	5.4	4.8	
IT	17.7	1.9	0.6	1.1	0.0	0.1	0.5	1.5
LU	0.4	6.1	3.3	4.2	4.0	5.4	5.7	
NL	6.3	3.7	0.8	1.7	1.1	1.3	2.0	2.1
AT	3.1	3.0	1.5	2.4	1.8	1.5	2.0	2.3
PT	1.8	4.1	0.6	1.1	0.3	0.4	0.7	
FI	1.9	4.7	2.2	3.6	2.1	2.5	2.9	2.9
Euro area	100.0	2.7	1.4	2.1	1.3	1.6	1.7	1.9
CZ	0.9	1.5	3.6	4.7	6.0	5.8	6.9	
DK	1.9	2.9	1.4	1.9	3.1	4.4	3.4	
EE	0.1	5.6	7.6	7.8	9.8	10.4	11.5	
CY	0.1	3.8	3.2	3.9	3.8	4.0	3.6	
LV	0.1	5.7	8.1	8.5	10.2	11.4	10.5	
LT	0.2	4.5	7.6	7.0	7.5	8.1	8.1	7.9
HU	0.8	4.2	4.1	4.6	4.1	4.4	4.2	4.3
MT	0.0	5.3	0.0	−1.5	2.5	5.4	2.5	
PL	2.2	5.4	3.0	5.3	3.3	3.6	4.7	4.6
SI	0.3	4.7	3.3	4.2	3.9	4.0	5.1	
SK	0.3	3.8	4.6	5.4	6.1	6.3	7.4	6.3
SE	2.7	3.2	2.2	3.7	2.7	2.9	3.1	3.9
UK	16.3	3.2	2.3	3.1	1.8	1.9	1.8	2.2
EU	100.0	2.9	1.7	2.4	1.6	1.8	1.9	2.2

Source: Eurostat
as in Table 1., pp. 37.

10. POST-CRISIS PERSPECTIVES ON THE FUTURE OF THE EU[1]

In this chapter we attempt to evaluate the consequences of 2004, when the EU–15 was enlarged by ten new members. Having discussed the challenges enlargement has caused in the preceding four chapters, we now turn to the often subsumed, but rarely formulated question: *if enlargement is a cause, or just a mere symptom* of the crises of the European project in its current form. A survey of the 'state of the Union' follows. The third section asks if new members develop into a 'colition of the nasty'. Finally, part four concludes with a normative vision of the future drafting possible scenarios, including *further* enlargement.

There is a high degree of gloom and depression in the discourse over the European Union. The languague used by politicians and the press alike, tends to be confrontational visions of the European 'super-state' as well as of egoistic net contributors, dominate. Attempts by the British Presidency in the second half of 2005 to reshape expenditure priorities and push long overdue reforms as part and parcel of the 2007–2013 Financial Perspective failed. Representatives of the four Visegrád countries rejected the British suggestions with great vigor, without even considering these as basis for negotiations. When a modified version was made public, the Hungarian PM first issued a statement rejecting it before even having considered what was a complex set of interrelated propositions, with reference to the projected diminishing of the size of the bugdet. It seems that the 'bigger the better' approach of the socialist period is returning. And while one has sympathy with Commission President José Manuel Barroso in his anger over cuts of the inflows, it would surely be politically simplistic and academically unfounded to contend that a bigger EU budget were equal to a stronger Europe, and conversely, by definition, a smaller budget to a weaker integration. Being aware of the large number of critical studies on EU spending (Midelfart-Kravnik and Overmas, 2002, Swinbank and Daubjerg, 2004), as

---

[1] A previous version of this chapter was published in the Italian quarterly, *Est-Ovest*, vol. 35. no. 6 (2005), pp. 33–50. Parts of the text re-used with permission. I also benefited from critical comments by János Martonyi, when he introduced the Hungarian edition of the book at Budapest Corvinus University, 13 December 2006.

well as the growing role of nationally funded joint projects, such as in the field of environmental protection, or even the deployment of the rapid reaction force in Macedonia, the identification of the financial perspective as a share of GDP with European policies and institutions and the committment thereto seems hasty at best.

In reality, the eastward enlargement of the EU can be qualified as *the single greatest success of European integration* to date. At the negligible cost of 0.15 per cent of the GDP of the EU–15, counting with Romania and Bulgaria by 2007, twelve formerly Communist countries could be brought to the family of European nations. The process of Europeanization, i.e the interplay of EU-level and domestic institutions and policies has been underway for over 15 years. This has helped to shape the workings of new democracies, the evolution of market institutions, and not least to bring about the critical minimum of policy consensus that has been needed for the shaping of relevant institutions and the conduct of policies that may run counter to vested interests, such as trade liberalization and ensuring price stability via an independent central bank.

Despite all conceivable criticism about the quality of the market order or of the functioning of democracy which may well be legitimate, it is beyond doubt that the EU managed to stabilize its 'backyard', both in terms of security policy and in terms of economic conditions. A glance of the statistics on economic activity might suffice to prove that new members have been showing regularly more robust economic activity indicators than the incumbents. While GDP growth in the Euro area decelerated from the 1996–2000 period of 2.7 per cent to 1.3 per cent in 2001–2004, Slovakia registered 3.7 and 4.6 per cent respectively, Hungary 4.0 and 3.6 respectively, Latvia 5.4 and 7.5 per cent, Lithuania 4.3 and 7.7 per cent, Estonia 5.6 and 7.0 per cent (source: ECB: *Statistics Pocket Book*. Frankfurt M, October, 2005, p. 37). The post-Communist economies have put their house in order out of their own initiative, *prior to joining the EU* – a great difference from the experience of Southern enlargement, when significant sums, on occassion reaching up to 4 per cent of local GDP were provided by the EC in terms of assistance. Moreover, these countries have clearly brought vitality in terms of new trade and investment opportunities, whereas inflated fears of mass migration – 370 to 650 thousand per year in some forecasts – have proven unfounded. The actual outflow of people was in the hundreds and thousands, not even reaching ten thousand in the case of Hungary. This happened for the simple reason that all those, who wanted to leave have already left in the 1989–2004 period.

The original 1957 project of the founding fathers has been by and large *completed*. Although some countries have decided not to join, or the EU has not yet agreed to their inclusion. Still the idea of creating a community where war is unthinkable, where common values rule, where rule of law and parliamentary democracy are no longer subject to doubt, where the market economy has been re-established, i.e the original agenda of the Treaty of Rome is basically accomplished. All these have been taking place in a period of sustaining growth. In the new member states, inflation has been arrested. While this time might eventually be a longer period than most of us would have liked it to be, still, from the long run perspective, this accomplishment defies most of the skeptical tones that were voiced at the onset of systemic change.

However, the *perception* of European integration differs fundamentally from the facts and figures. In the East, the bargains over macroeconomically insignificant sums, as well as over forms of support that defy the basics of public finance, such as direct income support to farmers, have created an atmposphere of frustration. The latter has been overshadowing the major accomplishment of having entered into a regulatory frame which creates, for the long run, much more favorable conditions for sustainable growth, than that of anybody left out. As this is already being factored in the calculations of investors, portfolio and FDI alike, this circumstance is already welfare enhancing in and for the new members.

Three Overlapping Crises and Enlargement

Meanwhile, in the West, enlargement has coincided with *three overlapping crises*. In fact, as we shall show below, enlargement has though not triggered these, still, given its modalities, it *has undoubtedly contributed* to these crises, rather than to their solution. Volumes have been written on this complex matter, for the sake of brevity I shall confine myself to listing these.

A. The *identity crisis*. For the generation of the founding fathers, but also for those of the Mitterand-Kohl-Delors cohort, the meaning of European integration, the move towards *finalité politique* was a given, not requiring special justification in terms of cost-benefit analysis. The idea of the 'ever closer union' has never been seriously questioned and this helped overcome deadlocks and crisis situations that have always followed the evolution of European integration (Dinan, 2004). However, with a generation of politicians born after World War II, this intuitive and intrinsic pro-integrationism or federalism has become questioned. When Baroness Thatcher wanted 'her money back' in 1984 and attained the unfamous British rebate, this was seen as a smallish price to be paid for the queer British to be kept inside Europe. Two decades later, Germany, and also Scandinavian, Southern and Benelux members tend to see the EU in purely financial terms. While this is mistaken in analytical terms, *perceptions shape policies more than facts do*, especially in a world dominated by electronic media. While the emergence of soft law, the progress of European policy transfer, the emergence of meso-level coordination together have turned the deepening project a reality (Wagener-Eger-Frtiz, 2006), most policy-makers have gradually but unambigously been converted to the intergovernmentalist, *minimalist perspective*. In so doing, the question of 'why Europe?' and 'what is the value added of jointly doing things that may be done separately' have been more frequently been raised. The median voter and also the median policy-maker considers European integration as a fact of life, *a given*, not worthy of reflecting about. In a way, having accomplished the original objectives, the EU has fallen *vic-*

244

tim to its own success. The attempts to create new visions, be that through the three successive conferences of Turin, Nice and the Convention in Laeken, or via the Lisbon Strategy, have failed to master this task. If we have no answer to what Europe stands for, it is difficult to come up with visions. Without visions, there is no strategy, without strategy no grand project, without project there is no schedule to be implemented. *Muddling through* remains the name of the game.

B. *Policy Crisis.* The EU has clearly underwent a set of policy crises. Except for the single currency, all major policy areas have been saddled with failures and forward looking projects, such as that of European financial regulation of the Lámfalussy Committee of 2001 or of opening up the services sector, as proposed by the Bolkestein Directive of 2004, have suffered serious setbacks. But this is not the whole story. All traditional major EU policy areas tended to end up in a dead alley. The Common Agricultural Policy, accounting for still over 40 percent of Community spending in the internet age, could be reformed in a very incremental manner only (Daubjerg, 2003), despite ever more radical reform proposals that have come from the Commission and net contributors ever since 1988.

Strucural funds have proven to be of limited avail in fostering regional convergence. While some convergence, especially nominal, could be observed in the 1990s, per capita GDP of the regions have not been converging (Rodokanis, 2003). Also in those cases, when convergence could be observed, it is difficult to *disentangle* the contribution of EU spending as against the overall economic environment and the disproportionately much more powerful national fiscal and monetary incentives. The existence of Cohesion funds was reightly put in question already back in 1999, with all four original cohesion countries having attained their objective of qualifying for the Euro-zone. Despite this the fund remained and new members anxiously fighting for their survival. In the area of common foreign and security policy, the Helsinki headline goals of setting up a 60 thousand strong rapid reaction force have clearly been missed, despite the war on terror.

The Lisbon Strategy of catching up with the USA has been trimmed during its re-launch of March 2005. Last but not least, the ups and downs of the Stability and Growth pact, as discussed in the two preceeding Chapters, has weakened the *credibility and efficiency* of the entire regulatory frame of the EU. In particular, the Eurostat, as well as the ECB have been under constant pressure from politicians to accomodate the tendency towards soft, populist policies.

In the political arena, the Constitutional Treaty was meant to signify a new beginning, by consolidating the status quo and creating a limited room for further deepening. However, it has been clear for participants of the Convention from the very outset (Haensch, 2003) that the disagreement among member states is such, that any radical proposal will be thwarted by somebody, with reference to 'vital' national interest. Also, *the atmosphere of overall distrust,* that emerged during the unlawful boycott of the right wing Austrian government and exacerbated by the wars in Afghanistan and Iraq, has proven unfavorable to a meaningful text.

In a way, the Constituional Treaty was lacking operational significance. It has not paved the way for further enlargement, it has not made decision-making simpler, it has not related to most what pertains to money. Therefore its rejection by the French and Dutch electorates in the first half of 2005 does not necessarily have unfavorable policy repercussions for the daily conduct of affairs. Much of the *meso-level and spontaneous, bottom-up activities*, such as environmental groups, the creeping legislation by the Commission and the European Parliament, obliging member-states in an ever growing set of fields, *has been going on uninterrupted ever since.* However the rejection, triggered basically by fears and perceptions, emotions rather than calculation, has been a clear signal. This says no to further deepening or further enlargement, for the rejection reflected basically the fears triggered by the racial strains, that have later became manifest in violent suburban riots in both countries.

C. *The Institutional Crisis.* Perhaps the most visible crisis sign of the EU is the inability to manage its decision-making structures. The very fact that Council Sessions last for two-three days and nights, that top politicians bargain over macroeconomically insignificant issues, or of questions totally unrelated to the daily lives of their electorate, speaks for itself. The informal institutions of the EU that used to work and allow for the bridging of irreconcilable positions, namely *informalism and collegiality have been eroding.* This has to do both with the increased number of actors as well as the steeply diminishing levels of mutual trust among these. The fundamentally intergovernmentalist structure of the EU has not been reformed prior to enlargement. Suggestions to cut back the size of the Commission, the Parliament and of working languagues and veto gates, have all foundered in the three conferences cited above.

As a consequence, an 'intimate circle' of the Council session can hardly be below 100, with PMs, foreign ministers, one person taking notes each, and one interpreter per delegation constituting it. The more EU politics has been perverted into showbiz for domestic audiences, the longer the secrecy of voting sustains, the more each player plays for the domestic audiences Brussels bashing, *the slimmer are the chances of meaningful – or indeed, any – compromise.* Regular attempts by Ecofin members to influence ECB, the weakening of the Commission, the open rivalry between Commission and Parliament, the extension of the co-decision mandate of the latter, that makes it capable to spoil any party, without, however, the chance of setting up a new one have all contributed to the laming. This has been exacerbated by the divergent courses of the member-states on a number of vital issues, from Iraq to fiscal sustainability. And the EU is known to be a club built on voluntary compliance, rather than sanctions and court-style enforcement. If a club is no longer composed of gentlemen, the oversight, even the operation may be endangered. Neither the joint monetary policy, nor the common foreign policy line might be effective, if voluntary compliance can no longer be taken for granted.

New members, on their part, were perhaps even *too quick to emulate* the (mal)practices of incumbents in terms of intergovernmentalism, in terms of maximizing their own *percieved benefit*, in terms of rejecting any vision that would go beyong immediate political gain. This has, of course, contributed to the crises that have already been alive and well by the time the accession of 2004 and 2007 has materialized.

Taking Stock and Looking Ahead

1. The state of the Union at the threshold of the two Financial Perspectives, marked by the rejection of two major documents that were meant to shape its future: the Constitutional Treaty on the political field and the Financial perspective for 2007–2013 as elaborated by the Luxemburgian and British. Though the Constitution, as discussed above, has been largely inoperative, given the amount of time and energy invested into its elaboration and also given the fact that not only governmental representatives from the new members were already involved in its elaboration, thus the rejection by the electorate of two of the original founding six members could not be seen but a *slap in the face of the entire political elite*, whose laboring has been turned down as irrelevant by the citizens.

There are at least two ways one may want to look at this largely unexpected outcome. Looking from a political perspective, one can't but wonder what made top politcians, especially in France, venture into this exercise. The consideration of splitting the Left was obviously a miscalculation, as the Right in France has been traditionally equally split over European matters. Likewise, the Dutch constitutional order does not require a referendum over something, which is esssentially an international treaty, *by no means replacing the basic law* of Holland. The blind faith of the political class in the integrationist tradition of the Dutch did not take into account the sea change that was observable by the first years after 2000. But looking from the sociological perspective, the rejection might be interpreted as a sign of healthy democratic features. More precisely it provided an unexpected, but unmistakeable *feedback to the political class,* uncovering the well known, but never acknowledged drift between the political class and the 'men on the street'. In a way, the EU, in its seclusive, exclusionist and often self-centered intergovernmental bargains has been unmasked to be involved in issues that are of no relevance to the electorate, and conversely, deeply disinterested in matters that are of concern to the electorate, such as immigration, unemployment, slow growth and a system of education neglecting the needs of the labor market.

Likewise, the rejection of the Financial perspective for 2007–2013 and the lasting inability to come to a quick and mutually acceptable correction *may be read in two ways*. At the immediate level it might be seen as a failure to reach agreement by two subsequent presidencies despite the fact that bargaining positions have been quite near by June 2005. Also, in purely technical and diplomatic terms, the chances of a major overhaul were dim, since the outcome has been a result of several years of dovetailing national positions. This translated in the Brussels compromise of December 2005 when three features were of relevance. First, the actual sum – 1.045% of common

GNI for 2007–2013 – is only a fraction away from the original 1.03. Second, the reformers did manage to secure an expenditure overhaul by 2009, even if preparations for the latter are less than intensive. Third, *major patterns of redistribution*, with farming and regional development dominant and IT/Lisbon Agenda and CFSP/JHA marginal, *survived*.

On the other hand, the defining feature of a crisis is precisely the *discontinuation* of the previous practices, emergence of new rules of the game and the formation of new priorities in response to the challenge. This is called 'the benefit of crisis' (Drazen and Grilli, 1993) which is seen by the literature of policy reform as a window of opportunity. Just owing to the cataclysm, vested interests previously opposing any change may be overrun. Unless we look at it from this perspective, and follow the initiatives of the British, but on a number of issues also of other net contributors, we can no longer take it for granted that e.g the bilateral Chirac-Schröder agreement over not touching farm subsidies until 2013 can, and should, indeed, survive 2009. The idea to launch a major overhaul, if for no other reason, because of the pressures coming from the WTO talks and the need to conclude at some later dote, the Doha Round on world trade liberalization, such changes might become simply unavoidable (Hertel and Winters, 2005). We may only speculate in political terms and advance academically better substantiated normative views with no immediate significance for policy-making, if we were to sketch the outcomes that may come. But a *de-emphasis of farming*, especially the still dominant production-related subsidies, and the appreciation of Lisbon related tasks, as well as of spending on justice and home affairs is a most likely outcome. Also the common foreign and security policy, to be discussed later, requires additional funding over and above the curently envisioned sums.[2]

2. It would be wrong to depict an entirely gloomy picture of the Union only because of recent political setbacks. In reality, *the history of the EU is also one of the crises*, and despite – even among – these, the process of deepening has been going on, and has gained irreversible dimensions. The more we appreciate new theories of Europeanization, stressing the relevance of contructivist elements as well as of the non-governmental actors of various sorts, from regions to citizens' movements, the more we appreciate the role of ongoing regular get together and coordination by technocratic agencies and the state administration of member states, *the less we feel the loss of a not very operational document*, or the voting down of a normatively poorly founded financial perspective, *as a serious defeat*. Activities of EU organs and also the inter-action among various fields has not been stopped by the stalemate. For instance, the rulings of the European Court of Justice continue to exert direct and implementable influence over individial members. Likewise, the recent ruling of the European Central Bank of rate hike, defying the calls from

---

[2] Given the inefficiency of current expenditures and the imperative to do something tangible for poorest nations in terms of market opening, the traditional French/Hungarian position of protecting CAP as an accomplishment is already unsustainable at the time of writing anyway.

Ecofin and major parts of the press has shown that *the logic of integration has not been stalled*. Likewise, the ever expanding role of social and environmental legislation is hard to overlook.

Most important among these, however, is the ongoing development of the Single market, triggered by the ovrall drive to deregulation. The IT revolution and global processes, such as those in the airline inustry or in the evolution of global financial markets. There is no way to stop these at the borders of the EU. By contrast, the functioning of the Euro allows for citizens and corporations to make more cross border comparisons, the ICT to foster cross border shopping and sourcing, enlargement allows for enhanced reliance on outsourcing. The veto players – mostly bureaucrats, unions and some monopoly producers – can no longer resort to easy protectionism as they used to in the first decade after adoption the Single Market Act. It will be hard to push the ghost of liberalization back to the bottle, despite the temporary defeat of the Bolkestein Directive in the summer of 2005 at the EU level. Services, accounting for three fourth of wealth creation, can no longer be excluded from the workings of the single market, the more regulated and fast track way, the better. True, as referred to it earlier, the ruling of the European Parliament of March 2006, adopting the basically protectionist GATS standards, and exempting most 'sensitive' sectors, from banking to construction, has made a tiny step ahead, but the deliberations basically go in the wrong direction of prohibitionism, rather than of free enterprise and free market access.

3. The *single currency* has proven to be a unanimous success. Technically speaking though the European Central Bank has continuously missed its headline goal, as defined in its 2003 May interpetation of 'below but close to 2 per cent per annum', still, price stability has been secured for all practical purposes. While in 1991–95 the harmonized index of consumer prices grew by 3.2 percent on average, preparation for the single currency has delivered an improvement to 1.6 per cent in 1996–2000. Following the attainment of /or qualification to the Euro club, a degree of consolidation fatigue emerged, exacerbated by such major external shocks as terorism, the burst of the bubble of the new economy, the increase of oil prices from 12 to 60 dollars a barrel and many more. Under these circumstances the 2.2 percent average HICP in 2001–2004 and the 2.2% for 2005, and below 2.5% for 2006 is a great achievment (all data from: ECB: *Statistics Pocket Book*, June, 2006. Frankfurt, M: p.36). The Euro, having lost first sizeably its external value, has gained strength against the Yen and the Dollar, with 2004–2006 seeing years of complaint against its excessive strength (then around 1.30 dollar per Euro), turning it into a core issue in the French Presidential campaign in late 2006. Price stability could be maintained, and the Euro has become an internationally accepted legal tender and store of value as well as a means of transactions, especially in the private sector.

This achievment is all the more remarkable, since the *fiscal framework* that was to ensure and support its smooth functioning has undergone *serious shocks*. The Stability and Growth Pact, as elaborated in our preceding chapters, remains a binding part of the acquis. However, the political pressure to find exemptions and excuses for postponing fiscal adjustment has been continuous, among old and new members alike. In short, this reinterpretation has taken the wind from the critical voices that would have called for more fiscal stringency from the new members, where fiscal deficits were bloated. For instance in the Czech Republic, once a bastion of fiscal conservatism, deficits attained 5.9% in 2001, 6.8% in 2002, 12.5% in 2003 and 3.0% in 2004. In Hungary the same data were 3.5%, 8.5%, 6.5% and 5.4 per cent in 2001–2004. In the case of Slovakia, the same data run as follows: 6.6%, 7.8%, 3.8% and 3.1%. In Poland, the general government deficit in 2001–2004 ran at 3.7%, 3.3%, 4.8 per cent and 3.9 per cent (according to ECB: op.cit. pp.42). In short, in the good years, when their growth was regularly more robust than of core EU, the Visegrád countries have *also missed the opportunity for fiscal corrections*. On the contrary, they replicated old and large members' digressions which have nothing to do with laying the groundwork for their sustainable development.

Fiscal profligacy has had *different repercussions for the old and new members*. For the old ones, already incumbent in the club, fiscal laxity has not brought about imminent punishment. At the political level, since it has been the three biggest states which were not playing by the rules in 2001–2005, that account for over 67 per cent of joint GDP of the Euro-zone, punishing these via the excessive deficit procedure has proven politically infeasible. Markets by contrast were more concerned about the instability in the USA and Iraq than with the EU states. In relative terms it was the instability and vulnerability of the US and Japan that lent support to ailing Europe, therefore the punishment that might otherwise have been expected from capital markets has not materialized. It is also true that the numbers of the SGP and their observance (or non-observance) bear only indirect relation to the issue of price stability that was the major objective. By contrast, for new Europe the missing of targets has become more of a problem. They are not yet members of the club of the single currency. They see their current account and fiscal deficits growing. For these economies, joining the stability club, i.e the Euro-zone, would be a great plus, in political and business terms alike. However, *the distance to this has been increasing*. The moving of the target date of entry by the Visegrád countries to 2014 at the time of writing, is a clear acknowledgement of their inability to cope. The drift is all the more embarassing, since the small Slovenia joined already in 2007. Bulgaria with its currency board regime may well qualify by 2009. Being left out for these postcommunist countries is *not so innocent as it is for Sweden or Denmark*, not to speak of Britain, where robust economic data ensure the continued interest of capital markets in these economies.

4. *The Lisbon Strategy* of the EU has been an attempt to modernize Europe and to provide a vision for the period, when the earlier visions of the Delors-Mitterand-Kohl period of parallel deepening and widening seemed about to be accomplished. The original strategy, as adopted in 2000 contained a number of utopian elements, such as becoming the most competitive club of the

earth, or the extension of the social rights, without caring much about productivity and structural reforms. As reflected in the soul-searching report of Wim Kok Commission, as well as in the Council deliberations of March 2005, a more realistic assessment had to be elaborated. First, instead of having over 170 indicators to be assessed, a more business-like strategy was elaborated. Second, the proper sequence between growth first and social improvement next was decided. Third, in order to operationalize the strategy, national programs had to be elaborated and submitted, together with semiannual progress reports.

In the current phase the revised strategy aims at the spread of ICT in the traditional branches as well as in improving education, so as to help young people to enter the job markets. With support to lifelong learning, elder people are meant to be retained (or re-enrolled) to the labor market. However, none of these commendable goals can be implemented, if member states continue to eschew painful, but necessary labor market reforms and welfare streamlining, that would allow to diminish the *disincentives to work and the disincentives to employ* new personnel. At the time of writing, quite timid measures are being made in most EU countries, except for Britain and Scandinavia. For this reason in some members, such as Poland and France unemployment continues to be public enemy number one, with their 2006 levels of 16.5 and 8.9% respectively, above the euro area avearage of 8.0% (ECB: op.cit. pp. 41).

5. Finally, as discussed in the previous section of this chapter, the wholesale *rethinking of major expenditure policies* of the EU has been underway. This applies to the common agricultural policy, to regional spending and common foreign and security policy. In each of these areas ideas abound, but political will seems to be limited at best. For this reason, the programmed overhaul of the Financial Perspective may perhaps trigger some more forward looking solutions than the ones currently contemplated in the corridors of power. The inability to find compromises along the old lines is perhaps the best incentive to think over the basics anew. It is also true, that limited amount of public spending is just one, and perhaps not even the most formidable obstacle to enhancing European competitiveness in general and in the R+D arena in particular (cf also Török, 2005).

Do New Members Really Form a Coalition of the Nasty?

By the coalition of the nasty we mean, as explained in preceding chapters, a behavior that is denoted in the more academic European studies literature as intergovernmentalism. In practical policy terms it implies a single-minded focus on the unilateral defense of what is percieved to be the national interest, without any of the idealism/Community spirit of the first decades. This is deeply rooted in a materialist perspective of *Realpolitik,* that considers the ideational component of European integration and most of the initiatives of the founding fathers as filthy talk, and focuses on the tangible material benefits, mostly in terms of official transfers and the net blance of those. As long as this is the success indicator, EU bargains are seen as zero sum games, therefore the chances of bridging the diametrically opposed views are minimal. The coalition of the nasty means a set of ad-hoc coalitions, where those disinterested in any change of the status quo find allies among neutral parties in order to ensure *the blockage of any major change* that may bring about uncertain benefits in the future – in other words policy and institutional reforms. Looking through the angle of social learning, new members have been perhaps even too quick in learning the 'established practie' of incumbents, at least as far as the past 15 years were concerned.

This lack of vision has to do with *a variety of factors.* First, in the long period of accession, new members were told not to come up with new ideas. Indeed, the stipulations of the Amsterdam Treaty, precluding any new opt-outs has been a clear signal, as was the acquis screening. The useful tactics have always been to keep low profile, in order not to hurt anybody inside the club who might veto. As a consequence, the stance of not getting involved in visionary debates, not to comment on principles, has become one of the strongest features of all those who had anything to do with EU matters in the new member states. Experiencing the disharmony among incumbents participation in the Constitutional Convention has only strengthened this feature. Second, the populist turn in politics made new members' poiliticians all too eager to emulate incumbents in 'protecting the national interest against Brussels', with a mere 0.94 per cent of joint GDP being redistributed via Union channels. Third, the materialist perspective that neglects and even negates those truly idealist views, that prompted the founding fathers to launch the entire exercise, has become dominant. The EU is seen, despite repeated claims to the contrary, as a milking cow for the new members, who tend to identify in their domestic policy games the actual size of net recipient position with the net contribution of EU to their well-being. This is understandable from the point of view of mass media, however it is plainly wrong, as the major gain is the improvement of their quality as a secure investment spot, via *enhanced credibility* of their regulatory system. Last, but not at all least, the resultant general euro-scepticism prompts players to adopt non-compromising stances also over matters of minor importance.

Given the growing number of players assertive 'intergovernmentalism' is bound to produce deadlocks and uneasy situations. The three day three night sessions of the Council are just the tip of the iceberg, but quite telling of the outcome. Likewise, the foot-dragging over policy outcomes that bare no relationship, in theory or practice, to the declared principles, such as the Lisbon Strategy or solidarity, is unlikely to produce sustainable outcomes. One of the most weighty innovations brought about by the British presidency has been the initiative to change the rules of the game for the 2007–2013 Financial Perspective, including the Schröder-Chirac deal of 2002 on farming. The latter is a must anyway, as discussed in the chapter on Globalization and Europeanization. Since it is well known that over 80 per cent of farm subsidies accrue to large farmers, over 2000 hectares, ones whose income position is by no means below average, the sustainability of the regime on grounds of tradition and sectoral concerns does not seem to be warranted (Swinbank and Daubjerg, 2004). Likewise, it is unlikely that regional spending may be justified and sustained, if the principle of solidarity, represented by the Commission only, is not being observed. Since it is competitiveness and administrative capacity, rather than level of development of regions that matter, it might be just as well to turn to global financial markets. This is so that the simple reason that less bureaucracy and less political predetermination may – and often does – imply significantly less transaction costs for most corporations, municipalities and individuals alike.

The situation is all the more paradoxical since the lack of vision/pragmatism/low key approach to EU matters is an imminent reflection of the myopia saddling domestic policies of the member-states, old and new. While the challenges of globalization, both economically and socially are imminent (cf.eg. more recently Kolodko, ed, 2005), the nature of media politics is such that important issues tend to be crowded out by entertaining ones. In the age of infotainment, weighty issues, such as terrorism, the spread of infectious diseases, vulnerability of the IT system, migration, but even such traditional concerns as the Balkans or the Middle East tend to be crowded out from popular attention. As a consequence, not many informed decisions can be taken. The priority of the oft-invoked 'median voter' is precisely *not to face* these serious, embarrassing and often unresolved challenges, where no easy answers are at hand. The rejection of the Constituional Treaty, the adverse publicity of Lisbon Strategy, the ritual mockery of the common foreign and seurity policy not confined to the tabloids, together do not bode well for more *forward-looking policies*. However it is precisely the latter that are in demand should Europe wish to establish itself as a major player of international relations, and avoid the regression into a free trade area. While the latter seems less likely, given the irrevocable ties that have emerged in the process of Europeanization across the areas, from legally binding pieces of legislation to activities of regions and the civil society, it is an age-old insight that *anything that does not grow is likely to regress*. Therefore the currently observable stagnation of political integration, as well as of the deepening project (especially in the area of services) is a cause for concern.

It is therefore hard to overlook the *drift between descriptive and normative* planes of our analysis. In the first dimension, the emergence of the coalition of the nasty seems to be an accomplished fact, judging by the tone and substance of the policies adopted by the new members. These clearly focus unilaterally on maximizing official transfers, whereas all other items, be that of political integration, future oriented plans or the advocacy of further enlargement seems to have been pushed to the background. On the other hand, the theory of 'benefit of crisis' quoted above draws on the broad historical experience of overcoming deadlocks owing to an unexpected breakdown and/or unconventional political initiatives that allow for previously non-realistic solutions to materialize. For the new members, their recent experience with the implosion of the Soviet Empire might be a case in point.

The Potential for Institutional Innovation and Further Enlargement

It is the nature of the *cumulation of strains* and the resultant crisis that does not allow for any forecast over how and when changes might occur. The only thing we can advance in terms of prediction, based on the unsustainability of the status quo, is that it must change under any event. There is no way how we can get meaningful answers to new questions, such as future enlargement, e.g with Turkey and Ukraine, if the analysis is based on the usual *ceteris paribus* assumptions, as it has become customary in the public administration as well as in most research institutes. There is *not even a relevant question to ask*, if the enlargement by Turkey is, e.g assessed on the base of weighting of votes as elaborated in Nice, or in terms of extending the current dairy quotas on a large country. Although it is true, that in terms of per capita GDP and agricultural employment, Turkey is not less advanced than Romania with about 5000 dollar per capita GDP measured on purchasing power parity and about 30 percent of the population employed in farming. However this is more of a drawback for Romania than an argument in favor of Turkey. It is equally certain that merely by joining in the social and economic model of Romania and Bulgaria, are unlikely to become less Southeast European than before. The experience with Greece in the 1980s as well as with Portugal in the past decade is indicative of the possibility and probalility of lengthy adjustment periods that may last for decades.

In order to be able to be meaningful, European analysts are well advised to adopt a post-materialist – rather than a postmodernist – vision, where value judgements and long term considerations of the European security order regain their original significance. It is hard not to reckon with the fact that the current disinerst in broader issues and the focus on material gain reflects the *diminished fear* that followed the collapse of the Soviet Union with its mighty army, and the underestimation of the threat of terror up until at least the Madrid and London attacks. In the light of the latter, a gradual reassessment may occur, with the Barcelona process of cooperating with Mediterranean countries gathering new momentum. The issue of further enlargement, especially with such large and diverse countries as Ukraine and Turkey, becomes feasible only after thorough *reforms of internal arrangements* of the EU will have been accomplished. These are unlikely until a new vision, following that a new strategy, from which a new enlargement project is being elaborated. Likewise the successful management of the Western Balkans, where state building, nation building and Europeanization should, in theory, *form an integrated strategy*, that would require basically more innovative and pre-emptive strategy, not so much more money. For assistance injected to areas where *uncorrupted* and *fair* government is *not yet secured*, can only be *wasted*. The ability to provide a realistic European perspective could induce local governments to *commit themselves to European values*, and then the process of association and finally accession could, in the long run, provide answers to the unfinished business of Balkan peace building.

It goes without saying that such a far-sighted policy is infeasible as long as the threat – or implicit tendency – to relegate the EU in a free trade area, which is at the root of intergovernmentalist approaches, can be overcome. As long as the EU is unable to overcome its identity crisis, it is unlikely to be able to advance new staregies. *Identity* in this plane implies a straightforward answer to what the EU stands for, the reassertion of the basic principles of the founding fathers, and their operationalization on a new area at a time when the original goals have been accomplished, while globalization triggers new challenges.

In concrete terms *internally*, there are at least three issue areas where major breakthroughs are required, both per se, and in order to be able to meet the new global challenges. *First,* there is a need for leaner and more functional decision-making structure, freed from national egoism and from the currently dominant prestige considerations. A Commission composed of about six members, could perhaps better serve the purpose than the current arrangement, where Commissioners are employed for areas where the Union has no immediate competences (as research and development and taxation), or duplications are obvious, as in the case of four foreign affairs Commissioners. Making the minutes of Council session public would rob politicians from their toy of instrumentalizing intra-EU deals for domestic audiences. The extension of qualified majority voting and the limitation of working languages would also be of assistance. *Second,* it could be declared that intra-EU redistribution is unlikely to grow, as net contributors will not foot the bill. In so doing, the requirement of spending for such activities that *add value to national activities* should be observed. For instance, development aid to advanced countries could be discontinued. Similarly, the budget for common foreign security policy and for justice and home affairs should grow, with farm spending declining. *Third,* but not least the need to regulate less, that is the continuation of the deregulation drive started by the Barroso Commission in September 2005 should be extended. Thereby a large number of unnecessary regulations that provide food for criticism only, but do not contribute to common good, can be avoided. In each and every case of new legislation, those proposing it should elaborate a) how it would contribute to the common good an b) who would foot the bill, how much the proposed legislation would cost.

On the *external,* front, improvements might be urgently needed, if the EU is to come close to a role the second largest economic power of the globe must play, if for no other reason, by default. It is inconcievable that for instance the EU position on global trade should fall victim to special interest politics of some member states, especially if the macroeconomic significance of the issue is not demonstrable. More recent cases of the inadequate reform of the banana and sugar regime, triggering immediate threat from developing countries of bringing it to WTO dispute settlement[3] is just a case in point. The EU is a major player in the international trade arena and there is no way how the EU could be eschewed if any major progress in terms of the Doha Round were to be attained (Charlton and Stiglitz, 2005).

---

[3] This has materialized in the summer heat of 2006 (*Neue Zürcher Zeitung,* 25 July, 2006.)

The second major area, where the EU has responsibilities is in common foreign and security policy. With the obvious de-emphasis of Europe during the two Bush administrations, *the anchor both for Southeast Europe and the Caucasian countries*, but to a degree also for Russia (in economic terms) has become the EU. There is no way to shrug off the responsibilities that emanate from the geographical, cultural and historic position of the EU–27, as the currently promulgated neighborhood policy seems to do. The 'anything but institutions' offer of June, 2004 was actually next to nothing, since the EU is basically about institutions. The European Neighborhood Policy (ENP) of 2005, integrating the basically dissimilar Southern and Eastern dimensions, seems to be yet another exercise in incoherent policies following mutually exclusive targets. The special relationship to Russia, brought about by the insistence of the largest military power in Europe, has been translated in the development of four common spaces. Analysis of the endeavor (Tyazhov, 2006) has shown that all items going beyond free trade in energy were bound to remain at the realm of declarative diplomacy. Similarly the Mediterranean dimension requires far more innovative and cooperative solutions than the ones focusing on policing unwanted migrants. While the ENP attempted to create an overall framework supportive of evolutionary and democratic change, this initiative foundered on the lack of cooperation from local elites, that continue to control any external influence to the smallest detail. For this reason democratization, if ever happens, is an outcome of *local enlightenment* rather than of extended European influence (Ganchev, 2006).

This unfortunate state of affairs follows from some of the inherent *ambiguities of the ENP as a policy instrument*. For one, the EU applies multiple and only partly overlapping criteria. Second, it clearly lacks the carrot of eventual membership, which has played, as we have indicated in several chapters, a pivotal role in bringing about elite consensus over contested issues. Finally, as in the case of Mediterranean and NIS countries, the non- or only partially democratic local leadership has other incentives than the ones favoring co-operation (more on these in Kelley, 2006). Thus ENP is unlikely to be the way to replicate the success of systemic change, where precisely those rewards and punishments were *instrumental* in fostering Europeanization, *that are missing* from the current instrument (more on that in: Csaba, 2004). Finally mending the transatlantic relationship, both in the economy and in politics, will require efforts, imagination, and not least internal coordination, much more than in 2000–2006.

Finally the question frequently arises if, and under what conditions, new EU members are to become *likely advocates of further enlargements?* For the time being, as long as the 'materialist' and 'realist' perspective dominates, the answer is a clear no. However, should the above sketched reassessment be forthcoming, with or without crises, this might trigger a more *forward-looking approach* on the side of new members. Once they will be able to see the issue of further enlargement through different lenses, than the one prompted by their fear of immediate loss of regional and farming transfers, this will allow them to *adopt a broader perspective*. In the latter, security of European order and democracy is not ensured as long as large countries and unsettled areas are not taken care of. This holds even allowing for the dominance of domestic balance of forces in settling the bills and setting the final outcomes. In the latter perspective, new members will assume their historic responsibility that comes from their geographical and historic position. In so doing, they can indeed *contribute something palpably* new to the rethinking of the common foreign and security policy of the EU. If one takes for granted the old insight, that times of internal stagnation are the times for external activity, there is no way how the following decade could eschew the implementation of at least some of the insights that may follow from the above sketched normative analysis. Instead of regressing into a free trade area, Europe, with the contribution of new members, may be on its way to be reborn as a *community worthy of voluntary emulating,* not only in the economy.

In conclusion, we have, again, come to the relevance of regulation and more generally to the quality and shape of institutions, as well as to the relevance of *institutional innovation* in the form of fundamental reforms. In the line of reasoning, presented up till now, institutional reforms are the key to overcoming developmental deadlocks. But what if not? We do have two impressive cases, one in Europe, one outside Europe, but with a potentially much stronger global outreach, which seem to defy this wisdom. Both Russia and China have been growing at impressively high rates despite their stagnant or at best hybrid reforms in the sense we defined systemic change in the first chapters. In order to test the more general considerations, whereto we shall return in the concluding chapters of this monograph, first we are compelled to interpret, within the same analytical frame, the alternative paths of 'institutionless growth', as exemplified by contemporary Russia and China in some detail.

References

CHARLTON, A. and STIGLITZ, J. (2005): A development-friendly prioritization of the Doha round proposals. *World Economy,* vol. 28. no. 3. pp. 293–312.

CSABA, L. (2004): Transition in and towards Europe. *Zeitschrift für Staats- und Europawissenschaften,* vol. 2. no. 3. pp. 330–350.

DAUBJERG, C. (2003): Policy feedback and paradigm shift in EU agricultural policy: the effects of MacSharry reforms on future reforms. *Journal of European Public Policy,* vol. 10. no. 3. pp. 421–438.

DINAN, D. (2004): *Europe Recast: a History of the European Union.*Boulder/Col./USA: Lynne Reiner.

DRAZEN, A. and GRILLI, V. (1993): The benefit of crises for economic reform *American Economic Review,* vol. 83. no. 4. pp. 598–607.

GANCHEV, V. (2006): 'Short-term problem-solving or lasting political transformation? Norms, values and interest in ENP's Mediterranean dimension' – MA Theses defended at the IRES Department of CEU, June.

HAENSCH, K. (2003): 'Beschreiben was sein kann': das Verfassungsenturf des Europaeischen Konvents. *Zeitschrift für Staats-und Europawissenschaften,*vol. 1. no. 3. pp. 299–312.

HERTEL, TH – WINTERS, L. A. (2005): Estimating the poverty implications of a prospective Doha development agenda. *World Economy,* vol. 28. no. 8. pp. 1057–1072.

KOLODKO, G. W. ed (2005): *Globalization and Social Stress.* New York: Nova Science Publishers.

MIDELFART-KRAVNIK, H. and OVERMAN, H. (2002): Delocation and European integration: is structural spending justified? *Economic Policy,* no 35., pp. 323–358.

RODOKANIS, S. (2003): Fifteen years of structural fund intervention/1988–2002/: a critical evaluation. *European Union Review,* vol. 8. nos/1–2/, pp. 65–106.

SWINBANK, A. and DAUBJERG, C. (2004): The CAP and EU enlargement. *Journal of Common Market Studies,* vol. 42. no1. pp. 99–120.

TÖRÖK, Á. (with TELCS, A. and BORSI, B.) (2005): *Competitveness in Research and Development.* Cheltenham/UK and Northampton/MA/USA:E.Elgar.

TYAZOV, A. (2006): 'The four common spaces between Russia and the EU- the nature of the project and prospects for successful implementation' – MA Theses defended at the IRES Department of CEU, June.

WAGENER, H.-J. – EGER, TH. – FRITZ, H. (2006): *Europaeische Integration. Recht und Ökonomie, Geschichte und Politik.* München:Verlag Vahlen.

11. RUSSIAN TRANSFORMATION: FROM STATE FAILURE TO MARKET FAILURE?[1]

There are a number of justifications why to insert something like a country study in a book devoted to theoretical issues. First, Russia used to be the focal point of the Soviet empire, therefore salient features of the old regime tended to generalize the Russian experience. This was only right since the Soviet Union, especially in the Stalin period, but also following the Brezhnev Doctrine of 1968 on limited sovereignty, had been keeping a watchful eye on what happened within the individual socialist countries and what not. Second, systemic change in Russia has been in the focus of attention of policy analysts and academic economists alike. Therefore, to some degree understandably, Russia continued to serve as a model for much of the transition literature as well.[2] Third, there seem to have been a fundamental clash between the universalist claims of the social sciences, adopted directly by Western policy advisors and part of the Russian *intelligentsiya*, and the reality that emerged on the ruins of the empire. Fourth, by the same token, the Russian experience allows for addressing some of the *basic categories of economic analysis*. For instance, what constitutes a market, what defines the quality of a market, what matters for economic growth, and last but not least, what the political economy conditions of turning these insights into policies are that are supportive of sustainable growth in the long run.

In this context we define the market as in classical economics, i.e. as a set of institutions that enable and co-ordinate exchanges based on private initiative in order to attain economic gains, at the end of the day, following price signals and maximizing wealth. In Russia numerous cases are known that are usually discussed under the heading of *'state failure'*, such as lack of co-ordination, inability to raise taxes, or provide law and order for everyone. This is contrasted with *'market failure'*, a term usually associated with predatory pricing, externalities, consumer myopia or free riding. In this chapter we adopt a *broader understanding*, where outcomes usually expected rationally from market games

[1] Useful comments by Huricihan Islamoglou, the late Kamilla Lányi, Silvana Malle, Gur Ofer, Vladimir Mau and Tauno Tiusanen are appreciated, with the usual caveats.
[2] A powerful example of this surviving tradition the twin volumes edited by Susan Rose-Ackerman and János Kornai (2004) whose approach is truly holistic.

259

fail to materialize. For instance if all or most goods behave like club goods, free prices generate less profits than fixed prices and many others. In extending the established category of market failure we hope to convey a mass phenomenon, namely that in the view of the overwhelming majority of Russian citizens and analysts market order equals to kleptocracy. In other words, market seems to be a failure on Russian soil. Since the co-evolution of state and market is a unifying theme of our monograph, this innovation in terminology is perhaps a sensible shorthand to facilitate the better structuring of our ideas that revolve around the same axis in all across the various subject matters of individual chapters.

Let us be clear from the very outset: this chapter does not attempt for a monographic country study of Russia. Rather it uses the case study to *illustrate the more general points* raised in our fourth set of questions. In terms of analysis, we rely on country studies/analyses as prime sources, not wishing to replicate them. Furthermore, we may re-iterate the need for a most often lacking *comparative perspective,* that we adopt and endorse. Russia watchers too tend to be selected from the defense community and among those having mastered the Russian language, that is classical area studies' persons. Those working on Russia quite rarely follow developments in other transition economies, thus the entire debate on the different routes of transition and the ensuing theoretical plurality is quite often missing. By contrast in this book we take the insights presented in the preceding chapters as given, and rely on these when addressing the Russian material. Thereby we hope to be able to convey at least some less conventional insights into a never ending debate, conducted with unchanged vigor over the past two centuries, inside Russia and internationally alike.

In the following, we shall present empirical/statistical evidence first, in order to be able to assess the major long-term processes. This is important since Russia has been the country where poetry and reality, to use Goethe's phrase, tend to be the most divorced in Europe. Then we survey major turning points of institutional change and try to interpret these. In turn, we look into the results of the first and second Putin Presidency and try to understand if and to what degree it failed to bring about conditions for sustained economic growth, as the findings of our comparative and empirical chapter already foreshadowed. This will allow us to enter into the generalizations on market and growth, as the basic subject of our analyses proper.

Russian Economic Change: A Bird's Eye View

Following our practice adopted in preceding chapters, we try to draw the macro picture by offering the long-term view and abstracting from the bits and pieces, readily available from country studies and continuous media reporting. In so doing our starting point is the insight developed in our previous monograph (Csaba, 1995) and supported by other analyses (Aslund, 2002; Mau and Starodubrovskaia, 2001) with different arguments. The collapse of the Soviet empire could not be attributed to unquestionable policy mistakes, external factors and other coincidental circumstances: it was inevitable. Furthermore, as explained in the monographs cited above, the first period of 1992–1993 was entirely spent on trying to recreate the Russian state, its borders, its state administration, and to avoid large scale disintegration along the Yugoslav lines. These *historic factors dominated* economic projects, diligently produced in contemporary workshops in Moscow and abroad; *crisis management* was the name of the game.

In economic terms, a systemic vacuum emerged (cf. also Popov, 1998, pp. 446–447) though this applies only at the level of formal institutions; thus *informal institutions dominated the scene.* Therefore, unsurprisingly for anybody familiar with the oeuvre of Douglass North and Friedrich August von Hayek, unintended *side-consequences have regularly proven more relevant in shaping outcomes,* than formal priorities as reflected in government documents, fiscal plans or privatization strategies. The problem has become multidimensional insofar as the Empire used to be a kind of 'natural order' for most agents, in terms of ideology and operation alike. Furthermore, following the failed coup of August 1991, no new Constitution had been elaborated, that could have set the tone for change in the decades to come.[3] Then could have been the ideal time to declare the discontinuity with the Soviet era, promulgating multiparty democracy, private property and freedoms in political and economic areas to be the cornerstone of the new Russian statehood.

Lacking such a clear signal allowed, basically up to the 1996 re-election of Boris Yeltsin to the Presidency, to question any measure that would follow the mainstream of transition: the stabilization, liberalization, institution-building and privatization (SLIP) strategy in each and every of its element. For instance Communists could rightfully resist land privatization, actually any major privatization, with reference to stipulations of existing legal and constitutional order. Thus whatever the reformist government did, they could only conduct with bad conscience, behind the scenes, in a defensive style, needing to justify the obvious. This is in sharp contrast to Hungary – but not the rest of Central and Eastern Europe –, where legal foundations and political compromises allowed for co-operative games to evolve – in part as a conscious strategy of the reformist wing of the outgoing regime (cf. also Kulcsár, 1995). The *commonality of values,* a degree of *social consensus,* that has been shown to play a pivotal role in the successful transformations in Central Europe, *has been conspicuously missing from the Russian society and from Russian democracy,* rendering it much more conflict-ridden even on basics (not to speak of detail). Rule by decree, a practice adopted by Yeltsin from Soviet and Tsarist era, made things

---

[3] One of the most active participants (Mau, 1999, pp. 114–116) also underscores this point in a self-critical tone, listing the long row of ensuing ramifications for reform policies. Actually, *rule by decree,* which was a feature of the entire post-revolutionary period, is *not to be mixed up with a strong state* (as it is a sign of an *activist-interventionist* administration, usually associated with weak, rather than strong core state). Also the idea that constitution-drafting takes time does not seem to hold, if we compare it to the Hungarian experience, explained by an insider – minister of justice at the time of systemic change (Kulcsár, 1995).

only worse, since not even the appearance of a common standard, a common point of reference has been left. Therefore, everything and the opposite of everything remained questionable and questioned – until the time of writing, indeed. Erratic policies of the President(s) allow for even more confusion to sustain and even less consensus to emerge.

All in all, these circumstances may justify that our starting point is *state failure*.[4] It is all the more important to highlight this aspect as much of the – local and international – literature critical of the reform policies (e.g. Kotz and Weir, 1997; Stiglitz, 2000) – attribute to the neo-liberal zeal of the reformers a feature that they had, in fact, *inherited from the crumbling Soviet Empire*. If the crisis is given, calls for 'more active policies', or 'resolute action in the area of x, y and z' simply miss the point and have been practically irrelevant. Let us stress: the core state remained much too 'embedded' in the web of vested interest. Thus it has been weakened in its main capacity to *act as a referee* rather than one of the players. This is clearly the *starting point*, rather than a consequence of whatever polices conducted during the very same period, thus the criticism of circular reasoning does not seem to hold. The direction of causality, to follow the classical argumentation of János Kornai (1992, subchapter 15.1.), *remained unchanged*, from the state to the market rather than vice versa, if for no other reason, than because of the fundamentally unreformed nature of the Soviet system until its very last days.[5]

Reference to the policy reform literature that was surveyed in our chapter on the Developmental dimension may suffice to support the claim that *a weak core state is hardly able to institute major changes*. Already the first step, stabilization is likely to founder, if pressure groups can create an effective counter-weight to the monetary authority. The latter in turn is unable to control money supply, aggravating the non-negligible technical difficulties of doing so, even on paper. Furthermore, if erosion of central power undermines one of the basic functions of any state, the ability to raise revenue via taxes, while lobbies protect their acquired rights for continued central financing, the *softening up of fiscal policy is also given*. Through this simple mechanism, the logic of stabilization is turned to its head. No matter how much preaching on stabilization happens (or happened in Russia in 1992–1994), it remained a declaration of good will, not of operational policy. The presence of vested interest groups had been manifest, with their power to print money: extreme cases are reported in detail in (Gaidar, ed., 1998; Mau, 1999). This feature is hard to doubt, since the same Viktor Gerashchenko, depicted customarily as the Evil himself, could skilfully manage different policies in 1998–2000, when he was instrumental in averting

---

[4] This concept is well developed in the political science and the development literature and describes a situation where the public authorities, or as the policy reform literature calls it, the core state, *proves unable to perform those elementary functions* that are ascribed to it by any theory. These include the provision of public order, enforcing laws and contracts, stability of prices and property rights, ability to defend the borders and all citizens under legislation of the country, smooth functioning of public services (transport, health care, education), fighting natural catastrophes etc.

[5] For a summary of evidence cf. a contemporary piece of the author (Csaba, 1992).

hyperinflation. If money remained irrelevant, control by and through money, which is at the heart of macroeconomic management in any market economy, was becoming *formal and ineffective*. Mind it, that these features have been recurring in developing countries, and have nothing to do with the Russian soul or other peculiarities of the country (that are numerous, indeed). In the Russian case, the predominant role played by *local power* (Hanson and Bradshaw ed., 2000) already foreshadowed the limitations on quick and efficient stabilization. By contrast, the strengthening of central authority under both Putin Presidencies allowed for a much more prudent monetary and fiscal policy to be conducted, irrespective of ideological undertones. True, learning by doing and structural changes in the preceding period, especially in 1996–1998, must have contributed to this outcome.

In the following, we shall provide an overview of macroeconomic developments based on the reporting of the EBRD and Economist Intelligence Unit, in order to avoid the reliance on over-politicized Russian reporting, further to make the numbers internationally comparable. Both sources give assessments of institutional reforms as well.

As can be seen from *Table 2. in chapter Three, the Empire left with sharply contracting GDP*. No consumption data is provided, still it is common knowledge that the crisis of food supplies played a major role in bringing opposition to the open in the 1989–1991 period. 1992–1993, often referred to as the period of 'monetarism', has in reality been a period of futile struggle for the unattainable. In this period central power was lacking and internally divided, between the Presidency and the legislation. 1994 was the first year when the first real attempt to stabilize was made, and this contributed to the steep fall of output. From 1995, inflation comes down from hyper to high inflation, but the limited success was followed by a further 4 per cent drop of GDP. 1996, the election year – basically its second half – brings down inflation to the moderate level of 47.8 per cent, reflecting the emergence of an uncontested power center. In this year a further 3.4 per cent drop was registered – a drop smaller than in the last Soviet year. *1997 can be seen as a turning point*, with inflation coming down to 14.7 per cent and GDP growing for the first time in many years. All in all, the four years of *transformational* recession, and the ensuing 20 per cent drop in GDP (against the 1993 levels) are *neither longer nor deeper than in Central Europe*. In this respect avenue Russia followed the 'main' of transition.

The cyclical recession of 1998 in Russia can only be seen in the context of *contagion of the emerging market crisis*, starting from Thailand and ending in Brazil, but catching Russia with its just emerging capital markets in the middle of its transformation (for the similarities cf. the lucid analyses by Lámfalussy, 2000; Kaminsky et al, 2003). True, this crisis was partly home-made, with the 'virtual economy', that is de-monetization aggravating the consequences of lax fiscal policies, co-existing with overly tight monetary policies. Still, this drop, like the Czech currency crisis of 1997 (Horvath, 1999) was by and large a 'normal' *cyclical downturn*, not attributable to peculiarities of post-Communist development. Also, the fundamental peculiarity, of mismatch between over-tight monetary and quite lax fiscal policies, is not particularly post-Communist in nature.

Unfortunately, this distinction tended to go under in the contemporary debates, thus the gloomy view, ascribing only failures to Russian transformation prevailed, domestically and internationally alike.

Notwithstanding the (still) majority view, it would be a *fallacy*, in academic terms, to add up *three different crises*, with three different sets of causes, into one, for the simple reason that there was a *timely sequence* among them. As can be seen, the devaluation of the ruble to 25 per cent of its pre-crisis levels helped to ward off the worst, and did put Russia on a growth path from 1999 onwards. Already the first year showed a growth exceeding the drop of 1998, a factor supportive of our reading of affairs, especially if we also see the four consecutive years of growth that followed. Also in line with our observations on Central Europe inflation has come down to the moderate levels, 20.8 per cent in 2000, 21.6 by 2001, 15.8 in 2002 and 14 per cent in 2003. These numbers are higher than those of the frontrunners, however Russia remained a large country with many lobbies, meanwhile *the anchor function of the European Union has been missing*. Therefore, moderate inflation is a convenient way of bridging over some of the strains that result from extended bargaining over scarce resources. Importantly, also for the more general perspective, *disinflation and growth has been going hand in hand,* no trade-off between the two is demonstrable[6] in the Russian numbers over the past fifteen years (when prices gradually have regained their signaling function).

If we look at the numbers of the 'government sector', some interesting insights emerge. First, contrary to some old-fashioned Keynesian theories, sustaining deficits could not act as stabilizers of economic activity, *either in the short or in the long run*. By contrast, economic recovery has also produced more government revenue, thus the consolidated or general government balance also started to improve. Reliance on seigniorage revenue and the ability to melt down politically pressured additional transfers could not compensate for the overall disorganization created by sustaining high inflation. By contrast, when the economy and fiscal policy is in healthy shape, reliance on seigniorage and on inflating away incomes also has become largely superfluous.

Yet another myth about Russia is the idea of *state desertion,* discussed in part in the comparative chapter. Numbers collected by the EBRD and EIU *(Tables 1 and 11)* do not support this widely spread claim. Consolidated government expenditure at 36 per cent of GDP is somewhere half way between the United States and Scandinavia, the two extreme numbers. These certainly do not reflect Latin American (or more generally, developing country) conditions. For instance, in Peru it is only 11 per cent, in Morocco 18 per cent, according to the World Bank tables already quoted several times.

Looking at the utilization of GDP it is easy to see that *collapse of investments* until 1999 had been a dominant factor. Seeing this it is hard to overlook that

---

[6] Peter Bofinger (1994, p. 77) shows and later proves by a comparative analysis of Central European experience, different degrees of 'tough' monetary policies brought about similar drops in output in the region. This proves that a large part of credit creation had been endogenous, thus any direct impact of monetary policy on output is hard to establish.

investment used to be bloated under the socialist period, thus some decline must have come as healthy correction of a previous distortion. Also not allowing for the inefficiencies, or correcting at least some of those, must have led to less investment. However, as seen in *Table 11*, the bottom of 14.4 per cent was increased to 17.9 per cent only by 2002, which is perhaps less than a country still significantly below its pre-crisis production level needs for the long run. The good news in the bad news is that once recovery started, investment grew and so did consumption, with the usual lag of about two years. On the other hand, if we consider the level of investments low, than *both the sustaining surplus in the current account and the occasionally negative FDI numbers give grounds for grave concern.* If locals do not find a good idea to invest home, why should others do so, provided locals are by definition better informed than outsiders?

Stagnant exports and imports are no signs of good: *stagnant exports are recorded sometimes even at times of high oil prices.* Recovery of overall economic activity, particularly in industry, *should have triggered a surge in imports* if this growth were to be over and above the levels provided by the temporary protection ensuing from devaluation. Cautious exchange rate policy in the early 2000s also provided some protection to domestic output. If neither FDI nor import grows, while export values stagnate, this is indicative of an out of date export pattern. The latter is unlikely to produce sufficient revenue, furthermore is unlikely to sustain as a growth engine in the long run. The *stagnant share of machinery and equipment* at 17 per cent of total exports is a clear sign of that. *Table 11* is indicative of a *diminishing openness* of the Russian economy, moreover the export/GDP ratio fluctuates widely, year by year, as in developing countries relying on primary commodity exports only. The stagnant share of imports in GDP is a sign of caution: revenues are *expatriated rather than spent on modernizing domestic fixed assets.* True, some partial, rather defensive modernization and upgrading of services is observable on the sites. Finally, import penetration, stagnant at 24 per cent of GDP or a third of Central European levels is a clear sign of how limited the role of imports creating competition is in the still fairly monopolized Russian economy.[7]

Analyzing the export performance of Russia in the 1998–2005 period Blank et al (2006, esp. p. 24) doubt, if the situation qualifies as Dutch disease, since export volumes are stagnant and the basic factors of competitiveness are low wages and depreciated rate of exchange.

The share of industry has gone down from 46 to 22 per cent in GDP. This is in line with the numbers observed in Central Europe and *should by no means*

---

[7] As Sergei Vasiliev (2000, pp. 248–249) notes, reforms of the natural monopoly sectors has come to a halt since 1997, and have been restarted in 2003 only, with OECD (2004) qualifying it still a wound point of reforms. Protecting monopoly positions could have been a strategy of luring investors through protected markets, as was the case in Hungarian energy sector in 1995; however investors, with a few exceptions, have not shown up. Ahrend and Thompson (2005) rightly qualify this as the wound point of Russian reforms under Putin, limiting potential improvements in several related areas.

qualify for de-industrialization. By contrast, the share of agriculture in GDP dropped to 8 per cent, while in employment its share is still over 13 per cent. This is an indication of continued inefficiencies, furthermore this rate of employment is very high for European standards. The forecast is indicative of the continued growth, led by the fuel sector and import substitution, with activity levels improving the employment situation, without endangering disinflation (yet another case when the Phillips curve is vertical). The deceleration of inflation reflects, inter alia, the strong fiscal position. However, the policy of the *Centrobank* does not move towards the lower single digit levels of Poland and the Czech Republic. The virtues of moderate inflation as a means to manage political compromises remained intact in the Putin era. *The slowdown of growth rates however, when the windfall component is filtered out, is perceptible, even though the pre-crisis levels have long not been attained.* Moreover, issues of overall – technological and organizational – modernization and *the structural problems do not seem to have been fundamentally addressed in the 'good years',* when ample domestic and external financing could have been available. External debt and its financing do not seem to pose a major problem for Russia any longer.

On balance, Russia seems to have been stuck as an 8–10 thousand $ per capita GDP country, without any indication of a lasting catch-up period, *but also without signs of the catastrophe scenarios,* once produced diligently in a number of research centers. The one-time factors of growth seem to dominate, and additional factors of structural modernization are not trivially forthcoming. The rate of investment is rather low, so is FDI. The system of capital allocation, via banking and the capital market, have not been showing signs of major improvement (a point we shall address below). Therefore the trajectory of 6–7 per cent annual growth rate, first envisaged in the Gref Plan in 2000 for a decade-long period, and re-iterated in the presidential address in May 2003 for the decade starting up then seems to be widely optimistic. This is nothing more and nothing less than a mechanistic extrapolation of the recovery of the 1999–2003 period of high fuel prices, yielding an average growth rate of 6.7 per cent. Still, there is considerable way to regain the 1989 levels in per capita terms. On the other hand, the dooms-dayers have also proven to be wrong in so far as there is no sign of Russia returning to what they described as a 'depression'. In a way, especially if foreign entry remains as limited as in the first decade of changes, Russia is more likely to follow a path *typical of a 'peripheral' developing economy than any of the extreme scenarios.* In this sense – but only in this limited sense – we accept the overall evaluation of Shleifer and Treisman (2004) calling Russia a 'normal country' and blaming analysts for their inflated expectations in terms of democracy and market type environment. But having opted for a *different alternative* than emerging Europe also has a price, especially in the long run developmental perspective. At the end of the day, this finding may be supported, if we look into the salient features of the Russian economic system as evolved over the past decade.

The Russian Market Order: The Wild East and/or State Capitalism?

Few subjects have generated such a broad debate without boundaries and rules as the economic system of Russia. It is not our intention even to attempt at summarizing the subject requiring monographs, or to rehash our previous writings. Instead, an attempt is made to present the *stylized facts*, first as these evolved, than as they show up in statistics.

Let us recall: the drift between poetry and reality was perhaps the greatest during the Gorbachev period. Then large-scale reform projects, a Russian leader who has been very popular in the West (not least because of his performance as a speaker) dominated the agenda. In reality, disintegration and crisis-management was the name of the game: without this, the defeat of the Soviet Army in Afghanistan and its enforced withdrawal (as late as in 1989) cannot be understood. This historic defeat, the first since 1918, had surely undermined the social consensus and the legitimating power of the military, whose might equals to Russian fame. A contemporary observer (Naishul, 1991) described the late days of the Soviet Union as a bargaining society, where finally any private interest could be attained at the cost of the public purpose. In a way, the 'genetic program' of the system has been broken, with neither stick nor the carrot remaining in the hands of the rulers. Gorbachev's belated attempt to reform the system unleashed suppressed forces, while his ability to control and manage them has already gone. This is why the system ended first with a *putsch* orchestrated by the then second and third in command (around General Secretary Yanayev), later by the officially appointed representatives of (formally still Communist ruled) three Slavic Republics in December 1991. Procedurally seen, there was *a process of self-elimination*, truly unprecedented in history (not triggered by either conquest or popular uprising).

As discussed above, the years 1992–1993 have been spent on redefining power, borders, political and economic structures, while 1994–1997 was a period of transformational recession. This was the time, when most of the *new economic structures evolved*. 'Evolution' stresses the largely spontaneous nature of change, that had little direct resemblance to the privatization programs diligently published each year by various governmental and advisory bodies. Without wishing to present a comprehensive account (as e.g. by the bulky volume of Gaidar, ed., 1998; or more analytically by OECD, 1997) let us just recall the major items.

First and foremost, it has turned impossible to follow the original line adopted in 1992 to make privatization an instrument of getting rid of *nomenklatura*. Rather, a compromise solution has been found, where those parts, especially in the energy sector, banking and the security apparatus (overseeing inter alia foreign trade), who were willing to join in, were actually co-opted and *turned into the new asset owner class*. It has been clear from relatively early on (Hare, 1994) that what looked formally employee-manager ownership with a flavor of self-management, was from the very outset, in reality, *manager-ownership of firms*.

Fearing a Communist comeback in the presidential elections of July 1996, the group around Yeltsin decided to hit two flies in a single stroke. First, they needed cash to manage disinflation, if Russia was to remain governable from the center. Second, they wanted to make sure that by the time the new President is elected, the crown jewels of the property of 'everybody and nobody' are in safe hands. This has prompted the replication of the 1905 practice, first adopted in the aftermath of the lost war against Japan, that is crediting the government in a mortgage loan technique. This is the (un)famous *loans for share program*, that created a class of big capital owners in a few months. The outcome allows for at least two readings. In a less conventional way Han (2006, pp. 100) explains this as a rent, appropriated by industrialists, previously fed by soft loans and soft fiscal practices. In a more traditional analysis, however, the parallel is drawn to Brazil (Baer and Bang, 2002) in terms of *efficiency and social outcomes*, since the private property that emerged from this process had little resemblance to the textbook models of a civilized Western economy. But that has not been the purpose of the exercise either.[8]

The *second* turning point, as shown by the macroeconomic trends was in 1997, when inflation came down to moderate levels and growth, even if very modestly, did resume. It could be documented by the detailed survey of contemporary policy measures, particularly ones on institution building, that this change was *not coincidental*, since, among other things, oil prices were low (Csaba, 1997). In this phase, the ruling coalition consolidated its power and its economic base, by creating the basic institutions of market type control.

This process was halted, though not, as many of us feared, reverted by the *third major phase*, triggered by the currency crisis of August 1998, when the contagion caught Russia in the middle of its recovery. The ensuing *devaluation did restore the solvency of the country and created a room for economic activity* by providing across the board protection of domestic markets. This one time measure was later supported by an other windfall, the hike in oil prices in 2000–2006, which allowed the fiscal position to consolidate and provided additional export revenues, even though structural change was sluggish. We can take this period, 1998–1999 as a third phase.

As fourth, the two phases of the first *Putin Presidency* should be mentioned. In the first stage, measures to consolidate central power, by relying on the secret police and the introduction of presidential envoys to control local power dominated. This was seen by many (e.g. Bruszt, 2000) as a legitimate attempt to regain the independence of state from business interests. Others highlighted the contradictory nature of centralizing policy while conducting, in theory, radical economic liberalization. It is not the place to replicate the evidence presented in (Csaba, 2002) to show that the first deliberation inevitably prevailed over the other. If for no other reason, than because centralized controls cannot be restrained to one activity area, while letting a related area free. We shall come back to this point in a minute.

---

[8] In his overview of the process Wladimir Andreff (2004, pp. 73 and pp. 75–77) rightly calls attention to this factor that made the then customary reference to the Coase Theorem instrumental at best. Unlike in the original model, in Russia virtually nobody was interested in triggering *turnaround* in privatized firms. If anything asset stripping resulted, as a side effect, in a more efficient utilization of previously publicly owned assets, one way or another.

Finally, *as fifth*, the 2003–2006 period can be seen as one in which Russia, *being a normal country*, became manifest. Preparations for the legislative elections in December 2003 and the Presidential elections in March 2004 has not allowed for major changes to materialize. A usual pre-election year, where 'oligarchs' have conspicuously been disciplined, support for the pro-presidential alliance shored up in all conceivable means. The building up the needed media, financial and organizational support for a President (basically without an operational economic program) prevailed over reform projects. On one level of abstraction, this may seem as a *lost opportunity*, since reforms are best introduced when no major opposition can be mounted. The ease by which the President could handle/drive out of business his real or conceived adversaries in 2000–2006 suggests that if any operational reform program were to emerge in the first four years, *a large part of it could well have been implemented*. This holds despite the election year, had it been so high on the agenda as say, the loans for shares program in late 1995 (also prior to presidential elections). On the other hand, we do not know of multiparty systems, where rulers can unexpectedly lose out (despite opinion polls to their favor), where experimentation prior to elections and the ensuing consolidation of power would be the rule. What is less normal is that *no major economic strategy* as different from the set of improvisations emerged *even after a landslide victory* for the President. Alas, this puts the performance of the 1995–1997 period in a more favorable perspective, with the benefit of hindsight.[9]

Let us look at *Table 12* containing the EBRD assessment of progress in *structural and institutional indicators* to control our major findings. The fact that the Bank has not been able to establish the share of centrally administered prices speaks for itself, for the EBRD has been involved in Russia, both as an investor and in technical assistance programs ever since its establishment. This speaking silence reflects the reality, where theoretically free prices are being controlled and managed by local authorities in a variety of hidden manners, irrespective of central intentions, basically with reference to social needs. This of course is, by implication, a serious constraint on the market nature of Russian economic order.

EBRD indicators show, in line with our own assessments, that privatization waves in reality *have not followed official pronouncements*. In the period of voucher privatization, progress in property reform was slow. The big jumps are observable in 1996–1997 and 1998–2000. The private sector reached its peak in GDP by 1997 and *has not grown ever since*, despite a large number of bold statements of intention. Also the index of price liberalization stagnates since 1993, whereas trade liberalization even diminished. Quite in line with this the tax levy on imports account for no less than 18.5 per cent, which is typical of a

---

[9] This certainly does not imply, as our perhaps most critical reviewer, Dr. Halm (2006, p. 280) attributes, 'turning a blind eye with amazing generosity to these features of Russian development that are unacceptable by European standards'. Whatever one may want to think about ideal ways of massive privatization at the desktop, the fact of the matter remains, that the share of private property ceased to grow by 1997 and, a decade later has shrunk by nearly 5 percentage points, following a decade of 'reformist zeal' (EBRD: *Transition Report*, 2006 November).

developing country, not of an advanced market economy. Lacking trade liberalization implies the *lack of microeconomic incentives for restructuring* that would be particularly important for manufacturing branches.[10]

Numbers on industrial productivity indirectly prove our claim that stabilization and hardening the budget constraints of enterprises started in 1995, when hyperinflation started to subdue. Also, unemployment started to be open. Later the jobless rate diminishes with the rebound of economic activity. The major improvements in labor productivity, however, evaporate since 1999, indicating the limits of improvements available by *passive restructuring,* that is by sacking people and selling off non-essential assets. The phase of active restructuring does require new investment and new managerial skills. Neither of the two seems to be forthcoming, with old nomenklatura managers/insiders turned owners, and *FDI purposefully constrained from any major market entry that could endanger the positions of incumbents.* The red tape surrounding the FDI and the lengthy lists of exceptions from firms to be privatized, regularly passed by the State Duma reflect the success of this endeavor. In turn, lacking new investment and new management allow for a gradually diminishing growth of productivity – no good sign for sustaining growth.

Turning to the banking sector the radical decline in the number of financial establishments, from 2297 in 1995 to 1329 by 2002 according to the Economist Intelligence Unit (*Country Profile, 2003,* p. 61) is a good news. This reflects that, as a benefit of the crisis of 1998, much of the non-viable pocket banks of firms and individuals had to close down. On the other hand, competition among financial service providers has also declined, with the limited if any presence of major foreign credit institutions. This feature, as elaborated in previous chapters, may pose a serious *dynamic constraint on the evolution of capitalism* as a non-state run business order in Russia in the long run.

It is important to note that in the 1999–2003 period the *'virtual economy'* of Russia, based on barters and other non-money forms of transactions *gradually disappeared.* The share of bad loans peaked in 1998 by 39.8 per cent, and have come down to 12 per cent by 2001. This development has dispelled much of the theorizing about a new brand of market order emerging on the base of money surrogates. However, the very low EBRD index of banking reform reflects that, except for administrative measures, precious little has been done to tackle the ills of a mis-developed banking sector in the country. A detailed study of Berglöf et al (2003, pp. 108–112) has found that foreign ownership accounts only for five per cent of Russian banking assets (against over 80 per cent in Hungary, Croatia or the Czech Republic).[11] Meanwhile, the Central Bank of Russia applies lax regulation serving insider interests, thus further discouraging foreign bank

---

[10] Typically for a developing country, market protection does not take place primarily through tariffs; the average tariff level was only 11 per cent in 2003. But this is not the major issue, as is known from Japan, China, Turkey, or even France for that matter.

[11] Foreign ownership is similarly low in advanced OECD countries. However, the latter are *exporters* of know-how and institutions currently *missing* in Russia; this shortage causes allocation inefficiency and multiple drawbacks, as shown in the chapter on 'Transnational markets'.

entry. In turn, the *room for new ventures to get externally funded and thus innovations introduced in industry remains limited*, as the declining share of credit granted to the domestic sector indicates. This is no good news for major enterprise restructuring, or for endogenous, innovation-based development of Russian industry. Others see the closure of big private banks on non-trivial grounds as a sign of cumulating strains, reflecting ongoing mismanagement, rather than yet another element of single-handedness (*Handelsblatt*, 6 July 2004).

Last but not least, the GINI coefficient of inequality is reported to be at 48 per cent by the *World Development Report* (2003, p. 237), by two percentage points above (!) that in Peru, one of the most unequal Latin American societies, and slightly below Mali, yet another unequal society in Africa. This means that Russian economic change has produced strains that are unlikely to be explained away by reference to general indicators, themselves being less than impressive anyway. The share of Russian population living on less than $2 a day was 25 per cent in 2001 according to the same source, a very high portion for an urbanized European country where traditional society with its social safety valve is no longer around. Thus the improvement, owing to the regular payment of wages and pensions under the Putin years, as reported in the empirical chapter, implied a sea change, with poverty halved by 2005.

How could we, in sum, describe the *peculiar features of the Russian market economy* that makes it distinct from other market economies? In addressing these contentious issues, it seems more expedient to take *developing country models as starting point*, rather than the welfare capitalist models of Scandinavia and Western Europe. This might be justified on grounds of GDP levels, on grounds of still very strong role of industry and agriculture in the society, as well as on grounds of salient features of functioning of the Russian market, to be addressed in some detail below. In doing so, we do not condone what we see, this is just part of a descriptive approach.

Perhaps the most distinctive feature of the Russian economy, making the parallel to developing countries imperative, is its *dual structure*. In short, what has been said about local power explains, that *islands of capitalism* exist in the sea of stagnant, decaying late state socialist structures. The concentration of FDI to Moscow – normally two thirds of inward FDI is implemented in the Moscow region, and the rest in the oil and gas fields – is per se a proof of this feature. Furthermore, it is known that in some regions – like Nizhnii Novgorod, or Samara – market oriented reforms are implemented, while in the Far East or in the red belt, the inherited structures try to adapt to the new realities. This is the reason why field work in Russia is so difficult and the results are even harder to generalize than in other countries: what is generalized for Moscow is a picture of flourishing development, the same surveyed in, say, Novosibirsk or Chukotka, is a view of decay and poverty. Both pictures are correct, as in Brazil, China or South Africa.

A different, though by no means less relevant dimension of dualism – plaguing actually most, if not all transforming economies – has been highlighted by a recent analysis of Yevgeny Yasin (2003). He calls attention to the fact that *the non-tradable sectors, accounting for about 70 per cent of Russian GDP remained largely unreformed.* These areas include the fuel and energy complex, housing, health (two big market sectors in the West), the budgetary sector (including public services across the board) and not least transport (airways, railroads, and the rest). He called for radical marketizing measures in order to facilitate improved efficiency and create funding for the long run growth of the entire economy. Reforming these sectors seems to be a precondition for improved allocation of resources through the financial sector, currently repressed by the 'needs' emanating from the survival tactics of these unreformed areas. On the other hand, it would be one-sided to remain silent on the evolving competition and cost-cutting, demonstrated by recent empirical studies in some other areas, particularly in retail chains (Radaev, 2003, pp. 60 and pp. 77). In a way, this could be taken as the most important sign of an existing and functioning market system. It is truly starting to observe that unchallenged, unconstrained presidential power in the 2003-2006 has not translated into any major reform of any areas of the non-tradable sectors listed above.

The Russian market economy in the first decade of the 2000s has further strong parallels to developing country models. These include: a dominant role of a weak state and a resultant *high degree of informalism and low degree of transnationalization.* As we tried to explain in the chapter on 'Transnationalization', this is likely to lead to a low level steady state equilibrium. In other words, growth rates do not correspond to those envisaged by various models of unconditional convergence, that derive 'required' or potential growth rates from a target state that is equated to that in current leading economies. Slow growth that allows for the state administration to exist and avoid major famines may well qualify as 'equilibrium' level. With the state being weak, it often falls hostage to business interests and is vulnerable to corruption. Though the first Putin Presidency was self-portrayed (and seen by some outsiders) as an attempt to change this sorry state of affairs, comparative empirical surveys on corruption (Raiser and Hellman, 2004) have shown *this attempt to fail.* In other words, it was a *change in clients* rather than a change in *modus operandi* that was observable in 2000–2006 period.

What we observe in Russia is well described by the established term of *'political capitalism'* of the development literature, denoting a situation, where entertaining good relations to the state administration is more important for the activity to be profitable than pleasing the customers.[12] Examples that in Russia this is the case abound, the once more the Presidency singles out oligarchs for setting precedents of examplary punishment. The latter included the media magnate Gusinskii, head of the major opposition NTV channel, the attempt to get the extradition of Boris Berezovskii, once counting among the 'inventors' of the political career of Putin on charges that British courts found inadequate, the jailing of fuel magnate Khodorkovskii, or the de facto expulsion of Chelsea

---

[12] The most recent OECD country study of Russia, published at the time of final proof-reading for the present edition, comes out with an unusually critical language blaming the growing political control over the Russian economy in the 2004-2006 period, as reported in: *Financial Times*, 1 December, 2006.

owner Abramovich, openly supportive of opposition parties. The more the public condones this type of 'serving justice' by the good king, the more internalized the behavior wishing to please the government will be. This is, of course, not a new phenomenon, but path dependency this time allows for shortcut solutions to be practiced. Furthermore, these cases are supportive of the apt claim by Stefan Hedlund (2001) describing Russian capitalism as 'property without rights', a thesis that leads him to elaborate on the pivotal role of the judiciary in bringing about and sustaining the West European type of market economy over the centuries, an issue we shall come back in the concluding chapter on the role of institutions in growth.

Distrust of the courts has also been traditional in Tsarist Russia and the Soviet period alike. With weak courts and non enforceable laws (often inherited from Soviet period, like the ones punishing profiteering) recreate the environment of low trust and extralegal law enforcement, that was once called by Boris Nemtsov (then Deputy PM) as *maffia capitalism*. The more we have to do with the 'paradox of plenty' the higher the probability of an authoritarian solution is to be lasting. For this – *the resource-based economy – neither needs nor requires more sophisticated forms of control.* Money thus matters, but not just money alone; allocation continues to be distorted at the macroeconomic level. Non-market forms of co-ordination (other than ethical) play a lasting role in managing affairs. This is a market economy (as we shall show below), still a specific one, definitely not a free market economy, nor welfare capitalism.

A second major feature of Russia is *regionalized authoritarianism*. This reflects the age-old tradition whereby enlightenment tends to come from the center, while local power is often more conservative and backward looking. This also implies that *many central decrees and laws aimed at liberalization are openly being sabotaged.* The most common practice is reference to shortage, special circumstances, or the need to sustain local supplies. In doing so, the local authorities have introduced de facto customs barriers, 'export' and 'import' stops from and to their areas, obliged producers to supply the goods locally rather than selling it to the highest bidder; not allowing foreigners to start business in areas allowed for by the national laws.

Similarly, local power tended to be involved in privatization deals, especially in spontaneous privatization, or management buy-outs. Local politicians, on occasion even the local administration, retain shares in the firms, and micromanage their activities. This feature *makes it difficult to establish what is (or is not) private, and if private, what that means in reality.* Whereas in the West privatization is the act of making firms independent of state bureaucracy, in Russia it may or may not be the case. As it seems, the attempt by President Putin to overrule local power by simply appointing the central presidential envoys has not changed much of the balance of power.

Under these circumstances rule of law, transparency, objective evaluation of asset value and the like remain abstract concepts. The Russian *stock exchange, that emerged from the very outset as an instrument of financing the government, not the corporate sphere* (cf. Réthi, 2003), continues to defy the name 'capital market' that should have lent itself to be the constituent of the new order.

If we describe these mixed forms of control as 'equilibrium solution' in any way, this implies, that the 1998–2006 period has proven: *Russia no longer faces disintegration, nor there is a threat of an all-out reversal to the Soviet model*. This is demonstrable by the discontinuation of all secessionist movements except for Chechnya, and local governors supportive of the President in reshaping the upper house in his own favor. The Communist Party, for its part, having always voted for the budget in the Duma, is obviously more of a movement of protest and a rallying point of the disenchanted, united by nationalism and populism, than a classical Marxist movement of any sort, with its vision of the future better world. The original capital accumulation, that has taken place in the 1989–2000 period could not be undone. However, the dynamics of change could be tempered and the scope of winners considerably restructured in the 2001-2006 period. Statist features, or nontransparent political/proprietory inter-twinings, exemplified by GAZPROM, or by the Union of Airlines established under governmental tutelage in 2006 among public firms are telling examples for the new trend, resembling to some extent the East-Asian market models.

Summing up what has been said, the 'Wild East' can neatly co-exist with state capitalism, since *these define different aspects of the same structure*, a feature well known from Latin American countries. An *assertive* state power should not be mixed up with the East Asian type of *developmental state*, though the intertwining between business and the administration is equally strong in the latter case. However, the basic difference is that a weak and captive state is *unable to launch and organize big development projects* that could change the landscape of the macro-economy. The liberalization project, elaborated under the technical assistance of the OECD is yet to take off. Even if private investment possibilities to infra-structure is liberalized, the continued harassment of major 'tycoons' is unlike-ly to build confidence among those who have anything to invest there, be there local residents or foreign strategic investors. The numbers presented in *Table 2*, showing that only 20.3 per cent of revenues accrues to the central state, does not allow for that. On the contrary: *one of the major challenges for Russia is likely to come from the inadequate and inefficient public investments into physical infrastructure, environment and health care*. Lacking these public goods may act as an additional constraint on economic development, which is a broader concept than growth.

How Can We Test If Russia Is Indeed a Market Economy?

This seemingly naive question has far reaching repercussions. For one, mem-bership in the World Trade Organization, where Russia lost out the contest in 2002 against China, it is a fundamental question to define the fate of application and the related disciplines, if and under what conditions the applicant is accept-ed as a fully-fledged market economy. Likewise, the main trading partner of Russia, the European Union applies a series of protective measures against state trading countries. While much of the original *rationale* of these is gone, the arse-nal hits all the more those outside the global trading framework and its disci-plines. Finally, both in policy literature and in the more academically oriented comparative economic systems literature it is a relevant theoretical issue if we can establish the existence of a market order or conversely, the lack of it.

If we avoid the ideological posturing present in a large section of the literature, there are a couple of points to be established. First, it is beyond doubt, that in Russia *the maximization of asset value is a dominant concern*, over and above other considerations. If clashing with competing concerns economic agents, in the vast majority of cases, and unless pressurized by force, follow strategies that maximizes their personal wealth. If and when conditions are insecure, this wealth is transferred to safe havens abroad. The recurring Russian current account surplus, against the background of mostly investment unfriendly local conditions, exacerbated by regular attacks on the 'oligarchs', only make this strategy rational, well known from developing countries. In a way, *capital flight is the best indicatior* that it is not ideology (of patriotism) or bureaucracy (calling for local investments) that dominate, but the *private microeconomic rationality*. And this was what we were after.

Second, *allocation* follows basically *price signals*. This is clear, if we compare 'poetry', that is economic policies in general and industrial policy in particular, with reality. In poetry, investments should have flown to high value added sectors, capitalizing in R+D and military conversion. In reality, investments flew basically to the primary sector and restructuring in high value added branches has been limited, as shown in our tables in the appendix a for this chapter. Also if we think about privatization or FDI, the processes have been dominated by *spontaneity* rather than by the elaborate projects of various state organs.

Last but not at all least, prices have indeed regained their *signaling functions*. Shortages that used to prevail in the late Soviet years disappeared, for *money can buy everything*, even foreign currency. This means that prices are dominant, though as seen above, by no means to the degree free pricing would imply. Meddling in pricing thus is not the same as state pricing, the former is also a practice known in developing nations like India. While not condoning any financial repression, it is a world of difference to state that the financial sector is *repressed* by state controls, versus the state where public authorities *set* all prices. Arbitrage, one of the textbook examples of what happens if one commodity has two prices, has been massive, and the widespread trade of shuttlers (*chelnoki*) is a prime example of this.

In sum, where asset value maximizaton is the name of the game, where microeconomics has been re-instituted as the logic defining economic actions of firms and households, finally where prices do convey basic signals about scarcities and motivate sellers and buyers to act accordingly, the market economy, in its broadest sense is given. *In this primary sense the Russian transformation has been a major success*, since this was the purpose of the exercise and it has been attained without major bloodshed.[13] Knowing the horrendous costs of

---

[13] Let us repeat: colonial wars in Chechnya or Abkhazia or Tajikistan do not count amongst the 'social costs of transition'. Most casualties result from these, not from the conquest of the Supreme Soviet, or from crushing demonstrations against price hikes or privatization. Inadequate investment in health started in the Brezhnev era, thus should not be blamed exclusively on the post-1992 period.

imposing the Soviet regime in terms of human lives (the exact number is still a subject of debate among historians, but it definitely ran in the millions) this is no small achievement.

It is a different, though related issue, if we want to know *what defines the quality of the market economy*, in other words, what type of market economy emerged on the ruins of the Soviet empire? This is a relevant issue, and lays at the heart of most debates in the social sciences. László Bruszt (2000) considers the captiveness of the Russian state to be at the root of market imperfections, the continued dominance of monopolies and the inability of the state to regulate. As we have seen in the chapter on 'Transnationalization', the *quality and strength of the core state* is indeed a defining feature of the market order, including its efficiency and social qualities in the long run.

Once we accept the Russian state's being traditionally weak and internally divided, first between lobbies, and second in territorial terms, it is no surprise to establish that it is hardly in a position *to provide the public goods and services* associated with a modern market order. Even some basic functions of the core state remain unattended. We have shown the limited ability of the central state to raise revenue. This has been a source of troubles, as regular reports of explosions of pipelines, of extreme forms of environmental degradation unknown in other European societies, the sad state of health of the Russian population, or the decay of physical infrastructure, primarily the railroad system indicates. Reports on these phenomena abound in the daily press, and it makes no sense to single any one of the cases.

An even more fundamental task of any state is to provide public security, *law and order* in an uncorrupted fashion for all citizens. This seemingly simple maxim cannot be ensured, inter alia for the continuous under-funding of police. Reform of the armed forces has though been declared several times, but not much has been implemented. The decade-long war in Chechnya is a good example of the limitations on the Russian army. The jungle of regulations and lack of civil control is a hotbed for arbitrariness, thus a basic function of the core state suffers.

A related, but not less important state function, appreciated by all economic theories is performed by the *judiciary*. The enforcement of contracts, at affordable costs and time, impartial and professional implementation of deals is a prime function in any civilized society. This function has a major role for the market economy, else extralegal forms of enforcement, such as corruption, the use of force and the like turn the market into a maffia economy. Organized crime is a widespread phenomenon in Russia, and this is immediately related to the weaknesses of the core state.

A following, perhaps most important feature defining the nature of the market is the *enforcement of property rights* and their security. Libraries have been written on the focal role of this formal institution in the market economy, and a separate school emphasizing it has emerged (Pejovich, ed., 2001, contains a summary of major contributions to this field). Development theory has shown that lacking private property rights and enforcement mechanisms render most of Sub-Saharan Africa a stagnant region, defying its richness in natural resources and other favorable endowments (Collier and Gunning, 1999).

In the case of Russia, the *property right system is particularly weak*. Not only is private property not protected from the state, but similarly, public property is often unprotected from grabbing. The evolution of a non-transparent mix of property structure explains why issues of *corporate governance* remain chronically *unattended*. By the same token, *restructuring in large corporations* is bound to remain slow – a feature that has been conspicuously showing up in the meager export performance of the Russian engineering sector. If one gives credit to the intellectual capacity having produced *sputnik*, ballistic missiles and still capable of operating new spaceships and space stations, the lack of improvement of export performance of Russia is becoming all the more perplexing. True, *institutions are the mediators* between endowments and market outcomes. Once the central role of property rights is accepted, the causal chain seems straightforward indeed. In short, lacking both sticks and carrots managers may be induced to asset stripping rather than maximizing the asset value of an owner, who is not always different from them. The flux between their private and managerial capacity distorts the usual incentive structure and leads to low level equilibria. Survival, rather than expansion is then the name of the game. Or alternatively, as Pekka Sutela (1998) formulated, the *secondary market* for assets remained non-existent, thus the control mechanisms remained extinct, thus the *built-in inefficency* has become constant feature at the macro-level.

One can only speculate if, and to what degree, the weakness of property rights and related institutions is *historically given*. The customary reference to the shadowy privatization deals – 'the theft of the century' – does not seem to hold, once we consider the experience of the United States. Not only is there a social norm not to ask for the origins of the first million dollars. The role of gold miners, robber barons and the like has richly been documented, to the point of being a commonplace about 19th century America. On the contrary, theory would expect the emergence of civilizing institutions, once *the need for transferring, bequeathing, securing, splitting etc. of wealth becomes real*, which are elementary functions of human social behavior. In our view, policy neglect, lacking traditions (both from Tsarist and Soviet periods) and the *ongoing lack of investment*, joined by the low social status of law enforcing agents, contribute to this phenomenon.

Lack of clear division between central and local state, between state and private, as a lasting phenomenon undermines the efficiency enhancing qualities of the market order, *without* however, *transforming it into some historically unknown social construct* (often postulated by Russia-watchers and Russian social scientists). An inefficient market economy – Bolivia as the standard reference in American debates – is by no means an exception. The emphasis of the post-Washington Consensus on *institution building and good governance* is a clear reflection of this insight. It has already found its way to the policy literature as well. To be fair, the continued failures of top-down, designed reform packages in Russia (to attain what the designers wished) have had a major sobering role for the entire economics profession, and in the gradual rediscovery of policies, institutions and values.

Liberalization and deregulation has long been seen as a major side condition for making the market economy more efficient. Ever since the 'counter-revolution' of Thatcher and Reagan, deregulation and liberalization have been on the agenda, also for established market economies. Leaving the ideological components aside, it is easy to accept, on the grounds of microeconomic theory, why liberalization is good for efficiency and adjustment. In the case of Russia, as summarized in *Table 12*, this has proven to be the *least advanced side of systemic change*. Interestingly and importantly, lack of liberalization in an environment with big arbitrage possibilities, such as in foreign trade or currency transactions, or privatization, is *a direct call for the non-law-abiding behavior*, so widespread in contemporary Russia.

Limited liberalization is problematic in more than one respect. First, lack of entry supports monopoly positions and diminishes efficiency gains from privatization. Second, monopolistic markets dominated by networks of producers call for different type of public policies, in terms of competition, than contestable markets do (Török, 2001). Third, with lacking liberalization the *microeconomic incentives* for change become extinct, therefore *improvement in the future may well not be forthcoming under self-regulation*. This may explain in part the continued *low efficiency* of many activities in Russia, not only in industry, but in banking, trade and services.

Finally, the *rule of law* is though a value on its own right, but is also constituent for the type of market economy that emerges. As any broad concept – from social intangibles to conscientious behavior of a tradesman – it covers a variety of formal and informal institutions and their interaction. The less conditions are conducive to a law abiding behavior becoming a social norm, the higher the probability is that capitalism equals to wheeling and dealing for the small scale, and theft or corrupting the state for the macro-level. And though one should not take these features of Russia as historically given, the outcomes can indeed be explained by a *single chain of reasoning*. This is based on the type of intertwining between the state and the market, policies and institutions. From this angle, the ongoing attempts of the first and second Putin Presidency to 'liberate the state from the capture by the oligarchs' has further *diminished the credibility* of any policy based on the rule of law. By contrast, the tradition of 'might is right' and that it is the top political leader who is the final judge on all major issues has been revived. If our previous line of reasoning holds, at least to some degree, we must see this tradition as one of the components leading to the chain of low efficiency and *low level steady state equilibrium* in the Russian market economy. It is in this context that Alexander Radygin (2004) interprets the changes in terms of a move toward a *model of state capitalism*.

What Matters for Growth?
Prospects for the Russian Economy

What we have argued until now may suffice to advance the thesis that the big question of Russian market transition, that dominated the debates in the 1990s is settled in the affirmative. Russia has become a market economy, though not the type dreamed of by most reform-oriented observers. There remains a different, not less important follow up question, namely what this market transformation will mean for the largest European state in the long run? What are the prospects for economic development of a country, based on an economic system that differs in some major aspects from the model of OECD countries?

This matter has long been figuring high on the agenda of policy-makers. Lenin wanted to catch up and overtake capitalism – an idea that has been re-stated by Khrushchev at the time of the perhaps over-ambitious atmosphere having followed the launch of the first satellite, the *sputnik* in 1957. Later on, Andropov's criticism of 'corrosion' and later his disciple, Gorbachev attempt-ing to accelerate the Soviet economy all aimed at saving great power status. Under Putin acceptance of the middle power status has obviously taken place. However in economic terms, the President in his ritually referred May 2003 address to the legislation called for a doubling of Russian GDP in a decade, prescribing thus a 7.2 per cent growth rate for the country. This is seen – even by the Ministry of Economy – as over-ambitious, with the latter agency work-ing with 4.5–5.0 per cent growth forecasts in its various materials. External observers (Sutela, 2004, pp. 222–225) put the growth rate at 2.5–4.0 per cent only, based on the quite optimistic Levine–Renelt growth coefficients most widely in use in growth accounting.

It is difficult, even next to impossible, to establish ex ante the actual growth rates of any economy. It is known that econometric models can establish only consistency criteria and probabilities under the constraints set by those calibrating them. However, it would be hard to disagree with Yegor Gaidar (2003, pp. 309–310) that the fundamental question is not so much the actual rate attainable in one year or another, but the long run trajectory; in his view under this angle the automatic continuation of the 1999–2003 period short of new windfalls, is not secured. Furthermore, as he correctly observes, it is time to change the quite traditionalist preoccupation of setting sectoral priorities, that keep on being redefined in the course of ongoing bureaucratic bargains. Industrial policy in the post-industrial age should mean *growth promotion through an enabling and business friendly regulatory environment* and providing rule of law.

This question becomes all the more relevant since the Putin Presidency seems to have opted for the 'Chilean way' of combining authoritarian political methods with market friendly rhetoric and measures. True, in a formal sense Putin has attained by his second term the exclusive power of the General. We also have yet to see the high quality radical market reforms. These have not been materializing during his entire first presidency, and several months following his landslide victory inaction, fear of committing any mistake were still the name of the game in his administration (Aslund, 2004). The cited analyst also mentions that the banking crisis of July 2004 already foreshadows that laming, lack of decisions may become an independent source of trouble, amplifying per se minor difficulties. This is by and large the opposite of what a comparable time span, in optimistic, reformist scenario would presuppose and require. Meanwhile in Chile 1978 was already a time of second generation reforms, such as those in banking and the pension system.

The combination of political authoritarianism with free market policies in a country, rather than a city-state, remains an intriguing theoretical puzzle. Can this policy mix work in an urbanized, post-industrial European society, and if yes, how? For there seems to be no doubt that the second Putin presidency continues to be based on the idea of a strong power, that may, in the optimistic reading,[14] be supported by further measures of institution building and improving the conditions for a market economy.[15] With the benefit of hindsight, pessimists, again, tended to be the well-informed optimists.

What we do know for sure is that the *allocation of resources plays a pivotal role*. The jury is still out on the most appropriate model of the capital market. More recent corporate governance literature highlights the importance of cultural factors in choosing the locally most appropriate options. Still, what we can see is that the *investment rate in Russia is currently at least by 5 percentage points less than in other transforming economies*. This circumstance sustains, while the country runs a regular surplus on its current account and FDI remains low.

Let us suppose that one way or another, additional resources can be mobilized for investment purposes. Our analysis of the collapse of the Soviet model and of the comparative developmental theories and experience definitely call into attention the focal role played by *the system of allocation*, be that through the stock exchange or the banking system. In the case of Russia it is a commonplace to observe, that the capital market is dominated by the issuance of government bonds, therefore it finances government needs, not the economy in its bulk. Russian analyses (Sizov, 2003, pp. 31 and pp. 42) complain that the stock exchange does not perform the role of providing external finance to post-privatization restructuring, nor does it provide reliable information of asset valuation. Moreover, less than 5 per cent of investment needs of the corporate sector is financed from the capital market according to the same source. Likewise, the banking system has long been subordinate to industrial interests, for it were the big industrial firms that established their home banks by making their financial units independent. The market clearing that followed the currency crisis of August 1998 has lead to the closure of many small local/real private banking establishments. This improved the *solidity* of the system, but

---

[14] In the pessimistic reading, as of Satter (2003) only the centralizing tendency and lack of democracy that sustains for sure.

[15] With the benefit of hindsight, it has proven correct to note (Mau, 1999, pp. 184–187) that the 1993 Constitution attained the maximum of legislating liberal principles that still are in need to be defended and implemented across the predominant policy of improvisations.

diminished competition. The smaller banking crisis of July 2004 had similar effects. Also the big survival was seen at the old, established state banks like Sberbank or Vneshekonombank, and the ones backed by big firms like Gazprom. Therefore, it is hardly surprising that these tend to serve their parent organizations primarily, not the purpose of resource allocation at the macroeconomic level. The latter function thus remains largely unattended – bad news for long run growth.[16]

What we know, in sum, allows for *a pessimistic assessment of the possibilities of improved resource allocation.* The obvious signs of what the development literature calls *'financial repression'* have been spotted. The stock exchange and banking, especially in the large scale sector, have built-in interest to support pre-existing structures rather than initiate divestment of inefficient, loss making activities and regroup the capital regained from here to more profitable areas. Russia is therefore, for structural and institutional reasons, confronted with a phenomenon known to lay at the heart of slow growth equilibrium in underdeveloped countries. Here we have to refer back to the line of earlier reasoning, explaining why it would be pivotal for letting major inflows of FDI in the banking sector if this structural weakness were to be overcome. Since insider dominance has been a defining feature of Russian capitalism, furthermore governmental policies in the past 15 years were positively aimed at sustaining and strengthening this, by creating market protection through a variety of ways, it is unlikely to be changed quickly. The *constituency for a sustainingly inward-looking option has been created and even strengthened* through the economic and power politics consolidation period in 1998–2004. Dyker (2004) rightly finds this as the major obstacle to Russian road to WTO.[17]

A related issue is financial intermediation and corporate governance. As long as savings are not secure and the incentive to invest them abroad is great, capital shortage, in the form of low investment rates, has to be taken as given. In the peculiar intertwining that emerged between banking and industry, with the dominance of industrial interest, problems of non-transparent forms of corporate governance, widely discussed in the literature on Asian crisis (Dyck, 2001) are likely to be reproduced. This renders the chances for accelerated modernization, *microeconomic restructuring* and market-led recovery *quite slim,* indeed, despite the sizeable human capital and technical skills accumulated in the Soviet period. Lacking micro-economic incentives are likely to pose a hindrance to a more optimistic scenario.

A closely related issue is the much-discussed problem of *resource dependent growth.* Contrary to declarations of intent, Russia has been unable to move away from the primary sectors and upgrade its manufacturing base. Once the built-in conservatism of the financial sector is understood, it is rational

---

[16] Russian analysts (Fedorenko and Simchera, 2003, p. 40) report of the halving of labor productivity in 1990–2002; meanwhile, a unit of GDP is produced by no less than 70 per cent more material input than in the last Soviet year.

[17] Preliminary agreement on the latter issue was reacted in December, 2006. But the structural constraints on FDI-led structural upgrading remain.

to expect slow changes *in the long run*, whatever the governmental structural priorities may be. The *low level of intermediation* and the *shallowness of financial markets* are both unique for Russia, even among the emerging economies. Furthermore, with the delay of restructuring, it is becoming increasingly costly, and the inherited human capital and technological skills are likely to be depreciated. The less management relies on the ICT revolution and the related organizational changes, discussed in the Transnationalization chapter, the more industrialism becomes a synonym of a museum in the 21st century.

Foreign direct investment has been shown to be a way of overcoming technological and organizational bottlenecks. The large scale inflow of *FDI* is, however, *unlikely to be a defining feature* of the decade to come, for the overall business unfriendly atmosphere, because of the vested interests of the insiders, and because of the nationalist accents of the government policies.[18] The strength of local power only strengthens the unfavorable phenomena, and so does the lack of clearly defined and enforceable property right structure. Without major inflows of FDI, endogenous growth is dependent exclusively on local innovation, as embodied in technological change applied in the business sector. The latter is known to have been the traditional wound point of the Russian industry all across its history. Moreover, as the comparative study of Piatkowski (2003, p. 6) indicates, per capita ICT spending in Russia remained at one third of the Hungarian levels, thus its influence on labor productivity could be marginal at best.

In the above said, we tried to offer concrete formulations of what in the more abstract literature is called *conditions for spillover* effects, also in terms of technology, products and organization. The more we believe in endogenous or neoclassical growth theory, *the less we can give credence*, even at the most abstract level of modelling, to *claims that governmental activism can and should be able to replace, even in part, the lacking micro-foundations of sustainable economic growth*. In his comprehensive analysis Weigert (2003, pp. 194–206) blames the lack of competition for this feature and makes propositions on how to overcome the deadlock. His list includes an active and less partisan anti-trust of independent regulatory organization, the support of bottom-up privatization through new entries, improving physical infrastructure and limiting the arbitrariness of authorities, making fiscal federalism explicit and submitting Russia to WTO disciplines. This is a next-to-exhaustive list, hard to disagree with at a normative level. Meanwhile, it is hard to overlook, that as long as the resource-based economy allows for earning an investment grade for Russia, the leadership is likely to see these deeper reforms as ones that may well be delayed. The ongoing campaign against the oligarchs may well be a move aimed at

---

[18] Arguing in the same vein Kalotay (2004, pp. 125–127) calls attention to the fact that much of reported FDI – in his calculation up to 27 per cent in the 2000s – has been round tripping, i.e. a form of capital flight transaction, without any palpable impact on corporate governance. Since this is related to the overall business unfriendly atmosphere and lack of property safety (especially following the war on oligarchs) the UCTAD specialists consider the forecasts of rapid take-off of FDI in Russia as 'premature' (pp. 130–131).

diverting attention to the stagnant structural reforms,[19] a fact acknowledged, at least in private conversation, by all well informed Russian officials.

Further delaying reforms though may be feasible as long as oil prices grow and strategic partnership with the US will mute loud criticism of the Russian leadership domestically and abroad. Still, this option may prove to be a *self-deception* much earlier than it may currently look, and the slow growth phase may be attained well before the pre-crisis level of activity could have been regained. Recent analyses (Bobylev, 2004, pp. 45–47) for instance call attention to some of the warning signs. Russia is one of the very few countries with *negative net rate of savings*. Moreover, the energy- and natural resource intensity of a unit of output in the 1990–2003 period grew by a coefficient of 1.6–2.6, while Western economies could grow with diminishing energy and fuel use in the same period. Perhaps even more *unfavorable* are the *structural changes in the macroeconomy.* The share of electric energy production, for instance grew from 3.5 per cent in 1980 to 8.5 per cent (!) by 2002; fuel industries grew from 6.5 to 16.4 per cent; non-ferrous metal production from 6 to 10.5 per cent, while the share of light industry went down from 16.6 to 1.7 per cent.

These changes are clearly indicative of the *serious and inherent structural limitations on sustaining the growth* much hailed by the government dominated Russian daily press, and business interests in the West, as a major accomplishment of the first Putin Presidency (although still below the pre-crisis level). As one of the close advisors of the Russian government (Mau, 2004, pp. 7 and pp. 13–14) observed, the lack of trust, uncertainty over the rules of the game, as well as the resultant search for those sabotaging quick results in the economy together have created an atmosphere of *overall restraint, distrust* among the agents of change, that is politics, business, banks, foreigners, the administration and civil society. The outcome of the latter is bound to exert unfavorable influences on the sources of growth in Russia in the long run.

Translating the theoretical insight into policy, it means that *prospects for a less resource dependent growth must be seen as dim,* for both internal and external reasons. While international markets for resources grow only slowly, those for technology intensive items and services expand. Meanwhile recent analyses (Bashmakov, 2006, pp. 86) put the growth performance of the non-fuel sectors of the Russian economy for 2008–2012 only at the range of 0.2 to 1.1 per cent per annum. Likewise the more ICT is the defining element of development, the more wealth creation becomes largely independent of the resource base. The latter is more likely to become a curse in terms of environment and in terms of returns alike. Therefore, the 'resource curse' so obviously present in Russia, is

---

[19] In a different reading Hishow (2004, pp. 104–105) considers these to be the two sides of the same coin. However, in reality, the fight against the oligarchs is made possible by the same resource rent, that allowed for Putin, comfortably live with a lack of an operational economic strategy, years after taking office. It also creates the disincentives to change, in line with the theory of petro-states quoted above. Therefore, it is naive to expect that a captive and resource-reliant power center should act both against the oligarchs and the resource curse, as the self-justification of the Putin Presidency would let us believe.

not a minor problem from the point of view of long-term developmental prospects of the country. The question therefore is not so much, whether Russia should be 'saved' from its oil and gas wealth (Köves, 2005, pp 394-398). Rather one wonders, that Russia could, indeed, become the sole economy of the globe whose secular prosperity is based on fuels, although the country has entered the phase of post-industrialism and IT revolution.

What is bad news in the long run may well come just as well in the medium run. For the room for the Pinochet-type policies, favored by the Putin Presidency is *more feasible under conditions of limited structural change.* The less civil society evolves, the less complex the economic structures are, the higher the chances for 'developmental dictatorship', or a policy of top-down modernization. As Vladimir Mau (2004, p. 14) puts it, from the plurality of conceivable development models only a *dirigiste* and an old-fashioned 'institutionalist' option remained politically viable. As we have shown above, this is not good news for *development* as distinct from questitative *growth*. Institutional reforms in the 2000-2005 period have hardly contributed to improved total factor productivity (Voigt, 2006, pp. 135-6) as distinct from making use of windfall gains, what secularly growing oil prices have secured.

Meanwhile, it is hard to overlook the *contrast* between the rather static *Russian way* and the much more dynamic Central European model, that was called *'emerging Europe'* in the Foreword. This insight may prompt major reassessment of Russian political and strategic plans, the potential role of Russia in the future European and global architecture. Whereas the adaptation to the status of a middle power has taken place under the first Putin Presidency, the ramifications of lasting marginalization in the global economy are not yet reflected in the thinking in and about Russia. *The inability of the core state to attend some basic functions may soon become problematic*[20] in terms of environment, health, smuggling, crime, fighting terrorism and even migration (with Russia being one of the biggest *recipient* of immigrants, primarily from post-Soviet states). The urbanization crisis and the decay of physical infrastructure pose major challenges, that are though foreseeable, still their solution is by no means imminent. For if we just consider that many cities and industries have been located in open defiance of natural endowments (Gaddy and Hill, 2003), the idea of market clearing transport tariffs, or market clearing energy prices do not seem to be realistic. Russia still has to develop a way of how to operate a state more *devoted to public purpose in the narrow sense,* than national glory in the broad sense. And this is indeed a cultural challenge for any nation – as we observed with France, Britain or postwar Germany.

In a lecture, Douglass North (2003) has brought up Russia as an example defying all existing theories. If there is a modicum of truth in our speculations

---

[20] This assesment is shared by the OECD (2004) highlighting, besides the resource curse, the traditional inability of the Russian state to deliver, implement and control even available enlightened *legislation* as a major *obstacle* to further *development* (as different from short-term quantitative growth in line with the broad interpretation adopted in various chapters of this monograph).

above, this would point to a different direction, since the limitations of Russian transformations could be explained within the *same theoretical frame* as the success of Central Europeans. Moreover, we hope to have contributed to the formation of *rational expectations* relating to what is, or is not, likely to work in terms of policy options and institutional arrangements, and also provide a rationale for why it should be the case. Therefore, if we include the neo-institutionalist theory of North into the broad church of economics, as we certainly do, then we are a step closer to an *explanatory theory* of economic development in the world and in the largest European country alike. Agreeing with his second major conclusion, that in sustainingly growing economies, the *informal norms* and the *enforcement mechanism matter more* than copying or not of patterns working well in advanced societies, our own forecast is likely to be supported. For it is *lagging behind the latter two dimensions that make Russia manifestly different* from its fellow transition economies in Central Europe. This may explain, at least in part, the new dividing line between emerging Europe and the laggards.

In concluding this chapter, we must directly answer the question raised in the title in the negative. It is *rather the form than the nature* of state failure and state capture that has undergone a basic change in the past twenty years. Following the breakdown of imperial bureaucratic co-ordination mechanisms a weak state emerged. It is this feature as well as the way of its intertwining with markets that lay at the heart of low efficiency-slow growth trap plaguing the Russian economy. All this does not mean that 'capitalism' in Russia 'failed', as some observers (Kagarlitsky, 1995) were too quick and eager to pinpoint. Its evolution just happened to be *different* from the projects and dreams of system designers. Unsurprisingly, it has proven to be an outcome of 'human action rather than human deliberation' (Hayek, 1995).

References

AHREND, R. and THOMPSON, W. (2005): Unnatural monopoly: the endless wait for gas sector reform in Russia. *Europe-Asia Studies*, vol. 57. no. 6. pp 801–822.

ANDREFF, W. (2004): Rossiskaia privatizatsiiia: podkhodi i posledstviiia. (Privatization in Russia: approaches and outcomes). *Voprosy Ekonomiki*, vol. 75. no. 6. pp. 57–78.

ASLUND, A. (2002): *Building Capitalism.* Cambridge and New York: Cambridge University Press.

ASLUND, A. (2004): Lonely at the top. *Moscow Times*, 13 July.

BAER, W. and BANG, J. (2002): Privatization and equity in Brazil and Russia. *Kyklos*, vol. 55. no. 4. pp. 495–522.

BASHMAKOV, I. (2006): Ne-neftegazovoi VVP kak indikator dinamiki rossiiskoi ekonomiki (Non-fuel GDP as an indicator of Russian economic growth). *Voprosy Ekonomiki*, vol. 77. no. 5. pp. 78–86.

BERGLÖF, E. – KUNOV, A. – SHVETS, Yu. – YUDAEVA, Ks. (2003): *The New Political Economy of Russia.* Cambridge/Mass. and London: The MIT Press.

BLANK, A. – GURVICH, E. – VILYUKAEV, A. (2006): Obmennii kurs i konkurentnosposobnost' otraslei russiiskoi ekonomiki (Exchange rate and competitiveness of Russian economic sectors). *Voprosy Ekonomiki*, vol. 77. no. 6. pp. 4–25.

BOBYLEV, S. (2004): Rossia na puti anti-ustoichivogo razvitiia? (Is Russia on a road of non-sustainable growth?) *Voprosy Ekonomiki,* vol. 75. no. 2. pp. 43–54.

BOFINGER, P. (1994): Macroeconomic transformation in Eastern Europe: The role of monetary policy reconsidered. In: HERR, H. – TOBER, S. – WESTPHAL, A. eds: *Macroeconomic Problems of Transition.* Cheltenham/UK and Northampton/USA: Edward Elgar Publishing Co., pp. 77–95.

BRUSZT, L. (2000): Constructing markets: the case of Russia and the Czech Republic. In: DOBRY, M. ed.: *Democratic and Capitalist Transformations in Eastern Europe.* Dordrecht-London-New York: Kluwer Academic Publishers, pp. 197–220.

COLLIER, P. and GUNNING, W. (1999): Explaining African economic performance. *Journal of Economic Literature,* vol. 37. no. 1. pp. 64–111.

CSABA, L. (1992): Russia beyond perestroika. *Communist Economies and Economic Transformation,* vol. 4. no. 3. pp. 33–359.

CSABA, L. (1995): *The Capitalist Revolution in Eastern Europe.* Cheltenham/UK and Northampton/MA/USA: Edward Elgar Publishing Co.

CSABA, L. (1997): Az új orosz kormány gazdaságpolitikája. (Economic policies of the new Russian government). *Valóság,* vol. 40. no. 8. pp. 16–35.

CSABA, L. (2002): Russia's political economy. In: BUGAJSKI, J. ed.: *Toward an Understanding of Russia.* Washington, D. C.: a book published by the Council on Foreign Relations, pp. 27–44.

DYCK, A. (2001): Privatization and corporate governance: Principle, evidence and future challenges. *World Bank Research Observer,* vol. 16. no. 1. p. 59–84.

DYKER, D. (2004): Russian accession to the WTO: Why such a long and difficult road? *Post-Communist Economies,* vol. 14. no. 1. pp. 3–20.

FEDORENKO, N. and SIMCHERA, V. (2003): K otsenke effektivnosti ispolzovaniia natsionalnikh resursov Rossii. (On the evaluation of the efficiency of use of natural resources in Russia). *Voprosy Ekonomiki,* vol. 74. no. 8. pp. 31–40.

GADDY, C. and HILL, F. (2003): *The Siberian Curse: How Communist Planners Left Russia Out in the Cold.* Washington, D. C.: The Brookings Institution Press.

GAIDAR, Ye. ed.: (1998): *Ekonomika perekhodnogo perioda.* (The economics of transition period). Moscow: a book published by the Institute of the Economy in Transition.

GAIDAR, Ye. (2003): Recovery growth and some peculiarities of the contemporary economic situation in Russia. *Post-Communist Economies,* vol. 15. no. 3. pp. 299–312.

HALM, T. (2006): A liberal credo? *Public Finance Quarterly,* vol. 51. no. 3. pp. 373–382.

HAN, B-J. (2006): Russia's macroeconomic stabilization revisited. *Journal of International and Area Studies,* vol. 13. no. 1. pp. 89–102.

HANSON, Ph. and BRADSHAW, P. eds: (2000): *Local Power and FDI in Russia.* Cheltenham/UK and Northampton/USA: Edward Elgar Publishing Co.

HARE, P. G. (1994): Privatization in comparative perspective: An overview of key issues. In: HERR, H. – TOBER, S. – WESTPHAL, A. eds: *Macroeconomic Problems of Transformation.* Cheltenham/UK and Northampton/USA: E. Elgar, pp. 192–214.

HAYEK, F. A. (1995): Emberi cselekvés, de nem emberi terv eredménye. (An outcome of human action, but not of human deliberation). In: HAYEK, F. A.: *Piac és szabadság.* (Market and freedom). Budapest: Közgazdasági és Jogi Könyvkiadó, pp. 292–301.

HEDLUND, S. (2001): Property without rights: Dimensions of Russian privatization. *Europe-Asia Studies,* vol. 53. no. 2. pp. 213–238.

HISHOW, O. (2004): 'Resource Curse' und ökonomische Entwicklungsoptionen Russlands. *Osteuropa Wirtschaft,* vol. 49. no. 1. pp. 81–105.

HORVATH, J. (1999): The Czech currency crisis of 1997. *Post-Communist Economies,* vol. 11. no. 1.

KAGARLITSKY, B. (1995): *Restoration in Russia: Why Capitalism Failed.* London and New York: Verso.

KALOTAY, K. (2004): Will FDI take off in the Russian Federation? *Journal of World Investment and Finance,* vol. 5. no. 1. pp. 119–138.

KAMINSKY, G. – REINHART, C. – VEGH, C. (2003): The unholy trinity of financial contagion. *Journal of Economic Perspectives,* vol. 17. no. 4. pp. 51–74.

KORNAI, J. (1992): *The Socialist System. The Political Economy of Communism.* Oxford: Clarendon Press.

KOTZ, D. and WEIR, F. (1997): *Revolution from Above: The Demise of the Soviet System.* London and New York: Routledge.

KÖVES, A. (2005): Oil and economy. A contribution to the discussion on Russian economic development. *Acta Oeconomica,* vol. 55. no. 4. pp. 371–402.

KULCSÁR, K. (1995): *Kontinuitás és átmenet.* (Continuity and transition). Szombathely: Savaria University Press.

LÁMFALUSSY, A. (2000): *Financial Crises in Emerging Economies.* New Haven and London: Yale University Press.

MAU, V. (1999): *Ekonomicheskaia reforma: skvoz prizmu konstitutsii i politiki.* (Economic reform seen through the prism of Constitution and politics). Moscow: Ad Marginem.

MAU, V. (2004): Itogi 2003 goda i itogi chetirokhletiia: politika protiv ekonomiki. (The results of 2003 and of a four-year period: Politics versus the economy). *Voprosy Ekonomiki,* vol. 75. no. 3. pp. 4–23.

MAU, V. and STARODUBROVSKAIA, I. (2001): *The Challenge of Revolution.* Oxford: Oxford University Press.

NAISHUL, V. (1991): *The Supreme and Last Stage of Socialism.* London: a book published by the Center for Research into Communist Economies.

NORTH, D. (2003): 'Understanding the Process of Economic Change' – keynote delivered to 7th convention of the International Society for New Institutional Economics, entitled *Institutions and Change,* Budapest Corvinus University, 11 September.

OECD (1997): *The Russian Federation.* Country studies series, published by the non-member states division, Paris.

OECD (2004): *The Russian Federation.* Country studies series, Non-member States Division, Paris, July.

PEJOVICH, S. ed.: (2001): *The Economics of Property Rights,* vols. I. and II. Cheltenham and Northampton: Edward Elgar Reference Book Series.

PIATKOWSKI, M. (2003): The contribution of ITC investment to economic growth and labor productivity in Poland in 1995–2000. Warsaw: *TIGER Working Paper* no. 43. available online: www.tiger.edu.pl

POPOV, V. (1998): Will Russia achieve fast economic growth? *Communist Economies and Economic Transformation,* vol. 10. no. 4. pp. 421–450.

RADAEV, V. (2003): Izmeneniiie konkurentnoi situatsii na rossiiiskikh rynkakh. (Changes in the competitive environment of Russian markets). *Voprosy Ekonomiki,* vol. 74. no. 7. pp. 57–77.

RADYGIN, A. (2004): Rossia v 2000–2004 godakh: na puti k gosudarstvennomu kapitalizmu? (Russia between 2000–2004: heading towards state capitalism?) *Voprosy Ekonomiki,* vol. 75. no. 4. pp. 42–65.

RAISER, M. and HELLMAN, J. (2004): The economics of corruption in transition economies. In: ROSE-ACKERMAN, S. and KORNAI, J. eds: *Honesty and Trust – The Experience of Transition Economies,* vol. Two. Houndmills/Basingstoke/UK: Palgrave/MacMillan.

RÉTHI, S. (2003): Az orosz értékpapírpiac kialakulása es fejlődése a kezdetektől napjainkig. (Emergence and development of the Russian stock exchange from its inception to nowadays). *Competitio,* (Debrecen), vol. 2. no. 1. pp. 56–74.

ROSE-ACKERMAN, S. and KORNAI, J. eds.: *Honesty and Trust in the Light of Post-Socialist Transition,* vols. I-II.. New York, Palgrove.

287

Satter, D. (2003): A low, dishonest decadence. *National Interest,* no. 72. pp. 75–84.

Shleifer, A. and Treisman, D. (2004): A normal country. *Foreign Affairs,* vol. 83. no. 2. pp. 20–38.

Sizov, Yu. (2003): Aktualniie problemi razvitiia rossiiskogo fondovogo rynka. (Topical issues in developing the Russian stock exchange). *Voprosy Ekonomiki,* vol. 74. no. 7. pp. 26–42.

Stiglitz, J. E. (2000): Wither Reform? In: Pleskovic, B. and Stiglitz, J. eds: *Annual Bank Conference on Development Economics 1999.* Oxford University Press for the World Bank, pp. 27–46.

Sutela, P. (1998): But…does Mr. Coase go to Russia? In: Sutela, P.: *The Road to the Russian Market Economy.* Helsinki: Kikimora Publications, pp. 167–182.

Sutela, P. (2004): *The Russian Market Economy.* Helsinki: Kikimora Publications.

Török, Á. (2001): Piacgazdasági érettség többféleképpen? (Is there a variety in terms of market maturity?) *Közgazdasági Szemle,* vol. 48. no. 9. pp. 707–725.

Vasiliev, S. (2000): Reforms in Russia. In Brzeski, A. and Winiecki, J. eds: *A Liberating Economic Journey.* London: Cromwell Press for CRCE, pp. 233–250.

Voigt, S. (2006): Russia's way from planning to market: a success story? *Post-Communist Economies,* vol. 18. no. 2. pp. 123–138.

Weigert, R. (2003): *Transformation, Wachstum und Wettbewerb in Russland.* Heidelberg-Berlin-New York: Physica Verlag.

Yasin, Ye. (2003): Strukturnii manevr i ekonomicheskii rost. (Structural change and economic growth in Russia). *Voprosy Ekonomiki,* vol. 74. no. 8. pp. 4–30.

Table 1.

Consolidated budget of Russia in 1999–2003
(Rb bn unless otherwise indicated)

	1999	2000	2001	2002	2003
Consolidated budget[a]					
Expenditure	1,258	1,960	2,419	3.422	3,955
Revenue	1,214	2,098	2,684	3,519	4,136
Balance[b]	–54	207	267	112	180
Ratios (% of GDP)					
Expenditure	26.1	26.8	27.1	31.6	29.7
Revenue	25.2	28.7	30.0	32.5	31.1
Balance[b]	–1.1	2.8	3.0	1.0	1.4

Source: Economist Intelligence Unit: *Country Profile Russia, 2004/2005, Main Report* (online version). London, July

Table 2.

Consolidated budget of Russia in 1998–2002
(Rb bn unless otherwise indicated)

	1998	1999	2000	2001	2002
Consolidated budget					
Revenue	903	1,619	2,711	2,685	3.520
Expenditure	1,119	1,769	2,482	2,423	3,400
Balance	–216	–150	229	262	119
Ratios (% of GDP)					
Revenue	33.4	34.0	38.4	29.7	32.4
Federal government	10.9	12.8	16.0	17.6	20.3
Local gobernment (net of transfers)	14.0	13.4	14.3	n/a	n/a
Extrabudgetary funds (net of transfers)	8.2	8.2	8.2	n/a	n/a
Expenditure	40.8	37.2	35.1	26.8	31.3
Federal government	16.7	17.1	15.1	14.6	18.8
Local governments	17.1	15.1	15.1	n/a	n/a
Extrabudgetary funds	9.4	7.0	7.1	n/a	n/a
Balance	–7.4	–3.2	3.3	2.9	1.1

Source: EIU: *Country Profile Russia, 2003/2004, Main Report* (July)

[a] Comprises federal, regional and local budgets, and extrabudgetary funds.
[b] Does not sum in source.

Table 3.

Economic Structure of Russia

	1999	2000	2001	2002[a]	2003
GDP at market prices (Rb bn)	4,823	7,306	8,944	10,834	13,285
GDP (US$ bn)	195.9	259.7	306.6	345.6	432.9
Real GDP growth (%)	6.2	10.5	5.1	4.7	7.3
Consumer price inflation (av; %)	85.7	20.8	21.5	15.8	13.7
Population (m)	146.3	146.2	145.8	145.3	144.7
Exports of goods fob (US$ m)	75,549	105,034	101,885	107,302	135,929
Imports of goods fob (US$ m)	–39,537	–44,862	–53,763	–60,965	-75,436
Current-account balance (US$ m)	24,611	46,840	33,795	29,116	35.845
Foreign-exchange reserves excl gold (US$ m)	8,457	24,264	32,542	44,054	73,175
Total external debt (US$ bn)	174.8	160.0	152.5	147.5	167.6
Debt-service ratio, paid (%)	13.6	9.9	14.3	11.2	10.0
Exchange rate (av) Rb: USS	24.62	28.13	29.17	31.35	30.69

Source: EIU: *Country Report Russia*, September 2004, *Main Report*, London (online edition)

Table 4.

Origins of Russian Gross Domestic Product 2003

	% of total
Agriculture	5.2
Industry	35.2
Services	59.6

Soruce: ibidem

Table 5.

Components of Russian Gross Domestic Product 2003

	% of total
Private consumption	50.6
Public consumption	16.9
Fixed investment	18.2
Stockbuilding	2.4
Net exports of goods & services	11.4

Source: ibidem

Table 6.

Principal Exports of Russia 2003

	% of total
Oil, fuel & gas	51.6
Metals	12.8
Machinery & transport equipment	7.9
Chemicals	6.2

Source: ibidem

Table 7.

Principal Imports to Russia 2003

	% of total
Machinery & transport equipment	25.8
Food, beverages & agricultural products	14.8
Chemicals	12.1
Metals	4.8

Source: ibidem

Table 8.

Main Destinations of Russian Exports 2003

	% of total
Germany	8.2
Italy	6.1
Netherlands	5.8
Italy	6.1
China	6.2
Ukraine	5.6

Source: ibidem

Table 9.

Main Origins of Russian Imports 2003

	% of total
Germany	12.9
Belarus	6.4
Ukraine	5.9
China	4.1
Kazakhstan	3.9
US	3.9

Source: ibidem

Table 10.

Russian Growth Forecast (% change, unless otherwise indicated)

	2002	2003	2004–11–04	2005
Real GDP growth	4.7	7.3	7.0	5.8
Industrial production growth	3.8	7.0	7.1	5.7
Gross fixed investment growth	3.0	12.9	14.0	11.0
Unemployment rate (av)	8.0	8.5	8.3	8.2
Consumer price inflation (av)	15.8	13.7	10.8	9.9
Consumer price inflation (year-end)	15.1	12.0	11.2	9.2
Central bank refinancing rate (year-end)	21.0	16.0	14.0	12.0
Federal budget balance (% of GDP)	1.7	2.4	2.4	1.3
Exports of goods fob (US$ bn)	107.3	135.9	162.5	171.6
Imports of goods fob (US$ bn)	61.0	75.4	92.9	107.7
Current-account balance (US$ bn)	29.1	35.8	46.0	40.1
Current-account balance (% of GDP)	8.4	8.3	8.4	6.4
External debt (year-end; US$ bn)	147.5	167.6c	169.6	168.5
Exchange rate Rb: US$ (av)	31.35	30.69	29.10	29.50
Exchange rate Rb: US$ (year-end)	31.78	29.45	29.49	30.49
Exchange rate Rb: E (year-end)	33.33	37.15	37.01	40.40
Exchange rate Rb: SDR (year-end)	43.21	43.77	43.92	46.70

Source: EIU: *Country Report Russia,* September 2004, Main Report, London (online edition)

Table 11.

Russian Macroeconomic Indicators, 1996–2004

	1996	1997	1998	1999	2000	2001	2002	2003 Estimate	2004 Projection
Output and expenditure				*(Percentage change in real terms)*					
GDP	–3.8	1.4	–5.3	6.4	10.0	5.1	4.4	7.3	5.5
Private consumption	–4.7	4.8	–3.3	2.9	7.2	9.7	8.5	7.3	na
Public consumption	3.1	–2.4	1.0	3.1	2.0	–1.7	2.4	2.2	na
Gross fixed capital formation	–21.2	–7.9	–12.4	5.4	18.1	10.2	3.0	12.9	na
Exports of goods and services	3.7	–0.5	1.9	11.2	9.5	–3.6	10.2	na	na
Imports of goods and services	1.3	0.4	–17.4	–17.0	32.4	18.0	19.1	na	na
Industrial gross output	–4.5	2.0	–5.2	11.0	11.8	4.9	–3.7	7.0	na
Agricultural gross output	–5.1	1.5	–13.2	4.1	7.7	7.5	1.7	na	na
Employment				*(Percentage change)*					
Labour force (end-of-year)	–0.6	0.1	–0.3	–0.5	–1.6	0.1	0.4	1.0	na
Employment (end-of-year) (In percent of labour force)	–0.7	–1.8	–1.6	–0.9	1.5	1.3	0.6	–0.8	na
Unemployment (end-of-year)	9.3	11.1	12.3	12.6	9.8	8.9	6.6	8.5	na
Prices and wages				*(Percentage change)*					
Consumer prices (annual everage)	47.8	14.7	27.6	88.1	20.8	21.6	–15.7	13.7	10.8
Consumer prices (end-of-year)	21.8	10.9	84.5	36.8	20.1	18.6	15.0	12.0	10.6
Produces prices (annual average)	50.8	15.0	7.1	58.9	46.6	19.2	14.0	15.6	na
Producer prices (end-of-year)	25.6	7.5	23.2	67.3	31.6	10.7	17.1	13.1	na
Gross average monthly seamings in economy (annual average)	87.3	20.2	10.7	47.7	43.2	45.8	36.2	24.6	na
Government sector				*(in per cent of GDP)*					
General government balanca	–9.4	–8.5	–8.2	–3.1	2.7	2.9	1.4	1.0	1.5
General government expenditure	45.3	47.8	42.6	36.7	34.3	34.5	37.0	35.5	na
General government debt	47.1	52.5	79.0	90.2	62.5	48.2	41.4	32.4	na
Monetary sector				*(Percentage change)*					
Broad money (M2, end-of-year)	30.6	29.8	19.8	57.3	82.4	40.9	32.4	50.5	na
Domestic credit (end-of-year) (In per cent of GDP)	48.3	22.2	68.2	34.1	13.7	30.0	29.6	22.7	na
Broad money (M2, end-of-year)	14.4	16.0	17.0	14.6	15.7	18.0	19.7	24.1	na

Table 11 (continued)

	1996	1997	1998	1999	2000	2001	2002	2003 Estimate	2004 Projection
Interest and exchange rates				*(In per cent per annum, end-year)*					
Central Bank refinance rate (uncompounded)	48.0	28.0	80.0	65.0	25.0	25.0	21.0	16.0	na
Treasury bill rate (all maturities)	33.6	36.6	48.1	na	na	na	na	na	na
Lending rate	146.8	32.0	41.8	39.7	24.4	17.9	15.6	13.0	na
Deposit rate	55.1	16.6	17.1	13.7	8.5	4.9	5.0	4.5	na
(Roubles per US dollar)									
Exchange rats (end-year)	5.6	6.0	20.7	26.8	28.2	30.2	31.8	29.4	na
Exchange rate (annual average)	5.1	5.8	10.0	24.6	28.2	29.2	31.4	30.7	na
External sector				*(In millions of US dollars)*					
Current account	10,846	−81	218	24,815	46,839	33,934	29,520	39,100	23,000
Trade balance	21,593	14,912	16.429	38,014	60,171	48,120	46,335	59,600	42,000
Merchandise exports	39,686	86,895	74,444	75,551	105,033	101,884	107,301	134,400	122,000
Merchandise imports	68,092	71,983	58,015	39,537	44,862	53,764	60,966	74,800	80,000
Foreign direct investment, net	1,656	1,681	1,492	1,102	−463	216	−48	−200	2,000
International reserves, excluding gold (end-of-year)	11,276	12,895	7,601	8,457	24,264	32,542	44,054	73,175	na
External debts stock	143,600	180,800	185,700	177,100	158,300	150,400	152,100	165,000	na
			(In months of imports of goods and services)						
International reserves, excludinggold (end-of-year)	1.6	1.7	1.3	1.9	4.8	5.3	6.3	8.6	na
			(In per cent of current account revenues, excluding transfers)						
Public debt service due	16.7	12.4	14.4	18.4	9.9	15.1	11.6	9.5	na
Public debt service pald	6.4	5.6	12.0	13.6	9.8	14.4	11.6	9.5	na
Memorandum item	*(Denominations as indicated)*								
Population (end-year, million)	147.5	147.1	146.4	145.6	145.2	144.4	145.3	144.9	na
GDP (in millions of roubles)	2 007 800	2 342 500	2 629 600	4 823 200	7 305 600	8 943 600	10 834 200	13 304 700	15 559 204
GDP per capita (in US dollars)	2,647	2,743	1,802	1,347	1,787	2,120	2,375	2,992	na
Share of industry in GDP (in per cent)	29.5	28.3	29.9	30.8	31.4	28.1	26.5	na	na
Share of agriculture in GDP (in per cent)	7.3	6.6	5.7	7.7	6.7	6.8	6.1	na	na
Current account/ GDP (in per cent)	2.8	0.0	0.1	12.6	18.0	11.1	8.6	9.0	4.4
External debt − reserves (in US$ million)	132,324	167,705	177,899	168,643	134,036	117,858	108,046	91,825	na
External debt/ GDP (in per cent)	36.7	44.6	70.4	90.3	61.0	49.1	44.1	38.1	na
External debt/ exports of goods and services (in per cent)	139.5	178.9	213.9	209.3	138.1	132.7	125.8	109.8	na

Source: EBRD *Transition Report Update,* April, 2004, page 65

Table 12.

EBRD Structural and Institutional Indicators of Russia, 1995–2003

Liberatisation
Current account convertibility – **full**
Interest rate liberalisation – **full**
Wage regulation – **no**

Privatisation
Primary privatisation method – **vouchers**
Secondary privatisation method – **direct sales**
Tradability of land – **limited de facto**

Infrastructure
Independent telecoms regulator – **no**
Separation of railway accounts – **no**
Independent electricity regulator – **yes**

Social reform
Share of the population in poverty – **23.8 per cent (2000)**
Private pension funds – **yes**

Stabilisation
Share of general government tax revenue in GDP – **38 per cent**
Exchange rate regime – **managed flost**

Enterprises and markets
Competition Office – **yes**

Financial sector
Capital adequecy ratio – **8 per cent**
Deposit insurance system – **no**
Secured transactions law – **yes**
Securities commission – **yes**

	1995	1996	1997	1998	1999	2000	2001	2002	2003
Liberalisation									
Share of administered prices in CPI (in per cent)	na	na	na	na	na	na	na	na	na
Number of goods with administered prices in EBRD-15 basket	5.0	5.0	5.0	2.0	2.0	2.0	2.0	na	na
Share of trade with non-transition countries (in per cent)	68.2	67.0	65.4	66.9	70.5	68.5	71.4	71.6	na
Share of trade in GDP (in per cent)	43.0	37.9	37.6	48.3	59.4	57.8	50.3	48.5	na
Tariff revenues (in per cent of imports)	10.7	7.9	7.2	7.1	6.9	18.5	21.1	16.9	na
EBRD index of price liberalisation	3.7	3.7	3.7	3.3	3.3	4.0	4.0	4.0	4.0
EBRD index of forex and trade liberalisation	3.0	4.0	4.0	2.3	2.3	2.3	2.7	3.0	3.3

Table 12 (continued)

	1995	1996	1997	1998	1999	2000	2001	2002	2003
Privatisation									
Privatisation revenues (cumulative, in per cent of GDP)	1.5	1.7	23.7	3.4	3.5	3.8	4.2	4.6	na
Private sector share in GDP (in per cent)	55.0	60.0	70.0	70.0	70.0	70.0	70.0	70.0	na
Private sector share employment (in per cent)	na	na	na	na	na	na	na	na	na
EBRD index of small-scale privatisation	4.0	4.0	4.0	4.0	4.0	4.0	4.0	4.0	4.0
EBRD index of large-scale privatisation	3.0	3.0	3.3	3.3	3.3	3.3	3.3	3.3	3.3
Enterprises									
Budgetary subsidies and current transfers (in per cent of GDP)	na	na	na	na	5.3	na	na	na	na
Share of industry in total employment (in per cent)	24.1	22.8	21.7	20.7	22.4	22.7	20.5	19.6	na
Change in labour productivity in industry (in per cent)	12.2	2.9	8.6	0.8	7.3	7.2	5.0	6.6	na
Investment rata/GDP (in per cent)	20.9	21.0	19.1	18.0	14.0	16.0	18.0	18.0	na
EBRD index of enterprise reform	2.0	2.0	2.0	2.0	1.7	2.0	2.3	2.3	2.3
EBRD index of competition policy	2.0	2.0	2.3	2.3	2.3	2.3	2.3	2.3	2.3
Infrastructure									
Fixed-line (mobile) penetration rate (per 100 inhabitanis)	17.0 (0.1)	17.5 (0.2)	19.2 (0.3)	19.9 (0.5)	21.0 (0.9)	21.8 (2.2)	24.3 (3.8)	24.2 (12.1)	na
Internet penetration rate (per 10,000 inhabitants)	na	na	1.1	1.2	6.3	22.5	24.5	28.4	na
Railway labour productivity (1989=100)	58.8	54.8	58.6	60.9	72.1	78.8	85.0	90.1	na
Electricity tariffs, USc kWh (collection rate in per cent)	2.33 (50)	3.00 (50)	3.20 (50)	2.7 (87)	1.1 (na)	0.9 (85)	na	2.4 (102)	na
GDP per unit of energy use (PPP in US dollars per kgoe)	1.4	1.3	1.4	1.4	1.5	1.6	na	na	na
EBRD index of infrastructure reform	1.7	2.0	2.0	2.0	2.0	2.0	2.0	2.3	2.3
Electric power	2.0	2.0	2.0	2.0	2.0	2.0	2.0	2.3	3.0
Railways	na	na	na	2.3	2.3	2.3	2.3	2.3	2.3
Roads	1.0	1.7	2.0	2.0	2.0	2.0	2.0	2.3	2.3
Telecommunications	2.3	2.7	2.7	3.0	3.0	3.0	3.0	3.0	3.0
Water and waste water	1.7	1.7	2.0	2.0	2.3	2.3	2.3	2.3	2.3

Table 12 (further continued)

	1995	1996	1997	1998	1999	2000	2001	2002	2003
Financial institutions									
Number of banks	2,297	2,029	1,697	1,476	1,349	1,311	1,319	1,329	na
(foreign-owned)	(21)	(22)	(26)	(30)	(32)	(33)	(35)	(37)	
Asset share of state-owned banks (in per cent)	na	na	37.0	41.9	na	na	na	na	na
Bad loans (in per cent of total loans)	12.3	13.4	12.1	30.9	28.1	16.1	12.2	11.4	na
Domestic credit to enterprises (in per cent of GDP)	8.7	7.4	9.5	12.8	10.9	11.9	15.4	17.3	na
Stock market capitalisation (in per cent of GDP)	4.6	9.7	31.0	16.2	41.7	15.3	26.7	38.5	na
EBRD index of banking sector reform	2.0	2.0	2.3	2.0	1.7	1.7	1.7	2.0	2.0
EBRD index of reform of non-bank financial institutions	2.0	3.0	3.0	1.7	1.7	1.7	1.7	2.3	2.7
Social sector									
Expenditures on health and education (in per cent of GDP)	6.3	7.4	8.7	7.4	6.6	6.3	6.3	6.6	na
Life expectancy at birth, total (years)	64.8	66.0	66.7	67.0	66.0	65.3	65.6	65.3	NA
Basic schoool enrotment ratio (in per cent)	88.4	88.7	88.7	88.5	86.8	89.4	90.1	na	na
Earnings inequaliti (GINI-coefficient)	47.1	48.3	na	na	na	na	52.1	na	na

Source: EBRD *Transition Report*, November 2003, pp. 186.

12. MARKET SOCIALISM: THE VIABLE IMPOSSIBLE?

In this chapter we try to address one of the more puzzling features of the political economy of emerging countries: the experience of China. The Asian giant at the time of writing, is already the seventh largest economy of the globe, with its export performance and import capacity on par with such members of the G-8 as Canada or Italy. The People's Republic of China is still a single party system. The Congress of the Communist Party, convened in January 2004, endorsed private property as constitutional. However, in reality the majority of firms operate *in a long continuum of mixed property,* in varying distance from the two ideal types, public and private. In the 2005 meeting of the American Economic Association a special session was convened for trying to figure out and interpret who, in fact, the Chinese enterpreneurs are and what economic logic they follow.[1] Thus one of the most successful emerging economies of the contemporary global economy seems to defy all theories of comparative economics. The latter would require a coherent economic order. By contrast, the Chinese experience allows for frequent calls, both in the academic and policy literature to look Eastward, rather than Westward in search of a successful model of development.

It would be futile to attempt to elaborate this complex matter in a single chapter exhaustively. However, a monograph on emerging economies could hardly aspire for being recognized in the field of new political economy, as defined in our Foreword, if it were to leave the most contentious issue unanswered. In the following pages we try to answer the question if, and to what degree, China can be considered, *in descriptive terms,* as *an alternative model of development.* Our hypothesis, to be tested, is that it bears a lot of resemblance to the experience of market socialism, an issue well known for Central and Eastern Europe. Therefore in the first, longer part we try to present *a comparative overview* of what is known today, with the benefit of hindsight of market socialism. We shall define market socialism in detail later. For now it may suffice to note that forms of socialism, both in theory and practice, that *deviate from the classical model,* gen-

---

[1] *American Economic Review,* vol. 96. no. 2.

eralizing Soviet experience (most exhaustively described in: Kornai, 1992; but also in: Hanson, 2003) are called this way. These attempt at, and also realize, to varying degree, *more reliance on horizontal, market type of co-ordination*, against the predominance of vertical, bureaucratic co-ordination, typical of the Soviet model. Our contention, to be substantiated later in this chapter, is that empirical experience has shown this model to be unstable. In the second part of the chapter we try to specify *the Chinese features of market socialism*. Finally, in the third part we try to offer an answer to the two fundamental questions about the Chinese model. First, is the Chinese model of market socialism *sustainable for many decades*, as official analysts in Beijing maintain, or is there a threat of implosion? Second: is it true, and if yes, to what degree, that *the Chinese experience defies all ideas of economic theory*, particularly growth theory and development strategy, as summarized in terms of the post-Washington Consensus? Those having read the preceding chapters may already suspect that our answer is in the negative. But at this point we may formulate it as a working hypothesis only.

China – A Challenge to the Post-Washington Consensus

At the outset of transformation, there has been almost a consensus view that the market system has no alternative. While this insight has found its place in the current mainstream on development economics, the new Washington consensus or post-Washington consensus, (Kolodko, 2000, pp. 119–141 and pp. 348–356; Williamson, 2000; Srinivasan, 2000), very few would venture to repeat in an academic writing the once famous dictum of Václav Klaus: the third road leads to the Third World. Much of Western Europe has remained within the framework of the welfare state, despite its obvious limitations. Also in the transforming economies, the rollback of the state has proven to be much less than the tough normative language adopted by early reformers would have indicated. Actually, as explained in the context of fiscal sustainability, it is the structure rather than the size of public spending in these countries that may lead to social and economic strains by providing less than optimal conditions for sustaining economic growth. And even in the United States, the Clinton period did not produce an era of 'unbridled capitalism'.[2] Thus the 'do what I say, not what I do' policy advice stemming from the international agencies and much of the academe has lost its original appeal. Last, but not at all least, the return of the Right in the US and in most of Europe by the first half of the first decade of the 2000s has not produced a free market backlash, neither in core Atlantic economies, nor in the emerging countries. Besides creating macroeconomic disequilibria, the combination of tax cuts and spending increases of the conservative governments of Berlusconi, Bush and Chirac have not changed the fundamentals of the status quo ante. Rather these have been saving the salient features of the *mixed economy*

[2] The then active participant, and later Nobel Prize winner Joseph Stiglitz (2001) positively attributes the success of the Clinton period to the disregard of rigid academic approaches in the policy-making process, primarily, but not exclusively, by FED Chairman Alan Greenspan.

models that shape all modern economies of the globe (more on that in Bornstein, ed. 1994; Bara and Szabó, eds, 2000).

It is against the background of this model of 'real capitalism', that is of a modern mixed market economy, that we are faced with the 'Chinese miracle'. This is defined mostly in terms of aggregate growth statistics. According to international data, the GDP of China has been growing by a staggering rate of 10 (!) per cent in the 1990–2001 period, with merchandise exports reaching $262 bn in 2001, that is equivalent to that of Canada, and outpacing imports by nearly 20 bn, making China one of the few trade surplus countries in the globe.

But the specifics do not stop there. The net private capital inflow attaining *close to $60 bn in 2001* makes the country, *with 52 per cent of GDP originating from industry,* very unlike any model of an underdeveloped country (sources for all data: *World Development Report 2003,* World Bank, Washington, 2003, pp. 234, 238, 240). Let us note that the slowdown in 2002–2004 still leaves China with a growth rate of 9 per cent, that many observers in China and abroad consider overheated. It is a surplus country and also one ruled by an unreconstructed Communist party (not reformed in the sense of Western European Communist or Eastern European post-Communist parties).

Thus, we find *a series of puzzles to be addressed,* especially in view of the naive or optimistic expectations, reflected in part in our previous writings, on the *inevitable nature of the rollback of the state* and the strengthening of market and ethical forms of co-ordination. This has not happened, although processes of transnationalization, as discussed in a preceding chapter, might well have called for that. From our perspective, this is important both from the academic and the policy perspective. It is also puzzling in a number of ways, but most importantly, *the Chinese experience needs to be explained.* Mainland China has always been and remains a puzzle in a number of ways. The big question to be addressed is if and to what extent, *China can serve, also in normative terms, as a more efficient alternative model for all emerging economies, but the post-Communist countries in particular,* as suggested among others by Nolan (1995) and Shlapentokh (2002). If the latter contention were to hold, the Chinese experience would, indeed, offer a viable alternative to the post-Washington consensus.

The puzzle is the sustaining success of the Chinese practice, that seems, for many, to have defied all theories, mainstream and Marxist-radical ones alike, in the past 30 years or so. Three decades certainly constitute a period long enough to deserve even historical analysis. Furthermore, it does require clarification why both growth and marketization has been so impressive.

This leads to a follow-up research question of ours. Is it *because of* market socialism that China succeeds, as one part of the literature holds, or conversely, *despite* these arrangements? The controversy is important not only because of China being the seventh largest economy of the globe and accounting for one fifth of humankind. From our perspective, it also matters, if there has been/could have been a realistic alternative to the post-Washington Consensus and what many decry as 'market fundamentalism' (e.g. Poznanski, 1999).

Let us be clear from the very outset: it would be a fallacy to mix up the *abstract theoretical models* of non-market systems developed in the academe over the past 200 years or so, often exclusively out of *intellectual curiosity* rather than intending any *practical application,*[3] with the policy experience of a limited number of countries in a limited period of time. All the more so, as Leszek Balcerowicz (1995, p. 36 and pp. 47–48) observes, the Western theoretical debates on alternative models of socialism, ever since the 1910s, and partly still ongoing, have *nowhere* immediately and demonstrably *influenced* the institutional and *policy choices* of system designers in Eastern Europe. This applies a fortiori for China, where the study of the Hungarian New Economic Mechanism had been elevated to the official policy level by the 1980s.

However, the collapse of the Hungarian model must have made it clear, that even the most extended/liberal form of market socialism has inherent limitations, irrespective of levels of development and of cultures. On the other hand, as the now classic monograph of János Kornai (1992, chapter 24) has eloquently proven, the efficiency losses, the motivational weaknesses, lacking innovation and finally the collapse of the Soviet model have been intimately related to the socialist features of it, in terms of ideology and orientation. Why socialist reforms try to improve what in Kornai's term is genetically deficient, their limited outcome cannot and should not be ascribed to coincidental factors, such as the policies of Gorbachev or the geopolitical constraints put by the Empire on local reformers. This analysis, based on empirical and ex post analysis, is supportive of earlier abstract insights of Friedrich August von Hayek (1940) on *the inherent limitations* of any such model that wishes to centralize *information* and switch of capital markets as a major mechanism of resource allocation.

On the other hand, it is hard to overlook the continued strong presence of the undercurrent of third way thinking in economic theory. Joseph Stiglitz (1994), for one, has always been critical of market triumphalism. Similarly Anthony Giddens (1998) and the ensuing theory and policy of New Labor sustains its skeptical overall assessment of the market as the sole coordinating mechanism. As the German and French social democrats put it, while transnationalization requires a yes to market economy, as no other viable economic alternative has yet been found anywhere in the globe, they never condone market society (cf. also Szentes, 1999, pp. 106–108). The survival of the welfare state in Western Europe and of the state redistribution in transforming economies, coupled with the Chinese experience do require a rethinking of what we should think about the appropriate mix of bureaucratic and market co-ordination, of institutions and policies. These issues are discussed in our chapters on Development, Regulation and the concluding chapter on Institutions and growth.

---

[3] This applies to the famous model of Edmond Malinvaud (1967) showing an arithmetically feasible equilibrium solution in the lack of private property. Similarly, as Ernő Zalai (2001, pp. 41–55) shows, the Arrow-Debreu model is institutionally neutral, thus general equilibrium may be attained in market and non-market systems alike. Cf. also Srinivasan (2001, pp. 506) for a similar interpretation.

In the following pages, we do not attempt to offer a critical survey of most of non-methodological part of economic theory, which would be close to impossible in a single chapter. Allowing for the inevitable pluralism in all big questions of the discipline, we try to achieve a more modest goal. Namely to present a summary of evidence, *at the level of models applied in comparative economic systems,* of what is known about market socialist systems in historical perspective, and then *compare to it the Chinese experience,* also at the level of stylized facts. This may help explain what is indeed peculiar about China, a factor frequently over-emphasized and indiscriminately accepted in much of the area studies literature. In doing so, we rely on analyses by other scholars, and do not aim at writing up yet another China monograph, or yet another book on the other successful market socialist experiment, to be found in Hungarian economic history of the 1953–1988 period. Our discussion remains at a more abstract level of stylized facts, while country-specific and time-specific circumstances tend to be abstracted away in order to underscore the systemic, inherent or structural features that lend themselves to generalizations.

Why Marketize Socialism?
Salient Features of the Classical Model

Much has been written on the possible role of market co-ordination in a Soviet economic model. Here we offer a brief schematic rehash of what economics now has to say about the starting point. In doing so, we rely on the classical monograph by János Kornai (1992), Leszek Balcerowicz (1995) and our previous monograph (Csaba, 1995) and avoid repeating arguments in the literature. In a way, this is the axiomatic part for the rest of the chapter, interpreting China in terms of a market socialist model (in line with the self-description offered by the official economists).[4]

Salient Features of the Soviet Model: Poetry and Reality

In the following, we present those features, that apply to several countries and several periods, over and above historic contingency. We also try to limit our observations to what most researchers of comparative economics and of area studies would concur.
1. The classical socialist system was based on *mono-archy, that is a single chain vertical unilateral dependence.* In other words, there was no functional differentiation, characteristic of modern and post-modern societies. Ideological representation was merged with functions of governmental administration. Similarly, in the Soviet type economy, interest representation was merged with party and economic functions. Bureaucratic forms of co-ordination dominated, though do not fully replaced, other forms of co-ordination. What

[4] Cf. eg. (Zhu, 2006)

János Kornai termed 'the genetic program' of the system was *hierarchical subordination and ideological leadership*, that sustain, though both ideologies and the forms of subordination may change.[5] The defining feature, for the economic structure, was always and in every country the uniform/undifferentiated socialist property, belonging to 'the people', i.e. to nobody, but managed by the party-state *nomenklatura*. Oppression and command were organizing principles. True, at times incentives, moral suasion and identification with goals also did have their place, though only as additional factors. Therefore it was nowhere easy to privatize, not easy to set up joint ventures, not easy to introduce exit of firms, hardening the budget constraints, as the hierarchy dominated, and various functions of property ownership (even *usus, usus fructus* and *abusus*, as known from Roman law have been missing). It was less than clear, for instance, who owned a Soviet or a Yugoslav or a Hungarian enterprise once Communism collapsed.

2. *Allocation* of resources followed *central deliberations,* bureaucratic deals/bargains, ideological postulates, but by no means market or price signals. This is not a 'socialist' or 'Russian' feature, as can be observed in the classical East Asian developmental dictatorships as well. It is particularly important to underscore this point, as known from Ludwig von Mises (1920/1976), the existence of capital markets, is *the defining feature of any market system.* If allocation of resources at the macroeconomic level follows bureaucratic, rather than market signals, sooner or later the dominance of bureaucratic and political-oppressive forms of co-ordination prevail. This theoretical insight had been amply demonstrated by the re-centralization tendencies of all socialist reforms, when decentralizing tendencies had invariably been reverted. Similarly, the sustaining authoritarian political features of the developmental dictatorships, as became clear in the wake of the 1997–1999 East Asian crisis. No socialist reform could surpass this point, otherwise the switch 'from Marx to market' (Brus and Laski, 1989) becomes inevitable.

3. *Insulation of domestic processes from the global economy is a must for socialist systems to survive.* In the opposite case, feedback from the world market crosses over the 'autochtonous' or arbitrary priorities set by the planners/politicians, overruling consumer sovereignty. It should be stressed, that it is not the *volume of foreign trade* that really matters, though centrally planned / Soviet type economies tended to trade significantly less than market economies of a similar size and at a similar level of development. This under-trading had, of course, been an additional source of welfare loss, at least in comparison to countries at similar level of development and/or of similar size. Still, what really matters for the salient features is that classical socialism is its *institutionally closed nature*. It matters less if a country exports

---

[5] For instance in the Brezhnev period Great Russian imperial thinking clearly dominated egalitarianism; likewise then nobody was seriously persecuted, let alone executed (even Solzhenitsyn could leave the USSR in 1970). Phil Hanson (2003, p. 254) blames this feature for the disintegration of the hierarchic command structures; my own view is that neither sticks nor carrots remained by the time Gorbachev acceded to power in 1985.

a lot or less. The crux of the matter is if prices on external markets influence domestic investment decisions. In concrete terms it implies a state monopoly on foreign trade as well as on currency transactions.

It is relatively easy to see that if trade were free, if currency were just another commodity to be purchased and sold at will, 'central planning', i.e. bureaucratic hierarchical co-ordination would turn to a farce. In this case, the socialist nature of planning (and the vitality of one party rule) would become hollowed. If planners chose A, but B is more profitable, people and corporations will arbitrage as to circumvent and undermine 'scientifically set' policy priorities. In a typical fashion 'infant industries' in most countries (not just socialist) tend to be unprofitable for longer initial periods. Since Soviet type industrialization was about military might rather than catching up and improving the well-being of the masses, *structural priorities* – such as the predominance of the military sector and its needs – actually *mattered more than anything else*. This resulted in an army being much stronger than the economic might of Russia/Soviet Union, but also that of North Korea, Yugoslavia or Albania or Vietnam would have justified. The dominance of defense and of ideological priorities over human needs and market signals has been a constant in all known socialist experiments to date.

4. An inevitable by-product of the first three arrangements had been that feature of the Soviet model that used to be least understood by outsiders, that is, *the passive, subordinate, instrumental role of money*. Money does NOT make the world go round under socialism. It is rather the import license, the plan directive, the bargain with the higher standing authority, or the incorporation of the firm's priorities in the formal national economic (and supply) plan that really mattered. Thus the reported/historic profitability of individual activities and branches did not really matter, either by themselves or comparatively. As a consequence price liberalization, that was always one of the standard propositions of mainstream economists, was simply missing the point; so did the idea to impute shadow prices.[6] In both cases (in the latter only for planners), a simple miraculous mechanism would have re-introduced *microeconomic rationality* (that is calculus and efficient management) in a system, where economic decisions were never based on price signals anyway.

This applied particularly to investments, that were decided by the planners following ideologically set priorities. Therefore, the attempts at re-calculating Soviet GDP at market prices, industriously conducted by mainstream researchers originating from the region, or the big debate of the '70s and '80s over who subsidizes whom within the Soviet trading block Comecon, and also within the Soviet economic complex, have often missed the point by taking prices too seriously. There has been a tendency to attribute much

---

[6] Wilhelm (2003) gives a powerful account of how prime insights and reliable information had been suppressed, even at the CIA, but also at the academe, with reference to the need for academic and methodological rigor.

more importance to these abstract and often over-politicized calculations (such as the famous Marrese–Vanous implicit subsidy theory)[7] than they could ever had in reality, which is though psychologically understandable, methodologically is plainly wrong.

As a consequence much of the ongoing controversy over the size of transition costs, or the size of actual output decline in the post-Soviet period, covered in Chapter Three, is based on shaky footings at best. This follows from the elementary insight that in the distorted world of the Soviet economy we did not have (and most probably will never have) an exact view of the status quo ante. Merely taking official Soviet numbers of say, 1988, and comparing these to those of 1992 or 1997 are simply out of line with professional minimum standards (a practice widely applied in much of the transition-related literature, especially in the more critical writings on the failure of transition as a whole).

We certainly are in grave need of quantitative estimates, but what we have is often not more than a guesstimate. If for no other reason, because of major structural changes and their impact on the GDP, long run historical statistics in general and socialist statistics, even recalculated, in particular tend to reflect *trends rather than exact magnitudes.* This is bad news for the entire profession of economists as well as for historians and other quantitatively oriented social scientists as well. If for no other reason, because of the policy relevance of establishing when the transformational recession is over, and when convergence to the West begins (if at all).

5. *Bureaucratic coordination dominated* over all other forms of coordination in all socialist countries in all periods of time, including the reformist periods. This is an important and lasting insight of the famous book of János Kornai (1980), *Economics of Shortage*, which explained in great detail why predominant contemporary concepts (such as the command economy, or modernization theory) proved incapable of explaining the crux of why and how a 'moneyless' economy could function at all for several decades. For instance, it was the deep conviction of contemporary economists and policy-makers, who created plans, over-ambitious catching-up projects, that the over-emphasis on the defense sector and related industries was central to lack of economic well-being. The ideology of overtaking capitalism, populist promises to let consumption grow in par with investments/needs, and the politically motivated oppression of the rural sectors were also among the traditional explanatory factors offered by the profession. By contrast, Kornai showsed that neither the legitimating principle of any socialism, that is central planning, nor policy mistakes, nor even 'distorted' prices may explain the reproduction of shortages: it was systemic.

By adopting less extreme policies or more conservative pricing, problems could indeed be alleviated, but not solved. The best illustration of this point is the comparison of Czechoslovakia with Romania or Poland. The Czecho-

---

[7] These issues are detailed in one of my previous monographes (Csaba, 1990. pp. 73–85).

Slovak leadership did pay a great deal of attention to preserving the coherence of the system and avoiding disequilibria on product markets, or to the avoidance of running big external and internal deficits. Therefore, they could preserve power, though the indirect costs of a stagnant economy, in terms of innovation and relative 'competitiveness' were even bigger than elsewhere. By contrast, Polish policies of the 1970s, where none of these conservative maxims were adhered to, have led to the disintegration of the economic (and later the political) system of socialism, long before the collapse of the Soviet Empire (basically by 1980, when the Solidarity mass movement could emerge and was tolerated for over a year).

Let us add: bureaucratic coordination alone cannot give a full explanation to the question *why such an obviously irrational system*, running counter to the basics of any school of economics, *could survive for so long*. While the prophecy of von Mises on the decay of the socialist system ultimately, proved right, his estimate of the time it would take (a few years rather than decades) has proven wrong.[8] Besides the crucial role of *one-time supportive factors*, such as the lend-lease agreement during World War Two, the oil price windfalls of 1973 and 1979, or the lavish external financing of the 1980s and many others, several *additional circusmtances* helped the long survival. *First* of all, what was described in textbooks as a command economy, worked in reality through all-encompassing bargaining. This has bridged the split between perceived/planned and actual processes, however it has annihilated the ex ante coordination claim of the planned economy. While it ran counter to ideological claims, it however did allow for corporate and regional interest articulation and interest representation. Thereby it was *softening up the irrationalities* and strains stemming from what was formally a purely hierarchic system of subordination (a colorful account of this is the bulky volume by Tamás Bauer, 1981).

Second, campaigns, that is politically orchestrated movements, supported by initiative from below, played recurringly a major role in attaining a few major policy priorities, from the construction of the Dnieper Dam to the conquest of the non-black-soil areas in Russia. *Third,* the focal role of *material incentives* (for individuals: bonuses, shops with special prices with special supplies; for corporations: preferential prices, priority in the supply of scarce inputs) were though denied, especially in the early idealistic period, but were widely used. Later, the use of closed shops open to certain people, like party bosses or miners, or the Intershop chain in East Germany where officially earned Western currency could buy most scarcity products, became

---

[8] Being a Viennese intellectual of the *fin de siècle* before migrating to Chicago, Ludwig von Mises could not even conceive the brutality of oppression and the cruelty of the Soviet regime. Very few people if any could have such Orwellian insights at the time. Orwell himself benefited from later insights gained from his participation in the Spanish civil war of 1936–1939. Also a backward Russian society, not possessing a strong tradition of checks and balances, nor with a strong and organized middle class, offered a much better laboratory for Bolshevik ideas and practices, than say France or Spain in the 1930s, or Portugal in the 1970s.

parts of normalcy. The large monograph of Attila Soós (1986) shows how campaigns and money continued to play a major role in the reform Communist periods as well. Lacking these the slowdown of economic performance, readily observable in countries of consolidated Communist rule, such as East Germany, Czechoslovakia or the Soviet Union during the 1980s, became inevitable, threatening the continued existence of these regimes.

These and other insights make it clear, that the *raison d'être* of socialism cannot be found in the realm of ideology or self-justification. 'Real socialism' has been shown to be a fry cry from its postulates. Socialism often worked in conjunction with *nationalist and/or imperial ideology*. Since these needed and justified territorial expansion and ideological assertiveness, the resultant *military needs could dominate* more mundane concerns typical of the 'rest of the world', such as welfare maximization or civil liberties. As long as both the anti-capitalist sentiment and military might could be credibly used as legitimating principles, bureaucracy, aided by campaigns, bargains and incentives, could use both *sticks* and *carrots* to manage complex industrial, and later post-industrial societies. *When both gradually evaporated, the system collapsed.*[9]

It is important not to overlook the big *discrepancy between the ideology* of socialism and the *realities of the Soviet model*, if for no other reason than because of the lasting influence of the *idealized image* of the period *surviving the system,* inter alia through the prime sources, that were produced invariably under censorship. Over and above these retrospective views, that are voiced by the elder generation, and tend to enhance the image the 'good old days', implicit in many analyses is the assumption that transition *should have delivered* all the goodies that the *ancien régime* had promised, and many people liked, such as an extended welfare system, free provision of services, tolerable living standards attained at low working hours etc. These claims are still represented strongly in the political platforms of various parties in all post-Communist countries, despite mounting evidence that these aims are either non-attainable, or never produced by the very socialist arrangements (first in Bence and Kis, 1972/1992; more recently Gedeon, 2003, pp. 37–39).

The ideology of the classical Soviet system was based on eight major features:
1. Promotion of equality among all members of society;
2. Planned and proportionate development, through steady and non-oscillating growth of GDP;
3. Ex ante regulation of macroeconomic and social processes;[10]
4. The promise of 'surpassing and overtaking the West', that is catching up, which materialized nowhere;
5. The evolution of a more human society than the market system;

---

[9] This was the subject of the previous monograph of the present author (Csaba, 1995, pp. 3–50).

[10] This claim has been proven plainly wrong by the cited works of Kornai, (1980) Soós (1986) and Bauer (1981); even if their contemporary counter-claim on the cyclical movement of the socialist economy has proven to be an over-interpetation by the later volume of Mihályi (1992) and the long empirical study of Schweitzer (2002).

6. Social self-management replacing the power of impersonal laws of the market;
7. A pattern of development that is self-contained, thus independent of 'harmful' influences of the global economy;
8. Finally a social progress, where well-being and human development is superior to the West, also in material terms (as the old slogan 'surpass and overtake' suggested).

The results of applying the Soviet model is as follows (without again aiming to be exhaustive):

1. The more advanced the country, *the more deleterious* the consequences of socialist experiments are. In developmental terms thus was Eastern Germany – the one-time *Mitteldeutschland* – and the Czech Republic, the countries that lost the most with respect to their relative position in the inter-war period. On the other hand, development in poor countries like Mongolia or Albania was more favorable in terms of human development indicators. Still, not even their evolution produced such economic structures that *allow for the continuation* of the socialist pattern of growth, once the Soviet Union and Yugoslavia disintegrated. In contemporary parlance, it was implicitly acknowledged by the calls for 'switching from extensive to intensive patterns of growth'. This phrase of party-language meant in economic terms the call for discontinuation of a factor intensive pattern. It also aimed at endogenous growth based on innovation rather than more inputs, without however bringing about any of its conditions.

2. *Allocation* of resources had proven *inefficient* with respect to that of market economies. This is no surprise knowing the elimination of capital markets, banking and the signaling function of prices. By the same token, the secular trend of lagging behind comes as inevitable, rather than coincidental. By the calculations of Bernhard Heitger (1991), in the 1950–1985 period the same unit of GDP required an annual *additional* investment of 5–7 percentage points for the socialist economies to yield the same. Simply adding up the numbers arithmetically, and even not allowing for – otherwise major – differences in quality, choice and availability – this feature reflects *a built-in tendency for socialist economies to lag.*[11] Even if we discount policy mistakes, such as the over-industrialization and the neglect of the services sector, or disregard for a moment the extreme decisions, openly criticized also during the Communist period, such as the introduction of the plantation of orange trees and cotton to Hungary, or the big computer program of Bulgaria, the long term comparative decline could not be avoided.

---

[11] GDP per head, for obvious reasons, does not reflect the major items of wellbeing, a major issue in contemporary mainstream economic theorizing, as documented in the Foreword to the current edition. Thus the more recent turn toward the comprehensive assessment of human development indicators (also by the international agencies) is rather overdue. But the level of development per se tells precious little about *quality of life* – a point regularly omitted when comparing the socialist and capitalist systems.

3. Given that the mono-archic system means the switching off all feedback mechanism and their subordination to the party-bureaucracy, *there is no room for corrections of major mistakes,* either at the macro- or the micro level. Major corrections in particular run counter to the nature of any bureaucracy. Inevitable minor corrections take place in the form of delays, additional costs and other deviations from planned processes. Neither incentives nor pressures for change had been imminent, not even in the reformist periods, as best illustrated by the Trabant car. The Trabant was considered a miracle of technology, introduced as a replacement for the Volkswagen of the '30s, but based on much poorer resources in an innovative fashion. The innovation included less weight and low petrol use. The car was renewed only twice in its 35 years of life span (compared to 5–6 years in contemporary Western models). Still a queue of 8–12 years existed in all socialist countries including East Germany (where the car was produced), as late as 1989.[12] *The inability to adjust,* either technologically and organizationally, *to Star Wars* was a major factor in Soviet military decline during the 1980s.

4. Disregard for quality, choice, dynamic changes and innovation in general thus also implies that *socialist welfare as always and everywhere been inferior* to what otherwise could be attainable at the given level of development. The latter implies given technology and given resource constraints. This follows already from the lack of capital markets and the lack of signaling and incentive function of prices at the microeconomic level. This insight was best illustrated in the Soviet military sector. In this priority area, in order to attain the same performance, sizeable quantitative superiority had been needed (both in terms of manpower and in terms of ammunitions and technology). In terms of European conventional forces that implied a 3:1 ratio in the 1980s.[13] We may take this as an indication of the overall level of comparative efficiency of the priority sector.

5. It is a sociological and business commonplace to observe that any bureaucracy is inherently *hostile to innovation.* The more we believe in neoclassical and/or endogenous growth theories, the more severe the problem of low innovative capacity we will consider. Innovations are known to matter in three planes: *organization, technology and product levels.* Without wanting to repeat the established findings of the business management literature, each of these can and does pose major problems for the competitiveness of firms.

This is the 'micro-foundation' of macroeconomics, the *hostility to innovation* has been a *major source of decay* in all existing socialist systems known today.

---

[12] For obvious reasons shortage produces shortages. It was customary to enroll for a new car before the one already ordered had arrived in order to work with the 12-year-queue. Because of the well-known phenomena of multiple hoarding strategies by all consumers and intermediaries it is hard to tell, also ex post, how big actual shortage had been. Lacking this information it is next to imposible to recalculate meaningful equilibrium prices that could deliver those retroactive GDP numbers that could be realistic.

[13] Paul Gregory (2003) published an empirical piece proving through archival material that the superior productivity and performance of Soviet defense industry was yet another myth.

The comparative performance of split countries (Korea, Germany, for a time Vietnam, but also Hong-Kong and mainland China) leaves no doubt as to the weight of this argument. The downfall of the Soviet Empire was also intimately related to its inability to mobilize resources that would have been needed to keep pace with a technology-inspired military program, such as Star War.[14]

By the same token, socialist lagging behind was inevitably *cumulative*. Contrary to some 'revisionist' contemporary views, advantageous features of the socialist system could not compensate for its less advantageous sides. This could be observed even in the priority defense sector, but also in many other areas and in the subsequent difficulties of conversion to peaceful aims. The true size of this problem is still being uncovered by the unfinished process of German re-unification,[15] where despite major injections of official and private capital flows, the massive presence of Western managerial and administrative skills, cultural commonalities, and a quick integration into a stable monetary frame, catching up virtually came to a halt by 1997. In the past twenty years we do not know of any major endogenous success story in larger scale in East German industry, banking, or various services, let alone universities and research centers.

Reform Socialist Models

Reforming the system or introducing market socialism instead of the classical Soviet model is defined as an attempt to avoid changes in the construction of the machinery (the macro-system as a whole), even at a high cost of changing each and every nut and bolt. Reforms are thus always initiated from above and aim at *preserving rather than transforming* the logic of the socialist system.[16] In the following, we survey major alternatives to the Soviet model, that emerged in the course of crises, such as in the mid-60s, and as a response to these. Thus *we do not know of cases where, enlightenment or insight, rather than political and economic exigency* would have triggered the introduction of these alternatives. In the following, we survey the policy alternatives that emerged in various times and countries.

Bukharin's New Economic Policy

In this and other subchapters, we do not aim at historical accounts, but attempt to distill socialist *institutional and policy models* from various episodes. Therefore, historians are likely to continue discussing the role of individual person-

---

[14] Contemporary analysts spoke of *Totrüsten* (waging an arms race to death) in describing the Reagan strategy of undermining Soviet economic power by the defense program

[15] According to the decisions of the *Bundestag* the major transfers to eastern provinces will continue at least until 2014.

[16] This, of course, has been setting severe limits to how far market coordination could go, and how relevant money could be, as recurringly underscored in the synthetic account by Balázs Hámori (2000).

alities or the exact conditions that triggered given reforms. It is unlikely to be disputed, however, that in 1921, following the uprising of Kronstadt, when the base turned against the Bolsheviks, that Lenin changed sides from among the hard-liners, led by Trotskiy, to the 'doves', led by Bukharin. Following his switch, the Bolshevik leadership made allowances for 'petty burgoise elements', the peasantry and abolished War Communism. The *series of improvised measures* added up to what all historians and comparative systems' theorists consider *a practical alternative to the original (naive) Marxian ideas*, ones that Fully negate the role of market coordination. This practice was in existence in 1921–1928 in Russia, thus empirical evidence can back up the theory. Let us survey the main features/stylized facts of the emerging first market socialist system.[17]

1. *Agriculture* has been *de-collectivized, though by no means privatized.* One of the first decrees following the Bolshevik takeover has been the famous *Dekret o Zeml'e*, the Decree on Land, that has played a symbolic, even ritual role, defining for common people and party-folk alike what made Soviet Russia *different from the rest of the world.* Relying on the long standing tradition of communal land ownership, only partially abolished by the land reforms of the 1860s and '90s, the Decree began with the programmatic sentence: Land belongs to the people.[18] While collective farms, created forcibly by the Bolsheviks in 1918–1920 were abolished, *private property was never restored.* Only *usus fructus* had been transferred to the peasants, who accounted for over 90 per cent of the Soviet population.

    There was no possibility of trading land, thus *no possibility of concentration of ownership* and emergence of scale economies, which is vitally important to some (though by no means all) sectors of agricultural production. Capital accumulation was severely restrained through state regulation of most prices and the need to pay taxes in kind (*prodnalog*) that left little room for major accumulation of wealth. Meanwhile, the *incentives* to produce, and thereby to overcome imminent famine, did emerge. The state tended to control machine purchases, and from 1924 on procurement prices served industrial accumulation, not the enrichment of successful farmers. Thus *spontaneity* returned through the backdoor, and the idea of a society without money finally abandoned.

2. *Services tended to be liberalized across the board.* This deregulation was instrumental in bringing about limited reconstruction in a country still in war, in some places as late as 1927, from 1914 onward. Mobilization of the Hayekian decentral knowledge, that is initiative of a large number of unconnected people interacting irrespective of plan and policies, did help reconstruct the

---

[17] This survey is based on Nove (1992, pp. 39–158); Carr and Davies (1974); Szamuely (1974); Brus (1972) and Balcerowicz (1995, pp. 19–141).

[18] This might explain why land could not be privatized in the entire Yeltsin period. Even Vladimir Putin needed over two years to gain approval from the State Duma for land privatization in June 2002, that is eleven full years after the collapse of Soviet Communism.

cities and trade. Services and petty business have been wide-spread, from shoe repair to prostitution, and the word *nepman* (denoting a wheeler-dealer) found a lasting place in Russian vocabulary. The novels of Ilf and Petrov (primarily the *Golden Calf*, as well as many other literary examples) give vivid illustrations of how bustling a society emerged in a spontaneous fashion over a very short period of time. This experience, in my view, invalidated from the very outset the concept of *Homo Sovieticus*, the image of a stagnant, order-waiting and obeying person, that is inherent in the totalitarian regime, once having played an illustrous role in social sciences. The repetition of the same experience in the 1990s, with the emergence of *noviie ruskiie* (new Russians) supports our claim, namely that *it is unfounded to treat Russians as a fundamentally market hostile species.*

3. *The management of state enterprises was largely deregulated.* The specific – non-translatable – technical term *khozraschet*[22] described the crux of innovations. While firms remained in the hands of the state, management was allowed to take independent decisions on current issues. What a 'current decision' is of course a fluid category, like 'small matters' in a marriage, routinely decided by the wife. In the 1921–1924 period, *khozraschet* stood basically for a harmonious marriage, with no 'big issues' emerging as a rule. Contrary to the 1929–1989 period planning was not meant to implement state orders, but mostly a forecasting exercise. Furthermore, no decision to give priority to the military sector existed. On the contrary, reconstruction and improving the living standards in the already conquered parts of Russia was on the agenda of Bolsheviks. Therefore, no matter how haphazard it looks, de-centralized socialism worked. New Economic Policy and *khozraschet* were code-words for *diminishing, on occasion abolishing, direct party control* by uncultivated cadres and a return of intellectuals – engineers and accountants – to overseeing the process of production.

Small business also flourished, improving supply-demand relations and overcoming bottlenecks. Although profits were taxed, partly could be retained, and depreciation reintroduced. All these measures allowed firms to stand on their own financial footings. The blossoming of private and uncontrolled, centrally non-directed activities had 'over-shooted' as most of *the booming part of the economy became independent of politics and planning.*

For this very reason, party loyalists immediately started to question the type of socialism NEP produced. The ideological backlash against the 'socialism of the nepmen', against 'petty-burgoise tendencies' represented by the market socialist practices, was followed by a political one (neatly doc-

---

[19] This is a shorthand for *khoziaistvennii raschet*, literally meaning economic accounting. This, however, has little in common with the concept as understood in market economies, where accounting is the financial side of business administration. The Soviet term implied the ideological turn away from the Marxian concept of a fully non-monetized, only commodity-based economy, that proved unworkable in 1918–1920, and was seen to be at the root of economic ills by Nikolai Bukharin, the chief ideologue of the time. More on that in (Szamuely, 1974).

umented in Nove, 1992, pp. 133–158), since the two logics obviously clashed. While loyalty to the Party and meeting ideologically selected plan targets were economically non-rewarding, business elites emerged quite independent of the Party. Thus the idea of one-party rule, the romanticism of revolutionary governance and the reality of day-to-day survival in Russia have come to an open clash by the middle of the 1920s.

4. *In foreign trade,* the practice of extending *concessions to foreigners and previous owners* was the name of the game. These old-new owners, relying on their knowledge and contacts could re-establish, basically from scratch, foreign trade contacts disorganized by the world and civil wars and the ensuing chaos. Specialized knowledge, capital and contacts were found. This contributed significantly to *overcoming of bottlenecks* created by war and War Communism, as well as the international isolation of Soviet Russia and the non-convertibility of the ruble. Shortage of food, of industrial intermediate products, construction materials and the like could gradually be overcome, thus the country could *return to normalcy.*

Concessions, similarly to land reform, implied the transfer of *usus fructus* only, and even that for a limited period of time. This arrangement was viable as long as no central planning and industrialization, as defined from 1927–1929 existed.[20] Thus the option was deemed a temporary concession (a form Lenin used to describe the entire NEP policy). State control over foreign trade, as well as over land, and over long-term issues, such as concentration and capital accumulation had been preserved all across the period.

5. *Investments were to be centralized, but central investment* – such as the reconstruction of railroads, or sustaining the bureaucracy – *accounted only for a fraction of overall investments.* This had been inevitable as long as reconstruction and fighting famine, rather than the later introduced industrialization priorities were put on the agenda. However, similarly to any mixed economy, *the border between central and decentral,* between investment and current expenditure *remained fluid* and thus politically and bureaucratically contestable.[21] The contest actually started from the very outset, with the left wing opposition declaring the NEP as treason of principles.

Bureaucracy and party bosses also felt immediately their loss of importance and control. Thus NEP was generally seen in party circles, although not among the population, as a step back. While the population saw these as a compromise with reality of a country composed of over 85 per cent by peasantry and another 10 per cent by petty producers (traders), money lenders, not by the large-scale industrial proletariat. Therefore they saw it as an attempt to introduce a *modicum of rationality.* By contrast, ideologically motivated revolutionary leaders saw it the other way around. The conflict

[20] How industrialization was defined is the subject of the two volumes by Carr and Davies (1974) and Carr (1976).

[21] Contestants included corporate bosses versus ministerial officials, party people in the regions versus private and semi-private enterpreneurs etc.

had been built in, from the very outset, due to the clash of two conflicting logic: that of the market and that of bureaucracy (ideology).

6. The outcome of *the clash of two logics* could hardly be questionable as long as the Bolsheviks managed to consolidate their power, both within the borders of what remained of the Tsarist Empire and internationally. The latter followed the separate deal with Germany in Rapallo in 1922. After the economy had recovered and the opposition crushed, the ideological faithful, supported by the very traditional *balance of power logic* (of trying to regain what had been lost in terms of territories and influence in the period after World War One) *took over*. With the benefit of hindsight, there can be no doubt that the change had hardly been coincidental, attributable to ideological or personal factors, or the need to overcome backwardness (usually invoked in contemporary and later political science and history works).

Once the almighty, uncontested bureaucratic-political center could be established, its need *to switch off all possible feedback* or forces of protest could easily dominate other considerations.[22] Once the priorities of industrialization and military build-up had been established, the death sentence of NEP was passed. Similar turns in policies produced similar outcomes in Hungary in 1955 and 1959, in Poland in the '60s and the '70s, as well as in Romania in the 1970s.

More importantly, one does not need these priorities to get market reforms rolled back. As has been seen in the economic reforms of Poland in the 1980s and of Czechoslovakia in the 1967–1971 period, *once the uncontested power of the Communist party emerges,* and the power of bureaucracy by and large consolidated, *reversion of market reforms is a practicality,* irrespective of an all-out political *démarche* or the lack of it. This was seen in the Hungarian experience, which will be discussed below. Whether intentionally or not, the New Economic Policy has never proven to be that major ideological re-assessment market socialists later attributed to it (Szamuely, 1974; Brus, 1972). *It never acquired any degree of ideological approval,* a normative dimension other than a necessary step back, a tactical concession. Instead, what János Kornai (1992, chapter 15.3) later termed as 'the genetic program of the system' prevailed. The lesson for the general argument thus is, that the Russian market socialist experiment was though *workable,* but it produced an unstable system. It has proven to be *unable to reproduce itself.* Thus stability, a core component of any economic order/model was missing. It ceased to exist due to the internal contradictions of the model, not because of external intervention or because of the spillover of the Great Depression.

---

[22] Given that the same story has been replicated several times under different historical conditions, such as in Hungary in the post-1972 period, or in China in the post-1958 and post-1989 periods, the logic of the system is hard to overlook, and the coincidental explanations remain of little analytical value.

The Yugoslav Model: Decentralization and Self-Management

A second market socialist model, combining plan and market, that came in existence for a long period of time[23] is that of the former Yugoslavia. Similar to the NEP in Russia the model of Yugoslav Communists never related in any form to the debates on market socialism, conducted with great fervor in the 1920–1948 period in the Western academe. Though the latter have produced some interesting theoretical and methodological insights, these never influenced policy-makers in Belgrade to any significant degree.[24] In fact, Marshall Tito as a fully fledged Communist, acknowledged Soviet practice as the only feasible, only possible, only acceptable model that each country needs to emulate. While this insight followed from the over-centralized and uniform nature of Cominform/Comintern, the international movement of Communist parties, actually a side-condition for anybody to survive the great purges of 1937–1938, or remain committed to the idea outside Soviet Russia.

Marshall Tito, relied on his homegrown guerilla army, delivering the victory against fascism, and not allowing the free formation of non-Communist parties, nor free elections in the postwar period. Therefore, on ideological grounds and using policy opportunity *building socialism in Yugoslavia started already*, by and large, *in 1945*. This included large-scale nationalization of pre-war private property, attempts to organize collective farms, persecution of non-Communists, limitation of civil society, brutal oppressions of dissidents and supporters of alternative options. Oppressions were extended to Croat and Hungarian nationalities (collective responsibility principles). These measures were hardly extraordinary if seen in the context of contemporary Soviet domestic practices, or later the East European experience. However, in 1945–1947 Stalin felt still constrained by Yalta. He was hoping for consolidating the government position of Communist parties in the West of Europe. Thus the idea of 'people's democracies' with multiparty system, private property and avoiding the all-out elimination of all non-Communist forces remained his top priority. Against this soft line, because of his hard-line Sovietization policies in 1945–1947, *Tito tended to be a left wing extremist*, not a right wing 'revisionist', customarily portrayed in later periods. This matters insofar as the drawbacks *of transplanting Soviet practices to a different environment began to be felt earlier* in Yugoslavia. By the time the Sovietization of Eastern Europe could be started (in 1948), Yugoslavia already faced the troubles that were similar to the ones

[23] Yugoslav economists at the time and external analysts have been divided over the timely limits: some put the Yugoslav model already to 1952, others, more convincingly, to 1965 (when a second, radical phase was introduced). The final stage should be put to 1989–90, with the Markovic Government attempting to impose reforms far beyond any conceivable limits to market socialism. In a contemporary lucid account, Szegvári (1991) highlights this point in terms of the convertibility projects and criticized these as being unfeasible and incoherent with contemporary systemic options. This criticism of course applied to all those projects that aimed (implicitly at least) at transforming rather than reforming market socialism.

[24] These include the limits to centralization, the focal role of information, the relevance of mathematical methods for planning and many others.

East Europeans experienced in 1951–1953 only, i.e. also in 3-4 years following the transplantation.

1945–1947 was the period, when the conflict of Tito with Russia started. It was idiosyncratic to emulate domestic Soviet practices in 1945–1947, when Stalin had a different shop-window, and potentially also a different strategy in the context of his continental strategy. In these years, he did not aim at conquest, but followed the more traditional imperial Russian line of regaining influence, lost after 1918–1922. This would have been much better served by keeping the French, Italian and Greek Communists in government positions, demilitarizing Germany and rendering it neutral 'forever', as was the case of Austria by 1955. It could realistically be complemented by joining the IMF and Marshall Plan for assisting reconstruction of the war-destroyed Soviet economy. The attempts by Tito and the equally influential Bulgarian leader, Dimitrov to form a customs union that would have covered Albania, and, if Communists won the civil war, also Greece, was too *obviously a challenge to the imperial nature of Soviet power.* The split had been inevitable. Since Yugoslavia was seen in the West as yet another Communist country by 1948, the split seemed lethal. It was anything but trivial that a homegrown Communist regime could survive anywhere in Europe,[25] especially during the American policy of containment.

In order to find an answer to the challenge to the basics of his power, the domestically based *Tito regime was forced to innovate. The outcome was a new socialist model, that is not a carbon copy of the Soviet one,* but addresses some of the peculiarities of Yugoslavia. This happened via a series of experimental steps and reached full maturity by the reforms of 1965.

Since this is not a country study, let us briefly sum up the salient features of this model. The model, let us recall, had not relied on theories of socialism or self-management, as developed in the West, such as the co-operatives, co-decision or *kibbutzim.* It emerged via trial and error, out of local experiences and power struggles among the Yugoslav Communists.[26] The features of this model include:

1. *The party of the Communists ceased to be organized by a nomenklatura,* i.e. a central list of cadres and competence, but was reorganized on a territorial principle. This was a requirement in terms of defense (a similar decentralizing option explained the long resistance of Khmer Rouge in Cambodia against the Vietnamese invasion of 1978). Modern industrial organization theory supports the insight that attenuated hierarchical structures are more efficient in managing decentralized systems by saving information and mobilizing local knowledge. It also accomodated the ethnic diversity of the forcibly reconstituted Yugoslav Federation, from which Croatia and Macedonia seceded during the Second World War. As Serbs accounted only

---

[25] The Hungarian, Bavarian, Slovak Communist experiments, as well as the Spanish Republican regime collapsed in the preceding decades.

[26] The following account is based on Soós (1986), Mencinger (1991), Tyson (1980 and 1983), Gligorov (1998), Uvalic (1992), Saks (1994), Burkett (1994).

for 40 per cent of the population, this arrangement was of immense significance.

Furthermore, the League of Communists ceased to exert immediate petty control over firm management, which was customary in the Soviet model. Former partisans continued to exert considerable influence; however, this was a far cry from the feudal dependencies of the Soviet Union. Finally *kolkhozes*, that were at the root of chronic inefficiency and supply bottlenecks across the entire Soviet period, *have been abolished. Self-sufficiency in foodstuffs*, a major priority all across Europe in the postwar period, *was attained* in Yugoslavia in a period, when Soviets had to import fodder and grain continually from 1963 onward. Allowing for small shops and other forms of 'petty capitalism' made contemporary Yugoslavia the envy of the rest of the socialist camp.

2. *Decentralization took two turns: territorial and firm level. Territorial* decentralization implied, contrary to Soviet or Czechoslovak practice, that member republics have not been relegated to a formal existence. As time passed, local ministries of finance, local planning boards, local party organizations gained in importance, and *the influence of Belgrade was constrained to areas of defense and security.* By contrast, ideological intolerance had been bigger and more lasting than in many other Communist countries.[27] The conflict between Belgrade and Zagreb, Belgrade and Ljubljana, Belgrade and Pristina or Novi Sad have enjoyed high publicity all across the Yugoslav period after 1965. Therefore the idea of a unified Yugoslav nation (and state), as postulated by the contemporary ideology and some retrospective accounts, have never existed.

There were two major *innovations at the firm level.* First, with the abolition of Soviet type central planning, the operational independence of managers – referred to as *khozraschet* in the Russian subsection – was instituted without much controversy. Self-management of workers was also introduced. This was motivated more by military than economic concerns. *A firm owned by workers is harder to overtake,* by any outside power, be that invaders or former owners. From the incentive side, if 'the firm belongs to you, you build it for yourself', then identification with the regime can be more personal. This translates into *job security,* which was important following the massive unemployment of the inter-war period. Though self-management in contrast to co-operatives or *kibbutzim,* has been mostly formal, the arrangement created a peculiar system.

For insiders, identification with the firm and maximization of wages turned into a reality. On the other hand, newcomers could easily find themselves without jobs from the '60s onward. Also, *resource allocation* was severely distorted by the incentives to invest in one's 'own' company rather than

---

[27] Glirgorov (1998 pp. 350–351) blames therefore Yugoslavs for having taken their home made, self-management ideology too seriously for too long, also in the 1980s, thus incapacitating themselves for preparations to a capitalist order.

in a most profitable use; or in one's own republic, rather than searching for the nationally or globally most interesting options. This explains why despite high investment rates, Yugoslavia *showed signs of decreased competitiveness and market shares from the early 1970s onward.*

3. Although Yugoslavia had a more open economy and society than the other Communist countries, it was still institutionally closed. Foreign trade was dominated by publicly owned firms. Trade was conducted in a variety of ways, thus shortages were milder, although exchange rate policies remained subordinated to central controls and the financial system was suppressed. Investment priorities never followed market signals – this is why each republic had its own oil refinery by the mid-1980s. On the other hand, external relations were helpful in overcoming some of the weaknesses of the Yugoslav system. Unemployment, which exceeded West European levels, could be alleviated by exporting labor. Guest workers to the welfare states of Europe could earn money for starting up their own business upon returning to their home country. The large-scale *movement of people thus helped remedy the inefficiencies of an insider dominated arrangement.*[28] Regular devaluations helped to inflate away excessive wages and stimulate exports, including revenues from tourism (an important source of revenue since the 1960s).

4. It follows that contrary to the classical Soviet model, where price stability was a given,[29] *inflation was an inherent feature of the Yugoslav model.* The leadership soon understood the advantages of moderately inflationary policies as devices to alleviate strains on consumer goods markets ever since the early 1960s. Contemporary critiques in East and West alike tended to overplay the relevance of this feature until the 1980s, when other socialist countries started to emulate it. As inflation *helped sustain existing structures,* laxity on price rises was coherent with the model. Meanwhile, it is hard to overlook that they continued to use a soft, inconvertible currency. Thus the role of the dinar resembled to the non-relevant, passive money, discussed in the case of classical Soviet model.

5. As could be expected, the *political and business logics defining the system were in historic conflict with one another.* The bureaucratic logic, supported by power interests of Belgrade, called for regular reversals, most intensively in 1971, in 1984 and in 1990. In each of these cases, the primacy of politics, so openly formulated by Lenin, could be observed. In each of these cases, the Communist politicians managed to overrule reforms of various sorts, emanating basically from the business elite and the intellectuals. Whereas in the period

---

[28] Madzar (2000, pp. 358–362) ascribes to the survival of this feature most of the inefficiencies of all Serbian reforms of the 1990s.

[29] As prices were mere accounting units, keeping them stable helped the technology of planning immensely. It had also been elevated to the level of political accomplishments, especially in periods when this stability could be contrasted with inflation in the West. The shortage component was either denied, or as later, its relevance played down (similarly to issues of choice, quality and innovation).

until the rule of Tito's army and secret police – the backbone of the regime – were efficient, centralization could be re-established. Nobody was able to question the primacy of the Belgrade leadership until the late 1980s. In 1990, however, these and other differences turned into major inter-ethnic economic, political and cultural clashes culminating in the disintegration of both Yugoslavia and the economic system. We have already addressed the diversity among successor states that also reflects their economic systems, with Slovenia being an EU member and a net contributor, and Kosovo being still a quasi-state, where subsistence farming and mafioso activities help avert famine. It seems, that *the external conditioning* of both Yugoslavia and the self-management system played a major role in sustaining this arrangement over the decades. In a more general level of analysis, thus the Yugoslav experience has also shown *market socialism to be an unstable economic order.*

The Hungarian Alternative[30] – The New Economic Mechanism

To make a long story short, the initial conditions for socialism in Hungary *were completely different from those in the case of Yugoslavia.* Hungary experienced partly free multiparty elections in 1945, with the Smallholders' Party, integrating all major non-socialist forces attaining 57 per cent of the votes. This was a clear message on the limitations on the speed and forms of how a regime loyal to the Soviet Union could be introduced. Hungarian Communists never got more than 22 per cent of the votes. Even this best result was attained only in 1948, when all major competitors have already been marginalized with the help of Soviet troops.

This prompted the Rákosi leadership to adopt an *overzealous* pro-Soviet stance, trying to imitate even those features of Stalin's rule that were obviously at odds with Hungarian realities. These included building up a strong defense industry, aiming at economic autarky, or introducing ideological and lifestyle uniformity. Introducing the crude Soviet methods to an *already urbanized and industrialized country was counterproductive,* even from the regime's perspective. This is why immediately following the change in Soviet leadership in 1953, a large-scale experimentation with reforms began.

The loss of political control, partly triggered by the open contest between the two major factions of the Communist Party, and partly by a growing popular dissatisfaction with the regime, culminated in the revolution of 1956. This was crushed by the Soviet troops. However, the insight that *overdoing Soviet practices might harm the colonial power itself gained acceptance.* Khrushchev, himself inclined to some change, supported the idea of cautious experimentation. János Kádár, a victim of oppressions of the Rákosi group between 1951–1955, earnestly believed in the merits of the original reform platform of Imre Nagy (the Communist Prime Minister, who turned in to the leader of the uprising).

[30] This formulation is borrowed from Tamás Bauer (1983).

Thus the ideas and the initiatives have gradually been *put in practice, later radicalized* when confronted with new challenges.[31] Below we follow the previous practice and list *stylized facts only*; the reader interested in bits and pieces should consult the references given under footnote 35. It is important to recall, that most Hungarian actors were just as ignorant of the debates on market socialism, as their Yugoslav counterparts. This held definitely in 1957, when the Commission of Economic Experts, headed by the non-Marxian Professor István Varga elaborated the original model. This aimed at abolishing much of the command features of socialism, while retaining central control over investments.

What are the major features of the Hungarian reform socialist model?

1. *The kolkhoz system had been given up.* This reform took place in response to supply bottlenecks and re-introduction of 'private' farming, as in Russia in the 1920s. This implied the abolition of compulsory deliveries (kept both in the NEP and in China, to be discussed below). *Khozraschet* was introduced. This relatively liberal model had to be given up in 1959–1962, when agriculture had to be collectivized, in line with the decision of Moscow. However, Hungarian collective farms from the mid-60s on, no longer resembled their Soviet counterparts. The scope of obligatory targets was limited. Formerly rich farmers/*kulaks* were integrated, sometimes given leading positions to the co-ops. Their non-farming activities flourished. They became the *breeding ground for petty capitalism.* Moreover, they were capitalizing on tax benefits supporting the farm sector. By the late '80s, a typical co-op earned over 80 per cent of its profits of such activities (from cleaning to printing). This helped the structural change from first to tertiary sector. It also explains why there were no food shortages in Hungary, a circumstance openly envied by other Communist countries. It contributed to the first priority of the Kádár regime, to sustain peace domestically.

2. *The New Economic Mechanism was introduced in 1968,* which implemented the across-the-board *abolition of command planning.* Not only were the numerous obligatory plan targets abolished (this freed the output side of firms). Moreover, also the more controversial input side was freed, with central allocation of inputs giving way to wholesale trade. The latter measure was introduced only by the outgoing government of Yegor Gaidar, in September 1992, in Russia. This is clearly indicating how important this arrangement is for centralized control. Once liberated from the slavery of central planning and petty tutelage by party bosses – or delivered to the mercy of circumstances, as contemporary managers felt – Hungarian corporate bosses ceased to be party appointed political supervisors: *they turned into businessmen by default.* They and nobody else were held responsible for bottlenecks of supply, shortages, quality problems and the rest, all vividly exposed by

---

[31] Libraries have been produced on this process. The best monographic account is still Berend (1990), drawing on a large number of still unpublished sources/archive materials. For a more critical assessment and literature survey, covering the bulk of English language sources and current evaluation of projects cf. Kornai (1986), Szamuely and Csaba (1998) and Csaba (2002).

a press whose freedom was constrained to criticizing economic mal-prac-
tices.

In systemic terms, these moves amounted to *decentralization without property reform*. What is beyond doubt – and amply documented in the contemporary sources surveyed in the works cited under footnote 35 – is that it
changed the system fundamentally by *modifying the rules of the game*. When
external constraints triggered a return to command practices, these immediately translated into enhanced bargaining and efficiency losses, reminding
the leadership of the limitations of its power (Antal, 1983).

3. The debt crisis of 1981–1982, largely brought about by spillover effects of
   declaring martial law in Poland, triggered another wave of liberalization.
   This time the *irregular economy* had been freed up, with all ensuing consequences. The latter included the emergence of a business elite, which, like in
   Yugoslavia or in Russia, was only partly overlapping with the Communist
   hierarchy, its rules of success were different. On the one hand, from the mid-
   70s on, Hungarian people were openly told to rely on themselves, rather
   than expecting anything from 'Daddy State'. Entrepreneurships of different
   variety flourished. Long working hours/taking up second and third jobs
   became the norm. In the social sphere, much of what other countries experienced in the transition period had already begun from the late '70s. This
   resulted in *a sizeable supply response, since prices were partially freed up*. Money,
   prices, interest rates, access to hard currency, and thus market forms of coordination started to matter. On the other hand, these 'socialist entrepreneurships' had indeed carried a series of socialist features. For example, *using
   public assets to create private profit* had become the norm. Similarly *eschewing
   rather than abiding rules* developed, which is not conducive to a market economy based on the rule of law. Transparency of the system, especially in economic matters further diminished. Enterprising abilities that are oriented at
   finding loopholes and cheating are hardly the ideal training ground for civilized market behavior.
4. Analysts developed a second, more radical market reform project in 1983.
   However, the leadership rejected most of its substance and had chosen to
   rely on external funding. Still, a part of reforms were introduced in the
   1984–1987 period. Most importantly, *enterprise councils* were relatively freely
   elected. In this way, managers became legitimate and even *quasi-owners of
   assets*. In the following years, firms were corporatized. A (soft) bankruptcy
   law stipulating exit was implemented in August 1986. The two tier banking
   system emerged, in 1987. All this laid the foundation for *a real market economy
   by creating a legal and institutional infrastructure*.
5. Finally, in order to avoid an open crisis, the government introduced a three-
   year-program of *liberalization and external opening* in 1989. Therefore it abolished quantitative restrictions, such as import quotas and licensing of hard
   currency transactions. Thereby, it abolished the state monopoly on foreign
   trade and currency transactions, abolished price and wage controls in most
   of the economy. The stock exchange was recreated. Spontaneous privatization started. FDI surged. In short, the switch from a socialist to a market

economy was smooth. The process of systemic change was though initiated by the outgoing but completed by the democratically elected government. Both acted in by and large the same line in 1989–1992.[32]

The general lesson is again that as long as the central bureaucratic power of the Communist party is intact, the socialist features of reforms constrain their effects. With the decline of economic performance, market coordination has gradually been gathering momentum. The change of the system was by and large *spontaneous and endogenous.* It was supported by the enlightened part of the ruling class, preparing its place in the new regime. The spread of market forces took a turn and gradually eliminated the socialist features of the market economy. The Hungarian experience, similarly to the other two cases, has proven, as a mirror image, the consistency of the Soviet model, as *allowing for inconsistency did lead to collapse.* Meanwhile, it also has shown the vulnerability of the mixed market socialist model. The latter *required special circumstances to sustain,* which is not the case with the market order.

The Chinese Model

China observers tend to be split in two camps. On the one hand, we find traditional area specialists, with a focus on language and culture, obviously stressing the peculiarity of the field of their study. More often than not, area specialists do not engage in any serious comparisons, or if they do, these remain often formal/perfunctory. On the other hand, we find international policy-makers and global analysts, who base their judgements on a few selected indicators and on officially reported figures – a practice that is quite dangerous in any Communist country. The commonality of both camps is the tendency to *overlook those features of Chinese market socialism that are though not identical, still comparable in systemic dimension to the previously presented cases.* We first offer *the stylized facts,* as a preliminary overview before we turn to a more extended discussion of China as a developmental alternative. Many endogenous institutional innovations in China bear great resemblance to substantive features of other market socialist models. The fact that Chinese policymakers have often been ignorant of these, which applies to much of Chinese researchers and China watchers, is not a paradox. As we have seen, this has always been the case with socialist policy-makers.

1. Chinese reformers *followed the path of others in similar situations.* When confronted with a deep crisis threatening the base of Communist rule, the strong ideological stance changed and they showed flexibility. In China, the 'four modernization' of Deng, declared in 1979, his proverbial dictum 'it does not matter if the cat is black or white, what matters is if it catches the mouse' is the one side. This represents the limitations to ideological ortho-

---

[32] This point, of course, has always been controversial. I tried to offer a detailed documentation in a contemporary article (Csaba, 1992), confronting my point with differring views. A recent, more detailed reconfirmation of this thesis was offered in the book of Muraközy (2004).

doxy. The slaughter on the Tienanmen Square in June 1989, setting clear limits to democratization is the other side of the same coin.

The 'Cultural Revolution' of 1966–1969 *disintegrated the Chinese party and state structures,* as well as supply chains, while famine threatened the most populous country of the globe. The challenge was indeed comparable to that faced by the Bolsheviks in 1920. Therefore, it is hardly surprising that the ideas developed for addressing these issues bore great resemblance to one another. The Communist party *de facto de-collectivized agriculture.* This measure, like in Russia in the 1920s, did not include deregulation. It also did not allow for *the creation of private property rights for land.* It stopped short of allowing for the ensuing trade in land and fixed assets.[33] Also, in line with the long forgotten NEP, petty capitalism was tolerated in the cities, helping to overcome shortages, particularly of daily necessities in both commodities and services. It is unsurprising to see that the rulers profit from petty capitalism, overcoming shortages and the improvement of living conditions. Contrary to ideological fears, *the leading role of the party only strengthened* from these changes, similarly to the Hungarian and Yugoslav cases.

Unlike in Russia, China has not adopted a vigorous industrialization policy that follows centrally set priorities that focus on the defense sector. Also, Chinese leaders never aimed at diminishing the dependence on the outside world, as the various anti-capitalist schools of import substitution advised. At the same time, the leadership adopted *a conservative, mercantilist stance,* not allowing for the so-called 'modernization deficits', approved by most development theories. Rather, they opted for the mercantilist view seeing trade and finance surpluses as a guarantee against potential external crises.

2. *Decentralized resource allocation* is a major difference between the Chinese and the Soviet model. In Soviet Russia, the major aim was to recreate the central state. In China, in line with several millenia of tradition, a strong omnipresent central state is not seen as the precondition of the survival of the state. On the contrary, decentralization served as a way of sharing burdens and responsibility. The Chinese central state, according to the *World Development Report 2003* (op. cit. p. 234) collects spends only 12 per cent of GDP, a number akin to European states of the Middle Ages, rather than to the Soviet Union. Therefore central taxes need not be high. Municipal budgets and taxes are of course higher, but being a developing country, China does not operate an extended welfare state. Therefore, it does not need to levy the public dues that such a model requires. Allocation is not in the task of the central bureaucracy, but rather of local bureaucracies. The term 'local' denotes the provinces, some of which like Sichuan are comparable to medi-

---

[33] Detailed analysis (Jacoby et al, 2002) has shown this feature to be of chief responsibility for explaining the quite restrained propensity of Chinese households to invest. However, investment for growth is what makes any plot or plant an enterprise in the economic sense.

um sized states with their population over 90 million (bigger than reunified Germany).

Likewise, as Carsten Herman-Pillath (1993b) argues, the role of *the Chinese cultural community* transgressing all state borders has been pivotal in the allocation of financial resources and of know-how alike. From its special function, it follows that the 'genetic program of the system' is modified. Problems arising from big centralized projects in the Soviet Union or in Romania do not show up in China. In short, it is no longer the 'central planner', but the Chinese business network interacting with local and central Party officials who decide over major investments. By contrast, problems of lack of central coordination do emerge, as the deepening urbanization crisis, regular blackouts, or the floods already indicate.

3. China is often mistaken for having an open and *export led* economy (cf. also Nolan, 2001). This surely is *not the case in terms of the theory of open economy and outward orientation*, discussed in (Balassa, 1993). Although China does export quite a lot (as we have seen, on par with Canada in dollar terms), however the equal treatment of exporting and import substituting industries, or more importantly, the influence of price signals on investment decisions is not given at all. In development theory outward orientation is not the same as export promotion. Therefore, the regular *surplus* in the Chinese trade balance cannot *qualify as a sign of export-led growth*. Rather, what we see the continued presence of insulating and filtering role of centralized trade regime and centralized currency management, typical of all socialist economies. This is in itself a sign of a *closed regime*. This has lead to the inconvertibility of the yuan.

In a nutshell, while China opened itself up in microeconomic terms, it remained a closed economy in macroeconomic terms. This has been indicated by the slow and conditional admission to the World Trade Organization, as late as 2002, nearly quarter of a century since the reform started. The big question is, of course, to what extent joining the WTO in 2002 is likely to change the overall landscape in systemic terms. Conditions of Chinese accession prescribe a gradual liberalization and proscribe the continuation of bureaucratic practices that used to ensure the surpluses in the Chinese current account. It remains to be seen, whether the WTO has the capacity to assist and monitor liberalization. In the case of Hungary, similar hopes were frustrated in the 1973–89 period. However, if WTO-led liberalization succeeds, it would be lethal to the socialist nature of the Chinese market economy, for the same reasons as explained in the Yugoslav and Hungarian cases.

4. Since 1984 *a stock exchange has been open* in Shanghai. In theory, it may well have sounded as the death knell to socialism. However it has not been the case. The reason is simple: *the market economy is a complex set of institutions, none of which functions on its own*. The stock exchange requires sound and solid accounting, controlling and auditing practices, else it is turned into a pyramid game. Whereas in the USA, the scandals were due to mal-practice partly remedied, following the propositions of the Sarabanes Commission, in China 'creative accounting' is the name of the game. It is hardly by chance

that residents are not allowed to trade in Hong Kong, and non-residents are not allowed to trade in yuan-denominated shares.[34] Lacking bankruptcy regulation, soft banking, continued Party involvement in the business affairs ensure the continuation of soft budget constraints for the Chinese enterprises. As a result, *financial results do not decide* over death and survival of the firm and the position of its top management. Moreover, due to weak disclosure and lacking enforcement, financial accounts can be manipulated. Therefore, the stock exchange cannot serve as a major instrument of capital allocation. Existence of a stock exchange therefore *does not even allow for evaluating asset prices.* Thus the stock exchange continues financial gambling more than it does macroeconomic control.

5. As an important innovation to comparative economic systems, we could learn from China, that *bureaucratic co-ordination* does not necessarily equate centralized command and control: *it may well be decentralized.* Analysts sympathetic to the Chinese strategy explain, that the clarification of property rights implied that 'authority tends to gravitate to the lower level of government' (Jefferson and Rawski, 2002, pp. 595). The same analysis has shown that government directed restructuring, such as – though not exclusively – the initiative to create 100 colossal enterprises dominate market based adjustment. As the authors put it (op. cit. pp. 612) high transaction costs limit the scope for market mediated exchanges and big governmental programs dissipate financial resources. In a way China has arrived to a crucial choice if it is to retain centralized management, or to opt for more market based solutions.

This insight emerged already in the late socialist period in Hungary, Russia, Poland and Yugoslavia. However, contemporary analysts tended to ascribe it to the failure and disintegration of the Communist hierarchy. By contrast, in China in the quarter of a century, devolution of decision-making has contributed to the preservation of the system by decentralizing economic and political strains. The analytical volume by Huang (2003, esp. pp. 309) addresses the question how bureaucratic co-ordination may co-exist with FDI, which is by definition profit driven. His conclusion is that *the local state does manage FDI*, diverting it to the least efficient state owned firms and in forms of joint ventures that are controlled by the local polity. This leads to the fragmentation of market and low efficiency.

On the other hand, empirical analyses (OECD, 2000) have long ago called attention to the problems that result from *excessive decentralization.* The under-provision of public goods, lack of control over management, macroeconomic disequlibria that cannot be covered forever, bankrupt firms whose lack of performance is covered by soft credits, that is bound to show up sooner or later in the books of banks. As the need to re-capitalize the two leading commercial banks of China in October 2003 (by a sum of $45 bn)

---

[34] Furthermore in the yuan market itself, A shares (open to domestic investors) trade with a large premium over B shares (open to foreigners only). Zhang (1999) develops a formal model explaining the trends and size of this liquidity premium.

indicated, covering up structural problems is neither cheap nor everlasting. The 150 m strong 'roaming population' (people no longer residing in the villages, but not yet registered in cities) is just the tip of the iceberg.

6. Our summary of the salient features of the Chinese system does allow for qualifying it as yet another model of market socialism. On the one hand, the common features of this arrangement, such as retaining party control and a closed economy, can be clearly observed. On the other hand, *Chinese characteristics, such as the long tradition of decentral control, or the predominantly rural society, allowed for different solutions than the one in Eastern Europe.* Furthermore the sustained high rates of economic growth may lend some popularity to a non-elected regime, and provides room for manoeuvre in both political and economic areas. It remains to be seen *if China will prove to be an exception* to the rule of the non-sustainability of market socialist systems.[35]

Is China a Developmental Alternative?

The Chinese experience is very rarely analyzed in comparative terms. While close to 30 years of sustained growth is indeed impressive, one should not forget that, for similar periods, following 1921, 1929 or even 1945, *the Soviet economy did register similarly high growth rates.* Official Soviet growth in the post-1929 period has been comparable to the numbers reported by China. Therefore past growth should not be taken as evidence for further growth in the future. All the less so, since growth rates, especially for the long run, cannot be chosen at will, following abstract 'optimality' criteria. These result from a complex *interaction* of factors, leading to *slower* trend rate of growth in more developed societies (Erdős, 1989; Barro, 1997). Still, the forecasts portraying China as Asia's next giant, the biggest economy of the globe by 2020 and the like, are often based on mechanistic extrapolation of past growth and an indiscriminte use of official Chinese statistics (Wu, 2003). Allowing for this – widespread though methodologically problematic-approach would come close to defying the fundamental insights, called the post-Washington Consensus, that are gained in the past three decades of policy reforms (Buiter et al, 1996).

China may thus look like a realistic alternative to the current 'conventional wisdom' in development theory, a suggestion frequently evoked in the policy debates on NIS (e.g. Nolan, 1995), but also in the wider community of development economists. Below we shall try to address the puzzle, *China growing sustainingly under Communist rule*, without however venturing for a country study. The latter is beyond the scope of a monograph on emerging Europe, while not addressing the issue would leave this argument unduly narrow and removed from global context.

---

[35] In his usual cautious tone, János Kornai (2000, pp. 33–35) assessing the Chinese experience more optimistically than the present author as a 'leadership no less friendly to the market and hostile to democracy than Pinochet', makes it clear, that even in the world of mixed systems there is a qualitative difference between a genuine market and a socialist market economy.

Our hypothesis goes as follows: when taking into consideration the level of development, economic structures and the catch-up potentials in each case, and given the distorted nature of official statistics (well known from other socialist periods and countries) there remains nothing truly puzzling about China (cf. also Chow and Lin, 2002). When we take into account the special circumstances that make China different from Russia, the remarkable Chinese growth, that allowed, among other things, for two peaceful leadership transitions since the death of Deng, *can be explained with the standard theories of development.*

1. A) For the Soviet Union and, later, Russia the role of *central state bureaucracy* has been formative ever since the period of Peter the Great. Likewise, ideological inspiration and legitimacy has been vital for sustaining the power structures. By contrast, in China the Marxian ideological legitimacy has gradually been giving way to nationalism. Furthermore Mao's 'Great Proletarian Cultural Revolution' in 1966–1969 crushed the almighty party and state apparatus. In the following period, especially during the consolidation period of 1976–1979, it could never regain its earlier standing. The government in Beijing could never regain full control in the provinces in the south and in the coastal areas. Ideology itself tended to be discarded, owing to the destruction of cultural,[36] educational and bureaucratic establishments and famine brought about by Mao's revolutionary zeal. *This made a lasting impact on the 'genetic program of the system',* since a mono-archic organization could not be re-instituted. *A decentralized bureaucratic system emerged.*

B) Furthermore, the egalitarian Communist ideology has gradually been replaced by a combination of *nationalism and materialism,* where the ends justify the means. China no longer portrayed itself as the vanguard of the Third World, whose vocation is to support revolutionary movements from Bolivia to South Africa. Even the relations with the one-time war ally, Vietnam turned sour by 1978 (up to the point of armed border clashes). Enrichment and material greed, once portrayed as the mortal sins against the socialist way of life/official ideals have not only become tolerable but even worth emulating, that is elevated to the status of a 'civic virtue'. Enterprise managers emerged as equals (and de facto stronger partners) vis-à-vis party bosses, though the latter have never lost their influence entirely. This had been helpful insofar as the borderlines of what is or is not compatible with socialism can be *continuously re-interpreted* in the course of time. *Ideology, the driving force of the regime also has been changing.*

C) Not aspiring to be a military power well beyond the economic potential of the country, China could avoid the trap of the priorizing large-scale and continuous redistribution of resources in favor of the defense sector. This lasting change *saved it from* one of the worst (surviving) legacies of the Soviet

---

[36] Fighting the music of Beethoven, the 'symbol of capitalist decay' culminated in putting LPs on fire in public gatherings. Universities were closed down. Leading scientists and politicians were sent to re-education camps; Deng himself was being re-educated as a manual worker at a pig farm. Similar practices were emulated in Vietnam, Cambodia and Laos.

model and the resultant *impoverishment of the rural areas*. Certainly, the 'liberalizing' changes do not make Chinese villages rich. But where the issue of famine has resurfaced over the pre-1979 period, the change has been important to Chinese society. On the one hand, petty enterpreneurship could flourish in the villages, allowing for a much better use of potential resources. This is quite important in a country where investment rate is close to 40 per cent in 2006 even reached 46 (!) pc.[37] By the same token, the efficiency of the limited resources remaining for consumption matters much more for living standards than official growth rates. This is why many observers consider 'rural capitalism' as a defining feature of China. On the other hand, field work (Chen, 2002, pp. 359–360) has shown a very partial emergence of what could be called a market for land, and that contributes to *continued low productivity* of the sector. This is therefore a 'socialist market economy', in line with the official dogma. In standard economic terms: *limited market without private property rights*. This is the third major feature of Chinese reforms.

2. Ever since Max Weber, the *'commercial spirit'* has been seen to be at the heart of capitalism as a macro-system. Abolishing the commercial spirit, that used to be one of the supreme ideological objectives under any Communist regime, has largely been accomplished in the Soviet Union. By the same token it is often seen as a major impediment to change in rural Russia, or even in East Germany. By contrast, China conducted lenient policies vis-à-vis small business up until 1958.[38] *Only two decades later*, the reforms of Deng abolished collective farms and allowed for petty capitalism along the NEP lines. This policy may well have failed in Russia, *but in China the commercial spirit was alive and well*. I recall a long discussion with a leading Chinese professional in 1985 in Vienna, where he insisted that I explain how the stock market is compatible with socialism. When I turned to technicalities, he stopped me saying: 'Enough, my son, this is what I remember from my youth'.

This example highlights an important aspect of China[39]: the continued availability of *social capital/social intangibles/tacit knowledge* that play a crucial role in the operation of any market economy (at least in the neo-institutionalist interpretation). It is easy to see why similar arguments can be extended to trade, services and agriculture, requiring much less sophisticated technical knowledge, survival of the commercial spirit could have been even more vigorous.[40] *Therefore, bottom-up evolution of trade and other market forms of*

[37] Economist Intelligence Unit: *Country Report China – Update*, London: November, 2006 (online edition).

[38] The fourth star in the Chinese flag is 'national burgeoisie', reflecting the fact that small business as *not* nationalized in the first decade after the Communist victory in 1949.

[39] These features are conspicuously missing in the countries most eager to emulate the Chinese experience, that is the Central Asian dictatorships and other New Independent States.

[40] Let us not forget that the business community in most of South-East Asia is ethnically Chinese, cultivating intensive relations with mainland brothers and sisters. 90 per cent of FDI in China is overseas Chinese.

exchanges, later more sophisticated transactions, could be relied upon in the course of decentralization as a means of economic policy reform. *Institution-building and the accompanying long learning periods*, plaguing for instance banking reforms in Eastern Europe, *did not need to play a similarly vital role in China.* They could rely on available local knowledge. This is a factor obviously hardly replicable in most other developing countries.

It is an interesting open question whether and to what degree market reforms of large-scale industry and farming as opposed to emergent de novo firms account for the vitality of the Chinese economy. Beyond doubt, the latter do play an important role, and from the point of view of long run dynamics of the evolution of market order.

3. *Regions in China have been largely autonomous.* This is in line with millennia-old Chinese traditions,[41] but is at odds with the way we conceptualize a socialist economy. The latter has traditionally been a centralized management concept ever since Marx, up to attempts to generalize the Soviet experience. In a way, the idea of *competing systems*, developed originally by Hayek, has become a reality. Already in the 1970s the radical reforms in Sichuan Province have gone much farther in allowing for market co-ordination and cutting back party tutelage than the national economic system in China allows nowadays. Abolishing ideological taboos was no major sacrifice as long as the *People's Army*, managed from Beijing, *poses a credible threat* to anybody attempting a violent overthrow of the rulers. Meanwhile, as long as no central ideological approval was needed, in backward Western provinces stone-age Communist command and control practices could be continued.[42] Similarly in the North-East, where most military and related industry is located, more centralized and less tolerant forms of management survived up until today.

All in all, China today is conspicuously lacking the *ideological* and *imperial* features that dominated the Soviet model. The latter required checking the substance of 'the only right way' and its ideological substantiation. Not having the philosophers' stone, even in theory, Chinese Communists can easily live with the continued *co-existence of various management forms within a single diverse country.* As it is cultural community rather than military power that keeps the nation together, this is a viable, though non-replicable policy reform option.

4. *Special economic zones (SEZ)* were created in the late '70s in the coastal areas. An off-shore regime is operating in these areas, thus 'laws of socialism', in their direct and indirect meaning, have been largely suspended. The blossoming of Shenzhen, itself a tiny village in the mid-70s, is a nice example of an attempt to emulate Singapore rather than Hong Kong in development

---

[41] More on that in the bulky summary of Gernet (2001).

[42] As late as in October 2003 computer specialists were imprisoned for transmitting non-approved contents. The ongoing practice of reading aloud the editorials of the party paper, or the use of public executions for punishing corrupt bankers are just a few examples.

terms. While political freedoms continue to be curtailed, economic freedoms are basically observed and public dues remain low. The relevance of these zones is shown by the fact that some calculations attribute no less than 70 per cent of Chinese value creation to them. These also represent the shop-window of modern and prosperous China under Communist rule also for the domestic population. However, analysts find *little or no convergence among the regions inside China.* As Bhalla et al (2003, pp. 37–38) explain, capital resources tended to be disproportionately allocated to the coastal provinces, thus the potential trickle down has actually been *diminishing.* The neglect of infrastructure and transport facilities continued and the provision of public goods in the West remained inadequate. Similar conclusions are reached, with a difference in emphasis, by the analysis of Dayal-Gulati and Husain (2002). In their empirical study of the spillover effects FDI though does contribute to intra-regional convergence, thus limited spillover is demonstrable. However, given the strong concentration of FDI to the coastal regions the development *level* across the regions has been *diverging.* The classic colonial *dual structure* has thus been reproduced under (or despite of) Communist rule.

Unsurprisingly there is no free transit for ordinary citizens to these zones. All the less so, since the spillover effects from labor intensive, processing and export-oriented FDI has been minimal to date according to empirical analyses (Fu, 2004); therefore, as the source quoted above notes these only *exacerbated the relative backwardness* in inland areas. If we abstract away from the problems ensuing form a dual structure, well elaborated in traditional development economics, SEZ constitute a success. Here, the tradeoff between economic and political controls did work, as the transitory nature of special concessions did not yet allow for any countervailing force to the Communist Party to emerge. On the other hand, as the analysis of Wen (2004, p. 341) highlights, public policies have immediately contributed to the increased geographical concentration of activities. In other words, the disadvantages of Western provinces, originating in location, poverty and lack of infrastructure have only been *exacerbated* by this option.

5. A further feature of Chinese development, highlighted by some analysts (Sun, 1997) is the pivotal role played by *a long continuum of non-state activities that are by no means private.* This fact is often overlooked in large panel/global comparisons of privatization, also in the ones quoted in the comparative empirical chapter, where non-state property – de-statization – is automatically counted as part of the private sector. The role of township-village enterprises, managed by locally appointed managers, or agricultural ventures dealing in part, on fixed prices and set routes, but in part in free prices and free trade channels are cases in point. However, as Xia (2003) explains, even in joint stock form of TVE stocks are non-tradable, thus they may be seen as *a promise of, rather than an embodiment of* private property rights. A number of China watchers attribute the success of China to these non-public forms of ownership

It is hard to measure their performance, and *it is equally hard to settle,* even in theory, *where state property ends and private property begins* (Yu, 2000). More importantly, save for intensive field studies, it is hard to determine the extent to which these work according to the logic of the market. The TVEs and farming units are, for instance, severely constrained in their ability to accumulate and invest. Thus in microeconomic terms they were hard to describe as asset value maximizing ventures. Empirical studies of over 80 firms have shown (Chang et al, 2003) that the effect of managerial incentives on the returns on assets remained quite small. By contrast performance was significantly better with better defined private property rights. Still, despite their obvious limitations, TVEs are obviously not the model bureaucratic units either, caring only about public purpose, ideology, or their own convenience.

On the other hand, as the extensive empirical study by Huchet and Richet (2002) has shown, the Chinese corporate sector can no longer be described through a single model of top-down control; a variety of forms and methods emerged, party control is varying – often to nominal. The two French authors differentiate not less than seven models along the continuum and report of a variety of new, market-oriented methods and *a great variety of hybrid forms*. However, in their conclusion they also *caution against the idea that competition alone, short of tackling issues of transparency, accountability and property rights could 'take care of the issues'*. Also Party control, they claim, put limitations to the ways and strength of competition, though more in the large-scale state-owned sector than elsewhere.

6. Mention has already been made of *foreign direct investment* that ranges from $40 to 45 bn a year. This is *twenty times that of Russia* in the 2000–2004 period, and one of *the largest inflows to any developing country*. Since Chinese per capita GDP at the exchange rate was only $1131 in 2001 according to the World Bank, *such a major inflow could substantially influence, even define the pattern of investment allocation*.

This is good news from the point of view of efficiency and welfare, since it explains favorable differences against the centralized and ideologically prejudiced practices of the Soviet model. It is bad news if we consider that non-central allocation implies the involvement of local party bosses, rather than the capital market. Thus some of the most trivial gigantic prestige projects – such as the reversion of Siberian rivers in the Soviet Union – may be aborted at an early stage. However other, less gigantic, but equally poorly founded ones may be realized. No economic control over these is exerted, the rule of law and transparency remain non-existent. The accounting problems would only multiply under this model.

Since local banks are, at the end of the day, in the hands of the local party bosses, the practice of soft crediting and rolling over any debt in a major priority investment is given. According to a central thesis of the monograph by Lin (2001), success in Chinese market positively requires the manipulation of the (local) state. This process is what he terms 'favor seeking', a bargaining process well described in the reforms of Hungary (Antal, 1983) and Yugoslavia (Soós, 1986) in the reform socialist period. These practices have been at the root of collapse of market socialism in Yugoslavia, Poland and Hungary in the 1980s. Therefore this feature should not be so benevolently overlooked as has become customary among China watchers.

Generalizing the experience of frontrunners of transition Michael Keren and Gur Ofer (2003, pp. 254–256) highlight the interconnection of *legal infrastructure and foreign bank entry*, that may be the final solution. On the one hand, if legal arrangements are inadequate, FDI in the banking sector remains limited. On the other hand, Central European experience has shown a strong positive correlation between foreign bank entry and performance of the financial sector. Foreign entry has also helped to upgrade the originally backward financial legislation and improve prudential supervision. This component seems to be entirely missing in China at the time of writing. While the dynamic consequences of this circumstance are clear and call for downward revisions of Chinese growth potential, in the short and medium run this does not necessarily show up in the numbers of economic activity. Therefore it is congruous with our assessment to underscore that *the success of Chinese exports is attributable to a large degree to the special zones and FDI flowing therein.*

7. *Fiscal federalism* has been a major feature of Chinese development since the mid-80s. This implies limited central interference in many affairs, corporate and political alike. This is good news for the center, able to devolute thus responsibilities for strain. Political and economic problems are thus less likely to cumulate into a single big bang. But it is also good news if seen from the point of view of firms and independent-minded regions. On the other hand, as seen in Yugoslavia, Hungary and Yeltsin's Russia, *decentralization without responsibility* for the outcomes of economic activity (especially in the banking sector and at the stock exchange) may create trouble for many reasons. The responsible conduct of professional fiscal and monetary policy does require central supervision, central implementation powers, and yes, control over lower level organs. Otherwise, money creation becomes decentralized and un-controllable as does tax collection. The latter may become a problem for the central state as seen in Russia between 1992 and 1998. Moreover, the *inflation and lack of transparency that is covered up in an arbitrary financial system may explode,* sooner or later creating a crisis known from inter-war proportions and seen again in both the cases of Soviet Union and Yugoslavia.

At the time of writing, as noted above, the Chinese government was forced to engage *in the fourth consecutive re-capitalization of the banking system* in the past twenty-five years. The fact, reported in Xia (2003) that the role of stock exchange has been diminishing both in absorbing private savings and in financing corporations. This is due to lack of transparency, lack of enforceable regulation and the resultant series of scandals. The outcome would be hard not to interpret as a writing on the wall. This is also a major reason for the extremely low overall efficiency of investments stressed by IMF studies (reported in Wolf, 2003), that contrast the capital intensive period of Korean development, when the ICOR was around 2.5 with those of current China, where the ICOR[43] is close to 5 (sic!). In macro-economic terms it means that the *efficiency of Chinese growth is only half of the Korean standard*.

8. In a system dominated by hybrid forms and non-transparency in basically all aspects of the economic system, *contract enforcement is anything but trivial*. Lack of formalization does not allow litigation and court decisions to play a formative role in conflict management. The special Chinese arrangement filling this gap is called '*guanxhi*,' which is the Asian equivalent of private enforcement mechanisms, known in 19th century US and Italy as maffia. In a recent analysis of this institution Schramm and Taube (2003) highlight the club good character of the arrangement: it works until the number of participants is small. In the Chinese case it means that the *guanxhi* developed into a network of networks. Anybody wishing to be sure of contract enforcement must be a member, otherwise not even high spot prices or bribes may do the job. The above quoted analysis also highlights the inherent reasons why this arrangement is *unlikely to be transformed into a formal legal system*, despite WTO membership of China. The tradition of avoiding law that is perceived as a tool of state repression strengthens this likelihood. Thus informalism, a feature that is known to be a component of laggards, is unlikely to change soon.

9. The sustainability of market socialist systems is questionable because of the theory and empirical material summarized earlier in this chapter. Not only is this so for abstract reasons of theory, that is the inevitable clash between the logic of bureaucratic and market co-ordination. Country evidence has also been showing toward the inherent instability of all forms of market socialism. These regimes either tend to regress into centralized bureaucratic control, or evolve into free markets. In the Chinese case *regionalism defining the overall state structure allows for a long period of sustainability*, since local power is not directly a function of central state structures, as was the case both in Yugoslavia and the Soviet Union. Financial repression did create a crisis in East Asia in 1997–1999, and has left many casualties. A roaming population close to 10 per cent of overall citizenry rarely bode well for public security. Living in a country with one of the worst Gini coefficients is by no means conducive to political stability. The urbanization crisis has been a source of discontent in all developing nations.

10. We can only speculate, for how long and in what form the centralized Communist power structures, lacking transparency and rule of law, will be compatible with the market forces. *If China does meet WTO obligations, i.e. if it makes its currency convertible, and makes its accounting practices transparent, it is unlikely to retain the socialist features of its economy for long*. The big question is if this change can be peaceful and orderly, or will happen

---

[43] Incremental Capital-Output Ratio/ICOR is the standard measure of showing how much investment is needed to get an additional unit of output, at the margin; thus this is the conventional measure of investment efficiency in growth theory.

via a bloody *revolution that was the case in the 17–20th centuries in the Middle Empire.*[44]

One should not forget that China is located in the region where the developmental state emerged and survived for decades. Where it has collapsed, per capita GDP levels way above the current Chinese value hare been attained. Nor is any of the newly industrialized countries any longer a predominantly rural society, as China has been. In other words, we may agree with the IMF analyses quoted above in seeing *yet another decade for fast* (8–9 per cent) *GDP growth for China plausible,* even under Communist rule.

However, in the long run *development perspective,* this potential alone *does not tell too much.* In poor countries, where the room for relocating hundreds of millions of people from low productivity farming to high productivity industry is given, relatively high rates of factor intensive growth is in line with what one would expect on the basis of standard growth theory (an argument first advanced by Paul Krugman (1994) and proven in academic terms by Alwyn Young (1995). But we also know from economics that growth based on structural effects is a one-shot exercise, as was the case in the Soviet Union or Japan for that matter. Later, however, conditions of endogenous growth require more sophisticated forms of management, and more diversified sources of sustainable development. Therefore *the long run perspective is likely to differ from the short and medium term view*: market socialism is viable in the medium run, even though a comparison to free market Hong Kong speaks for itself (in terms of development alternatives).

11. The question of the *developmental sub-state* needs to be addressed. Is not a provincial government in China by and large equal to the developmental state in Taiwan or Malaysia? The question is if the theories generalizing the experience of newly industrializing countries may be adopted to Chinese provinces. These are, as we have seen the major non-market actors of development in the most populous country of the globe. We tend to doubt the validity of this comparison. At the end, the core state always put limits on what is feasible for any province staying within its limits, as explained in our chapter on 'Transnational markets and local politics'. The Tienanmen massacre in 1989, and its softer follow-up, the crushing of the pro-democracy movement in 2002 already indicated this. Meanwhile the *role of networks and other informal institutions* of the Chinese ethnic community (Hermann-Pillath, 1993b) over and above the state borders may be seen as a very modern phenomenon, in line with the growing role of networks in orchestrating economic activity in the information age (an issue discussed in several other chapters of this book) These help overcome the cumulative lagging behind that daunted the countries of the Soviet model.

---

[44] In the extensive and critical assessment of the Hungarian edition László Muraközy (2006, p. 81) raises the serious point that China, as of now, has already transgressed the borderline of market socialism. In view of the limitations, especially on formal institutions and private property, listed in our 14 points above, we perhaps have to agree to disagree.

By the same token, these forms may lend support to the continued existence of an unchanged status quo (while changing structures at the micro-level), and act as lubricants of pro-market change, *undermining the centralized control* in both the economy and society. It is objectively impossible to predict what way the interactions will produce an outcome. However field work on the role of informal structures (Wang, 2001 esp. p. 174) indicate that these are likely to remain dominant over formal rules, basically over any form of Westernization, and more likely to *inhibit any change towards open markets* and open society.

12. Finally, we should address some of the *academic debates on the nature of the Chinese model*. These revolve around the role of competition and hardening of budget constraints. Tian (2002) argues that lacking a competitive environment can produce situations, where public firms outperform their private competitors. His conclusion is that creating competition is a precondition to successful privatization. By contrast Li et al (2000) conclude that the competition on commodity markets, already strongly present, supports performance-oriented selection of both firms and their managers. Banks, according to the evidence completed by Park and Shen (2003) turn their backs to public and semi/public firms and focus on the private sector and follow considerations of return, not informal expectations of party bosses. This process creates a counterweight to bureaucracy. Similarly, the emerging competition among regions will impose severe limitations on attempts at regional autarky.

In the same line, Cull and Yu (2000) report the growing role of credit finance in corporate decisions and the resultant hardening budget constraints. In the same line Yu (2000) describes the growing role of meritocracy in setting manager pay. Later analyses of the same authors (Cull and Xu, 2003) underline a paradox in this evolution. While corporate independence and access to bank credit are growingly correlated, the intertwining between crediting and profitability is *diminishing* because of the ever more frequent rescheduling of corporate bad debts by the banks. In other words, competition on the product markets fell short of hardening the budget constraints of enterprises and banks alike. These changes though clearly represent a move towards more market coordination, still, as OECD (2000) notes, *fall short of addressing the problems of corporate governance, fiscal reforms and lack of transparency.*

Therefore, what we face is an atypical Janus faced market socialist process, where the internal dynamics of reform moves toward free markets, even though these are a long way off (cf. also Gang, 2003 and the discussion of this point below). If there is any lesson from the three market socialist experiments surveyed in the preceding sections, it is the clear empirical evidence that in developmental/historical perspective *the issue of property cannot be avoided*. Sooner or later, the need to evaluate assets correctly, allocate these in chunks, allow for heritage emerges (that may allow for the adoption of long time horizons in terms of asset value maximizing). The latter will either call for actual, rather than virtual private property, or the suppression of competition to narrowly defined limits so that it should not undermine bureaucratic control.[45]

13. We have quoted Douglass North (2003) highlighting the crucial importance of *formal institutions* against informal solutions *in turning the market*, a millennia-old institution, into a modern capitalist institution and *the engine of growth*. In his theory, it is impersonal contacts, formalization that allow for the locomotive role of accumulation and exchange (a view shared by the late Lord Peter Bauer (2000) and others). If this is the case, the continued informalism that has been a defining feature of Chinese institutional system is a paradox. The real paradox, according to this view, is much less why China can grow under Communist role, but a different one. In our interpretation, *if the market remains a pre-modern institution,* due to its culturally determined mode of functioning, than the spread of market co-ordination should not be equated with overall modernization. Field work by Susan Whiting (2001) in three provinces seem to indicate that this is indeed the case. *Informal command structures,* often related to the Communist Party matter more than free market considerations of various sort, though the latter of course are growing in importance.

This state of art hardly allows for the reading (as in Shevchenko, 2004, pp. 180) describing this type of Communist Party involvement in economic administration as 'productive and socially efficient' under the angle of second bet theory, that is known to be superior in addressing real world situations than abstract normative approaches like ours. Though the presence of the party does mean that institutional vacuum, a problem of early transition period has not emerged. However the involvement of party bosses in entrepreneurial activities is anything but helpful from the point of view of modernizing considerations, let alone plain efficiency at the micro level.

It is rather telling that the same journal issue carrying the above cited – and in some circle majority – interpretation of the Chinese experience two ethnic Chinese scholars conduct an analysis of a more mundane side of the same, which is corruption. Gou and Hu (2004, esp. pp. 272 and 277) explain, that the monopoly position of the Communist party creates a strong incentive to create rents. This takes place through administrative monopoly. The latter exists in the sectoral and regional dimensions alike. The peculiarity of the situation is the *incentive to create and sustain rents* at the cost of consumer welfare. The outcome is a sizeable and proven inefficiency of redistribution of wealth and income to 'directly unproductive profit seeking activities', to use the established term of Bhagwati. Furthermore, as the authors show, this contribute to the lasting segmentation of the Chinese market, that is giving up one of its more obvious advantages.

14. It might be interesting to test *if lack of formal judicial institutions will constrain growth and property reform in China, and if yes, how.* A recent agnostic paper

---

[45] This point is demonstrated in detail in the two large international projects assessing the lessons of market socialism, as presented in Wagener (ed., 1998) and (Kaase–Sparschuch–Wenninger (eds, 2002).

by Feld and Voigt (2003, esp. pp. 516–518) has indicated that, similarly to central banks, real rather than formal independence of courts is what matters. While formal independence has been shown to have no effect on growth in a panel of 71 countries, by contrast, real judicial independence has shown favorable results in 57 of these. But this finding is also contingent upon the influence of other economic and institutional factors. This may prompt decision-makers to delay legal reform, that *may well backfire by sustaining the unclear status of private property rights and of formalization of impersonal relations.*

This is precisely the line taken by official reform economists (Gang, 2003) that consider the continuation of the process, short of political reforms, and relying on improvisation – the only way open to them. But these are long run constraints. The 'unlimited supply of labor' a la Singer and Lewis still allows for China to grow in a factor intensive manner for a decade at least. Still, it is hard to overlook the fact that in the first years of 2000s, a healthy dose of *fiscal stimulus* rather than the market, allowed for the sustaining dynamism. The quality of this growth, however, and the move towards real market, may be a different matter. For one, Ahrens (2001, chapter 7) highlights the limits to ad-hoc solutions. This point may be especially valid in the future, with the Chinese economy and society growing not only in quantity, but turning itself into *more complex structures* that need more sophisticated forms of regulation.

Marketization without modernization might therefore be a shorthand form for the Chinese paradox. As long as we accept that countries like Bolivia, Moldova, or for that matter, Sri Lanka as market economies, that may and do function without 'necessarily' producing social, cultural and other 'by-products' of modernity in the sense of Max Weber, this is not so much perplexing.[46] For it is not the mere existence of certain institutions, rather *their quality which is decisive for the long term economic and social outcomes* (Srinivasan, 2003). By the same token, the Chinese paradox is in need of major redefinition against the majority view in the literature. The question is therefore neither growth nor Communist ideology, or not even the usefulness of neither public nor private forms of property. The big unresolved issue is modernity, and if there is a movement toward that direction.[47]

Concluding Remarks

The jury is still out over the merits and de-merits of the Chinese model. What we tried to argue in this chapter is a broad generalization in comparative economic systems, non-country-specific view of analytical economics. We adopt a comparative approach. In so doing, we addressed the Chinese experience of policy reform in terms of market socialism. We have demonstrated the funda-

[46] On the lasting and important differences among models see the book of Dore (2000).

[47] In her account of Chinese charges Csanádi (2006) qualifies China as a case of self-exploitative model that is sound to be stretched to its inherent limitation soon.

mental similarity of this model to other forms of market socialism. We have also highlighted the special circumstances that allow for China to grow within such an eclectic system, that seems to defy all theories.

On the other hand, it would be hard to overlook major *similarities of China with the experience of other East Asian developmental states,* especially of Japan in the 1950–1990 period, but also South Korea or Taiwan or Singapore.[48] If we accept that large country size allows for less opening, thus a longer life span of a functionally closed system, this should apply to China. While this consideration may in part explain the past, it remains to be seen to what extent WTO membership will change this side condition. The Chinese experience looks, indeed, if torn out of this broader context, as defying all pre-existing theories and country experiences. *But it does not, and existing theories allow for explaining what we observe in China in empirical terms.*

The success of China over the past three decades seems to have been driven by *a series of factors that are not replicable in other countries.* Most important of these include the millennium long tradition of decentralization, the survival of the commercial spirit and the major role of the cross-border cultural community of ethnic Chinese. It is worth calling attention to statistical analyses (Wu, 2003) that question much of the official reporting by the Chinese government. Friedrich Wu also shows that *very high factor inputs and non-replicable structural factors* explain the high growth rates (cf. the evidence provided in Chow and Lin, 2002).[49] This was also seen in the Soviet Union in the 1930s, '40s and '50s. Economic theory is quite clear about the limitations of a growth pattern based on high factor inputs only (Easterly and Levine, 2001). Others (Lo and Tian, 2002) explain that if accounted properly, the superiority of private property over all other property forms in China, in terms of efficiency can already be proven. This is in line with 'conventional economic wisdom' and challenges culturalist claims of Chinese exceptionality.

Finally, it is time to answer the original question. *There does NOT seem to exist something called the Chinese puzzle.* Our finding received a strong empirical backing from a basically statistical-empirical analysis by Alwyn Young (2003) of Stanford, disentangling the component of growth in China for the 1978–1998 period. He finds that systematic understatement of inflation accounts for 2.5 per cent of growth per year. Likewise, the 'usual suspects' for high growth in poor countries, such as rising participation rates, improvement in educational attainment, the transfer of labor from agriculture to industry account for most

[48] One of the very few comparative perspectives is offered by the volume edited by Maria Weber (2001), exploring the issue from the point of view of corporate governance.

[49] In the EACES conference where the preliminary version of this chapter was presented as a keynote, a lively debate emerged if Chinese statistics indeed overstate growth, or due to lack of controls and the expansion of SMEs rather underreport, or the two tendencies may eventually even out, as Silvana Malle suggested. Whatever is the case, the sources quoted in the main text offer a detailed methodology for the *downward revision*. The well-known fact of under-investment in infrastructure and environmental protection would certainly deduce from the developmental, but also from the growth performance in any meaningful calculation.

of the remainder. Sustained labor productivity gain in the range of 2.6 per cent (op. cit. pp. 1259) is respectable though, but 'can be seen nothing short of miraculous'. He also interprets the findings as 'a testament of misguided nature of plan policies that kept the peasantry tied up in agriculture, by restricting rural – urban migration and limiting the development of non – agricultural activities, while saddling it with inefficient and alien organizational structures'.

Given the dominance of farming in employment much of the growth originated in agriculture. In view of the specifics, including level of development and complexity of social structure, the parallel drawn between China and Central or Eastern Europe seems basically misplaced. While everything may well be compared to anything, in meaningful analyses attempts must be made to compare structures/cases of identical level of development, complexity and the like. The call to 'look Eastward for a successful model' (Nolan, 2001) is not well established, since this normative cannot be followed. Unless falling back to a pre-industrial structure, or developing something comparable to the Chinese cultural community, *no country in transition, and definitely none of the NIS should look to the East for a developmental alternative.*

Also if we draw the historical parallel, it is unlikely that a more professional Khruschev or a more reform-minded Brezhnev could have adopted the Chinese way, since the peculiar driving forces have always been missing from the Russian context (for good or bad). By contrast, Chinese reformers can still gain a lot from studying mature and overripe socialist reforms in Central Europe in the 1980s as well as the failures of their transition. Notwithstanding our theoretical skepticism it is beyond doubt that the way China will settle its problems will be an issue to be watched for decades to come, and not only for the two traditional groups of China analysts, but also for academic economists with a comparative orientation.

References

AHRENS, J. (2001): *Governance and Economic Development: a Comparative Institutional Approach.* Cheltenham/Glos/UK and Northampton/MA/USA: Edward Elgar Publishing Company.

ANTAL, L. (1983): Conflicts of financial planning and regulation: On the nature of restrictions. *Acta Oeconomica,* vol. 30. no. (3–4), pp. 199–224.

BALASSA, B. (1993): Outward orientation. In: BALASSA, B.: *Policy Choices for the 1990s.* Basingstoke and London: MacMillan, pp. 3–55.

BALCEROWICZ, L. (1995): The 'socialist calculation debate' and reform discussions in socialist countries. In: BALCEROWICZ, L.: *Socialism, Capitalism, Transformation.* London-New York-Budapest: Central European University Press, pp. 35–50.

BARA, Z. and SZABÓ, K. eds (2000): *Gazdasági intézmények, országok, rendszerek.* (Economic institutions, countries and systems). Budapest: Aula Publishing Co.

BARRO, R. (1997): *Determinants of Economic Growth: A Cross-Country Empirical Study.* Cambridge/Mass. and London: The MIT Press.

BAUER, T. (1981): *Tervgazdaság, beruházás, ciklusok.* (Planned economy, investments, cycles). Budapest: Közgazdasági és Jogi Könyvkiadó.

BAUER, T. (1983): The Hungarian alternative to Soviet-type planning. *Journal of Comparative Economics*, vol. 7. no. 3. pp. 304–316.

BENCE, Gy. and KIS, J. (1972/1992): *Hogyan lehetséges kritikai gazdaságtan?* (How to construct critical economics?). Budapest: a book originally published in *samizdat* in 1972 and later made available by a joint edition of T-Twins and Lukács Archives, Budapest.

BEREND, T. I. (1990): *A History of Hungarian Economic Reforms, 1953–1988*. Cambridge and New York: Cambridge University Press.

BHALLA, A. – YAO, Sh. – ZHANG, Z. (2003): Regional economic performance in China. *Economics of Transition*, vol. 11. no. 1. pp. 25–39.

BORNSTEIN, M. ed (1994): *Comparative Economic Systems: Models and Cases*. 7d edition. Burr Ridge – Sidney etc.: IRWIN.

BRUS, W. (1972): *The Market in a Socialist Economy*. London: Routledge and Kegan Paul.

BRUS, W. and LASKI, K., (1989): *From Marx to Market: Socialism in Search of an Economic System*. Oxford: Oxford University Press (reprinted in 1992).

BUITER, W. – LAGO, R. and STERN, N. (1996): Promoting an efficient market economy in a changing world. London: *CEPR Discussion Paper* no1468 (October).

BURKETT,J. (1994): Self-managed market socialism and the Yugoslav economy, 1950–1991.In: BORNSTEIN, M. ed.: *Comparative Economic Systems: Models and Cases*. Burr Ridge etc.: Irwin, pp. 322–352.

CARR, E. (1976): *Foundations of a Planned Economy*, vol. II. Harmondsworth/UK: Penguin Books.

CARR, E. and DAVIES, R. (1974): *Foundations of a Planned Economy*, vol. I., (1926–1929). Harmondsworth/UK: Penguin Books.

CHANG, Ch. – MCCALL, B. – WANG, Y. (2003): Incentive contracting versus ownership reforms: evidence from China's township and village enterprises. *Journal of Comparative Economics*, vol. 31. no. 3. pp. 414–428.

CHEN, Ch.-H. (2002): Property rights and rural development in China's transitional economy. *Economics of Planning*, vol. 35. no. 4. pp. 349–363.

CHEN, K. – JEFFERSON, G. – SINGH, I. (1992): Lessons from China's economic reforms. *Journal of Comparative Economics*, vol. 16. no. 2. pp. 201–225.

CHOW, G. and LIN, A. (2002): Accounting for economic growth in Taiwan and mainland China: a comparative analysis. *Journal of Comparative Economics*, vol. 30. no. 3. pp. 507–530.

CULL, R. and YU, L.-C. (2000): Bureaucrats, state banks and the efficiency of credit allocation: the experience of Chinese state-owned enterprises. *Journal of Comparative Economics*, vol. 28. no. 1. pp. 1–31.

CULL, R. and XU, L.-C. (2003): Who gets credit? The behavior of bureaucrats and state banks in allocation of credit to Chinese SOE. *Journal of Development Economics*, vol. 71. no. 2. pp. 533–559.

CSABA, L. (1990): *Eastern Europe in the World Economy*. Cambridge and New York: Cambridge University Press.

CSABA, L. (1992): Macroeconomic policy in Hungary: poetry versus reality. *Soviet Studies*, vol. 44. no. 6. pp. 947–964.

CSABA, L. (1995): *The Capitalist Revolution in Eastern Europe*. Cheltenham/UK and Northampton/USA: Edward Elgar Publishing Co.

CSABA, L. (2002): Economics: Hungary. In: KAASE, M. – SPARSCHUCH, V. – WENINGER, A., eds: *Handbook of Three Social Sciences in Central and Eastern Europe. Economics, Political Science, Sociology*. Berlin-Budapest-Brussels: a book jointly published by GESIS Center for Information, Collegium Budapest and the Fifth Framework program of the EU Commission, pp. 83–101.

CSANÁDI, M. (2006): *Self-Consuming Evolutions*. Budapest: Akadémiai Kiadó.

DAYAL-GULATI, A. and HUSAIN, A. (2002): Centripetal forces in China's economic takeoff. *IMF Staff Papers*, vol. 49. no. 3. pp. 364–394.

DORE, R., (2000): *Stock Market Capitalism: Japan and Germany versus the Anglo-Saxons*. Oxford and New York: Oxford University Press.

EASTERLY, W. and LEVINE, H. (2001): It is not factor accumulation: stylized facts and growth models. *World Bank Economic Review*, vol. 15. no. 2. pp. 177–220.

ERDŐS, T. (1989): *Growth Rate and Growth Path*. Budapest: Akadémiai Kiadó.

FELD, L. P. and VOIGT, S. (2003): Economic growth and judicial independence: Cross-country evidence using a new set of indicators. *European Journal of Political Economy*, vol. 19. no. 3. pp. 497–527.

FU, X.-L. (2004): Limited linkages from growth engines and regional disparities in China. *Journal of Comparative Economics*, vol. 32. no. 1. pp. 148–164.

GANG, Fan (2003): The dual transformation of China: Past 20 years and 50 years ahead. In: KOLODKO, G. W. ed.: *Emerging Market Economies: Globalization and Development*. Aldershot/UK and Burlington, VT/USA, pp. 169–186.

GEDEON, P. (2003): *Piac és demokrácia*. (Market and democracy). Budapest: Aula Publishing House.

GERNET, J. (2001): *A kínai civilizació története*. (History of Chinese civilization). Budapest: Osiris Kiadó.

GIDDENS, A. (1998): *The Third Way and Its Critics*. London: Polity Press.

GLIGOROV, V. (1998): Yugoslav economics facing reform and dissolution. In: WAGENER, H.-J., ed.: *Economic Thought in Communist and Post-Communist Europe*. London: Routledge, pp. 329–361.

GREGORY, P. (2003): Soviet defense puzzles: archives, strategy and under-fulfillment. *Europe-Asia Studies*, vol. 55. no. 6. pp. 923–938.

GUO, Y. and HU, A. (2004): The administrative monopoly in China's economic transition. *Communist and Post-Communist Studies*, vol. 37. no. 2. pp. 265–280.

HANSON, Ph. (2003): *The Rise and Fall of the Soviet Economy, 1945–1991*. London: Pearson Education.

HAYEK, F. A. (1940): Socialist calculation: the 'competitive' solution. *Economica*, new series, vol. 7. no. 26. pp. 125–149. In: Hayek, F. A.: *Individualism and Economic Order*. Chicago: Chicago, Regnery, 1948, pp. 181–208.

HÁMORI, B. (2000): Reformszocialista kísérletek. Piaci szocializmus, avagy a reformok korlátai. (Reform socialist attempts. Market socialism or the limits to reform). In: BARA, Z. and SZABÓ, K. eds: *Gazdasági rendszerek, országok, intézmények*. (Economic systems, countries, institutions). Budapest: Aula Publishing House, pp. 269–325.

HEITGER, B. (1991): Wirtschaftliches Wachstum in Ost und West, 1950–1985. *Die Weltwirtschaft*, no. 1. pp. 173–192.

HERMANN-PILLATH, C. (1993a): Informal constraints, culture and incremental transition from plan to market. In: WAGENER, H.-J. ed.: *On the Theory and Policy of Systemic Change*. Heidelberg and New York: Physica Verlag, pp. 95–120.

HERMANN-PILLATH, C. (1993b): China's transition to the market: A paradox of transformation and its institutionalist solution. In: WAGENER, H.-J. ed.: *The Political Economy of Transformation* . Heidelberg and New York: Physica Verlag, pp. 209–241.

HUANG, Y.-Sh. (2003): *Selling China: Foreign Direct Investment During the Reform Era*. Cambridge and New York: Cambridge University Press.

HUCHET, J.-F. and RICHET, X. (2002): Between bureaucracy and the market: Chinese industrial groups in search of new forms of corporate governance. *Post-Communist Economies*, vol. 14. no. 2. pp. 170–201.

JACOBY, H. – LI, G. – ROZELLE, S. (2002): Hazards of expropriation: Tenure insecurity and investment in rural China. *American Economic Review,* vol. 92. no. 5. pp. 1420–1447.

JEFFERSON, G. and RAWSKI, Th. (2002): China's emerging market for property rights. *Economics of Transition,* vol. 10. no. 3. pp. 585–617.

KAASE, M. – SPARSCHUCH, V. – WENNINGER, A. eds: (2002): *Handbook of Three Social Sciences in Central and Eastern Europe, 1989–2001 (Political Science, Economics, Sociology).* Budapest-Berlin-Brussels: a book jointly published by Collegium–Budapest, Gesis–IZB Berlin and 5th Framework Program of EU Commission, Brussels.

KEREN, M. and OFER, G. (2003): Globalization and the role of foreign banks in economies in transition. In: KOLODKO, G. W. ed.: *Emerging Market Economies: Globalization and Development.* Aldershot/UK and Burlington/VT/USA: Ashgate Publishing Ltd, pp. 237–266.

KOLODKO, G. W. (2000): *From Shock to Therapy: The Political Economy of Post-Communist Transition.* Oxford etc.: Oxford University Press for WIDER.

KORNAI, J. (1980): *The Economics of Shortage.* Amsterdam: North Holland.

KORNAI, J. (1986): The Hungarian reform process: visions, hopes and the reality. *Journal of Economic Literature,* vol. 24. no. 4. pp. 1687–1737.

KORNAI, J. (1992): *The Socialist System: The Political Economy of Communism.* London etc.: Clarendon Press.

KORNAI, J. (1995): Market socialism revisited. In: KORNAI, J.: *Highway and Byways.* Cambridge/Mass. and London: The MIT Press, p. 1–34.

KORNAI, J. (2000): What the change of system from socialism to capitalism does and does not mean. *Journal of Economic Perspectives,* vol. 14. no. 1. pp. 27–42.

KRUGMAN, P. (1994): The myth of Asia's miracle. *Foreign Affairs,* vol. 73. no. 6. pp. 62–78.

LI, Sh. – LI, Sh. – ZHANG, W. (2000): The road to capitalism: Competition and institutional change in China. *Journal of Comparative Economics,* vol. 28. no. 2. pp. 269–292.

LIN, Y.-M., (2000): *Between Politics and Markets: Firms, Competition and Institutional Change in Post-Mao China.* Cambridge and New York: Cambridge University Press.

LO, V. and TIAN, X. (2002): Property rights, productivity gains and economic growth: The Chinese experience. *Post-Communist Economies,* vol. 14. no. 2. pp. 245–258.

MADZAR, L. (2000): A singular constraint on the economic development on the FR of Yugoslavia. In: BRZESKI, A. and WINIECKI, J. eds: *A Liberating Economic Journey.* London: The Cromwell Press for CRCE, pp. 339–365.

MALINVAUD, E. (1967): Decentralized procedures for plannig. In: BACHARACH, M. and MALINVAUD, E. eds: *Activity Analysis in the Theory of Growth and Planning.* Houndmills/UK, MacMillan and New York: St. Martin's Press, pp. 170–208.

MENCINGER, J. (1991): From socialism to capitalism and from dependence to independence: the double transition of Slovenia. *Est-Ovest,* (Italy), vol. 22. no. 5. pp. 57–92.

MIHÁLYI, P. (1992): *Socialist Investment Cycles: An Analysis in Retrospect.* Dordrecht and New York: Kluwer Publishers.

von MISES, L. (1920/1976): Economic calculation in the socialist commonwealth. In: NOVE, A. and NUTI, M. eds: *Socialist Economics.* Harmondsworth/UK: Penguin Books, pp. 75–91. – originally published In: *Archiv für Sozialwissenschaft und Sozialpolitik,* vol. 47. no. 1. (1920), pp. 86–121.

MURAKÖZY, L. (2004): *Yet Another Change of Regime.* University of Debrecen: Faculty of Economics, Competitio Book Series, no. 3. (September).

MURAKÖZY, L. (2006): A történelmi puzzle (The historic puzzle). *Competitio,* vol. 5. no. 3. pp. 69–82.

NOLAN, P. (1995): *China's Rise, Russia's Fall: Politics, Economics and Planning in the Transformation from Stalinism.* New York: St. Martin's Press.

NOLAN, P. (2001): *China in the Global Economic System*. Cambridge and New York: Cambridge University Press.

NORTH, D. (2003): 'Understanding the Process of Economic Change' – keynote address to the 7th Convention of the International Society for New Institutional Economics, entitled '*Institutions and Change*', Budapest Corvinus University, 11 September, 2003.

NOVE, A. (1992): *An Economic History of the USSR. (Last and Final Edition)*. Harmondsworth/UK-Sidney etc.: Penguin Books.

NOVE, A. and NUTI, M. D. eds (1976): *Socialist Economics*. Harmondsworth/UK: Penguin Books.

OECD (2000): *Reforming China's State Owned Enterprises*. Paris: A publication of the Industrial Economics Division.

PARK, A. and SHEN, M. G. (2003): Joint liability lending and the rise and fall of China's TVE. *Journal of Development Economics*, vol. 71. no. 2. pp. 497–531.

POZNANSKI, K. (1999): Transition as large-scale institutional disintegration. *Acta Oeconomica*, vol. 50. no (1–2), pp. 1–36.

SAKS, S. (1994): The Yugoslav firm. In: BORNSTEIN, M. ed.: *Comparative Economic Systems: Models and Cases*. Burr Ridge etc.: Irwin, pp. 300–321.

SCHRAMM, M. and TAUBE, M. (2003): 'On the co-existence of guanxi and a formal legal system in the PR of China – an institutional approach' – paper presented to the 7th Convention of ISNIE entitled '*Institutions and Change*', Budapest Corvinus University, 13 September.

SCHWEITZER, I. (2002): A hazai beruházások alakulásának főbb irányzatai az elmúlt évtizedekben és néhány tanulság (Major trends of investments in Hungary and some lessons) – parts I and II. *Külgazdaság*, vol. 46. no. (7–8), pp. 4–32 and no. 9. pp. 4–30.

SHEVCHENKO, A. (2004): Bringing the party back: The CCP and the trajectory of market transition in China. *Communist and Post-Communist Studies*, vol. 37. no. 2. pp. 161–185.

SHLAPENTOKH, V. (2002): Post-Mao China: An alternative to the end of history? *Communist and Post-Communist Studies*, vol. 35. no. 3. pp. 237–268.

SOÓS, K. A. (1986): *Terv, kampány, pénz*. (Plan, campaigns, money). Budapest: a book jointly published by Kossuth Kiadó and Közgazdasági és Jogi Könyvkiadó.

SRINIVASAN, T. N. (2000): The Washington Consensus a decade later: Ideology and the art and science of policy advice. *World Bank Research Observer*, vol. 15. no. 2. pp. 265–270.

SRINIVASAN, T. N. (2001): Neoclassical political economy, the state and economic development. In: SRINIVASAN, T. N.: *Economic Policy and State Intervention*. (edited by V. S. N. NARAYA). Delhi: Oxford University Press, pp. 504–530.

SRINIVASAN, T. N. (2003): 'Globalization, growth, inequality and poverty' – paper presented to the international conference of TIGER Institute '*Globalization and Social Stress*', Warsaw, 22–24 October

STIGLITZ, J. E. (1994): *Whither Socialism?* Cambridge/Mass and London: The MIT Press.

STIGLITZ, J. E. (2001): The roaring nineties. *The Atlantic Monthly*, no. 3. pp. 75–89.

SUN, L. X. (1997): Emergence of unorthodox ownership and governance structures in East Asia: An alternative transition path. Helsinki: WIDER *Research for Action*, no. 38.

SZAMUELY, L. (1974): *First Models of Socialist Economic Systems*. Budapest: Akadémiai Kiadó.

SZAMUELY, L. and CSABA, L. (1998): Transition in Hungary and in Hungarian economics. In: WAGENER, H.-J. ed.: *Economic Thought in Communist and Post-Communist Europe*. London: Routledge, pp. 157–214.

SZEGVÁRI, I. (1991): Systemic change and convertibility: A comparison of Poland, Hungary and Yugoslavia. In: CSABA, L. ed.: *Systemic Change and Stabilization in Eastern Europe*. Aldershot/UK and Brookfield/Vermont/USA: Dartmouth Publishing Co. pp. 33–44.

SZENTES, T. (1999): The transformation of CEE: A study on the international context of the process. In: TEMESI, J. and ZALAI, E. eds: *Back to a Market Economy*. Budapest: Akadémiai Kiadó, pp. 91–108.

TIAN, G. (2000): Property rights and the nature of Chinese collective enterprises. *Journal of Comparative Economics*, vol. 28. no. 2. pp. 247–268.

TYSON, L. A. (1980): *The Yugoslav Economic System and Its Performance in the 1970s.* Berkeley; Institute of International Studies.

TYSON, L. A. (1983): Investment allocation under market socialism: Hungary and Yugoslavia compared. *Journal of Comparative Economics*, vol. 11. no. 3.

UVALIC, M. (1992): *Investment and Property Rights in Yugoslavia: The Long Transition to a Market Economy.* Cambridge and New York: Cambridge University Press.

WANG, H.-Y. (2001): *Weak State, Strong Networks: The Institutional Dynamics of FDI in China.* Oxford: Oxford University Press.

WEBER, M. ed.: (2001): *Reforming the Economic Systems in Asia.* Cheltenham/UK and Northampton/MA/USA: Edward Elgar Publishing Co.

WEN, M. (2004): Relocation and agglomeration of Chinese industry. *Journal of Development Economics*, vol. 73. no. 1. pp. 324–347.

WHITING, S. (2001): *Power and Wealth in Rural China.* Cambridge and New York: Cambridge University Press.

WILHELM, J. H. (2003): The failure of the American Sovietological profession. *Europe-Asia Studies*, vol. 55. no. 1. pp. 59–72.

WILLIAMSON, J. (2000): What should the World Bank think about the Washington Consensus? *World Bank Research Observer*, vol. 15. no. 2. pp. 251–264.

WOLF, M. (2003): The long march to prosperity: Why China can maintain its explosive rate of growth for another two decades. *Financial Times*, 9 December.

WU, F. (2003): Chinese economic statistics: Caveat emptor! *Post-Communist Economies*, vol. 15. no. 1. pp. 127–145.

XIA, Y-L. (2003): 'Globalization and China's institutional progress during transition' – paper presented to the international conference of TIGER entitled *'Globalization and Social Stress'*, Warsaw, 22–24 October

YOUNG, A. (1995): The tyranny of numbers: Confronting statistical realities of the East Asian growth experience. *Quarterly Journal of Economics*, vol. 110. no. 3. pp. 641–680.

YOUNG, A. (2003): Gold into base metals: productivity growth in the People's Republic of China. *Journal of Political Economy*, vol. 111. no. 6. pp. 1220–1261.

YU, L. C. (2000): Control, incentives and competition: The impact of reform on Chinese state-owned enterprises. *Economics of Transition*, vol. 8. no. 1. pp. 151–174.

ZALAI, E. (2001): *Matematikai közgazdaságtan.* (Mathematical economics). Budapest: KERSZÖV Jogi és Üzleti Kiadó.

ZHANG, J. H. (1999): Stock price premia and Chinese equity market separation. In: DIMITROV, M. – ANDREFF, W. – CSABA, L., eds: *Economies in Transition and the Varieties of Capitalism.* Sofia: Gorex Press for the European Association for Comparative Economic Studies, pp. 281–302.

ZHU, Y. (2006): 'Economic growth and reforms in the P.R. of China' – paper presented at the conference of the Brenthurst Foundation and Konrad Adenauer Stiftung entitled *Globalization and Economic Success*, Cairo, 13-14 November, available at: www.thebrenthurstfoundation.org

13. PRIVATIZATON, REGULATION AND REGULATED MARKETS

Several decades elapsed since the onset of the Thatcher–Reagan Revolution. By now, the superiority of private property over non-private forms, be that co-operatives, workers' managed firms, NGOs or plain public is no longer a subject of serious controversy in the empirically oriented literature. Kikeri and Nellis (2004) for instance survey the broad and controversial literature on developing, post-Communist and Western economies and find overwhelming evidence in favor of this claim. What is, however, less certain, is the set of *side-conditions that ensure the meeting of the efficiency criterion* of the privately owned firms at the social level. Since one of the classical issues of political economy has been the issue of rent-seeking (Krueger, 1974), and directly unproductive profit-seeking activities (Bhagwati, 1998), all emerged and studied in the context of private market economies.

Privatization, Regulation and Efficiency

Post-Communist transformation has proven to be a most interesting laboratory for testing ideas about economic change in general and of property structures and the role of regulation in particular. The loans-for-shares program in Russia in 1995/1996 has, for instance proven, that though the fast redistribution of property is feasible, it is not a socially (or even micro-economically) efficient arrangement, neither in the short, nor in the long run. Likewise, the continued existence of small private plots in Polish farming, their growing significance in terms of employment in countries like Bulgaria and Romania, has by no means been contributing to enhanced macro-economic efficiency and improved social welfare. On the other hand, the broader comparison of empirical evidence (Djankov and Murrell, 2002) has proven, that if put in the proper context, that is if privatized to outsiders, if supported by appropriate financial sector reform and corporate governance structures, *private enterprise has been predominantly more efficient in the post-Communist context as well.* In none of the cases surveyed in the studies summarizing case studies, could we find evidence for the long continuum of non-private forms of property actually having delivered better, or at least as good results as did private property. This finding holds, provided *external ownership* and accountability were dominant and *competition* controlling for the activities of private agents. Here, as highlighted in the Russia and China chapters, *enforcement* rather than the formal availability of rules that matter.

In other words, it is the degree to which agents internalize the formal/new rules of the game what matters. In deciding over if and how learning is effective, experience – of learning by doing – seems to be vital. If and when for instance bankruptcy regulations are enforced, the phenomenon of the 'virtual economy', or queuing, or inter-firm barter simply disappears. This experience has gained support first in Hungary, later in the Czech Republic and Poland (in the second half of the 1990s). Under the Putin Presidency even Russia ceased to be a 'virtual economy', where money settlements pay a subordinate role at best and enterprises settle their mutual claims via deliveries in commodities or in convertible currency cash. If however non-payments remain recurringly unpunished, there is no incentive for players to change. Thus soft budget constrains are likely to sustain long after political changes, or after the promulgation of new policies. This is the experience of several South-East European countries as well as many New Independent States. As a consequence, the ability to tax remains limited, the 'core state' becomes weakened and in some cases even corrupted, and the vicious circle of underdevelopment, well described in traditional development literature re-emerges. This is finally what the poor indicators of economic activity in the majority of transforming economies reflect. In other words, private property is though a *necessary*, however, by no means a *sufficient* condition for sustainable economic development in general, and in the post-Communist context in particular.[1]

While in the Western literature on privatization, introducing private property in place of public and semi-public ownership implies, by definition, the introduction of *competitive arrangements*, in emerging economies it is not always the case. This, of course, is to be understood in a normative way. Analyzing network industries in European perspective, Pál Valentiny (2004) reports of the sustaining problem of predatory pricing and price squeezing (the latter aiming at pricing the competitor out of business so as to make way for later, sustaining price increases by the winner). Combining legal and political approaches, the analysis shows a fair degree of agnosticism, as far as practice of the courts are concerned, not least because of difficulties of proof. West European competition policy, in general, moves toward analyzing hypothetical solutions, expected behavior and strategic practices.

This is, by and large, the opposite of the *emerging market experience*, as we shall illustrate in the case of Hungary. The Office for Economic Competition has consequently adopted a stance of staying out of privatization deals, rejected any suggestion that they should consider hypothetical situations and mar-

[1] Heitger (2004, pp. 399–400) finds a strong causal link between property and welfare: a unit of improvement in the property rights indicator yielded two units of increase in welfare for the 1975–1995 period.

ket behavior that is to be expected, and shied off making any judgement on strategic practices (Voszka, 2003, pp. 118–124). This function has not been taken over, neither by the State Property Agency (later State Property Holding and Privatization Inc), nor by the Ministry of Finance, nor by sectoral authorities. As long as privatization remained 'the responsibility vested in the government as a whole', the task of creating competition as part and parcel of privatization) transformation, remained by and large unattended. Kravtsenniouk (2002) in a condoning tone, presents a similar picture for the other Central European economies, allowing us to use Hungary as a representative case. Let us give a few examples!

Privatization of the energy sector in Hungary has, for instance, often resulted in transferring property title to foreign state-owned firms, such as *Electricité de France,* or even more glaringly, in the airline industry *Malév* Hungarian Airlines was 'privatized' to the currently still state-owned *Alitalia* in 1992. Unsurprisingly, especially in the latter case, when sheltered monopoly positions have been sustaining, the efficiency improvement expected from privatization has *failed to materialize,* since the incentive structure as well as the 'stick and the carrot' provided by real competition have not been brought about. A mere transfer of the title has not triggered any change in corporate behavior or efficiency.

This point is exposed in great detail in the monograph by Éva Voszka (2003, chapter II), explaining that in Hungary the conflict between the abstract need to create competitive arrangements has, at least in industry, often been subordinate to immediate pressures to raise budgetary revenues. Alternatively, the dominant concern was to *create private proprietors who would act against any attempt to revert the process of systemic change.* The latter is rightly considered to be a defining feature of post-Communist transformation. It is easy to see, also in abstract terms, that lack of competition may and does cause efficiency and welfare losses. Thus the traditional public policy function of protecting competition as a public good *remains valid even after transition is by and large over.*

This consideration is most relevant, as we have indicated in several empirical chapters, in the field of financial intermediation, for this has an immediate bearing on macroeconomic *allocation* and thus the *actual,* versus potential, *growth rate of the given economy.* Two separate studies, conducted independent of each other, but published simultaneously (Várhegyi, 2003, 1046–1047; Móré and Nagy, 2003, pp. 33–34) have shown that the relative market power of banks in Central Europe has led to sustainingly high margins, low intermediation and high financing costs and sizeable efficiency losses. Meanwhile, direct trust-busting is, for understandable theoretical and practical reasons, not advocated by any of the literature quoted above. The concern over the inadequate evolution of competition, as well as the insufficiently contestable market structure has been shown to be a source of allocative *inefficiencies* and consumer *welfare losses* all across the front-runner emerging economies.

This negative finding is of immense significance in bringing back the issue of regulation and *redefining the role of the state.* It would be cheap to re-iterate the propositions voiced by famous representatives of mass privatization, as well as of adherents of the minimal state having denounced the calls for regulation as a covert form of statism. Interestingly, if anything, the opposite conclusion emerges from the study of privatization in East and West. Whereas in the West, privatization has always been a *regulated process* with clearly set priorities, thus controllable and foreseeable outcomes, the fundamental reason of the lack of legitimacy and lack of popularity of privatization in the East rests with its *unregulated, non-transparent and thus incalculable outcomes.*

Banking crises in Albania, Romania, Latvia and Russia during the 1990s, or alternatively, the recurring need for bailing out banks in China have provided ample evidence that similar consequences may, and indeed do, occur under quite dissimilar historic, cultural and economic conditions, provided *third party enforcement, prudential* regulations and *transparency* is missing from the financial sector. Private banks could just as easily go under as public ones, while big ones have always had a longer grace period thus a tougher ending than the small ones. The 'too big to fail' argument, developed originally in the context of US banking – most recently with the Savings' and Loans crises in the late '80s – *has proven relevant* in the post-Communist and developing country context as well. This factor explains why *soft budget constraints of banks*, both private and public, *could last for so long after systemic change.* And if one recalls how Western governments treated crises of such financial institutions as *Credit Lyonnaise* or *Mediobanca,* let alone the house banks of German *Ländern,* it is clear that the issue is there, irrespective of the Communist legacy, but importantly for any modern economy.

As it has emerged from the experience of 19th century America, as well as of post-Communist economies, primarily in the New Independent States and in South-East Europe, unregulated processes trigger a series of events known in the broader literature as *market failure.* These include predatory pricing, private enforcement, use of force, corruption, misuse of dominant market power, asset stripping and the like. Meanwhile, in economies, like those of the United States or the United Kingdom, where free markets are accepted as formative principle, far reaching *regulation,* and even severing *enforcement* ensures the civilized nature, and also the efficiency gains of the market arrangements. From the stock exchange to banking, the energy sector and airlines or pharmaceuticals, regulation is *all-embracing.*

This does not imply, by any means, a reversal to the idea of mixed economy a la Tinbergen or any third road concepts. Subscribing to the need for regulation implies no more and no less than accepting insights from more general theories of systems, namely that following *individual rationality* does not automatically lead to *collective rationality.* Experience of the past twenty years has re-enforced the insight: precisely in order to be able to reject the 'productive state' one needs a 'protective state', to use the old terminology of James Buchanan. In other words, the funeral for macroeconomics might have been too early a call by those advocating the micro-foundations of macroeconomics, since the early 90s. While such link, beyond doubt, needs to be established, the simple *submerging of macro-economics into micro-economics would seem hasty* at best.

Private Property and Multi-Level Governance

Post-Communist and broader emerging market experience, including that of the East Asian crisis of 1997–1999, have called attention to the importance of regulatory embeddedness of the institution of private property. The recurring misuses in the accounting profession, from Enron to Parmalat, have lent support to the view calling for the *complex set of pre-conditions,* created by rules and informal institutions, for the efficiency and welfare enhancing qualities of private property to reveal themselves.

In trying to address the issue of how exactly the mechanics of private property functions, if it works, two strands of the literature have been emerging. One of them is the *corporate governance literature,* which addresses issues pertaining to the principal-agent problems. Namely, how a distant, and in case of publicly traded corporations, dispersed ownership structure may provide those incentive and control functions, that are associated with private property. This, as the broad empirical overview of Dyck (2001) proves, implies important regulatory functions, such as constructing institutions that constrain and control both the *grabbing hand of the state,* as well as the *grabbing hand of managers,* that are likely to engage in asset stripping, if overall conditions of uncertainty and lack of transparency together provide opportunities and incentives for this type of behavior.

It might be interesting to recall that this insight *is not confined to* the post-Communist or broader *emerging market experience.* Privatization of the British Rail has not proven to be extremely helpful, and has been reverted by New Labor, in the context of a generally market-friendly, decentralizing and pro-competitive policy line. Likewise 'privatization' of public utilities in France, implying a mere regionalization of servivces that continue to be run along the lines of *'service publique'* rather than any kind of cost-effectiveness or new public management principles, have brought little improvement. Calls for privatization of water supply, for instance, may have proven to be an extreme move of the shuttle, since conditions for creating competitive conditions in this market are unlikely to be given. Therefore Swiss, British and developing country experience support the insight that the 'one size fits all' approach might not be workable. Furthermore, in each of the above listed cases *privatization and regulation together* deliver the outcome. Thus it might be cheap to blame any one side for the joint performance that serves as a base for social acceptance or resistance.

By the same token, the task of *governance* emerges quite soon, both at the macro- and at the microeconomic level. At the *macro-economic level,* the task is straightforward: while everybody is interested, as an individual, at higher prices, society as a whole is interested in price stability. Thus the need for a monetary authority emerges. Likewise everybody, as a producer, is interested in obtaining or retaining monopoly positions/secure markets, while society as a whole is interested in competition. Also at the *micro-economic level,* there is a need to protect interests of property owners/shareholders, of not allowing for predatory practices, but also of ensuring reliable information, be that of statistical reporting, tax declarations or solid accounting for that matter. As in their overview of related literature Glaeser and Shleifer (2003, pp. 422) put it, establishing the rule of law itself has become an economic problem. This has given birth to the *regulatory state*.

While this – and the need for auditing each of these pieces of information by independent agents with unquestionable integrity – may sound trivial, the World.com and Ahold scandals and their successors, propping up every month ever since they have been unmasked, how *vulnerable* even the most sophisticated society may be against malpractices. The latter included typically three areas: the multiplication of off-budget items, the growing reliance of financial derivatives and the valuation of immaterial goods. Analyzing the lessons of these developments Bélyácz (2004) correctly underscores that in each of the previously listed items, especially in the valuation of non-material assets, there exists *intrinsic ambiguity*. There is no way how – basically static – accounting procedures could properly 'put a price on' the *future* value creating *potential* of any such intangible, be that in the new economy or be that just a conventional industrial innovation, or a new brand name or a new marketing method. As there is no benchmark to measure against, no analogy, no previously known case, it is hard to make judgements that, with the benefit of hindsight, would not prove naive, over-optimistic, or simply wrong. This is the *nature of business risk* that cannot be excluded from any such activity.

It goes without saying that the need for regulation is a quite abstract concept, that may, though *does not have to, boil down for calls for more state intervention* with reference to market failures. These references tend to be involved more often than empirically justified; however it is hard to avoid regulation if monopoly practices emerge. On the other hand, the much-publicized Microsoft case has proven, that abstract considerations may or may not hold. In the computer industry consumer welfare is bound to be significant, once the trend of *falling prices* and improved performance is *demonstrably outpacing any other industry* or service sector. What we claim here is supportive of an insight that has long formed competition policies in the European Union, namely that trust busting *may or may not* be conducive to improved *consumer welfare* in each and every market. The idea of forcing corporations to disclose company specific (asset specific) strategy-related information disregards the fact that it is precisely these items that constitute *the core of potential profit making* and market power. These constitute the competitive edges over other players on the same market. Thus the likelihood of the latter being fully disclosed in due time, that is prior to major market events, is very limited indeed. The calls for more central/state intervention and regulation thus cannot be justified with the ritual reference to the scandalous cases.

Therefore in contemporary economic and regulatory literature more sophisticated claims are being advanced. For one, regulation does not necessarily imply state regulation, since the collusion between political considerations (especially in competitive democracies) and professional concerns over the long run may easily emerge. Thus the increased role for *independent regulatory agencies*, with their management appointed for periods longer than the election cycle.[2] But similarly important is to guard caution against 'outsourcing' public functions to the private sector, where *impartial enforcement* and following *the public purpose* (as different from partisan interest, or business interest) cannot be secured. Controversial experiences with private provision of health care in the United States (in terms of lack of universal coverage), or of privatization of railways in Britain (in terms of security) have called attention to the multitude of paradoxes of applying a per se valid insight indiscriminately. True, the art of policy-making is one through learning by doing, still the far-reaching repercussions in terms of wealth and social wellbeing call for moderation and reflection.

The *farther we move*, in terms of theory and policy, from the competitive product *markets of simple commodities*, that lay at the heart of initial econometric modelling markets, *the more comprehensive the task of regulation,* understood to be fundamentally different from interventionism, becomes. Regulation of drug prices, or more generally of finding the proper balance between the private and public provision of health care, have undoubtedly become the truly most challenging issues for regulation.[3] On the one hand, market failure here may be a valid argument, as most people tend to be myopic while young and healthy, and tend to underestimate the costs of their medication, especially under the contemporary medical technologies. On the other hand, the state provision of health, as the British NHS, has also proven unsustainable. Reform of this public service by New Labor implied a fair degree of decentralization, in the name of democratization and accountability. True, it remains to be settled if these measures indeed followed the political aim of bringing services closer to the citizens, making them aware of the potential of their municipalities and individual responsibilities, or just followed considerations of managerialism/administrative efficiency.

The British case has not proven to be a major success story, insofar as the problem of allocation of scarce resources, or the evolution of a new mixture of public and private provision of similar services has remained unresolved. Likewise, health reform in Germany until 2004 (if this deserves the name) has introduced some transparency and cost-consciousness on the side of service providers. It lacksed, however any major overhaul of a fundamentally statist system run on the principles of command and control (and public funding for the vast majority of services, with private insurance playing a marginal role at best).

Meanwhile, cost explosion could hardly be constrained in either case by fiat (that is by quotas). Furthermore, it looks unreasonable to assume, that market incentives, that fit best for most of human activities, should simply be switched

---

[2] Broader analysis has shown: this policy option may be of limited avail. In the words of Aghion et al (2004, pp. 583) particularly developing countries may find themselves 'between a rock and a hard place'. High institutional insulation – such as of the ECB – may lead to expropriation and tyranny, while low insulation – as with proportional representation and competitive media democracy – means that reforms hurting anybody are not implemented.

[3] This is the reason why health economics has evolved into a major field, with most unconventional approaches and issues, as documented in the over-arching volumes edited by Cluyer and Newhouse (2000).

off, when the 'subject' is our lives and our health. Furthermore, as long as health is a function of lifestyles, individual efforts, consciousness as much (or even more) than of the health care system, the *meritocratic component* of what used to be described as a classic public good comes to the fore. In more general terms, the *dividing line between public and private is diminishing*.

The longer people live in societies, the more acute these problems become. On the other side of the same coin, health has undoubtedly become *a major factor in attaining economic performance* at the macro-level. On the one hand, sociological studies on unemployment recurringly relate the crowding out from labor markets with health issues (either as a cause or as a consequence of joblessness). By contrast, macro-economic analyses (Bloom, Canning and Sevilla, 2004) have demonstrated a positive, sizeable, and statistically significant positive impact on output, even if controlling for all conceivable distorting variables.[4]

But over and above its major economic significance, health is *a value for human beings on its own right*, thus its provision deserves as much attention as any other aspect of economic activity, including the ever growing sector of services. Finally, it is equally justified to note (Ofer, 2004), that if it is a social norm and expectation to have a freedom to choose our jeans, than it should be equally a norm to be *free to choose* our doctor and other conditions of medication. The more we think of *privacy as a major asset of human condition,* the more weighty this argument is. This should make it clear, that the call for regulation is by no means equal to denying the role of competitive market arrangements. On the contrary, regulation makes sense if and to the degree it is based on market principles, that allow for an open ended outcome, without however, making allowance for the 'might is right' type of settling competitive issues.

Likewise, in the area of *environmental protection*, serious economic matters prop up for immediate consideration. In the very moment we leave the world of wishful thinking, typical of the Club of Rome three decades ago, and take the environmental challenge seriously, the more sustainability matters. By the same token, the more the latter will be seen as a task for regulation *to create the incentives for business to endogenize* these considerations in their microeconomic decisions. Furthermore, the environmental industry, too has evolved into a special interest group, with demands and considerations that may or may not follow the public choices. Thus it is anything but trivial, which mechanisms of deliberations would allow for the democratic accountability[5] of the environmental industry and related wide-spread services alike.

---

[4] By contrast, Péter Mihályi (2003, pp. 85–86) suggests that this correlation exists in low levels of development only, not however for advanced economies, where health care behaves like a luxury good.

[5] Accountability is one of the most controversial issues in IR theory. One of the basic insights is, however, that legitimacy of international organizations, or of independent/technical regulatory agencies *cannot and should not be equated* with directly legitimated elected politicians. More on that in (Keohane and Nye, 2003, pp. 394–408), explaining the wide variety of accountability models that may describe the interrelationships among different levels and dimensions of actors (including networks and clubs).

The less sustainable public pensions become, due to ageing and the slow-down of growth, the higher the priority for *privatizing the pension system* and the spread of life insurance is. These areas are obviously in great need for regulation, due to their very *long gestation period*, and due to the numerous *accounting uncertainties* inherent in our not knowing our life span, nor our material, mental and physical conditions in advance for decades. If private pension funds can vary in their performance in great numbers, while they must invest to government bonds, as has been the case in Hungary in 1997–2006, there must be something fundamentally wrong with their regulation of accounting and reporting/disclosure. By the same token such arrangement, though meeting the Friedmanian requirement of individual pension accounts, still does not allow for the formation of rational expectations. For whatever expectations any of us form in terms of return may be built on sand, as it may reflect innovative accounting techniques only.

Interrelationships between Welfare and Financial Sector Reforms

The prospects for private provision of old age pension and health care are directly linked to the issues of regulating non-banks. All the more so that the *raison d'être* of these is to provide better and safer returns than the normal banking business, thus improving the efficiency of using those funds that are (can be) allocated for old age and for times of illness. The problem in this area is multidimensional. On the one hand, financial intermediation is less and less performed by formal banking institutions; on the other hand, banks themselves increasingly earn their living on a variety of related, but *non-banking activities*. Some analysts (Llewellyn, 2002, pp. 224–225) go as far as asking if banks are necessary at all for banking, and if the integrated banking structure is likely to survive? With the spread of information technology and with the new wave of diversification among financial activities even such, previously hardly conceivable forms as virtual banks emerge (they have already emerged in the Anglo-Saxon world). Meanwhile, non-banks intruded the area traditionally reserved for banks, the more lucrative parts of financial services. Banks though may survive as *information managers* and *service providers*, however the traditional 'Chinese Walls' separating banking from insurance, from brokerage, or even consultancy businesses of various sorts has been dramatically disappearing. This means a fundamental challenge for *regulation*, that used to be *tailored to the segmentation of the financial markets* and based on the assumption of different logic of functioning in each of these areas. The more IT allows for de-localization of activities and *de-materialization* of financial flows, and not only in the derivatives markets, the tougher the life of regulators is bound to be.

On the one hand, many of the traditional ideas built on the assumption of the ability of public authorities to 'throw a bit of sand in the machines of financial markets', that laid the groundwork for the once famous Tobin tax, are simply out of touch with contemporary realities. Even such an authoritarian regime as that of Russia has been failing, for over fifteen years, in even diminishing capital flight from a country allegedly plagued with capital shortages. On the other hand, these 'footloose industries' are also hard to tax. The latter is not just a practicality – that is a big challenge for the welfare state built on regular social security contribution collected by the big firms – but also an academically open question. It is namely impossible to localize where in an international network value added is being created and in what proportion. Thus it is hard to establish what would be a 'fair tax rate' to be levied on any of these activities.

Our basic contention is that with the paradigmatic changes brought about by the ICT revolution and the process of transnationalization, i.e. of two irreversible processes defining the 21st century, the very *fundamentals of regulation have been shaken*. This is a paradox, since as we have seen, self-regulation, or to properly put it, the spontaneous interaction of self-interested players may only produce sub-optimal outcomes. The case for some form of regulation is obvious. In this respect self-regulation, self-enforcing rules and such well-known examples as the previously discussed *lex mercatoria* can serve as examples. Self-regulation is often-times tougher and more intrusive, moreover more sophisticated than governmental/administrative actions may ever be, if for no reason because it is a product of interested parties/professionals. The lucrative component of this arrangement is that it exempts participants from legal liabilities, whereas it allows for the necessary *flexibility in technology and the choice of strategies* that may be brought in line with business interest (Haufler, 2003, p. 250). True, experience has indicated that such self-regulatory arrangements are of *varying intensity and efficacy*.

The trouble with all these is, especially in the light of the accounting scandals and the response by the Sarabanes Commission is, that these cases have shaken the *integrity* of major players. This initiative has gathered momentum by the formal proposal of the US government to impose the same arrangement across the board in the European Union as well. The European Commission, though not having the right to legislate directly, has elaborated a tight framework regulation that would basically copy all major elements of the US innovations, such as imposing individual accountability for each item, or the obligatory rotation of auditing partners, or the obligatory separation of auditing and approving organs in each firm (as reported in: *Financial Times*, 15 March, 2004). The old question of the Romans, 'who guards the guardians' have obtained immediate policy relevance. Since as long as the auditing firms are seen (or even portrayed by ill-meaning observers) as greedy and self-serving actors in a large-scale gambling game, there is little hope that considerations of fairness, equity, transparency are enforceable. On the other hand, central regulation on a global scale is clearly not to be organized, thus such ideas as the even farther going International Fiscal Authority with the right to tax (Taylor, 2002) stand even poorer chances of implementation. Likewise, the inability of the international banking community to agree on the Basle Two Accords to remedy the mechanistic, and in many ways inappropriate Basle

One[6] until as late as April, 2003,[7] is indicative of the diversity of interests, that in theory would call for some sort of regulation.

This is not to declare the 'end of the state' in line with naive utopian anarchist-Communist lines, or by contrast, following the libertarian creed. In reality self-regulation could be shown to be oftentimes *pre-emptive*, that is aimed at avoiding action to be taken by public authorities on such diverse matters as safety, environmental protection or child prostitution, to list some of the examples addressed in the source quoted below (Haufler, 2003, pp. 233–235). As long as NGOs are in a position of undermining the reputational capital of major firms, this becomes a very real threat, especially for firms in industries characterized by a high degree of asset specificity and thus of high exit costs. The examples of Nike, or of Exxon, for that matter, are well known and much publicized stories that need no reiteration at this point.

In both the financial sector and in health reform some truly fundamental paradoxes emerge. On the one hand, *transparency is a public good* that needs to be promoted. On the other hand, *information* equals to *power and money*. Thus this is the most valuable *private good* any market player may possess with. In fact, many loss-making activities, such as retailing, is needed for banks not so much per se, as for the additional information these provide on the overall state and standing of their clients. The latter may be extremely valuable in a seemingly unrelated operation, such as a mortgage loan, to be extended, for convenience, by the same bank to its client. Thus any idea that would artificially compel banks to share these with their competitors, let alone with their regulators, is bound to fail.

The mirror side of the same coin is related to a competing consideration, where *privacy is also seen as a highly valuable public good to be protected by law*. Both in financial and in the physical health aspects, let alone psychical considerations, sexual habits, alcohol or drug problems, family instability and the like, information that may be vital for proper economic assessment of health risks may turn out to be intrusive, per se. Potential damages from disclosure via storage, observance and communication may be even more exacerbated. On the other hand, no classical insurance agent is likely to offer any contract to a 85- year-old, suffering from a variety of diseases, and lack of stable income from property. Thus the *conflict of interest is hard to resolve.* Beyond doubt, formal regulations, be these state-imposed or self-regulatory, will make sense only to the degree their enforcement is ensured, the latter being crucially dependent upon *internalization* by agents, or in broader sense, *social acceptance* of these. Experience with high tax-high service economies points towards the same.

---

[6] For instance the stipulation of 8 per cent capital adequacy ratio is clearly inadequate for higher risk environment, such as the emerging economies. Czech and Hungarian banks currently voluntarily provision 16 to 18 per cent of their outstandings for unforeseen eventualities. Likewise in the East Asian crises, the Basle One principles proved irrelevant and unable to warn of risks in advance. Furthermore, as Eichberger and Summer (2004) prove in a formal model, imposing capital constraints on banks may increase systemic risk, raise interest rates and diminish liquidity, thus constraining economic activity in the real sector.

[7] For a detailed analysis of Basle Two cf. (Mérő et al, 2003).

The latter conflict is also multi-dimensional. On the one hand, at the micro-level, all of us have an interest in peeping into the other players' cards, thus our advocacy of transparency is sincere. On the other hand, when it comes to our own cards, our zeal may be less than maximum. If it is a higher standing authority that may decide over disclosure, we may rightly feel, with the horrible experience of totalitarian states in the 20th century, that we need to be protected, primarily from the Leviathan. On the other hand, the next to unlimited trade with personal data, related to internet use and e-shopping, is already foreshadowing the *dangers if privacy is delivered to the mercy of business interest.* Unsolicited calls in our Sunday night pushing 'very special deals' on us, uninvited phone calls by insurance, travel and banking agents in our peak working time, or massive spamming of our electronic correspondence[8] are just the tip of the iceberg. Access to our health and other privacy related information, though in theory sheltered by privacy laws and policies of firms alike, may severely endanger our potential for employment, or even the rate our insurer may charge for the health services we may need in the future.

Self-regulation, which may be the customary solution may not be efficient, since one of the crucial elements of formal institutions, *impartial third party enforcement is not being secured.* If war is too serious a thing to be left to the generals, data protection may be too serious a thing to be left over to internet service providers, bankers or health bureaucrats, let alone journalists and politicians. Moreover, there is no trivial procedure or principle to resort to, as the ICT revolution has created new paradigms. Scarcity, which used to be the basic point of orientation has given way to over-abundance (of information), which is exactly the opposite of what economic theories have been built upon. *The dividing line between public and private has become porous.* Free access to inform-ation and the need to use it as a private good are clearly in conflict. Further, as long as entering the market presumes reliance on all the best and newest accomplishments of IT, the practice of managing sensitive pieces of information *regularly precedes* the formation of laws and even of *informal institutions,* such as (moral and professional) standards, sanctioned by the guild. This is a fundamental and non-sector-specific, non-country-specific challenge that is yet to be addressed.[9]

This feature, *the withering away of the delineation between public and private spheres is perhaps the biggest challenge for regulation in the decades to come.* These changes are much more profound and go much deeper in the fabric of economy and society, than the traditional idea of public-private partnership, or the outsourcing of some public functions to private agents would suggest. No

[8] US regulations as of January 2004, having turned spam into a criminal offence, are seen as non-enforceable by the majority of computer specialists and service providers.

[9] Clark (2004) reports of a new coding system in softwares that allows only limited and non-transparent ways of connecting various databases. For instance only the fact that somebody is on the list of intelligence agencies and of hotel customers is uncovered. Then authorities need a judicial permission to decode (but only a single piece). The rest remains covered in signs and numbers. The limited opening by the program and coding of the rest is the innovation that, if practicable on the large scale, may be one of the solutions to the conflicts between privacy and security interests.

doubt, when the Defense Department in Britain entrusted Morgan Stanley to organize its procurement, the idea of 'strategic sectors', often invoked in the literature on industrial policy has become very relative one, indeed. Likewise the 'hollowing' of the traditional structures, be that through the outsourcing of activities in a global network in industry, or the virtualization of banking in a multi-functional information management center, has already posed major challenges for regulation and public policies alike.

On the one hand, the entire base of the traditional community, that generates legitimacy for wielding power in the democratic process has been shaken (more on that in: Salzberger, 2002). As long as we cannot clearly locate the firm, be that industrial or financial, *there is no clear principle according to which public dues could be levied.* The classical ideas of civil society and self-help, the ensuing provision of public goods and welfare services on citizens' rights is hard to operationalize, as long as it is finally in the discretion of economic agents to comply or not to comply with taxation rules. While indirect taxes, as value added tax and consumption related duties are easy to collect, it is hard to imagine, with an angle of the well-known trends of ageing societies, that voluntary contributions and fully funded private provision, of both health and old-age pension services could be sustained on any acceptable levels. On the other hand, de-materialization of operations does not allow for the more traditional coercive measures to operate. Furthermore, the competition among localities and among regulatory systems put severe limits to what can and what cannot be imposed upon the millions of players in the transnational economy.

In short, both subjects and objects, principles and procedures, that is the entire *philosophy and the tool-kit of regulation need to be redefined.* One of the few things we may know for sure is that purely national solutions, that is sector specific regulations adopted by national legislations would surely not do. Moreover, as experience has shown, not even regional arrangements, such as the *acquis communautaire* of the European Union are in a position of withstanding the transnational processes and challenges, that are sometimes, though by no means always, global.

Regulatory Regimes: The Case for Transnational Solutions

One may well wonder under this angle, for how long the fortress Europe mentality, still dominating most of the EU may survive, and if yes, with what kind of repercussions for the efficacy of any legislation ensuing from these deliberations. If one only thinks about the challenges listed above, or about the emergence of such truly global problems as tens of millions of displaced persons, desertation, deforestation, the re-emergence of infectious diseases, migration, multicultural societies, mass poverty, the digital divide and ensuing split in advanced societies and among societies of the globe, or the erosion of the multilateral trading system, reflected in the regular failures of the Millennium or Development Round since 1999 (most recently in July 2006), there is reason to be concerned.

357

If we remain only with the WTO framework for a moment, it is quite clear that it is the changing nature of transnational exchanges that has triggered an ever thicker, broader set of regulations, constraining sovereignty in the 19th century sense. Since it has long been impossible to delineate where 'industrial commodities' end and 'non-industrial ones', to be protected begin, furthermore, the more general dividing line between 'tradables' and 'non-tradables' is equally on the verge of withering, the mandates of multilateral arrangements needed to be extended. With transforming the GATT into WTO in 1994 the very first steps have been made. No matter how critically one may be inclined towards the rules adopted, it is better to have, in the light of the above said, *any multilateral rules than none*. This applies primarily to the small and weaker partners.

It would be hard to deny that implementation of the 1994 understandings has been less than perfect in the decade that followed. Primarily, in the field of agriculture, but also in some areas of industry as steel and textiles, most relevant to poor countries, protectionism survived more than it could be justified. However, the turning over the table, as happened in Cancún in September 2003, is surely not a solution. The failure of the Multilateral Investment Agreement in 1999 in the OECD was already a warning sign, that *even among the rich countries narrow-minded interest representation is likely to dominate broader, let alone global, concerns for regulation*. This would have been all the more urgent, since the 1997–1999 financial crisis has already shown the need for action in the area of international financial architecture (Summers, 2000). The more important role is assigned by development theory to foreign investments in generating growth, the more pressing is the need to elaborate multilaterally agreed and approved *codes of conduct*. Regretfully, the latter issues have been simply swept away from the agenda of the Doha Round in the WTO, which is likely to produce a major shortcoming for the years to come.

It would be hard to overlook, that the more networking is becoming the name of the game, the greater the need for regulating *competitive behavior at the global scale will be*. The easiest solution could be to extend the mandate of the WTO,[10] which, having long ceased to be concerned with customs duties only. It does have the expertise and the access to information, as well as the co-operation among governments needed for this. The technical – non-political – nature of WTO dispute settlement mechanism, as well as the quasi-automatic nature of most of the procedures make this forum best suited to arbitrate among competing claims on complex matters. The special fund allocated for assisting developing country claimants is an additional feature in its favor. However, with the erosion of WTO, in part due to advanced country practices in the traditional trade area, in part due to developing country reactions in form of more protectionism and more rigid negotiating stances, the medium-term chances for this most needed arrangement, must be seen as dim.

[10] These were the so-called Singapore issues, such as investment, competition policy, public procurement laws and trade promotion means.

Without aiming at being exhaustive, our broad overview of the emerging issues points towards at least *two puzzles*. One is the economic one: if there is a modicum of truth in the above listed paradoxes, it may be necessary, still insufficient, to follow the advice of the mainstream (Barro, 2002) to apply economic calculus to all walks of life. While this might well be the crux of the problem in overcoming some of the insurmountable financing difficulties, especially in the welfare sphere, by the same token a number of regulatory tasks emerge. For the *self-interest of the players may be inadequate as a control and screening mechanism* to avoid trivial abuses, let alone bring about socially acceptable (perhaps even optimal) outcomes (whatever way we define optimality in a democratic process of public choice). If that is the case, *the regulatory task needs to be redefined in transnational terms.*

The second challenge follows from the simple fact that most of the regulatory theory, policy and institutions tended to be nation-specific, country-specific. At the end of the day all theories presume the existence of a *core state* that is able and willing to use force as *ultima ratio,* has a monopoly on this, and is democratically accountable. This is not always the case in the transnational arena. The UN for instance is accountable but not efficient. The EU by contrast is though fairly efficient in a number of areas, notably in ensuring monetary stability, however it has long been struggling with democratic deficit. In the case of independent regulatory agencies, be that a competition office or the WTO dispute settlement mechanism, democratic legitimacy is anything but trivially secured.

Herewith, we bump into a third major problem, the above discussed *withering the boundary between public and private spheres*. It is hard to delineate and establish what is a fully private sphere, and what is fully public, the closer we move to real world situations, the less so. For instance if medical care is provided in a mixed system, it is hard to imagine the Chinese Walls between public and private provision. In the case of pharmaceuticals, for that matter, the drive for cheap medication – supported among others by the South African President Mbeki at the 2002 Johannesburg Forum – would surely reproduce, if taken literally, the shortcomings well known from Communist provision of medication, allegedly free of charge and provided as universal entitlements of all citizens. Short of this digression, the elementary economic consideration that would allow for the R+D costs of transnational pharmaceutical firms to recoup, and provide further incentives to new entrants, should somehow be reconciled with the established fact that most pharmaceutical products are being sold on an *administrative market*. This is the case even today, where publicly approved budgets, publicly controlled prescriptions, set prices and the rest are the name of the game.

Likewise, the ongoing privatization of such previously 'strategic' areas as airlines, water management, or the provision of electricity via an emerging spot market and exchange regulating the fluctuation of prices, it would be hard to establish the border-lines. Moreover, the broader the IT reshapes trade, the more trans-border online shopping, from air tickets to mass customized furniture becomes the rule, the more prices tend to be individualized, that is tailored to the needs and level of information of the individual customer (more on that in the volume of Kocsis and Szabó, 2003). This implies that *traditional economic assumptions, such as the law of one price, or the impersonal nature of market exchange, may undergo serious modifications.*

From the above stated it follows, that the entire way of thinking about the public sector needs to be re-assessed. On the one hand, there are less and less activities that may be assigned exclusively or primarily to the public domain, if for no other reasons, because of the cost explosion on the one hand, and slow trend rate of growth in advanced countries on the other. In a way, due to the withering away of borders, and because of the anchoring of the trend to liberalization in the irreversible processes of IT revolution and transnationalization, there is no way to force the ghost back to the bottle. On the other hand, the emerging new type of market, based on networks, power derived from information, inherent tendencies of decentralization and deregulation, lack of protection of data is a very different one from the customary, modelled on the 'market for lemons'. *This new structure of the transnational market is in need of transnational third party enforcement and provision of public purpose.* And here is a function, which is either public or non-private, else impartiality of enforcement is no longer secured. Likewise, the democratic legitimacy of the emerging new rules need to be ensured, perhaps not in the same manner as in the Greek city-state (as explained in footnote 5).

The more authoritarian a political system is, the less the paradigmatic shift in corporate governance, away from Fordism to Toyotism has materialized, *the graver the challenges* for the individual economies and corporations are. In other words, it is not so much the type of ownership as *the model of managing assets* that is to set the pace of changes. Meanwhile the move toward private property, while it does require the abolition of red tape and cutting back of bureaucratic barriers to entry, it also poses *new challenges to regulation.* As the post-Communist experience has shown, unregulated banking sectors are unlikely to perform better than over-regulated and suppressed ones. Even if the former lead to big crises, as in Latvia and Albania in 1995 or in Romania in 1998, these may shatter the confidence in the domestic financial system and lead to long term low levels of savings and investment.

In a way, the traditional dichotomy between free and regulated markets is likely to be a matter of the past. *At the end of the day, all markets become regulated ones,* even in cases we preach the opposite. While most micro-economic textbooks take agricultural commodities as examples for simple products traded on free markets, in the real world there are few less regulated markets than those for farm products, and not only in Japan, Switzerland, or in the European Union. Financial markets, often blamed for de-stabilizing the vulnerable national economies of the South, all work under strict rules. The current debate is precisely about *the way these should be globally re-shaped* in order to overcome misuses and fraud. And as long as pensions are provided, at least in part, by private funds, capital markets and welfare reforms directly overlap.

In order to be able to come up with forward-looking suggestions rather than the mere re-iteration of the extensive litany on the ills of our 'brave new world', more *innovative approaches to transnational regulation* need to be adopted. These include ideas of how to ensure *contestability of markets*, since networking also may imply closing out new entry (as in the case of Microsoft). A second task is to ensure *transparency*, which is important not only in the financial sector examples, mentioned above, but in the simpler exchanges of commodities and services, where the law of one price is no longer valid. Individualized pricing may though increase, but equally decrease and arbitrarily disperse, *consumer benefit*, which is, in the end of the day, the opposite of what anyone would expect of the competitive order. A third, seemingly old-fashioned, but related requirement is that of *equal and fair treatment*. This issue might well have been long forgotten, but individual pricing and the freedom to contract may turn to its extremes.[11] The more we consider the partial privatization of health care and old-age pensions as inevitable, the higher importance we are likely to attach to this issue.

An equally important dimension is related to transnationalization. Most, if all of these regulations, at least in an ideal world, should aim at least having *global validity*, else the competition among localities and among regulations may easily undermine any attempt to regulate. Recent experience has shown, that it is *not* a hopeless exercise. Gunning et al (2003) report of the first successes of the so-called Kimberley process, where the origin of diamonds sold by major players on the global markets need to be testified. This helped to counteract rebel groups that used to pressurize producers for providing finance for their activities. The ebbing of civil strife in several sub-Saharan African countries is a good indication of this process in the making. Likewise, the arrest and later conviction of former Ukrainian Premier Lazarenko in Switzerland on charges of money laundering, or the freeing up the fortune of former Philippine dictator Marcos to international court claims by Switzerland, or the enforcement of the 2001 OECD regulations outlawing the tax deduction of money paid out for corrupting local officials by multinational firms, are all pointing towards some hope. *Co-operative games* are thus already seen *more rewarding in the international arena*, than fully non-cooperative ones, as postulated by the realist school of international relations.

Under this angle, several items can be listed that contribute positively to our agenda. Transnational pieces of regulation include a number of innovations. Strengthening the WTO framework and deepening the discipline, enforcement of Basle Two, the enforcement of the IMF Code of Good Fiscal Practices or the OECD Code of Conduct for Corporate Behavior are pointing towards those items of regulations, that are already in the making and may constitute steps to settling the set of issues we raised. However, it would be hard to overlook

---

[11] Subcontractors, for instance, not agreeing to predatory pricing of wholesale chains may simply be blacklisted. Individual pricing of, say, airfares, often lead to cases when five passengers in the same row are charged five different prices for the identical service (with the sixth left on ground due to overbooking, although the EU directive of January 2004 penalizes the latter practice). Roma applicants may be automatically turned down in job search on the basis of visibility or even typical names.

that *regulation is clearly lagging behind reality.* Regulation of IT trade – over and above the 1994 GATT chapter – is nowhere close to the challenges already present in contemporary business practices. Likewise, accounting rules are nowhere close to where they should be, and the shaken credibility of the profession is likely to render self-regulation questionable in public perceptions. Also the dispute settlement mechanism within the WTO has often proven to be either too rigid, or too strongly related to particular business interest so as to gain general acceptance.

The spread of *lex mercatoria,* as discussed in the chapter on Transnational markets, and the growing reliance of business partners on elected arbitration instead of going through the costly and time consuming formal legal procedures is an indication that what we have at our disposal is *rather just a skeleton than a fully developed body of transnational regulation.* Reforming the entire formal structure of international relations, starting up with the United Nations, is perhaps a too challenging idea. However it is hard to deny that 'non-choices are also choices'. So the spontaneous emergence of second and third best options though allow for the trial and error, so much needed to find out what is feasible and what is optimal. On the other hand, it is also a sign of growing *erosion of the formal regulatory structures built on the 19th concept of sovereignty and the related superstructure of public international law in its entirety.* From the emergence of such new forms as 'The Coalition of the Willing' to Basle Two Accords, where provisioning for risks should be weighted on the base of discretion by the (accountable) banker, we are already well into a process of *total redefinition of the rules of the game,* along which the process of transnational economic and political interchanges may and should be analyzed.

One may wonder what the optimal mix of regulation and self-regulation may be by the sector/issue area. It is common knowledge that voluntary agreements have a much higher probability of implementation – this is why corporate self-regulation figures higher on the agenda (Graham and Woods, 2006). However the above cited research also underscores the indispensable role of governmental oversight for good outcomes.

The European Dimension

If our quite densely presented agenda holds – and perhaps should be substantially extended – then it poses a major challenge to the *acquis communautaire.* For the time being the *acquis* is more a halfway-house solution among national arrangements, than an independent, truly transnational, and primarily *globally oriented* set of rules. More often than not, the presence of vested interests – polished up as national interests – shape its actual implementations. Considerations of yesterday rather than of tomorrow shape priorities of Community spending as much as areas that are declared to be of common concern.

In order to overcome the present stagnation it would be necessary to strengthen the federalist component of the EU (Hallström, 2003) at the expense of inter-governmentalism. The more the challenges are likely to occur on a global scale – not only in the fight against terrorism – *the graver the danger of marginalization of the European Union structures is.* This, of course, would imply, among others, a lost opportunity for Europe in general, and for the new member-states in particular.

Our conclusion is thus pointing toward two interrelated directions. On the one hand, mainstream insights about the uses of *deregulation* on both product and labor markets remain valid. By deregulating both, product prices fall and even stagnant real wages earn more purchasing power, thus product market deregulation directly increases the real wage. Labor market deregulation has similarly been shown to be beneficial: by reducing the barriers to entry it lowers unemployment (Blanchard and Giavazzi, 2003). Thus the policy of *privatization*, that is normally associated with both, is likely to bring about tangible benefits. The more we understand that current pay-as-you go *pension* systems and state managed *health care systems* are unsustainable from the financial point of view, while these are inefficient and unfair from the social point of view, the more we can advocate and forecast in the same time that privatization is likely to be *extended to ever new areas,* in old and new EU members alike.

Experience in the post-Communist world and elsewhere has indicated, that the chain between private property and improved efficiency, especially in the social sense, is a fairly long one. A set of institutions and regulations need to be in place in order to provide the benefits most models simply assume. Thus in real world situations policy relevant analysis must also stress regulation.

In this chapter, drawing on previous empirical analyses, we advocated *a brand new agenda for regulation.* Overcoming the traditional dichotomy of public sector equalling with regulated markets, and private sector with free market, we contended, that the IT revolution and processes of transnationalization *have fundamentally changed the rules of the game.* The ongoing, in part spontaneous, in part policy-induced, privatization of formerly publicly provided goods and services call for addressing the consequences of withering away of the boundaries between public and private. ICT has also brought about new questions and *trade-offs in terms of privacy and transparency.*

The challenge is further increased by the fact that the dichotomy between the public and the private sector has become a matter of the past already by now, i.e. long before the changes indicated above could unfold in their entirety. It has less to do with the infrastructure projects on public-private partnerships, that enjoyed currency in the physical infrastructure developments for a long time. It has more to do with the fact that service providers, producers and market agents in general arise in *the long continuum in between.* For instance in health services it would be hard to find purely public or purely private systems at the macro-level. Between the two side models, we find a variety of in-betweens, such as charity foundations, volunteer groups, church run establishments, self-help organizations and even co-operatives. The same applies basically for the entire non-tradable sector, from printing to funeral services. Reforms in the welfare systems in the Netherlands, Sweden or Britain have all extended this grey zone. The expansion of the above mentioned intermediate forms are also clearly discernible in the welfare services of emerging economies as well.

The true challenge that follows from this blurring of the boundaries is not so much the growing complexity, but the changes in the *modus operandi*. As known from research on small business, which has also long been struggling with the unevenness of the subject of its analysis, these broad categories cover activities of entirely different nature. The charity organizations of churches, for one, do not aim at maximizing asset value, *their efficiency cannot and should not be measured against microeconomic criteria*. Likewise, the sound conduct of business implies an entirely different set of indicators in the non-profit sector than in normal businesses, or in the traditional budgetary logic (where cost minimization is the name of the game). Co-operatives and other non-business partnerships *may or may not operate on the business principle*.

This of course poses a series of major challenges for regulation, not least because of the public finance and *burden sharing perspective that remains valid*. Once business establishments pay up to two thirds of their wage costs for public dues of various sorts (such as pension and health care contributions, unemployment taxes, environmental tax and the like), as in the case of Hungary at the time of writing, being re-classified as a non-business or simply not-for-profit venture may be the easiest way *to eschew over-taxation*. Once this incentive is given and is strong, the fiscal authority can hardly avoid over-regulating the non-business sphere, or put up with substantially lower tax revenues. This is not a major challenge if society is in favor of *free market* solutions including a small state. This however is *not the case in continental Europe* in general and in the emerging economies in particular. Only parties promising more rather than less, public services, more rather than less state redistribution, more rather than less social protection and provision could win elections since democracy has been restored or introduced in the emerging economies.

It goes without saying that the large, and in our forecast ever growing sector of the in-betweens *cannot be forced into the customary public finance textbooks' regulatory pattern of either state/public or private/business establishments*, since it is the crux of the matter that these are neither fish nor flesh. Whereas the group of subsistance ventures can, in practice, be left on their own, with reference to the self-help element in their activity (that by definition implies a saving on public expenditure on social safety), this is not necessarily the case with the more elaborate in-betweens. For instance, since pharmaceuticals are treated as 'normal' products to be traded and controlled for safety only, it is hard to justify that private ambulance or care services for the elderly be fully exempted from public dues, as well as excluded from public subsidies state-owned providers regularly receive. On the other hand, it may be absurd to levy a public due on activities of self-help, such as child care organized by the neighborhoods. The broader is the scope of the welfare state, the more difficult to draw a dividing line. Furthermore activities that do not pursue profit motives, and activities that may well do, are equally hard to delineate in most of the services. If one thinks only about the 'gratis economy' of the internet (Bitzer et al, 2006) it is hard to think of applying the traditional bivariate model to go by.

In the traditional business sector, especially in the business of going around with risks, some workable solutions have already been emerging. The idea of *reinsurance* has long become a reality, thereby exempting individuals from conditions that are not under their influence. Doing so, for instance, can help overcome the otherwise non-soluble problem of women having to pay either higher fees, or accept lower services, for the simple reason of their working shorter and living longer, besides the gender-specific higher risks and needs of their medical care. According to empirical studies of West European countries, at the practical level inefficiencies resulting from these problems may be negligible, once the principle of reinsurance within the risk community is accepted.

Under this angle European regulation and public policy should become *all-embracing, though by no means interventionist*. The new regulatory agenda must be transnational, preferably a global one, with multilateral institutions and meso-level associations playing a major role. The latter – the mechanism of enforcement and self-enforcement – may be vital, else the competition among localities and regulations will thwart any similar effects. We have brought examples to show, that commonality of interest has already been bringing about more co-operative games.

One of the more obvious avenues for change could be a major *deregulatory drive within the EU*. For the time being, EU regulation tends to be used by national bureaucracies for attaining various particular objectives. What comes or does not come to be regulated at EU level is rarely judged on the base of its merit, i.e. if this is to be more efficient than national or global regulations. Oftentimes disagreement over major issues, such as the budget or SGP or Iraq pushed some less relevant issues to the fore, as a kind of *ersatz*. The infamous EU debates on the definition of chocolate, or the optimal shape of cucumber are better publicized cases in point.

What is trivially efficient from the macro-perspective would, however, *rob several interest groups from their bargaining chips*. While the EU does not have a mandate in social policy, or no supranational authority in matters of environment, in both areas tendencies to extend/relocate competencies have been observable. There is little hope to see these changing for the better in the future, as long as regulation in the EU remains hostage to sectoral interest, national politickling and backward-looking approaches, the three issues we tended to be critical of. Revoking out of date regulations and a thorough efficiency-check, by contrast, could bring *palpable results without major costs*.

Sticking to inter-governmentalism might have been self-serving in the *short term interest* of the negotiators. However, this may turn to be *self-defeating* in the long run. This happens by allowing for, and indeed, inviting more bureaucratic regulations – *ones that have barely anything to do with the arrangements we have advocated* all across this chapter. On the other hand, as we tried to argue earlier (Csaba, 2003) it would be premature to bury the 'benefit of crisis' thesis of political economy. With sabotaging all changes, laming is a foreseeable outcome, one that is unlikely to be sustainable on political grounds. Likewise the potential disintegration of SGP, followed by a decay in all of the non-economic regimes, such as environment and justice and home affairs, present such a credible threat that no responsible European politician may want to live with. The time for policy reforms then comes – though nobody knows whenexactly. Thus *radical EU reforms may well be on the cards,* much more than the customary extrapolation of the short-term processes – or a rational choice model – would indicate.

References

AGHION, Ph. – ALESINA, A. – TREBRI, F. (2004): Endogenous political institutions. *Quarterly Journal of Economics,* vol. 119. no. 1. pp. 565–612.

BARRO, R. (2002): *Nothing is Sacred: Economic Ideas for the New Millennium.* London and New York: The MIT Press.

BÉLYÁCZ, I. (2004): 'A vállalati részvények belső és piaci értékének konfliktusáról.' (On the conflict between the internal and market valuation of corporate stocks) – a paper presented to the scientific conference on the occasion of the 173th General Assembly of the Hungarian Academy of Sciences entitled *'Corporate Bankruptcies in the Early 2000s: The Failure of Traditional Financial and Legal Control?'* Budapest, 11 May.

BITZER, J. – SCHRETTL, W. – SCHRÖDER, PH. J. J. (2006): Intrinsic motivation in open source software development. *Journal of Corporative Economics,* vol. 31. no. 4. pp. 1–11.

BHAGWATI, J. (1998): Directly unproductive profit-seeking activities. In: BHAGWATI, J.: *Writings on International Economics.* (edited by V. N. BALASUBRAMANYAM). Delhi: Oxford University Press, pp. 134–151.

BLANCHARD, O. and GIAVAZZI, F. (2003): Macroeconomic effects of regulation and deregulation in goods and labor markets. *Quarterly Journal of Economics,* vol. 118. no. 3. pp. 843–878.

BLOOM, D. E. – CANNING, D. – SEVILLA, J. (2004): The effect of health on growth: A production function approach. *World Development,* vol. 32. no.1. pp. 1–14.

CLARK, D., (2004): Software may offer help for clash between security and privacy. *Wall Street Journal Europe,* 15 March.

CLUYER, A. and NEWHOUSE, J. eds (2000): *Handbook of Health Economics,* vol. s. 1A and 1B. Amsterdam etc.: Elsevier.

CSABA, L. (2003): Enlargement – for crisis or reform? In: KUKLINSKI, A and SKUZA, B. eds: *Europe in the Perspective of Global Change.* Warsaw: Ofycijna Wydawnicza 'Rewasz' for the Club of Rome, pp. 189–195.

DJANKOV, S. and MURREL, P. (2002): Enterprise restructuring in transition: A quantitative survey. *Journal of Economic Literature,* vol. 40. no. 3. pp. 739–792.

DYCK, A. (2001): Privatization and corporate governance: principles, evidence and future challenges. *World Bank Research Observer,* vol. 16. no.1. pp. 59–84.

EICHBERGER, J. and SUMER, M. (2004): Bank capital, liquidity and systemic risk. Vienna: Austrian National Bank *Working Paper* no. 87. (May).

GLAESER, E. and SHLEIFER, A. (2003): The rise of the regulatory state. *Journal of Economic Literature,* vol. 41. no. 2. pp. 401–425.

GRAHAM, D. – WOODS, N. (2006): Making corporate self-regulation effective in developing countries. *World Development,* vol. 34. no. 5. pp. 868–883.

GUNNING, W. et al (2003): *Breaking the Conflict Trap.* Washington and Oxford: Oxford University Press for the World Bank.

HALLSTRÖM, L. (2003): Support for European federalism? An elitist view. *Journal of European Integration,* vol. 25. no. 1. pp. 51–72.

HAUFLER, V. (2003): Globalization and industry self-regulation. In: KAHLER, M. and LAKE, D.

eds: *Governance in a Global Economy*. Princeton and Oxford: Princeton University Press, pp. 226–252.

HEITGER, B. (2004): Property rights and the wealth of nations: a cross-country study. *CATO Journal*, vol. 23. no. 3. pp. 381–402.

KEOHANE, R. and NYE, J. (2003): Redefining accountability for global governance. In: KAHLER, M. AND LAKE, D. eds: *Governance in a Global Economy*. Princeton and Oxford: Princeton University Press, pp. 386–411.

KIKERI, S. and NELLIS, J. (2004): An assessment of privatization. *World Bank Research Observer*, vol. 19. no. 1. pp. 87–118.

KOCSIS, É. and SZABÓ, K. (2003): *Digitális paradicsom vagy falanszter?* (A digital heaven or a phalanster?) Budapest: Aula Publishing House.

KRAVTSENIOUK, T. (2002): Merger regulation in central and eastern Europe: evidence from Hungary, Romania and Slovenia. *Acta Oeconomica*, vol. 52. no. 3. pp. 327–346.

KRUEGER, A. (1974): The theory of rent-seeking society. *American Economic Review*, vol. 64. no. 3. pp. 291–303.

LLEWELLYN, D. (2002): Financial intermediaries in the new economy: will banks lose their traditional role? In: SIEBERT, H. ed.: *Economic Policy Issues of the New Economy*. Heidelberg and New York: Springer Verlag, pp. 215–240.

MÉRŐ, K. et al (2003): *Tanulmányok az új bázeli tőkeeegyezmeny várható hatásairól.* (Studies on the expected impacts of Basle Two capital adequacy accords). Budapest: *MNB Műhelytanulmányok*, no. 27. (October).

MIHÁLYI, P. (2003): *Az egészégügy gazdaságtana* (Economics of health care). Veszprém: Egyetemi Kiadó.

MÓRÉ, Cs. and NAGY, M. (2003): A piaci struktúra hatása a bankok teljesítményére: Empírikus vizsgálat Közép-Kelet-Európára. (Impact of market structure on the performance of commercial banks: An empirical analysis of central and Eastern Europe). Budapest: National Bank of Hungary, *MNB Füzetek*, no. 12. (December).

OFER, G. (2005): Globalization and the welfare state: developed, developing and transition countries In: KOLODKO, G. W. ed: *Globalization and Social Stress*. New York: Nova Science, pp. 91–118.

SALZBERGER, E. (2002): Cyberspace, governance and the new economy. In: SIEBERT, H., ed: *Economic Policy Issues of the New Economy*. Heidelberg and New York: Springer, pp. 168–208.

SUMMERS, L. (2000): International financial crises: causes, prevention and cures. *American Economic Review*, vol. 90. no. (2–3). pp. 1–16.

TAYLOR, L. (2002): On global macroeconomic management. In: NAYYAR, D. ed.: *Governing Globalization: Issues and Institutions*. Oxford and New York: Oxford University Press for WIDER, pp. 73–103.

VALENTINY, P. (2004): Árprés és felfaló árazás. Közgazdasági elmélet, bírói szabályozói gyakorlat. (Price squeezing and predatory pricing. Economic theory, legal practice and regulation). *Közgazdasági Szemle*, vol. 51. no. 1. pp. 24–45.

VÁRHEGYI, É. (2003): Bankverseny Magyarországon. (Competition in banking in Hungary). *Közgazdasági Szemle*, vol. 50. no. 12. pp. 1027–1048.

VOSZKA, É. (2003): *Versenyteremtés – alkuval?* (Creating competition through bargains?). Budapest: Akadémiai Kiadó.

14. INSTITUTIONS AND GROWTH: WHAT IS THE NEXUS?

As has been shown in the preceding chapters, the issue of institutions in generating growth remains a major and controversial topic in the literature on the new political economy of emerging economies. Ever since the publication of the World Bank report, *From Plan to Market* (1996) and ever since the Nobel Prize of Douglass North in 1993 and of Joseph E. Stiglitz in 2001, it is no longer trendy to downgrade institutionally informed analyses as 'poetry'. Likewise policy failures in post-Communist and developing economies over the past two decades, the crises in east Asia and in the ITC sector have triggered new interest in institution-related and policy-relevant academic research. Judging by the output of major publishing houses and of leading journals in the international economics profession this seems to be a lasting trend. And a fore-fighter of the mainstream, Robert E. Lucas (1988, p. 5) established some time ago, that numbers on long run development were hard to interpret in other than institutional terms.

In the first decade of the 2000s the question, it seems, is no longer if institutions matter, rather the question needs to be re-formulated: *how do they matter?* The preceding analyses have supported the claim by Havrylyshin and van Rooden (2003), namely that institutions do matter, but only in the context of supportive policies. And conversely, policies matter and sustain only if the rules of the games – institutions – are supportive of certain economic insights.

In addressing this field, we enter on a slippery slope: similarly to many other evergreens in the social sciences in general and in economics in particular, there is no consensus view on which we could rely upon. The nexus between investment and growth remains largely unanswered, or likewise, the interrelationship between human capital accumulation and growth remains largely unclear. Conditions that trigger innovation and endogenous technological progress are also at best approximated in the negative – that is in listing what is *not* conducive to innovation, rather than being positive about it. Therefore our subject has also more unknowns than equations. However, it may make sense to sum up, without aiming at being exhaustive, of what we may claim to know about the role of institutions in promoting growth. In doing so, it is not our intention to replicate the thorough and detailed literature review provided by Aron (2000), that also concludes with a slightly agnostic tone on the ways academic findings may be channeled into policy-making. However, even a rudimentary summary may worth a try, in attempting to *generalize what our analysis contributed to more general knowledge,* that is which insights have been supported and which ones not.

Endowments, Policies and Culture

Our analysis is supportive of previous research by Martha de Melo et al. (2001) or Addison and Rahman (2005) highlighting the over-emphasis on geography and (instrumentalized) path dependence in the policy discourse explaining failures and successes. We may join these researchers in underscoring the role of *microeconomic incentives for restructuring,* and the resultant emphasis on bringing about and sustaining such rules of the game, that are conducive to high domestic *savings* – high domestic *investments* scenario, with due emphasis on the efficiency of resource *allocation* and prudential *regulation* of the financial sector (not only of banking). We also have found, that *weak institutions* are often *path dependent,* and conflict-ridden political situations, namely civil wars, but also milder but lasting forms of civil conflict are harmful. Even lack of consensus over the fundamental values and strategies of development and ongoing power struggle among major social actors, vested interest goups and political agents, is conducive to *sustainingly weak core state.* This ensues in the lack of anchors for sensible, growth-oriented policies.[1] This is the reason, as we tried to document, why laggard countries are unable to operationalize those academic insights that could, in theory, lead to improvement.

The agenda of good governance, local ownership of reform and the anti-corruption drive all point toward the need for a strong, technocratic and *professional administration,* committed to the public good and thus *disembedded from vested interest groups.* However this maxim is hard to adhere to. In societies, where it has traditionally never paid investing into civil service, where rule-abiding always resulted in losses, where informal rather than formal institutions and dispute settlement mechanisms have been dominating, it is hard to see how the fixed point of change, the anchor may emerge. We do have convincing historical examples, from Kemal Atatürk to Lee Kuang Yew of Singapore that charismatic personalities can change the name of the game. Also, the democratic transitions – the famous Huntingtonian third wave – have lent support to the more normative claims that changes for the better might be

---

[1] Dornbusch (1993) assigned the following tasks to the core state in orchestrating policy reform: a) provide a good ideology; b) ensure strong administrative capacity; c) target instruments according to well defined objectives; d) ensure decentralization and accountability, that is features that are bound to be built up in a decade or longer; e) open up the economy; f) make it attractive to FDI; g) restore regular access to global financial markets. From this it follows, that lack of consensus over fundamentals may render even a strong state ineffectual.

feasible.[2] Others (Williams, 2003) have highlighted the role of technocrats, policy advice, and the ability to create *independent agencies* where technocratic considerations are provided with a degree of autonomy, if not insulation, from countervailing pressures. In short, the long term or collective rationality is *institutionalized* against vested interest politics, based on individual rationality, inevitably dominating daily politics in a democratic society. However, this is unlikely to be quick and unlikely to produce results in a single electoral cycle.

This finding might explain why macro-economic policies have proven *less* relevant in the *longer run* than they looked. *Unless macro-policies are anchored in some institution* – be that balanced budget rules, privatization plans, constitutions supportive of private enterprise, EU accession, international accounting standards etc. – *these are unlikely to survive the counter-reaction of vested interest groups.* Likewise, unless sound macro-polices are supported by micro-economic foundations, brought about in part by domestic legislation – such as the rules on bankruptcy, solid finances, or regulating network industries and deregulating product and factor markets – these are bound to 'lose teeth' and be rolled back. Experience with the inefficiency of these polices lends support to claims of national uniqueness and to justifications for not even attempting to attain what in academic terms may look the obvious goal.

Foreign assistance, once highlighted by Gunnar Myrdal (1971) and his followers as the core component of development policies, has proven to be inefficient in countries, like in many states of sub-Saharan Africa, where the *domestic* institutional infrastructure has proven inadequate for absorbing these (more on that in van der Walle, 2001). A similar finding is emerging through the observation of the quasi-states of Bosnia-Herzegovina, Kosovo and the like among the NIS. In these cases a culture of aid dependency has already emerged, without however any prospect of self-sustaining development. In other words, *lack of progress cannot and should not be blamed on inadequate external financing,* the lack of a new Marshall Plan for Eastern and central Europe, or for the Balkans for that matter. Empirical analysis (Ovaska, 2003, p.186) has found that in the period of 1975–1998 in a sample of 86 developing countries one percentage point increase in aid as a percent of GDP *decreased* per capita growth by 3.65 per cent, since aid has not contributed to better governance, but allowed for postponement of adjustment.

The focal role of institutions is also highlighted by the insight (Easterly and Levine, 2001; Erdős, 2003) that questions whether factor accumulation would be the ultimate driving force of development. As we have seen in the case of South-East Europe, Azerbaijan and also Russia, more investment, even plenty of new investment may well lead to more waste, *provided the mechanisms of effi-*

---

[2] Interestingly a leading East Asian analyst (Jung, 2003) considers as weakening the core state the measures that diminish the previous executive overweight and create checks and balances in Japan and South Korea in the turn of the millennium, such as the abolition of 'head of family' position in the public administration. In the European perspective, the interpretation would run the other way around.

cient resource allocation, control of expenditures, incentives for recoupment are not being created. The existence of capital flight in all countries at lower level of development is a plain warning, since it is not realistic to expect foreigners to risk their property when better informed locals do not venture for the same.[3] As we have shown, in some economies the low absolute level of investment is also a cause for concern. But in the majority of cases it is rather efficient allocation and lack of transnationalization that may be at the root of prolonged economic difficulties.

Finally special mention should be made of the *resource curse* (as elaborated in, inter alia in Ross, 1999; or in Karl, 1997, pp. 44–67 on petro-states) which seems to be particularly relevant for the new independent states but also in South-East Europe. While some analysts (Jones-Luong, 2003) develop sophisticated theories of why this is not a strong pre-determination, empirical studies are not supportive of the latter claim. Empirical evidence, provided recently, inter alia, by Kim (2003, pp. 31–34 and 41–45) has been indicative of the immediate relevance of the revenues from fuel extraction in *sustaining authoritarian methods* of control, both politically and in terms of corporate governance. This works by providing windfall revenue to the government, thus relieving it from the burden of painful adjustment. Growth could, indeed be recovered without major privatization and liberalization measures, thus the incentive to change must have been diminishing also during the Putin Presidency. What could be observed in the oil producing monarchies in the three decades following 1973 oil price hike (Glasser, 2001, pp. 4–26 and p. 109) seems to have been replicated in Russia and Kazakhstan since the late 1990s. As simple products do not *require* sophisticated management techniques, nor do they *allow* for these. And while neither historical determinism nor economic structuralism is by any means our perspective, it is hard to overlook the strong interrelationship. Thus we may only join those (Atkinson and Hamilton, 2003) observing two items. First the significant negative correlation between resource abundance and slow growth is a statistical fact, hardly to be disputed away. Second, the *inability of governments to manage revenues* is at least as important an explanatory factor, as the availability of quick/cheap money on its own right. The two together culminate in regularly low savings, that in turn translate into low investment and low growth in the long run scenario.

In a broader context, it would be hard to deny that institutions are the intermediaries between endowments/resource richness and policies. Therefore, contrary to early modernization theories, is not the change in the pattern of production that triggers a change in society. Rather it is the public choices embodied in the rules of the game that decide if factor abundance is a curse or blessing. Resource abundance may further *deteriorate* already poor institutions, but never *cause* their emergence (Mehlum et al, 2006).

---

[3] True in exceptional cases, such as start-up situations, transnationals with large bargaining power may well venture in areas where locals are suppressed by governments. But this colonial type of intervention hardly produces the forward and backward linkages a la Hirschman (1981).

The interaction between the sophistication of social structures and efficiently deployable management techniques has been one of the eldest insights in sociology. Likewise in management literature it has been among the established facts to ascertain that more sophisticated intertwining, better educated workforce, more ICT, generally what is known as Toyotism, requires different incentives and different forms of control (including less hierarchy, more collective rather than individual incentives etc.). Thus, the burden of proof remains on the shoulders of those who advance theories doubting such fundamental insights.

In reality, our empirical and analytical survey of the post-Communist economies has clearly pointed towards the *traditional lines*. The prolonged rule of despotic regimes of Central Asia, or the less pronounced forms of authoritarianism in other Newly Independent States would be hard to explain, if we abstracted away from the lack of structural change, lack of post-industrialism and lack or weakness of civil society. As long as most of wealth creation requires simple management methods, well suited to the endowments of the fuel and energy sector, the incentives to change may come from the diplomatic arena, owing to the broadening of the focus of international agencies. These adopted, already during the second Clinton Presidency, a vigorous anti-corruption stance, advocacy of universal human rights and the like. Over and above this, the entire approach to poverty alleviation and development has undergone a change. As the volume of the then chief economist of the World Bank (Stern, 2002) illustrated, the international agencies have internalized those insights from the new generation in development economics, that had been critical of the earlier view that treated recipients as objects of action. Rather than following the earlier passive approach, the idea of *empowerment* has come to the fore. Here the major objective is not to remedy certain static shortcomings, but facilitate change and learning, spread knowledge, and foster entrepreneurship. In this approach, *bringing about the abilities that allow for future value creation and innovation* come to the fore, and the issue may be broader than resources: actually any state capture and monopolism may be a danger (Havrylyshyn, 2004).

By contrast, if resource abundance allows for rents to be appropriated, even if these are in part shared with the population, there is no receptive environment for the empowering approach. Rather the traditional *culture of dependence* and self-reinforcing processes of *patriarchal approaches* and policies are likely to cement themselves. By the time the resource boom will have been over, the challenge will be all the greater. Still, this will hardly change the overall landscape. The more a country sustains the *economic base of a traditional society*, be that resource dependence, or control over foreign trade, or over a few revenue generating sources, such as smuggling, public monopolies, control over ports, transit routes, or tourist places, the *less sophisticated* the economic and the ensuing *social structure* remains, the better the chances for *enduring authoritarianism are*. Trivial economic costs of opting for the inferior are unlikely to change the balance of forces on their own, short of external influences.

The light at the end of the tunnel comes with *transnationalization* and the *ICT revolution*. Those features that we discussed in previous chapters are unlikely to leave despotic states unaffected. Therefore while in the short run features of path dependence render the continuation of authoritarianism probable, and when fuel prices are high, this may even work, *in the long run it is unlikely to remain so*. Rather, those processes that have triggered the implosion of the Soviet Empire and the collapse of authoritarian regimes worldwide will exert influences on the resource dependent authoritarian states of the Middle East and Central Asia alike. In the case of Russia, the European orientation of society and of the elite, as well as the ongoing process of integration in the global organizations, such as WTO, the political priority enjoyed by G 8 and the IMF, membership of many international agencies, altogether will exert a strong *demonstration effect* with the time passing.

Formalization and Enforcement

Institutions are known to be rules of repeated games (more on that, also in game theoretic terms in: Aoki, 2001). Both formal and informal institutions, such as norms, habits, value judgements and perceptions are important for shaping outcomes. As we have also seen, copying formal institutions is though easy, still in most cases *ineffective* in bringing about improvements. Institutions emerge in part as an outcome of human deliberation – system design – and in part spontaneously, in ways that are not yet properly understood by the various social sciences. From the perspective of North-inspired neo-institutionalist approach *formalization and enforcement* have been shown to be formative in the Russia, China and Transnationalization chapters.

From the point of view of economic development, the defining moment is if, and under what conditions, new institutions may contribute to the better combination of the factors of production, better allocation of resources and a generally innovation-friendly environment. We have shown the importance of rule of law considerations and property rights regimes. The longer horizon we take,[4] the more convincing the insight is that security of savings, the possibility to transfer property (and bequeath it), the solid allocation of financial resources in a flexible and safe financial system *constitute a single chain*, what German economists term as the *economic order*.[5] This approach implies that there is a strong *interdependence among the individual elements* of the macro-system, and changing only one of them, while keeping all the rest intact, is unlikely to be effective. Privatization in the Czech Republic in the early nineties, or severing monetary policy in Russia in the mid-1990s are cases in point.

[4] This is precisely what is often missing, especially if and when nationalism and the related ideology of catching up turns haste into a virtue in the eyes of the public – a big change over the pre-18th century period, as explained by Landes (1998).
[5] Heitger (2004, pp. 399–400) in his posthumus article rightly draws the conclusion from empirical statistical analysis, that if properly accounted for indirect impacts, private property counts among the *ultimate sources of economic growth*.

Neither social sciences in general, nor our empirical analysis in particular have produced anything that can be termed as *a cookbook of optimal policies*, including sequencing and monitoring, that could serve as a general guide to any country in any period of time. What is particularly remarkable is the wide variety of interplay among formal and informal institutions, as well as the different ways institutions and policies may interact. It seems that, in some cases, the *self-reinforcing logic* of *virtuous circles*, in other cases those of *vicious circles* are demonstrable. Testing the empirical validity of suggestions by Olson and North, Mark Gradstein (2004, pp. 516–517) has found a self-reinforcing tendency between the protection of property rights and growth, with *law enforcement being crucial*. Likewise in the vicious circle scenarios the lack of these mechanisms can be blamed for the self-propelling processes in the opposite direction. While we share his conclusion about law enforcement being a public good, we definitely do not subscribe his second finding, that would consider formal enforcement to be a luxury of rich countries. On the contrary, as we have indicated in several places, *poor countries should actually value even more public administration and the independent judiciary as a scarcity good*. Therefore they are well advised to spend more lavishly on these (in order to pre-empt other private agents, such as TNC or maffiosi to do the same to an underpaid and demoralized administration). In triggering the outcomes, as well as in the potential change of trajectory, the interaction of transnational markets with local politics has been shown to be the key. Major components of development, such as good governance, rule of law, accountability, trust, social intangibles are all soft categories, that are known to emerge slowly and in ways that are non-trivial for the formal economic analysis. The limitations of the latter must herewith be clearly acknowledged.

Some new empirical analyses have supported our reading of causality. In a seminal article Acemoglou and Johnson (2005) prove that property rights have *first order effects* on long run growth and institutional development, whereas contractual rights matter mainly for the evolution of the financial sector.

Finally, mention should be made of a quickly changing institution, that has been playing a pivotal role in shaping the outcomes of the past fifty years: *the European Union*. Through its existence and changing policies the EU has been shown to play a pivotal role in shaping institutional change and in orchestrating policy consensus in the frontrunner countries. Meanwhile, among the laggards the lack of this anchor has allowed for the reproduction of inefficient and path dependent structures, recombinant property and of inward looking coalitions. As we have tried to prove, especially in the chapter on the 'Limits to accession driven transformation' and on 'The non-stability pact', EU arrangements are far from perfect. Nor do they serve the purpose of maximum competitiveness. Still, EU arrangements have been and still are, as a rule, superior to locally developed alternatives, if for no other reason than *their superior enforcement and monitoring mechanism*. This explains why opting for the suboptimal may be a shortcut solution in policy-making for many years, even if not forever. By providing the anchor and monitoring functions, the EU has helped to change the rules of the game in the frontrunner group. Here path dependent forms of management could be overcome primarily via FDI, and on the macro-economic level, via harmonizing laws to the EU arrangements, the acquis. All this explains why it has *not* been *the official fiscal transfer component* through which the EU assisted the more successful cases of transition. Likewise, it is *the EU perspective* rather than any other arbitrary criterion that *has created a dividing line* among transforming economies. In one group, we find those for whom Communism is no longer a defining feature of their development. In the other group, by contrast, those where this weighty heritage still matters for structural change and policy options alike.

Meanwhile, it is equally important to re-iterate that the EU *has never been meant to be a growth promoting organization* in its main functions. The EU, remains primarily a political architecture. This implies a stronger *emphasis on primarily non-economic matters,* such as citizenship, the common foreign and security policy, or environmental protection. While EU has contributed to bringing about sound macroeconomic policies in a number of its incumbents and also in the new member states, the ongoing debate on the modification of SGP is a clear indication that it has been built on *voluntary compliance.* In other words, independent enforcement mechanisms are and will remain limited, by virtue of its predominantly, though by no means exclusively, *inter-governmental nature.* Therefore it remains within the competence of *each and every member-state,* old and new, *to bring about conditions favorable to innovation and growth.* Some of the regulatory frame, including monetary regulation, fiscal codes of conduct, and many detailed regulations is allocated to the Community level and enforcement is secured by the European Court of Justice and the ECB, two supra-national organizations. Still, this framework may or may not be conducive to growth, as the juxtaposition of Ireland and Germany in the 1990s would clearly illustrate. As the empirical analysis of Hughes-Hallet et al (2003, pp. 59) show, the disciplinary effects of the SGP might have been eroded already by 2004 and the consolidation fatigue of large countries could not be overcome by the international (non-enforcable) rules alone.

Policies and Transnationalization

We have seen, in the comparative empirical chapter as well as in the chapters on the European Union, that *policies clearly matter.* While macro-economic theory clearly advocates non-inflationary growth, as the only sustainable solution for the long run, prudence and solid fiscal stances are easier preached than practiced. Macroeconomic stability *cannot* be taken as given, *it needs to be recreated from time to time.* Fiscal sustainability, though easily conceptualized, is hard to attain under democratic framework, unless what the Germans call *Stabilitätskultur* emerges. This term implies that none of the major actors conduct policies and pursue agendas that are in open conflict with the virtue of price stability. Furthermore, wage restraint may be attained if monetary targets are credible. On the other hand, the expenditure side of general government can be calculated so that it would not offset the maxim of price stability.

Irrespective of the role ascribed to cyclical fine-tuning, fiscal policies can remain solid. Likewise, state administration should not be seen as pork to be handed out for *clientele*. Rather a technocratic (British style) approach is required. This lengthens horizons, especially if rule-based rather than discretionary decision-making becomes dominant.

As we have illustrated in the empirical chapters, these *normative considerations cannot be taken as given,* not even within the European Union. While in academic terms the overall policy frame, what Walbroek (1998) aptly termed the 'one world consensus' is no longer subject to serious professional debate,[6] myopic policies and parochial public debates do allow for recurring populist pressures, from Poland to France. *Policies* in a democratic environment are inevitably, at least to some extent, *the independent variable* in the growth equation, even if there is no absolute freedom of choice ('sovereignty' in the old sense).

Policies and policy agents may be instrumental in bringing about, or torpedoing, change by way of their contribution to *institution building*, or conversely, by avoiding action even if it is overdue. The Swedish Social Democrats' policies under Göran Persson in the post-1999 period indicate, that even the most entrenched structures, such as the investment funds administered by trade unions, or the previously purely public and overly lavish pension system may be reformed. By contrast, the experience of Poland and Hungary in the 1997–2006 period is indicative of the dangers of falling to victim to one's own success. In both of these countries, high growth rates brought about by early reforms allowed for a prolonged policy of doing nothing in terms of institution building. Only the latter that could have laid the groundwork for further convergence to EU levels. Similarly, policies play a pivotal role in either strengthening/internalizing, or conversely, watering down and marginalizing the new institutions that emerged in various stages of systemic change.

There are a couple of areas where policies and institution-building go hand in hand in bringing about improvement in the virtuous circle scenario. Prudential regulation and enforcing the appropriate, that is impartial, rules of the game do run counter to the immediate interests of the businesses concerned. When network industries are privatized, the role of regulation of entry comes to the fore. Here again, incumbents do have a vested interest in prolonging market opening, and if they manage to get their agenda through, the entire society pays the bill. Sluggish opening of European electricity markets, or the creeping liberalization of the European airline industry is just as indicative of this issue, as the inability of the EU to agree on the joint regulation of European stock exchanges, thereby depriving the region of one of the more obvious advantages of economies of scale and scope alike. Some

---

[6] This is in part, at least, due to the rather general, non-specific formuli and approaches, allowing for adjustment to different contexts. In fact, already beginning with the East Asian financial crises of 1997–1999 international financial organizations, such as the IMF and the World Bank, have also adopted this differentiated approach, in contrast to their previous rigid standardization attempts.

of the new challenges for regulation in the context of ever greater dimensions of privatization have been addressed in our chapter on 'Privatization and regulation'.

One of the recurring themes in the related debates is, as discussed in a separate chapter in some detail, if, and to what extent, regulatory functions could be outsourced from the government, in order to keep it lean and avoid the hypertrophy of public agencies. While entrusting public functions to private firms obviously carries the danger of partisan enforcement and degrading regulation, the emergence of independent regulatory agencies, not under immediate government supervision, with technocratic leaders elected or appointed for much longer periods than a single electoral cycle, show the tendency toward *institutionalizing sustainable policies*. On the other hand, it would be hard to deny that this option puts some fairly strong limitations on contest as a major component of democratic decision-making. The way public choices are made in these ever extending areas are anything but trivial, nor is the way how these agencies should co-ordinate their activities with elected, thus directly legitimated governments.

Policies are crucial in *promoting or hindering transnationalization, primarily through FDI and involvement in global institutions,* such as WTO, and in applying or diluting such meso-level regulations as international accounting standards, transparency enhancing measures and empowering policies. True, mere formal adoption (promulgation) of WTO compatible rules, or joining in this organization for diplomatic reasons (as NIS coutries seem to do) will be of no avail, unless the rules are internalized and enforced, quite in the sense of Douglass North. But being outside of the multilateral framework may be yet another attempt to reinvent the wheel, or a mere waste of scarce academic and administrative resources on establishing a frame that is likely to be overrun by the existing global rules of the game anyway, at least in business practice.

As we tried to document in various chapters, relying on FDI is crucial for microeconomic modernization and restructuring. Likewise it is hard to see how the capital power and professional knowledge, furthermore the needed personal integrity of bankers and fund managers may come around, unless Western experience and players are allowed to penetrate the markets of emerging economies. True, knowing the accounting scandals in the USA and elsewhere, not even this seems to be a truly safe bet. What we can and do maintain is *a weaker proposition.* We do know that lacking these close ties no modernization and catch-up is feasible, whereas the inversion of the thesis does not automatically yield good results. One of the reasons explaining this is, that owing to conflict of interest, especially in the financial sector, but also in terms of micro-economic integration (regulating networks, health care, rural development, environment etc.) *the regulatory and monitoring function cannot be outsourced from the domain of public policy.* This is so, if for no other reason than the need for a referee in any games that are often zero sum in the short run. Thus while most of the tacit knowledge, capital and learning by doing is bound to come from the corporate sector, the *monitoring* and *macro-economic steering function* remain inherent Features in public policies.

Finally, it would be hard to disagree with a conclusion by T. N. Srinivasan (2003) that it is *a quality, rather than the sort of institutions which is decisive* for long term economic performance. The example of the stock exchange in Moscow and Shanghai clearly illustrate, that simply introducing a formal institution with well known characteristics per se, is a long way from bringing about the *outcomes* normally associated with these. It is the social and overall context that determines the outcomes, though as frontrunner emerging countries and the newly industrialized economies have demonstrated, the 'tyranny of history' is no longer a general all-valid argument for justifying any failure. From this insight, it also follows that any *external influence*, should this come from the EU or transnational agents, *is bound to be limited in any non-disintegrating society.*[7] It is precisely the ability to adjust and adopt new forms of organization and the concomitant values and behavioral norms that is the name of the game. In a way, there is no way to eschew organic change, that is 'domestically owned' and supported by societies, if good policies are to survive one election cycle.[8]

The Politics of Economic Reform

Already early analyses, such as those coordinated by Bates and Krueger (1993, pp. 444–472) have highlighted how little is known about the precise inter-relationships between the economics and politics of institutional reforms. Reforms in a broad sense are understood to be more than administrative tinkering. Thus they involve *comprehensive overhauls of how the system and its defining institutions operate* on the base of policy initiative from above, and conducted in an organized, rather than spontaneous, manner. Experience with policy reform is varied. It is indicative of the *feasibility* of such project under a variety of socio-economic conditions in all emerging economies. However, as the authors rightly warn, it would be *simplistic* to postulate an *immediate relationship* between poor economic performance and 'ensuing' corrective reforms. As many stagnant developing economies, and more recently Japan (Saxonhouse and Stern, 2003; Hoshi and Kashyap, 2004) and Germany and other core European economies (Siebert, 2002) testify, there is no 'inevitability' to change. Also there is no pre-ordained way of overcoming a predatory state, that continues to maximize distributional objectives rather than public welfare. What is known for sure that doctrines (ideas) perceptions play a *much bigger role* than customarily assumed. Furthermore, it is also known that such major change never comes

---

[7] This explains, alas, why so little can be done even through pre-emptive wars and humanitarian interventions to overcome consequences of dictatorships in a sustaining and human manner. It also explains, why various international organizations tend to be more silent than they should, when encountering problems of oppression and obvious mismanagement/corruption among their member states. But usual cowardice, lack of principles to speak up, as most recently in the Sudan, in the name of diplomacy, also has been a persistent feature.

[8] The contextuality of good policy is an issue highlighted by the summary chapter by Stiglitz (2000, pp. 556–561).

about when interest groups dominate the scene. Therefore the classic insight of Mancur Olson (1982) is also valid for emerging economies, the more they become mature democracies, the more so.

What policy reform means, in broad terms, is the institutionalization of 'the public purpose', or in political science terms 'collective rationality'. This may happen by the adoption of rules of fiscal discipline, limitation of immediate, electorally motivated distributory policy, cut public spending back to limits set by considerations of fiscal sustainability, redirect expenditure priorities according to the bottleneck principle. It may further require enhanced transparency, and extend the role of technocratic or independent regulatory agencies, not under the control of daily political games. In standard economic terms, we may speak about *the public good character* of the above listed principles and practices. This is so, since the substance of these is the non-exclusive, non-excludable nature, further that each member of the society benefits, while no single individual is directly interested in attaining these qualities.[9]

In short, policy reform is the *set of actions,* usually triggered by political exigencies, such as revolution, recession, balance of payment crises and the like, that *re-tailor the rules in repeated economic games.* Policy reform is excluded by definition in public choice approaches to political economy. Still, these could be observed among others, in the reality of frontrunner countries and other emerging economies, like Mexico, Argentina, Turkey, Korea and Israel. Despite the voluminous literature, we know precious little about the exact *mechanics of successful change,* that would go over the anecdotal evidence and case description, which in one group of countries ended up in success, and in an other group in failure and reversal. Given the crucial role of social, historic, cultural and other contextual factors, *it is impossible to elaborate in abstract/analytical terms a cookbook that would contain the ingredients of optimal policies* that could be resorted to in any country and under any circumstances. As the overview (Nijkamp and Poot, 2004, pp. 118) concludes, 'there remain severe limitations on what can be learned for policy from highly aggregative models of endogenous growth'. In their reading of the evidence governmental activity through education and infrastructure[10] is rather positive, on investment and growth is rather weak, if any. Thus policies *cannot be assigned* with the task of generating growth through immediate action.

---

[9] For instance, each producer is interested in higher rather than stable prices, while the community as a whole is not interested in other than stable price levels. Thus a central bank ensuring price stability is neither 'embedded', nor representing any particular interest, rather the public purpose only. In this respect, new international political economy literature uses even such terms as 'international public goods' when talking about transparency, or properly audited government and corporate reporting. These, of course, can never obtain 'microeconomic foundations', as overzealous analysts would require from any macroeconomic category in recent years.

[10] The latter point is obviously contestable. Physical infrastructure projects are prime examples of 'cathedrals in the desert', from the Brazilian highways crossing the Amazon rain forests to the Danube Bridge of Szekszárd, serving two hundred (sic!) cars a day in its year of construction. In general big prestige projects may be the hotbed of corruption at the phase of their planning, implementation, completion/controls and retrospective evaluation alike.

This implies, *inter alia,* that adopting EU regulations in the course of harmonization of legal and regulatory systems *may or may not provide additional impetus for improved developmental perspectives* in the new member countries. If and when local conditions, at the end of the day, translate these formal rules in the old, established inefficient practices, this 'inculturation' may actually deprive these arrangements of their civilizing and monitoring functions. It is clear, for instance, that no amount of harmonization and external monitoring will *substitute* for an administratively efficient core state, a lean and non-corrupt civil service, high levels of professionalism in financial regulation and non-partisan enforcement of existing laws by an independent, properly paid judiciary. Likewise, many of the categories re-discovered in recent political economy theorizing, such as regulatory quality, prudence, good governance, transparency or fair trading practices, social intangibles *hardly lend themselves to quantification.* By contrast, some *other features* of sound policies, such as fiscal sustainability, or a pension system not carrying over implicit debts, clearly *can and should be phrased in quantitative terms only.* These dual insights show up in the earlier quoted corporate governance literature where advocacy of particular, culture-dependent, contextually well functioning models has given way to insights (primarily in Aoki, 2001) over the inevitability of *lastingly diverse forms* that lead to success.

The Role of Financial Institutions

We may venture to formulate some of the *necessary, though by no means sufficient conditions* for an environment that is *favorable to sustainable economic growth.* The earlier surveyed, and generally the more technical, literature on growth is inconclusive over the mechanics of its generation. Thus we can only refer to those policy-relevant insights that definitely count among the necessary components of success, without being able to deliver the *sufficiency* conditions for emerging economies.

One of the emerging new consensus points in the literature is the *focal role of savings.* This used to be part of the conventional wisdom. However, with the triumph of Keynesianism, the per se true insight, that savings always equal to investments at the macroeconomic level, has been too easily translated into a policy where savings did not really matter.[11] By contrast, the studies on underdevelopment, surveyed in our chapter on the Developmental dimension have clearly indicated the enhanced policy relevance of savings. Unless the domestic savings' rate can be kept sufficiently high, there is no way how FDI could replace this, nor could activist state policies compensate for the loss. The East Asian growth miracle (Nelson and Pack, 1999) but also our comparison of

---

[11] Analyzing the role of savings in the Hungarian economy Tibor Erdős (2004) calls attention to the frequent occurrence of forced savings, primarily in the corporate sector, as well as to limitations to increasing household savings in a transition economy, especially through interest rate policy.

China and Russia in the respective chapters, further the contrary experience of South-East Europe and Central Europe analyzed in the empirical and comparative chapter, also has drawn attention to the crucial importance of savings. Not only savings in general, *but savings in monetary form, preferably in domestic currency and kept in the domestic system of financial intermediation that is needed.*

Each component of the above normative has been shown to matter. Savings may well be high, but kept 'under the pillow', or invested into housing, or kept in the form of precious metals, paintings and other objects of art. These phenomena are well known from developing economies struck at a low level steady state equilibrium. The reason for this may be in the generally business unfriendly environment, governmental policies hostile to financial investments,[12] that are often portrayed as particularly exploitative in the public perceptions. Under these circumstances, savings often *do not take place at all* (people produce less and immediately consume it). Alternatively, they treasure what is needed for unforeseeable events in such forms that are *not accessible* to external agents. Therefore *financial intermediation is bound to remain shallow* and the resources for investment meager. Low tax revenues and the tradition of not investing in the state administration, that is often seen as a handout for loyalty, result in *low state capacity*, particularly low capacity to tax, but equally low capacity to implement policies.

Under these circumstances, the room for participatory development (Dalay-Clayton – Dent – Dubois, 2003) is bound to remain limited, for bottom up development and co-decision capacity would *pre-suppose* the existence of the lean and technocratic bureaucracy. African, South Asian and Latin American experience thus lends support to our claim on the focal role of the core state. This in turn can conduct policies favoring savings and developing the *formal system* of financial intermediation,[13] primarily of banking and the stock exchange. Actually, experience with the Russian 'virtual economy', when in the 1995–1999 period mutual non-payments of bills had become the norm in the exchanges among Russian corporations, has lent support to the insight that de-monetization is a fairly successful way of *keeping the 'grabbing hand' of the state away from private pockets*. This in turn reinforces our claim that the inability to tax, the lack of incentives to save, the lack of formal institutions of finance, and the low level of investments constitute *a single chain* in explaining under-development.

Savings therefore need to be in *monetary form*, that is as deposits in the banks, stocks and government bonds. If this norm is violated, the corporate sector has to rely exclusively on retained profits and depreciation for financing its expansion. Particularly if taxes are high – say for concerns of re-distribution

---

[12] Ideological considerations and the tradition of predatory state have been combined to deliver the above outcome in Africa in the post-decolonialization period, as reported in (Tangri, 1999).

[13] As Lord Peter Bauer (2000) recurringly noted, there is always an informal system of trading and money lending, else famines and shortages become extreme. A similar argument is advanced in a more general level in Hayek (1989), while Bauer provides empirical evidence, primarily from West Africa.

– firms will *sustain low profitability*. They turn to 'costing', including various items of consumption among the operating expenses of the establishment. This is not only distortive, that is not allowing for the best use of resources, but leads to massaging the signals of the price system. It also provides an incentive to invest within the fences of the firm only, rather than searching for the best returns across the board (nationally and abroad). In turn, *the low level of efficiency, rooted in the misallocation of resources will sustain*, therefore we are back to square one of the vicious circle of underdevelopment. Even if in this less pessimistic scenario investments will be higher than in a 'pure socialist' solution, like the one experienced recently in Zimbabwe, and previously in Mozambique and Ethiopia, growth is unlikely to be impressive. It may not even be attaining potential trend rates of growth, because of the built-in inefficiencies in the system. This is the situation typical of most sub-Saharan and Latin-American small economies. As we have seen in the various chapters, South-East Europe, the Caucasus and Central Asia is clearly trapped in a situation reflecting the above listed stylized facts, but recent analysis (Mérő, 2004) has indicated lack of financial depth to emerge as a long run constraint on growth of the frontrunners as well.

Even if financial savings are high enough, say, because of the dominant precautionary motive that allows for poor societies like China or Vietnam to sustain high savings rates, that need to be *in domestic currency*. If that is not the case, there will either be dis-intermediation, or the function of mediating between savings and investments will be taken over by *foreign financial institutions*. The latter might well be inevitable to some degree, say at the *early phases* of transformation, as discussed before, or in countries where policy reform is *initiated in a low trust-low credibility environment*. However, this should *not become a lasting feature* of the system, else the chain of savings-investments-taxation-public goods and services – more incentive to produce and generate revenues (even if that is taxed) will be broken. Moreover foreign banks obviously cream off the best clients and more profitable business, since these are no charity foundations. Therefore much of the profit that should be re-invested for building up the financial sector and its costly physical infrastructure in the emerging/poor economy will never be made. The second best option thus may turn to be not at all so lucrative. In this context, reference should be made to the old insight, namely that anybody using other countries' currencies is in the end *financing the deficits of the issuing government*. That is not a very lucrative perspective for any poor country, trapped in stagnation, among others due to its low rate of savings.[14]

What has been unfolded does not contradict to our previous favorable assessment of the role of foreign banks in the process of bringing about conditions of sustainable growth and its financing in emerging economies in general, and in post-Communist countries in particular. Nor should these ideas be interpreted as counter-arguments to introduce full currency convertibility.

---

[14] This explains why, despite its recent popularity in the financial literature, so few economies have resorted to full dollarization (actually Panama, Ecuador and Grenada being these).

Arguments favoring transnationalization allow for the full capacity and the full scope of micro-economic optimization decisions to unfold. In reality, due to non-negligible transaction costs, it is unlikely that in a normal economy profits would be immediately turned into currency and re-patriated abroad, *unless the threat of a (return of the) predatory state is very real.* Short of this policy option it is rather likely that foreign investors will *increase* the scope of their local sourcing – an experience shared by Hungary, Ireland, the Czech Republic and Portugal. The strengthening of domestic tacit knowledge allows for *deepening and broadening of financing.* The latter in turn allows for *more efficient combination of factors,* and better external financing of expansion projects of local businesses, small and large alike. Growth in turn allows for *more revenues to be channeled to public coffers.* If for no other reason, because big foreign banks (and investors in general), according to Hungarian and other experience, are unlikely to undermine their brand name by under-the-counter dealings, or not paying public dues. This holds, if the host country, following the principles of optimal taxation, levies lower burdens than in the country of origin. The resultant inflow, in turn, *allows for the broadening of public services,* for improving tax collection, professionalizing the state administration, and replicate the *virtuous circle scenario* we described in the empirical section and in the chapter on transnationalization.[15] It goes without saying, that secure property rights, law and order, contract enforcement and generally rule of law considerations matter even more in the financial sector. This finding is in line with those of Calderón and Liu (2003, pp. 331–332) stressing that *the causality goes from financial sector development toward growth,* however financial liberalization and institution building is helpful only if supplemented by other supply side policies. In their panel of 109 countries, the mechanics of change works through the chain of capital accumulation, allocation and technological upgrading, stressing the need for financial development already at lower and intermediate levels of development.

In his broad analysis of the role of capital markets in emerging Europe Pálosi-Németh (2006) reinforces earlier cited results of Berglöf and Bolton (2002) on the limited role of financial intermediation in fostering growth. However, as the same analysis demonstrates, this reflects the inability of the financial sector to perform some of its basic functions. Furthermore, it is likely to contribute to the foreseeable deceleration of the trend rate of endogenous growth, long before catching up with EU 15. This is in line with the findings of the recent monograph of Tibor Erdős (2006) elaborating this point in detail.

Once we accept the insight that *rule of law* and a *deep financial sector* definitely count among the defining conditions that allow for innovation and endogenous growth, *we can assign this task to public policy.* There is a world of difference between two concepts. One is the assignment the task of growth *generation,* particularly of attaining quantitative targets – such as high growth rates, above the average of OECD countries – to economic policy, normally also charging it with

---

[15] Similar finding is presented via different reasoning by Tanzi (2005).

the task of ensuring full employment. It is a different one to hold it responsible for *bringing about and sustaining those side-conditions that are known to contribute positively to growth.* An overall business-friendly atmosphere does contain a number of non-quantifiable tasks, but definitely includes priorities on price stability, rule of law, fiscal sustainability, cutting back red tape and the like.

It has long been a contentious issue in the literature, not least in the context of financial globalization, if and to what degree countries at a lower level of development or at lower level of institutional maturity should *liberalize* and *deepen their financial sector.* Also, the traditional East Asian developmental state did not rely on deep financial markets. However the latter model has not proven to be sustainable. In a recent study, Rioja and Valev (2004) have shown on a panel of 74 countries, that *the finance/development nexus does change with the level of development.* At low level of development, financial improvements have uncertain effects. At intermediate level of development, *large and positive* impacts on growth were demonstrable. Finally, at high level of development the influence is still positive, but smaller. The conclusion from this analysis may be twofold. First: *emerging economies eminently need* improvements in their financial sector if they are to enhance efficiency of the use of their limited resources. Second, at higher levels of development, long term factors of growth are not conducive to equally high rates of further improvements for reasons detailed in growth theory. Therefore it might be *unjustified to extrapolate* mechanistically the efficiency gains of the intermediate levels to the long run.

Freedom in this context is not just an instrument of attaining the supreme technical objective, growth, as Amartya Sen (1999) reminds us in his seminal monograph. Yet another Indian economist, T. N. Srinivasan (2001) calls attention to the fact that dictatorships, in historical and statistical evidence, have *not proven to be more efficient in generating higher rates of savings and growth, let alone welfare,* than democratic societies. Actually, historic experience over the past thousand years has been exactly the opposite. While most technological innovations originated in China, their massive application invariably happened in Europe and North America, reflecting the defining role of institutions supportive of freedom (Landes, 2006). Moreover the more we appreciate the insight of the new developmental paradigm, that it is not physical capital accumulation that is the engine of growth, but a broad set of policies and institutions that *together add up to a favorable environment,* the less likely we shall see any virtues of authoritarian regimes. The insights on the growing role of ICT, on the changing business paradigm, on the growing importance of decentral tacit knowledge and endogenous innovation, all point toward the non-replicable role played by various forms of market co-ordination, as well as of state policies and regulations *supportive of these.* Economic freedoms are therefore positively required for growth to take off, while political freedoms need not be postponed – a finding supported also by the empirical study of Vega-Gordillo and Álvarez-Avce (2003).

One may wonder to what extent the traditional savings – intermediation – investment chain, and to what extent freedoms drive growth. Recent econometric evidence (Daculiagos and Ulubasoglu, 2006) has shown the contribution of freedoms as *relevant* and *positive,* even if previous studies (including the

384

ones we cited in the previous edition) tended to overstate this role and unduly de-emphasized the traditional role of physical capital. On the other hand, a unit of physical capital produces 74 to 150 per cent more output in free countries with good quality institutions, whereas the existence of growth itself could be a disincentive to change. The causal link thus is *just the reverse* of what early modernization theory had (Gwartney et al, 2006).

Finally, special mention should be made of the crux of *micro-economic restructuring* and the entire system of incentives, which is the set of institutions and rules *regulating entry and exit*, which together define the type of market economy we are addressing. As illustrated in preceding sections, one of the major unresolved problems of both socialist, post-socialist and statist developing economies has been the *lack of market/social control over the arbitrary selection of winners*. Furthermore this initial failure tended to be aggravated by the lack of monitoring and retroactive correctives by the consumers, local and international alike. The more we move away from textbook-like tasks of the SLIP agenda, and approach what has become customarily termed third generation reforms, such as those in the health and pension systems, in network industries, in former natural monopolies, in many previously publicly provided services as waste management or water management, the greater the importance of the quality of regulation is, or as the international agencies christened it, of *good governance*.

It is equally important, on the one hand, to sustain gate-keepers, following the earlier described consideration of public purpose in regulating *entry* into such sensitive systems as finances, pipelines, air transport or health care. These should follow the prevention and pre-emptive principles. On the other hand, it is equally important to provide a regulated *exit possibility* for those failing, and not only (not even primarily) in the small business sector. This call for updated and sharpened bankruptcy legislation, anti-trust activities, strict enforcement of accounting and transparency rules, and also discretionary intervention when big crises are in the making. Experience in the United States in the 2001–2004 period has provided new evidence of the need to act, even if the government adopts a general non-interventionist stance.[16] Whereas expansion is more often than not taking care of itself, *divestment often requires assistance from public authorities*, for considerations of employment and regional development alike.

Self-Correction and Coordination in Complex Systems

One big complex of unknowns revolves around *the political-institutional preconditions of sustainable policies for growth promotion. This includes issues pertaining to self-correction and the coordination issues in complex systems.*

Sustainability has gained prominence both in the more academic and in the more policy-oriented literature in the 1980s and 1990s for a simple reason. The

[16] Crisis management in the auditing sector, managing the crisis of airline industries, of insurance and many others, rather than the narrow-minded and old fashioned steel quotas that show the direction of both academic and policy reflection, over discretion.

more the focus of attention turns away from issues of fine tuning and managing the business cycle, that used to figure prominently in Keynes-inspired thinking, the more the *longevity of policies,* rather than their coherence comes to the fore. Simply put, if one contemplates the vices and virtues of changing the pension system, from pay-as-you-go to fully or partially funded, the horizon of analysis is bound to involve the *overlapping generations,* their diverse interests, and not least the several decades long period in which the processes take place. Similar – in part identical – issues emerge during the partial privatization of health care and related services.

Likewise, the more we include such items in economic analysis as *trust* and *credibility, social norms* and the like (in the context of informal institutions and considerations of implementation and enforcement), the more we have to face the fact that *these do not change overnight.* One may even argue that these are the fruits/final outcomes of these solid policies that are, in the end, built on the availability of these. For this simple reason, but also with reference to frequent policy reversals, experienced not only in Latin America, the consideration of *how to orchestrate* policies and arrangements that last long enough to bite, has become *endogenized* in the economic analysis. While traditional economics considered these outside the scope of its attention, the nature of things has changed so that it can no longer be the case.

The more we consider *democratic environment* as given, the less we can employ the traditional concept of the benevolent dictator and that of the black box of politics, both being extraneous to economic analysis. Balanced budget rules and independent regulatory agencies may though help, but unlikely to save the laborious task of building up and sustaining *reform constituencies.* The more the deliberations need to be continuous, like in health care, where no obvious solutions are at hand, the more important this component is bound to be. Also the availability of a *lean and non-partisan state administration* devoted to the public purpose rather than to vested interest representation, is a condition that needs to be *continuously recreated.* The more complex the areas of regulation grows, the longer it takes and the more costly it will be to find and sustain high professional level in the macro-regulation and in the operation of formal institutions.

We have already seen (Srinivasan, 2001) that *increased participation may or may not improve the quality of governance.* The experience of water management projects in India, where – non-representative – local elites pursued their own agenda, or the presence of equally non-representative but vocal NGOs in various international negotiations, are clearly indicative of the limitations of a 'the bigger the better' approach. Meanwhile, in a democratic society there surely is a – perhaps changing – limit to freeing up regulatory agencies from immediate (day-to-day) political accountability, at least in the long run. The more these rules and nominations follow some principle of qualified majority – be that two thirds or three fourths – the higher may be the legitimacy and their ability to withstand cyclical policy pressures.

True, the reverse problem of *the ability for self-correction* is equally important in a quickly changing world. This requires, among others, observance of the principles of transparency, accountability, contestability and the continuous operation of various checks and balances that constitute the heart of democracy.[17] While all this looks straightforward, nothing is more difficult to deliver in practice than adherence to these simple maxims. *Transparency* of general government accounting may seriously inhibit the discretionary handing out of pork to constituencies, creative accounting and cover up of practices that deviate from the principle of serving public purpose only. *Accountability* tends to be an abstract category if turnover in the state administration is high, and by the time of finishing investigations nobody, that could be held responsible, is available any longer. Likewise, decisions taken in collective, like in cabinets and behind closed doors, without taking votes, may never be fully turned to controls, as everybody tends to remember in a different way. Last, but not at all least, political *contestability* is an important issue. As long as one group or line of thinking may monopolize the floor – as for instance the Italian and Austrian Christian Democrats and Socialists, or Japanese Liberal Democrats could for over four decades – this is likely to enhance the chances for ossification, cumulative cover-ups, and general inability to correct mistaken decisions.

This issue was focal in the Nobel lecture of Prescott (2006), who took issue with the traditional view, considering economics *as an instrument only*. He emphasizes the need for democratic deliberation over those constitutional rules that can only infrequently be changed, and with a lag, so as to ensure the solution to the problem of time inconsistency.

Finally, with the growing complexity of economic and social system, in part due to transnationalization and the ICT revolution, *problem of macro-coordination is becoming the crucial issue*. This insight, highlighted already in the now classic Bates and Krueger (1993, pp. 470) volume has several planes. First, it relates to the *administrative* capacity of public administration. Second, it relates to the *analytical* capacity of think tanks supportive of the government. Third it relates to the *political* ability of the governing group to deliver *coherence and commitment* for sufficiently long periods of time.[18] In order to attain these reliance on such *meso-level arrangements*, as the international accounting standards, enforced auditing requirements, widespread reliance on public procurement and the like may be of assistance. However these can by no means replace discretion and careful case-by-case assessment of the situation – a consideration all practicing policy-maker – or as John Williamson (1994) called them *technopol*[19] – stresses in their analytical accounts.

---

[17] In his influential book, based on his famous article, Fareed Zakharia (2003) revived this old insight, calling attention to the dangers of the tyranny of 50 per cent plus one.

[18] International political economy literature tends to allocate a focal role to the Ministry of Finance. However, as the vivid account of Greskovits (2001) explains, in emerging economies the relationship between the Prime Minister, following general political or even historic aims, and his Minister of Finance, following a narrow economic logic and fiscal crisis management, more often clashes than coincides.

[19] This is a merger of the words technocrat and politician, and the article refers to the need of exceptional professional technocratic knowledge combined with charismatic political abilities to communicate the professional agenda. Such public figures as R. Barre, A. Ciampi, J. Stiglitz, L. Balcerowicz, D. Cavallo, O. Issing or T. Padoa-Schioppa may serve as points of reference.

Rules, Ideas and Policy Discretion

An immediate follow-up question that may arise from the above said if, and to what degree, *institutions are able to replace policies and exclude discretion?* This is all the more relevant, as rules, by definition, act as *constraints on deliberation.* Thus whatever rule is introduced limits 'sovereignty', 'democratic deliberation', 'relying on the popular mandate', or just pragmatism understood as 'common sense'. For instance the rules not allowing parties under 5 per cent of the popular vote to gain representation regularly exclude 15 plus per cent of valid votes from Hungarian legislation. The 3 per cent ceiling of the Maastricht Treaty does not allow for a government to be involved in growth generating – 'counter-cyclical' – policies in bad times irrespective of the performance of this government in good times. Adoption of a regime of inflation targeting does not allow for monetary authorities to accommodate lax fiscal policies (without their loss of credibility).

By contrast, academic economics is concerned with long run phenomena, such as non-inflationary growth, good governance, credibility and sustainability in a number of planes. Therefore it becmes compelling to provide certain, consensus-based *insights to be supported by rules and institutions that are hard to change* (and by no means to be changed overnight). Rule-based behavior certainly enhances calculability, thereby allowing for a better interaction between regulators and market players, thus enhancing the efficiency of policies. In concrete terms these allow *major changes* to be accomplished with minor, *soft policy measures,* that of course further increase credibility and efficiency of both policies and institutions.[20] This is the reason why the idea of rule-based behavior enjoys growing popularity in the analytical literature worldwide.

On the other hand, assessment of each and every situation cannot be saved. In the period between 1999–2006 we could observe a number of occasions when the governing board of the FED, of the ECB and of the Bank of England and of the Bank of Japan have all come to quite *different conclusions* on the measures that were deemed necessary to attain their quite *similar goals.* The ongoing idiosyncratic behavior is per se a proof of discretion, a fact that has never been denied by any of the major actors, from Duisenberg and Trichet to Greenspan.

How can we know that policies are also irreplacable? Besides the earlier quoted insights, recent analyses of ongoing crises (Collier et al, 2003) call attention to the danger of *reproducing the weak and predatory state,* in part because of sheer disintegration, in part because of the tradition of *not investing in the public administration.* The latter may turn into a self-fulfilling prophecy, with revolving power groups misusing the administration as their self-service shop, thereby further diminishing its efficiency. In some developing countries, mostly in Africa, kinship and political loyalty matters more than professional

---

[20] Gottlieb (2000) presents the case of Israeli monetary policy reacting to the East Asian and Russian financial crisis with deregulation and opening up, thus saving a lot of money otherwise needed for intervention, plus restoring the exchange rate of the *shekel* to the pre-crisis level in only eight weeks.

knowledge; administration also serves as an *employment buffer*. This is why the above quoted analysis is also calling for the creation of lean and professional civil service as a precondition for further improvements.

One of the recurring themes in the policy reform literature is the *unfavorable experience with transplants*. Arrangements, both at the level of corporate governance and of public policy, that work well under one set of conditions, often fail to deliver under different settings. Once formal institutions become defunct or watered down, the functions of co-ordination is taken over by informal institutions. This, as seen with the laggard group of emerging economies, is about the opposite of what rule of law and credibility considerations would require. Once institutions borrowed from abroad remain on the surface, or function only superficially, there is a grave danger of their being eroded. South-East Europe is one of the regions, together with the NIS, where formal rules tend to be dominated by informal ones. As we tried to show in the case of both China and Russia, this is a sign of inadequate modernization and carries the *danger of inefficiency and lasting slowdown*. In this context, Silvana Malle (2004, pp. 42 and pp. 47) rightly draws attention to the contrasting experience in Central Europe. She is indicating that institutions take root better if and where they had a certain legal and political pre-history, as common law in former British colonies. This insight also means, as she explains, that those transplants that are fundamentally alien to the cultural context are most likely to be rejected by the social fabric and the democratic political process alike.[21]

We know fairly little about how institutions may be successfully transplanted. It seems that processes of transnationalization in general, and of ICT in particular may, at a certain level, contribute to this. Also meso-level, institutions were shown to have emerged for settling differences and collisions among various national rules. In a way, progress in the Millennium Round of trade talks, pertaining to several areas outside commodity trade, like intellectual property, public procurement, export promotion measures and investments, would have been crucial to create *civilized rather than archaic ways of conflict resolution*. As seen in the cases of China and Russia, WTO membership may well serve as an incentive to streamline and modernize their respective institutional infrastructure.

An equally important, though much less explored area is the *mechanism of self-correction*. Once an insight gets institutional backing, it will be hard to change. This is the plus and the minus about it. On the one hand, this allows to act it as a bullwark against policy reversal. On the other hand, *priorities and insights may and do change*. Public choice, for instance, favoring more egalitarian provision of services may give way to insights favoring more self-help and vice versa. Professional insights, especially in the social sciences can rarely be taken as given *forever*. The 1960s was molded by the belief in technological progress – called in German *Machbarketisglaube*. By contrast, the current age is formed by post-modernist and post-structuralist approaches, and by uncer-

---

[21] A similar conclusion is formulated in an even more pronounced manner by (Winiecki, 2003).

tainty pertaining to the powers of what any administration is up to. It goes without saying that the two approaches translate into different institutions, that are much more difficult to change than policies are. For instance the moving wage setting of *scala mobile*, itself a source of chronic inflation in Italy in the 1970s had been possible to change only at the cost of major social unrest and several years of fights. Likewise, the current slow reform of the pension system in Western Europe is a case in point. The idea of inter-generational solidarity, when one generation is significantly more populous than the other, and when perspectives for growth are dim, is hard to sustain, but also hard to change. The more myopic and vested interest dominated political processes are, the longer it will take to institute those changes that ensure elementary rationality from the public purpose perspective.

Last but not at all least *ideas seem to matter*, much more than it was customarily thought in a few decades' time span. If this holds, there obviously is a *trade-off* between *flexibility* needed by the open-ended nature of social and economic change on the one hand, and stability, *calculability and credibility*, provided by the *institutionalization* of insights and behavioral norms. Ideas shape policies in a trivial fashion, but so do their institutions. As we have seen in both China and Russia, the big role of *informal institutions* is intimately related to the deep rooted, historically conditioned *distrust* in the state in general and of the judiciary as a politically instrumentalized arm of the executive in particular. Perceptions and norms are slow to change, which of course is yet another justification for why spending on education, of the judiciary and of the state bureaucracy (ensuring its lean and technocratic qualities) need to be treated as *investment* rather than consumption or social expenditure.

This circumstance may explain the empirical findings of Linda Weiss (2003, pp. 294–298) that contrary to widespread claims, *the taxing power of states has not diminished*. The tax burden – especially on capital – even grew by several percentage points since the 1960s, while difference in the tax/service structures remained decisive. The real change, as the case studies of her collection prove, has been from statism to governed interdependence. In other words, the room for Keynes inspired demand management has diminished. Still the process of transnationalization has been enabling the state for a variety of new functions and activities (like the regulatory ones discussed in our chapter on Privatization and regulation). How enabling these processes work, is a function of *the quality of the institutional framework in the respective society*, as well as on the values governing public choices, among other things, on funding and reforming public administration.

The Democratic Development Alternative

What do we know and what should we know? First and foremost the jury is still out on the mechanics of growth, a major field of general economics. In short, neoclassical theories of Samuelson, Barro, and Solow tend to attribute up to 75 per cent to factors extraneous to the analytical frame, such as technological progress and innovation. Endogenous and especially evolutionary theories, by contrast, are much better at explaining processes, not however at 'putting numbers' on the factors of growth. We do know that institutions, rule of law, property rights and the like matter. However, while the *direction*, as elaborated in the previously cited works of Bauer, Olson, de Soto, Heitger or North is clear, *it is hard to establish exactly which is the chain through which they work*. More precisely, what we know are bits and pieces, we are able to explain failures, not however able to create a cookbook to go by.[22]

The study of emerging economies has, perhaps contributed, though to a limited degree, *to clarifying and understanding these more general considerations of economic theory.* In our analysis we hope to have been able to show that in the majority of cases it is *not the Communist heritage, but factors common to other countries at similar level of development* that are decisive. For instance the level of transnationalization, the broadness and deepness of capital markets, sound banking, incentives to save and to invest, context-specific methods of corporate governance and the like are the 'usual suspects'. Cultural and local specifics *modify rather than redefine* the logic of its functioning. Therefore both successes and failures of emerging and other post-Communist economies can be interpreted *within a single theoretical framework.*

While we have found many cases that go along the standard line of explanations, *we have not found any single counter-case.* In all those cases when empirical findings do not seem to be supportive of the general claims, we could spot a specific set of circumstances that explain derailment. For China, Russia and the Balkans *the standard set of explanatory variables do seem to deliver acceptable results,* once modifying factors such as path dependence and the weak core state are accounted for. This is the standard way of proof for any abstract thesis in the natural sciences, and paradigms need to be re-assessed *only if the exception becomes the rule.* Although we have seen and cited many claims describing transformation and re-emerging growth in terms of puzzles, we could not find empirical and analytical support to substantiate these claims. The latter look thus *rather widespread than soundly substantiated.*

The predictive power of the findings, such as the interrelationship between FDI and export patterns, or financial soundness and growth, seem to hold in line with the general claims (not invented, merely applied by the present analysis). Thus, as Antoni Kuklinski (2001, pp. 130–133) explained, the mere fact of Hungary and Poland each losing ten places in the Philadelphia Index of Scientific Output between 1981–1998 is unlikely to have left the innovative capacity of the respective economies unaffected. The latter is known to translate directly into the trend rate of economic growth. The less policies counteract the anti-innovative bias of transition societies, that has been manifest anyway, *the longer and deeper the period of slowdown is bound to be.* Likewise, the low level of revealed technological progress is unlikely to leave the Russian growth

---

[22] Lucas (1988, p. 5) notes that figures must be seen as *potentials* and reflections of *social interchange* rather than extraneously *given* variables following a predetermined path.

potential intact, once oil windfalls fail to reemerge in a regular fashion. Decades long neglect of R+D and of quality higher education is far from being a forgivable omission from the perspective of what rates of growth will be *sustainable* in the coming decades. Claims to the contrary, repeated endlessly by self-justifying public figures, are unlikely to invalidate the basics of growth theory, neoclassical and endogenous, institutional and evolutionary alike.

The list of conditions for emerging from the ruins of the Soviet empire, presented here is not meant to be exhaustive. However, it does contain at least some of the *necessary, even though not all the sufficient conditions*. One of the reasons for this is the fact that the broader developmental literature also struggles with the normative view it may offer on small, land-locked countries located in big distances from the major growth poles – an obvious disadvantage, currently stressed again by the new economic geography. Therefore we too fell short of offering trivially available *remedies* for the multiplication of ills in Central Asia and South-East Europe alike.

Our findings on the emerging economies, both the descriptive and in the normative planes, *point to the same direction as the broader developmental literature,* as represented by the volume of Todaro and Smith (2003). They are stressing the importance of decentralization and democracy. They also urge to *create stakeholders.* They stress the importance of bottom-up, *organic development* and participation. The latter applies at least in two planes. *First:* participation of the population in the process of *macro-political deliberation,* through voice and representation. People since Amartya Sen (1999) are no longer seen as a mere object of 'benevolent dictators', even at the abstract level of the theory of optimal economic policy. *Second,* participation in the processes of *transnationalization,* rather than rejecting it by way of seclusion, de-linking or searching, in vain, for 'national ways and models' has been shown to be able to produce superior outcomes in terms of wealth creating and well being alike. Likewise, one of the widespread hypotheses about the vices of democracy and the virtues of enlightened authoritarian regimes in poor countries, a platitude in many sociology and economic textbooks, *has proven to be a myth.* Panel analysis of Rodrik and Waciorg (2005) has not fund a single case when this point would have applied over the past 15 years.

Similarly, the great historical overview of David Landes (1998, pp. 217–218) highlights: that besides institutions committed to 'larger goals' over and above vested interest representation, the provision of personal and proprietary freedom, freedom of contract *responsive, honest government, free of any predation* have been the major components of economic success across the centuries. Furthermore, as Johann Lambsdorff (2003, pp. 468–469) indicates, corruption in poor counties lowers productivity by 2 percentage points per annum on average. For Tanzania for instance, he finds that improving its level to that of the United Kingdom would yield no less than 10 per cent increase of the capital stock. Later studies, however, highlighted the endogeneity of this factor. As Mendez and Sepulveda (2006, pp. 95–6) show, corruption – does not act on its own, but as part of aggressive practices. Thus only *broad liberalization,* not a focused vigorous anti-corruption drive may help. Therefore, at least in part, it is the *lack of professional and non-corrupt government* that may explain why non-European civilizations fell short of capitalizing on their frequent, but temporary, edges in terms of education or technological innovation.[23]

As we have seen through the publications of the international agencies, as well as of the development literature (as exemplified by the representative volume of Meier and Stiglitz, eds, 2001) a large number of fundamental issues are being re-assessed. The role of policies, institutions, of policy reform and sustainability have put a number of previously settled questions back on the agenda. It is reassuring to observe, that also in political science and international relations a parallel development takes place. The empirically based comparative methodology evolves toward *a neo-institutionalist synthesis,* that builds though on the rational choice model, without however staying at that level of abstraction (cf. the broad overview of Saxonberg and Linde, 2003, p. 14). *It is an entire new research agenda that is in the making.* The good news is that emerging economies fit into this picture. The bad news is that the process seems to be much *more open ended* than it was thought even a couple of years ago, be that from the angle of growth theory, or from the angle of development studies, or even from the perspective of new institutional economics for that matter. Attempting even to take stock of these is a task of a subsequent monograph.

References

ACEMOGLOU, D. – JOHNSON, S. (2005): Unbundling Institutions. *Journal of Political Economy,* vol. 113. no. 5. pp. 949–995.

ADDISON, T. and RAHMAN, A. (2005): Capacities to globalize: Why are some countries more globalized than others?, in: KOLODKO, G. W. ed: *Globalization and Social Stress.* New York, Nova Science, pp. 45–56.

AOKI, M. (2001): *Comparative Institutional Analysis.* London and Cambridge (Mass.: MIT Press.

ARON, J. (2000): Growth and institutions: A review of the literature. *World Bank Research Observer,* vol. 15. no. 1. pp. 99–136.

ATKINSON, G. and HAMILTON, N. (2003): Savings, growth and the resource curse hypothesis. *World Development,* vol. 31. no. 11. pp. 1793–1807.

BATES, R. and KRUEGER, A. eds: *Political and Economic Interactions in Economic Policy Reform.* Oxford: Basil Blackwell.

BAUER, P. (2000): *From Subsistence to Exchange and Other Essays.* Princeton, N. J.: Princeton University Press.

BERGLÖF, E. – BOLTON, P. (2002): The great divide and beyond: Financial architecture in transition. *Journal of Economic Perspectives,* vol. 16. no. 1. pp. 77–100.

CALDERÓN, C. and LIU, L. (2003): The direction of causality between financial development and economic growth. *Journal of Development Economics,* vol. 72. no. 1. pp. 321–334.

[23] This means no more and less, that the era of traditional factor input and endowment-based analyses is over. Only empirical concepts encapsulating various aspects of economic freedom, that is a new Austrian school approach, may produce relevant and quantitatively robust explanations of the rise and decline of nations in the past 50 years or so (for a good summary cf Czeglédi, 2006).

COLLIER, P. – ELLIOT, V. L. – HEGRE, H. – HOEFFLER, A. – REYNAL-QUEROL, M. – SAMBANIS, N. (2003): *Breaking the Conflict Trap*. Oxford and Washington: Oxford University Press for the World Bank.

CZEGLÉDI, P. (2006): A gazdasági szabadság mint az intézményi környezet indexe (Economic freedom as an index of institutional quality). *Külgazdaság,* vol. 50. no. 2. pp. 54–75.

DALAL-CLAYTON, B. – DENT, D. – DUBOIS, G. (2003): *Rural Planning in Developing Countries: Supporting Natural Resource Management and Sustainable Livelihoods*. London: Earthscan Publications Limited.

DOCONLIAGOS, CH. – ULUBASOGLOU, M. A. (2006): Economic freedom and economic growth: does specification make a difference? *European Journal of Political Economy,* vol. 22. no. 1. pp. 66–81.

DORNBUSCH, R. (1993): *Stabilization, Debt and Reform*. New York: Harvester Wheatsheaf.

EASTERLY, W. and LEVINE, H. (2001): It is not factor accumulation: stylized facts and growth models. *World Bank Economic Review,* vol. 15. no. 2. pp. 177–220.

ERDŐS, T. (2003): *Fenntartható gazdasági növekedés*. (Sustainable economic growth). Budapest: Akadémiai Kiadó.

ERDŐS, T. (2004): Mekkora lehet nálunk a fenntartható növekedés üteme? (What is the plausible rate of sustainable growth in Hungary?) Parts I and II. *Közgazdasági Szemle,* vol. 51. no. 5. pp. 389–414. and no. 6. pp. 530–559.

ERDŐS, T. (2006): *Növekedési potenciál és gazdaságpolitika* (The potential rate of growth and economic policy). Budapest: Akadémiai Kiadó.

GLASSER, B. L. (2001): *Economic Development and Political Reform: The Impact of External Capital on the Middle East*. Cheltenham (Glos.) UK and Northampton/MA/USA: Edward Elgar Publishing Co.

GOTTLIEB, D. (2000): Globalization and world financial turmoil: a test for Israel's economic policy. In: BARA, Z. and CSABA, L. eds: *Small Economies' Adjustment to Global Tendencies*. Budapest: Aula Publishing House for the European Association for Comparative Economic Studies, pp. 213–244.

GRADSTEIN, M. (2004): Governance and growth. *Journal of Development Economics,* vol. 73. no. 2. pp. 505–518.

GRESKOVITS, B. (2001): Brothers-in-arms or rivals in politics? Top politicians and policy-makers in the Hungarian transformation. In: KORNAI, J. and HAGGARD, S. and KAUFMAN, R. eds: *Reforming the State: Fiscal and Welfare reform in Post-Socialist Countries*. Cambridge and New York: Cambridge University Press, pp. 111–144.

GWARTNEY, J. – HOLCOMBE, R. – LAWSON, J. (2006): Institutions and the impact of investments on growth. *Kyklos,* vol. 59. no. 2. pp. 255–273.

HAVRYLYSHIN, O. (2004): 'Unchartered waters, pirate raids and safe havens: a parsimonious model of transition progress' – paper presented at the Tenth Dubrovnik Economic Conference, 24–25 June.

HAVRYLYSHIN, O. and van ROODEN, H. (2003): Institutions matter in transition, but so do policies. *Comparative Economic Studies,* vol. 44. no. (2–3) pp. 1–32.

HAYEK, F. A. (1989): *The Fatal Conceit: Errors of Socialism*. Chicago: The University of Chicago Press.

HEITGER, B. (2004): Property rights and the wealth of nations: A cross-country study. *CATO Journal,* vol. 23. no. 3. pp. 381–402.

HIRSCHMAN, A. (1981): *Essays in Trespassing: Economics to Politics and Beyond.* Cambridge and New York: Cambridge University Press.

HOSHI, T. and KASHYAP, A. (2004): Japan's financial crisis and stagnation. *Journal of Economic Perspectives,* vol. 18. no. 1. pp. 3–26.

HUGHES-HALLETT, A. – LEWIS, A. – von HAGEN, J. (2003): *Fiscal Policy in Europe, 1991–2003: an Evidence-Based Analysis.* London: Center for Economic Policy Research.

IBRD (1996): *From Plan to Market. World Development Report.* Oxford and Washington: Oxford University Press for the World Bank.

JONES-LUONG, P. (2004): 'Rethinking the resource curse: ownership structure and institutional capacity' paper presented to the conference of TIGER Institution *Globalization and Social Stress'*, Warsaw, 22–24, Oct. 2003.

JUNG, Y.-D. (2003): 'Re-juvenating statehood: Japan and Korea compared' – paper presented to the international conference on the occasion of the 50th anniversary of re-launching the Alexander von Humboldt Foundation, entitled *'The Public Sector in Transition: East Asia and the European Union Compared'* Berlin, 7–10 December.

KARL, T. L. (1997): *The Paradox of Plenty: Oil Booms and Petro-States.* Berkeley – Los Angeles-London: University of California Press.

KIM, Y.-K. (2003): *The Resource Curse in a Post-Communist Regime: Russia in Comparative Perspective.* Aldershot,/UK and Burlington/VT/USA: Ashgate Publishing House.

KUKLINSKI, A. (2001): Strategic triangle: R+D – innovation – economic growth. In: BÜNZ, H. and KUKLINSKI, A. eds: *Globalization – Experience and Prospects.* Warsaw: Oficyjna Wydawnicza 'Rewasz' for the Friednrich Ebert Foundation, pp. 124–137.

LAMBSDORFF, J. (2003): How corruption affects productivity. *Kyklos*, vol. 56. no. 4. pp. 457–474.

LANDES, D. (1998): *The Wealth and Poverty of Nations: Why Some are So Rich and Some So Poor?* New York: W. W. Norton & Co. Inc.

LANDES, D. (2006): Why Europe and the West? Why not China? *Journal of Economic Perspectives*, vol. 20. no. 2. pp 3-22.

LUCAS, R. E. (1988): On the mechanics of economic development. *Journal of Monetary Economics*, vol. 22 .no. 2. pp. 3–42.

MALLE, S. (2004): Institutional diversity and economic performance. *Competitio*, (Debrecen), vol. 3. no. 1. (special English language edition), pp. 32–48.

MEHLUM, H. – MOENE, K. – TORVIK, R. (2006): Cursed by resources or by institutions? *World Economy*, vol. 29. no. 8. pp. 1117–1132. – in a more academic version also in: *Economic Journal*, vol. 116. no. 508. pp. 1–20. (Jan. 2006).

MEIER, G. and STIGLITZ, J. E. eds (2001): *Frontiers of Development Economics: The Future in Perspective.* Oxford: Oxford University Press.

de MELO, M. – DENIZER, C. – TENEV, S. (2001): Circumstance and choice: patterns of transition. *World Bank Economic Review*, vol. 13. no. 1. pp. 1–32.

MENDEZ, F. – SEPULVEDA, F. (2006): Corruption, growth and political regimes: cross-country evidence. *European Journal of Political Economy*, vol. 22. no. 1. pp. 82–98.

MÉRŐ, K. (2004): Financial depth and economic growth – the cases of Hungary, the Czech Republic and Poland. *Acta Oeconomica*, vol. 54. no. 3. pp. 297–322.

MYRDAL, G. (1971): *The Challenge of World Poverty: A World Anti-Poverty Program in Outline.* New York: Vintage Books.

NELSON, R. and PACK, H. (1999): The Asian miracle and growth theory. *Economic Journal* vol. 109. no. 457. pp. 416–436.

NIJKAMP, P. and POOT, J. (2004): Meta-analysis of the effect of fiscal policies on long run growth. *European Journal of Political Economy*, vol. 20. no. 1. pp. 91–124.

OLSON, M. (1982): *The Rise and Decline of Nations: Economic Growth, Stagflation and Social Rigidities.* New Haven: Yale University Press.

OVASKA, T. (2003): The failure of development aid. *CATO Journal*, vol. 23. no. 2. pp. 175–188

PÁLOSI-NÉMETH, B. (2006): 'A tőkepiacok szerepe a feltörekvő országok gazdasági fejlődésében' (The role of capital markets in the economic growth of emerging countries). – Ph. D theses submitted to the Faculty of Economics of the University of Debrecen, October.

PRESCOTT, E. (2006): Nobel lecture: The transformation of macroeconomic policy and research. *Journal of Political Economy*, vol. 114. no. 2. pp. 203–235.

RIOJA, F. and VALEV, N. (2004): Does one size fit all: a re-examination of the finance-growth relationship. *Journal of Development Economics,* vol. 74. no. 2. pp. 429–447.

RODRIK, D. – WACIORG, R. (2005): Do democratic transitions produce bad economic outcomes? *American Economic Review,* vol. 95. no. 2. pp. 50–56.

ROSS, M. (1999): The political economy of resource curse. *World Politics,* vol. 51. no. 2. pp. 297–322.

SAXONBERG, S. and LINDE, J. (2003): Beyond the transitology–area studies debate. *Problems of Post-Communism,* vol. 50. no. 3. pp. 3–16.

SAXONHOUSE, G. and STERN, R. (2003): Japan's bubble economy and the lost decade. *World Economy,* vol. 26. no. 3. pp. 267–281.

SEN, A. (1999): *Development as Freedom.* New York: Knopf.

SIEBERT, H. (2002): Europe – quo vadis? *World Economy,* vol. 25. no. 1. pp. 1–32.

SPAHN, H.-P. (2001): *From Gold to Euro.* Heidelberg and New York: Springer Verlag.

SRINIVASAN, T. N. (2001): Democracy, market and development. In: SRINIVASAN, T. N.: *Economic Policy and State Intervention* (edited by T. N. NARAYANA). Delhi: Oxford University Press, pp. 531–550.

SRINIVASAN, T. N. (2003): 'Globalization, growth, inequality and poverty' – paper presented to the TIGER conference on *'Globalization and Social Stress',* Warsaw, 22–24, October

STERN, N. (2002): *A Strategy for Development.* Washington: The World Bank.

STIGLITZ, J. E. (2000): Reflections on the theory and practice of reform. In: KRUEGER, A. E. ed: *Economic Policy Reform: The Second Stage.* Chicago and London: The University of Chicago Press, pp. 551–584.

TANGRI, R. (1999): *The Politics of Patronage in Africa: Parastatals, Privatization and Private Enterprise.* Cheltenham/UK and Northampton, /MA/USA: Edward Elgar Publishing Co.

TANZI, V. (2005): The economic role of the state in the 21st century. *CATO Journal,* vol. 25. no. 3. pp. 617–638.

TODARO, M. and SMITH, S. (2003): *Economic Development 8th edition.* Boston: Addison Wesley.

VEGA-GORDILLO, M. and ÁLVAREZ-ARCE, J. (2003): Economic growth and freedom: a causality study. *CATO Journal,* vol. 23. no. 2. pp. 199–215.

WAELBROEK, J. (1998): Half a century of development economics. *World Bank Economic Review,* vol. 12. no. 2. pp. 323–352.

WALLE, N. van de (2001): *The Politics of Economic Reform in Africa.* Cambridge and New York: Cambridge University Press.

WEISS, L. (2003): Is the state being 'transformed' by globalization? In: WEISS, L, ed: *States in a Global Economy.* Cambridge and New York: Cambridge University Press, pp. 293–317.

WILLIAMS, M. E. (2003): Market reforms, technocrats and institutional innovation. *World Development,* vol. 30. no. 3. pp. 395–412.

WILLIAMSON, J. (1994): In search of a manual for technopols. In: WILLIAMSON, J. ed.: *The Political Economy of Policy Reform.* Washington, D. C: Institute for International Economics, pp. 9–48.

WINIECKI, J. (2003): Determinants of catching up or falling behind: interaction of formal and informal institutions. *Post-Communist Economies,* vol. 16. no. 2. pp. 137–152.

ZAKHARIA, F. (2003): *The Future of Freedom: Illiberal Democracy at Home and Abroad.* New York: W. W. Norton.

15. SUBJECT INDEX